Spirited, Skilled and Determined:
The Nineteenth Century Boat and Ship Builders of Battery Point

Nicole Mays

Navarine Publishing

Navarine Publishing

First published in 2024 by Navarine Publishing
GPO Box 2178, Hobart, Tasmania 7001
www.navarine.net

Copyright © Nicole Mays
Typesetting by Nicole Mays

Printed in Australia by IngramSpark

All rights reserved. No part of this publication may be produced, stored in a retrieval system or transmitted in any form by any means without the prior permission of the copyright owner.

Enquiries should be made to nicmays@gmail.com

ISBN: 978-1-7637259-0-4

A catalogue record for this book is available from the National Library of Australia

Please note that while I have intended to provide a definitive and accurate history and profile of Battery Point's nineteenth century boat and ship builders, and their families, as well as the vessels they built or were involved with, some events, names, dates and locations may have been unintentionally incorrectly stated or omitted. Vessel measurements may also be different or incorrect, particularly between those dimensions reported in the press versus those listed in registration papers. I apologise for any errors or omissions.

COVER IMAGES: *Genevie M. Tucker* on the patent slip at R. Kennedy and Sons' shipyard (Tasmanian Archives, NS1013/1/372).
SS *Warrentinna* at Battery Point (Tasmanian Archives, NS1013/1/22).
Barque *Eucalyptus* below Secheron (W L Crowther Library, State Library of Tasmania, AUTAS001126070440W800).
Battery Point boat and ship yards, 1880s (Tasmanian Archives, NS73/1/1/2).
Map of Battery Point (Tasmanian Archives, AF819/1/135).

SS *Warrentinna* on the stocks at Battery Point (c1883).
Courtesy Tasmanian Archives (NS1013/1/22).

Spirited, Skilled and Determined

Map of Hobart Town and surrounds, including Battery Point (c1839).
Courtesy Allport Library and Museum of Fine Arts, State Library of Tasmania (AUTAS001131821480).

Contents

Introduction	1
Historical Context	3
Battery Point	7
Daniel Callaghan	13
William Williamson	23
John Watson	41
Peter Degraves	63
Joseph Risby	75
Jacob Chandler	87
James Mackey	117
John Ross	135
John Lucas	151
Charles Miller	173
George Whitehouse	189
Lachlan Macquarie	205
Robert Inches	217
Other Builders	233
Synopsis	263
Finale	273
Index	275

Spirited, Skilled and Determined

Battery Point boat and ship yards (circa 1880s).
Courtesy Tasmanian Archives (NS73/1/1/2).

Introduction

> 'And of course there were the Hobart yards of Samuel Gunn, Degraves, John Watson, John Ross, John McGregor, Purdon and Featherstone, John and Charlie Lucas and Percy Coverdale. It would all make interesting reading if the history of these and all the other yards could be written.'
>
> Harry O'May (1957).

Owing to Tasmania's remote island location and the fact that it is surrounded by some of the world's most treacherous waters, much of the state's written maritime history is focused on tragedy with gruesome tales of convict escapades, shipwrecks and loss of life. However, in this history there is also perseverance, dogged hard work and achievement.

Tasmania's boat and ship builders were (and still are) spirited, skilled and determined entrepreneurs. The nineteenth century builders of Battery Point, near Hobart, especially, were tenacious risk takers, successfully using endemic timbers and scant resources to create vessels they adapted to new and emerging trades. Hundreds of Battery Point-built ketches, schooners, barques and brigs traversed local rivers and waterways, the unrelenting waters off Tasmania's coast, the perils of Bass Strait, and beyond. They were employed in local trade, in coastal trade, in intercolonial trade, as well as trade with New Zealand, Europe, Asia, and the Americas. Smaller craft, including whaleboats, lifeboats and dinghies, were constructed for use locally, as well as to supply visiting colonial and international vessels. A plethora of waterman's boats were built for use on the River Derwent for a growing pleasure and passenger trade. Racing craft were also built for use by local and visiting crews with often high stakes on offer.

As commercial boat and ship building enterprises at Battery Point expanded to encompass more builders and more yards, Battery Point-built vessels developed a reputation both individually and collectively and were highly sought by buyers locally, regionally, in other colonies and overseas. All the while the builders remained on the shore of this slight neighbourhood perfecting their craft, building new vessels, and maintaining and improving existing ones.

Strengthened by the legacy of those who had gone before them, boat and ship building at Battery Point continued well into the twentieth century, with recreational vessels, including yachts and motor launches, taking prime position on the stocks. As boat and ship building at Battery Point celebrates nearly 200 years of history, this book highlights one of the many successes in Tasmania's maritime history by profiling and analysing boat and ship building at Battery Point during the nineteenth century: the men and the vessels they built.

This book signifies a significant revision of one published by the author in 2014 titled *Spirited, Skilled and Determined: the Boat and Ship Builders of Battery Point (1835 - 1935)* that is now out of print. In the decade since its publication, additional records have become available detailing construction of many more vessels at Battery Point, as well as the existence of Battery Point's first commercial boat builder, Daniel Callaghan, who began operation there in 1830. As such, this edition now profiles over 20 builders, as well as more than 720 vessels built at this location during the nineteenth century; the latter an increase of over 170 from the previous volume. Updates have also been made to the history of many of the craft included in the first volume as more information has become available. Whereas the first edition profiled boat and ship building through to 1935, this revised edition ends at 1903 in consequence of the twentieth century boat builders of Battery Point being highlighted in a follow up book published by the author in 2017: *Industrious, Innovative, Altruistic: the 20th Century Boat Builders of Battery Point*.

Please note: For historical significance and consistency, the book uses imperial measurements rather than metric. Consistent with the nomenclature of the day, it also refers to Tasmania as Van Diemen's Land up until 31 January 1854, and Hobart as Hobart Town up until 31 December 1880. Intercolonial trade is defined as trade between the various states (once colonies) of Australia; trans-Tasman trade refers to trade between Australia and New Zealand.

View of Sullivans Cove, Hobart Town (1804). Watercolour possibly by G. W. Evans.
Courtesy State Library of New South Wales (SV6B/Sull C/1).

Historical Context

'... but for some time to come a Boat will be the only Vessel I shall have occasion to construct.'

Lieutenant-Governor David Collins (1803).

By necessity the first vessels built at Hobart Town, Van Diemen's Land, following the arrival of Lieutenant-Governor David Collins and his contingent of convicts, marines and free settlers in February 1804, were small purpose-built boats required to convey passengers and cargo across the River Derwent and to outer lying farms and settlements along its reaches. Recognising the need for the building of smaller vessels, Collins had appointed Samuel Gunn to direct Hobart Town's Department of Shipwrights.[1] Though a convict sentenced to seven years transportation for stealing a saddle and bridle, Gunn had served as a shipwright in the Royal Navy and was the only member of Collins' 400+ retinue to arrive in the Derwent with any boat building experience.[2] In a letter to his supervisor, Governor Philip Gidley King of New South Wales, dated 16 December 1803, David Collins stated that he had little need for a shipwright, ' ... *for some time to come a Boat will be the only Vessel I shall have occasion to construct*'.[3]

[1] Historical Records of Australia. Series III. Volume 1.
[2] M. Tipping (1988). *CONVICTS UNBOUND. The Story of the Calcutta Convicts and their Settlement in Australia.*
[3] Historical Records of Australia. Series III. Volume 1.

Hand-drawn map of Hobart Town (c1805) by G. P. Harris, showing buildings and other locations of interest.
Courtesy National Library of Australia (nla.obj-135224422).

Collins' intention to only build smaller vessels was swayed by several factors. First, larger craft being built in Sydney were well-suited to supply provisions and communiqué between his infant colony and New South Wales. Second, his hands were tied by authority. Since Van Diemen's Land was under the jurisdiction of the Government of New South Wales, any vessels intended to be built at Hobart Town had to be approved by Governor King, with King under strict instruction that colonial-built vessels not infringe upon the East India Company's monopoly on trading routes in the Indo-Pacific region. Third, drawing on his experience as deputy judge advocate in the early years of the New South Wales settlement, Lieutenant-Governor Collins was likely concerned about the possibility of illegal trade by members of his party with visiting ships, particularly shrewd free settlers and marines out to make a quick profit. As such, trade between merchant vessels and the populous of Hobart Town was forbidden. Finally, Collins wanted to limit the number of watercraft at Hobart Town to lessen the possibility that they could be used as a means of escape by ambitious convicts.

The restrain and apprehensiveness of Lieutenant-Governor Collins toward the building of new vessels for the River Derwent was also likely an artefact of the population, in its infant years, being constantly on the verge of starvation. Due to its involvement in the Napoleonic wars, England had little time and resources to direct to the establishing colony and, as such, Hobart Town remained somewhat of a neglected child. Still, Collins reiterated his priority for boat building in a letter addressed to his superiors in London dated 6 August 1804 in which he included, in a list of much needed supplies, '*sheet copper, copper bolts and nails, and sail needles*'.[4] Making the most of his lot, Lieutenant-Governor Collins' delicate balancing act between encouraging commerce and industry, securing his convicts, and prohibiting illegal trade, continued throughout his six-year tenure. Combined these factors meant that Samuel Gunn likely spent the colony's early years building a few small boats, and repairing and maintaining what existing craft the settlement possessed.

As the settlement of Hobart Town grew, three men can be identified as providing the impetus for boat and, subsequently, ship building in the region. They were William Collins, Dr Thomas Birch and Captain James Kelly. A late master in the Royal Navy, William Collins arrived in Hobart Town in 1804 as part of David Collins' entourage and immediately set about finding his niche in the developing settlement.[5] Audacity and opportunity saw him quickly appointed to the position of Harbour Master of Hobart Town, with one of his first tasks being to report on the possibility of establishing a local whale fishery.[6] Sensing Hobart Town could play a pivotal role in the South Seas whaling industry, William Collins recommended that a whaling station be established close by.[7]

Following through with his recommendations, in 1806 William Collins built and outfitted a bay whaling station at Ralphs Bay on the south-east shore of the Derwent, approximately seven miles from Hobart Town.[8] Though the station was soon abandoned, likely owing to regulations prohibiting the landing of any cargo at Hobart Town, as well as an embargo on the station's men from visiting Hobart Town, the enterprise not only marked the germination of the colony's involvement in the industry, but also encompassed the building of several smaller whaleboats for its operation.[9]

The growth of Hobart Town's water-based industries, including boat and ship building, however, remained stagnant in the succeeding years. The

[4] *The Mercury*, 6 August, 2004.
[5] M. Tipping (1988). *CONVICTS UNBOUND. The Story of the Calcutta Convicts and their Settlement in Australia*.
[6] J. F. Philp (1936). *Whaling Ways of Hobart Town*; J. B. Walker (1950). *Early Tasmania: The Walker Memorial Volume*.
[7] J. E. Philp (1936). *Whaling Ways of Hobart Town*.
[8] J. E. Philp (1936). *Whaling Ways of Hobart Town*.
[9] K. M. Bowden (1964). *Captain James Kelly of Hobart Town*.

Lieutenant-Governor David Collins (1756 - 1810).
Courtesy Allport Library and Museum of Fine Arts, State Library of Tasmania (AUTAS001125646778w800).

prohibition of trade by merchant vessels, restrictions related to the building of both small and large craft, and the untimely death of Lieutenant-Governor David Collins, were just three of several presiding factors.[10]

In 1812, eight years after Hobart Town's founding, restrictions on the building of larger vessels were finally lessened, though government permission was still required for the building of boats in excess of 14 feet (ft) on the keel.[11] The first vessel of any significance built at Hobart Town was the 40-ton schooner *Henrietta Packet*, launched in late 1812 to the order of Dr Thomas Birch, a prominent merchant who had arrived in Hobart Town in 1808 as medical officer on board the whaler *Dubuc*.[12] The next vessel built at Hobart Town was the *Campbell Macquarie*, a brig of 133 tons constructed by Samuel Gunn for R. W. Loane, local merchant, and launched in January 1813.[13] Both vessels were immediately engaged in intercolonial trade; their success a direct result of the easing of regulations prohibiting the discharge of cargo at minor Australian ports in 1813.[14]

Expanding his involvement in intercolonial trade, Dr Thomas Birch next purchased the brig *Sophia*.[15] With Captain James Kelly at its helm, the *Sophia* was not only instrumental in conveying cargo and passengers between Hobart Town and New South Wales, but was also one of the first local vessels to be successfully employed in the whaling industry; an industry from which the population of Hobart Town would generate much success, and consequently wealth, in the decades to come.

The 1820s saw the settlement of Hobart Town (and Van Diemen's Land, generally) mature, with commerce and industry spurred by the increasing availability of convict labour. Free settlers began arriving to take advantage of vast expanses of land made accessible for farming and the cultivation of wheat and wool began. The era also saw the building of a few more larger vessels, primarily for employment in developing local and intercolonial trades, and the newly established whaling industry.

Apart from a government shipyard established in 1824 at Macquarie Harbour on Van Diemen's Land's remote west coast, boat and ship building during this period was still quite informal. Besides a hub of activity related to boat building at the Hobart Town wharf, there was no concentrated or private shipbuilding locus in the colony. Compounded by the need for long lengths

[10] J. B. Walker (1950). *Early Tasmania: The Walker Memorial Volume*.
[11] *Historical Records of Australia*. Series III. Volume 1.
[12] adb.anu.edu.au/biography/birch-thomas-william-1782; *The Sydney Gazette and New South Wales Advertiser*, 31 October 1812.
[13] W. Lawson and the Shiplovers' Society of Tasmania (1949). *Blue Gum Clippers and Whale Ships of Tasmania*.
[14] K. M. Bowden (1964). *Captain James Kelly of Hobart Town*; en.wikipedia.org/wiki/Young_Lachlan.
[15] K. M. Bowden (1964). *Captain James Kelly of Hobart Town*.

Painting of Sullivans Cove, Hobart Town looking over at the Old Wharf (1829).
Courtesy Tasmanian Archives (NS1013/1/1635).

of timber to form the keel, instead many vessels were built in an *ad hoc* manner along various pockets of the River Derwent's shoreline and connecting waterways, including at Austins Ferry, at Browns River (now Kingston), at North West Bay, and at Canadian Point (now Rosny). Taking advantage of growing demand, industrious settlers also began importing smaller vessels from England and subsequently advertising them for sale. Many of these craft were advertised as '*English-built*', suggesting that they enjoyed a reputation superior to locally built vessels. With regular trade now established between the two countries, the importation of smaller boats from England likely also proved cost-effective.

The early 1830s saw the formality of Hobart Town's boat and ship building industry starting to take shape. Several vessels were built around the 'Old Wharf' area, now Hunter Street. These included the schooner *Contest*, launched in April 1828 to the order of Thomas Lucas and intended for bay whaling; the cutter *Industry*, completed in April 1829 for William Young and Bernard Walford and also intended for bay whaling; a sloop of about 50 tons named *Tasmanian Lass*, launched in May 1830 and built for the same partnership's bay whaling activities; and the 28-ton schooner *Maria*, launched in 1831.[16,]

However, the construction of warehouses for merchants and the establishment of commercial businesses in this area, as well as the proposed development of a 'New Wharf' along the current location of Salamanca Place, led Hobart Town's boat and ship builders to look further afield for suitable shoreline to establish their businesses. It was likely the proposed New Wharf development, and the close proximity of Battery Point to this area, that led enterprising builders to consider Battery Point. Opportune was the sale of several waterfront allotments during this time in the locale. Battery Point's shoreline was also conducive to boat and ship building: the site was reasonably sheltered, the water was of adequate depth for vessels, and the ground provided enough space for the housing of stocks and other infrastructure.

The narrative that this 170-acre envelope of land has to tell is now unparalleled. Since 1830 boat and ship builders have plied their trade on the edge of this slight suburb of Hobart, in the nineteenth century alone producing upwards of 720 vessels.

[16] *The Tasmanian*, 18 April, 9 May 1828; *The Hobart Town Courier*, 25 April 1829; *Colonial Times*, 19 March 1830; *The Tasmanian*, 28 May 1830; *The Hobart Town Courier*, 29 May 1830, 24 September 1831; G. Broxam & M. Nash (2012). *Tasmanian Shipwrecks. Volume 1: 1797-1899*.

Painting of Hobart Town from the Old Wharf looking towards the New Wharf (c1839). Courtesy State Library of Victoria (H22568).

Battery Point

'... the story of the Battery Point slips appears as a rapidly changing kaleidoscope of men and ships. Names come and go, slips move from place to place, boats are launched and sail out of the story...'

Amy Rowntree (1968).

Since its establishment in the early years of Hobart Town's development, Battery Point has been an eclectic neighbourhood — a melting pot of industry and commercial activities peppered with grand houses, villas and working class cottages. Predominantly lower-to-middle class for most of its existence, in recent decades Battery Point has become a highly sought after suburb, popular for its historical charm, quaintness and walking distance to Hobart. However, situated along part of its shore are the boat and ship building yards that, though today lie somewhat dormant with only a few slips in operation, can claim a history rich with commercial industry, entrepreneurism, competitiveness and camaraderie.

For many thousands of years the traditional owners and custodians of nipulana (Hobart), the Mouheneener band of the South East Nation of Tasmanian Aborigines utilised the land now known as Battery Point, including its headlands and beaches. Following European settlement in 1804, the Revered Robert Knopwood first moved into the area, on 1 January 1806 receiving a land grant of 30 acres upon which he built his home Cottage Green on the site's north-west corner, spending £1,000 on its construction, as well as other improvements.[17] His grant bordered the burial ground (St David's Park) and extended to the shoreline along Sullivans Cove, with an allowance made for later construction of a roadway. The property encompassed much of present-day Salamanca. Owing to financial difficulties, in March 1816 Knopwood sold 25 acres of the 30-acre parcel to Captain William Townsend Jones, including Cottage Green, its buildings, gardens and fruit trees, for the hefty sum of £2,000. The transaction was on the proviso that £1,000 be paid up front and the other £1,000 a year later.[18] Jones also took immediate possession of the remaining five acres as a separate transaction.[19]

The bulk of Battery Point, however, remained largely undisturbed until 1818 when a 90-acre land grant was given to William Sorell, the colony's newly-arrived Lieutenant-Governor.[20] A small portion of land located at the southern point of the harbour had also been cordoned off by the Crown for use as a battery which was in use early in the settlement's founding.

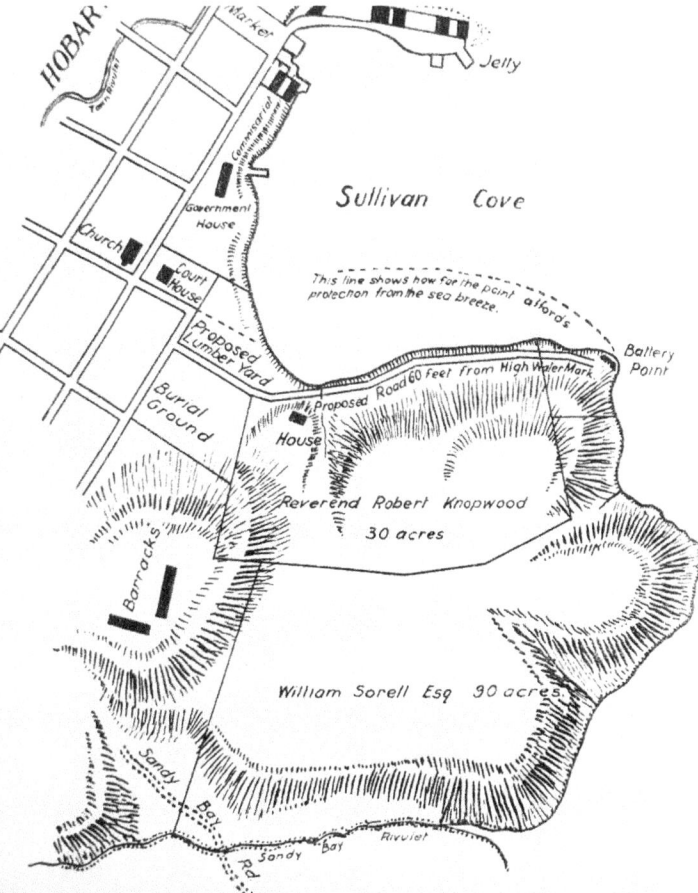

Map of Sullivans Cove, showing land grants given to Knopwood and Sorell (c1826). Courtesy A. Rowntree (1968). *Battery Point Today and Yesterday*.

---

[17] W. H. Hudspeth (1945). *Note on Cottage Green*.
[18] *The Sydney Gazette and New South Wales Advertiser*, 7 April 1821.
[19] *The Sydney Gazette and New South Wales Advertiser*, 7 April 1821.
[20] adb.anu.edu.au/biography/sorell-william-2680; A. Rowntree (1968). *Battery Point Today and Yesterday*.

Early sketch of Sullivans Cove, Hobart Town (c1810), showing location of Cottage Green and the battery (later Mulgrave Battery). Courtesy Tasmanian Archives (AF394/1/170).

In July 1818, by command of Lieutenant-Governor Sorell, the Mulgrave Battery was officially named in honour of the Earl of Mulgrave.[21] Up until this point in time, the location had been coined 'Knopwood's Point' by the European settlers.[22] Works were then under construction, including a guard house and home for the signalman. Guns located on a platform at Government House were to be removed to Mulgrave Battery as soon as the site was ready.[23]

In May 1820 the five-acre allotment Captain Jones had purchased four years prior from Reverend Knopwood, situated between the latter's property and the Mulgrave Battery, was advertised for sale as part Jones' deceased estate.[24] The parcel was purchased by Robert Carns who cautioned those from taking stones from the property for use as ballast.[25] That same year Lieutenant-Governor Sorell issued regulations stipulating that special permission was required to land boats between the Mulgrave Battery and Sandy Bay Creek.[26]

In March 1821 Knopwood's financial problems continued and he was bordering on insolvency. The administrator's of Captain Jones' estate were also unable to meet the final payment of £1,000 owed for Cottage Green.[27] Knopwood appears to have avoided immediately having to vacate the property in order to salvage his fortune, however in October 1823 the inevitable occurred with the local press publishing that the, '... *valuable property at Cottage Green, so eligibly situate for merchants' residences, store-houses, &c,*' was to be auctioned.[28] Failing to sell, the land was subsequently re-surveyed and in March of the following year an advertisement in the press stated that up to 20 lots, part of the Cottage Green property, were advertised for sale on behalf of J. T. Collicott, auctioneer.[29] The purchasers appear to have been predominately merchants, namely James Grant, Captain Andrew Haig, Mr Hamilton, Captain Kelly and G. F. Reid.[30] While Knopwood managed to retain ownership of a smaller allotment that included and surrounded the site of his home Cottage Green, the property itself was advertised for sale by the Sheriff's Office in December 1828.[31] The eight-acre site was purchased by Henry Jennings for £710 (he was later found to be somewhat nefariously acting as agent

---

[21] *The Hobart Town Gazette and Southern Reporter*, 1 August 1818.
[22] *The Van Diemen's Land Gazette and General Advertiser*, 18 June 1814.
[23] *The Hobart Town Gazette and Southern Reporter*, 18 July 1818.
[24] *The Hobart Town Gazette and Southern Reporter*, 20 May 1820.
[25] *Hobart Town Gazette and Van Diemen's Land Advertiser*, 5 May 1821; 12 August 1825.
[26] *The Hobart Town Gazette and Southern Reporter*, 21 October 1820.
[27] *Hobart Town Gazette and Van Diemen's Land Advertiser*, 17 March 1821.
[28] *Hobart Town Gazette and Van Diemen's Land Advertiser*, 11 October 1823.
[29] *Hobart Town Gazette and Van Diemen's Land Advertiser*, 5 March 1824.
[30] Libraries Tasmania (NS1013/1/1794).
[31] *The Hobart Town Gazette*, 13 December 1828.

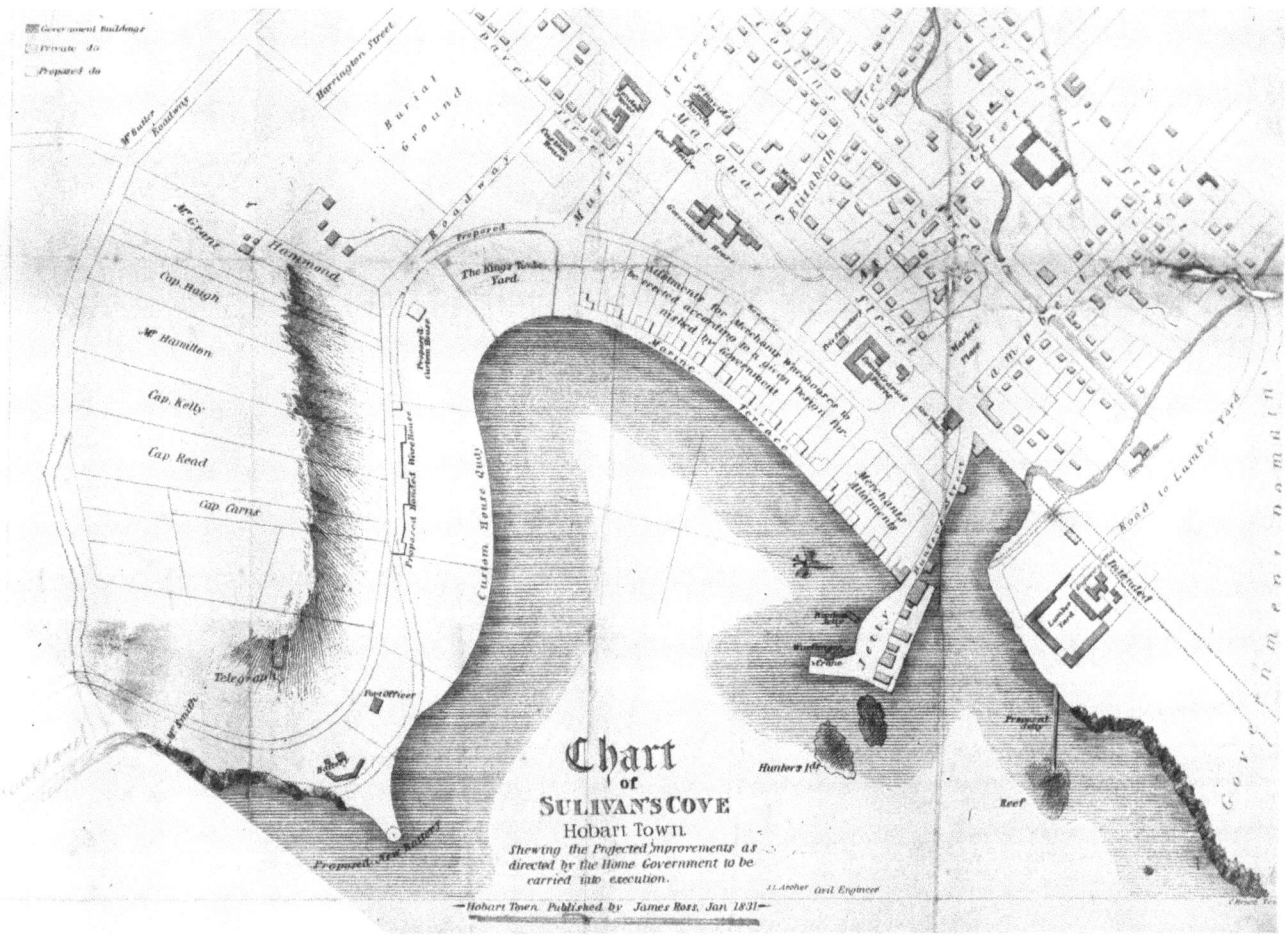

Map of Sullivans Cove, Hobart Town (1831).
Courtesy Tasmanian Archives (NS1013/1/1794).

for Van Diemen's Land's then Lieutenant-Governor, George Arthur, with Knopwood relocating across the River Derwent to Clarence Plains.[32] It was the start of a period of immense redevelopment and subsequent subdivision of Battery Point into smaller and smaller allotments, mainly at the hands of commercial and mercantile interests, primarily those associated with trade and shipping.

This boon was in part due to a survey of the harbour undertaken in mid-1825 which revealed a good depth of water along the eastern side of Sullivans Cove as well as the sheltered south side of the Mulgrave Battery.[33] The survey inspired the proprietors of nearby properties to offer to the government a portion of their land for construction of a road 60ft in width.[34] The road was to travel along the front of Cottage Green to the Mulgrave Battery and was deemed of valuable use should the government propose to construct a public wharf in the vicinity, as well as for ships sheltering in the basin by Mulgrave Battery. Expanded to travel from Davey Street, across Cottage Green to the Battery, the road was well underway in June 1826 with convict gangs noted to be employed on the project.[35] Several months later, a road from Browns River, a small settlement located on the edge of the River Derwent some 10 miles to the south, to the Mulgrave Battery was also under construction.[36]

With all of this development came further subdivision of Knopwood and Sorell's original parcels of land. As stated, part of the former's property was divided into allotments suitable for building mercantile stores in association with the New Wharf. With the proposed construction of this shipping precinct, parcels within Knopwood's old land grant suddenly jumped ten times in value in 1832, much to his chagrin.[37]

Meanwhile, during the period 1818 to 1824, there had been little activity or development associated with William Sorell's 90-acre land grant at Battery Point. Upon the Lieutenant-Governor's recall back to England in 1823 he had attempted to sell the property but failed to find a buyer. Instead, the parcel was transferred to William Kermode, a recently-arrived English merchant, apparently in lieu of monies owed, with Kermode cautioning persons from taking loam or stones from his land adjoining the Mulgrave Battery and the Military Barracks in February 1824.[38] Two years later, the entire

[32] *Colonial Times*, 16 January 1829.
[33] *The Hobart Town Gazette*, 10 September 1825.
[34] *The Hobart Town Gazette*, 15 October 1825.
[35] *The Hobart Town Gazette*, 11 February, 24 June 1826.
[36] *The Hobart Town Gazette*, 19 August 1826.
[37] *The Colonist and Van Diemen's Land Commercial and Agricultural Advertiser*, 7 December 1832.
[38] *The Hobart Town Gazette and Van Diemen's Land Advertiser*, 20 February 1824; Rowntree A (1968).

Painting of Hobart Town and Sullivans Cove, showing Mulgrave Battery, by Edward Duncan (1830).
Courtesy State Library of Victoria (H31992).

portion was advertised for lease, its suitability for use as a dairy touted for potential lessees.[39] In November 1828 Kermode opted to subdivide the land, with building allotments between one and 20 acres offered for sale.[40] Indicating the lack of desirability of the area, or perhaps the state of the local economy, only some of the parcels sold. The bulk of what we now know as the suburb of Battery Point would remain in the possession of the Kermode family for several more decades.

Of Kermode's allotments that did sell, the initial purchasers included Messrs Horne, Butler, George Frankland, Clarke, Reid and Mason, as well as Lieutenant-Governor George Arthur.[41] Thomas Horne's parcels, comprising 20 acres in total and purchased in September 1830, included the area that would later become the boat and ship building yards located between Napoleon Street and the shore of the River Derwent.[42] Another site used for commercial boat and ship building operations was located at the bottom of present-day Finlay Street adjacent to the Mulgrave Battery. This stretch of shoreline, made up of two separate allotments, was purchased by Stephen Adey and Thomas Smith, respectively in 1830 and 1831.[43]

In the succeeding years, more allotments at Battery Point were advertised for sale with further subdivision occurring amongst the original and subsequent property owners such that within a few decades all that remained were small building sites. More roads were constructed, parsing through the developing suburb, connecting Battery Point to Hobart Town and the New Wharf area, as well as to Sandy Bay and beyond.

Construction of a pier forming the New Wharf, extending from Sullivan's Cove to the Mulgrave Battery began in July 1830.[44] This ambitious project further enhanced Battery Point's appeal to merchants and shipowners. The wharf was first noted to be in use in April 1831.[45]

It was in this context that Battery Point's first commercial boat builder established himself in 1830. Newly-arrived Irish immigrant Daniel Callaghan set up a small operation on Thomas Smith's property near the Mulgrave Battery.

The following chapters detail the next 70 years of boat and ship building at Battery Point: the men and the vessels they built, beginning in 1830. The chapters are presented in chronological order, starting with Daniel Callaghan, who launched two sailing boats from Battery Point in early 1831. Included at the end of each chapter is a table summarising the vessels known to have been built at Battery Point during the nineteenth century by each builder.

---

[39] *Colonial Times and Tasmanian Advertiser*, 10 February 1826.
[40] *The Hobart Town Courier*, 1 November 1828.
[41] Libraries Tasmania (AUTAS001136187713).
[42] www.thelist.tas.gov.au (Historical Deed 01/0714).
[43] www.thelist.tas.gov.au (Historical Deeds 01/0852 and 03/2832).
[44] *The Hobart Town Courier*, 3 July 1830.
[45] *The Hobart Town Courier*, 9 April 1831.

Map of Battery Point and Sullivans Cove (c1830s).
Courtesy W L Crowther Library, State Library of Tasmania (AUTAS001136187713).

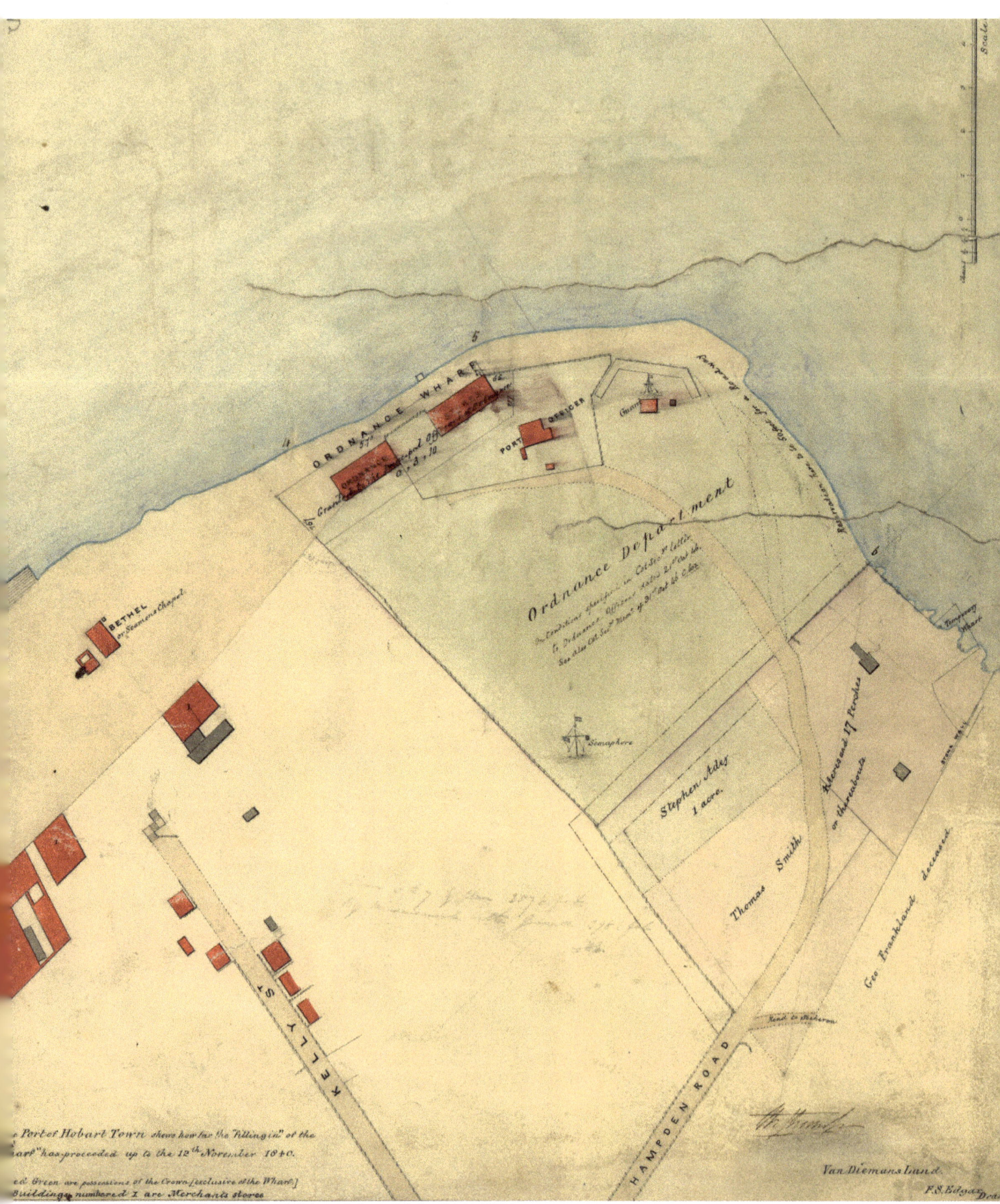

Map of the New Wharf (Salamanca), Mulgrave Battery and Battery Point (c1840s).
Courtesy Tasmanian Archives (AF394/1/171).

Daniel Callaghan

'... intends to commence Ship and Whale-boat building, in all its branches.'
Colonial Times, 19 February 1830.

Having left Cork, Ireland, in July 1829, Daniel Callaghan, sometimes rendered as O'Callaghan or Callahan, and his wife Mary arrived in Hobart Town on board the ship *Medway* on 16 February of the following year.[46] Obviously keen to establish his business, three days later an advertisement in the *Colonial Times* was published stating that Callaghan intended to 'commence ship and whale boat building in all its branches'.[47] The same advertisement was carried by *The Hobart Town Courier* the following day, and repeated over several weeks in other publications, on one such occasion with Callaghan calling for an apprentice.[48]

> **To Merchants, Whalers, and others.**
> DANIEL CALLAGHAN begs leave to announce to the Public of Hobart Town, his arrival by the Medway in this Colony, where he intends to commence Ship and Whale-boat building, in all its branches. His references will be found most satisfactory as to properly and capability.—Apply at the Derwent Distillery.
> February 19, 1830.

Colonial Times, 19 February 1830.

Callaghan provided his place of contact as the Derwent Distillery. This business, located on Hobart Town's rivulet off Macquarie Street, likely in the vicinity of the bottom of current-day Gore Street, had been taken over by James Hackett, Callaghan's cousin on his maternal side, in early 1829.[49]

Hackett and his wife Maria (nee Donovan) had arrived in Hobart Town from Ireland by the brig *Coronet* in October 1828.[50] Hackett had been born in 1800, some three years after Callaghan. While Hackett's father had originally been involved in tanning, in 1825, he along with his four sons (Bartholomew, William, Dominck and James), had established a distillery at Midleton near Cork.[51] The family's upward trajectory saw them embrace society, mingle in politics, support the Catholic Church and encourage innovation and education. For James Hackett, in particular, a keen interest in emerging technologies during the mid-1820s saw him become a member of the Cork Mechanics' Institute where he was noted as constructing and presenting a *'beautiful steam engine'* for a future lecture on mechanics.[52]

While the distilling business had bode well for the Hackett family initially, they appear to have invested too heavily in a short space of time, becoming burdened by debt. James Hackett's relocation to Van Diemen's Land may have been because of the family's financial constraints. The Irish liquor industry was also being hindered by the increasingly vocal temperance movement, as well as regulatory pressure and political interference.

The production of liquor and spirits, however, must have proved a more worthwhile exercise for James Hackett in Hobart Town as in June 1829 the *Colonial Times* praised him not only for his industry and wealth, but also for the purchase of 200 head of fat oxen which were to be butchered and then exported back to Ireland.[53] The following month Hackett was congratulated in the local press for the quality of his clove, cinnamon and peppermint cordials.[54] He also joined Hobart Town's intellectual class. Later in 1829, for example, Hackett gave a lecture on the steam engine to members of the Mechanics' Institution.[55] Those in attendance included Lieutenant-Governor George Arthur and his wife, as well as other esteemed members of Hobart Town's society.[56] The lecture discussed the construction of the barometer and the principle of atmospheric pressure by experimentation.

---

[46] *Colonial Times*, 19 February 1830.
[47] *Colonial Times*, 19 February 1830.
[48] *The Hobart Town Courier*, 20 February 1830; *The Tasmanian*, 5 March 1830.
[49] *Colonial Times*, 9 January 1829.
[50] *The Tasmanian*, 10 October 1828; *Colonial Times*, 9 January 1829.
[51] Ireland, Catholic Parish Registers, 1655-1915. National Library of Ireland, Dublin, Microfilm 04778/02; *The Constitution or Cork Advertiser*, 12 January 1858.
[52] *Southern Reporter and Cork Commercial Courier*, 1 October 1825.
[53] *Colonial Times*, 19 June 1829.
[54] *The Hobart Town Courier*, 11 July 1829.
[55] *The Hobart Town Courier*, 14 November 1829.
[56] *The Hobart Town Courier*, 14 November 1829.

Moulins a ble dans les environs d'Hobart-Town, Van-Diemen.
A lithograph by artist Louis Auguste de Sainson showing the Hobart Town Rivulet/Gore Street location and the site of Hackett's Distillery (c1833).
Courtesy Allport Library and Museum of Fine Arts, State Library of Tasmania (SD_ILS:608938).

The year closed with Hackett being elected a director of the Derwent Bank, though he resigned a few months later, coinciding with his appointment as an auditor of the Mechanics' Institution.[57]

With James Hackett enjoying the opportunities afforded by his relocation to Van Diemen's Land, Callaghan, upon his own arrival in Hobart Town, would have found himself greatly advantaged by Hackett's well-resourced and influential network. There was also a new family member to meet, with Callaghan and his wife Mary serving as witnesses to the christening of Hackett's son Bartholomew on 25 April 1830.[58]

Both Daniel Callaghan and his cousin James Hackett, as well as their respective wives, hailed from Passage West, Ireland, a port town located on the west bank of Cork Harbour some six miles south-east of Cork's city centre. It was predominantly a working class area, populated by small tenant farmers and those associated with maritime trades. Callaghan was the oldest of at least three children, all boys, born to Michael and Catharine Callaghan (nee Hackett) and was baptised on 31 July 1797.[59] While his father remained a tenant farmer of Carrigaline West, Callaghan had spent his late teens and early 20s learning the craft of shipbuilding, likely with the support and encouragement of the Hackett family.[60] Though improvements in vessel design and construction, and steam propulsion, as well as the implementation of new tools and technologies, such as patent slips, were beginning to filter through the shipbuilding industry in Cork, the local economy was in a general state of decline leading into the late 1820s, in part the result of free trade with the more industralised nation of England reducing demand for Irish exports; a situation likely bolstering Callaghan's decision to search for work further afield.[61] Belfast was also quickly overtaking Cork as the centre for Irish shipbuilding, with ship and boat building ultimately giving way to repair work as the decades wore on.

On a personal level, Callaghan married Mary Ryan in Cork, likely in the months leading up to their departure. As free immigrants the couple set sail for Australia in mid-1829, brimming with a sense of optimism and the hope of new opportunities. It was to be an interesting decision the pair made to start a new life in Australia. History reveals that Callaghan's trajectory may have been set on a completely different course had he stayed in Ireland.

Besides being involved in the tanning and distilling industries in and around Cork, the Hackett family soon became involved in local politics, helped in part by their expanding resources and business connections. Capitalising on this affluence, Callaghan's younger brother Eugene went on to become an extremely successful and wealthy businessman in the nearby county of Limerick, operating a tannery and shoe-making business that was still in existence well into the twentieth century. In 1864 he was elected Mayor

---

[57] *Colonial Times*, 4 December 1829, 26 March 1830; *The Hobart Town Courier*, 27 March 1830.
[58] Libraries Tasmania (RGD21/1/1 no. 3486).
[59] Ireland Roman Catholic Parish Baptisms, Passage West Parish (1797, 1799); *Evening News*, 2 September 1882.
[60] Ireland, Valuation Office Books, 1831-1856 (Cork, Carrigaline West).
[61] *Cork Constitution*, 2 December 1828.

of Limerick.⁶² The well-respected family, now referred to as O'Callaghan, would play an important role in Limerick and its politics for generations to come.

Daniel Callaghan was also a cousin of Sir William Bartholomew Hackett (1800 - 1872), a merchant of Cork who became the largest manufacturer of leather in Ireland.⁶³ He served as the Mayor of Cork and was knighted in 1852. Another relation was Sir William Hackett (1824 - 1877), barrister-at-law who died at Colombo of cholera while serving as the Chief Justice of Ceylon. He had been knighted in 1866 and had previously held the position of Chief Justice of Fiji.

Advertisement for Eugene O'Callaghan's business.
Source: H. Oram (2010). *Bygone Limerick: The City and County in Days Gone By*.

Following in these familial entrepreneurial footsteps and those of his cousin James Hackett, then living at Hobart Town, and likely buoyed by the latter's resources and connections, Callaghan soon established a boat building business at Battery Point. The yard was in the vicinity of current-day Finlay Street, near the Mulgrave Battery and in close proximity to the developing New Wharf area. It was very likely located on property then owned by Thomas Smith.

From its founding, the construction and repair of whaleboats and other smaller vessels would have occupied the bulk of Callaghan's time at his Battery Point yard. The early 1830s saw Hobart Town fast becoming a hub for whaling vessels en route to the southern seas. Several of the town's more prominent merchants had also joined the industry, commissioning or purchasing ships, barques, brigs and other large vessels to enter the trade. All required a complement of whaleboats, usually between four and six craft per vessel; all of these boats additionally required fitting out and repair.

Another outlet for Callaghan's expertise was local sailing races. The 1831 Hobart Town Regatta, held in late February of that year and one of the first well-organised regattas to take place on the River Derwent, saw two sailing boats built by Callaghan compete amongst a fleet of eleven. These were the *Helena* and *Tri-Color* which finished second and third, respectively. The press noted that, '... *Mr. Callaghan, the industrious ship-builder, of the Battery Point, was so successful in the first operations of his vocation as to build two of three winning boats at the late "Regatta" ... thus showing that in Van Diemen's Land, ability and industry will always receive every possible encouragement*'.⁶⁴

Capitalising on this success, Callaghan was asked by the organiser of a follow-up regatta, Lieutenant Hill of the Royal Navy, who at the time was working as Hobart Town's port officer, to build a sailing boat to be awarded to the race winner.⁶⁵ Dubbed *The Prize*, the vessel measured 24ft overall with a beam of 7ft 4in, was valued at just under £100 and took a little over two months to complete.⁶⁶ Notably referred to as the '*Grand Regatta*', the event was held on the River Derwent on 22 August 1831 with 14 competitors, all in craft under 30ft in length, paying the £1 1s entry fee.⁶⁷ After a challenging race, the first vessel across the line was *The Wave*, owned by Peter Buchanan.⁶⁸ He was subsequently rewarded with *The Prize*, while the second and third place-getters received considerable monetary-based purses.

Continuing to build his business, Daniel Callaghan advertised for two apprentices throughout April and May 1831.⁶⁹ Just over six months later, on 5 January 1832, a large boat was launched from his Battery Point yard.⁷⁰ Stated to be '*one of the finest modelled craft that ever was built in Van Diemen's Land*', the 28-ton schooner *Charlotte* was built to the order of Samuel Henry Thomas specifically to trade between Oyster Bay, Maria Island and Spring Bay on Van Diemen's Land's east coast.⁷¹

The 1832 Hobart Town Regatta, convened in late February of that year, saw a six-oared galley boat built by Callaghan to the order of Captain Dance featured in the pulling race, manned by personnel from HMS *Sulphur*. The race was held over a distance of six miles with Captain Dance's boat finishing a credible third despite the disadvantage of only being launched that day.⁷² The same disadvantage befell a four-

---

⁶² *Limerick Reporter*, 1 December 1863.
⁶³ F. Boase (2018). *Modern English Biography (volume 1 of 4), A - H*.
⁶⁴ *The Tasmanian*, 4 March 1831.
⁶⁵ *The Tasmanian*, 4 March 1831.
⁶⁶ *The Tasmanian*, 11 March, 11 June 1831; *Colonial Times*, 22 June, 17 August 1831.
⁶⁷ *The Tasmanian*, 20 August 1831.
⁶⁸ *The Tasmanian*, 3 September 1831.
⁶⁹ *The Tasmanian*, 29 April, 14 May 1831.
⁷⁰ *Colonial Times*, 4 January 1832.
⁷¹ *Colonial Times*, 4 January 1832; *The Hobart Town Courier*, 28 January 1832.
⁷² *The Tasmanian*, 25 February 1832.

oared gig which Callaghan had built to the order of a Mr Melville. Manned by a team of whalers, this particular craft finished the race in third though was elevated to first as the winner and second placed vessel did not comply with the race rule that all of the boats 'should be either Colonial built or Colonial property'.[73]

In April 1832 Callaghan was stated to be building a four-oared gig for the express purpose of competing in a pulling match against the celebrated boat *Auriga*. The race was to be worth fifty sovereigns, a significant sum for the time.[74] Callaghan, however, could have used the prize purse himself as he was likely suffering financial duress owing to lack of payment from Samuel Henry Thomas associated with the newly completed schooner *Charlotte*. The vessel was first advertised for sale by auction in late April.[75]

SALE BY AUCTION,
BY MR. ELLISTON,
At his Mart in Argyle street, on Thursday the 17th day of May :—
If not previously disposed of by Private Contract.

THAT beautiful little schooner the CHARLOTTE, burthen 28 tons, measurement and equal to cant the largest whale; she is allowed to be one of the fastest sailing vessels in the port, built by Mr. D. Callaghan, and is completely found.

TERMS :—Approved Bills, at 4, 8, and 12 months.

Application to Mr. Elliston, Auctioneer, or to Mr. Pinker, Elizabeth street.

The Hobart Town Courier, 28 April 1832.

The *Charlotte* failed to sell and Callaghan remained unpaid. More than a year then passed with the vessel unused. Still failing to make payment, in August 1833 Samuel Henry Thomas was sued by his creditors in the Hobart Town Supreme Court. Callaghan was listed as one of seven men owed substantial amounts of money, predominately in default of mortgage payments made on property.[76] The *Charlotte* was advertised for sale by the Sheriff's Office a few weeks.[77] Some agreement for its purchase appears to have then been made for the craft was noted as loading for Swanport in late September under the command of Captain Henry Matthison.[78] The vessel would remain on this route for several years, also making at least three trips to New Zealand in 1834, a trade partnership then in its infancy.[79] In August of that year, for example, the *Charlotte* returned to Hobart Town from New Zealand with four passengers and a cargo of pork, potatoes and flax.[80]

The colourful history of the small schooner *Charlotte* continued for a number of years. By January 1836 the vessel was in the possession of local innkeeper John H. Thompson who, owing to debts that he was unable to pay, took it upon himself to flee Hobart Town in the vessel loaded with provisions and cargo. His creditors, collectively owed several thousands of pounds, upon learning of the *Charlotte*'s stealth departure '*occasioned a lively sensation throughout town*', ultimately ending with the issuance of a sheriff's writ.[81] Two bailiffs then proceeded down the River Derwent in the *Eliza* in pursuit of the craft and its wanton owner. Fortunately, the *Charlotte* was found at anchor in Safety Cove and its owner agreed to sail the vessel back to Hobart Town to face the wrath.[82] The *Charlotte* was advertised for sale in Hobart Town the following month.[83] The craft subsequently disappears from the records, though may have been the vessel advertised for sale at Hobart Town in October 1843 that, two years later, was involved in the Pittwater trade under ownership of J. Chipman.[84]

Despite the uncertainty of payment for construction of the *Charlotte*, Callaghan continued to eke out a living at his Battery Point boat building enterprise. During this period James Callaghan, likely a cousin who had recently immigrated from Ireland, also joined the enterprise; the duo operating as 'Messrs Callaghan'.[85] In May 1832 the pair were noted as assembling and planking a steam boat of 65ft to the order of Dr Alexander Thompson, a Scottish medical practitioner who had only recently arrived in Hobart Town after making several trips on board convict transports to the colony in the 1820s.[86] The vessel's machinery had been imported from England and once complete, it was the intention of Dr Thompson to employ the vessel between Kangaroo Point and the New Wharf.[87] Named *Governor Arthur*, the steam boat was launched on 12 June 1832 to the enthusiasm of a large concourse of spectators.[88]

The speculation of a steam-powered vessel by Dr Thompson came at great risk and expense, however. The development of steam-propelled craft was only in its infancy. Not dissimilar, the world's first public steam railway had only opened a few years before. The technology used to propel the *Governor Arthur* was akin to a rudimentary paddle steamer. Impressively, the vessel's maiden voyage, which took place on 10 September 1832, saw the craft travel the three mile distance across the Derwent from Hobart Town to Kangaroo Point in a matter of 12 minutes.[89] Internally,

---

[73] *The Tasmanian*, 25 February 1832.
[74] *Colonial Times*, 11 April 1832.
[75] *The Hobart Town Courier*, 28 April 1832.
[76] *The Hobart Town Courier*, 9 August, 6 September 1833.
[77] *The Hobart Town Courier*, 6 September 1833.
[78] *The Tasmania*, 27 September 1833; *Colonial Times*, 1 October 1833.
[79] *Colonial Times*, 25 March 1834.
[80] *The Hobart Town Courier*, 8 August 1834.
[81] *Bent's News and Tasmanian Three-Penny Register*, 9 January 1836.
[82] *Bent's News and Tasmanian Three-Penny Register*, 9 January 1836.
[83] *The Courier*, 20 October 1843; *Colonial Times*, 2 February 1836.
[84] *Colonial Times*, 17 May 1845.
[85] *Colonial Times*, 9 May 1832.
[86] *Colonial Times*, 9 May 1832; adb.anu.edu.au/biography/thomson-alexander-2731.
[87] *Colonial Times*, 9 May 1832.
[88] *Hobart Town Courier*, 15 June 1832.
[89] *The Hobart Town Courier*, 14 September 1832.

there was much to report on too. The cabin was stated to be *'very commodious, with seats all around, and females may now cross with the greatest safety and comfort, free from the presence and rough language of ruder passengers, a desideratum long and much felt on this now much frequented ferry'*[90].

Remarkably, the *Governor Arthur* represented the second steam vessel to service the River Derwent. The 58ft steamer *Surprise*, which had been built in Sydney by R. Millard and launched in April 1831, had been relocated to Hobart Town in February 1832 after being purchased by Dr Thompson.[91] Notably the first steam boat launched in Australia, the *Surprise* was placed on the Kangaroo Point to Hobart Town ferry service, becoming a pioneer of the route even after being sold by Dr Thompson in 1833.[92]

Unfortunately there was little need for two vessels to traverse the River Derwent and the enterprise was short-lived. Dr Thompson transferred the *Governor Arthur* to the River Tamar in June 1833 where he and his family had elected to settle.[93] This relocation, however, proved only temporary with the vessel returned to the River Derwent. In March 1835 it was notably involved in recovery efforts associated with the wreck of the convict ship *George III*. Still one of Tasmania's worst maritime disasters, resulting in the loss of 134 lives, mostly convicts held below deck, the vessel had come to grief on submerged rock near Southport while attempting to navigate the D'Entrecasteaux Channel between Bruny Island and the colony's mainland.[94]

The *Governor Arthur* would later be transferred to Melbourne where, in 1847-48, it was converted to a schooner and involved in the coastal trade. Following, it went to New Zealand. The craft was ultimately broken up at Port Chalmers with its register closed in 1872.

With the construction and fitting of the *Governor Arthur*'s machinery complete, nearly six months passed before another vessel built by Messrs Callaghan of Battery Point was launched. This was the 35ft cutter *Emerald*. Built on speculation, the craft was advertised for sale between May and October 1833.[95] A sailing boat was next launched and first noted on the River Derwent in August of that year. Witnesses of the craft's performance were noted to be '*astonished*' at its speed. The press stated, '*We should much like to see her sail against the Fox, belonging to the Derwent Yacht Club*'.[96]

[90] *The Hobart Town Courier*, 14 September 1832.
[91] *The Sydney Monitor*, 2 April 1831; *Colonial Times*, 15, 22 February 1832.
[92] *The Sydney Monitor*, 2 April 1831; *Colonial Times*, 15, 22 February 1832, 19 February 1833.
[93] *Colonial Times*, 4 June 1833.
[94] en.wikipedia.org/wiki/George_III_(ship).
[95] *Colonial Times*, 21 May, 18 June 1833.
[96] *Colonial Times*, 13 August 1833.

Governor Arthur Registration Papers.
Register of British Ships: Main register prior to Merchant Shipping Act 1854, Port Melbourne (1839 - 1855), National Archives of Australia.

Regrettably, this time period coincided with Daniel Callaghan's law suit against Samuel Henry Thomas for payment associated with construction of the schooner *Charlotte*. He was very likely strapped for cash. In August 1833 Messrs Callaghan's assets were advertised for sale by auction. These included a four-oared boat built of English oak, a galley boat, and a nearly-new pleasure barge.[97] Separately advertised for sale was a 12-ton sloop, the *Perseverance*, which Messrs Callaghan had built to order, along with a new dinghy.[98]

On 16 October 1833 the creditors of Daniel Callaghan were requested to meet at George Hesse's office in Argyle Street with a statement of their claims.[99] Callaghan was also subject to legal action from his business partner and relative James Callaghan.[100] Less than two weeks later he left Hobart Town on board the barque *Ann* for Sydney.[101] Daniel Callaghan's wife Mary likely followed several months or possibly years later, in the interim remaining in Hobart Town with the Hackett family.

The cutter *Emerald* was eventually sold by the Sheriff's Office to Louis Beaurais then to Craven Johnson.[102] In April 1834 the vessel took its maiden voyage to New Zealand's Bay of Islands with a cargo of sundries.[103] Sadly, Craven Johnson was on board when the *Emerald* went missing, most likely on its return leg from New Zealand.[104]

Settling in New South Wales, Daniel Callaghan established a shipbuilding enterprise on the Macleay River, located on the mid-north coast. Now known as Kempsey, the region was even more remote than Hobart Town and had a population of significantly less, predominantly convict gangs and labourers. It was the forests of cedar, however, that drew the shipbuilders. Here, in partnership with John Barclay, a master shipwright formerly of Canada, Callaghan, now often referring to himself as O'Callaghan, launched at least three vessels.[105] First was the 58ft schooner *Eliza*, built to the order of Francis Girard who owned a wharf and steam-powered flour mill at Darling Harbour, Sydney, that was completed in early December 1836.[106] Girard also owned land along the Macleay River from which he exported cedar to Sydney.[107] Such was the novelty of the *Eliza*'s launching in the region that the press, reporting on the event, stated that it was attended by '*many of the inhabitants of the district as were able to devote a day to this peculiar attraction; ... it is no slight gratification to the builder, that men of known professional acquirements were loud in applauding the excellent proportions of this elegant vessel, and her evident adaption to the purposes for which her enterprising owner had determined to devote her. ... She has a large and highly ornamented cabin, appropriated to the accommodation of such passengers as may be induced to visit the banks of the McLeay, for which she will be laid on as a regular trader*'.[108] When describing details regarding the *Eliza*, the press also reported that, '*Another vessel by the same builder is about to be commenced for Mr. Girard; another is but slowly progressing for Mr. T. H. James, of Sydney, under the direction of a Mr. Bartley; and a third will be forthwith built by several Scotch artizans on their own account*'.[109] It continued, '*As a place for such pursuits, the extensive navigation of the McLeay, capable of carrying a vessel of 80 tons full fifty miles from its entrance, at Trial Bay, offers numerous inducements. The timber on its banks consisting of stupendous cedar, rose wood, and all that class of timber, for which the Colony is eminently noted for, so much as to present an inexhaustible field, either for natural architecture of speculation*'.

The second vessel Messrs Callaghan and Barclay constructed on the banks of the Macleay River was the cutter *Rob Roy*, built to the order of T. H. James and launched on 27 January 1837.[110] Next came the schooner *Francis*, built to the order of Francis Girard and completed in July of that year.[111]

The cedars, however, were soon exhausted and by the early 1840s the resource all but depleted. Daniel Callaghan moved to Sydney where he and his wife Mary welcomed what appears to have been their second child, a daughter named Maria, born in 1839.[112] Though no registration of her birth has yet been found, it is likely that the couple's first child, Catherine, was born somewhere in New South Wales in 1837.

With his movements from this point forward somewhat hard to trace, it was around 1838 that Callaghan found work at Captain Fotheringham's patent slip in Sydney. Employed in some kind of supervisory role, on 4 September 1840 he placed an advertisement in the local press offering a reward of £2 for the apprehension of his 18-year-old apprentice William Shea.[113]

The first Australian colony to be installed with such a device, Sydney's patent slip had arrived on board the ship *Governor Halkett* from England in September 1832.[114] The property of Captain Alexander Fotheringham, it was laid down at the bottom of Sussex Street, Darling Harbour, and in operation by May 1833.[115] The local press eagerly reported on the

---

[97] *Colonial Times*, 10 September 1833.
[98] *Colonial Times*, 10 September 1833.
[99] *Colonial Times*, 15 October 1833.
[100] *The Hobart Town Courier*, 8 November 1833.
[101] *The Hobart Town Courier*, 1 November 1833.
[102] *The Hobart Town Courier*, 8 November 1833.
[103] *The Hobart Town Courier*, 2 May 1834.
[104] R. Parsons (1983). *Ships of Australia and New Zealand Before 1850: Part One A - J*.
[105] *The Sydney Gazette and New South Wales Advertiser*, 6 May 1837; *Dungog Chronicle: Durham and Gloucester Advertiser*, 5 August 1927.
[106] *The Sydney Gazette and New South Wales Advertiser*, 12 January 1837.
[107] *The Sydney Gazette and New South Wales Advertiser*, 14 October 1837.
[108] *The Sydney Gazette and New South Wales Advertiser*, 10 December 1836.
[109] *The Sydney Gazette and New South Wales Advertiser*, 10 December 1836.
[110] *The Sydney Gazette*, 11 February 1837; *The Sydney Gazette and New South Wales Advertiser*, 18 April 1837.
[111] *The Sydney Gazette and New South Wales Advertiser*, 18 April 1837; *The Australian*, 16 June 1837; *The Sydney Gazette and New South Wales Advertiser*, 9 January 1838.
[112] Ancestry.com. Australia, Birth Index, 1788-1922.
[113] *The Sydney Monitor and Commercial Advertiser*, 4 September 1840.
[114] *The Sydney Gazette and New South Wales Advertiser*, 18 September 1832.
[115] *The Currency Lad*, 27 April 1833; *The Sydney Gazette and New South Wales Advertiser*, 23 May 1833.

Darling Harbour showing the Patent Slip (1843). Painting by John Skinner Prout. Courtesy Mitchell Library, State Library of New South Wales (DG SSV1A/25).

innovation, which in time would prove to be a boon for ship repair and maintenance. '*The body of the slip is constructed in the form of a ship's bottom, and runs on coffed iron rollers along the bed, which is also cased with iron, after the manner of the rail-roads. The slip extends sufficiently into the water, to allow of a vessel of heavy burthen being floated on it, when she can be removed high and dry, by means of tackles. The great advantages of the patent slip is, that loaded vessels may be hauled off and examined, without removing the mast or cargoes, which could not be done under the old plan of careening.*'[116]

Captain Fotheringham's patent slip remained in constant operation until late 1839 whereby it was advertised for sale without reserve.[117] It was then sold to Messrs Samuel Peek & Co. for £5,200, with Captain Lister to be the manager.[118] Callaghan appears to have remained employed at the site for a number of years, though by the mid-1840s was residing at Twofold Bay on the New South Wales far south coast. This area's first settlements, Eden and Boyd Town, were then only in their infancy, however shore-based bay whaling had commenced over a decade prior, and it was likely this industry and its demand for shipwrights that drew Callaghan to the region. He is assumed to be the '*D. Callaghan*' that was noted as a passenger on board the schooner *Harlequin* that left Sydney for Boyd Town on 30 March 1844.[119] Also on board was a '*J. Callaghan*' perhaps referring to Callaghan's short-term business partner and likely relative James Callaghan who had remained in Hobart for some time following Daniel's relocation to New South Wales in 1833. James had married Mary Fenton, spinster, on 22 May 1835 at the Hobart Town Roman Catholic Chapel.[120] Remaining in Van Diemen's Land for a number of years, in 1840 he was noted as launching the 44-ton bay whaler *Mary*, built at Hobart Town's Old Wharf in conjunction with John Gray to the order of a Mr Witton.[121]

Daniel Callaghan's wife Mary appears to have sailed to Twofold Bay sometime after his arrival. The couple's third child, a son named Michael Eugene, was born in the region in 1845.[122] It is not known how long the family then remained in the Boyd Town area, though they were likely the '*Mr and Mrs Callaghan, and three children*' that arrived back in Sydney on 17 September 1845 as passengers on board the barque *Rebecca*.[123]

While it is not known where Daniel Callaghan found work upon his return to Sydney, it is probable that he was the '*Callaghan*' that won a sailing race at a Pyrmont regatta held in May 1848. The boat in question, *Sprig of Shillelah*, was a skiff not exceeding 17ft on the keel with the prize being six guineas.[124] Later that year, a list of unclaimed letters published in the *New South Wales Government Gazette* notes that one addressed to '*Callaghan, Mr. D., shipwright, Port Macquarie*' was waiting to be claimed, perhaps indicating that he was at the time, or had recently been, working in this area.[125]

In December 1849 Daniel Callaghan testified in Sydney as part of a case heard in the Supreme Court involving the underwriters of the barque *Isabella Anna*

[116] *The Sydney Monitor*, 11 May 1833.
[117] *The Sydney Gazette and New South Wales Advertiser*, 21 September 1839.
[118] *The Sydney Gazette and New South Wales Advertiser*, 2 November 1839.
[119] *The Australian*, 1 April 1844.
[120] *Morning Star and Commercial Advertiser*, 29 May 1835.
[121] *Tasmanian Weekly Dispatch*, 10 January 1840.
[122] Ancestry.com. Australia, Birth Index, 1788-1922.
[123] *The Australian*, 18 September 1845.
[124] *The Australian*, 26 May 1848.
[125] *New South Wales Government Gazette*, 6 October 1848.

and its owner; an action to recover the amount of a policy of insurance on the vessel which had been condemned and abandoned in New Caledonia.[126] The arguments centred on the vessel's seaworthiness with claims that its deteriorated condition had been concealed prior to its final voyage.

The *Isabella Anna* had left Sydney in February 1848 after undergoing extensive repairs at the Patent Slip, valued at £800. However, en route to New Caledonia, the vessel began to leak. Barely making the journey, upon arrival the *Isabella Anna* was deemed too far gone to repair and was subsequently sold by its captain for a diminutive £50.[127] While Callaghan's involvement in the court case was minimal, his presence as a witness indicates that he had once more found work at the Darling Harbour Patent Slip, which again appears to have been at least part-owned by Captain Fotheringham.[128]

Showing more entrepreneurial spirit than perhaps he had in the past decades, and indicating that he had some capital to fund a new build, in late 1854 Daniel Callaghan advertised a clipper-built schooner for sale that he had recently constructed on the banks of the Georges River.[129] The vessel measured 55ft overall with a beam of 15ft and a depth of 6ft. It was stated to be well-supplied with a complete suit of sails, standing and running rigging, anchors and cables, etc. Originally named *Emma*, though changed thereafter to *Emerald*, Mort & Co. sold the vessel at auction on 13 December to a Mr Corcoran for £700.[130] This appears to have been the last large vessel built by Callaghan. He likely returned to shipwright work, based locally in and around Sydney, for the remainder of his career.

Callaghan's wife Mary died on 9 October 1857, aged 49, at the family's home, 62 Cumberland Street, Sydney.[131] Her death notice, published in the *Sydney Morning Herald*, stated that she was '*niece of Sir William Hackett, Knight of Cork, Ireland*', somewhat of an over exaggeration of the actual relationship between the pair.[132] Sir William Hackett was her husband's cousin.

Daniel Callaghan died on 2 September 1872 at his residence, 66 Cumberland Street, Sydney, at the age of 75.[133] He was survived by at least two of his five children. His eldest daughter Catherine (born 1837), died in August 1906 in Balmain, Sydney.[134] His eldest son Michael (born 1845), died in September 1914 in Liverpool, Sydney.[135] Of note, the latter also worked as a shipwright.[136]

The biographical details of Callaghan and his wife Mary's additional children, Maria (born 1839), Margaret (born 1849) and Edward (born 1852) have as yet not been determined.

> O'CALLAGHAN.—Of your charity pray for the repose of the soul of Daniel O'Callaghan, who died at his residence, 66, Cumberland-street, Sydney, September 2, 1872, aged 72 years; also Eugene O'Callaghan, J P, brother of the above, who died at his residence, Lutuworth-street, Limerick, Ireland, May, 1881, aged 72 years. "Eternal rest give unto them, O Lord, and may perpetual light shine on them."

Evening News, 2 September 1882.

While recognised as Battery Point's first commercial boat builder, Daniel Callaghan only spent a few years working from this location before relocating to New South Wales. Still, plying his trade from an allotment in the vicinity of the Mulgrave Battery, he built at least 15 vessels, ranging from smaller sailing boats to larger cutters and sloops, as well as the colony's first steam boat, the *Governor Arthur*.

---

[126] *The Sydney Morning Herald*, 13 December 1849; *The Shipping Gazette and Sydney General Trade List*, 15 December 1849.
[127] *The Sydney Morning Herald*, 13 December 1849; *The Shipping Gazette and Sydney General Trade List*, 15 December 1849.
[128] *The Sydney Morning Herald*, 14 December 1849; *The Shipping Gazette and Sydney General Trade List*, 14 April 1849.
[129] *Empire*, 9 December 1854.
[130] *The Sydney Morning Herald*, 15 July 1854; *The Maitland and Hunter River General Advertiser*, 16 December 1854.
[131] *The Sydney Morning Herald*, 13 October 1857.
[132] *The Sydney Morning Herald*, 13 October 1857.
[133] *Evening News*, 3 September 1872; *The Sydney Morning Herald*, 4, 6 September 1872.
[134] *The Sydney Morning Herald*, 27 August, 25 October 1906.
[135] *The Sydney Morning Herald*, 1 October 1914.
[136] *The Sydney Morning Herald*, 1 October 1914.

Vessels built by Daniel Callaghan, his partners and employees at Battery Point (1831 - 1833)

Year	Name	Type	Description
1831	*Helena*	Sailing boat	Built by Daniel Callaghan to compete in the sailing race at the 1831 Hobart Town Regatta, held in February of that year. Helmed by a Mr Melville, finished second out of a fleet of eleven.
1831	*Tri-Color*	Sailing boat	Built by Daniel Callaghan to compete in the sailing race at the 1831 Hobart Town Regatta, held in February of that year. Helmed by R. L. Murray, finished third out of a fleet of eleven.
1831	*The Prize*	Sailing boat	24 (oa) x 22 x 7.3ft. Built by Daniel Callaghan as first prize for a sailing race to be held as part of a regatta convened on 22 August 1831. The race was won by Peter Buchanan in *The Wave*.
1832	*Charlotte*	Schooner	41.2 x 12.7 x 5.5ft. 28 tons. Built by Daniel Callaghan and launched on 5 January 1832. Built to the order of Samuel Henry Thomas and intended for the Van Diemen's Land east coast trade. Advertised for sale by auction in April 1832 shortly after completion. Remained in Thomas' hands for over a year and the subject of court action by creditors, of which Callaghan was one party. First noted as loading for the east coast in September 1833, by this time owned by Messrs Clowder and Buckles. Remained in the east coast trade for a number of years, also making several trips to New Zealand in 1834. Advertised for sale by auction without reserve in August 1834. By January 1836 owned by J. H. Thompson. Advertised for sale the following month. Disappears from the record thereafter, with its register later closed with the statement '*Lost*'.
1832	--	Galley boat	Six-oared galley built by Daniel Callaghan to the order of Captain Dance and launched on the day of its first race at the Hobart Regatta (held on 25 February 1832). Manned by personnel from HMS *Sulphur*.
1832	*Little Helena* (?)	Gig	Four-oared gig built by Daniel Callaghan to the order of a Mr Melvile and launched on the day of its first race at the Hobart Regatta (held on 25 February 1832). Possibly named *Little Helena*.
1832	--	Gig	Four-oared gig built by Daniel Callaghan to compete in a pulling match against the *Auriga* with a prize of 50 sovereigns on offer.
1832	*Governor Arthur*	Steam boat	63.2 x 10.9 x 4.6ft. ON 31695. 113 tons. Assembled by Daniel and James Callaghan from materials imported from England for Dr Alexander Thompson to ply between Hobart Town and Kangaroo Point. Completed in mid-1832. Undertook its maiden voyage in September 1832. Transferred to the River Tamar in June 1833 and advertised for sale there a few months later. By December 1833 still for sale and returned to Hobart Town. Purchased by Captain William Wilson and placed on the Derwent ferry run, receiving a new engine in late 1834. Involved in rescue attempts from the convict ship *George III* in March 1835. Several subsequent owners in quick succession. Transferred to Melbourne in 1841 by owner T. Walker to run on Port Phillip Bay. Damaged by fire on 23 December 1841 while moored at the Queen's Wharf, Melbourne. Repaired and returned to service in February 1842. By 1846 owned by Captain Cole, its engines transferred to a new vessel (the *Diamond*) launched in 1847. Converted to a schooner and placed in the Victorian coastal trade. By the late 1850s transferred to New Zealand and operating in the coastal trade. Broken up at Port Chalmers with its register closed on 31 December 1872.
1833	*Emerald*	Cutter	35 x 13.5 x 7.1ft. 32 tons. Built by Daniel and James Callaghan on speculation. Advertised for sale between May and November 1833. Sold by writ to Louis Beaurais and then sold to Craven W. Johnson. Lost on the return leg of its maiden voyage from Hobart Town to New Zealand, with owner Craven Johnson on board. The craft had left Hobart Town in April 1834.
1833	--	Sailing boat	Built by Daniel and James Callaghan and noted to be a '*new smack*' sailing on the River Derwent in August 1833. Witnesses were stated to be '*astonished*' by the craft's performance and sailing qualities.
1833	--	Four-oared boat	Built by Daniel and James Callaghan of English oak and copper-fastened. Advertised for sale as part of an auction of their assets held at the New Wharf on 19 September 1833. Stated to be '*built to order without regard to expense, and is unequalled in any part of the world for durability and value*'.
1833	--	Galley boat	Built by Daniel and James Callaghan. Advertised for sale as part of an auction of their assets held at the New Wharf on 19 September 1833. Stated to be '*built at the expense of his Majesty's Government of the very best materials the dock yard afforded, is better than when first set afloat, and will prove a bargain to the fortunate purchaser*'.
1833	--	Pleasure barge	Built by Daniel and James Callaghan. Advertised for sale as part of an auction of their assets held at the New Wharf on 19 September 1833. Stated to be '*quite new, and [built] upon a very safe principle, exactly similar to the late Prince of Wales' barge, and is of important value to any family fond of aquatic excursions*'.
1833	*Perseverance*	Sloop	12 tons. Built by Daniel and James Callaghan. Advertised for sale as part of an auction of their assets held at the New Wharf on 19 September 1833. Stated to be '*A very superior twelve ton sloop ... built to order by Callaghan - of the best materials the country affords - well found with anchors, cables, sails, rigging, and all neccessaries*'.
1833	--	Dinghy	Built by Daniel Callaghan. Advertised for sale as part of an auction of his assets held at the New Wharf on 19 September 1833. Built for the sloop *Perseverance*.

Map of Hobart, incorporating Battery Point drawn by George Frankland (c1830s). He named Colville Row (later street) after his mother's family. Courtesy State Library of Tasmania (AUTAS001139593859).

William Williamson

'It is much better to have vessels built here than to go to England and buy half-worn out vessels, which is too often done, and in some instances vessels that are almost unseaworthy.'

The Hobart Town Advertiser, 20 October 1846.

While Daniel Callaghan was Battery Point's first commercial boat builder, the area's first shipbuilder was William Williamson. He was born on 10 July 1805 in Leith, Scotland, the second eldest of at least six children born to James and Agnes Williamson (nee More or Moir).[137] Though Williamson's father was a grocer by trade, the family lived close to the Leith docks where Williamson would soon find work.[138] Now considered a suburb of Edinburgh, Leith in the early nineteenth century was a locus for shipbuilding with at least eight yards in operation, including Sime and Ranken, one of Scotland's oldest and most respected firms. Beginning work in his teens, Williamson would have received formal shipwright training and experience at one of these yards.

In 1826, at the age of 21, Williamson was noted as living at Sime's Court, North Leith. That year he married Henrietta Williamson, daughter of Donald Williamson, a farmer from Thurso in the Scottish Highlands. Just under a decade later, likely sensing opportunity for skilled and resourceful tradesmen, Williamson, Henrietta and their two children emigrated from Scotland to Van Diemen's Land.

Williamson and his family arrived in Hobart Town sometime in 1834. Here they joined Henrietta's brothers, Ramsay and George Williamson, who had emigrated from Scotland several years prior.[139] Involved in wine and spirits, another of Leith's famous industries, the duo had become successful wine importers and publicans. Another brother, Sinclair, had also spent some time in the colony, initially operating a butcher shop in partnership with John Muir in the mid-1820s before establishing the Edinburgh Wine Vaults in Elizabeth Street in 1829.[140]

In July 1833 Sinclair announced his intention to depart Hobart Town.[141] By December of that year, he had transferred the licence for the Edinburgh Wine Vaults to William Wilson and sailed for Scotland taking twenty bales of wool with him; he would return to the colony several years later.[142] By July 1834 the Edinburgh Wine Vaults was under licence to his brother Ramsay who was previously licensee of the Green Man Inn (Glenorchy) and then the Berriedale Inn.[143] George Williamson was nearby, as proprietor of the Royal Oak in Murray Street.[144]

Upon arrival in Hobart Town, instead of securing work with his brothers-in-law, William Williamson opted to continue with his niche of shipbuilding. The first record we have of his newly-established enterprise comes from an advertisement published late in 1834.

Damaged Masts, Sails, &c.
BY MR. T. Y. LOWES,

On Friday, the 26th instant, at Mr. Williamson's Yard, near the Hulk, at the New Wharf, at 12 o'clock,

THE Damaged Masts and Sails of the Ship *Henry Clay*, for the benefit of the Underwriters.

Terms—Cash. [4504]

Colonial Times, 23 December 1834.

Courtesy National Records of Scotland, O.P.R. Marriages 692/01 Leith North.

[137] Scotland, Select Births and Baptisms, 1564 - 1950.
[138] digital.nls.uk/directories/.
[139] *Hobart Town Gazette and Van Diemen's Land Advertiser*, 22 November 1823, 10 September 1824; *Colonial Times*, 5 June 1832.
[140] *The Hobart Town Courier*, 21 February 1829; *The Hobart Town Gazette*, 3 October 1829.
[141] *Colonial Times*, 23 July 1833.
[142] *The Tasmanian*, 6 December 1833; *The Hobart Town Courier*, 14 February 1834.
[143] *Colonial Times*, 21 September 1831; *The Colonist and Van Diemen's Land Commercial and Agricultural Advertiser*, 22 July 1834.
[144] *The Tasmanian*, 5 September 1834.

As the year 1835 began, William Williamson continued developing his shipyard on the edge of the River Derwent *'below Mulgrave Battery'*.[145] It was almost certainly the same location that Daniel Callaghan had used for his boat building enterprise prior to his departure from the colony in October 1833. Owned by Thomas Smith, a wharf had been built on the four-acre site, optimising its use for shipbuilding and repair work.[146]

Smith's wharf was part of a continued period of development for Battery Point. Further subdivision of large land plots had occurred, resulting in new streets being built and homes being constructed. The area's new residents had also coalesced to improve their neighbourhood, noted in April 1834 as forming a subscription for the erection of a church.[147] Not all were impressed by the rapidity in which improvements were being made, however. *The Colonist and Van Diemen's Land Commercial and Agricultural Advertiser* in May 1834 criticised the use of 200 convicts as part of a chain gang at the time *'employed in making a road near the Battery; along the whole extent of which there is not one single house, or one single inhabitant. The only reason which can be assigned for thus uselessly employing this large body of men at this spot, while the principal streets of the town, thickly studded with houses, and densely populated, are left impassable, from the immense traffic of the inhabitants cutting the surface into mud, knee deep, to the great injury of the tax-paying people, is, that the ****** and other Crown Officers of the Colony, have speculated largely in the purchase of the included land, which the cutting of these roads will force into immediate value!!!'*[148] This reproval may have been directed at George Frankland, the colony's surveyor general, who had purchased two allotments of land at Battery Point from William Kermode, comprising nearly ten acres, that had originally been part of William Sorell's 90-acre parcel.[149] Named Secheron, and overlooking the bay on the south side of the Mulgrave Battery, here Frankland designed and built a substantial residence that still exists today as one of the more impressive and historic colonial houses of Battery Point.[150]

Needing help at his own yard, though likely with little resources to pay for labour, Williamson advertised two ship carpentering apprenticeships to *'stout lads'* between the ages of 14 and 15. Successful applicants were to be *'taught ship building and boat building in all its branches'*.[151]

The first vessel noted as being at Williamson's Battery Point shipyard was the Sydney-built cutter *Emma Kemp*. Williamson spent the first few months of 1835 lengthening and widening the craft, in effect doubling its capacity.[152] The craft's owner was Thomas Horne, a politically vocal Hobart-based solicitor and speculative merchant and shipowner who also owned a large chunk of land in the area of Battery Point that would become the Napoleon Street boat and shipyards (refer to map on page 11, surname noted as Horn).[153] The *Emma Kemp* was advertised for sale in late March 1835 by Messrs McDougall and Stracey with a note that, *'This Vessel preserves her original name, together with a few of her former fortunate timbers, &c., with that exception, she is entirely new'*.[154] It was re-launched the following

[145] *The True Colonist*, 12 June 1835.
[146] *The Hobart Town Courier*, 11 September 1835.
[147] *The Hobart Town Courier*, 11, 18 April 1834.
[148] *The Colonist and Van Diemen's Land Commercial and Agricultural Advertiser*, 27 May 1834.
[149] Tasmanian Government, Historical Deed 01/1001; *The Tasmanian*, 29 September 1837.
[150] *Colonial Times*, 30 September 1834.
[151] *Colonial Times*, 27 January 1835.
[152] R. Parsons (1983). *Ships of Australia and New Zealand Before 1850: Part One A - J*.
[153] Tasmanian Government, Historical Deed 01/0714; adb.anu.edu.au/biography/horne-thomas-3798.
[154] *Colonial Times*, 31 March 1835.

The Secheron Estate at Battery Point prior to its subdivision in 1925.
Illustrated Tasmanian Mail, 21 October 1925.

month.¹⁵⁵ Next on the stocks was the schooner *Maria*. Built at Hobart Town in 1831 by John Gray, the craft had received a thorough overhaul prior to being advertised for sale in June 1835.¹⁵⁶

The first vessel built by Williamson at Battery Point was the 33ft schooner *Alligator*, launched from his shipyard towards the end of 1835.¹⁵⁷ The craft was advertised for sale in late January of the following year, stated to have a carvel bottom and *'built of the very best material'*.¹⁵⁸ However, appearing to have been unable to sell the *Alligator* outright, Williamson partnered with John Eason, David Mackey and Samuel Kendall to retain a quarter-share; the group trading under the auspices of 'William Williamson and Company'. The craft was placed in the intra-coastal trade, sailing to Great Swanport in late 1836 with William Hollis as master.¹⁵⁹ The *Alligator* was then placed in intercolonial trade, sailing to Twofold Bay, New South Wales, with general cargo and salt in May of the following year.¹⁶⁰

By 1839, however, the *Alligator* had been transferred to Sydney.¹⁶¹ The following year saw the vessel trading on the New South Wales south coast. Two years later, in late August 1843, the *Alligator* was reported to be ashore at Bulli, just north of Wollongong, *'with two or three holes through her bottom'*.¹⁶² The vessel disappears from the records thereafter.

Considering Williamson had built the *Alligator* on speculation, his failure to find a buyer forced him into a business arrangement with three other partners, likely only recouping some of the funds he had outlayed for its construction. This decision also forced him into not only becoming a shipbuilder but also a ship owner involved in trade, a rather risky decision. It was also not the best of times to enter a new enterprise. Van Diemen's Land's economy was suffering during the mid-1830s due to a reduced demand for wool, which was fast becoming the chief component of the export market; the result being a lowering of prices for the commodity in England. This downturn also affected the Hobart Town real estate market, including allotments situated at Battery Point. Following a period of speculation that had yielded positive results, the well-heeled were being forced to consolidate their assets. For example, in October 1835 Benjamin Guy advertised a one-acre allotment for lease located between the River Derwent and current day Napoleon Street.¹⁶³ Four allotments neighbouring the Secheron estate were advertised for sale in January 1836.

Fronting the Derwent and located near the Mulgrave Battery, they constituted the parcel of land then owned by Thomas Smith, a portion of which had been used by both Daniel Callaghan and William Williamson for shipbuilding purposes. The sales advertisement stated that the four allotments were *'apportioned with a view to the construction of wharves and warehouses and offering the peculiar advantage of laying vessels of large burthen alongside jetties to load and discharge. Adjoining lot 1, is the only place in the harbour calculated for laying down a patent slip'*.¹⁶⁴

Despite these financial setbacks, there was also continued development of the suburb of Battery Point itself, with James Luckman erecting a wind mill along Cromwell Street, and subscriptions still incoming for the construction of a church, with the first stone laid in October 1836.¹⁶⁵ In terms of the former, the press described the wind mill's construction as, *'that perfect kind common round London, in which the circular roof and sails balance and adjust themselves to the wind by means of a fan wheel on the opposite side. It is about 50 or 55 feet high, and forms a striking object to vessels coming up the river'*.¹⁶⁶

James Luckman's windmill at Cromwell Street, Battery Point, built in 1836 behind which stands St George's Anglican Church, consecrated in May 1838 (c1860s). Courtesy Tasmanian Archives (NS73/1/1/8).

It was in this context that Williamson continued to ply his trade on the shore of Battery Point, though he too was a casualty of the harsh economic times. In April 1836, for example, he advertised for all claims for and against him to be settled.¹⁶⁷ The following month he advertised the new schooner *Alligator* for sale, along with two vessels partly in frame, a punt, and numerous shipbuilding equipment, timbers, tree nails, blocks and supplies; the disposal of Williamson's assets likely an effort to rein in his finances, as well as the possibility of being forced to seek new premises.¹⁶⁸

Remaining at his shipyard located in the vicinity of the Mulgrave Battery, given that Thomas Smith's

---

¹⁵⁵ *Colonial Times*, 28 April 1835.
¹⁵⁶ *The Hobart Town Courier*, 12 June 1835; R. Parsons (1983). *Ships of Australia and New Zealand Before 1850: Part Two K - Z*.
¹⁵⁷ *The True Colonist*, 29 January 1836; R. Parsons (1983). *Ships of Australia and New Zealand Before 1850: Part One A - J*.
¹⁵⁸ *The Tasmanian*, 29 January 1836.
¹⁵⁹ *The True Colonist*, 25 November 1836.
¹⁶⁰ *The Tasmanian*, 19 May 1837.
¹⁶¹ R. Parsons (1983). *Ships of Australia and New Zealand Before 1850: Part One A - J*.
¹⁶² *The Sydney Morning Herald*, 1 September 1843.
¹⁶³ *The Hobart Town Courier*, 23 October 1835.
¹⁶⁴ *The Hobart Town Courier*, 8 January 1836.
¹⁶⁵ *Bent's News and Tasmanian Three-Penny Register*, 13 February 1836; *The Hobart Town Courier*, 21 October 1836.
¹⁶⁶ *The Hobart Town Courier*, 18 March 1836.
¹⁶⁷ *The True Colonist*, 8 April 1836.
¹⁶⁸ *The Tasmanian*, 6 May 1836.

allotments went unsold, in March 1837 Williamson advertised for three shipbuilding apprentices.[169] He then began construction of two large vessels. In early May 1837 the local press reported that he was building a craft of 40-tons burthen, purchased by Captain Andrew Haig, merchant of Hobart Town, whom Williamson would have an ongoing partnership for many years. The other vessel was quite substantial, being of 200 tons, and conceivably an enormous financial risk since it was being built on speculation.[170]

Intended for intercolonial trade, Captain Haig's 39ft schooner *Lady Franklin* was launched on 18 May 1837.[171] Of note, the infamous bushranger Martin Cash states in his autobiography that he was employed on the *Lady Franklin* during the week of its launch.[172] A convict from County Wexford, Ireland, sentenced to seven years transportation to New South Wales for shooting a man, Cash had only arrived in Hobart Town from Sydney three months prior in an attempt to thwart a new charge of stealing cattle.[173]

Like Cash, the subsequent history of the *Lady Franklin* would also be newsworthy. The vessel spent less than a year conveying passengers and freight between Hobart Town and Victoria. On 20 April 1838 the craft left Hobart Town for Port Phillip Bay carrying fifteen passengers and a cargo of rum, tobacco, furniture, apparel, sugar, tea, potatoes, flour, timber and shingles.[174] The following day Captain John Crocker diverted the *Lady Franklin* to Port Arthur to replace the vessel's jib-boom. Continuing on its passage to Victoria six days later, the vessel failed to arrive with no trace of it ever found.[175]

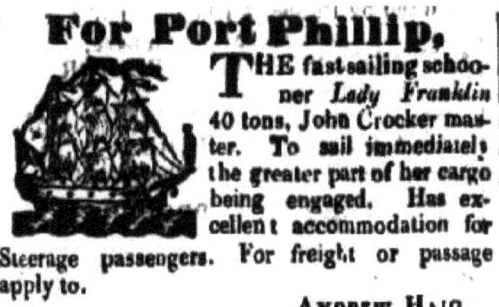

The Austral-Asiatic Review, Tasmanian and Australian Advertiser, 20 February 1838.

While construction of the larger 200-ton vessel being built at Williamson's Battery Point shipyard during this period was piecemeal, there was work on hand. Seemingly finding it difficult to retain his apprentices, Williamson advertised for *'Two stout Boys, from 14 to 15 years of age, as apprentices to ship building'* in August 1837.[176] On 14 April of the following year, the same month that the *Lady Franklin* was lost, he launched a second vessel built to the order of Captain Haig, the 40ft schooner *Fanny*.[177] Like the *Lady Franklin*, the craft was intended for intercolonial trade. Rather alarmingly, however, during the launching process it was found that, *'some kind friend, doubtless of Mr. Williamson's'* had bored a hole in the vessel's bottom allowing for an influx of water.[178] The issue was soon remedied, *'and thus the malice of the felonious actors timely thwarted'*, though set the tone of the *Fanny*'s career.[179] Leaving Hobart Town on 30 May 1838 en route to Western Australia on its maiden voyage, with Captain James Gill at the helm, the vessel went ashore between Cape Jaffa and Cape Northumberland, South Australia.[180] While its passengers and crew managed to make it to safety, and ultimately onto a whaling station located at Encounter Bay, the *Fanny* was a complete wreck. The Adelaide press reported on the mishap. *'The particulars of the loss of the "Fanny", are not fully known. She was bound from Hobart Town to Swan River, with a general cargo; she is on shore between Cape Jaffa and Cape Northumberland, a total wreck, crew and passengers saved, but it is reported that not a particle of cargo will be recovered. We cannot understand how the "Fanny" could have so deviated from her course as to be near the southern coast, but we hope soon to be enabled to report full particulars. A Wesleyan Missionary and his lady, lately from England to Hobart Town, passengers by the "Fanny", to settle in Swan River, had a narrow escape, and have lost every particle of their baggage. They are now most kindly entertained at the fishery at Encounter Bay. We are glad to hear that instructions have been forwarded to the stations and captains of the Company's ships there, to furnish every possible assistance and everything that may conduce to their comfort, and to afford them the means for their reaching Adelaide as soon as possible.'*[181] Subsequent reports revealed serious flaws in the statements provided by the *Fanny*'s master, Captain Gill, regarding the vessel's course, as well as suspicion regarding his sudden exit from Adelaide upon being pressed on the issue.

With Williamson's Battery Point shipyard entering its sixth year of operation, its total output to date had been the launch of three small schooners for intercolonial trade. The late 1830s proved busy too, particularly in terms of the construction of new vessels but also with regards to the repair and refit of existing craft. In August 1838, for example, the 242-ton ship *Louisa* (built at Calcutta, India, in 1823) was advertised for sale by Williamson having undergone a thorough repair.[182] Also advertised for sale were three new whaleboats, 16 tons of water casks, and 50 tons of iron ballast.

---

[169] *Colonial Times*, 21 March 1837.
[170] *Bent's News and Tasmanian Three-Penny Register*, 6 May 1837.
[171] *The Hobart Town Courier*, 19 May 1837.
[172] M. Cash (1929). *Martin Cash, the Bushranger of Van Diemen's Land in 1843-4*.
[173] en.wikipedia.org/wiki/Martin_Cash.
[174] *The Tasmanian*, 27 April 1838; *The Hobart Town Courier*, 27 April 1838.
[175] G. Broxam & M. Nash (2012). *Tasmanian Shipwrecks. Volume 1: 1797-1899*.
[176] *Colonial Times*, 29 August 1837.
[177] *Colonial Times*, 17 April 1838.
[178] *Colonial Times*, 17 April 1838.
[179] *Colonial Times*, 17 April 1838.
[180] *The Advertiser*, 1 June 1838.
[181] *Southern Australian*, 11 August 1838.
[182] *The True Colonist*, 10 August 1838.

Painting of the ship *Sir George Arthur*.
Courtesy Maritime Museum of Tasmania (P_1984-504).

The *Louisa* was purchased by Captain Haig for £1,500; Haig having an immediate need to replace the schooners *Lady Franklin* and *Fanny*, both lost in mid-1837 and 1838, respectively.

However 1838, by and large, continued a general period of financial melancholy for Hobart Town's residents, with many local merchants and businessmen struggling to keep afloat while others went insolvent. This downturn adversely affected Williamson's customer base, a general feeling of unease leading to less speculation on the building of new vessels. Many of Hobart Town's upper echelon, prosperous through the years of Lieutenant-Governor George Arthur's rein, opted to return to England, potentially not in favour with the new governor, Sir John Franklin, who had arrived with his wife, daughter, nieces and their entourage the previous year to begin his tenure.[183] George Frankland advertised his Secheron estate for sale in January 1838, comprising the '*substantial, elegant, commodious, and unique*' residence and eight acres of land, established as gardens.[184] Advertised for sale separately was '*the ground bordering the river* [to] *be sold in separate portions; and from its very convenient and sheltered situation, merchants, ship-builders, and others, are invited to give due consideration to the opportunity this afforded them, since no other waterside premises can embrace the same numerous advantages*'.[185] Ironically, also advertised for sale that very day in the same publication was Thomas Smith's property located on the edge of the River Derwent; he too indicating a want to return to England. Of particular note, despite its present use for shipbuilding, the latter parcel was described as, '*most desirably situate as building ground, between the Battery and Mr. Frankland's residence, consisting of 300 feet frontage on the River Derwent, and 1330 feet frontage on the curved road, out of which thirty good allotments could be formed*'.[186] Indicative of a lacklustre economy, both parcels of land took many months to sell, Frankland being forced to lease his Secheron estate to the colonial government. His separate allotment, suited to merchants, shipbuilders and others, was still being advertised for lease in September 1838.[187]

It was at this juncture in time that an interesting event took place in Hobart Town: the launch of a 387-ton ship, the *Sir Governor Arthur*. Built over several years across the River Derwent at Kangaroo Point by John Johnson to the order of John Petchey, local merchant, the spectacle was widely reported in the local

[183] *The True Colonist*, 6 January 1837.
[184] *The Tasmanian*, 5 January 1838.
[185] *The Tasmanian*, 5 January 1838.
[186] *The Tasmanian*, 5 January 1838.
[187] *The Austral-Asiatic Review, Tasmanian and Australian Advertiser*, 21 August 1838.

press, one publication giving a lengthy description, 'owing to the irregularity of the tide the ceremony which had been fixed for 10 A.M. did not take place until half past 4 P.M., during which delay we never saw so large a concourse of people more, orderly, more well-behaved, or more patient. His Excellency, Sir John Franklin, attended by his Aide-de-Camp, and accompanied also by the Colonial Secretary and Chief Police Magistrate, Major Ryan, the Port Officer, &c., and very many others, with their families, were amongst the first who landed at Kangaroo Point, at 10 o'clock; and from this time the two steam vessels, and all the boats and small craft in the harbour, kept incessantly discharging their cargoes of living souls during the forenoon, until, we imagine, there could not have been less than three thousand persons present. Hobart Town appeared deserted - business was at a stand - with one consent all seemed inclined to make a holiday upon the occasion. The ships in harbour hoisted their colours; whilst the Eliza government vessel, which conveyed a numerous party across the river, decorated with flags from her deck to her trucks, and with the new ship, also covered with flags, tended much towards the enlivenment of the scene. The fine band of the 21st Fusiliers was in attendance. Tents were pitched in various parts, and the liberality of Mr. Petchey provided substantial refreshment for his visitors. At length the signal gun announced all to be in readiness. Sir John Franklin stood ready to christen her, and at the first perceptible motion of the vast fabric threw a bottle filled with wine at her bows, but failed to break it, and it fell unhurt to the ground. It was immediately picked up and handed to Sir John, who, with the true ardour of a sailor resolved to do his duty, laid hold of a rope with his left hand which was hanging from her bows, and again hurled the bottle against her, which was dashed in pieces. At this moment a flag hoisted at the mainmast announced her name to be the Sir George Arthur, amidst the cheers of the spectators. She went off in gallant style, but did not succeed in getting quite afloat, in consequence of the yielding of the ways to the enormous pressure of her weight, owing to which her stern bedded in the mud with about thirteen feet of water. We have since learnt from Mr. Petchey, that she is perfectly safe and uninjured, and will be easily warped off ... We cannot conclude our notice of this interesting event, without remarking, that at the moment of her going off Sir John Franklin was for a short time in imminent peril. We observed, that in the ardour of the moment, Sir John had seized hold of a rope, (attached to the ship) by which he was dragged several yards along the ways. Sir John was, however, determined not to relinquish his hold until he had christened her in the usual style, by breaking the bottle against her bows, the consequence of which was, that as soon as he let go of the rope, the impetus ceasing, His Excellency received rather a severe fall, but fortunately unattended by any serious personal injury. Major Ryan also had a narrow escape of injury from a large log of wood that fell down. His Excellency, Sir John Franklin, quitted Kangaroo Point in his barge shortly after the launch, and was loudly and heartily cheered by the people on the shore and in the various crowded vessels as he passed by them, to all of which Sir John returned the compliment hat in hand, and with the zest and energy of a true son of the ocean. The day terminated, we are happy to add, without any accident beyond the minor disasters usually incidental upon such occasions when honest citizens determine "to make a day of it." The boat which contained the band lost her rudder, and was carried down the river a considerable distance; the men succeeded in reaching the shore about five miles down, having, however, to wade through the water, and carrying their musical instruments on their heads'.[188]

Though another large vessel, the 290-ton fully-rigged ship *Maria Orr*, had been built at the Old Wharf, Hobart Town, for William Orr by William Pender and Charles Chessell, and launched in January 1838, it was the debacle surrounding the launch of the *Sir George Arthur* that would prove a blessing for the establishment and continued development of Battery Point's shipbuilding industry in the many decades to come.[189] This realisation, along with the availability of suitable parcels of land, likely going cheaply at the time, saw more than one shipbuilder capitalise on the location. A letter to the editor of *The Hobart Town Courier* published on 9 November 1838 echoed this sentiment. Following a genial and eloquent introduction, the writer, James Grant, agent for Lloyd's, opined, 'I have been present at launches of first-rate ships from Her Majesty's Dock Yards on the Thames, and do not remember that any of them went off in better, or more beautiful style, than did the Sir George Arthur; but unfortunately the want of sufficient depth of water prevented her from fairly floating. She stopped about mid-ships, I think, and this is the circumstance which induces me now to trespass on your space, with a view to obviate such an occurrence in future; and which I understood happened to the beautiful Maria Orr, launched some little time since, when I was absent from Town, and built by one of the earliest founders of our navy, Mr. Orr of this Town. Ship building is so important a pursuit to this island, and it being expedient that every protection and assurance should be afforded to those who embark in it, I wish to impress on them that the risk of launching can be included in an insurance from the Derwent to London, and easily provided against, at a very moderate cost, if the sites for building yards, and all "appliances to boot" are selected with reasonable care. It is evident that such a weight as a 400 ton ship, slipping, however gently, from an inclined plane, requires a much greater depth to float her than would be necessary in ordinary to float her, and without ample depth the stern may strike either rock or hard ground; if the former the keel may be broken, or the stern posts so shattered as to make her unfit for sea, or doubly hazardous, and altogether great expense and discomfort to both owner and builder! - happily in the present instance "all is right." Under these circumstances, and as in my own opinion there is now the fairest prospect for success here, (indeed I should not be surprised to see Great Britain forming a naval arsenal in the Derwent, the English forests

---

[188] *The Hobart Town Courier*, 19 October 1838.
[189] *The Tasmanian*, 19 January 1838.

of oak are getting exhausted, and, with the dense population of our native land, it is impossible to expect that space can in future be spared for replanting) - I most anxiously recommend it to all concerned to secure proper sites, while the opportunity remains to them. Round the Battery Point, and about Secheron Bay, the land meets the water, (which is very deep) abruptly, and as the materials in a manner overhang the river, the labour of making "docks, slips, and ways" for every purpose of building, repairing and heaving down ships for examination, will be exceedingly easy, and the expense, consequently, light, while, as I understand, Mr. Frankland and others are willing to give leases on reasonable terms, or even to sell portions; there is yet too, in that direction, ample space left in the grounds behind for rope walks, (the best of New Zealand flax is almost at our doors), the construction of forges for anchor smiths, and the whole contiguous to every trade in the Town attached to shipping, &c., and connected by regular links to the Wharfs round Sullivan's Cove, and the entire harbour!'

Of note, here we have Hobart Town's representative to Lloyds of London, tasked with supplying local shipping information, casualty intelligence, vessel surveys and insurance claims and adjustments, advocating not only for the development of a shipbuilding industry in Hobart Town, but for the suitability of Battery Point and the Bay of Secheron for its establishment. Though not disclosed, perhaps there was also some personal incentive for the choice of Battery Point as an ideal shipbuilding location. Grant owned property contiguous to the Secheron estate which perhaps he had purchased on speculation.[190]

With regards to our subject at hand, William Williamson continued his commercial shipbuilding activities at Battery Point. February 1839 saw him advertise the cutter *Ariel* for sale, described as, '*almost new, about 14 tons burthen, new sails, chain cable, dingey, two sweeps, all in excellent order, and fit for immediate work*'.[191] It is not known if Williamson built the craft or was merely tasked with managing its sale.

In 1839 Williamson completed two more vessels. These were the 56ft schooner *Truganina* launched in May 1839, and the 60ft schooner *Lillias* launched on 4 October 1839. Undoubtedly constructed on speculation, the former was '*rebuilt on a former model*', very likely a hulk.[192] Upon completion, *Truganina* was chartered by Kerr, Alexander, and Company at a cost of £50 per month to transport supplies and provisions to their whaling stations at Southport and Recherche Bay, and to carry timber to Hobart Town on its return leg.[193] By the end of 1839 the vessel was under Captain Haig's management and being used to convey passengers and freight between Hobart Town and Port Phillip Bay, at the time a developing trade route. The following year saw *Truganina* trading between Adelaide, Port Phillip Bay, and Hobart Town. It was wrecked in late November 1842 at Lady Bay, Victoria.[194]

In contrast to *Truganina*, Williamson built the schooner *Lillias* to the order of James Strachan, wool merchant of Hobart Town, specifically for the Port Phillip Bay trade.[195] The craft was described as a '*beautiful little*

---
[190] *Colonial Times*, 20 November 1838.
[191] *The Tasmanian*, 22 February 1839.
[192] *Colonial Times*, 7 May 1839; *The Hobart Town Advertiser*, 4 October 1839; *Port Phillip Patriot and Melbourne Advertiser*, 5 December 1842.
[193] *Colonial Times*, 7 May 1839; *The Tasmanian*, 17 May 1839.
[194] *Port Phillip Patriot and Melbourne Advertiser*, 5 December 1842.
[195] *Colonial Times*, 8 October 1839.

Painting of the schooner *Lillias*.
Courtesy www.wikitree.com/genealogy/Strachan-Photos-58/.

vessel, built after Scotch plan'.[196] Another article detailing its launch noted, 'The model and workmanship of this little vessel do the builder credit, and the order and conduct of the launch afford ample proof of his adequacy to the business'.[197]

Under Strachan's ownership, Lillias spent 10 years conveying passengers, livestock, timber and general cargo between Hobart Town, Melbourne and Geelong on a regular schedule. Considering the perils of Bass Strait and Port Phillip Heads, the craft was extremely lucky to have maintained such a consistent timetable for so many years without incident.

During this period Williamson was also involved in repairing larger vessels. The French whaler Elizabeth, for example, was noted in the press as undergoing repair and refit at his yard in August 1839 in an article concerning an application for the erection of a patent slip that had supposedly been made to the government; Williamson's yard being noted as, 'an instance of the want of a more convenient place for repairing vessels'.[198] However, it would be another 15 years before a patent slip was installed at Battery Point.

In late October 1839, a few weeks after the launch of the Lillias, the Colonial Times carried an article detailing the establishment of a new shipbuilding company. Composed of George Bilton, Captain Edward Goldsmith, Captain Haig, John James Meaburn and William Williamson, the group combined resources to purchase two one-acre waterside allotments located off Napoleon Street, Battery Point, previously owned by H. W. Mortimer.[199] The first property had a frontage on the River Derwent of approximately 115 feet with a depth of about 300 feet and, at the time it was advertised for sale in September 1839, was noted to be undergoing considerable improvements, 'principally consisting of the construction of a wharf'.[200] A four-room weatherboard structure, capable of being converted 'at a trifling cost' into a house, was also erected on the allotment.[201] Located next door, the second property was of similar dimensions. Operating as the Derwent Ship Building Company, the group intended to develop the properties into an 'extensive and well sheltered building yard, and patent slip'.[202] Williamson likely spent the next month or two relocating his plant and equipment to this new location. Sadly, however, he spent the bulk of this time grieving. His wife Henrietta died on 1 November 1839, likely due to complications from childbirth.[203]

The year 1840 dawned and the Derwent Ship Building Company began operation. Its first tender was unfortunately a politically charged issue. In 1838, when several businessmen in Hobart Town contracted with the Van Diemen's Land government to have a steamship built for them by convict labour at Port Arthur, because it was cheaper than having it built privately, the notion that the government should be encouraging private enterprise instead of taking 'the bread out of their mouths' was touted in the press by several esteemed citizens.[204] This rhetoric was fuelled even further by the fact that when the contract was signed, the press noted that at least 30 local shipwrights were out of work.[205] The resulting vessel (the Derwent) was so poorly built and not to specification that the press hinted that the government forfeit its right to payment.[206] Instead, the government charged Williamson's newly formed company with undertaking repairs on the Derwent.[207] With 10 shipwrights employed on the vessel, the public versus private debate was amplified even further.[208]

Following the Derwent's relaunch, Williamson, under the guise of the Derwent Ship Building Company, began work on several new vessels, built on speculation, including those that would become the schooner Queen and the brig Diana. An employee during this period, the boat builder William Williams, also advertised for sale a near-new square-sterned 16ft pleasure boat from the company's Battery Point yard in April 1840.[209]

The 36-ton schooner Queen, built on speculation, was launched on 16 September 1840.[210] Sadly, however, its launch resulted in the death of Samuel Kendall, the Derwent Ship Building Company's foreman, who was crushed underneath the vessel while preparing it for launch.[211] This accident was just the start of a chequered career for the Queen, in which the craft failed to find a consistent owner and trade route.

Though advertised for sale on many occasions immediately after its launch, the Queen remained in the hands of various partners of the Derwent Ship Building Company, including George Bilton, who first registered the craft in August 1841.[212] It then disappears from the records until mid-1846 when the vessel was purchased by Thomas Patterson and placed in the Pittwater to Hobart Town river trade.[213] By April 1848, however, the Queen was once again advertised for sale.[214] A series of short-term owners soon followed, including John Jackson, George Perriman, James Morling, William Dawson and, finally, in April 1853, James Garth of Port Cygnet.[215] Under Garth's patronage the Queen solidified its involvement in the river trade, sometimes going by the moniker Queen of Sorell.

---

[196] The Hobart Town Courier, 4 October 1839.
[197] Colonial Times, 8 October 1839.
[198] The Hobart Town Courier, 30 August 1839.
[199] Colonial Times, 29 October 1839; www.thelist.tas.gov.au (Historical Deed 02/3002).
[200] Colonial Times, 24 September 1839.
[201] Colonial Times, 24 September 1839.
[202] Colonial Times, 29 October 1839.
[203] Colonial Times, 5 November 1839.
[204] Colonial Times, 31 December 1839.
[205] Colonial Times, 31 December 1839.
[206] Colonial Times, 31 December 1839.
[207] Colonial Times, 31 December 1839.
[208] Colonial Times, 31 December 1839.
[209] The Hobart Town Advertiser, 10 April 1840.
[210] The Courier, 22 January 1841.
[211] The Hobart Town Courier and Van Diemen's Land Gazette, 18 September 1840.
[212] The Courier, 22 January, 19 November 1841; Colonial Times, 25 January 1842; R. Parsons (1983). Ships of Australia and New Zealand Before 1850: Part Two K - Z.
[213] R. Parsons (1983). Ships of Australia and New Zealand Before 1850: Part Two K - Z; Colonial Times, 21 April 1846; The Courier, 3 March 1843.
[214] The Courier, 29 April 1848.
[215] R. Parsons (1983). Ships of Australia and New Zealand Before 1850: Part Two K - Z.

Advertised for sale part-way through completion in July 1840, stated to have been *'built of the best blue gum timber with pine decks'*, the 162-ton brig *Diana* was launched by the Derwent Ship Building Company five days after Christmas in 1840.[216] The *Colonial Times* reported, *'The proportions and model of this vessel are as near as possible to those approved by the celebrated shipbuilder, Mr. Hedderwick, of Leith, who is universally admitted to stand at the head of British marine architects'*.[217] The shipbuilder in question was Peter Hedderwick who in 1830 had published *A Treatise on Marine Architecture*, containing the theory and practice of shipbuilding, with rules for the proportions of masts, rigging, weight of anchors, etc., as well as the inclusion of valuable tables calculated for the use of shipwrights and seamen, and the proportions, scantlings, construction, and propelling power with regards to steam-ships.[218] The book also included 20 illustrations containing plans and draughts of merchant-vessels from 50 to 500 tons, with mast and rigging plans.

Less than a month following its launch, the *Diana* was again advertised for sale.[219] The vessel eventually fell into the hands of the Derwent Ship Building Company's partner George Bilton, who advertised it *'for sale, freight, or charter'*.[220] The *Diana* sailed to Twofold Bay, New South Wales, on 7 February 1842 on is first intercolonial voyage, arriving back in Hobart Town in July with a cargo including 50 head of cattle and 400 wethers.[221] By 1843 the *Diana* had been placed in the Port Albert, Victoria, to Hobart Town livestock trade.[222] However, in early July 1843 the craft parted from its cables during a heavy gale in Portland Bay and became embedded in sand, all hands saved.[223] Though the vessel suffered minimal structural damage, following survey it was recommended that the *Diana* be immediately sold *'as is'* for the benefit of all involved.[224] The craft was auctioned off a day later and sold to Henty and Company of Launceston for £400.[225]

Within weeks, however, the *Diana* had been pulled from the sand and repaired. The vessel arrived in Launceston on 19 August 1843 with a load of bullocks and spars.[226] After spending the next 13 months trading between Launceston and Victoria, with occasional trips to Sydney, the craft was completely wrecked on 1 October 1844 at Port Fairy, Victoria, all hands saved.[227] Henty and Company received an insurance payment of £1,200, and pieces of the wreck were sold off individually.[228]

Unfortunately, the viability of the Derwent Ship Building Company was short-lived. On 3 March 1841, less than 18 months after its formation, the company was dissolved, likely a combination of its directors suffering financial hardship due to the wreck of several of their vessels, a general lack of interest in the building of new craft, the lack of sale of vessels built on speculation, and the poorly performing colonial economy.[229] Captain Haig, for example, having been a successful merchant and shipowner in Hobart Town since his arrival in 1833, was forced to sell his recently built home (Narryna at Battery Point), among other personal assets.

Correspondingly, assets of the Derwent Ship Building Company were sold at auction in April 1841. These included the barque *Eamont*, the cutter *Shamrock*, the schooner *Truganina*, the brig *Diana*, and the schooner *Queen*.[230] Also advertised for sale were two new launches, one whaleboat, one gig, and several smaller craft, along with spars and Huon pine logs.[231]

Showing resilience, Williamson continued shipyard operations at Battery Point stating profusely in the local press, over several weeks, that he was now in business *'on his own private account'* and that he intended *'to erect a patent slip in his yard'*.[232] He also returned to his previous shipyard located near the Mulgrave Battery, noted to back at this site by at least February 1841.[233] This property was still owned by Thomas Smith, despite numerous attempts over many years to dispose of it.

> **Notice.**
> Hobart Town, 3rd March, 1841.
>
> THE Co partnership hitherto carried on by the undersigned under the style or firm of "The Derwent Ship-building Company" has been dissolved as on this date.
>
> GEORGE BILTON
> for JOHN JAMES MEABURN
> GEORGE BILTON
> ANDREW HAIG
> E. GOLDSMITH
> WM. WILLIAMSON.
>
> Witness, ROBERT PITCAIRN.
>
> 561
>
> ---
>
> **Ship Building.**
>
> WILLIAM WILLIAMSON, Ship-builder, late Partner of the "*Derwent Ship Building Company*," *now dissolved*, begs most respectfully to acquaint his kind patrons and the shipping interest generally, that he has recommenced in his former Ship Building Yard, at Battery Point, ON HIS OWN PRIVATE ACCOUNT, where he will gratefully receive their orders, and endeavour, to the utmost of his humble ability, to execute them to their satisfaction. He intends to erect a Patent Slip in his Yard, which will enable him to repair ships of large size.
> March 4, 1841. 564

Tasmanian Weekly Dispatch, 5 March 1841.

---

[216] *The Hobart Town Advertiser*, 24 July 1840; *Colonial Times*, 5 January 1841.
[217] *Colonial Times*, 5 January 1841.
[218] catalog.hathitrust.org/Record/008604794.
[219] *The Courier*, 22 January 1841.
[220] *The Courier*, 19 November 1841.
[221] *Colonial Times*, 8 February 1842; *The Courier*, 8 July 1842.
[222] *Colonial Times*, 7 March 1843.
[223] *Launceston Examiner*, 19 July 1843.
[224] *Launceston Advertiser*, 3 August 1843.
[225] *Launceston Advertiser*, 3 August 1843.
[226] *The Courier*, 25 August 1843.
[227] *Launceston Examiner*, 30 October 1844.
[228] *The Courier*, 15 October 1844; *Launceston Examiner*, 30 October 1844.
[229] *The Courier*, 5 March 1841.
[230] *Colonial Times*, 30 March 1841.
[231] *Colonial Times*, 30 March 1841.
[232] *Colonial Times*, 9 March 1841.
[233] *The Courier*, 12 February 1841.

A snippet published in the *The Hobart Town Advertiser* on 2 April 1841 provided more personal details regarding the dissolution of the Derwent Ship Building Company. '*Mr. Williamson. - We perceive by an advertisement that this enterprising and industrious shipwright has, on the dissolution of the ship-building company, recommenced business on his own account. We believe Mr. Williamson did not find his connection with the company so advantageous as he expected; and therefore as he has a large family, and is generally esteemed as a worthy man, we trust he will now be liberally supported.*'

Despite this praise, business for Williamson, remained bleak. He built only one vessel in 1841: a gig pulling four oars named *The Arrow*. This particular craft was built specifically to race at the Hobart Town Regatta held in December of that year.[234] Repair work continued to provide income, however, with several large vessels noted at his yard during the year, including the brig *Brothers*.[235] With the whaling industry playing a more prevalent role in Hobart Town, the storage and export of whale oil began to impede on space at the New Wharf. To alleviate the strain, Hobart Town's Legislative Council met throughout mid-to-late 1841 to find a solution. One possibility discussed was the purchase of part or all of Thomas Smith's land next to the Mulgrave Battery in order to extend the new wharf and make it an area for storage of whale oil.[236] Given Williamson had only just returned to this location, he was likely concerned as to what impact any decision would have on his business. There was also likely renewed interest in the area as the Mulgrave Battery was undergoing extensive renovations and expansion at the time, with the battery itself, by now comprising 10 new 8-inch muzzle loading cannons, moved further up the hillside.[237] Following completion, it was officially renamed the Prince of Wales' Battery.[238]

Still, Williamson persisted. In early January 1842 he advertised for a small vessel or barge to convey 750 timbers and knees from 'Lawn Farm', located near New Norfolk, some nine miles down the River Derwent.[239]

However, the first half of 1842 was another poor period for Williamson. In February he sought the public's help in finding his 19-year-old indentured apprentice, John Williams, who had absconded.[240] In March Williamson appeared in the Supreme Court having brought a civil suit against Richard Armstrong, director of the Steam Boat Company, to recoup £20 owed to him for undertaking repairs on the steamship *Derwent*.[241] Unfortunately the case was awarded to the defendant. In April the sale of the '*splendid new schooner Scotia, 120 tons register*', took place at his Battery Point yard.[242] The craft had been built at North West Bay by John Eason. That same month, the behaviour of Williamson's apprentices was highlighted in the local press for '*grossly and wantonly*' insulting '*persons upon several occasions on the high-road, Sandy Bay*'.[243] In May 1842 Williamson was listed as a creditor in the insolvency of Richard Wilton, builder of Hobart Town.[244]

Persevering, Williamson diversified his business interests. In August 1842 he added rope making

---

[234] *Colonial Times*, 7 December 1841.
[235] *The Hobart Town Advertiser*, 23 April 1841.
[236] *The Courier*, 10 September 1841.
[237] *The Courier*, 4 March 1842; en.wikipedia.org/wiki/Hobart_coastal_defences.
[238] *The Hobart Town Advertiser*, 25 March 1842.
[239] *Colonial Times*, 4 January 1842.
[240] *Colonial Times*, 22 February 1842.
[241] *Colonial Times*, 22 March 1842.
[242] R. Parsons (1983). *Ships of Australia and New Zealand Before 1850: Part One K - Z*.
[243] *The Courier*, 17 June 1842.
[244] *The Cornwall Chronicle*, 7 May 1842.

Remnants of the Prince of Wales' Battery (previously named Mulgrave Battery) prior to dismantling (1880s).
Courtesy Allport Library and Museum of Fine Arts, State Library of Tasmania (AUTAS001144580578).

(under David Mackey's management) to his shipyard's commercial activities; the first operation of its kind in the colony.[245] He likely also realised some much needed capital from the sale, by auction, of more of the Derwent Ship Building Company's assets the following month.[246] The inventory included four valuable building allotments fronting on Napoleon Street; a comfortable cottage situated on a valuable plot of ground, adjoining the above, with an excellent wharf, and embracing many advantages; a large building allotment, contiguous to the latter, with extensive water frontage, and *well known as the property of the Shipbuilding Company*'; as well as four building sites on Colville Street.[247] Williamson's personnel issues continued however, with his apprentice William Sawyer being charged with misconduct; the case was dismissed in September 1842.[248]

In February 1843 Williamson advertised for a foreman *'to take the general and effective management'* of his shipyard; the successful applicant was to be provided with a residence on the premises.[249] The following month he launched the 73ft schooner *Sylvanus* from his yard.[250] Due to lack of interest from buyers, the craft was advertised for sale in May 1843, though Williamson retained ownership of the vessel and used it to convey general cargo, timber and shingles to the Victorian ports of Port Albert, Portland Bay, Geelong and Williamstown, returning to Hobart Town with livestock.[251]

Just over two years later, in June 1845, the *Sylvanus* became stranded on a sand bank near Cape Lodi on Van Diemen's Land's east coast while en route to Hobart Town from Port Albert.[252] Its small contingent of passengers, crew, as well as most of its cargo of cattle and sheep, managed to make it safely to land.[253] From the underwriters Williamson received £500 for the loss of his vessel and a few days later the *Sylvanus* was sold at auction.[254] Obviously believing the vessel had suffered only minor damage and could be got off the sand bank without too much trouble, Williamson subsequently purchased the craft for £310.[255]

Within a few weeks Williamson had managed to free the *Sylvanus* and found the vessel relatively unscathed from its misadventure.[256] After undergoing necessary repairs near the stranding, the *Sylvanus* was back at Battery Point in early October 1845.[257] Less than two weeks later, it resumed service to Port Albert.[258]

Three years later Williamson sold the *Sylvanus*. By 1848 the vessel was owned by August Kramer, David Hoy and Henry Brock, and in 1850 by William Boys, Frederick Hall and Matthew Absom.[259] However, the latter trio's possession of the craft only lasted a few months as the *Sylvanus* was completely wrecked on 2 July 1850.[260] While en route to Hobart Town, with a cargo of cattle, butter, and tallow, the vessel ran ashore at Port Albert, Victoria, in the channel that now bears its name, all hands saved.[261]

Much of 1844 was a quiet yet industrious period for Williamson, with new builds underway and repair work continuing. However, a fire at his shipyard in October that year destroyed a weatherboard building used by David Mackey for his rope making works.[262] Fortunately the vessel Williamson then had on the stocks and nearing completion was saved.[263] This craft proved to be the 81ft barque *Harriette Nathan* which was launched the following month for Nathan, Moses and Company, in partnership with William Young and Captain James Gardener, with the intention of employing it in the southern whale fishery.[264]

After spending a few years engaged in various whaling voyages, the *Harriette Nathan* joined the intercolonial trade, sailing between Hobart Town, Port Albert, Twofold Bay, and Adelaide. In 1850 it began sailing between Australia and San Francisco taking advantage of the need for provisions and supplies, particularly building materials, in high demand in California as a result of the gold rush.

Between 1851 and 1866 the *Harriette Nathan* was a regular in the Hobart Town to Port Phillip Bay trade, remarkably without major incident. In September 1866 the craft changed routes again and began sailing between Hobart Town and Auckland, New Zealand. The following year the *Harriette Nathan* was sold to Henry Peak of Hobart Town for £1,100 who intended to run it between Hokitika, New Zealand, and Hobart Town.[265] After several passages between Hobart Town and Hokitika, the vessel sadly vanished en route from New Zealand in April 1868 with the loss of eight hands.[266]

1845 saw more development taking place at Battery Point. With allotments close to Hobart Town becoming highly sought after, the estate of Secheron was

---

[245] *Colonial Times*, 23 August 1842.
[246] *The Courier*, 2 September 1842.
[247] *The Hobart Town Advertiser*, 22 July 1842.
[248] *The Hobart Town Advertiser*, 20 September 1842.
[249] *The Austral-Asiatic Review, Tasmanian and Australian Advertiser*, 10 February 1843.
[250] *Colonial Times*, 21 March 1843.
[251] *The Hobart Town Advertiser*, 23 May 1843; *Colonial Times*, 12 September 1843.
[252] *Colonial Times*, 4 July 1845.
[253] *Colonial Times*, 4 July 1845.
[254] *The Cornwall Chronicle*, 5 July 1845; *The Courier*, 5 July 1845.
[255] *Launceston Examiner*, 12 July, 1845.
[256] *The Courier*, 30 August 1845.
[257] *Colonial Times*, 10 August, 1845.
[258] *The Observer*, 28 October 1845.
[259] R. Parsons (1983). *Ships of Australia and New Zealand Before 1850: Part Two K - Z*; *The Argus*, 14 January 1850; *The Courier*, 5 August 1848.
[260] R. Parsons (1983). *Ships of Australia and New Zealand Before 1850: Part Two K - Z*.
[261] *Colonial Times*, 12 July 1850.
[262] *Colonial Times*, 29 October 1844.
[263] *The Courier*, 5 November 1844.
[264] *Colonial Times*, 16 November 1844.
[265] *Launceston Examiner*, 30 July 1867.
[266] *Colonist*, Volume XI, Issue 1126, 10 July 1868.

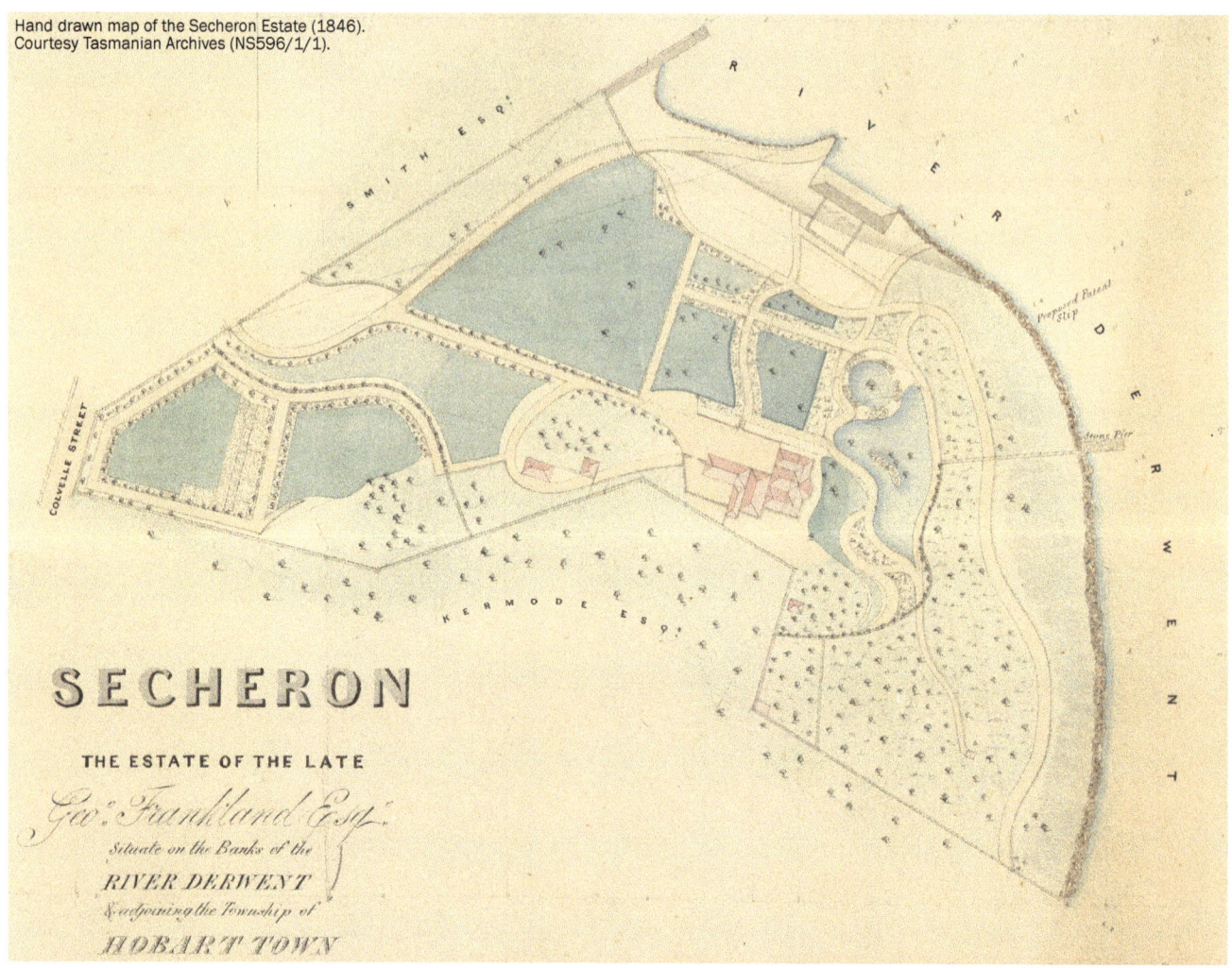

Hand drawn map of the Secheron Estate (1846). Courtesy Tasmanian Archives (NS596/1/1).

subdivided. Included in the sale were 19 allotments, the first comprising the stone residence and garden.[267] A further 10 wharf-side allotments were presented with frontage on the River Derwent of 100ft each, *'commencing at the stone wall which divides this property from Williamson's Ship Building Yard; the depth of water in front of this range of wharfs will admit of the largest vessels lying close aside'*.[268] The additional eight building sites were stated to hold commanding views of Hobart, the harbour and Sandy Bay.[269] The bulk of the land and the house was subsequently purchased by Arthur Perry, solicitor of Hobart Town, in February 1845 for £2,880; considering the low sum realised, the local press stated it was *'awful times for the landed proprietors'*.[270] As evident from the aerial photograph opposite, taken in late 1928, the Secheron estate would remain largely in tact for nearly another 90 years. Of note, the area within the square was the location of Williamson's shipyard, though by this point in time had undergone substantial in-filling and development.

Continuing to ply his trade, in early 1845 Williamson launched the 47ft schooner *Ariel*.[271] The vessel was advertised for freight or charter and described as being *'well adapted for the Launceston or Port Albert trade'*.[272] The weeks that followed saw Williamson involved in several difficult situations. First he faced court, charging Margaret Fay, a pass holder in his service, with stealing £5 from his pocket book which he had left in his jacket on the parlour sofa.[273] She was found guilty and sentenced to seven years' transportation. That same week Williamson had undertaken a fishing trip with George Whitby of the Whalers' Return Hotel to Betsy Island in company with a Mr Hunter of the New Wharf and Frederick Lovett. Preparing to depart from the island and return to Hobart Town, Whitby had taken his seat in the stern of the craft, *'nearly opposite the muzzle of a piece which lay along the thwarts, and, in endeavouring to get a dog on board, by some unfortunate accident the gun went off, and the charge passed through Mr. Whitby's knee; every assistance was immediately rendered by his companions; a messenger was despatched to Hobart Town for medical assistance, and the Guard-boat, with prompt alacrity, brought down Dr. Crowther at an early hour in the*

---

[267] *The Courier*, 1 February 1845.
[268] *The Courier*, 1 February 1845.
[269] *The Courier*, 1 February 1845.
[270] *Colonial Times*, 18 February 1845; *The Tasmanian and Australia-Asiatic Review*, 20 February 1845.
[271] *Colonial Times*, 1 April 1845.
[272] *Colonial Times*, 1 April 1845.
[273] *The Courier*, 10 April 1845.

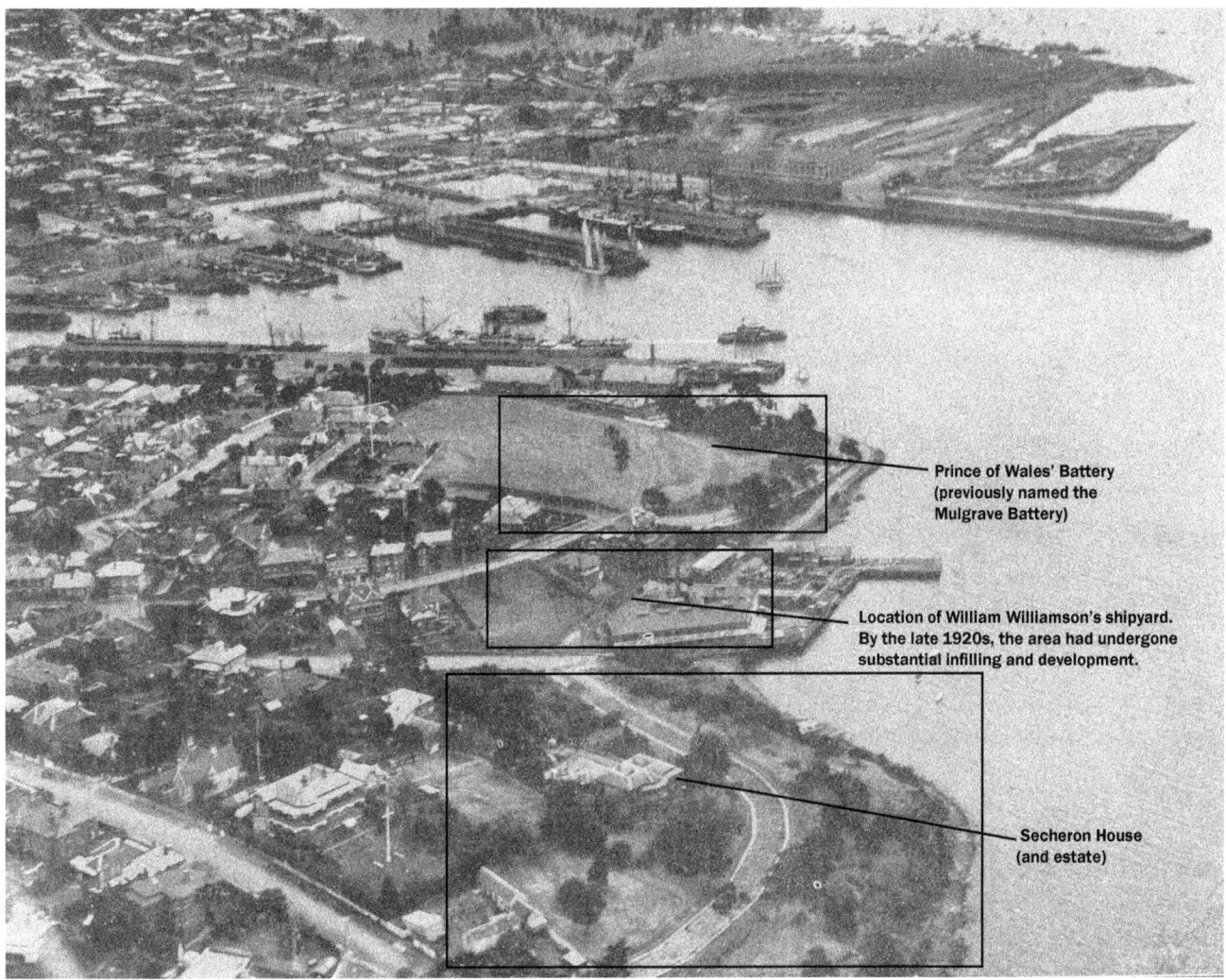

1929 aerial of Battery Point and Hobart wharves.
Illustrated Tasmanian Mail, 2 January 1929.

morning. Having been conveyed to his residence, Mr. Whitby has been unremittingly attended by Doctors Officer and Crowther, and this morning his leg was amputated, high on the thigh ... Sincerely do we regret to state, that the greatest fears are entertained for the recovery of Mr. Whitby'.[274] He died a few days later.[275] An inquest produced a verdict of 'Accidental Death', with several witnesses agreeing that prior to his death George Whitby had stated the accident was occasioned only by himself.[276]

There was likely more despondency when Williamson's new schooner *Ariel* failed to sell; no parties seem to have been interested in the craft and it sat redundant until July 1845, likely an indication of the depressed state of the economy.[277] Advertised for sale in early 1846, by August 1848 the *Ariel* was owned by David Lang of Pittwater and employed in the local river trade.[278] However Lang's possession of the craft was short-lived and the vessel was again offered for sale by auction in August 1851.[279] There are very few records for the *Ariel* during the 1850s and into the early 1860s, likely the result of the movement of coastal and local river traders not being routinely documented. The craft was then noted to be involved in the local timber and produce trade, sailing between Recherche, the Huon and D'Entrecasteaux Channel and Hobart Town. It was most probably the barge *Ariel* that was advertised for sale at Constitution Dock, Hobart Town, in October 1865 by the estate of G. H. Pink and sold to John Hargraves for £190; the same craft then went ashore during a gale at Recherche Bay in June 1866, all hands saved.[280]

Late 1845 and the bulk of 1846 was another busy time for Williamson. He was initially noted as repairing the steamer *Thames* and refitting the whalers *Nimrod*, *Cheviot* and *Marianne*, while much of the latter half of 1846 was spent working on a large vessel built to the order of August Kramer of Hobart Town.[281] However, he continued to have issues with some of

---

[274] *Colonial Times*, 12 April 1845.
[275] *Colonial Times*, 13 April 1845.
[276] *Colonial Times*, 15 April 1845.
[277] *Colonial Times*, 4 July 1845.
[278] *Colonial Times*, 10 March, 1846;
R. Parsons (1983). *Ships of Australia and New Zealand Before 1850: Part One A - J*.
[279] *Colonial Times*, 19 August 1851.
[280] *The Mercury*, 3 October 1865; *Tasmanian Morning Herald*, 20 October 1865; *The Mercury*, 13 June, 9 July 1865.
[281] *The Observer*, 25 November 1845; 6, 30 January, 3 February 1846.

his employees. In October 1846 Williamson took his apprentice Isaac Richardson to court, charging him with being absent without leave.[282] Undeterred, the 75ft brig *Esperanza* was launched from his shipyard on 24 December 1846, built at a cost nearing £3,000.[283] The craft's launch was well attended with much celebration and Christmas revelry had by all.[284]

With August Kramer on board, the *Esperanza* sailed from Hobart Town to the Philippines in February 1847, taking a cargo of meat, candles and cider.[285] The craft then sailed from Manila to Adelaide, arriving on 16 July 1847.[286] The *Esperanza* spent the next few years involved in intercolonial trade, also making occasional trips to Peru, Mauritius and New Zealand. In January 1850 the vessel was purchased by a Mr Cleburne for £1,250, who immediately placed it in the Australia to California trade.[287] Back in Hobart Town by the end of the year, the craft returned to intercolonial trade where it spent the next 18 years, mainly sailing between New South Wales and Victoria, under a plethora of owners.[288]

On 23 February 1868 the *Esperanza* was bound for Melbourne from Newcastle laden with coal. With Captain Baker, his wife, their child, one passenger and seven crew members on board, the vessel was wrecked on Bird Island on the New South Wales coast, the result of bad weather.[289] Sadly, with the exception of Peter Moss, a crew member who managed to make it to shore, all on board were drowned.[290]

Less than two months after the launch of the *Esperanza*, in February 1847 Williamson's Battery Point shipyard and surrounding property was sold at auction. After nearly two decades of ownership, and several attempts to sell during the interim, Thomas Smith, who by now resided in Sydney, relinquished his four-acre property.[291] The parcel was divided into three lots: the first, with 91ft of river frontage, was purchased by Williamson via a mortgage to David Hoy (late government shipbuilder) at a cost of £991; and the second and third lots, with a combined river frontage of 182ft, were purchased by Henry Degraves for £1,174.[292] Degraves also purchased two smaller allotments for £46 and £51, respectively.[293] Ten building allotments were also sold to various parties, located along Hampden Road, including four to Arthur Perry, then owner of the Secheron estate. The entire sale realised £3,361.[294]

With his purchase complete of the Battery Point shipyard that he had leased for many years, Williamson continued operations. Shortly after the auction he began building his largest vessel yet, a 245-ton barque that was launched on 22 August 1848.[295] Measuring 91ft in length, the vessel was purchased by Henry Brock and David Hoy for £2,120 (the latter likely did not provide payment given Williamson owed him a similar amount for purchase of the shipyard property), and named *Margaret Brock*.[296]

After a few trips to New Zealand early on in its career, the *Margaret Brock* settled into intercolonial trade, sailing primarily between South Australia and Hobart Town. On occasion the craft also sailed to California taking passengers to the booming goldfields. The discovery, shortly thereafter, of gold in Victoria also saw the vessel conveying passengers from Adelaide to Geelong in the early 1850s.

On 23 November 1852, while en route to Melbourne from Port Adelaide, the *Margaret Brock* struck a reef that now bears its name near Guichen Bay, South Australia. On ascertaining the seriousness of the situation Captain MacMeekan ordered the vessel's 44 passengers, including five women and three children, and crew, to shore in the craft's boats with a supply of provisions.[297] The contingent landed at Cape Jaffa and spent several days trekking northwards before meeting up with cattlemen who assisted them with the overland journey to Adelaide.[298] The *Margaret Brock* was completely wrecked.[299]

Sadly, construction of the *Margaret Brock* combined with the purchase and subsequent mortgage of his shipyard property likely tipped Williamson over the financial precipice. In March 1848, several months before the launch of this substantial vessel, he announced his insolvency and, in the months following, multiple claims were made against his estate.[300] In August 1848, in conjunction with the launch of the *Margaret Brock*, Williamson's shipbuilding yard, including a new and '*substantially built*' house and other buildings, was sold at public auction to John Watson (by now a well-known shipwright of Battery Point, operating from a yard off Napoleon Street) for £1,150.[301] Also sold was a 177-ton schooner named *Catherine*, a 20-ton schooner named *Jane*, as well as his one-third share in the schooner *Sylvanus*, and several boats.[302]

With his insolvency finalised in October 1848, Williamson was next noted as building '*a vessel down the river ... for parties engaged in the colonial trade ... of*

---

[282] *The Hobart Town Advertiser*, 6 October 1846.
[283] *Colonial Times*, 25 December 1846.
[284] *Colonial Times*, 25 December 1846.
[285] *Launceston Examiner*, 20 February 1847.
[286] *South Australian Register*, 17 July, 11 August 1847.
[287] *The Courier*, 9 January 1850; *Launceston Examiner*, 26 January 1850; *The Courier*, 9 February 1850.
[288] *Colonial Times*, 24 September 1852;
R. Parsons (1983). *Ships of Australia and New Zealand Before 1850: Part One A – J*.
[289] *The Sydney Morning Herald*, 29 February 1868.
[290] *The Sydney Morning Herald*, 29 February 1868.
[291] *The Courier*, 16 January 1847.
[292] *The Courier*, 10 February 1847.
[293] *The Courier*, 10 February 1847.
[294] *Colonial Times*, 9 February 1847; *The Courier*, 10 February 1847.

[295] *The Courier*, 26 August 1848.
[296] *The Courier*, 26 August 1848.
[297] *South Australian Register*, 1 December 1852.
[298] *South Australian Register*, 1 December 1852.
[299] *South Australian Register*, 1 December 1852.
[300] *The Hobart Town Advertiser*, 14, 21 March 1848; *The Courier*, 8 April, 20 May 1848; *Colonial Times*, 20 June 1848.
[301] *The Hobart Town Advertiser*, 1, 25 August 1848; *The Courier*, 23, 26 August 1848; *Colonial Times*, 25 August 1848.
[302] *Colonial Times*, 8, 25 August 1848; *The Courier*, 26 August 1848.

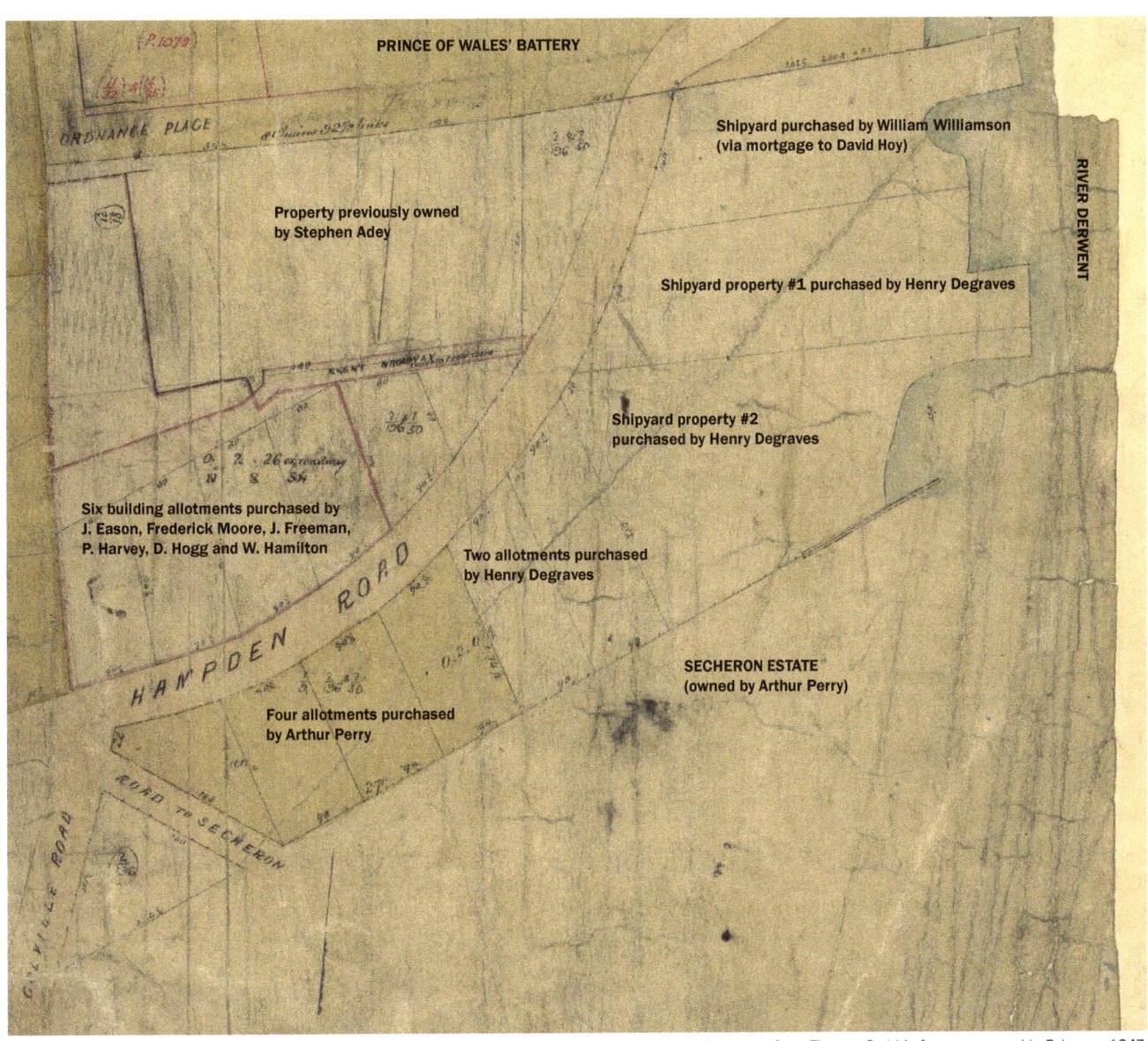

Adapted map showing location of William Williamson's shipyard and others that purchased property from Thomas Smith's four-acre parcel in February 1847. Original courtesy Tasmanian Archives (AF394/1/114)

about 200 tons'.[303] The craft was the brig *Union*, built at Surveyors Bay under '*the immediate superintendence of Mr. Williamson, the well-known shipbuilder, formerly of Battery Point, and is in every respect a credit to his judgement and workmanship ... We are glad his late effort adds so much to his credit; and we hope the owners will realise a good price at the ensuing sale, in order that encouragement may be given to our enterprising ship-builders, and that such men as Mr. Williamson may be constantly kept adding to the mercantile navy of Tasmania*'.[304] The vessel was built in conjunction with Samuel Biggins and launched in July 1849 and, upon being brought up to Hobart Town, was soon thereafter sold to Frederick Patterson.[305]

A few weeks later, on 24 July 1849, Williamson and his son Ramsay departed Hobart Town for Adelaide, South Australia, as passengers on board the barque *Cacique*.[306] Williamson's oldest son William had relocated to Adelaide from Hobart Town earlier in the year.[307] In late September 1849 the trio were joined by Williamson's daughter Catherine and youngest son Sinclair.[308] Now in his 50s, however, his greatest professional achievements were behind him. Owing to a lack of resources, particularly suitable timber, few vessels were built at Port Adelaide during the 1850s. Instead, Williamson spent the remainder of his career repairing and overhauling existing vessels alongside two of his sons, William (Jr), and Ramsay, who also became shipwrights.[309]

William Williamson died at the age of 63 on 9 July 1868 at the Port Adelaide residence of his daughter, Mrs Catherine Martin.[310] He was buried at Alberton

[303] *Colonial Times*, 13 October 1848; *The Courier*, 4 November 1848.
[304] *Colonial Times*, 13 July 1849.
[305] *Colonial Times*, 13, 24 July 1849.
[306] *The Hobart Town Advertiser*, 27 July 1849; *Adelaide Times*, 13 August 1949.
[307] *Adelaide Times*, 26 February 1849.
[308] *Adelaide Times*, 24 September 1849.
[309] *South Australian*, 5 March 1850; *Adelaide Times*, 4 April 1851; *Adelaide Observer*, 19 April 1851; *South Australian Register*, 9 November 1855.
[310] *South Australian Register*, 10 July 1868.

Cemetery, located just south of Port Adelaide.[311] As previously mentioned, Williamson's wife Henrietta died at Hobart Town in November 1839, aged 34, possibly due to complications from childbirth. Of the couple's children, their eldest daughter Catherine married Captain John Martin of Adelaide and died on 4 April 1901 at Birkenhead, Port Adelaide, aged 75.[312] Their eldest son William died at Castlemaine, Victoria, on 3 November 1893 leaving a wife and five daughters.[313] Their second eldest son Ramsay died at Adelaide on 29 January 1904.[314] The couple's youngest son Sinclair died of cancer aged 48 on 8 September 1888 at Birkenhead, Port Adelaide.[315]

Overall, William Williamson was an extremely capable shipbuilder. Born and raised in Scotland, many of his vessels were built off Scottish plans. More than a shipbuilder, however, Williamson was an entrepreneur, building vessels on speculation, retaining ownership or part-ownership in several of these craft, and forming partnerships with Hobart Town's more prominent merchants and businessmen to take advantage of growing intercolonial trade routes. Unfortunately his stint at Battery Point suffered from the economic climate and conditions in which he toiled. Demand for vessels during his career was quite low, particularly in the 1840s when the local economy was poor. In addition, the trades his craft were involved with were still in their infancy and often quite tenuous. The lack of initial sale of some vessels also meant that Williamson retained a share in them. This meant that he suffered twice as much financially when they were wrecked. Owing to the immature state of coastal charting and rudiments of navigation at the time, this occurred quite frequently. Still, Williamson can be favourably recognised as the first commercial shipbuilder of Battery Point. All told he built at least 18 vessels primarily at a yard located next door to the Mulgrave Battery, later Prince of Wales' Battery, between 1835 and 1848, 10 of which were employed in intercolonial and, occasionally international trade.

[311] *South Australian Register*, 11 July 1868.
[312] *The Advertiser*, 6 April 1901.
[313] *Evening Journal*, 23 November 1893.
[314] *Australian Death Index, 1787-1985*.
[315] *Evening Journal*, 8 September 1888.

Vessels built by William Williamson, his partners and employees at Battery Point (1835 - 1848)

Year	Name	Type	Description
1835	*Alligator*	Schooner	33.3 x 12.3 x 10.2ft. 20 tons. Built by William Williamson likely on speculation. Advertised for sale in late January 1836. By May of that year owned by Wm. Williamson & Company (comprising William Williamson, John Eason, David Mackey, Samuel Kendall). By January 1837 owned by Edward Lloyd, by May 1838 by Alexander Imlay. Transferred to Sydney and in 1839 owned by John Hawden and in 1840 by Jane Thompson of Broule (NSW). Subsequent short-term Sydney-based owners were Thomas Dunn; Thomas Dunn and William Aitkenhead; R. R. Ronald; and William Roden. Reportedly wrecked off Bulli (NSW) in late August 1843.
1837	*Lady Franklin*	Schooner	39.0 x 13.1 x 7.4ft. 26 tons. Built by William Williamson on speculation and purchased part-way through construction by Captain Andrew Haig, merchant of Hobart Town. Launched on 18 May 1837. Employed in intercolonial trade, sailing between Hobart Town and Victoria. On 20 April 1838 left Hobart Town for Port Phillip Bay carrying 15 passengers and a cargo of rum, tobacco, furniture, apparel, sugar, tea, potatoes, flour, timber and shingles. The following day Captain John Crocker diverted the craft to Port Arthur to replace the vessel's jib-boom. Continuing on its passage to Victoria six days later, the *Lady Franklin* failed to arrive with no trace of it ever found.
1838	*Fanny*	Schooner	40.0 x 12.0 x 7.6ft. 23 tons. Built by William Williamson and launched on 14 April 1838, built to the order of Captain Andrew Haig. Intended for intercolonial trade, its launch was marred by someone nefariously boring a hole in the vessel's bottom which was soon fixed. Left Hobart Town on 30 May 1838 en route to Western Australia, with Captain James Gill at the helm, on its maiden voyage. Went ashore between Cape Jaffa and Cape Northumberland, South Australia, and became a complete wreck, all hands saved.
1838	-	Whaleboat	First of three whaleboats built by William Williamson or his employees and advertised for sale in August 1838.
1838	-	Whaleboat	Second of three whaleboats built by William Williamson or his employees and advertised for sale in August 1838.
1838	-	Whaleboat	Third of three whaleboats built by William Williamson or his employees and advertised for sale in August 1838.

Year	Name	Type	Description
1839	*Truganina*	Schooner	56.2 x 17.2 x 10ft. 61 tons. Built by William Williamson likely on speculation and *'rebuilt on a former model'*. Initially chartered by Kerr, Alexander, and Company at a cost of £50 per month to transport supplies and provisions to their whaling stations at Southport and Recherche Bay, and to carry timber to Hobart Town on the return leg. By late 1839 under Captain Haig's management and being used to convey passengers and freight between Hobart Town and Port Phillip Bay. In 1840 trading between Adelaide, Port Phillip Bay, and Hobart Town. In January 1841 advertised for sale, freight or charter. Two months later listed for sale by auction, and by mid-1841 registered to George Bilton. Eventually fell into Duncan McPherson's hands, resuming its career in intercolonial trade. Wrecked in late November 1842 when, en route from Port Phillip Bay to Hobart Town, its master sought shelter from a storm in Lady Bay, Victoria, and in the dark it ran into nearby rocks, all hands saved.
1839	*Lillias*	Schooner	60.0 x 17.8 x 9.5ft. 88 tons. Built by William Williamson and launched on 4 October 1839. Built to the order of James Strachan, wool merchant of Hobart Town, specifically for the Port Phillip Bay trade. Built after a Scotch plan. Spent 10 years conveying passengers, livestock, timber and general cargo between Hobart Town, Melbourne and Geelong on a regular schedule. Sold in May 1849 to Captain Lovett for £1,000 with the intention of being sailed between Sydney and California. Either the press report was incorrect or Captain Lovett changed his mind as the vessel shortly thereafter was purchased by James Cook of Circular Quay, New South Wales. Under Cook's patronage, it spent the next three years transporting cargo and passengers between New South Wales, Victoria and Van Diemen's Land. In December 1852 purchased by a Mr Bostock of Warrnambool, Victoria. A few weeks later, blown ashore (on 30 December 1852) during heavy weather in Warrnambool Bay and wrecked (all hands saved).
1840	*Queen*	Schooner	38.0 x 14.4 x 5.1ft. 22 tons. Built by William Williamson as part of the Derwent Ship Building Company. Built on speculation and launched on 16 September 1840 from a newly-established Napoleon Street shipyard, its launch resulting in the death of the yard's foreman, Samuel Kendall, who was crushed while preparing it for launch. Advertised for sale on many occasions immediately after its launch, remained in the hands of various partners of the Derwent Ship Building Company, including George Bilton, who first registered it in August 1841. Disappears from the records until mid-1846 when purchased by Thomas Patterson and placed in the Pittwater to Hobart Town river trade. Advertised for sale in April 1848. A series of short-term owners followed, including John Jackson, George Perriman, James Morling, William Dawson and, finally, in April 1853, James Garth of Port Cygnet. Placed in the river trade, sometimes going by the moniker *Queen of Sorell*. In 1857 converted to a cutter. Wrecked at Sandy Bay, Tasmania, in October 1866, all hands saved. At the time of loss, owned by Edwin Picken of Port Esperance.
1840	*Diana*	Brig	75.0 x 20.1 x 14.6ft. 162 tons. Built by William Williamson as part of the Derwent Ship Building Company and launched on 30 December 1840. A month later advertised for sale, eventually falling into the hands of the Derwent Ship Building Company's partner George Bilton, who advertised it *'for sale, freight, or charter'*. Sailed to Twofold Bay, New South Wales, on 7 February 1842 on is first intercolonial voyage, arriving back at Hobart Town in July with a cargo including 50 head of cattle and 400 wethers. By 1843 placed in the Port Albert, Victoria, to Hobart Town livestock trade. In early July 1843 parted from its cables during a heavy gale in Portland Bay and became embedded in sand, all hands saved. Suffered minimal structural damage, however following survey it was recommended that it be immediately sold *'as is'* for the benefit of all involved. Auctioned off a day later and sold to Henty and Company of Launceston for £400. Within weeks, pulled from the sand and repaired. Arrived in Launceston on 19 August 1843 with a load of bullocks and spars. Spent the next 13 months trading between Launceston and Victoria, with occasional trips to Sydney. Completely wrecked on 1 October 1844 at Port Fairy, Victoria, all hands saved. Henty and Company received an insurance payment of £1,200, and pieces of the wreck were sold off individually.
1840	–	Pleasure boat	Square-sterned 16ft pleasure boat built by William Williams, an employee of the Derwent Ship Building Company. Advertised for sale in April 1840.
1841	*The Arrow*	Gig	Four-oared gig built by William Williamson. Competed at the 1841 Hobart Regatta, held in December of that year.
1841	*The Matchless*	Sailing boat	Sailing boat built by William Williams, likely at the yard of the Derwent Ship Building Company. Competed at the 1841 Hobart Regatta, held in December of that year, and won the first class sailing boat race.
1841	*The Merit*	Sailing boat	Sailing boat built by William Williams, likely at the yard of the Derwent Ship Building Company. Competed at the 1841 Hobart Regatta, held in December of that year.
1842	*Chase-all*	Gig	Four-oared gig built by William Williamson. Competed at the 1841 Hobart Regatta, held in December of that year. Also competed in a private race against the *Comet* for £5 in November 1843. May have been renamed *Atalanta* for the 1843 Hobart Regatta.

Year	Name	Type	Description
1843	*Sylvanus*	Schooner	73.9 x 19.2 x 7.1ft. 72 tons. Built by William Williamson and launched in March 1843. Advertised for sale a few months later though failed to sell. Williamson retained ownership and used it to convey general cargo, timber and shingles to the Victorian ports of Port Albert, Portland Bay, Geelong and Williamstown, returning to Hobart Town with livestock. In June 1845 became stranded on a sand bank near Cape Lodi on Van Diemen's Land's east coast while en route to Hobart Town from Port Albert. Williamson received £500 for the loss of the vessel from the underwriters and a few days later the craft was sold at auction, Williamson purchasing it for £310. Freed within a few weeks and found relatively unscathed from its misadventure, after undergoing necessary repairs near the stranding, the vessel was back at Battery Point in early October 1845. Less than two weeks later, resumed service to Port Albert. Sold three years later. By 1848 owned by August Kramer, David Hoy and Henry Brock, and in 1850 by William Boys, Frederick Hall and Matthew Absom. Completely wrecked on 2 July 1850 while en route to Hobart Town, with a cargo of cattle, butter, and tallow, it ran ashore at Port Albert, Victoria, in the channel that now bears its name, all hands saved.
1843	--	Sailing boat	Sailing boat built by William Williamson to compete at the 1843 Hobart Regatta, held in December of that year.
1844	*Harriette Nathan*	Barque	81.7 x 21.3 x 9.3ft. 126 tons. ON 31951. Built by William Williamson to the order of Nathan, Moses and Company, in partnership with William Young and Captain James Gardener, with the intention of employing it in the southern whale fishery. Launched in November 1844. Spent a few years engaged in various whaling voyages, then joined the intercolonial trade, sailing between Hobart Town, Port Albert, Twofold Bay, and Adelaide. In 1850 began sailing between Australia and San Francisco. Between 1851 and 1866, a regular in the Hobart Town to Port Phillip Bay trade. In September 1866 began sailing between Hobart Town and Auckland, New Zealand. The following year sold to Henry Peak of Hobart Town for £1,100 who intended to run it between Hokitika, New Zealand, and Hobart Town. After several passages between Hobart Town and Hokitika, vanished en route from New Zealand in April 1868 with the loss of eight hands.
1845	*Ariel*	Schooner	47.0 x 12.6 x 5.4ft. 26 tons. Built by William Williamson on speculation. Advertised for freight, or charter soon after launch, described as bring '*well adapted for the Launceston or Port Albert trade*'. Appears to have then sat redundant. Advertised for sale in early 1846, by August 1848 it was owned by David Lang of Pittwater and employed in the local river trade. For sale by auction in August 1851. Likely involved in the local river trader over the next decade, transporting timber and produce between Recherche, the Huon and D'Entrecasteaux Channel and Hobart Town. Most probably the barge of the same name that was advertised for sale at Constitution Dock, Hobart Town, in October 1865 by the estate of G. H. Pink and sold to John Hargraves for £190; this vessel went ashore during a gale at Recherche Bay in June 1866, all hands saved.
1846	*Esperanza*	Brig	75.1 x 23.3 x 11.1ft. 141 tons. Built by William Williamson to the order of August Kramer of Hobart Town and launched on 24 December 1846, built at a cost nearing £3,000. With its owner on board, sailed from Hobart Town to the Philippines in February 1847, taking a cargo of meat, candles and cider. Then sailed from Manila to Adelaide, arriving on 16 July 1847. Spent the next few years involved in intercolonial trade, also making occasional trips to Peru, Mauritius and New Zealand. In January 1850 purchased by a Mr Cleburne for £1,250, who immediately placed it in the Australia to California trade. Back in Hobart Town by the end of the year, the craft returned to intercolonial trade where it spent the next 18 years, mainly sailing between New South Wales and Victoria, under a plethora of owners. On 23 February 1868, bound for Melbourne from Newcastle laden with coal, with Captain Baker, his wife, their child, one passenger and seven crew members on board, the vessel was wrecked on Bird Island on the New South Wales coast, the result of bad weather. All on board except Peter Moss, a crew member who managed to make it to shore, were drowned.
1848	*Margaret Brock*	Barque	91.5 x 23.6 x 13.6ft. 244 tons. Built by William Williamson and launched on 22 August 1848. Prior to completion, purchased by Henry Brock and David Hoy for £2,120. Undertook several trips to New Zealand then settled into intercolonial trade, sailing primarily between South Australia and Hobart Town. On occasion also sailed to California taking passengers to the booming goldfields. Sailed between Adelaide to Geelong in the early 1850s. On 23 November 1852, while en route to Melbourne from Port Adelaide, struck a reef that now bears its name near Guichen Bay, South Australia. The vessel's 44 passengers, including five women and three children, and crew, managed to make it to shore in the craft's boats with a supply of provisions. The vessel was completely wrecked.

John Watson

'One great cause, if indeed not the principal, of the rapid development of this suburb [Battery Point], was the extensive ship–building trade formerly carried on here with Mr. John Watson, as the pioneer.'

The Hobart Town Mercury, 10 February 1858.

John Watson (circa 1870s).
Courtesy Tasmanian Archives (NS543/1/271).

Battery Point's second commercial shipbuilder, John Watson, was born in Beverley, East Yorkshire, England, on 1 November 1801, and baptised at Saint Mary and Saint Nicholas, Beverley, on 30 November that same year.[316] He was the eldest of two children, both boys, born to John (Sr) and Ann Watson, nee Galley.[317] A shipbuilder by trade, Watson's father undertook his seven-year apprenticeship beginning in 1793 at the Plymouth Dockyard in Devon and was likely one of several generations of his family involved in maritime trades.[318] Around 1800 Watson (Sr) moved to Beverley where, for more than a decade, he was involved with the building of vessels of several hundred tons.[319]

Following the demise of the Beverley shipbuilding industry coinciding with the end of the Napoleonic Wars, Watson (Sr) moved to Hampshire, establishing himself and his family at Southampton. It was likely in this location that John Watson undertook a shipbuilding apprenticeship with his father. Afterwards, an ambitious Watson then moved to Mill Wall, Poplar, near London—an area significant for its ocean-going port and a hub for shipbuilding activity—and found employment as a naval architect.[320] Dividing his time between Mill Wall and Southampton, by the mid-1820s Watson had partnered with his father and his younger brother George to form 'Watson and Sons Shipbuilders'.[321] Together the trio launched at least two vessels, including the 91-ton schooner *Orotava* and the 212-ton ship *Eutape*.[322] Both were launched from Northam, Southampton, in 1826, with the *Orotava* built for the Teneriffe, Cadiz, and Oporto wine trade, and the *Eutape* built for the West India trade; the latter to the order of a Mr Forest, merchant of London.[323] John Watson had also married during this period. On 2 April 1825 at All Saints Church, Poplar, he married Mary Middleton, a 21-year-old spinster from Tynemouth, Northumberland.[324] Their first child, a daughter, was born the following year.[325]

---

[316] England, Select Births and Christenings, 1538-1975; Australian Cemetery Index.
[317] England, Select Births and Christenings, 1538-1975.
[318] *Records of the Boards of Stamps, Taxes, Excise, Stamps and Taxes, and Inland Revenue: 1 August 1790 – 28 February 1796.* IR 1/67. The National Archives.
[319] E. Robin (2011). *John Watson (1801 1887): Pioneer Shipbuilder and 'Father or the Wharves'*; www.british-history.ac.uk/report.aspx?compid=36427.
[320] *1825 Pigot's Directory of London and Provincial Towns.*
[321] *Hampshire Chronicle,* 9 August 1830.
[322] *Hampshire Chronicle,* 10 April 1826.
[323] *Hampshire Chronicle,* 10 April , 26 June 1826.
[324] London, England, Church of England Marriages and Banns; England, Select Births and Christenings, 1538-1975.
[325] Australia Cemetery Index, 1808-2007 for Ann Galley Canaway.

The untimely death of John Watson (Sr) in 1830 prompted Watson and his brother George to relinquish the family's shipbuilding business.[326] Shortly thereafter they both made the decision to immigrate to Van Diemen's Land. George was first to leave, arriving in Hobart Town per the *Resource* late in 1830.[327] Within a few months he had established himself as a prominent merchant and was advertising the sale of various imported goods in exchange for local produce, including wheat, from a store located at the Old Wharf.[328] Most likely receiving assistance from his brother John still based in England, several vessels arrived from London with an assortment of cargo and goods consigned to George Watson.[329] Some of these items were conveniently sold to the Van Diemen's Land government, presumably at a more profitable price than could be realised in the open market, while other goods were forwarded to Sydney where their demand may have been higher.[330] Colonial produce such as wool, as well as seal skins were also shipped back to London on George's behalf.[331]

Sensing further financial opportunity, by July 1831 George had partnered with several of Hobart Town's merchants to charter a boat in the river trade, with loading and discharge taking place near his store on the Old Wharf.[332] Around this period he also became an agent for vessels heading to Sydney and London. Capitalising on a new and growing industry, he also began chartering vessels for year-long whaling voyages.[333] In the coming years George would not only invest heavily in this developing industry, including operating a whaling establishment at Recherche Bay, but also coalesce the merchants and traders of Hobart Town to join him in establishing local enterprises as opposed to allowing overseas-based merchants and shipowners to derive benefit from the much sought after resource.[334] Many of these early business transactions were likely conducted from afar as George was known to have been back in England by early 1832 when he married Anne Cunningham at All Saints Church in Poplar on 21 April of that year. A son, George Chale Watson, was born to the couple at Deptford in Kent in September of the following year. George, his bride and newborn son then appear to have sailed back to Van Diemen's Land. In time, George would solidify himself as a prominent merchant and agent of Van Diemen's Land, involved in local, intercolonial and international trade.

Following in his younger brother's footsteps, John Watson, his wife and children, by now comprising four young daughters, as well as his mother Ann, arrived in Hobart Town on board the barque *Norval* on 15 July 1832; Watson receiving a free passage via employment as the ship's carpenter.[335] The 395-ton vessel had left London in early February of that year under the command of Captain H. M. Friend.[336] Watson's wife Mary had given birth to their fourth daughter on board the vessel in late April.[337] The couple named the child Mary Friend Watson after the *Norval*'s captain.

While Battery Point's first commercial boat builder, Daniel Callaghan, had announced his expertise and availability to take on work in the Hobart Town press within days of his arrival back in 1830, it was some nine months after John Watson's arrival, in April 1833, that the *The Hobart Town Courier* finally declared, '*Among the numerous emigrants that have recently come to our shores, we have much pleasure in mentioning one, who is in every way calculated to be of essential service to the colony. We mean Mr John Watson, the shipbuilder, whose talents as a naval architect, from long tried experience and the highest testimonies at home, are completely established. Mr. Watson built several vessels of large burden at Southampton, London, and other ports, and in every instance with the most decided success, both as fast sailers & secure sea-boats*'.[338]

Given this lapse in time, it is apparent that John Watson did not immediately set himself up as a shipbuilder in Van Diemen's Land. Instead, he likely found employment managing his brother George's mercantile, trade and/or whaling enterprises. There was no doubt ample work for him given the intensity with which his brother was involved in the maritime industry and the fact that George is known to have been back in England by this time.

Vessels involved in both intercolonial trade and the whaling industry would have also required overhaul, repair and refitting, perhaps explaining how Watson spent some of his time employed. During this period, however, he is known to have built at least two boats; both were constructed 18 months after he had arrived from England and both were of a recreational variety as opposed to a commercial need. These were the *Fox* and *Daisy*, built specifically to compete at the Hobart Town Regatta held in February 1834.[339] Noted in the press as the '*most elegant and best equipped yatch* [sic], *we have ever had belonging to this port*', the *Fox* finished first in the race for decked boats.[340] Likewise, the *Daisy* finished first in the race for large open boats.[341]

Shortly following the 1834 Hobart Town Regatta, Watson found himself in favour with the colonial government. William Moriarty, port officer of Hobart Town, recommended him for the position of Master Shipwright at the newly-established shipyard of the Port Arthur penal settlement.[342] Accepting the position

---

[326] *Hampshire Chronicle*, 9 August 1830.
[327] *The Tasmanian*, 31 December 1830; *Colonial Times*, 31 December 1830.
[328] *The Tasmanian*, 11 February, 25 June 1831.
[329] *The Hobart Town Courier*, 9 April 1831.
[330] *The Tasmanian*, 28 May 1831; *Colonial Times*, 22 June 1831.
[331] *The Hobart Town Courier*, 16 July 1831.
[332] *The Tasmanian*, 2 July 1831.
[333] *The Hobart Town Courier*, 26 October 1832, 18 January 1833; *Colonial Times*, 3 September 1833.
[334] *The Hobart Town Courier*, 28 August 1835; *Colonial Times*, 25 September 1835.
[335] E. Robin (2011). *John Watson (1801 1887): Pioneer Shipbuilder and 'Father of the Wharves'*; *The Hobart Town Courier*, 20 July 1832.
[336] *Hampshire Telegraph and Naval Chronicle*, 13 February 1832.
[337] Libraries Tasmania (RGD32/1/2/ no 5296).
[338] *The Hobart Town Courier*, 12 April 1833.
[339] *Trumpeter General*, 7 March 1834.
[340] *Colonial Times*, 4 March 1834.
[341] *Colonial Times*, 4 March 1834.
[342] E. Robin (2011). *John Watson (1801 1887): Pioneer Shipbuilder and 'Father of the Wharves'*.

Port Arthur Penal Settlement (1847). The dockyard was located around the bluff on the left. Courtesy Tasmanian Archives (NS479/1/71).

at a salary of £150 per year plus rations, John Watson arrived at Port Arthur with his wife, children, now comprising five daughters, and mother per the *Isabella* on 12 April 1834.[343] His need to accept this position may have been driven by Watson temporarily closing his brother's retail business and selling all of the stock at an auction held at the Old Wharf in January 1834.[344] Upon George's return to Hobart Town, he would open another store at the Old Wharf.

After spending some months establishing a shipyard at Port Arthur, where he was master shipwright of up to 80 adult convicts and boys from nearby Port Puer, Watson settled into work, laying down the keel of a nearly 100-ton schooner in May 1834.[345] Between May 1835 and March 1836 he launched several vessels, including the 97-ton schooner *Eliza* and the 19-ton schooner *Emily*.[346] However, owing to an incident in which the welfare of his seven-year-old daughter was compromised, in early 1836 Watson resigned from his position at Port Arthur effective almost immediately.[347]

The 284-ton barque *Fanny*, which he was noted as building at the time of his resignation, was completed by his successor David Hoy in December 1837.[348]

By May 1837 Watson was noted as building a 40-ton vessel at Browns River, on the banks of the River Derwent south of Hobart Town.[349] A few months later he was employed at a whaling establishment at Southport, likely owned or part-owned by his brother.[350]

During these years George Watson had invested heavily in the whaling industry, including the purchase and provision of ships and the establishment of bay whaling stations at Southport, Recherche Bay and on Van Diemen's Lands' east coast.[351] George also invested in the building of vessels to furnish the developing intercolonial trade, including the 28-ton schooner *Victoria* built by John Watson at George's premises at the Old Wharf and launched in late 1837.[352] This particular yard had lately been in the possession of John Gray, shipbuilder.[353] The *Victoria* may actually have been the vessel noted under construction at Browns River that

---

[343] E. Robin (2011). *John Watson (1801 1887): Pioneer Shipbuilder and 'Father of the Wharves'*.
[344] *Colonial Times*, 14 January 1834.
[345] *The Hobart Town Courier*, 22 May 1834; portarthur.org.au/the-dockyard/.
[346] *Morning Star and Commercial Advertiser*, 26 May 1835; *The Sydney Monitor*, 23 March 1836; M. Nash (2001). *Convict Shipbuilding and the Port Arthur Dockyard*.
[347] E. Robin (2011). *John Watson (1801 1887): Pioneer Shipbuilder and 'Father of the Wharves'*; *Colonial Times*, 23 February 1836.
[348] M. Nash (2001). *Convict Shipbuilding and the Port Arthur Dockyard*.
[349] *Bent's News and Tasmanian Three-Penny Register*, 6 May 1837.
[350] *The Hobart Town Courier*, 14 July 1837.
[351] W. Lawson & the Shiplovers' Society of Tasmania (1949). *Blue Gum Clippers and Whale Ships of Tasmania*; *Colonial Times*, 4 August 1840.
[352] R. Parsons (1983). *Ships of Australia and New Zealand Before 1850: Part Two K - Z*.
[353] *Colonial Times*, 5 September 1837.

was subsequently completed at the Old Wharf, where the builders certificate notes that it was launched on 10 November 1837.[354]

Just under a year later, on 11 October 1838, John Watson launched another schooner, the *Bandicoot*.[355] Like the *Victoria*, this vessel was built to the order of his brother George at the Old Wharf.[356] Intended for the Port Phillip Bay trade, the craft was sold to William Young and Duncan McPherson in December 1839 and subsequently placed in intercolonial trade, also making occasional trips to New Zealand.[357]

The *Victoria* and *Bandicoot* were complemented by several small recreational boats built by John Watson, likely at the Old Wharf location. These included the four-oared gig *Wallaby* and the five-oared whaleboat *Tasman*.[358] Both competed at the 1838 Hobart Town Regatta, held in December of that year and given the title of the first 'Hobart Town Anniversary Regatta', where they won their respective races.

The Hobart Town Regatta would quickly become a popular and welcome social holiday for the local population, the offerings including entertainment, food and refreshments, as well as a highly-competitive series of races involving local competitors and those from visiting vessels. While the arrival of Van Diemen's Lands' new Lieutenant-Governor in early January 1837, Sir John Franklin, had unhinged several of its more prominent residents, mainly chief supporters of Lieutenant-Governor George Arthur, the new administration and its encouragement of aquatic sports resulted in a type of boat becoming a prolific boon for Hobart Town's resident boat builders for many decades: the smaller racing boat, whether it be yacht, gig, whaleboat or dinghy.[359] Sir John Franklin

[354] R. Parsons (1983). *Ships of Australia and New Zealand Before 1850: Part Two K - Z*.
[355] *Colonial Times*, 16 October 1838.
[356] *Colonial Times*, 16 October 1838.
[357] R. Parsons (1983). *Ships of Australia and New Zealand Before 1850: Part Two K - Z*.
[358] *The True Colonist Van Diemen's Land Political Despatch and Agricultural and Commercial ...* ; 7 December 1838.
[359] *The Tasmanian*, 6 January 1837.

Courtesy Tasmanian Archives (NS3431/1/16).

instigated his first government-backed regatta held on 1 December 1838 and from the get-go the local boat builders were quick to capitalise on its opportunities. With an estimated 12,000 assembled on shore and afloat, the event also proved a worthwhile investment for John Watson.[360] The four-oared gig *Wallaby* he likely built for his brother George won first prize in its race, collecting 15 sovereigns in prize money. Watson's five-oared whaleboat *Tasman* also won first prize out of 16 boats in its race; Watson being presented by the Sir John Franklin with a purse of 30 sovereigns.[361]

In mid-1839 John Watson moved his shipyard operations from his brother's property at the Old Wharf to his own yard at Battery Point.[362] Located on the edge of the River Derwent just off Napoleon Street, the parcel of land, comprising 3 roods and 19 perches, i.e., just under one acre, was then in the possession of Captain James Kelly, well-known Hobart Town mariner and whaler, along with R. O'Farrell, J. Montagu, Thomas Brown and William Knight.[363] The property had originally been part of the 90-acre parcel granted to William Sorell, conveyed to William Kermode and subsequently transferred to Thomas Horne.[364] After leasing the property for a number of years, in 1847 John Watson would petition for its ownership.[365]

Following establishment of his new shipyard, in October 1839 Watson was noted as having repaired the *Lord Hobart* at the property; a brig involved in intercolonial trade recently purchased by his brother George.[366] Another vessel he repaired around the same time was the barque *Samuel Cunard*.[367]

The Second Hobart Town Anniversary Regatta, held on the River Derwent on 3 December 1839 provided another opportunity for Watson to exhibit his smaller-built craft and to recoup some money. In the race for five-oared whaleboats, he entered the *Van Diemen*. Competing against a fleet of 19 craft, the vessel finished first, collecting a purse of £30.[368] Of note, this amount was equivalent to the annual salary of a tradesman or labourer in Van Diemen's Land at the time.[369] In presenting Watson with the prize, Sir John Franklin was reportedly, '*happy to learn that he was a person who abstained from an indulgence in ardent spirits; it gave him great pleasure to award to Mr. Watson a similar prize to that which he received last year, namely, the first whale-boat prize. After some observations on the advantages of encouraging boat-building, his Excellency presented the prize contained in an elegant purse of blue and white silk, ornamented with gold rings, to the successful winner, who retired amidst the cheers of the crowd; as did also the other successful competitors*'.[370]

Likely putting his prize money to good use, the first large vessel built by Watson at his newly-established Battery Point shipyard was launched in early 1840.[371] Built to the order of Thomas Lucas, whaler of Hobart Town, the 130-ton schooner *Sisters* spent over a decade employed in intercolonial trade, also making regular trips to New Zealand and occasional trips to Asia.[372] In 1847 the craft was purchased by Duncan McPherson and John Guthrie of Hobart Town for £1,780, and in 1848 by McPherson and Hugh Clark.[373] Five years later, on 8 April 1852, the *Sisters* was wrecked during a gale at Turanganui in Poverty Bay, New Zealand, all hands saved.[374]

On 12 August 1840, six months after completing the *Sisters*, Watson launched the 78-ton schooner *Flying Squirrel* from his Battery Point shipyard.[375] Built for himself in partnership with Alfred Garrett, the vessel was intended for the Port Phillip Bay trade.[376] Though a regular trader between various Victorian ports and Hobart Town for the next two decades, by December 1841 the craft was owned by J. S. and Arthur Willis.[377] A succession of short-term owners then followed.[378] By

George Frankland's Map of Hobart Town and Battery Point (c1830s), showing the location of John Watson's Battery Point shipyard off Napoleon Street. Courtesy Tasmanian Archives (AUTAS001139593859).

---

[360] *The True Colonist Van Diemen's Land Political Despatch and Agricultural and Commercial ...* ; 7 December 1838.
[361] *The True Colonist Van Diemen's Land Political Despatch and Agricultural and Commercial ...* ; 7 December 1838.
[362] *Colonial Times*, 24 September 1839.
[363] www.thelist.tas.gov.au (Historical Deeds 01/2858, 02/6081, 02/6082); *The Cornwall Chronicle*, 13 November 1847.
[364] *The Courier*, 12 November 1841.
[365] www.thelist.tas.gov.au (Historical Deeds 01/2858, 02/6081, 02/6082); *The Courier*, 12 November 1841.

[366] *Colonial Times*, 15 October 1839.
[367] *The True Colonist Van Diemen's Land Political Despatch, and Agricultural and Commercial ...* , 21 August 1840.
[368] *Colonial Times*, 3 December 1839; *The Hobart Town Courier and Van Diemen's Land Gazette*, 6 December 1839.
[369] Statistical Society (Great Britain) (1838). *Journal of the Statistical Society of London*.
[370] *Colonial Times*, 10 December 1839.
[371] R. Parsons (1983). *Ships of Australia and New Zealand Before 1850: Part Two K - Z*; *Colonial Times*, 5 May 1840.
[372] *Colonial Times*, 12 January 1841; *Launceston Examiner*, 5 July 1845.
[373] R. Parsons (1983). *Ships of Australia and New Zealand Before 1850: Part Two K - Z*; *Launceston Examiner*, 23 January 1847.
[374] *Otago Witness*, Issue 57, 19 June 1852.
[375] *Tasmanian Weekly*, 14 August 1840; *Colonial Times*, 18 August 1840.
[376] R. Parsons (1983). *Ships of Australia and New Zealand Before 1850: Part One A - J*.
[377] R. Parsons (1983). *Ships of Australia and New Zealand Before 1850: Part One A - J*.
[378] R. Parsons (1983). *Ships of Australia and New Zealand Before 1850: Part One A - J*.

the early 1860s the *Flying Squirrel* was embarking on whaling voyages, though with mixed success.[379] Several years later, and into the 1870s, it was a regular in intercolonial trade under ownership of Piggott Brothers and, afterwards, H. Haege.[380] Following a remarkable 35 years of service the vessel was wrecked off King Island in September 1875, all hands saved.[381]

Another boat completed by Watson late in 1840 at Battery Point was the gig *Hyacinth*. Built to compete at that years' Hobart Town Regatta, the craft finished third in the race for gigs pulling four-oars with Watson at the helm.[382] The following year saw Watson again compete in the gig race at the Hobart Town Regatta where he finished first in the *Centipede*.[383] He also won a whaleboat race in the *Opposition*.[384] Both boats were built by Risby and Son of Collins Street (later boat builders of Battery Point).[385] Watson was, however, named as the builder of a first-class sailing boat named *The Tasman* that was sailed by a Mr Wray in that year's regatta race.[386] During this period he additionally furnished the Government of Van Diemen's Land with vessels he had built, including a punt and a small boat upon which payment was granted in July and October of 1841, respectively.[387] In March of the following year two more boats were supplied to the Colonial Treasury.[388]

In early 1842 Watson's most ardent supporter, his brother George, became insolvent.[389] Like many of his peers, the decline in wheat prices combined with the outbreak of disease affecting the livestock and wool trades, and the costs associated with supplying and outfitting whaling stations and vessels, meant that George was financially strained and forced to sell off many of his assets.[390] In time, however, George would recover from this financial discord, continuing to operate his warehouse at the Old Wharf and manage vessels involved in intercolonial trade, as well as his commercial whaling interests.

Undeterred by these family-related events, John Watson continued apace. In May 1842 he launched a 69ft paddle steamer powered by a 20 h.p. non-condensing engine for use as a ferry on the River Derwent.[391] Intended to travel between Risdon, Bridgewater, Compton Ferry and Hobart Town, the *Native Youth* was built to the order of Henry Davidson and Alexander Clark.[392] The vessel spent the next few years transporting passengers, goods and produce across the Derwent; from 1846 owned by James Murdoch.[393]

In 1850 the *Native Youth* was purchased by William Green and ceased operating on the Derwent.[394] It was, however, back in James Murdoch's hands in 1853, trading between Hobart Town and New Norfolk.[395] By 1854 the *Native Youth* had been converted to a schooner and its engines removed.[396] Following a stint in coastal trade under various owners, primarily transporting coal, the *Native Youth* was wrecked at Goose Island, Bass Strait, on 22 November 1863 after delivering stores to the lighthouse station, all hands saved.[397]

The second large vessel built by John Watson in 1842 was the schooner *Flying Fish*, launched from his Battery Point shipyard on 29 November.[398] Built to the order of a syndicate of eight local merchants, including Alfred Garrett, John Clinch, J. W. Storie and himself, the craft was intended for the Port Phillip Bay trade.[399] Stated to be one of the fastest intercolonial schooners of its time, the 83ft *Flying Fish* spent nearly two decades trading primarily between Hobart Town and Victoria under various owners before being wrecked at Port Elliot, South Australia, after parting from its moorings during a storm on 3 December 1860, all hands saved.[400]

The mid-1840s proved the start of a busy period for John Watson. In early 1845 his Battery Point shipyard was busy overhauling and repairing the brig *Industry* at a cost approaching £1,000, recently purchased by a Mr Nathan for use in the whaling industry.[401] That same year his yard was also noted as refitting the *Harriette Nathan*, the *Ariel*, the whaler *Highlander*, and being entrusted with the sale of the schooner-rigged boat *Vestal* which had been built in Deal, England, and imported to Van Diemen's Land on board the barque *Kinnear*.[402] With the dual goal of sourcing timber and expanding his shipbuilding operations, in 1845 Watson applied to the Government of Van Diemen's Land, successfully receiving a land grant in the D'Entrecasteaux Channel. The property, comprising more than 500 acres, was named Middleton after his wife's family.[403]

Along with continuing to undertake refit, repair and overhaul work, the following year saw John Watson launch his largest vessel to date. On 20 October 1846 the barque *Flying Childers*, built to the order of his

---

[379] *The South Australian Advertiser*, 28 April 1860; *The Mercury*, 20 May 1861.
[380] *The Argus*, 11 October 1875.
[381] *The Argus*, 11 October 1875.
[382] *Tasmanian Weekly Dispatch*, 4 December 1840.
[383] *The Courier*, 3 December 1841.
[384] *The Courier*, 3 December 1841.
[385] *Colonial Times*, 7 December 1841.
[386] *Colonial Times*, 7 December 1841.
[387] *The Hobart Town Advertiser*, 27 July, 5 October 1841.
[388] *Launceston Examiner*, 19 March 1842.
[389] *Launceston Courier*, 10 January 1842.
[390] *The Courier*, 4 February 1842; *The Hobart Town Advertiser*, 25 March 1842.
[391] *Launceston Examiner*, 28 May 1842; *Colonial Times*, 31 May 1842.
[392] *Colonial Times*, 16 August 1842;
R. Parsons (1983). *Ships of Australia and New Zealand Before 1850: Part Two K - Z*.
[393] *The Courier*, 1 July 1846.
[394] *The Courier*, 20 April 1850.
[395] *Colonial Times*, 10 March 1853; Parsons (1983). *Ships of Australia and New Zealand Before 1850: Part Two K - Z*.
[396] *Colonial Times*, 16 March 1854;
R. Parsons (1983). *Ships of Australia and New Zealand Before 1850: Part Two K - Z*.
[397] *The Mercury*, 28 November 1863.
[398] *Launceston Examiner*, 3 December 1842.
[399] *Launceston Examiner*, 3 December 1842;
R. Parsons (1983). *Ships of Australia and New Zealand Before 1850: Part One A - J*.
[400] *The Mercury*, 23 January 1861; R. Parsons (1983). *Ships of Australia and New Zealand Before 1850: Part One A - J*; *The South Australian Register*, 4 December 1860.
[401] *Colonial Times*, 8 February 1845.
[402] *Colonial Times*, 21 October 1845; *The Observer*, 14 November 1845; *The Hobart Town Advertiser*, 6 January 1846.
[403] E. Robin (2011). *John Watson (1801 1887): Pioneer Shipbuilder and 'Father of the Wharves'*.

Flying Fish (circa 1850s).
Courtesy State Library of South Australia (B 22217).

brother George (by now recovered from his financial difficulties), was launched, the christening ceremony performed by John Watson's daughter Jane.[404] Intended for the whaling industry, the 229-ton vessel was estimated to have been built at a cost of £4,000.[405] With 21-year-old Captain Edward Lucas at the helm, the *Flying Childers* operated as a successful whaling vessel for many years in the South Seas.[406]

Less than two months following completion of the *Flying Childers*, the schooner *Miranda* was launched from John Watson's Battery Point shipyard on 15 December 1846.[407] This time the ceremony was performed by his daughter Ann, amidst the loud applause of a large concourse of spectators.[408] The Hobart Town press reported, '*We are gratified in having to notice the kindness, and liberality evinced by Mr. Watson, the ship-builder of Battery Point, toward the people of his establishment, on Thursday last. After the launch by him of the Miranda, he entertained them all, (nearly fifty in number, of all grades,) to an excellent dinner, and an abundance of wine, ale, &c., in fact, with anything the men themselves thought would contribute to their comfort and enjoyment. ... We like these acknowledgments, (after the old English fashion,) of the services of the employed, by the employers. ... The men should be known to the masters, and the masters to the men, not only in the hours of toil, but in those of rational happiness, and relaxation. We admit, that in this Colony, to carry these feelings into practice is difficult, but "where there is a will, there is a way," and, in this instance, as on previous occasions of the kind, it seems to be no very great difficulty with Mr. Watson*'.[409]

Flying Childers (circa 1850s).
Courtesy Maritime Museum of Tasmania (P_GSL143).

[404] *Colonial Times*, 20 October 1846.
[405] *Colonial Times*, 20 October 1846; *The Hobart Town Courier*, 20 October 1846.
[406] W. Lawson & the Shiplovers' Society of Tasmania (1949). *Blue Gum Clippers and Whale Ships of Tasmania*.
[407] *Colonial Times*, 15, 18 December 1846.
[408] *Colonial Times*, 18 December 1846; *The Hobart Town Herald and Total Abstinence Advocate*, 19 December 1846.
[409] *The Britannia and Trades' Advocate*, 24 December 1846.

Built to the order of Captain Godfrey Bentley and a John Reeve of Gippsland, Victoria, the 76ft *Miranda* was a regular in the Port Albert to Hobart Town cattle trade for several years.[410] The vessel was wrecked at Rabbit Island near Wilsons Promontory, Victoria, during a gale on 7 August 1852, all hands saved.[411]

1846 was a busy period in the development of Battery Point more generally. Homes and small cottages continued to be built as more people moved to the area. The presence of an increasing number of residents and commercial enterprises also resulted in the need for more roads, footpaths, drainage, sewer and services. Of significance, in early May 1846 Richard Burt was granted a licence for a public house to be called the Shipwrights' Arms.[412] Nearly 180 years later, the still-extant hotel has proudly remained in operation, located on the corner of Trumpeter and Colville streets.

Sandy Bay Baths from the bottom of Napoleon Street (circa 1860s).
Courtesy W L Crowther Library, State Library of Tasmania (Abbott Album, 136189370).

The Shipwrights' Arms Hotel (circa 1930s, before extensive enlargement).
Courtesy Tasmanian Archives (PH30/1/7587).

Also established just south of Battery Point during this period was the Sandy Bay Baths. In November 1846 the proprietor, George Cooper, advertised that in providing every necessary accommodation that may be required, a '*substantial bridge had been erected for the convenience of persons proceeding to the Baths from Battery Point, so that they can avoid what has heretherto been a great objection, namely, reaching the Baths with wet or damp feet*'.[413] Deemed '*rough*' in construction, the bridge provided a welcome gangway for those wishing to partake in a cold or hot bath at a rather moderate price.[414] However, there were also problems to deal with. Thistles in the New Wharf and Battery Point neighbourhood were noted as being plentiful and in need of removal.[415]

With so much development going on nearby, John Watson appears to have remained more than satisfied with his stake at Battery Point. Given his inclination to take care of his employees, it is believed that he helped orchestrate the construction of four adjoining cottages to be built along Napoleon Street for his workers, the tender for which was announced by the then landholder, James Peek Poynter, in late 1846.[416] Still standing today, the cottages are a poignant reminder of John Watson and his legacy. He would formally take possession of the parcel of land in June 1848.[417]

TO BUILDERS, &c.

FOUR adjoining Cottages are required to be erected in Napoleon-street, Battery Point, the plans and specifications of which may be seen on application to Mr. Poynter, on the New Wharf; and tenders for the same will be received by him until 12 o'clock on Friday the 1st January 1847.

The entire work to be comprised in one tender, and the contractor will be required to give security for the due performance of the contract.

December 21, 1846.   2458

Colonial Times, 25 December 1846.

---

[410] *Colonial Times*, 18 December 1846; *Launceston Examiner*, 30 December 1846.
[411] *The Argus*, 20 August 1852; *Colonial Times*, 27 August 1852.
[412] *The Courier*, 6 May 1846.
[413] *Colonial Times*, 13 November 1846.
[414] *The Hobart Town Advertiser*, 25 December 1846.
[415] *The Hobart Town Advertiser*, 27 November 1846.
[416] *Colonial Times*, 25 December 1846.
[417] www.thelist.tas.gov.au (Historical Deeds 03/3690, 03/4401).

Conjoined cottages located on Napoleon Street near the corner of Derwent Lane (c1970s).
Courtesy Tasmanian Archives, Margaret Bryant Collection (NS3373/1/201).

During this period John Watson and his ever-growing family, now encompassing eight daughters and three sons, was also living at Battery Point, at a house located on the corner of Napoleon and Sloane streets. John and his wife Mary's last child, a girl named Maria, would be born in 1847. With their eldest child born in England in 1826, many of their children were approaching adulthood and beginning to leave the nest. The first to marry was their eldest daughter, Ann Galley Watson. She married Phillip Cannaway, master of the Hobart Town Grammar School at the Wesleyan Chapel in Melville Street on 1 January 1847.[418] Witnesses to the event were John Watson and his brother George.[419]

Either as a wedding present or in kindness to the newly-wed couple, the *Colonial Times* of 13 August 1847 stated that, '*Mr. John Watson, the well-known ship-builder, is about to erect a very fine edifice on the allotment at the corner of Macquarie and Harrington-streets, and opposite the Catholic Church, which is intended for a seminary and dwelling-house for Mr. Cannaway. The building will be constructed with every convenience adapted to a commodious academy, and the situation is most favourable in every particular*'. With the property comprising 36 perches, the building was located on the current site of the Travelodge Hotel, on the corner of Macquarie and Harrington streets, directly opposite St Josephs Catholic Church.

[418] *Colonial Times*, 5 January 1847.
[419] Libraries Tasmania (RGD37/1/6 no. 1061).

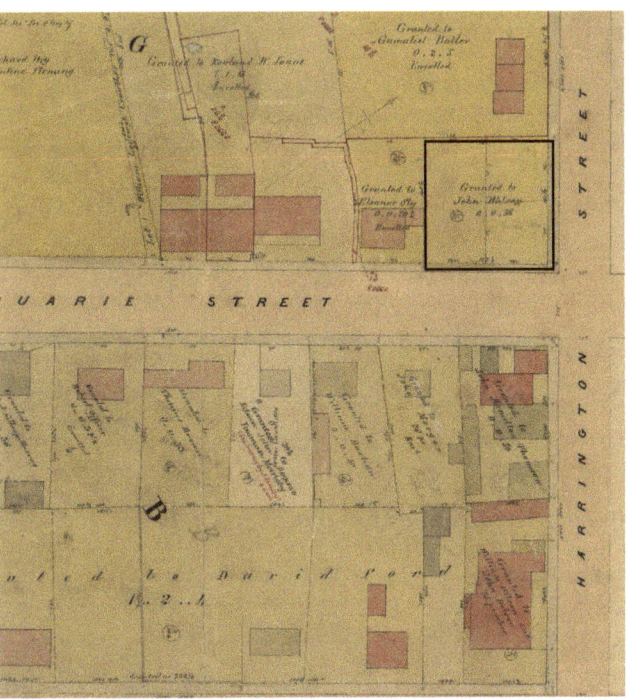

Map showing location of property (in bold box) granted to John Watson for his son-in-law Phillip Cannaway.
Courtesy Tasmanian Archives (AF393/1/54).

Map of Battery Point, showing location of John Watson's residential property and shipyard (circa 1850s). Courtesy Tasmanian Archives (AF93/1/39).

More real estate transactions soon followed. Having occupied his Napoleon Street shipyard for eight years, in 1847 John Watson petitioned the City of Hobart Town for its possession.[420] The near one-acre parcel was formally transferred to him the following year.[421]

With business continuing to thrive, an extraordinary occurrence took place at John Watson's Battery Point shipyard on 20 January 1848 with the launch of two vessels: the barque *Fair Tasmanian* and the schooner *Circassian*.[422] Intended for the Port Albert to New Zealand cattle trade, the former was built to the order of John Johnson, ship chandler of Hobart Town, while the latter was intended for the Port Phillip Bay trade and built to the order of Messrs Maxwell and Smith.[423]

With its figure head carved by William Duke, a noted '*master of the chisel as well as the pencil*', the 144-ton *Fair Tasmanian* was unfortunately damaged by fire at its mooring off Watson's shipyard in March 1848 and scuttled to extinguish the flames.[424] The vessel was soon repaired and sailed on its maiden voyage to Port Albert two months later.[425] The *Fair Tasmanian* spent the next 13 years employed in intercolonial and trans-Tasman trades, also making occasional trips to Mauritius, London and California.[426] It was wrecked after parting from its mooring at Warrnambool, Victoria, on 28 May 1864, all hands saved.[427] At the time of loss, it was owned by Valentine Wright of Melbourne.[428]

The 95-ton *Circassian* was a regular in the Port Phillip Bay trade for 15 years, under several different owners.[429] In August 1864 the craft was purchased by Piggott Brothers of Melbourne and placed in the Port Frederick trade.[430] Sadly the *Circassian* was wrecked several months later, on 6 October 1864, near Ram Head, Victoria, drowning three of its crew.[431]

1848 also saw John Watson continuing to establish saw milling operations at the 500-acre Middleton property he had acquired 30-miles south of Hobart Town on the D'Entrecasteaux Channel. Here, a variety of timbers were prepared, with the press noting that, '*a keel had been cut there 110 feet long in one piece. Everything, planks and all, were on the same scale*'.[432] Meanwhile, building works were on-going at the junction of Macquarie and Harrington streets, to be established as a school for his son-in-law.[433] Designed by Alexander Dawson and built by a Mr Roberts, some of the timber for the property's construction was likely transferred to Hobart Town from Watson's mill at Middleton.[434] The Tasmanian Academy opened its door to students in early February 1848.[435]

With the ability to source and prepare his own timber, another vessel built by John Watson in 1848 was the 187-ton barque *Flying Fox*, launched from his Battery Point yard on 2 November 1848.[436] It was the fourth vessel he had built to the order of his brother George, and was intended for employment in the whaling industry.[437]

The *Flying Fox* left Hobart Town for the South Seas on its maiden voyage on 16 January 1849 with Captain Chamberlain at the helm, returning on 14 November with 200 tons of oil and bone.[438] After being resupplied, the vessel left Hobart Town in January 1850, this time

---

[420] *The Cornwall Chronicle*, 13 November 1847.
[421] www.thelist.tas.gov.au (Historical Deeds 01/2858, 02/6081, 02/6082); *The Cornwall Chronicle*, 5 August 1848.
[422] *Colonial Times*, 21 January 1848.
[423] *Colonial Times*, 21 January 1848; *The Courier*, 19, 22 January 1848.
[424] *Hobarton Guardian, or, True Friend of Tasmania*, 22 January 1848; *Colonial Times*, 7 March 1848; *The Courier*, 24 May 1848.
[425] *Hobarton Guardian, or, True Friend of Tasmania*, 22 January 1848; *Colonial Times*, 7 March 1848; *The Courier*, 24 May 1848.
[426] W. Lawson & the Shiplovers' Society of Tasmania (1949). *Blue Gum Clippers and Whale Ships of Tasmania*.
[427] *The Mercury*, 9 June 1864.
[428] *The Argus*, 20 May 1863; *The Mercury*, 9 June 1864.
[429] R. Parsons (1983). *Ships of Australia and New Zealand Before 1850: Part One A - J*.

[430] *Launceston Examiner*, 18 August 1864.
[431] *Launceston Examiner*, 27 October 1864.
[432] *The Hobart Town Advertiser*, 21 January 1848.
[433] *The Hobart Town Advertiser*, 15 February 1848.
[434] *The Courier*, 13 May 1848.
[435] *The Courier*, 16 February 1848.
[436] *The Courier*, 4 November 1848; *Colonial Times*, 7 November 1848.
[437] *The Courier*, 4 November 1848; *Colonial Times*, 7 November 1848.
[438] *The Courier*, 17 January 1849; *Launceston Examiner*, 17 November 1849.

Barque *Runnymede*.
Courtesy Tasmanian Archives (PH30/1/997).

with Captain Brown at the helm.[439] However, in January 1851 word was received in Hobart Town that the *Flying Fox* had been wrecked off Sydenham Island in the South Pacific, all hands saved.[440]

Enthused by demand for new orders and the success of the vessels he had previously launched from his Napoleon Street shipyard, in August 1848 John Watson purchased the remainder of William Williamson's Battery Point shipyard at a cost of £1,150.[441] Located on the River Derwent adjacent to the Prince of Wales' Battery, the property had 91ft of frontage along the high water mark and included a house and several newly erected buildings.[442] Given his yard was heavily involved in the refit, repair and overhaul of vessels during this period, being able to work on multiple projects simultaneously, while also building new vessels, was considered to be a lucrative investment.

Now with three shipyards in operation (two at Battery Point and one at Middleton) John Watson embarked on a huge expansion of his shipbuilding empire. In early 1849 he was noted as building a whaler, upwards of 300 tons, for Askin Morrison at his Napoleon Street shipyard.[443] He was also noted, at his yard by the Prince of Wales' Battery, as having laid down the keel of a 100ft vessel.[444] At his Middleton property John Watson was noted as having several vessels in the course of construction, including a vessel of 350 tons, and was also building houses for the accommodation of workers.[445] As with the other two sites, this property was additionally being used to refit and repair existing vessels.[446] All told no less than 40 apprentices were noted as being in his employ, the press reporting that they were, '*young men of respectable parents, who will all be able, in the course of time, to assist in extending this truly national element of greatness*'[447] Significantly, though he had worked at Port Arthur, John Watson was by now staunchly against the hiring or employ of convicts, probationers and pass holders.[448]

Askin Morrison's 284-ton barque *Runnymede* was launched from John Watson's Napoleon Street shipyard on 21 March 1849.[449] The vessel left Hobart Town the following month for the whaling grounds under Captain Bayley's command, arriving back in June 1851 with a cargo of oil and bone.[450] A six month whaling voyage

---

[439] *The Cornwall Chronicle*, 9 January 1850.
[440] *Colonial Times*, 3 January 1851.
[441] *The Cornwall Chronicle*, 5 August 1848; *The Courier*, 26 August 1848.
[442] *The Cornwall Chronicle*, 5 August 1848; *The Courier*, 26 August 1848.
[443] *The Courier*, 7 February 1849.
[444] *The Courier*, 7 February 1849; *Colonial Times*, 23 February 1849.
[445] *The Courier*, 7 February 1849; *Colonial Times*, 23 February 1849.
[446] *The Courier*, 25 August 1849.
[447] *The Courier*, 7 February 1849; *The Cornwall Chronicle*, 28 February 1849.
[448] *The Courier*, 7 February 1849; *The Cornwall Chronicle*, 28 February 1849.
[449] *Cornwall Chronicle*, 31 March 1849.
[450] *The Courier*, 20 April 1850; *The Courier*, 18 June 1851.

next ensued with the *Runnymede* back in Hobart Town in December 1851.[451] Following 30 more years spent whaling, the *Runnymede* was wrecked during a gale at Frenchman's Bay, near Albany, Western Australia, on 19 December 1881, all hands saved.[452]

1849 saw Watson return to his patronage of the Hobart Town Regatta, held on 30 November of that year. He launched a sailing boat to compete in the race for first class sailing boats.[453] Given Watson's name was not listed on the event's program, it is likely this craft was built to the order of a specific customer rather than for his own use.

The steamer *White Hawk* was the next large vessel Watson built, launched from his Napoleon Street shipyard on 16 January 1850.[454] Built principally for transporting timber to Battery Point from his Middleton property, the 68ft craft was fitted with a 20 h.p. engine supplied by a local foundry owned by David Gillespie; the first condensing engine made in Van Diemen's Land.[455] The *White Hawk* made its inaugural trip to Middleton in mid-June 1850, with all parties pleased with its performance. Of note, the vessel was stated to have achieved a speed of 11 knots under steam, with not the slightest vibration in the engine.[456] Unfortunately, early in the morning of 18 June 1850, six months after its launch, the *White Hawk* caught fire while moored off Watson's Napoleon Street shipyard and suffered major damage.[457] The vessel's deck and cabin were burnt and its boiler destroyed.[458] Watson had built a shed for accommodation of a watchman on his property with directions to visit the steamer twice every night, however, the man unfortunately fell asleep and failed to check it on the night of the fire.[459] Alas, no-one was aware of the fire until significant damage occurred.

In late February 1850 Watson purchased a new brig for £800 that had recently been built by several of his ex employees, including Thomas Cullen and James Mackey, on the Huon River.[460] The 133-ton brig *Dart*, originally named *Aberdeen*, entered service the following year in the Port Phillip Bay trade.[461]

On 1 May 1850 the 312-ton barque *Panama* was launched from Watson's Napoleon Street shipyard.[462] Sold during construction to Burns, White and Company of the Old Wharf, at a cost of £5,000, the vessel was intended for the California trade.[463] Fitted out in less than seven weeks, the *Panama* sailed to California on 19 June 1850 with a full complement of passengers and cargo of timber intended for the gold fields; a voyage that took 80 days.[464] Returning to Hobart Town in July 1851, the vessel then made its way back to California.[465]

Less than two months following completion of the *Panama*, a brigantine was launched from Watson's Napoleon Street shipyard: the 154-ton *Sword Fish* built to the order of Captain John Clinch and Thomas Ogilvie and intended for the Port Phillip Bay trade.[466] The vessel's cabin, fittings, figure head and other ornamental work was carried out by a Mr Fairchild of Battery Point who was also licencee of the Shipwrights' Arms Hotel.[467]

With demand for new builds at a precipice, on 26 September 1850 the 188-ton schooner *Free Trader* was launched from Watson's Napoleon Street shipyard, built to the order of Captain Godfrey Bentley, previous owner of the *Miranda*, and W. A. Guesdon, both of Hobart Town.[468] Intended for the Port Albert livestock trade, the 87ft craft spent five years sailing between Port Albert and Hobart Town before being converted to a barque.[469] Under various owners the *Free Trader* traversed Victorian, Tasmanian and South Australian coastal ports, with occasional trips to New Zealand and California, until 21 July 1894 when it went ashore near Warrnambool, Victoria, and was subsequently wrecked, all hands saved.[470]

Wreck of the *Free Trader* at Warrnambool, Victoria, in July 1894.
Courtesy Corangamite Regional Library Corporation vis Picture Victoria.

---

[451] *The Courier*, 23 July, 24 December 1851.
[452] *The Mercury*, 27 January 1882.
[453] *The Hobart Town Advertiser*, 13 November 1849.
[454] *The Courier*, 4 November 1848.
[455] *The Courier*, 4 November 1848; *Colonial Times*, 22 January 1850; *The Britannia and Trades' Advocate*, 20 June 1850.
[456] *The Britannia and Trades' Advocate*, 20 June 1850.
[457] *The Hobart Town Advertiser*, 21 June 1850; *The Courier*, 22 June 1850.
[458] *The Britannia and Trades' Advocate*, 27 June 1850.
[459] *The Irish Exile and Freedom's Advocate*, 22 June 1850.
[460] *The Courier*, 27 February 1850; R. Parsons (1992). *Australian Shipowners and their Fleets. Book 12 (Hobart to 1859, A - L)*.
[461] *The Courier*, 27 February 1850; R. Parsons (1992). *Australian Shipowners and their Fleets. Book 12 (Hobart to 1859, A - L)*.
[462] *The Courier*, 4 May 1850.
[463] *The Courier*, 4 May, 8 June 1850.
[464] *Colonial Times*, 21 June, 10 December 1850.
[465] *The Courier*, 16 July, 2 August 1851.
[466] *Colonial Times*, 19 July 1850.
[467] *The Britannia and Trades' Advocate*, 25 July 1850; *The Hobart Town Advertiser*, 6 September 1850.
[468] *Launceston Examiner*, 28 September 1850; *The Cornwall Chronicle*, 3 October 1850.
[469] *Colonial Times*, 27 September 1850; R. Parsons (1992). *Australian Shipowners and their Fleets. Book 12 (Hobart to 1859, A - L)*.
[470] *The Mercury*, 24 July 1894.

Macquarie Street near Harrington Street

Buildings commissioned by John Watson for his son-in-law's school on the corner of Macquarie and Harrington streets. Courtesy W L Crowther Library, State Library of Tasmania (AUTAS001124075144).

Fast becoming a prominent citizen of Hobart Town, John Watson was also noted for his fairness and integrity. Well-respected, several events during this period highlight his upstanding character. For example, in September 1846 he was nominated as municipal commissioner of Hobart Town's Macquarie Ward.[471] In 1850 he was a committee member of the Female Emigration Society, a society formed to aid the reception of female emigrants of good character arriving from England.[472] That same year he was balloted for and elected to the Royal Society of Van Diemen's Land.[473] Later in 1850 Watson extracted a 146ft length of blue gum from his property at Middleton as a contribution to the Exhibition of the Industry of All Nations, to be held in London the following year.[474]

In early 1851 the 319-ton *Middleton* was launched from Watson's shipyard at Middleton, under the supervision of a Mr Smith.[475] Intended for international trade, the vessel set sail for London on 8 February 1851 under Captain Storie's command, taking a quantity of whale oil and wool.[476] Upon arrival back in Hobart Town later that year, Watson sold the *Middleton* to Thomas Chapman, MLC, for £2,600.[477] Continuing in the London trade, the vessel left Hobart Town in June 1852 with a full complement of passengers and cargo, including £100,000 worth of gold.[478] Back in Hobart Town in April 1853, the *Middleton* was then sent to Batavia.[479] It was wrecked the following month, on 29 June 1853, on a coral reef near Lombok, Indonesia, all hands saved.[480]

The next vessels off the stocks, launched from one of Watson's Battery Point two shipyards, were the 50-ton schooner *William* and the 70-ton schooner *Moscheto*; the latter almost certainly built from the hulk of the fire-damaged *White Hawk*.[481] Intended for coastal trade, both craft were advertised for sale by Maning Brothers around the time of their launch in February 1851.[482]

Shortly thereafter Watson's financial realities came to bear. On 20 March 1851 he conveyed and assigned his estate to Alexander McNaugton, Richard Burns and Charles Seal, all of Hobart Town, trustees for the benefit of themselves and all other creditors.[483] On 1 April the three trustees offered the following properties for sale: a stone mansion at the corner of Macquarie and Harrington Streets comprising 17 apartments,

---

[471] *Launceston Advertiser*, 24 September 1846.
[472] *Colonial Times*, 6 September 1850.
[473] *The Courier*, 12 October 1850.
[474] *The Courier*, 15 January 1851.
[475] *The Courier*, 8 February, 17 September 1851.
[476] *The Courier*, 8 February 1851.
[477] *Colonial Times*, 25 November 1851; *The Courier*, 20 December 1851.
[478] *The Courier*, 12 June 1852, 14 February 1853.
[479] *The Courier*, 27 April, 1 September 1853.
[480] *The Courier*, 1 September 1853.
[481] *Colonial Times*, 25 February 1851; *The Courier*, 12 March 1851; Graeme Broxam, pers. comm.
[482] *Colonial Times*, 25 February 1851; *The Courier*, 12 March 1851; R. Parsons (1992). *Australian Shipowners and their Fleets. Book 13 (Hobart to 1859, M - Z)*.
[483] *The Courier*, 29 March 1851.

including an exhibition room (this was the school he had built for his son-in-law Phillip Cannaway, though it had only been in use for a short-period of time); an unfinished residence fronting Macquarie Street and adjoining the latter, also comprising 17 rooms; an 11-room brick edifice located at the corner of Napoleon and Trumpeter (now Sloane) streets, originally intended for a public house, though the current residence of Watson and his family; two stone cottages located opposite Watson's Napoleon Street shipyard; and a cottage with a large garden, coach house and stables situated behind the two stone cottages previously mentioned.[484] Interestingly, the Watson family's home was located on property originally granted to Thomas Harbottle who had built a two-storey residence there intended for use as a public house.[485] The licence had been declined and in the late 1840s the ever-expanding Watson family moved in. The house, now earmarked with the address of 1 Sloane Street, still stands today and in itself has a remarkable history.[486]

Also offered for sale as part of Watson's estate was a one-fourth share in the brig *Dart*, now on its first voyage to Port Phillip Bay; the hull of a schooner, about 50 tons, with masts, just off the stocks; and a new marine steam engine manufactured by David Gillespie.[487] Perhaps an indication that the two brothers continued to be linked financially, shortly thereafter Watson's brother George also entered into insolvency.[488] His assets, including properties and vessels, were subsequently sold at auction.[489]

On 27 June 1851 more of John Watson's assets were advertised for sale, including his shipyard located adjacent to the Prince of Wales' Battery and an attached dwelling house.[490] This property was sold in early July for £1,600, while his family's home realised £410.[491] Also advertised for sale in conjunction with Watson's estate was a new barque of 323 tons built for the London trade.[492] Launched from Watson's shipyard adjacent to the Prince of Wales' Battery in July 1851, the vessel was purchased by Charles Seal of Hobart Town for £1,800 and subsequently named *Southern Cross*.[493]

Late 1851 proved to be a difficult time both professionally and personally for Watson and his family. On 23 November his 6-year-old daughter died of inflammation of the lungs.[494] Only a few weeks later,

[484] *Colonial Times*, 1 April 1851.
[485] *The Tasmanian Colonist*, 8 September 1851; also refer to map on page 50.
[486] www.batterypointhall.org.au/number-1-sloane-street.
[487] *Colonial Times*, 1 April 1851.
[488] *The Courier*, 5 April 1851.
[489] *Colonial Times*, 18 April 1851.
[490] *Colonial Times*, 27 June 1851.
[491] *The Courier*, 12 July 1851.
[492] *The Courier*, 12 April 1851.
[493] *Colonial Times*, 11 July 1851; 21 December 1852.
[494] Libraries Tasmania (RGD35/1/3 no. 1055).

John Watson's family home on the corner of Napoleon and Sloane Streets, Battery Point (2023). Courtesy author's collection.

on 4 December, his 10-year-old daughter Eliza also died. The cause of death was the same as for her younger sister.[495] Completing a trifecta of deaths, Watson's mother Ann died at Hobart Town on 19 December 1851 of 'Decay of nature'.[496]

Persevering, in October 1851 a dividend was paid to all of Watson's remaining creditors and his insolvency was finalised.[497] Fortunately able to retain possession of his Napoleon Street shipyard and his property at Middleton, Watson continued operations with the repair, overhaul, survey and refit of larger vessels, as well as the launch of two schooners in late 1851. These were the *Van Tromp*, launched from Battery Point and built to the order of Alexander Kerr, and the *Helen*, launched from Middleton and built to the order of Henry Cole.[498]

Between 1852 and 1854 Watson built at least three more schooners (the *Eclipse*, *Victory* and *Annie*) though work continued to be stalled owing to the scarceness of labour—a combination of the exodus of local men to the Victorian gold fields, and Watson's preference to not employ convict labour.[499] Still during this period, his yard was active with work involving existing vessels. Watson was also busy on a political level. In early 1853 he was a candidate for alderman of Hobart Town, though failed to receive enough votes to be elected.[500]

Of the three new vessels, the schooner *Victory* was launched from Watson's Battery Point shipyard and near-immediately advertised for sale by trustees of the estate of T. Stevens.[501] Becoming a regular trader between various Victorian and Tasmanian ports for nearly 15 years, the vessel sadly went missing near Port Phillip Heads, Victoria, en route from Table Cape to Melbourne in March 1866, with the loss of all hands.[502]

The schooner *Eclipse* was launched from Watson's Battery Point shipyard on Christmas Eve 1852.[503] Intended for the Port Albert to Hobart Town cattle trade, where it spent over a decade employed, the *Eclipse* was built to the order of John Johnson of the New Wharf.[504] Commanded by Captain Burgess, the vessel was noted as fitting out in preparation for its maiden voyage in May 1853.[505]

Intended for the river trade, the 60-ton schooner *Annie* was built by Watson at Battery Point yard on speculation and launched late in 1853.[506] Soon offered for sale, in 1854 the vessel began trading between Hobart Town and Southport.[507]

Unfortunately, Watson's financial health continued to be precarious with no new orders received in 1854, though he was still owner of several vessels involved in intercolonial trade, and was also exporting timber to Victoria.[508] Watson had also purchased the barque *Prince Regent* and fitted it out for whaling.[509] By December of that year his property at Middleton, including 150 acres of land, three brick cottages, four weatherboard cottages, various wharf buildings, 14 township allotments, and 400 acres of land adjoining the township, was advertised for sale.[510] Failing to find an immediate buyer the property was put up for auction in March 1855.[511]

By December 1855 Watson had defaulted on a mortgage taken out the previous year on his Napoleon Street shipyard and the property was advertised for sale by public auction.[512] All told the site consisted of two parcels of land—the first comprising one acre and seventeen perches and the second comprising one acre and four perches.[513] It was bounded on the north-east by land granted to Benjamin Guy.[514] Situated on the two parcels were several dwelling houses, workshops and jetties.[515]

The following month more of Watson's personal estate was advertised for sale, including the *Sword Fish*, the British-built *Wee Tottie*, the new schooner *Tommy*, the *Fire Fly*, the *William Hill*, a large punt, the hull of a barque, two new whaleboats and numerous shipbuilding and whaling implements and tools, as well as the whole of his stock in trade.[516] His Napoleon Street shipyard was purchased by Duncan McPherson for £4,000 who subsequently subdivided the property, leasing the allotments to various commercial and residential tenants over the succeeding decades, including shipbuilders John Lucas and Robert Jeffrey.[517]

In February 1856 the schooner *Tommy* was sold to T. D. Chapman and Company for £805.[518] The vessel was sold again the following year to Captain McLachlan with the intention of placing it in the coastal trade.[519] Another change of ownership occurred shortly thereafter and by the late 1850s the *Tommy* was trading between Tasmania, Victoria and South Australia.[520] Though its register was later transferred to the mainland, the vessel remained in intercolonial trade up until October 1892.[521] It was hulked in Melbourne and broken up in the early 1900s.[522] The *Tommy* was the last large vessel built by John Watson.

---

[495] Libraries Tasmania (RGD35/1/3 no. 1074).
[496] Libraries Tasmania (RGD35/1/3 no. 1110).
[497] *The Courier*, 20 August, 27 September 1851.
[498] *Geelong Advertiser and Intelligencer*, 11 January 1852;
W. Lawson & the Shiplovers' Society of Tasmania (1949). *Blue Gum Clippers and Whale Ships of Tasmania*.
[499] *The Courier*, 11 June 1853.
[500] *The Courier*, 3, 5 January 1853.
[501] *Colonial Times*, 9 March 1852.
[502] *Launceston Examiner*, 23 April 1866;
R. Parsons (1992). *Australian Shipowners and their Fleets. Book 12 (Hobart to 1859, A - L)*.
[503] *Colonial Times*, 21 May 1853.
[504] *The Cornwall Chronicle*, 21 May 1853.
[505] *The Courier*, 17 May 1853.
[506] *Colonial Times*, 10 December 1853.
[507] *Colonial Times*, 10 December 1853; *The Courier*, 7 March 1854.
[508] *The Hobart Town Advertiser*, 30 June 1854; *The Courier*, 20 July 1854.
[509] *The Hobart Town Advertiser*, 19 May, 5 September 1854.
[510] *The Courier*, 29 December 1854.
[511] *The Courier*, 22 March 1855.
[512] *The Courier*, 12 December 1855.
[513] *The Courier*, 12 December 1855.
[514] *The Courier*, 12 December 1855.
[515] *The Courier*, 12 December 1855.
[516] *The Courier*, 8 January 1856; *The Tasmanian Daily News*, 29 January 1856.
[517] *The Courier*, 30 January 1856; *The Hobart Town Gazette*, 8 February 1861.
[518] *The Courier*, 26 February 1856.
[519] *The Hobart Town Mercury*, 9 December 1857.
[520] *The Hobart Town Daily Mercury*, 17 January 1859; *Launceston Examiner*, 6 October 1859, 5 June 1860.
[521] *The Mercury*, 12 July 1883; *The Australiasian*, 15 October 1892.
[522] National Archives of Australia (Register of British Ships: Main Register subsequent to Merchant Shipping Act 1854, Port Melbourne [contains Volume 3 to Volume 4]).

Spirited, Skilled and Determined

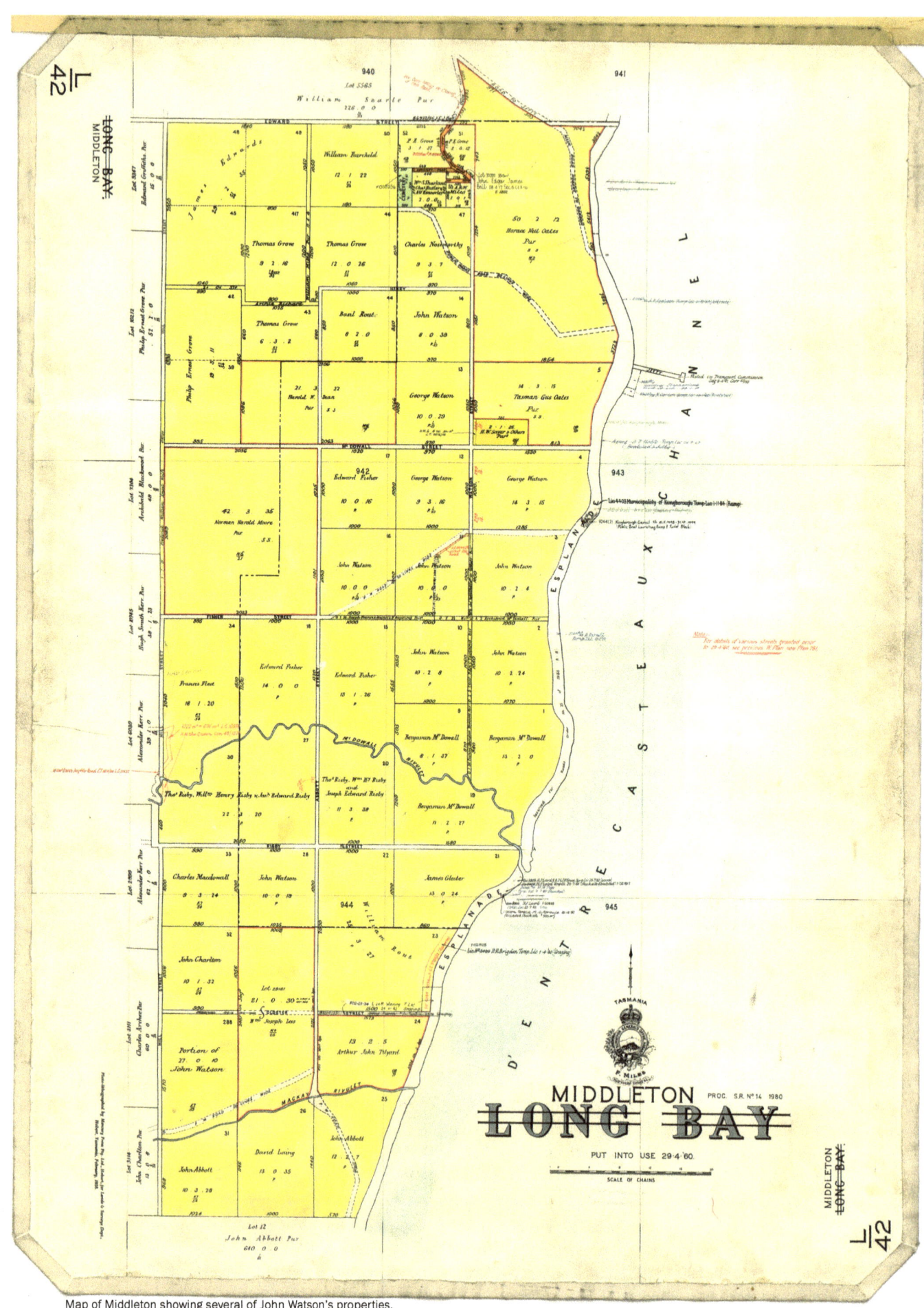

Map of Middleton showing several of John Watson's properties.
Courtesy Tasmanian Archives (AF819/1/212).

Cape Wickham Lighthouse and quarters (1880s).
Courtesy Museums Victoria Collections (1249613).

Needing to support his large family, Watson pressed on. His brother George was also suffering financially during this period and had been forced to give up his home, Barton Vale, located in Goulburn Street, Hobart Town, so there was little opportunity for Watson to gain employment or monetary support through familial vectors.[523] George Watson died on 24 May 1857.[524] Cause of death was epilepsy; he was 53 years of age.[525] He was survived by his wife Anne and several children, though one son (James) would be killed the following year in a shocking accident at Port Esperance whereby him and five others, including two children, lost their lives when a large tree fell on the hut they were sheltering in during bad weather.[526] The group had reportedly been planting potatoes in a paddock at the time.[527] James was 18 years of age.[528]

Persevering, John Watson was noted in the press as repairing a boat for the Tasmanian Government in mid-1857.[529] He also supplied timber to Thomas Cullen and James Mackey, shipwrights of Battery Point, for the building of their 100ft steamer *Emu* which was launched on 29 December of 1857.[530] However, more stable and distinguished employment opportunities were to come in the years that followed.

In June 1859, at the age of 58, Watson accepted a contract with the Hobart Marine Board (at a salary of £200 per annum) to superintend various construction projects, including at the New Wharf.[531] In May 1860 this work saw him temporarily appointed to the office of superintendent at King Island where he was tasked with overseeing construction of Cape Wickham Lighthouse; the building of which was undertaken by employees of a Melbourne-based firm.[532] Watson sailed with his wife Mary to the island in mid-1860, remaining there until the work was completed in late 1861.[533]

Political and humanitarian concerns continued to be of interest. In 1863 Watson testified before the House of Assembly's Joint Commission on Prison Labour on the good conduct of convicts under his supervision at Port Arthur stating that he found them very willing and able to learn.[534]

The late 1850s through to the mid-1860s coincided with more deaths in his immediate family, however. In October 1859 Watson's fourth daughter Mary died in St Kilda, Victoria; the wife of John Whitney.[535] Five

---

[523] *The Courier*, 5 September 1856.
[524] *Colonial Times*, 26 May 1857.
[525] Libraries Tasmania (RGD35/1/5 no. 262).
[526] *The Hobart Town Daily Mercury*, 19 October 1858.
[527] *Launceston, Examiner*, 26 October 1858.
[528] *The Hobart Town Advertiser*, 20 October 1858.
[529] *The Hobart Town Mercury*, 22 August 1857.
[530] *The Hobart Town Daily Mercury*, 1 January 1858; *The Courier*, 25 June 1858.

[531] A. Hudspeth & L. Scripps (2000). *Capital Port: A History of the Marine Board of Hobart 1858 - 1997*.
[532] *The Hobart Town Daily Mercury*, 11 May 1860.
[533] A. Hudspeth & L. Scripps (2000). *Capital Port: A History of the Marine Board of Hobart 1858 - 1997*.
[534] *The Mercury*, 28 August 1863.
[535] *The Hobart Town Daily Mercury*, 29 October 1859.

years later his youngest son George would die in Melbourne, where he had relocated with two older brothers, William and John.[536] He was 20 years of age.

Professionally, in 1864 Watson's association with the Hobart Marine Board saw him inspecting and approving tenders, including for the rigging, sails and fit-out of the new government schooner *Harriet*, recently built by John Lucas and Robert Jeffrey at Watson's ex Battery Point yard.[537] A few months later he reviewed and approved tenders for the construction of a new boat for the *Harriet*.[538] Still later that year Watson oversaw the repair of Franklin Wharf.[539]

In 1865 Watson superintended the repair and alteration of the entrance to Constitution Dock.[540] In 1867 he oversaw the tender process for the removal of Steamers' Jetty at the Hobart Town wharf, as well as improvements to the Kangaroo Point wharf.[541]

Continuing to undertake similar projects, the early to mid-1870s saw Watson superintending the construction of a causeway across Fisherman's Dock and construction of the Argyle Street Pier.[542] In 1874 Watson also became a widower. His wife Mary died at their home in Fitzroy Place, Hobart Town, in March of that year. Cause of death was '*Age and infirmity*'.[543] She was 70 years of age. Mary was buried at Queenborough Cemetery, Sandy Bay.[544]

In 1878 more improvements were made to the Hobart Town wharf based on a plan Watson had developed, which was subsequently adopted by the Hobart Marine Board.[545] That same year he was tasked with overseeing the work.[546] The following year Watson supervised improvements to the Bellerive wharf, as well as to Brooke Street Pier.[547]

In 1882, now in his early 80s, Watson prepared plans and supervised the lengthening of the Dunn Street Pier.[548] He also developed plans for the construction of a new guiding pier at Kangaroo Point.[549] As well, he prepared plans for a 48ft punt to hold a steam dredge.[550] The punt was built by James Mackey at Battery Point.[551] Also in 1882 Watson was tasked with administering the construction of a boarding boat for use by the Launceston Marine Board.[552] Built by Charles Miller

[536] *The Mercury*, 17 February 1864.
[537] *The Mercury*, 11 August 1864.
[538] *The Mercury*, 13 September 1864.
[539] *The Mercury*, 5 October 1864.
[540] *The Mercury*, 23 June 1865.
[541] *The Mercury*, 29 June, 29 July 1867.
[542] *The Mercury*, 24 July 1874; *The Cornwall Chronicle*, 28 April 1876.
[543] Libraries Tasmania (RGD35/1/8 no. 1939).
[544] *The Mercury*, 14 March 1874.
[545] *The Mercury*, 29 July 1878.
[546] *The Mercury*, 29 July 1878.
[547] *The Mercury*, 28 February, 9 June 1879.
[548] *Launceston Examiner*, 11 February, 5 April 1882.
[549] *The Mercury*, 15 April 1882.
[550] *The Mercury*, 8 July 1882.
[551] *The Mercury*, 7 August 1882.
[552] *Launceston Examiner*, 23 December 1882.

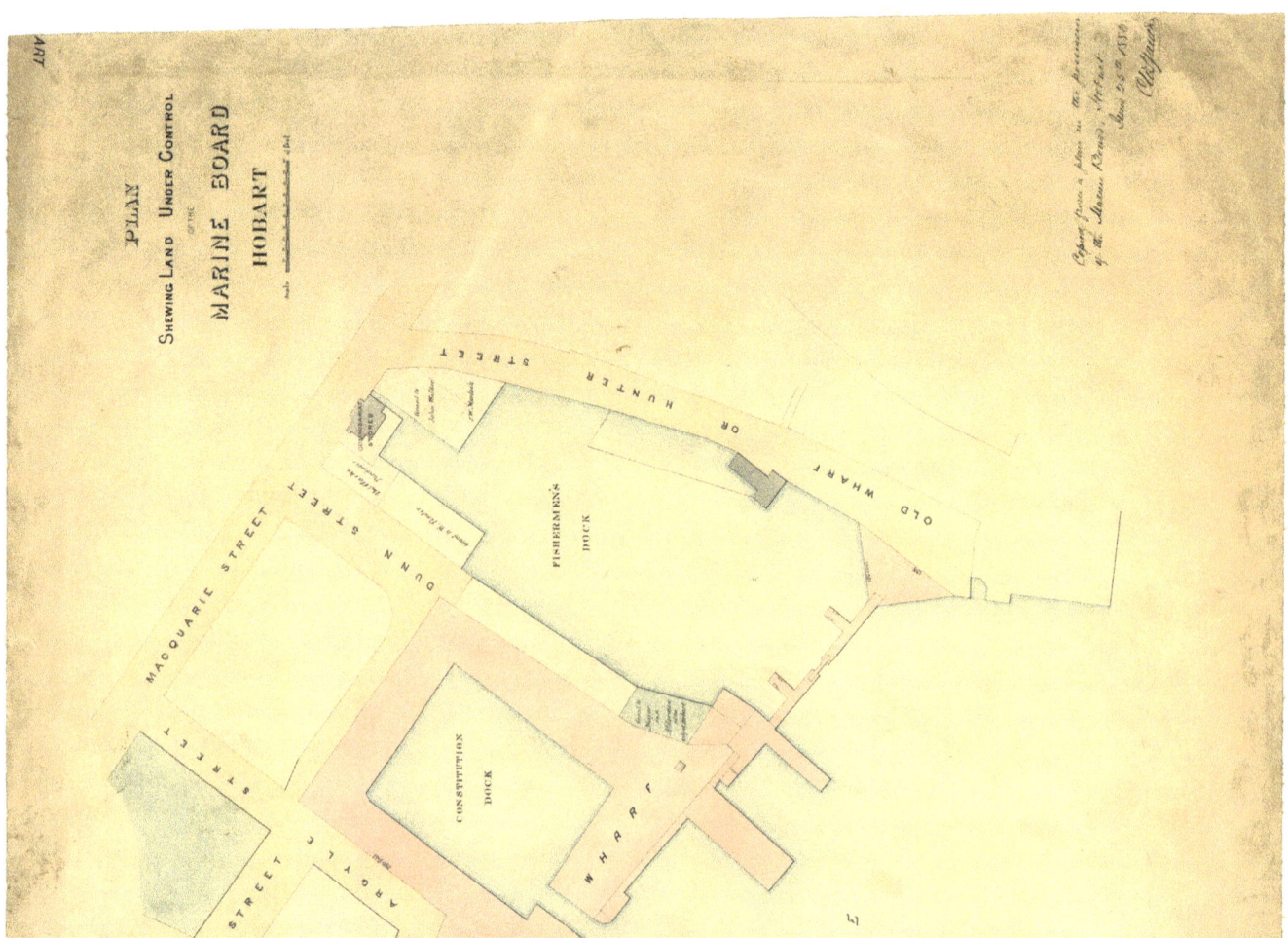

1880s map of the Hobart Wharves area showing land under control of the Marine Board of Hobart.
Courtesy Tasmanian Archives (AF394/1/87).

of Battery Point, Watson received five per cent of the boat's cost as remuneration.[553]

In 1883 Watson supervised the lowering of two sides of Constitution Dock.[554] In December 1883 he was noted for the valuable advice and assistance he had given to the Hobart Marine Board over several decades, particularly for the furnishing of plans and speculation *pro bono*.[555] As a result the Board recommended that he be given an annual salary of £100 in addition to the commission paid to him for his superintendence work.[556]

In 1884 Watson was commended for his involvement in improvements to Waterman's Dock, including completion of a platform on the Brooke Street side for use by the river steamers.[557] In 1885, likely due to his advanced age, Watson declined the Hobart Marine Board's appointment of him to Shipwright Surveyor, instead recommending Donald McMillan for the position.[558] During this year, however, and up until his death, he kept up with various maintenance and improvement works at the Hobart wharf.[559]

In addition to his work associated with the Hobart Marine Board, Watson further supplemented his income in the decades following the demise of his shipyard operations. Considered one of Tasmania's primary experts on local timbers, in mid-1862 he was contracted by the colonial government to survey for a new tram line at Southport.[560] He was also tasked with reporting on local timber in the vicinity of Esperance and Southport.[561] Shortly following, he was commissioned to undertake a similar examination of the timbers near the Don and Leven rivers, though was unable to complete this task due to illness.[562] In October 1862 Watson was again contracted by the government to inspect and report on timber production in the Cygnet region, as well as the building of a tram road between Cygnet and Sandfly.[563]

A third income source materialised in September 1862 when Watson was appointed marine surveyor of the Derwent and Tamar Assurance Company.[564] Like his appointment with the Hobart Marine Board, the position was on a contract basis though the work was regular. He retained this position up until his death.[565]

Watson died while on a family holiday at Browns River (now Kingston), Tasmania, on 16 March 1887, aged 85.[566] He was buried at Queenborough Cemetery, Sandy Bay, with his late wife Mary.[567]

Watson was survived by seven of his 12 children, including five daughters and two sons, as well as many grandchildren. His third eldest daughter Jane had predeceased him by six months. She died in Hobart on 7 September 1877 at the age of 47.[568] Watson left his estate chiefly to his youngest daughter Maria and her husband George Waterhouse. He also stated in the document, '*I express as a last wish that none of my relatives will feel it necessary to wear mourning at my death well knowing that my memory will always be fondly cherished by them without their showing their regret outwardly*'.[569]

In summary, John Watson was highly regarded for the quality of his work, as well as his honest and charitable conduct; his shipbuilding career spanned four decades, two countries, and at least five locations within Tasmania (i.e., the Old Wharf; Port Arthur; Napoleon Street and below the Prince of Wales' Battery, Battery Point; and Middleton). Watson first established a shipyard at Battery Point in 1839 where, up until 1855, he built 13 schooners, six barques and one brigantine, many of which furnished developing intercolonial and international trades. Smaller craft were also constructed, while several more vessels were built at a shipyard located at Middleton in the D'Entrecasteaux Channel. A third shipyard, located at Battery Point near the Prince of Wales' Battery, was also in operation between 1848 and 1851. Many of these vessels played important roles in the development of Australia's intercolonial trade, while others became pioneers of international trade and were among the first Tasmanian-built vessels to arrive in England. Regrettably only five of John Watson's vessels survived him. These were the barque *Free Trader* and the schooners *William*, *Moscheto*, *Annie* and *Tommy*.

Bequeathed with the moniker '*Father of Ship Building*' in Tasmania, Watson's legacy lies not only in the vessels he built but also in the men he taught the trade.[570] Some of his more noteworthy apprentices included John and Alexander McGregor, John Lucas, James Mackey and John Dalgleish.[571] However, owing to Watson's 28-year involvement with the planning and development of Hobart's waterfront area on behalf of the Hobart Marine Board, perhaps he is equally deserving of the moniker '*Father of the Hobart Wharves*'.[572]

---

[553] *Launceston Examiner*, 23 December 1882.
[554] *The Mercury*, 23 June 1883.
[555] *The Mercury*, 1 December 1883.
[556] *The Mercury*, 1 December 1883.
[557] *The Mercury*, 18 July 1884.
[558] *Launceston Examiner*, 21 March 1885.
[559] *The Mercury*, 28 March, 18 July 1885; 13 February, 15 May, 14 August, 13 November 1886; 29 January 1887.
[560] *The Mercury*, 3 June 1862.
[561] *The Mercury*, 22 July 1862.
[562] *The Mercury*, 25 July 1862, 13 March 1863.
[563] *The Mercury*, 17 October 1862, 6 March 1863.
[564] *The Mercury*, 20 August, 3 September 1862.
[565] *The Mercury*, 12 March 1887.
[566] *The Mercury*, 17 March 1887.
[567] www.findagrave.com/memorial/226963972.
[568] *The Mercury*, 8 September 1877.
[569] Libraries Tasmania (AD960/1/13 no. 2520).
[570] *The Mercury*, 11 June 1872.
[571] *The Mercury*, 11 June 1872; L. Norman (1938). *Pioneer Shipping of Tasmania: Whaling, Sealing, Piracy, Shipwrecks, etc. in early Tasmania*.
[572] E. Robin (2011). *John Watson (1801 1887): Pioneer Shipbuilder and 'Father or the Wharves'*.

Vessels built by John Watson and employees at Battery Point (1839 - 1854)

Year	Name	Type	Description
1839	Van Diemen	Whaleboat	Five-oared whaleboat built by John Watson to compete at the Second Hobart Town Anniversary Regatta, held on the River Derwent on 3 December 1839. Finished first in the race for five-oared whaleboats, competing against a fleet of 19 craft. First prize was a purse of £30.
1840	Sisters	Schooner	77.4 x 19.2 x 11.7ft. 130 tons. Built by John Watson to the order of Thomas Lucas, whaler of Hobart Town, and launched in early 1840; builder's certificate signed 28 March 1840. Involved in intercolonial trade, also making regular trips to New Zealand and occasional trips to Asia. Other owners were Duncan McPherson and John Guthrie (1847) and Duncan McPherson and Hugh Clark (1848). Wrecked during a gale at Turanganui, Poverty Bay, New Zealand, on 8 April 1852, all hands saved. At the time of loss, under the command of Hugh Clark, a part-owner.
1840	Flying Squirrel	Schooner	70.8 x 18.6 x 11.3ft. ON 31927. 78 tons. Built by John Watson for himself and Alfred Garrett, intended for the Port Phillip trade. Spent 35 years involved in intercolonial trade under a succession of owners, also making occasional trips to the whaling grounds in the early 1860s. Wrecked off King Island, Bass Strait, on 21 September 1875, all hands saved. At the time of loss, owned by John Johnston and registered in Melbourne.
1840	Hyacinth	Gig	Built by John Watson to compete in the gig race at the 1840 Hobart Town Regatta. Finished third with John Watson at the helm.
1841	The Tasman	Sailing boat	Built by John Watson to compete in the race for first-class sailing boats at the 1841 Hobart Town Regatta. Helmed by a Mr Wray.
1841	--	Punt	Built by John Watson to the order of the Government of Van Diemen's Land. Completed by July 1841.
1841	--	Boat	Small boat built by John Watson to the order of the Government of Van Diemen's Land. Completed by October 1841.
1842	--	Boat	First of two small boats by John Watson in March 1842 to the order of the Government of Van Diemen's Land.
1842	--	Boat	Second of two small boats by John Watson in March 1842 to the order of the Government of Van Diemen's Land.
1842	Native Youth	Paddle steamer	69.3 x 14.4 x 6.9ft. ON 31992. 51 tons. Built by John Watson to the order of Henry Davidson and Alexander Clark and launched in May 1842. Fitted with a 20 h.p. non-condensing engine. Intended for use as a passenger and freight ferry on the River Derwent. By 1846 owned by James Murdoch, in 1850 owned by William Green, in 1853 again owned by James Murdoch. Engine removed and converted to a schooner in 1854. Involved in coastal trade under various owners. Wrecked at Goose Island, Bass Strait, on 22 November 1863, all hands saved. At the time of loss, owned by Peter Oldham.
1842	Flying Fish	Schooner	83.4 x 18.9 x 10.0ft. ON 31926. 122 tons. Built by John Watson for a syndicate of eight local merchants including Alfred Garrett, John Clinch, J. W. Storie and himself. Launched on 29 November 1842. Involved in intercolonial trade for several decades, primarily sailing between Hobart and Port Phillip Bay. Driven ashore and wrecked at Port Elliot, South Australia, on 3 December 1860, all hands saved.
1846	Flying Childers	Barque	96.4 x 23.5 x 10.4ft. ON 32031. 229 tons. Built by John Watson to the order of his brother George Watson, intended for the whaling industry. Launched on 20 October 1846. Subsequent owners included Askin Morrison and the McGregor family. A successful whaling vessel for several decades, also periodically operated in intercolonial trade with occasional trips to Asia. Wrecked at Port Davey, Tasmania, on 16 June 1877 while seeking shelter during a gale, all hands saved.
1846	Miranda	Schooner	76.1 x 20.6 x 11.3ft. 127 tons. Built by John Watson to the order of Captain Godfrey Bentley and John Reeve of Gippsland, Victoria. Launched on 15 December 1846. For several years a regular in the Port Albert to Hobart Town cattle trade. Wrecked at Rabbit Island near Wilsons Promontory, Victoria, 7 August 1852 during a gale, all hands saved.
1848	Fair Tasmanian	Barque	87.7 x 22.4 x 12.0ft. ON 32001. 144 tons. Built by John Watson to the order of John Johnson of Hobart Town. Launched on 20 January 1848. Spent 13 years employed in intercolonial and trans-Tasman trades, making occasional trips to Mauritius and California. Wrecked after parting from its mooring at Warrnambool, Victoria, on 28 May 1864, all hands saved. At the time of loss, owned by Valentine Wright of Melbourne.
1848	Circassian	Schooner	77.3 x 21.3 x 9.9ft. ON 32044. 95 tons. Built by John Watson to the order of Messrs Maxwell and Smith. Launched on 20 January 1848. Involved in the Port Phillip Bay trade up until August 1864 when purchased by Piggott Brothers of Melbourne and placed in the Port Frederick trade. Wrecked near Ram Head, Victoria, on 6 October 1864; three crew drowned.
1849	Flying Fox	Barque	86.0 x 21.0 x 12.9ft. 187 tons. Built by John Watson to the order of his brother George Watson. Launched on 2 November 1848. Intended for the whaling industry. Wrecked off Sydenham Island in the South Pacific on its second whaling voyage in late 1850, all hands saved.

Year	Name	Type	Description
1849	*Runnymede*	Barque	103.6 x 23.2 x 15.5ft. ON 32032. 284 tons. Built by John Watson to the order of Askin Morrison. Launched on 21 March 1849. Intended for the whaling industry where it spent more than 30 years employed. Wrecked at Frenchman's Bay, near Albany, Western Australia, on 19 December 1881, all hands saved. At the time of loss, owned by James Bayley of Hobart Town.
1849	--	Sailing boat	Built by John Watson to compete in the race for first-class sailing boats at the 1849 Hobart Town Regatta.
1850	*White Hawk*	Steamer	68.0 x 11.6 x 5.8ft. 18 tons. Built by John Watson for his own use. Launched on 16 January 1850. Fitted with a 20 h.p. engine and intended to bring timber up to Hobart Town from the Huon and Channel. Burned while moored off John Watson's Battery Point shipyard on 18 June 1850. Hulk used to build the schooner *Moscheto*, see below.
1850	*Panama*	Barque	93 x 26 x 16.5ft ON 27189. 312 tons. Built by John Watson. Sold during construction to Burns, White and Company, of Hobart Town. Intended for the California trade. By November 1852 destined for London with a cargo of treenails, iron, wool, oil, coal and gold. Made several more trips between Hobart Town and London until March 1855 when sold to buyers from Wales and its register transferred to Newport. Following nearly two decades spent trading in the northern hemisphere, wrecked near Skagen, Denmark, on 11 March 1872 en route from Shields, Northumberland, England, to Copenhagen with a cargo of coal, all hands saved. At the time of loss, owned by James Wood of Blyth, Northumberland.
1850	*Sword Fish*	Brigantine	89.5 x 23.2 x 11.1ft. ON 31942. 154 tons. Built by John Watson to the order of John Clinch and Thomas Ogilvie. Launched in July 1850. Intended for the Port Phillip Bay trade. Later employed in intercolonial and trans-Tasman trades. Wrecked on 7 May 1882 at Tomahawk Island off the north-west coast of Tasmania, at the time en route from Kaipara, New Zealand to Melbourne, all hands saved.
1850	*Free Trader*	Schooner	111.0 x 22.2 x 11.0ft. ON 31959. 188 tons. Built by John Watson to the order of Captain Godfrey Bentley and W. A. Guesdon of Hobart Town. Launched on 26 September 1850. Intended for the Port Albert livestock trade. Later converted to a barque and involved in intercolonial trade with occasional trips overseas. Wrecked on 21 July 1894 near Warrnambool, Victoria, all hands saved. At the time of loss, owned by Henry Bowden of Hobart.
1851	*William*	Schooner	47.6 x 14.8 x 6.3ft. ON 31868. 25 tons. Built by John Watson. Advertised for sale in Hobart Town in February 1851. Register transferred to Geelong a few months later. Involved in intercolonial trade until 1863 when its register was transferred to Lyttelton, New Zealand. Following three decades spent in coastal trade, blown up in the early 1900s as part of a marine explosion display at the Lyttleton Regatta.
1851	*Moscheto*	Schooner	72.0 x 11.4 x 5.7ft. ON 31609. 33 tons. Built by John Watson from the hulk of the burnt steamer *White Hawk*. Advertised for sale in Hobart Town in February 1851, shortly after launch. Involved in intercolonial trade. Register transferred to Melbourne in 1853 and Sydney in 1856. In 1858 converted to a screw steamer. Spent several decades employed on Sydney Harbour. Broken up in 1905, at the time owned by Einerson Bros. of Balmain.
1851	*Southern Cross*	Barque	113.0 x 23.6 x 17.0ft. ON 32020. 323 tons. Built by John Watson and sold to Charles Seal of Hobart Town shortly after launch in July 1851. Employed in the London trade. Later traded to Europe, Asia, New Zealand and South America, under various owners. Wrecked on 17 January 1880 near Cape Douglas, South Australia, all hands saved. At the time of loss, owned by William Belbin and Charles Dowdell of Hobart Town.
1851	*Van Tromp*	Schooner	50.0 x 14.0 x 6.6ft. ON 31764. 32 tons. Built by John Watson to the order of Alexander Kerr of Hobart Town. Involved in the Port Phillip Bay trade. In 1859 transferred to Sydney and engaged in Pacific Island trade. Wrecked near Vanuatu in August 1872, all hands saved.
1852	*Eclipse*	Schooner	108.7 x 23.3 x 10.6ft. ON 31966. 180 tons. Built by John Watson to the order of John Johnson of Hobart Town. Launched on 25 December 1852. Intended for the Port Albert to Hobart cattle trade where it spent over a decade employed. Likely the vessel of the same name that was wrecked near Farquhar Inlet, New South wales, en route from Sydney to Gladstone, Queensland, in July 1866 with the loss of eight lives.
1853	*Victory*	Schooner	69.0 x 15.7 x 6.1ft. ON 32024. 51 tons. Built by John Watson on speculation and advertised for sale in July 1853, a month after its launch. A regular trader between various Victorian and Tasmanian ports for nearly 15 years under various owners, including Joseph Risby. Went missing near Port Phillip Heads, Victoria, en route from Table Cape, Tasmania, to Melbourne in March 1866 with the loss of all hands. At the time owned by John Jones and John Stark.
1853	*Annie*	Schooner	56.5 x 15.5 x 5.8ft. ON 31938. 30 tons. Built by John Watson. Involved in various Tasmanian-based coastal and river trades under many owners for six decades, including Robert Power, William Fisher, G. Jennings, Hugh McBride, and the Risby family. Condemned and broken up around 1920 at the request of the Hobart Marine Board.

Year	Name	Type	Description
1854	*Tommy*	Schooner	73.6 x 17.2 x 7.2ft. ON 32048. 59 tons. Built by John Watson. Advertised for sale in late 1855/early 1856 as part of his estate and sold to T. D. Chapman and Co. Sold again in 1857 to Captain McLachlan and in 1859 to John Gibson of Launceston. Spent four decades employed in intercolonial trade under various owners; its register transferred to Melbourne in 1863 upon sale to William Williams. Register transferred to Adelaide in 1867 and back to Melbourne in 1870. Remained in service until October 1892. Hulked in Melbourne and broken up in the early 1900s.
1855	–	Whaleboat	First of two whaleboats built by John Watson and advertised for sale as part of his assets in December 1855.
1855	–	Whaleboat	Second of two whaleboats built by John Watson and advertised for sale as part of his assets in December 1855.

Hobart from behind Cascade Brewery.
Courtesy Tasmanian Archives, J. W. Beattie Tasmanian Series 588b (NS4077/1/224).

Peter Degraves

'At three o'clock on Saturday afternoon, all the roads and avenues leading to Mr. Degraves's shipbuilding grounds were completely alive by the immense concourse of people who were merrily hurrying to the scene of action. Carriages, carts, and gigs, cakes, nuts, and lollies, seemed to be jostled together, and moved along in one enlivening mass.'

Colonial Times, 21 August 1849.

Peter Degraves (circa early 1850s).
Courtesy Tasmanian Archives (NS2511/1/217).

An educated, well-connected, shrewd and opportunistic industrialist, Peter Degraves arrived in Hobart Town with his family on board the ship *Hope* in 1824; a vessel he owned in partnership with his brother-in-law Hugh Macintosh. Following five years holed up in the Hobart Town Gaol, owing to past business transactions being of a less than honourable nature, Degraves spent two decades establishing himself as one of Van Diemen's Lands' wealthiest and more powerful businessmen, including through the operation of a timber mill, flour mill and brewery. Continuing to build his empire, in early 1847 Degraves, together with his oldest son Henry, established a shipyard at Battery Point near the Prince of Wales' Battery next door to land that had previously been leased to William Williamson by owner Thomas Smith.[573] The property, with a river frontage of 182ft, had been purchased by Henry Degraves for the sum of £1,174.[574] Here the determination and resolve of Degraves and his son saw them build the largest vessel yet constructed in Australia, the 562-ton *Tasman*. Between 1848 and 1853, eight additional vessels were launched from the Degraves family's Battery Point shipyard before the untimely death of both Degraves and his son in 1852 and 1854, respectively.

In terms of genealogy, Peter Degraves was born at the very fashionable address of Red Lion Square in London, England, on 24 November 1780 and baptised nearby at St George the Martyr, Queen Square, on 17 December of that year.[575] He was the eldest of two children, both boys, born to Dr Peter and Ann Degravers (later Degraves), nee Jones.[576] Of French origin, Dr Degravers was a medical practitioner who specialised in the treatment of the eye; one press report from 1788 notes that he was a Professor of Anatomy at the University of Paris.[577] He appears to have spent the greater part of Peter Degraves' childhood travelling England and Scotland giving consultations and lectures or employed as a surgeon on board vessels involved in the African slave trade.[578] Still, likely through resources provided by the maternal side of his family, Peter Degraves, his mother and younger brother Henry were well provided for in London. In the 1790s the family notably lived near Grosvenor Square in the exclusive Mayfair district.[579]

[573] *The Courier*, 16 January 1847.
[574] *The Courier*, 10 February 1847.
[575] London, England, Church of England Baptisms, Marriages and Burials, 1538-1812 for Peter Degravers.
[576] London, England, Church of England Baptisms, Marriages and Burials, 1538-1812 for Degravers.
[577] *Newcastle Courant*, 13 December 1788.
[578] *Reading Mercury*, 24 December 1781; *Caledonian Mercury*, 20 January 1787, 19 May 1788.
[579] Westminster Rate Books (1634 – 1900) for Degraves.

Baptism record of Peter Degraves (noted as Degravers), 17 December 1780, St George the Martyr, Queen Square, London. Courtesy www.ancestry.com.

In keeping with his upper-class childhood, Degraves was educated at Dr Lord's Academy, operated by Walter Lord of Tooting, Surrey.[580] It is also reported that he studied law at Gray's Inn and engineering under Rennie, the celebrated Scottish engineer, though the authenticity of these statements requires further investigation.[581]

After a period of apprenticeship, likely served in London, Degraves moved to Manchester, Lancashire; a rapidly emerging industrial and manufacturing hub known principally for its steam-powered cotton mills, the first of which had been built only 20 years prior. Here, buoyed by enthusiasm and supported by his family's capital, Degraves entered the mercantile trade.

By 1804 Degraves was involved in the manufacture of muslin and other articles in partnership with James Lane of London and George Dickinson of Kirby Stephen.[582] However, by May of the following year the partnership had been dissolved.[583] Shortly following Degraves partnered with Thomas Bainbridge to establish a warehouse business in Manchester, operating as 'Peter Degraves and Company'.[584] Unfortunately the success of this enterprise was also short-lived. By 1807 the pair filed for bankruptcy; Degraves opting to return to London where he established a warehouse business in Bread Street, Cheapside.[585] A dividend was paid out on the Degraves/Bainbridge estate in 1809.[586]

Some time during this period Degraves married Ann Macintosh, sister of Hugh Macintosh who was a major of the East India Company and had served with Degraves' younger brother Henry in India as part of the Eighth Regiment Native Infantry.[587] Degraves and his new bride settled in Cheapside where their first child Sophia was born in July 1808.[588] Sadly, she died one day later. Another daughter, Louisa Frances, was born the following year.[589]

Continuing a downward spiral in relation to his business dealings, in early 1810 Degraves was convicted of stealing £3,000 worth of French cambric and Irish linen, the property of John Parsons of Manchester (who had previously been in the employ of Degraves), from a warehouse then owned by Thomas Bainbridge.[590] Following an extensive and complicated trial which took place at the Lancaster Assizes in April 1810, and where in a *'long and eloquent defence'* Degraves professed his innocence stating instead that he had been grossly misunderstood, he was found guilty by jury and sentenced to a year in prison.[591] Astonishingly, and likely the result of his personal and/or family connections,

---

[580] *Morning Post*, 19 December 1807.
[581] W. Lawson & the Shiplovers' Society of Tasmania (1949). *Blue Gum Clippers and Whale Ships of Tasmania*; *The Mercury*, 12 April 1924; G. Jeffreys (2011). *Hugh Macintosh and Peter Degraves: the Story of an Officer and a Gentleman*.
[582] *The Derby Mercury*, 4 July 1805.
[583] *London Gazette*, 18 June 1805; *Oracle and the Daily Advertiser*, 24 June 1805.
[584] *Manchester Mercury*, 16 February 1808.
[585] *Morning Post*, 27 May 1807; *Bury and Norwich Post – Bury St Edmunds*, 2 May 1810.
[586] *Kentish Gazette*, 6 June 1809.
[587] UK, Registers of Employees of the East India Company and the India Office, 1746-1939 for Hugh MacIntosh; *Hampshire Telegraph and Naval Chronicle*, 29 January 1810.
[588] G. Jeffreys (2011). *Hugh Macintosh and Peter Degraves: the Story of an Officer and a Gentleman*.
[589] G. Jeffreys (2011). *Hugh Macintosh and Peter Degraves: the Story of an Officer and a Gentleman*.
[590] Report of Alexander Thomson. HO 47/45/3. The National Archives; *Lancaster Gazette*, 7 April 1810.
[591] *Lancaster Gazette*, 21 April 1810.

Degraves' case was discharged two months later by Royal Pardon upon advice of the presiding judge.[592]

Following his short stint in prison Degraves appears to have laid low, likely the result of his business affairs affecting his reputation. By 1813, and possibly with the help of his wife's Scottish family, he had established a business on the Isle of Lewis off Scotland's west coast curing large volumes of fish and was also involved in coastal trading.[593] The success of these enterprises, like Degraves' previous ventures, appears to have been brief. By April 1816 he was back in England where the birth record of his sixth child, a daughter named Sophia, lists him as a cotton merchant of Battersea Fields, near London.[594] Three years later, in 1819, coinciding with the birth of his seventh child Frances Deborah, Degraves was noted as a gentleman of Marlborough Street, Southwark, London, suggesting that he had acquired independent means to support himself and his growing family.[595] This 'support' may have been from his maternal aunt Deborah who had married a wealthy French merchant named John Decharme and, following his death in 1788, gained independent wealth.[596]

Continuing his resourceful ways, in 1820 Degraves partnered with his brother-in-law Hugh Macintosh, by now retired from the East India Company after being wounded during fighting in Seringampatam, to purchase the Venice-built 231-ton ship *Hope* with the intention of sailing the vessel to Van Diemen's Land; Macintosh likely providing the necessary capital for its procurement.[597] Apprised of the need for timber and the availability of land grants in the developing colony suitable for cultivation, the pair then purchased machinery to build a sawmill and a flour mill, as well as other equipment and merchandise which they intended to use or sell upon embarking at Hobart Town.[598] Macintosh also purchased agricultural equipment with the intention of establishing himself as a genteel landowner.[599] More revenue to furnish their trip and pay off debts was gained from fare paying passengers, of which there were approximately 90.[600]

Sailing from London in late October 1821, the *Hope* was forced back to port at Ramsgate, Kent, just 80 miles from London, owing to its leaky condition.[601] Here Degraves and Macintosh fell into a quandary when their ship was seized by the Comptroller of His Majesty's Customs, having been found in breach of the Passengers Act for having on board 50 more passengers than allowed by law.[602] What occurred next was dramatically played out in the English press with intending emigrants cautioned as a result of what transpired.[603] For it appears the *Hope* left London two months behind schedule, such that passengers who had rescinded their lodgings were forced to live on board.[604] By agreement with Degraves and Macintosh they were to be supplied with provisions and food.[605] No provisions were distributed to the passengers and the supply of food was stated to be grossly inferior in both quantity and quality as to what was promised.[606]

With no means to support themselves, no lodging other than on board, and no access to their belongings, the passengers were left destitute upon landing at Ramsgate. Fortunately their plight was taken up by several influential gentlemen, including Sir William Curtis, and by January 1822 the government had agreed to charter a vessel for those still willing to travel to Van Diemen's Land.[607]

The entire situation did not bode well for Degraves or Macintosh. Having recouped nearly £3,000 from their fare paying passengers, they were still unable to pay off debts prior to leaving London and, as such, were arrested for not only breaching the Passengers Act but also for monies owed to creditors.[608] Upon further investigation, the near-30 year old *Hope* was also deemed unfit for service.[609]

After spending several months in prison, during which time various court cases took place, Degraves and Macintosh were finally released.[610] At some point during this process, however, good news came in that Lloyds of London had agreed to their insurance claim regarding repairs to the *Hope*.[611]

With the *Hope* repaired and deemed seaworthy, the vessel finally sailed for Hobart Town on 19 September 1823; nearly two years after the first attempt.[612] Given the disastrous state of their finances and reputations, Degraves and Macintosh were likely more anxious than ever to leave the shores of England for Van Diemen's Land.

The *Hope* arrived at Hobart Town on 18 May 1824.[613] By June of the following year Degraves had been granted 2,000 acres of land at 'Cascade' in the foothills of Mount Wellington.[614] Significantly, the parcel encompassed sections of both the Hobart Town Rivulet and the Guy Fawkes Rivulet and their convergence near the current site of the Cascade Brewery.[615] Just three months later the Hobart Town press announced that Messrs Macintosh and Degraves' water-powered sawmill, erected near the Cascade on the Hobart Town Rivulet, was fully operational with the complex machinery noted for

---

[592] *Lancaster Gazette*, 30 June 1810.
[593] G. Jeffreys (2011). *Hugh Macintosh and Peter Degraves: the Story of an Officer and a Gentleman*.
[594] London, England, Births and Baptisms, 1813-1906 for Sophia Degraves.
[595] London, England, Births and Baptisms, 1813-1906 for Frances Deborah Degraves.
[596] *Kentish Gazette*, 21 October 1788.
[597] G. Jeffreys (2011). *Hugh Macintosh and Peter Degraves: the Story of an Officer and a Gentleman*; *Public Ledger and Daily Advertiser*, 30 January 1810.
[598] G. Jeffreys (2011). *Hugh Macintosh and Peter Degraves: the Story of an Officer and a Gentleman*.
[599] G. Jeffreys (2011). *Hugh Macintosh and Peter Degraves: the Story of an Officer and a Gentleman*.
[600] G. Jeffreys (2011). *Hugh Macintosh and Peter Degraves: the Story of an Officer and a Gentleman*.
[601] *Morning Chronicle*, 22 November 1821.
[602] *Morning Chronicle*, 22 November 1821.
[603] *Cambridge Chronicle and Journal*, 11 January 1822.
[604] *Cambridge Chronicle and Journal*, 11 January 1822.
[605] *Cambridge Chronicle and Journal*, 11 January 1822.
[606] *Cambridge Chronicle and Journal*, 11 January 1822.
[607] *Cambridge Chronicle and Journal*, 11 January 1822.
[608] *Cambridge Chronicle and Journal*, 11 January 1822.
[609] *Cambridge Chronicle and Journal*, 11 January 1822.
[610] G. Jeffreys (2011). *Hugh Macintosh and Peter Degraves: the Story of an Officer and a Gentleman*.
[611] G. Jeffreys (2011). *Hugh Macintosh and Peter Degraves: the Story of an Officer and a Gentleman*.
[612] *The Sydney Gazette & New South Wales Advertiser*, 27 May 1824.
[613] *The Sydney Gazette & New South Wales Advertiser*, 27 May 1824.
[614] M. Bingham (1992). *Cascade: A Taste of History*.
[615] Tasmanian Archives (AF396-1-120).

1820s map of Hobart Town and surrounds showing Peter Degraves' 2,000 land grant, incorporating the Hobart Town and Guy Fawkes rivulets.
Courtesy Tasmanian Archives (AF396/1/120).

its efficiency.[616] The pair were also noted to be in the process of erecting a steam engine at the Hobart Town wharf for use in grinding corn.[617] In addition, showing his engineering capabilities, Degraves was drawing up plans to supply Hobart Town residents with water.[618]

Though by now located over 10,000 miles from London, Degraves could not escape the shrewdness of his past business dealings and by early 1826 was being sued by local agents of his creditors back in England.[619] As a result the Hobart Town Sheriff's Office took possession of the Cascade sawmill, associated machinery and timber, as well as working bullocks, a small house and household furniture with the goal of selling the assets at auction.[620] To thwart the sale, Degraves and Macintosh dissolved their partnership by mutual consent with the latter taking sole responsibility for any outstanding debt.[621] Though successful at maintaining possession of their assets, including the sawmill at Cascade which soon began supplying timber for use in construction of Hobart Town's New Wharf, Degraves and Macintosh's financial problems were far from over.[622] In December 1828 the pair filed for insolvency.[623] Creditors, however, retaliated by having Degraves thrown into the debtor's section of the Hobart Town Gaol.[624] Resolved of his innocence a determined Degraves spent the next few years campaigning to all realms of government for his release. He was finally set free in July 1831.[625]

Not letting his incarceration affect his business operations, Degraves continued to manage his affairs from gaol, including his sawmill, as well as develop plans for new enterprises. Indicative of his consistent need to capitalise on every situation, regardless of how dire, he spent his incarceration also designing a plan for a new gaol.[626] His financial shrewdness was additionally echoed in the fact Degraves sent the Government of Van Diemen's Land a bill upon being released from the prison.[627]

In early 1832, just six months after his release, Degraves began building a brewery at his Cascade property. The business, including a malt house, was

[616] *Hobart Town Gazette*, 10 September 1825.
[617] *Hobart Town Gazette*, 10 September 1825.
[618] M. Bingham (1992). *Cascade: A Taste of History*.
[619] M. Bingham (1992). *Cascade: A Taste of History*.
[620] *Colonial Times and Tasmanian Advertiser*, 7 April 1826; *Hobart Town Gazette*, 8 April 1826.
[621] *The Hobart Town Gazette*, 21 October 1826.
[622] *The Tasmanian*, 25 October 1827; *Colonial Advocate, and Tasmanian Monthly Review and Register*, 1 May 1828; M. Bingham (1992). *Cascade: A Taste of History*.
[623] *The Tasmanian*, 12 December 1828.
[624] *The Tasmanian*, 25 October 1827; *Colonial Advocate, and Tasmanian Monthly Review and Register*, 1 May 1828; M. Bingham (1992). *Cascade: A Taste of History*.
[625] M. Bingham (1992). *Cascade: A Taste of History*.
[626] Tasmanian Archives, Colonial Secretary Correspondence for Peter Degraves.
[627] Tasmanian Archives, Colonial Secretary Correspondence for Peter Degraves.

operational the following year with the Hobart Town press noting, '*Mr. Degraves, in particular, does not only brew beer of a nutritious and wholesome kind, but also pays much attention that his beer is always clear*'.[628] The clearness of the product was obviously due to the enviable location of his brewery in the foothills of Mount Wellington and its access to uncontaminated fresh water.

Further spreading his interests and resources, in 1834 Degraves developed plans, partly financed and began building Hobart Town's first theatre — the Theatre Royal, now the oldest continually operating theatre in Australia; a project that was completed in 1837.[629] He also designed a wooden suspension bridge to be built across the River Derwent at New Norfolk, though this plan appears not to have been implemented.[630] These professional developments, however, were punctuated by sad family-related events. On 26 December 1834 Hugh Macintosh died at Cascade '*after a tedious illness*', aged 58.[631] In the years immediately prior, Degraves and his wife Sophia had also endured the deaths of their twelfth and thirteenth children, respectively. A daughter named Matilda had died in February 1829 aged just 10 days, while a daughter named Isabella had died in April 1833 aged only five weeks.[632]

By 1835, showing a remarkable turnaround, Degraves was being applauded in the local press for his industry and perseverance. His property at Cascade was stated to be a '*little town - a paragon of industry and perseverance*' whereby '*every branch of the family is employed more or less in the labour and drudgery of the concern, and richly deserve the sweets that arise from honest industry*'.[633] Finding himself also in favour with the government, Degraves applied for and was subsequently granted an additional 2,000 acres of land at Cascade.[634] Yet, continuing a life of contrasts, in December 1835 he was fined for breaching the Water Act, having diverted the Hobart Town Rivulet from its usual course for his own benefit, causing many of the town's inhabitants to be devoid of much of their supply.[635]

Continuing apace, in 1836 Degraves completed construction of a water-driven flour mill at Cascade, stated to be capable of grinding more flour than all of the other mills in Hobart Town combined.[636] He also applied for a land grant at the Hobart Wharf along Hunter Street.[637] This was likely to assist in his newly established timber export business which Degraves began operating in earnest in 1838.[638] Court cases still played an important role on his agenda, including in September 1838 when he successfully sued the government for compensation regarding the forced removal of his mill-dam at Cascade three years prior.[639]

By the early 1840s Peter Degraves was considered one of the most powerful and wealthiest men in Hobart Town. In May 1841 he also became a widower. His wife Sophia died at Cascade of a neck tumor.[640] She was 53 years of age. By now in his early 60s, however, it appears age did not slow Degraves down. With the help of his four sons, Henry, Charles, John and William, he was actively expanding his flourishing business operations, including establishment of an extensive baking operation.[641] He was also still busily engaged in engineering pursuits, including drafting plans (some of which were later implemented) to better supply Hobart Town with water; of course with his own water rights fully accounted for.[642] The saga for Hobart Town's water rights would continue to plague Degraves for many years, his battle to prioritise and service his personal and business interests at the detriment of thousands of residents reaching an apex in 1850.[643]

With the development of intercolonial trade, the export of Degraves' timber, beer and flour to the more lucrative mainland markets became a reality. In August 1841, for example, 23,500ft of timber, 134 bags of flour, 422 bags of potatoes and 90 bags of wheat were shipped to Sydney via the schooner *Sisters*.[644] Purchasing or building vessels to ply intercolonial trade, thus maintaining more control over the supply chain, was the next logical next step for Degraves.

Needing a suitable property with which to establish a shipyard, in early 1846 Degraves and his son Henry leased waterfront land at Battery Point, near the Prince of Wales' Battery and in the vicinity of William Williamson's existing shipyard.[645] Disregarding the need to build vessels to furnish intercolonial trade, however, the pair teamed up with local merchants Messrs Thomas Brown and Louis Nathan and laid the keel of a vessel in excess of 500 tons.[646] The ship was intended to eclipse all others built in the colony with the notion of showing '*the good people of England what we colonists can do*'.[647]

In February 1847, at auction, the Degraves' purchased their shipyard outright from William Williamson for £1,174; the property, consisting of two parcels of land, having a combined river frontage of 182ft (refer to map on page 37).[648] The following month, on 12 March 1847, the largest vessel ever built

---

[628] *The Colonist and Van Diemen's Land Commercial and Agricultural Advertiser*, 1 March 1833.
[629] M. Bingham (1992). *Cascade: A Taste of History*; *The Hobart Town Courier*, 25 July 1834; en.wikipedia.org/wiki/Theatre_Royal,_Hobart.
[630] *The True Colonist Van Diemen's Land Political Despatch, and Agricultural and Commercial ...* , 7 March 1835.
[631] Libraries Tasmania (RGD34/1/1 no. 3481); *Trumpeter General*, 26 December 1834.
[632] Libraries Tasmania (RGD34/1/1 no. 1896, RGD34/1/1 no. 2999).
[633] *Colonial Times*, 28 April 1835.
[634] *The Hobart Town Courier*, 27 November 1835; *The Hobart Town Courier*, 8 July 1836.
[635] *Colonial Times*, 29 December 1835.
[636] *The Hobart Town Courier*, 13 May 1836.
[637] *Launceston Advertiser*, 29 September 1836.
[638] *The Hobart Town Courier*, 18 May 1838.
[639] *Colonial Times*, 18 September 1838.
[640] Libraries Tasmania (RGD35/1/1 no. 1058).
[641] *The True Colonist Van Diemen's Land Despatch, and Agricultural and Commercial ..*, 7 June 1844.
[642] *Colonial Times*, 12 January 1841, 25 September 1846; *The True Colonist Van Diemen's Land Despatch, and Agricultural and Commercial ...*, 21 November 1844; *The Observer*, 1 July 1845.
[643] *Colonial Times*, 15 February 1850.
[644] *The Courier*, 20 August 1841; *The Sydney Monitor & Commercial Advertiser*, 1 September 1841.
[645] *Colonial Times*, 13 February 1846.
[646] *Colonial Times*, 13 February 1846; *The Hobart Town Herald and Total Abstinence Advocate*, 3 March 1847.
[647] *Colonial Times*, 13 February 1846.
[648] *The Courier*, 16 January, 10 February 1847.

in Australia to date was launched.[649] At 133ft overall, the 562-ton *Tasman* was built entirely of blue gum sourced from Degraves' property at Cascade.[650] The vessel's build was superintended by John Gray, local shipwright, who had previously worked out of a yard at the Old Wharf and later went on to build vessels on Bruny Island and down the Huon.[651]

With a figurehead featuring a carved kangaroo, the *Tasman* sailed on its maiden voyage to London, via Port Phillip Bay, in late August 1847 with a cargo predominantly of wool.[652] The vessel spent the next seven years taking various cargoes to England, returning to Australia with a much needed influx of immigrants. In September 1854 the *Tasman* was purchased by Perrin and Company and its register transferred to Bristol, England.[653] The vessel spent the next few years involved in international trade, primarily sailing between London and Calcutta, before being advertised for sale in London in August 1858.[654] It was again advertised for sale in November 1860, this time lying in the Salthouse Dock, Liverpool.[655] Unfortunately the fate of the *Tasman* remains unknown. It disappears from *Lloyd's Register of British and Foreign Shipping* in 1865, though two years later, in May 1867, was advertised for sale at Greenock, Scotland.[656]

> Unless previously disposed of by Private Treaty.
> On Thursday, the 22nd instant, at Three o'clock, at Cunard, Wilson, and Co.'s Saleroom, Exchange, Liverpool.
> The strong and burthensome ship
> TASMAN,
> 560 tons register. Built at Hobart Town in 1847, and classed A 1, 9 years, at Loyd's. Is copper fastened and sheathed with yellow metal, carries very largely on a light draft of water, and is well worthy of inspection. Lying in the Salthouse Dock. Apply to Messrs. Fletcher and Co.; or to
> CUNARD, WILSON, & CO., Brokers.

Liverpool Daily Post, 20 November 1860.

In 1848 two more vessels were launched from the Degraves family's shipyard at Battery Point, both intended for the whaling industry. These were the barque *Emu*, of 308 tons, launched on 2 March 1848 and built under the superintendence of John Gray, and the barque *Lady Emma*, of 230 tons, launched on 16 December 1848 and built under the superintendence of John Ross (who later operated his own shipyard at Battery Point).[657]

Built to the order of Thomas Brown of Hobart Town, the *Emu* spent five years employed in the whaling industry before being placed in international trade.[658] In 1855 the vessel was purchased by Gales and Company of London and its register transferred to England.[659] Like the *Tasman*, the vessel's subsequent fate remains a mystery; the *Emu* disappears from the British records after 1856.

Built on speculation and purchased by Burns, White and Company prior to launch, the whaling barque *Lady Emma* left Hobart Town for the South Seas whaling grounds in February 1849 with Captain William Young at the helm.[660] The vessel then spent four years employed in the whaling industry before being sold to Captain Gardener for £1,525 in January 1853 and placed in intercolonial trade.[661] Several more changes of ownership saw the *Lady Emma* back in the whaling industry in 1855 where it remained for more than a decade.[662] The *Lady Emma* was sold in October 1864 to E. M. Fisher of Hobart Town for £2,200 and again placed in intercolonial trade, making occasional trips to New Zealand.[663]

In August 1879, still involved in intercolonial trade, the *Lady Emma* struck Acteon Reef in the D'Entrecasteaux Channel, suffering a broken rudder, among other significant damage.[664] The vessel was perilously towed to Hobart Town and placed on McGregor's slip at the Domain.[665] Deemed beyond repair, the following week saw the *Lady Emma* advertised for sale by the insurance underwriters.[666] The craft was sold to John Perkins for £100 and dismantled.[667] Following, in October 1879, several lots belonging to the *Lady Emma* were sold at auction.[668] Coincidentally, its hull was purchased by John Lucas, shipbuilder of Battery Point, for £11 with the intention of using it to construct a jetty off his shipyard.[669]

On 18 August 1849 the 403-ton barque *Derwent* was launched from the Degraves' Battery Point shipyard, built to the order of Messrs Brown and Company under the superintendence of John Ross.[670] The press reported, quite playfully, on the launch event. '*How beautiful the new ship looks upon the stocks - how excellent the model! And what praise is due to Mr Duke, the carver of the figure-head, it being his first attempt of the kind. An how exhilarating to witness the many happy faces around you, waiting for the moment when the words shall sound upon the ear - "Off she goes!" The workmen have left off striking the wedges - the upright poles are removed - a bottle of Champagne is thrown by*

---

[649] *The Courier*, 6 March, 13 March 1847.
[650] *The Courier*, 6 March 1847.
[651] *Tasmanian Weekly Dispatch*, 10 January, 15 May 1840; *Launceston Examiner*, 24 October 1846; *The Courier*, 6 March 1847; *Colonial Times*, 10 September 1850, 31 October 1851, 9 August 1856; *Tasmanian News*, 12 February 1890.
[652] *The Hobart Town Advertiser*, 22 December 1846; *Colonial Times*, 27 August 1847.
[653] R. Parsons (1992). *Australian Shipowners and their Fleets. Book 12 (Hobart to 1859, A - L)*; *Lloyd's Register of British and Foreign Shipping*, 1855.
[654] *London Standard*, 23 January 1856; *Shipping and Mercantile Gazette*, 13 August 1858.
[655] *Northern Daily Times*, 17 November 1860.
[656] *Liverpool Daily Post*, 11 May 1867.
[657] *The Courier*, 4 March, 20 December 1848.
[658] *Colonial Times*, 3 March 1848, 7 November 1854; *The Courier*, 4 March 1848, 25 April 1853;

[659] *Launceston Examiner*, 28 January 1854.
[659] *Lloyd's Register of British and Foreign Shipping*, 1856.
[660] *The Courier*, 20 December 1848; *Colonial Times*, 16 February 1849.
[661] *Colonial Times*, 11 January 1853; *The Courier*, 18 January 1853.
[662] *Colonial Times*, 26 October 1855; R. Parsons (1992). *Australian Shipowners and their Fleets. Book 12 (Hobart to 1859, A - L)*; *The Mercury*, 10 October 1864.
[663] *The Mercury*, 31 October 1855, 18 October 1864, 10 April 1879.
[664] *The Mercury*, 20 August 1879.
[665] *The Mercury*, 1, 2 September 1879.
[666] *The Mercury*, 9 September 1879.
[667] *The Mercury*, 12, 22 September 1879.
[668] *The Mercury*, 4 October 1879.
[669] *The Mercury*, 4 October 1879.
[670] *The Courier*, 22 August 1849.

Lady Emma (right) and PS *Monarch* at the New Wharf, Hobart (circa 1865). Courtesy Tasmanian Archives (NS1013/1/1623).

the hair hand of Miss Davis (Mr Degraves's granddaughter) and not Miss Degraves, as stated in the Advertiser - a flag is immediately unfurled at the mast-head, bearing on it "Derwent" - and the ship glides gracefully into her future element, amidst the deafening shouts of the multitude on shore, re-echoed by those on board. The principal portion of the visitors now retired to a splendid banquet prepared by the worthy shipbuilder for the entertainment of friends. After the ladies had left the festive scene, the toast, the song, and the merry jest flew round the hospitable board, treading on each other's heels, like boys on a slide. And many an orator with laughing eye of that long-to-remembered-night, the next morning admitted with a grave countenance "the potency of Mr. Degraves's Champagne".'[671]

Intended for the London trade, where the vessel spent 11 years employed, in September 1850 noted to have made the London to Hobart Town run in a *'splendid'* 98 days, the *Derwent* was sold to Francis Dixon of London in 1860 and its register transferred to England.[672] After several years spent trading between England and the Middle East, the *Derwent* foundered off Cape de Galle in the Mediterranean Sea while on a voyage from Constantinople to Ireland on 8 April 1865, all hands saved.[673]

On 29 November 1849, less than six months following completion of the *Derwent*, the schooner *Jenny Lind* was launched from the Degraves' Battery Point shipyard.[674] Built to the order of Henry Degraves, likely under the superintendence of John Ross, the 135-ton vessel was intended for the Port Phillip Bay trade where it spent several years employed.[675] In November 1852 the *Jenny Lind* was sold to buyers from Melbourne for £1,600.[676] The vessel was sold a year later to buyers from Sydney for £2,250 and placed in intercolonial trade.[677] Nearly a decade later, in October 1862, the *Jenny Lind* was wrecked near the entrance to Port Curtis, Queensland, all hands saved.[678]

The next vessel off the stocks at the Degraves' Battery Point shipyard was the 138-ton schooner *Yarra*, launched on 19 July 1850.[679] It was a busy few days at Battery Point generally with John Watson launching the *Sword Fish* only the day before.[680] Of similar

[671] *Colonial Times*, 21 August 1849.
[672] *Colonial Times*, 10 September 1850; R. Parsons (1992). *Australian Shipowners and their Fleets. Book 12 (Hobart to 1859, A - L)*.
[673] *Shields Daily Gazette*, 15 January 1863; *Newcastle Journal*, 26 May 1863, 8 February 1864;

Elgin Courier, 21 April 1865.
[674] *The Hobart Town Advertiser*, 30 November 1849; *The Courier*, 29 December 1849.
[675] *The Courier*, 29 December 1849, 31 May 1851.
[676] *Colonial Times*, 2 November 1852; R. Parsons (1992). *Australian Shipowners and their Fleets. Book 12 (Hobart to 1859, A - L)*.
[677] *The Courier*, 19 October 1853.
[678] *The Sydney Morning Herald*, 13 October 1862.
[679] *The Courier*, 20 July 1850.
[680] *The Courier*, 20 July 1850.

Painting of the *Jenny Lind* off Gabo Island by Frederick Garling (circa 1857 - 1862). Courtesy Vaucluse House Collection, Museums of History New South Wales (V87/64).

dimensions to the *Jenny Lind*, being 85ft in length with a breadth of nearly 20ft and a depth of 10ft, the *Yarra* was also intended for the Port Phillip Bay trade where it spent a decade employed before being transferred to intercolonial trade under various owners.[681] More than 30 years following its launch, the *Yarra* was wrecked at Warrnambool, Victoria, on 23 October 1882 during a gale, all hands saved.[682]

A third schooner, the *Portland* (initially referred to as the *Miss Degraves*), was launched from the Degraves' Battery Point shipyard in late 1850.[683] It was near-immediately sailed to Melbourne and advertised for sale though appears not to have sold; the Degraves' retaining possession and employing the vessel in the Hobart Town to Port Phillip Bay trade run.[684] Four months later the *Portland* was purchased by Frederick Hitchins of Geelong, Victoria, for £950 with the intention of placing it in the Apollo Bay timber trade.[685] The *Portland* spent little time in this role, however. The craft was wrecked on 14 September 1852 while entering Port Phillip Heads, Victoria, all hands saved.[686]

Shortly following completion of the *Portland*, the brig *Melbourne* was launched from the Degraves' Battery Point shipyard. Built for the family's own employment in intercolonial trade, the vessel first arrived in Melbourne in May 1851.[687] Its construction came at a pivotal time for the Degraves family's Victorian-based businesses which were undergoing a large-scale expansion. The *Melbourne*'s arrival in Port Phillip Bay coincided with an article in the local press noting, '*The Messrs Degraves, a respectable and highly influential firm from the sister colony of Tasmania, have two splendid buildings on the way; one for a brewery and flour mill in Flinders Lane, and the other for stores in Queen-street*'.[688]

As demand for timber, grain, wool, produce, cattle and sheep in Victoria increased even further, the *Melbourne* continued to be involved in intercolonial trade for nine years. It was wrecked during a gale in the Kent Group, Bass Strait, on 15 August 1859, all hands saved.[689] At the time of loss, the *Melbourne* was owned by Robert Knarston of Victoria.[690]

The last vessel built at the Degraves' Battery Point shipyard, launched on 5 January 1853, was the paddle steamer *Bendigo* though it appears to have been

[681] *Colonial Times*, 23 July 1850; R. Parsons (1992). *Australian Shipowners and their Fleets. Book 13 (Hobart to 1859, M - Z)*.
[682] *Evening News*, 23 October 1882.
[683] *The Melbourne Daily News*, 20, 25 December 1850; *The Hobart Town Advertiser*, 3 January 1851.
[684] *The Melbourne Daily News*, 20, 25 December 1850; *The Argus*, 29 January 1851.
[685] *Geelong Advertiser*, 19 April 1851; *The Courier*, 7 May 1851.
[686] *Adelaide Morning Chronicle*, 27 September 1852.
[687] *The Argus*, 3 May 1851.
[688] *Geelong Advertiser*, 3 May 1851.
[689] *The Argus*, 30 August 1859.
[690] R. Parsons (2008). *Shipping Losses and Casualties concerning Australia and New Zealand. Vol. II*.

originally referred to as the *Faugh-a-Ballagh* at the time of completion.[691] Built under the supervision of its master, William Martin, and intended to ply between Melbourne and Williamstown, the craft was fitted with a 25 h.p engine made by Messrs Easby and Robertson and sent to Victoria a few months after launch.[692] The *Bendigo* was later owned by the Government of Victoria and operated by the Melbourne Harbour Trust for several decades.[693] Sold out of service in January 1878, the vessel was subsequently used as a barge before being broken up in May 1899.[694]

At the age of 73 and just one week prior to the launch of the *Bendigo*, Peter Degraves died on 31 December 1852 at his Cascade residence.[695] Cause of death was influenza.[696] His eldest son Henry was left to carry on the Battery Point shipyard, as well as oversee management of the family's sawmill, brewery, flour mills and theatre, in addition to his own fleet of international and intercolonial trading vessels. The early 1850s Victorian gold rush proved extremely lucrative for the mills; timber and flour could not be loaded onto vessels fast enough. This boon, however, resulted in a shortage of labour in Hobart Town which was particularly detrimental to the town's shipyards. As such, Henry Degraves closed the Battery Point shipyard, instead opting to focus on the more profitable areas of the Degraves' business empire. His brothers, Charles, John and William, were additionally tasked with managing different components of the family's operations, with William primarily based in Melbourne.[697]

Unfortunately Henry Degraves died unexpectedly in May 1854 at the age of 43 of '*apoplexy*', i.e., a stroke.[698] He had only just returned to Hobart Town from a trip to England via Victoria. The *Colonial Times* reported, '*The decease will be severely felt by the citizens, who universally esteemed him, as he was ever the cheerful and liberal supporter of the various objects of philanthropy and commercial enterprise for which Hobart Town has become proverbial*'.[699]

Despite Henry Degraves' death, the family retained possession of their Battery Point shipyard, though no new vessels were built. Instead, over the next few decades, the property was leased in parts to various shipwrights, including John Gray.[700]

In December 1865 the property was reportedly sold to the Tasmanian Pyrolignite Company Ltd. for £2,000; the organisation had been formed two years prior with the purpose of distilling acetate acid, and other analogous products, from species of Tasmania's hardwood.[701] By January 1867 *The Mercury* reported that the '*works of the Pyrolignite Company, on the River Derwent, were opened on Tuesday last, from which date the operations of the company may be said to have fully commenced. The object of the company is, we presume, well known, vis., the extraction of pyroligneous acid, and the manufacture of acetate of lime and other substances from the indigenous timber of this country. The site occupied by the company's new works is that formerly known as Ross's shipyards, Battery Point, and the land occupied comprises 1½ acres, purchased by the company from Mr. Degraves, besides about half an acre leased from Mrs Petty [Perry]. The land has been all securely fenced, and about five thousand tons of wood is now stored upon it, ready to undergo the process of retorting, and a stock sufficient to keep the works in active operation for the next six months. The actual works of the company may be said to commence at the water's edge, where a substantial jetty has been erected 45 feet long by 60 feet wide, run out to a depth of 12 feet, so that vessels of considerable draught may like alongside and discharge wood. The jetty is fitted with an iron crane and every facility for the speedy discharge of vessels*'.[702]

With so much invested in its establishment and so much promise, the Tasmanian Pyrolignite Company unfortunately failed to be a success. The business was voluntarily wound up in December 1867, with the Degraves family retaining possession of the land due to default of payment.[703] In late January of the following year, the whole of the plant, stock and property of the company was sold by the Sheriff of Hobart Town.[704] In the decades, part of the land would be leased to boat builder Benjamin Dyer. It then became the site of the Iron Smelting Works. Following the demise of this operation, between 1876 and 1885 it was leased to boat builder Lark Macquarie. Despite its use as a substantial shipyard where some of the largest vessels yet built in Tasmania were launched; its use for this industry were over.

In 1887 the property was purchased from the estate of John Degraves by Charles Featherstone and W. E. Watchorn, solicitors.[705] Two years later it was sold to Risby Bros. for use as a timber yard.[706] It later became the site of the Port Huon Fruitgrowers' Association.

Many words have already been published on Peter Degraves; his establishment of the Cascade Brewery being the primary focus. However, the shrewd, enterprising, culpable and calculating businessman leaves a legacy also entwined with Tasmania's maritime history. Though not shipbuilders *per se*, Degraves and his son Henry appointed qualified shipwrights, including John Gray and John Ross, to superintend the building of vessels at their Battery Point shipyard in

---

[691] *The Courier*, 6 January 1853; *Hobarton Guardian, or, True Friend of Tasmania*, 16 April 1853.
[692] *Hobarton Guardian, or, True Friend of Tasmania*, 16 April 1853.
[693] *The Argus*, 21 November 1877, 25 January 1878.
[694] *The Argus*, 25 January 1878.
[695] *The Courier*, 5, 6 January 1853.
[696] Libraries Tasmania (RGD35/1/3 no. 2005).
[697] M. Bingham (1992). *Cascade: A Taste of History*.
[698] *The Courier*, 15 May 1854; Libraries Tasmania (RGD35/1/4 no. 1270).
[699] *Colonial Times*, 16 May 1854.
[700] *The Courier*, 11 January, 14 February 1856.
[701] *The Mercury*, 23 May, 30 December 1865.
[702] *The Mercury*, 10 January 1867.
[703] *The Mercury*, 25 November 1867.
[704] *The Mercury*, 31 January 1868.
[705] *The Mercury*, 24 April 1888.
[706] *The Mercury*, 25 November 1889.

fulfillment of personal and/or business goals. Perhaps of greatest significance, their drive and competitiveness saw construction of the largest vessel ever built at Battery Point, the 562-ton *Tasman,* launched in 1847. It was also the largest vessel built in Australia at the time. Additionally launched between 1848 and 1853 were three barques, three schooners, one brig and one paddle steamer.

While Henry died only 18 months after his father, Degraves' three surviving sons Charles, John and William (the latter likely to a lesser extent as he appears to have been more interested in agricultural pursuits), continued operation of the family's businesses, which they had jointly inherited.

Following Charles and John's own deaths in 1874 and 1880, respectively, the Degraves' empire was broken up and sold by trustees. Neither Charles nor John had married and there were no subsequent heirs. Conversely, while William had married, there were no children born to him and his wife. William died in 1883.

Of Peter Degraves' surviving daughters, noting that five had pre-deceased him, sadly both Louisa and Ellen were drowned, along with eight of their children, in the wreck of the *Royal Charter* off the coast of Wales in October 1859. The vessel had been en route to Liverpool from Melbourne. More than 450 passengers and crew lost their lives in the disaster; only 40 men managed to make it to safely to nearby land.[707] All of the women and children on board perished.

The oldest surviving child of Peter Degraves and his wife Sophia was their ninth child Deborah. She had married James Milne Wilson, who for some years worked as a manager for the Cascade Brewery. He later became Mayor of Hobart Town and served as Premier of Tasmania from 1869 to 1872. Deborah died at Hobart in 1897. Her death marked the end of the family legacy of Peter Degraves and his empire.

---

[707] www.anglesey-history.co.uk/places/royal-charter/index.html.

Peter Degraves' Cascade Brewery and property (circa 1860s).
Courtesy Tasmanian Archives (LPIC147/3/148).

Vessels built by Peter and Henry Degraves and employees at Battery Point (1847 - 1853)

Year	Name	Type	Description
1847	*Tasman*	Ship	119.4 x 27.3 x 20ft. ON 13715. 562 tons. Built by Peter and Henry Degraves for Peter Degraves in partnership with Louis Nathan and Thomas Brown under the superintendence of John Gray. Launched on 12 March 1847, intended for international trade. Spent seven years trading between England and Australia. Purchased by Perrin and Company of Bristol in September 1854 and register transferred to England. Spent the next few years involved in international trade, primarily sailing between London and Calcutta. Advertised for sale in London in August 1858 and in Liverpool in November 1860. Disappears from Lloyd's Register of British and Foreign Shipping in 1865 though was advertised for sale at Greenock, Scotland, in May 1867.
1848	*Emu*	Barque	107.6 x 26.2 x 14.7ft. ON 24644. 308 tons. Built by Peter and Henry Degraves to the order of Thomas Brown under the superintendence of John Gray. Launched on 2 March 1848. Spent five years employed in the whaling industry before being placed in international trade. Purchased by Richard Gibson Gales of Gales and Company, London, in October 1855 and transferred to England. Fate unknown. Disappears from the British records in 1856.
1848	*Lady Emma*	Barque	91.8 x 23.3 x 12.8ft. ON 32030. 230 tons. Built by Peter and Henry Degraves under the superintendence of John Ross. Built on speculation, purchased by Burns, White and Company prior to launch. Launched on 16 December 1848. Involved in the South Seas whaling industry. Sold to Captain Gardener for £1,525 in January 1853 and placed in intercolonial trade. Several more changes of ownership saw it back in the whaling industry in 1855 where it remained for more than a decade. Sold in October 1864 to E. M. Fisher of Hobart Town for £2,200 and again placed in intercolonial trade, making occasional trips to New Zealand. In August 1879 struck Acteon Reef in the D'Entrecasteaux Channel, suffering a broken rudder, among other significant damage. Towed to Hobart Town and placed on McGregor's slip at the Domain. Deemed beyond repair, advertised for sale by the insurance underwriters. Sold to John Perkins for £100 and dismantled. In October 1879, several lots sold at auction, including its hull which was purchased by John Lucas, shipbuilder of Battery Point, for £11 for use constructing a jetty off his shipyard.
1849	*Derwent*	Barque	119.9 x 25.7 x 16.2ft. ON 625. 403 tons. Built by Peter and Henry Degraves to the order of Brown and Company under the superintendence of John Ross. Launched on 18 August 1849. Intended for the London trade, where it spent 11 years employed. Sold to Francis Dixon of London in August 1860 and transferred to England. After several years spent trading between England and the Middle East, foundered off Cape de Galle in the Mediterranean Sea while on a voyage from Constantinople to Ireland on 8 April 1865, all hands saved.
1849	*Jenny Lind*	Schooner	82.6 x 19.6 x 10.4ft. ON 32440. 135 tons. Built by Peter and Henry Degraves to the order of Henry Degraves, likely under the superintendence of John Ross. Launched on 29 November 1849. Intended for the Port Phillip Bay trade. In November 1852 sold to buyers from Melbourne for £1,600. Sold a year later to buyers from Sydney for £2,250 and placed in intercolonial trade. Nearly a decade later, in October 1862, wrecked near the entrance to Port Curtis, Queensland, all hands saved.
1850	*Yarra*	Schooner	85.0 x 19.1 x 9.9ft. ON 32019. 138 tons. Built by Peter and Henry Degraves under the superintendence of another shipwright. Launched on 19 July 1850. Spent 10 years employed in the Port Phillip Bay trade before being transferred to intercolonial trade under various owners. Register transferred to Adelaide in 1858, Melbourne in 1859, Launceston in 1867 and Melbourne in 1872. Wrecked at Warrnambool, VIC, on 23 October 1882 during a gale, all hands saved. At the time of loss, owned by Hugh R. Reid.
1850	*Portland*	Schooner	62.1 x 17 x 8ft. 72 tons. Built by Peter and Henry Degraves under the superintendence of another shipwright. Launched in late 1850. Purchased by Frederick Hitchins of Geelong, Victoria, in April 1851 for £950 with the intention of placing it in the Apollo Bay timber trade. Wrecked on 14 September 1852 while entering Port Phillip Heads, all hands saved.
1851	*Melbourne*	Brig	85 x 19.9 x 9.9ft. 149 tons. Built by Peter and Henry Degraves for themselves under the superintendence of another shipwright. Launched early in 1851. Intended for intercolonial trade. Wrecked during a gale in the Kent Group, Bass Strait, on 15 August 1859, all hands saved. At the time of loss, owned by Robert Knarston of Melbourne.
1853	*Bendigo*	Paddle steamer	80.8 x 14.3 x 6.7ft. ON 79504. 47 tons. Built by Peter and Henry Degraves under the superintendence of another shipwright, William Martin. Launched on 5 January 1853. Intended to ply between Melbourne and Williamstown, fitted with a 25 h.p engine made by Messrs Easby and Robertson and sent to Victoria a few months after launch. Later owned by the Government of Victoria and operated by the Melbourne Harbour Trust for several decades. Sold out of service in January 1878. Subsequently used as a barge before being broken up in May 1899.

Joseph Edward Risby (circa 1880s).
Courtesy Allport Library and Museum of Fine Arts, State Library of Tasmania (AUTAS001136192036).

Joseph Risby

'Another class of vessel, unknown a few years since, is now becoming numerous; we allude to the river barges ... A new one will shortly be added to their number, of a size exceeding that of any of the best. It is built by the Messrs Risby, the well known and unrivalled whaleboat builders.'

The Hobart Town Advertiser, 21 March 1848.

Joseph Edward Risby was born in 1826 at Clarence Plains (now Rokeby), Van Diemen's Land, and baptised on 21 August that year by the Reverend Robert Knopwood.[708] He was the fifth of seven children born to Thomas and Diana Risby (nee Morrisby) between the years 1816 and 1838.[709]

Thomas Risby had arrived in Van Diemen's Land with his parents and four siblings in October 1808, aged 16, per the *City of Edinburgh* as part of Norfolk Island's resettlement program.[710] While Thomas had been born 'free' on the island, both his parents were former convicts. His father Edward had arrived in Sydney with the First Fleet in 1788, while his mother Ann (nee Gibson) had arrived with the Second Fleet.[711] Both were subsequently transferred to Norfolk Island where they spent the remainder of their sentences, marrying in 1791 and going on to establish a family. Edward's good behaviour earned him a land grant on Norfolk Island; the growing Risby family farmed the property from the 1790s until their departure to Hobart Town in 1808.[712]

Having successfully cultivated his land at Norfolk Island, upon arrival in Hobart Town Edward Risby was granted twice the equivalent number of acres. His 30-acre parcel was located in the vicinity of what is now Tolosa Street, Glenorchy.[713] Upon reaching adulthood, Thomas Risby was initially granted land at Tea Tree.[714] However, he soon exchanged this parcel for more acres across the River Derwent going on to establish himself as a farmer at Ralphs Bay.[715] Here he grew crops and tended livestock, being noted as supplying fresh meat to the colonial government in 1818.[716]

In 1826, shortly after the birth of his son Joseph, Thomas Risby relinquished farming and moved his family to Hobart Town. Here he commenced work as a boat builder, operating out of a plot of land in Collins Street he had purchased from his father-in-law (John Morrisby) for £100.[717] The property backed on to the Hobart Town Rivulet, conveniently providing access to the River Derwent.

Thomas Risby's transition into boat building came at a pivotal time in Hobart Town's history. The whaling industry, including offshore and bay whaling, was rapidly developing. Boats for use in conveying passengers and stores on local rivers and waterways, as well as for fishing and recreational pursuits, were also in demand.

In addition, whaleboat races were becoming increasingly popular, with local crews often pitted against crews from visiting vessels. The popularity of these races led to more formal events being staged. By the late 1830s, the Hobart Town Regatta had been born and competition between the local and international whaling crews intensified with reputations at stake and much money changing hands between the competitors and those partaking in shore-side bets. During this period, the skilled workmanship of Thomas Risby was increasingly sought after such that he came to be considered one of the finest boat builders in Hobart Town.[718]

Having taught the craft of boat building to his three elder sons, Thomas (Jr), William and Joseph, 'Risby and Sons, boat builders', dominated the Hobart Town boat building landscape well into the early 1840s. Though little information is available on the commercial and recreational boats they built, the local press alludes to several racing boats completed by the family during this period. The five-oared whaleboat race at the 1840

---

[708] Libraries Tasmania (RGD32/1/1 no. 2235).
[709] Siblings were Thomas Risby born 1816; William Henry Risby born 1818, Mary Ann Risby born 1821, Eliza Risby born 1823, Henry Edmund Risby born 1829, and Lavinia Rose Risby born 1838 (www.findagrave.com/memorial/191720833; Libraries Tasmania: RGD32/1/1 no. 630, 1043, 1484, 3064; RGD32/1/2 no. 8337).
[710] Libraries Tasmania (CSO1/1/177 file 4306 p p. 222).
[711] W. H. L. Risby (2020). *Risby Ancestors: From Convict Beginnings*.
[712] W. H. L. Risby (2020). *Risby Ancestors: From Convict Beginnings*.
[713] W. H. L. Risby (2020). *Risby Ancestors: From Convict Beginnings*.
[714] W. H. L. Risby (2020). *Risby Ancestors: From Convict Beginnings*.
[715] W. H. L. Risby (2020). *Risby Ancestors: From Convict Beginnings*.
[716] *The Hobart Town Gazette and Southern Reporter*, 11 July 1818.
[717] *The Hobart Town Courier*, 15 August 1829; W. H. L. Risby (2020). *Risby Ancestors: From Convict Beginnings*.
[718] *Colonial Times*, 27 August 1831; A. Graeme-Evans (1995). *Against The Odds: Risbys – Tasmanian Timber Pioneers 1826-1995*.

Hobart Town Regatta, for example, featured at least four boats built by Risby and Sons. These were the *Schah*, built by William Risby which won first prize in the race; the *Native Cherry*, built by Thomas Risby which won second prize; the *Will-If-I-Can* and the *Tasman*, both built by Thomas Risby (Jr) and finished third and fourth, respectively; and the *Flying Squirrel*, which finished fifth and was built by William Risby.[719] Meanwhile, the race for six-oared whaleboats held at the same regatta featured three boats built by the Risby family: the *Maria*, *Camilla* and *Van Diemen*.[720]

Other racing boats built by the Risby and Sons at their Collins Street residence during this period included the four-oared gigs *Caterpillar* (later named *Beppo*) and *Centipede*; the five-oared whaleboats *James*, *Farmer* and *Delias*; and the whaleboat *Opposition*.[721] All of these craft were completed in time to compete at the 1841 Hobart Town Regatta held in early December of that year.

Showcasing not only their boats but their own sporting ability, it was around this time that the three Risby sons began participating in regatta races. By way of illustration, in 1842 Joseph Risby won the race for native youths under 16 years of age competing in the five-oared whaleboat *Bluebeard*, a boat he likely built.[722] Similarly, the four-oared gig *Coronella*, which first competed at the 1843 Hobart Town Regatta, was built and helmed by Thomas Risby (Jr).[723]

The success and quality of the Risby family's commercial, recreational and racing boats prompted the local press to congratulate Thomas Risby for finally putting a stop to the importation of boats from England.[724]

In 1844 a monumental event affecting the Risby family took place: they moved their boat building operation to Napoleon Street, Battery Point.[725] The parcel of land had briefly been used by the Derwent Ship Building Company before the enterprise disbanded.[726] It had been purchased from parties associated with the Company, including George Bilton, Edward Goldsmith and James Meaburn.[727] The property featured 112ft of frontage on the River Derwent and was situated next to land then owned by Benjamin Guy. The following year, Thomas Risby (Sr) retired from professional boat building, handing over the family's business to his three sons. Operating as 'Thos. Risby and Brothers', the trio first notified their customers, including local whalers, of the new establishment in January 1845.[728]

[719] *Tasmanian Weekly Dispatch*, 4 December 1840; *Colonial Times*, 8 December 1840.
[720] *Tasmanian Weekly Dispatch*, 4 December 1840; *Colonial Times*, 8 December 1840.
[721] *Colonial Times*, 7 December 1841; *The Hobart Town Advertiser*, 28 March 1843.
[722] *Colonial Times*, 6 December 1842.
[723] *The Courier*, 14 October 1846.
[724] *Colonial Times*, 7 December 1841.
[725] *The Hobart Town Advertiser*, 21 January 1845.
[726] *The Hobart Town Advertiser*, 22 July 1842.
[727] www.thelist.tas.gov.au (Historical Deed 02/6082).
[728] *The Hobart Town Advertiser*, 21 January 1845.

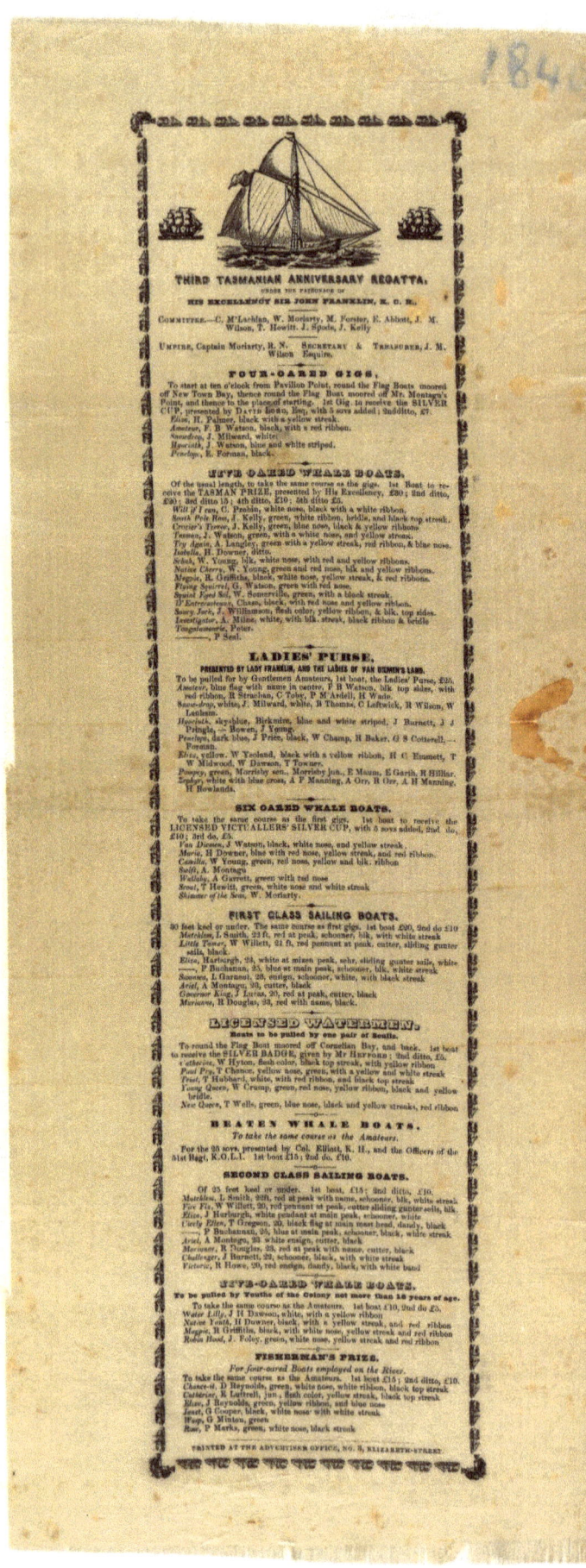

1840 Hobart Town Regatta Program.
Courtesy Tasmanian Archives (NS73/1/2).

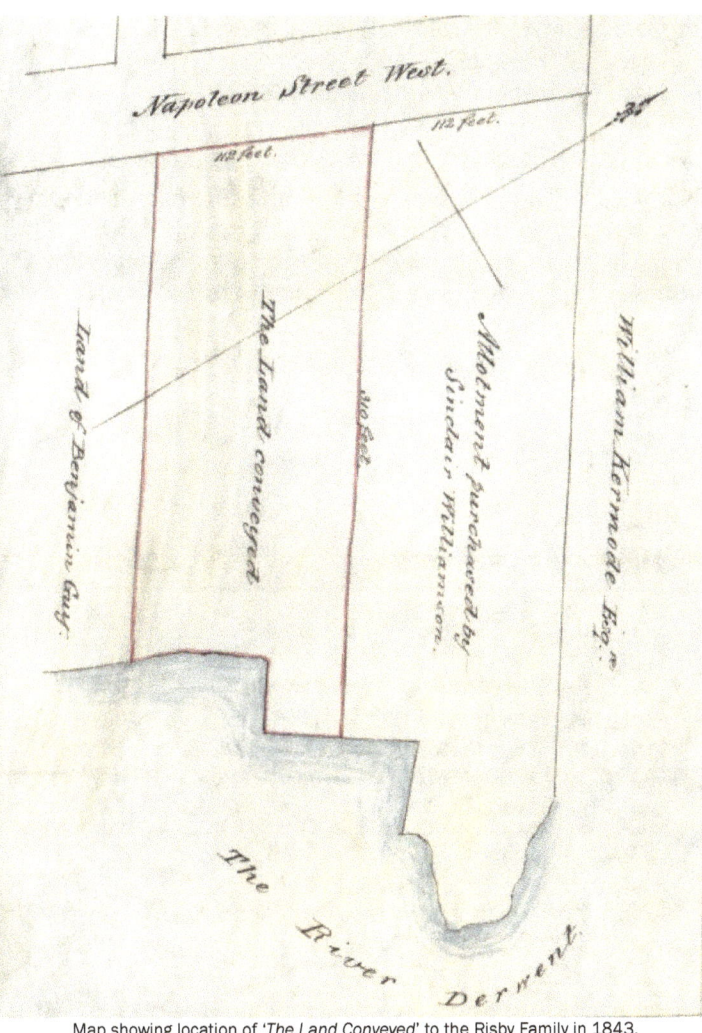

Map showing location of 'The Land Conveyed' to the Risby Family in 1843. Courtesy www.thelist.tas.gov.au (Historical Deed 02/6082).

Primarily involved in the building and repair of commercial whaleboats, as well as smaller recreational vessels, unfortunately little is known about this side of the Risby brothers' business; the building of whaleboats for racing deemed far more noteworthy by the local press. For example, the four-oared gig *Cupid*, was built in 1845 to compete at that year's Hobart Town Regatta.[729] A boat was also built by Risbys for the colonial government in 1846.[730] That same year they were noted as building a 'Thames wherry' on speculation though intended to compete at the upcoming Hobart Town Regatta.[731] The vessel was advertised for sale in November 1846 along with the pleasure schooner *Vestal* which they had recently overhauled and '*several other new gigs and boats*'.[732] The five-oared whaleboat *Harlequin*, launched in late 1846, was additionally constructed by Risby and Brothers at their Battery Point boat yard.[733] Helmed by Joseph Risby, the craft finished first in the race for native youths at the 1846 Hobart Town Regatta.[734]

The following year saw Risby and Brothers tasked with building the prize boat (a whaleboat) to be awarded to the first place crew of the five-oared whaleboat race at the 1847 Hobart Town Regatta.[735] They also built the wherry *Curlew* and the five-oared whaleboat *Pacific*, specifically for racing at that year's regatta. The former, '*modelled and built by Mr [Joseph] Risby*' was described as '*one of the prettiest wherries ever seen on the river*' when its owner-builder won the scullers' amateur race at the regatta.[736] Business at the Risby boat yard was more than brisk with the three brothers advertising for two apprentices late in 1847.[737]

The success at local regattas and in private rowing matches of racing boats built by Risby and Brothers was soon conveyed to the mainland and it was not long before intercolonial orders were received. Of significance, in December 1847 the whaleboat *Harlequin* and the gig *Cupid* were both purchased by William Dind of Sydney.[738] The two vessels were intended to compete at an upcoming regatta on Sydney Harbour. Notably, the *Harlequin* had '*been for some months at seas in the Fortitude*', indicating its use not just as a racing boat but also as a commercial craft.[739]

In early 1848 a square-sterned gig with sails built by Risby and Brothers was advertised for sale as part of Justice Montagu's estate.[740] The firm also supplied another boat to the Government of Van Diemen's Land.[741] The whaleboat *Lady Griffiths* was additionally launched from Risby and Brothers' Battery Point boat yard early in 1848.[742] Built to the order of Richard Griffiths specifically for racing, the vessel's first contest saw it compete in a race for £40 a-side against the *Lady Denison*, a whaleboat built by boat builder Jacob Chandler who operated the yard next door to the Risby's.[743] *Lady Griffiths* finished second in this match up.[744]

Also built by Risby and Brothers in 1848 were the whaleboat *Odd Fellow*, the scull *Kingfisher*, and the five-oared whaleboat *Little Wonder*.[745] All three boats competed at the 1848 Hobart Town Regatta.[746]

The late 1840s saw the Risby family begin developing another area of their family business; the sourcing, milling and exporting of timber. In 1848 Thomas (Jr) and Joseph Risby teamed up to build the 46-ton schooner *Spy* at Long Bay (now Middleton) in the D'Entrecasteaux Channel where they had been granted

[729] *The Courier*, 6 December 1845.
[730] *Launceston Advertiser*, 7 December 1843; *The Observer*, 5 December 1845; *Launceston Examiner*, 23 May 1846.
[731] *The Courier*, 14 October 1846.
[732] *The Hobart Town Advertiser*, 13 November 1846.
[733] *The Cornwall Chronicle*, 9 December 1846.
[734] *The Courier*, 5 December 1846.
[735] *Colonial Times*, 22 October 1847.
[736] *The Hobart Town Advertiser*, 3 December 1847.
[737] *The Hobart Town Advertiser*, 1 October 1847.
[738] *The Hobart Town Advertiser*, 14 December 1847.
[739] *The Hobart Town Advertiser*, 14 December 1847.
[740] *The Hobart Town Advertiser*, 4 January 1848.
[741] *The Hobart Town Advertiser*, 3 March 1848.
[742] *The Courier*, 15 March 1848.
[743] *The Courier*, 15 March 1848.
[744] *The Courier*, 15 March, 6 December 1848.
[745] *The Courier*, 15 November 1848; *Colonial Times*, 17 November, 5 December 1848.
[746] *Colonial Times*, 5 December 1848; *The Courier*, 6 December 1848.

11 acres of land.[747] The vessel was a significant departure from the smaller class of boats built by Risby and Brothers previously, as well as a strong indication of the direction of Joseph Risby's future business enterprises. *The Hobart Town Advertiser* provided additional detail. 'Another class of vessel, unknown a few years since, is now becoming numerous; we allude to the river barges. Several are already actively engaged in the carrying trade between the different settlements near the city. A new one will shortly be added to their number, of a size exceeding that of any of the best. It is built by the Messrs Risby, the well known and unrivalled whaleboat builders, who promise to be equally successful in this new branch of marine architecture. An important adoption in most of the modern barges has been applied to this one. Instead of lee boards, a wall in the centre of the vessel allows a false keel to play up and down, according to the depth or shallowness of the water'.[748]

While initially intended for the local river trade, instead the *Spy* began conveying passengers and freight from Hobart Town to Port Phillip Bay in March 1849.[749] On its return leg the craft often brought livestock or beef which was advertised for sale by Thomas (Jr) and Joseph Risby at Hobart Town.[750] Instrumental in the growth of the Risby family's timber operations, the *Spy* spent the next six years transporting timber, shingles, palings, laths and staves to Melbourne on a regular basis.[751] Beginning in January 1849 Joseph Risby also began advertising the sale of timber from Risby and Brothers' Battery Point boat yard.[752]

> **Macquarie Harbour Pine.**
>
> On Sale, at the Yard of the Undersigned, MACQUARIE HARBOUR PINE, cut or in log. Purchasers of Pine will do well to examine the timber at this yard, as it can be confidently recommended as the cheapest and best in Hobart Town.
>
> J. E. RISBY,
> Battery Point.
>
> January 30, 1849.   299

Colonial Times, 30 January 1849.

Shortly thereafter, on 24 March 1849, the three brothers dissolved their partnership by mutual consent. While Thomas (Jr) and Joseph remained put, William Risby relinquished his involvement in the firm. In June 1850 he advertised his boat building tools for sale, along with a quantity of pine and the four-oared whaleboat *Traveller*, which had won four prizes at the last regatta.[753] Around this period William Risby deserted his wife and four children.[754] He later moved to rural Victoria where he died in 1886.[755]

> **Dissolution of Partnership.**
>
> WE, the Undersigned, hitherto trading under the style or firm of Thomas Risby & Brothers, Boatbuilders, of Battery Point, do hereby mutually agree to a Dissolution of Partnership from this date.
>
> As witness our hands this 24th day of March 1849.
>
> THOMAS RISBY, Jun.
> WM. H. RISBY.
> J. E. RISBY.
>
> Witness—JOHN CASTLES.   971
>
> **Notice.**
>
> ALL CLAIMS against the late Firm of Risby & Brothers, boat builders, at Battery Point, are requested to be sent into Thomas Risby, jun., and debts owing to the said Firm to be paid to him without delay.
>
> April 24, 1849.   972

Colonial Times, 27 April 1849.

With William Risby's departure, Thomas (Jr) and Joseph Risby were left to continue operations of the family's Battery Point boat yard. In June 1849, two five-oared whaleboats and a five-oared gig built by the pair were advertised for sale.[756] Also built during this year were a boat to the order of the colonial government and three boats launched in time to compete at the Hobart Town Regatta, including a gig to compete for the Ladies' Purse and two five-oared whaleboats to compete for the Tasman Prize (one of which was named *Doctor*).[757] The four-oared gig *Eclipse* and scull *Gazelle,* raced by Joseph Risby at the Sandy Bay Regatta in early January 1850, were also likely completed towards the end of 1849.[758] The 1850 Hobart Town Regatta additionally saw Joseph Risby compete in the Amateur Scullers' Race in the *Swiftsure,* while in 1852 he competed in the same event in the *Interloper*.[759]

The early to mid-1850s coincided with Joseph Risby and his older brother Thomas (Jr) concentrating more on the growing timber trade, though operations continued at their Battery Point boat yard. In terms of the former, the two brothers purchased the barque *Cacique* in February 1851; the vessel joining the *Spy* in the Port Phillip Bay trade and also making occasional

---

[747] www.thelist.tas.gov.au (Historical Deed 03/5520);
R. Parsons (2008). *Shipping Losses and Casualties Concerning Australia and New Zealand. Vol. II (K - Z).*
[748] *The Hobart Town Advertiser*, 21 March 1848.
[749] *Colonial Times*, 23 March 1849.
[750] *Colonial Times*, 3 July 1849, 26 April 1850; *The Hobart Town Advertiser*, 31 July 1849.
[751] R. Parsons (2008). *Shipping Losses and Casualties Concerning Australia and New Zealand. Vol. II (K - Z).*
[752] *Colonial Times*, 30 January 1849.
[753] *Colonial Times*, 24 April 1849, 21 June 1850.
[754] *Hobarton Guardian, or, True Friend of Tasmania*, 14 August 1850.
[755] W. H. L. Risby (2020). *Risby Ancestors: From Convict Beginnings.*
[756] *The Courier*, 6 June 1849.
[757] *The Hobart Town Advertiser*, 13 November 1849; *The Colonial Times*, 4 December 1849.
[758] *Colonial Times*, 4 January 1850.
[759] *The Hobart Town Advertiser*, 3 December 1850; *The Courier*, 7 January 1852.

trips to New Zealand and Twofold Bay.[760] Now with two vessels transporting their timber products to the extremely profitable intercolonial markets, business was prospering. At their newly established timber yard located at the bottom of Murray Street, between the New Wharf and Franklin Wharf, Macquarie pine sourced from Van Diemen's Lands' west coast was also advertised for sale.[761] With the building of boats becoming less of a priority, Thomas (Jr) and Joseph Risby advertised part of their Battery Point boat yard for lease in June 1851 with immediate possession.

To Shipwrights, BOATBUILDERS, AND OTHERS.

TO LET, with immediate possession, a portion of the Building Yard, known as Risby's Boat Yard, at Battery Point.

☞ The allotment has an excellent water frontage, has a cottage and three boat sheds erected thereon, and ample room for ship-building purposes.

Apply to
T. & J. RISBY,
Timber Yard,
Murray-street.
Hobart Town, June 23, 1851.

Hobarton Guardian, or, True Friend, 25 June 1851.

In March 1853 Thomas Risby (Jr) moved to Collingwood, Victoria, where he supervised the sale of timber and other goods shipped from Hobart Town via the Risby brothers' vessels.[762] His wife Elizabeth (nee Birchall) and their five children followed a few months later.[763] Thomas (Jr) also established a timber yard in Little Oxford Street, Collingwood, and later owned and operated the Grace Darling Hotel nearby in Smith Street.[764] Both Thomas and his wife died in 1859.

With their business continuing to expand, in April 1853 Thomas (Jr) and Joseph Risby sold their schooner *Spy* to W. Burgess and T. Daws for £1,000.[765] On the same day they purchased the much larger Scottish-built schooner *Gem* for £1,800.[766] Several months later, Joseph Risby purchased an allotment with a frontage of 33ft at the Hobart Town Wharf from the Crown at a cost of £907.[767] Here he established an extremely lucrative steam sawmill.

On a personal level, Joseph Risby, aged 27 years, married 19-year-old Isabella Wilson at St David's Cathedral, Hobart Town, on 8 September 1853.[768] The newlywed couple moved into Joseph's house at Napoleon Street, Battery Point, where their first son Henry Edward Risby was born in May of the following year.[769] He sadly died on 18 August that same year of '*debility*'.[770] Ironically, Thomas (Jr) had also lost his youngest and only son two days prior; 2-year-old Joseph Thomas Risby died at the family's Smith Street home in Collingwood, Victoria.[771]

In terms of activity at the Risby family's Battery Point boat yard during the early to mid-1850s, business remained brisk with many boats known to have been built. These included at least 18 boats built for the Government of Van Diemen's Land (three in 1851, five in 1853, five in 1854 and five in 1855).[772] Another five-oared whaleboat built by Risby Brothers was found adrift at Risdon Ferry in 1853.[773] That same year a five-oared whaleboat built by the pair were discovered wrecked at Wedge Bay.[774] The 1854 Kangaroo Point Regatta, held in early January of that year additionally saw Joseph Risby competing in the race for Amateur Scullers' in a boat he more than likely built named *Gem*.[775]

Mainland demand for boats built by the Risby family also continued with one boat shipped to Melbourne on board the *Harriette Nathan* in March 1853, a five-oared boat built to the order of *The Argus* newspaper and conveyed to Melbourne by the *Sir William Wallace* in September 1853 (named *The Argus Express*), one whaleboat sent to Geelong on board the *Lady Emma* in August 1854, and one whaleboat sent to Melbourne on board the *City of Hobart* in December 1854.[776]

Another whaleboat built during this period, the *John Francis*, was advertised for sale in November 1854, described as a '*first-rate luggage boat, suitable for the expected opening at Macquarie Harbour, and in thorough repair*'.[777] A nearly new five-oared whaleboat built by Risby Brothers was advertised for sale a few months later.[778] Repair work on private and government vessels also continued during this period, as did Joseph Risby's involvement in local regatta races. The 1855 Hobart Town Regatta, for example, saw him compete in two races: the Amateur Scullers' Race in the *Grace Darling*

---

[760] *The Courier*, 1 March, 12 November 1851; *Colonial Times*, 29 April, 1 July 1851.
[761] *Colonial Times*, 27 June 1851; *The Courier*, 14 June 1853.
[762] *The Argus*, 12, 15 March 1853.
[763] *The Courier*, 15 July 1853.
[764] *The Argus*, 12 July 1854, 13 February 1855.
[765] *The Courier*, 13 April 1853.
[766] *The Courier*, 13 April 1853.
[767] *The Courier*, 29 August 1853.
[768] Libraries Tasmania (RGD37/1/12 no. 203).
[769] Libraries Tasmania (RGD33/1/5 no. 1051); *The Courier*, 5 April 1856.
[770] Libraries Tasmania (RGD35/1/4 no. 1434).
[771] *The Hobart Town Advertiser*, 21 August 1854; *Launceston Examiner*, 22 August 1854.
[772] *Launceston Examiner*, 15 February, 13 December 1851, 20 January 1853;
The Hobart Town Advertiser, 22 August 1851;
The Courier, 14 June, 27 December 1853, 10 January, 25 July, 29 August, 1 November 1854, 10 January, 27 March, 27 June 1855;
The Colonial Times, 21 August 1855.
[773] *The Courier*, 28 September 1853.
[774] *The Courier*, 8 October 1853.
[775] *The Courier*, 3 January 1854.
[776] *The Courier*, 26 March 1853; 30 August, 30 December 1854; *Launceston Examiner*, 10 September 1853.
[777] *The Courier*, 18 November 1854; *The Tasmanian Colonist*, 20 November 1854.
[778] *The Courier*, 16 January 1855.

and the Tasman Prize for five-oared whaleboats in the *Harlequin*.[779] While he finished runner-up in the former, Risby claimed victory in the latter race.[780] It is assumed that he had a hand in building both boats.

Around this period workers associated with Joseph Risby's pine operations at Macquarie Harbour discovered specimens of gold and conveyed the samples to Hobart Town on board the schooner *Gem*. The presence of the highly sought after metal sent many of Van Diemen's Land citizens into a tizz, with several meetings held in Hobart Town to discuss options and entertain prospects of finding more gold in the western parts of the island.[781] Joseph Risby was asked to detail the manner in which the pieces were found, in turn expressing his confidence that more could soon be discovered.[782] In haste, parties were proposed to be sent to the region to investigate further with Joseph offering the *Gem* free for use.[783]

While gold may have not been found in quantities large enough to spur commercial operations, the west coast timber industry was becoming more and more viable with Joseph Risby capitalising on the resource and expanding his involvement in the supply chain, through sourcing, milling, transporting and shipping ventures at Strahan, Hobart Town and Victoria. In June 1855 Messrs T. and J. E. Risby announced that they had moved their timber yard from the bottom of Murray Street to Argyle Street in Hobart Town, near the current site of the Royal Hobart Hospital.[784] Still, work continued at Risby's Battery Point boat yard with a nearly new fishing boat, with well, sails, oars and three nets, advertised for sale by W. Russell of the New Wharf that same month.[785] A five-oared whaleboat, nearly new, with two sets of oars, steer oar, mast, sail and anchor built by Risby's was advertised for sale in mid-January 1856.[786]

In February 1856 Thomas (Jr) and Joseph Risby announced the dissolution of their partnership by mutual consent.[787] With Thomas (Jr) now based permanently in Melbourne, Joseph took sole responsibility for the pair's boat building, timber and shipping operations.

NOTICE is Hereby Given that the Partnership hitherto subsisting between the Undersigned, Thomas Risby the younger and Joseph Edward Risby, in Hobart Town, as Boat Builders, Timber Merchants and Ship Owners, under the Style or Firm of "T. and J. E. Risby," has been this day dissolved by mutual consent. The said Joseph Edward Risby, who will henceforth carry on the said business on his own account, is authorised to receive and give discharges for all debts due to the said Copartnership, and he will discharge all its liabilities.

Dated this Eighteenth day of February in the year 1856.

Thomas Risby, Junior,
J. E. Risby.

Witness—R. W. Nutt, Solicitor,
Hobart Town.   713

The Courier, 19 February 1856.

[779] *The Hobart Town Advertiser*, 2 January 1855.
[780] *The Hobarton Mercury*, 3 January 1855.
[781] *The Hobart Town Advertiser*, 20 November 1854.
[782] *Colonial Times*, 21 November 1854.
[783] *Colonial Times*, 21 November 1854.
[784] *The Hobart Town Advertiser*, 16 June 1855.
[785] *The Hobart Town Advertiser*, 21 June 1855.
[786] *The Courier*, 16 January 1856.
[787] *The Courier*, 19 February 1856.

View of Lower Murray Street, Hobart Town, looking across at the New Wharf (circa 1857).
Courtesy W L Crowther Library, State Library of Tasmania (Charles Abbott album, Item 45, 136188992).

With regard to output at Joseph Risby's Battery Point yard, another boat was supplied to the Tasmanian Government in May 1856.[788] Later that year he commissioned construction of a boat dock, i.e., break wall/jetty at the site, in order to provide shelter to vessels moored inside it without the consequence of weather and tide.[789] Shortly thereafter a four-oared racing boat complete with oars was advertised for sale at his boat yard, the price being £20.[790] Next listed for sale was a 3-ton sailing boat, built by Risby, stated to be 20ft on the keel and complete with masts, sails, oars and gear; its current owner being a Mr Kirby of the Golden Fleece, Kangaroo Point.[791] The sailing boat race at the 1856 Hobart Town Regatta saw Joseph Risby finish fourth in the *Tommy*, another craft he very likely built.[792]

1857 saw two more boats, a five-oared whaleboat and a skiff, built by Risby advertised for sale in Hobart Town in May of that year.[793] A few months later, another whaleboat built at his Battery Point yard was advertised for sale, this time in Sydney.[794] This particular boat was stated to be '*quite new*' and imported expressly for the champion whaleboat race.[795] In October 1857 a pleasure boat with sails and four oars, 20ft in length, built by Risby, was advertised for sale at his Battery Point yard.[796]

The year 1857 was not without its disappointments, however. Joseph Risby's schooner *Gem* was wrecked in May of that year on Tasmania's wild west coast, carrying a load of timber from Macquarie Harbour. The vessel's master, four crew members and Risby himself, managed to make it safely to shore in the vessel's boats and from there on to Port Davey; a distance of some 60 miles.[797] The men were then picked up by the whaler *Reliance* and transferred back to Hobart Town.[798] The *Gem* was not insured. Fortunately, by this time in his career, Risby had several other vessels involved in coastal trade that could take up the slack produced by the lost vessel.

Continuing his involvement with local aquatic events, in late 1857 Joseph Risby completed building a schooner-rigged boat of about 3 tons named *Swift*.[799] The vessel was advertised for sale in November of that year. He also built the *Flirt*, a boat of a similar size and description that first competed in the sail boat race for vessels under 3 tons at the 1857 Hobart Town Regatta.[800] The craft went on to become a regular participant in

[788] *Colonial Times*, 21 May 1856.
[789] *Colonial Times*, 27 September 1856; *The Hobarton Mercury*, 29 September 1856.
[790] *The Tasmanian Daily News*, 24 October 1856.
[791] *The Courier*, 29 November 1856, 8 January 1857.
[792] *Colonial Times*, 8 December 1856.
[793] *The Courier*, 28 May 1857.
[794] *The Sydney Morning Herald*, 4 August 1857.
[795] *The Sydney Morning Herald*, 13 August 1857.
[796] *The Hobart Town Advertiser*, 22 October 1857.
[797] *The Courier*, 15 May 1857.
[798] *Colonial Times*, 16 May 1857.
[799] *The Hobart Town Mercury*, 25 November 1857; *The Courier*, 30 November 1857.
[800] *The Courier*, 4 December 1857.

The Battery Point boat and shipyards, showing Risby's Jetty in the middle of the image (circa 1860s). Courtesy Tasmanian Archives (NS179/3/1/195).

local sailing races for many years under various owners. In December 1857 Risby was noted as building a four-oared boat to be awarded as the prize for the five-oared whaleboat race at the upcoming Huon Regatta.[801] The boat was stated to be worth £40.[802] Finally, in April 1858, a new un-named boat built by Risby and pulled by a Mr Turnbull finished second in the dinghy race at the Kangaroo Point Regatta.[803]

With timber operations by now dominating the bulk of his time, in October 1858 *The Hobart Town Daily Mercury* announced that Charles Henry Miller, boat builder, had succeeded Joseph Risby at his Battery Point boat yard.[804] In relinquishing his business Risby thanked the public and his friends for their encouraging patronage over the past 30 years, including to '*the old established firm of "Risby and Sons"*'.[805] He noted that his boat yard had been transferred in its entirety to his former general manager and superintendent, Charles Henry Miller, an employee of 13 years, and stated that he had complete confidence in his successor's ability to execute all orders.[806]

In the decades that followed Joseph Risby built up his timber company through the establishment of a steam sawmill at the Franklin Wharf; the development of various bush mills, particularly on the west coast and the Tasman Peninsula; and the commissioning or purchasing of many more vessels to add to his fleet, including the schooner *Victory* (built by John Watson at Battery Point in 1853) and the steamer *Koonya* (built by William Bayes at Battery Point in 1887).[807]

[801] *The Hobart Town Mercury*, 11 December 1857.
[802] *The Hobart Town Mercury*, 11 December 1857.
[803] *The Hobart Town Daily Mercury*, 21 April 1858.
[804] *The Hobart Town Daily Mercury*, 12 October 1858.
[805] *The Hobart Town Daily Mercury*, 14 October 1858.
[806] *The Hobart Town Daily Mercury*, 14 October 1858.
[807] *The Hobart Town Daily Mercury*, 12 June 1858.

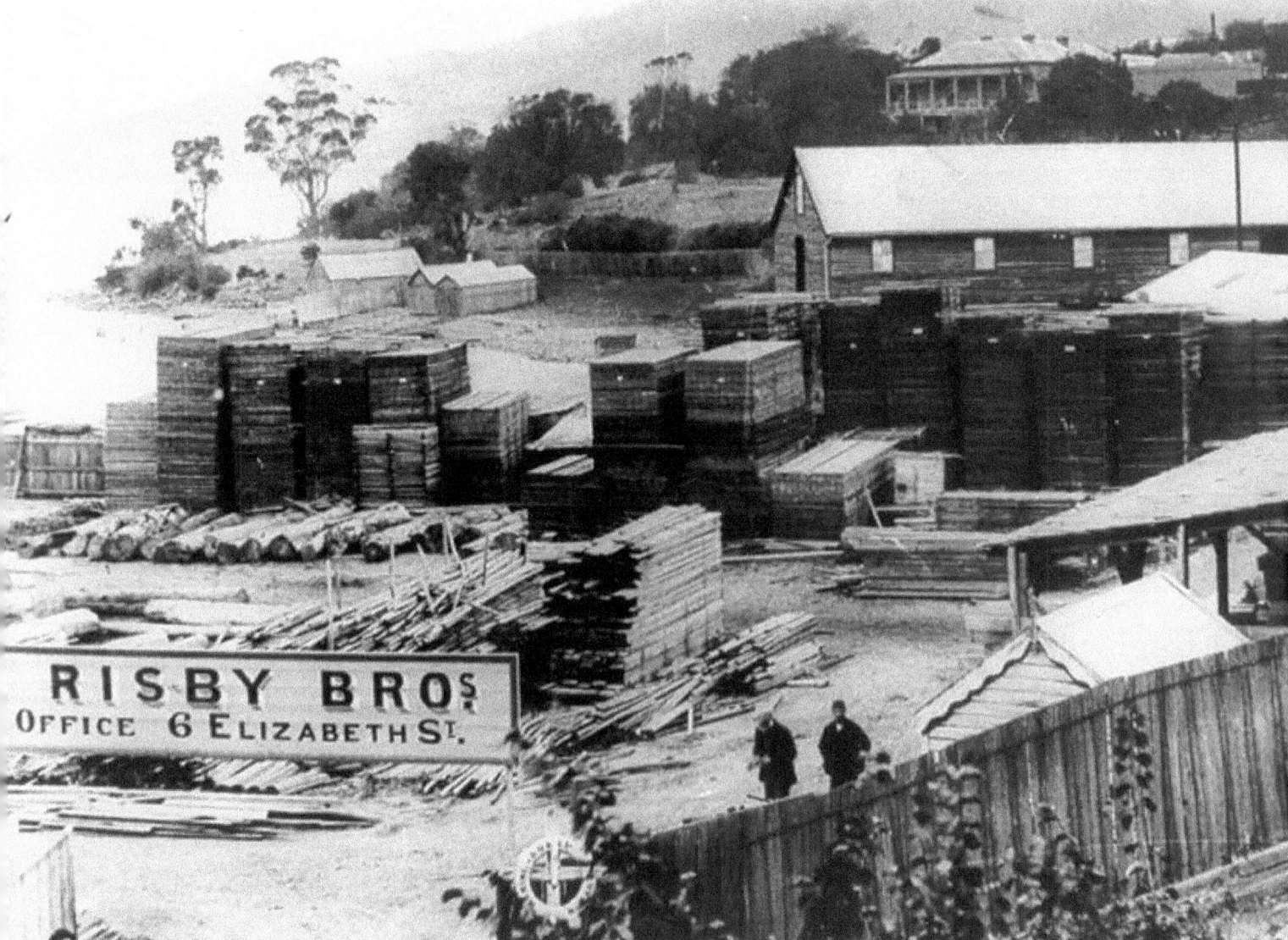

Risby's timber storage yard at Castray Esplanade, Battery Point (circa 1900s). Courtesy Tasmanian Archives (PH30/1/4949).

The company's success was helped in part by the New Zealand gold rush, the west coast mining boom, and the building of much needed infrastructure in Tasmania, including railways. Several of his sons later ushered in further development and expansion of the Risby's family business, notably establishing a timber storage site at Castray Esplanade, Battery Point, near where the first commercial boat and ship builders worked from beginning in 1830. Following nearly 150 years of operation the Risby family's company ceased operations in 1995.

A prominent citizen, Joseph Risby was also an extremely well-respected member of the Hobart Town community and was particularly connected with aquatic sports. For example, he was a founding member of the committee that established the Sandy Bay Regatta, and also served for several decades on the organising committee of the Hobart Town Regatta.[808] During the 1850s he served on the board of the Kangaroo Point Steam Navigation Company.[809] In 1862 Risby was elected Alderman of Hobart Town which he served until 1876.[810] This appointment ultimately saw him elected to the House of Assembly between 1877 and 1882.[811]

Joseph Risby died at his home, 14 Napoleon Street, Battery Point, on 30 October 1889 at the age of 63.[812] He was buried at Cornelian Bay Cemetery.[813] His wife Isabella had died in August 1865, aged 31, just nine days after giving birth to their ninth child.[814] The infant, a son named Louis John Wilson Risby, sadly died a few months later.[815] Now aged 39 years, Risby became a widower with five living children, three sons and two daughters. Nearly a decade later he formed a relationship with Sarah Jones who resided on the Tasman Peninsula. The couple had five children between 1875 and 1885. All were born in Hobart and registered with the surname of Jones. They later adopted the surname of Risby and were recognised in a codicil to Joseph Risby's will.[816]

Though the mainland gold rush saw Joseph Risby prioritise the development of his timber and intercolonial trading businesses over the family's Battery Point boat yard, between 1845 and 1858 at least 67 boats were built, many of which were prominent in local whaleboat races and regattas, while others were exported to the mainland. This number is likely a gross underestimate of the actual number of boats built by the Risby family owing to the unavailability of records related to smaller commercial craft, which likely numbered in the hundreds.

Like Peter Degraves, Joseph Risby's legacy is rich in industry and entrepreneurism, particularly in terms of the establishment of his timber company. Still, Risby leaves a legacy much aligned with the Battery Point boat and ship yards. In partnership with his father and two brothers, Joseph Risby established a boat yard at Battery Point in 1846 at a time when John Watson was the only other shipwright occupying property along the Napoleon Street corridor. Soon after, Jacob Chandler joined them, establishing his own yard next door, and the locus that became the Battery Point boat and ship yards was born.

---

[808] W. H. L. Risby (2020). *Risby Ancestors: From Convict Beginnings*.
[809] *The Hobart Town Mercury*, 4 February 1857; W. H. L. Risby (2020). *Risby Ancestors: From Convict Beginnings*.
[810] *The Mercury*, 12, 20 May 1862; W. H. L. Risby (2020). *Risby Ancestors: From Convict Beginnings*.
[811] en.wikipedia.org/wiki/Members_of_the_Tasmanian_House_of_Assembly,_1877.
[812] *The Mercury*, 31 October 1889.
[813] *The Mercury*, 31 October 1889.
[814] Libraries Tasmania (RGD35/1/7 no. 5472, RGD33/1/9 no. 7924).
[815] Libraries Tasmania (RGD34/1/2 no. 2374).
[816] W. H. L. Risby (2020). *Risby Ancestors: From Convict Beginnings*.

Vessels built by Joseph Risby, his family and employees at Battery Point (1845 - 1858)

Year	Name	Type	Description
1845	Gazelle ex Cupid	Gig	Four-oared gig built by Thomas Risby and Brothers to compete at the 1845 Hobart Town Regatta. Purchased by William Dind of Sydney in 1847 and transferred to New South Wales. Raffled off in January 1848 at the Custom House Hotel and sold to a Mr Nairne for £18. Renamed *Gazelle* and finished third in the race for amateur gigs at the 1848 Anniversary Regatta on Sydney Harbour. Finished second in the same race the following year.
1846	--	Boat	Built by Thomas Risby and Brothers to the order of the Government of Van Diemen's Land.
1846	--	Wherry	'Thames' wherry built by Thomas Risby and Brothers on speculation and intended for racing at the 1846 Hobart Town Regatta. Advertised for sale in November of that year.
1846	Harlequin	Whaleboat	Five-oared whaleboat built by Thomas Risby and Brothers and launched in late 1846. Finished first in the race for native youths at the 1846 Hobart Town Regatta, helmed by Joseph Risby. Purchased by William Dind of Sydney in 1847 and transferred to New South Wales. Had spent some months at sea on board the *Fortitude*.
1847	--	Whaleboat	Five-oared whaleboat built by Thomas Risby and Brothers at the request of the Government of Van Diemen's Land. Awarded as a prize to the winning crew of the five-oared whaleboat race at the 1847 Hobart Town Regatta.
1847	Curlew	Wherry	Built by Thomas Risby and Brothers to a model by Joseph Risby. Used by him in the race for amateur scullers at the 1847 Hobart Town Regatta, finishing first.
1847	Pacific	Whaleboat	Five-oared whaleboat built by Thomas Risby and Brothers to compete at the 1847 Hobart Town Regatta. Finished first in the race for the Tasman Prize, helmed by Captain Gardener.
1848	--	Gig	Square-sterned gig built by Thomas Risby and Brothers. Advertised for sale in early 1848 as part of Justice Montagu's estate, complete with sails.
1848	--	Boat	Built by Thomas Risby and Brothers to the order of the Government of Van Diemen's Land.
1848	Lady Griffiths	Whaleboat	Five-oared whaleboat built by Thomas Risby and Brothers to the order of Richard Griffiths. Raced in private pulling matches on the River Derwent.
1848	Odd Fellow	Whaleboat	Built by Thomas Risby and Brothers to compete at the 1848 Hobart Town Regatta. Helmed by Richard Wilson in the race for watermen, finishing third.
1848	Kingfisher	Scull	Built by Thomas Risby and Brothers to compete at the 1848 Hobart Town Regatta. Finished first in the race for amateur scullers, helmed by Joseph Risby.
1848	Little Wonder	Whaleboat	Five-oared whaleboat built by Thomas Risby and Brothers to compete at the 1848 Hobart Town Regatta. Finished second in the race for the Tasman Prize, helmed by Joseph Risby.
1849	Traveller	Whaleboat	Built by Thomas Risby and Brothers to compete at the 1849 Hobart Town Regatta. Finished first in the race for native youths, helmed by John Turnbull. Advertised for sale in 1850.
1849	--	Whaleboat	Five-oared whaleboat built by T. and J. Risby. Advertised for sale in June 1849.
1849	--	Whaleboat	Five-oared whaleboat built by T. and J. Risby. Advertised for sale in June 1849.
1849	--	Boat	Built by T. and J. Risby to the order of the Government of Van Diemen's Land.
1849	--	Gig	Built by T. and J. Risby to compete for the Ladies' Purse at the 1849 Hobart Town Regatta.
1849	--	Whaleboat	Five-oared whaleboat built by T. and J. Risby to compete for the Tasman Prize at the 1849 Hobart Town Regatta.
1849	Doctor	Whaleboat	Five-oared whaleboat built by T. and J. Risby to compete for the Tasman Prize at the 1849 Hobart Town Regatta. Competed in the race for the Tasman Prize.
1849	Eclipse	Gig	Four-oared gig built by T. and J. Risby to compete at the 1850 Sandy Bay Regatta, helmed by Joseph Risby. Finished second in the amateur gig race.
1849	Gazelle	Scull	Built by T. and J. Risby to compete at the 1850 Sandy Bay Regatta. Finished third in the race for amateur scullers, helmed by Joseph Risby.
1850	Swiftsure	Scull	Built by T. and J. Risby to compete at the 1850 Hobart Town Regatta. Finished second in the race for amateur scullers, helmed by Joseph Risby. Finished second in the race for amateur scullers at the 1851 Sandy Bay Regatta, helmed by Joseph Risby.
1851	--	Boat	Built by T. and J. Risby to the order of the Government of Van Diemen's Land.
1851	--	Boat	Built by T. and J. Risby to the order of the Government of Van Diemen's Land.
1851	--	Boat	Built by T. and J. Risby to the order of the Government of Van Diemen's Land.
1852	Interloper	Scull	Built by T. and J. Risby to compete at the 1852 Hobart Town Regatta. Finished second in the race for amateur scullers, helmed by Joseph Risby.
1853	--	Boat	Built by T. and J. Risby to the order of the Government of Van Diemen's Land.
1853	--	Boat	Built by T. and J. Risby to the order of the Government of Van Diemen's Land.

Year	Name	Type	Description
1853	--	Boat	Built by T. and J. Risby to the order of the Government of Van Diemen's Land.
1853	--	Boat	Built by T. and J. Risby to the order of the Government of Van Diemen's Land.
1853	--	Boat	Built by T. and J. Risby to the order of the Government of Van Diemen's Land.
c1853	--	Whaleboat	Built by T. and J. Risby and found adrift at Risdon Ferry in 1853.
c1853	--	Whaleboat	Five-oared whaleboat built by T. and J. Risby. Wrecked at Wedge Bay in 1853.
1853	--	Boat	Built by T. and J. Risby and shipped to Melbourne on board the *Harriette Nathan*.
1853	The Argus Express	Whaleboat	Built by T. and J. Risby and shipped to Melbourne in September 1853 on board the *Sir William Wallace*. Built to the order of *The Argus* newspaper.
1853	Gem	Scull	Built by T. and J. Risby to compete at the 1854 Kangaroo Point Regatta. Competed in the race for amateur scullers, helmed by Joseph Risby.
1854	--	Boat	Built by T. and J. Risby to the order of the Government of Tasmania.
1854	--	Boat	Built by T. and J. Risby to the order of the Government of Tasmania.
1854	--	Boat	Built by T. and J. Risby to the order of the Government of Tasmania.
1854	--	Boat	Built by T. and J. Risby to the order of the Government of Tasmania.
1854	--	Whaleboat	Built by T. and J. Risby and shipped to Geelong on board the *Lady Emma*.
1854	--	Whaleboat	Built by T. and J. Risby and shipped to Melbourne on board the *City of Hobart*.
c1854	John Francis	Whaleboat	Built by T. and J. Risby and advertised for sale in November 1854.
1855	--	Boat	Built by T. and J. Risby to the order of the Government of Tasmania.
1855	--	Boat	Built by T. and J. Risby to the order of the Government of Tasmania.
1855	--	Boat	Built by T. and J. Risby to the order of the Government of Tasmania.
1855	--	Boat	Built by T. and J. Risby to the order of the Government of Tasmania.
c1855	--	Whaleboat	Five-oared whaleboat built by T. and J. Risby and advertised for sale in January 1855.
1855	Grace Darling	Scull	Built by T. and J. Risby to compete at the 1855 Hobart Town Regatta. Finished second in the race for amateur scullers, helmed by Joseph Risby.
1855	Harlequin	Whaleboat	Five-oared whaleboat built by T. and J. Risby to compete for the Tasman Prize at the 1855 Hobart Town Regatta. Finished first in the race, helmed by Joseph Risby.
1855	--	Fishing boat	Built by T. and J. Risby. Advertised for sale in June 1855 complete with well, sails, oars and three nets by W. Russell of the New Wharf.
c1855	--	Whaleboat	Five-oared whaleboat built by T. and J. Risby. Advertised for sale with oars, steer oar, mast and sails in January 1856.
1856	--	Boat	Built by Joseph Risby to the order of the Government of Tasmania.
c1856	--	Whaleboat	Four-oared whaleboat built by Joseph Risby for racing. Advertised for sale in October 1856.
1856	--	Sailing boat	20ft. 3 ton. Built by Joseph Risby. Advertised for sale complete with masts, sails, oars and gear by Mr Kirby of the Golden Fleece, Kangaroo Point in later 1856/early 1857.
1856	Tommy	Sailing boat	Built by Joseph Risby to compete at the 1856 Hobart Town Regatta. Helmed by Joseph Risby, finished fourth in the sailing boat race.
1857	--	Whaleboat	Five-oared whaleboat built by Joseph Risby. Advertised for sale in May 1857.
1857	--	Skiff	Built by Joseph Risby. Advertised for sale in May 1857.
c1857	--	Whaleboat	Built by Joseph Risby and advertised for sale at Sydney in August 1857.
1857	--	Pleasure boat	20ft. Built by Joseph Risby. Advertised for sale in October 1857, complete with sails and oars.
1857	Swift	Sailing boat	Schooner-rigged. 3 tons. Built by Joseph Risby. Advertised for sale in November 1857.
1857	Flirt	Sailing boat	28 (keel) x 6.9ft. 6 tons. Built by Joseph Risby and raced by him at the 1857 Hobart Town Regatta. Also competed at the 1858 Kangaroo Point Regatta and in several private sailing matches. In existence until at least November 1897 when advertised for sale.
1857	--	Whaleboat	Four-oared whaleboat built by Joseph Risby to be awarded to the winning crew of the five-oared whaleboat race at the 1858 Huon Regatta. Stated to be worth £40.
1858	--	Dinghy	Built by Joseph Risby. Pulled by a Mr Turnbull in the dinghy race at the 1858 Kangaroo Point Regatta.

THE EIGHTH ANNIVERSARY
REGATTA,
IN COMMEMORATION OF THE DISCOVERY OF VAN DIEMEN'S LAND.
WEDNESDAY, THE 3RD DECEMBER, 1845.

UNDER THE IMMEDIATE PATRONAGE OF

HIS EXCELLENCY SIR JOHN E. EARDLEY-WILMOT, BART.

COMMITTEE:

Captain MORIARTY, R.N.	Mr. WILSON.	Mr. C. SEAL.	Mr. BIRDMYRE.
,, JACOMB.	,, T. MACDOWELL.	,, DOWSING.	,, GEORGE WATSON.
,, FORSTER.	,, GEORGE CHASE.	,, A. H. MANING.	Captain HAYLE.
Mr. POWER.	,, T. BROWN.	,, L. NATHAN.	,, ROSS.
,, KERR.	,, R. WEBB.	,, R. DOUGLAS.	,, M'PHERSON.
,, MORRISON.	,, J. KELLY.	,, MEABURN.	,, CROSBIE.
,, CHAPMAN.	,, CLEBURNE.	,, W. YOUNG.	
,, LEWIS.	,, PERRY.	,, R. GRIFFITHS.	

Judges—Mr. KELLY and Mr. C. SEAL.
Umpire—Captain MORIARTY.   Treasurer—W. ROBERTSON, Esq.
Secretary—Mr. ELLISTON.   Assistant Secretary—Mr. RONALD SMITH.

GIGS PULLING FOUR OARS,

To proceed round a boat moored off Cornelian Bay, from thence round a boat moored off Judge Montagu's Point, and back to the place of starting.

First boat, twenty sovereigns, presented by His Excellency Sir J. E. EARDLEY-WILMOT, Bart.; second boat, ten sovereigns.

Rose, G. R. Lewis; blue flag; black, gold riband.
Comet, J. C. Hall; blue, with name in gold; yellow bottom, black appersides.
Cornelia, Lovett; red and white; yellow, with black gunwale.
Cupid, Thomas Risby; red and yellow; black.
Fair Queen, G. R. Lewis.

SIX-OARED WHALEBOATS,

To take the same course as the Gigs.

First boat, a purse of thirty sovereigns from the Regatta Fund; second boat, twenty sovereigns; third boat, ten sovereigns.

Native Cat, M'Williams; blue; lead coloured, black riband and white nose.
Paul Pry, G. Chase; white, with "I hope I don't intrude;" lead-coloured bottom, yellow streak, black riband, white nose.
Albion, R. Griffiths; blue and white; white bottom, yellow and black streak, red and yellow bridle.
Bazzeetta, J. Gardiner; blue, white, and red; green, with black bridle.

FIRST-CLASS SAILING BOATS,

Keel not to exceed thirty feet, to take the same course as the Gigs.

First boat, twenty-five sovereigns; second boat, fifteen sovereigns.

Marian, O'Meagher; schooner; red pennant, white ball.
Terror, Buchanan; ditto; red.
Governor Wilmot, Petchey; ditto; red burgee at peak.
Matchless, H. Dawson; ditto; blue and white.
Nautilus, J. H. Dawson; cutter; blue at peak.

FIVE-OARED WHALEBOATS,

To take the same course as the Gigs.

First boat, a purse of twenty sovereigns; second boat, twelve sovereigns; third boat, six sovereigns.

Harriet, M'Williams; blue flag; black, red riband, white nose.
Tiger Cat, G. Watson; Union Jack; black, yellow streak, yellow bridle.
Arabaia, Gardiner.
Charleton, R. Griffiths; white and blue, horizontal; white bottom, red and yellow streak, red and yellow bridle.
Petrel, Moriarty; lead coloured.

SECOND-CLASS SAILING BOATS,

Keel not to exceed twenty-five feet, to take the same course as the Gigs.

First boat, twenty sovereigns; second boat, ten sovereigns.

Terror, Buchanan; schooner; red.
Matchless, H. Dawson; ditto; blue and white.
Young Prince, Petchey; ditto; blue burgee.
Moggy, Felder; ditto; blue.
Dolphin, Clark; ditto; red and white.
Nautilus, J. H. Dawson; cutter; blue at peak.

LICENSED WATERMEN,

Pulling in four-oared whaleboats with two oars, such boats having ferried at least one month previous to the Regatta, to proceed round a boat moored off New Town Bay and back to the place of starting.

First boat, ten sovereigns; second boat, six sovereigns; third boat, three sovereigns.

Blue-Eyed Maid, Davis; yellow flag; blue nose, green bottom, yellow riband.
Hope, Bushton; red; blue and white strips, red riband.
Susan, Grimston; blue; black, yellow riband.
Rampant Lion, Hansen; red and white, quartered; blue and white streaks.

RIVER CRAFT,

Not to exceed twenty-five tons, to take the same course as the Gigs.

First boat, twenty-five sovereigns; second boat, twenty sovereigns; third boat, ten sovereigns.

Flinders, William Martin; schooner; red, with ball white in centre.
Mary, D. Fisher; ditto; red ensign at peak.
Red Rover, W. Gard; ditto; red at main.
Prince of Wales, A. Glover; cutter.
Catherine, George Wickins; ditto; red and white at main.
Vulcan, Barnes; ditto; tricolor.
Terror, ——; schooner.
Folkstone, S. Biggins; cutter; blue peter.
Ariel, J. Foyle; ditto; blue, with white ball.
Victoria, H. Grubb; ditto; union at peak.
New Invention.

ELLISTON, PRINTER, HOBART TOWN.

1845 Hobart Town Regatta Silk Program.
Courtesy State Library of New South Wales (74VMb5WLKGE3).

Jacob Chandler

'At that time ... the principal boat builders were Messrs Chandler and Risby, and as pulling was mainly kept up through their agency ... their enterprise and tests of skill in trying to out vie each other in constructing speedy boats ended in producing a lighter and better class of boat year by year.'

Tasmanian News, 22 February 1887.

A young and ambitious boat builder by trade, Jacob Bayly Chandler is assumed to have arrived in Hobart Town from England some time between 1842 and mid-1843. There were numerous ships transporting skilled labourers from England to Van Diemen's Land at the time, some offering free passage. The *Sir Charles Napier*, for example, docked in Hobart Town on 28 November 1842 after a 130-day passage from London with 220 assisted emigrants on board.[817] The vessel's voyage had been sponsored by the Government of Van Diemen's Land with those on board also receiving a small payment upon arrival.[818] Alternatively, Chandler may have worked for his passage to Australia as a ship's carpenter on board one of the many intercolonial sailing vessels trading to and from England at the time.

Born in Dover, Kent, on 17 March 1822, Chandler was baptised at the Zion Chapel in Last Lane, Dover, on 28 April of that year.[819] He was the second of six children born to Thomas and Mary Chandler, nee Bayly, between the years 1820 and 1831.[820]

Situated 70 miles from London, Dover at the time of Chandler's birth was a bustling maritime community with a thriving port, helped in part by its close proximity to France. The town was also developing into a seaside resort, particularly for London's elite who sought the cleaner air that coastal Kent offered.

Chandler and his family lived in Strond Street in a working class neighbourhood of Dover, near the waterfront.[821] His father Thomas was a shoemaker, as was his maternal grandfather and namesake Jacob Bayly.[822] Still, it was a maritime rather than land-based trade that Chandler embarked on. This opportunity may have been predicated by the death of Chandler's mother Mary in 1832 and his father the following year. Now orphans, the couple's six children were handed over to various aunts and uncles on both the Bayly and Chandler sides of the extended family. Jacob Chandler himself appears to have been taken in by aunts and uncles associated with the Bayly family, based in nearby Deal. Here one uncle, Michael Bayly, operated a boat building yard.[823] Chandler more than likely became apprenticed to his uncle or a nearby yard around the age of 12.

A market town and sea port of approximately 8,000 people, Deal was well-known for its boat building expertise. There were several types of boats endemic

---

[817] *The Hobart Town Advertiser*, 25 October 1842; *Colonial Times*, 29 November 1842.
[818] *Colonial Times*, 25 October 1842; *Launceston Examiner*, 14 December 1842.
[819] England & Wales, Non-Conformist and Non-Parochial Registers, 1567-1970; England, Select Births and Christenings, 1538-1975.
[820] England & Wales, Non-Conformist and Non-Parochial Registers, 1567-1970; England, Select Births and Christenings, 1538-1975.
[821] Pigot's Directory of Kent, 1824; UK< Poll Books and Electoral Registers, 1538-1893 for Thomas Chandler; England & Wales, Non-Conformist and Non-Parochial Registers, 1567-1970.
[822] UK Register of Duties Paid for Apprentices' Indentures 1710-1811; Pigot's Directory of Kent, 1824.
[823] England, Andrews Newspaper Index Cards, 1790-1976 for Michaely Bayly.

Baptism record for Jacob Bayly Chander, Zion Chapel, Last Lane, Dover, Kent, England.
Courtesy England & Wales, Non-Conformist and Non-Parochial Registers, 1567-1970.

to the town; the four/five-oared galley punt, the 50ft galley, and the lugger, being the most celebrated of the local vessels.[824]

At the time of Chandler's apprenticeship, however, Deal was suffering from the effects of an economic downturn. The town's prosperity had peaked during the French Revolutionary and Napoleonic Wars when a naval yard was located nearby. There were also more than a dozen boat building yards in operation. By 1815, however, the naval yard had closed and the population of Deal had dropped accordingly. The boat building industry was also in a state of decline, though there were still at least five boat yards in operation in 1840, including the one owned by Michael Bayly, which he had run for many decades.[825]

In the early 1840s Chandler left England, probably working his passage to Australia on a whaling or merchant vessel. It was likely a lack of opportunity in Kent that most heavily influenced his decision; the waning Deal boat building industry had resulted in an over-supply of labourers with similar skills. By this time Chandler was also in his early 20s and likely yearning for adventure and new opportunities.

Chandler is first noted as being present in Van Diemen's Land via reports in the press of the 1843 Hobart Town Regatta held on 1 December of that year. Competing in the race for gigs pulling four oars, out of a field of seven competitors, he claimed victory in a new boat he had built named *Rose*.[826] Described as a '*capital race*', the *Colonial Times* reported that, '*the result appeared to give considerable satisfaction to the old marine hands, the owner and steerer of the winning boat Rose, Jacob Chandler, being known to them as an industrious, steady young man, who had been heretofore employed in repairing the whale-boats, chiefly belonging as we understood to Mr. Young's party, and who had built the gig for the express purpose of a trial at the Regatta. She is a well-made Deal-fashion boat, thirty-six fee long, and won the race by a long distance. ... Considerable interest was excited by this race, and particularly with regard to Risby's boat, Coronella, which being built by a crack builder, and well-manned to boot, was considered likely to win.*'[827] Chandler was awarded a substantial prize of £20 for his win from Lieutenant-Governor Sir John Eardly-Wilmot, himself only newly arrived in Hobart Town. The interaction was reported, '*young Jacob Chandler stepped modestly forth at the call. His Excellency briefly addressed him; that, he said, was the first time he had ever had the pleasure to present a prize in Van Diemen's Land, but he*

---

[824] L. F. Herreshoff (1956). *The Compleat Cruiser: The Art, Practice and Enjoyment of Boating*.
[825] England, Andrews Newspaper Index Cards, 1790-1976 for Michaely Bayly.
[826] *The Hobart Town Advertiser*, 1 December 1843.
[827] *Colonial Times*, 5 December 1843.

Deal luggers and a four-oared galley on the Beach at Port Arms Station, Deal, Kent, England in 1866.
Courtesy Wikipedia Commons.

sincerely hoped it would not be the last; he had great pleasure in presenting the winner of so good a race with a purse of twenty sovereigns. And the purse was presented accordingly, [notably] with a nautical bow from the receiver.'[828]

In what was fast becoming a regular occurrence on the River Derwent, in the weeks following the Hobart Town Regatta, a personal challenge was issued to Chandler by Thomas Risby (Jr) to privately race the *Rose* against the *Coronella* for £20 a-side.[829] While Chandler initially ignored the suggestion, by early February of the following year he published the following response, very likely instigated by Risby's persistence.

A Challenge.

I SEE by an Advertisement in last Tuesday's Paper, that Mr. Risby talks very large about his new gig, the *Coronella* losing, and lays the fault to the crew ; but I believe it is well known, by men who understand those things far better than I do, that he could not have got a better crew in the colony than pulled in her on that day so that's all bounce, as the wide awake lads say so I hereby challenge to pull my gig, the *Rose*; that beat her before, on the 10th day of March next, for the sum of Twenty Pounds a side, the same distance that they pulled before, as my crew will not be in town before. I hope this will put all bouncing to an end.

I remain your humble servant,
JACOB CHANDLER.

Feb. 8, 1843.

The Hobart Town Advertiser, 9 February 1844.

Chandler's crew was obviously made up of whalers, either involved in bay whaling or out at sea. Despite all the innuendo and hype, for reasons unknown the much anticipated private race between the *Rose* and the *Coronella* did not take place. The two craft did no meet again until the 1845 Hobart Town Regatta; the race for four-oared gigs was not held at the 1844 Regatta owing to only three entries being received whereby a minimum of four was required.[830] By this stage, however, Chandler had sold the *Rose* to George Lewis and Risby had sold the *Coronella* to F. Lovett.[831] Still, Chandler remained involved with the craft.

Competing in the race for four-oared gigs, the *Rose* again triumphed by a quarter of a mile margin with the *Coronella* finishing second.[832] The press relayed the scene that followed. '*The Rose, (a black boat), was carried shoulder high, by the crew to the front of the Pavilion attended by a band of music), where the* [Lieutenant] *Governor and a numerous party had taken their stand. His Excellency delivered the prizes in terms most laconic: - He said to the winner "here, take this purse, come again next year, and I'll give you another. Catch it." The Governor then threw it down, but so as that Mr Chandler did not catch it. ... The people gave three cheers for the successful competitors, whose names were, Rose; - Chandler, coxwain, with William Smith, and the two Bennett's, (brothers) and another. Coronella - Lovett, (coxwain), with John Smart, Timothy Bushton, Hugh Dogherty, and Thomas Atkins.*'[833]

Despite dropping the winner's purse, perhaps intentionally thrown off-target by a wayward Lieutenant-Governor Sir John Eardly-Wilmot who during this point in his tenure was finding himself more and more out of favour with the populous of Hobart Town, Chandler's day at the 1845 Regatta continued with two more successes. First, *Paul Pry*, a six-oared whaleboat he had recently built to the order of George Chase won the second race of the day, while another whaleboat built by Chandler for George Watson named *Tiger Cat* won the race for five-oared whaleboats.[834] Nearing the end of the day, the *Rose* won a private sailing match for £5 a-side against the *Comet*, both vessels pulled by crews consisting of locally-born youths.[835] This success was followed up a few months later when the *Rose* won the Subscription Silver Cup, valued at £5, at the New Norfolk Regatta, helmed by its owner George Lewis.[836]

With Chandler's boats proving victorious on multiple occasions, challenges for private matches became more and more frequent. In March 1846 a private race on the River Derwent, held over a three-mile distance, took place between the *Rose*, steered by Chandler, and Risby Brothers' *Cupid*; the former again earning the prize purse of £20.[837]

The 1846 Hobart Town Regatta saw two new vessels built by Chandler make their debut, with both expected to be competitive against the *Rose*. The first was a four-oared gig of unknown name, built to the order of John Dunn, Esq.[838] Unfortunately no additional details are known of this craft as it was not helmed by its owner. The second named *Ellen* was a four-oared gig built to the order of Messrs Westbrook that finished second in its race to Risby's *Cupid*.[839] Though the same length as the *Rose* (which was relegated to third place), this particular vessel was wider in the centre.[840] Also completed during this period at Chandler's yard at the Old Wharf, where he had established himself, was the waterman's boat *Rampant Lion*, built to the order of a Mr Burman (likely William) and intended to compete at the 1846 Hobart Town Regatta where it finished third.[841]

---

[828] *Colonial Times*, 5 December 1843.
[829] *The Hobart Town Advertiser*, 26 December 1843.
[830] *The Hobart Town Advertiser*, 6 December 1844.
[831] *The Hobart Town Advertiser*, 5 December 1845.
[832] *The Hobart Town Advertiser*, 5 December 1845.
[833] *The Hobart Town Advertiser*, 5 December 1845.
[834] *The Courier*, 3 December 1845; *The Hobart Town Advertiser*, 5, 16 December 1845.
[835] *The Hobart Town Advertiser*, 16 December 1845.
[836] *The Hobart Town Advertiser*, 20 February 1846.
[837] *Colonial Times*, 24 March 1846.
[838] *The Hobart Town Advertiser*, 28 August 1846.
[839] *The Courier*, 14 October 1846; *The Hobart Town Advertiser*, 4 December 1846.
[840] *The Courier*, 14 October 1846.
[841] *The Courier*, 14 October 1846; *The Hobart Town Advertiser*, 4 December 1846.

The latter months of 1846 coincided with personal joy for Chandler. On 3 October he married 20-year-old Hannah Macbeth at the private residence of the Reverend Samuel Hewlett, in Harrington Street, minister of Hobart Town's Baptist congregation.[842] Born in London, she had arrived in Hobart Town with her parents and four siblings in December 1834 per the ship *Eveline*.[843] Just three weeks after his marriage, on 24 October, Chandler's younger siblings William and Mary Selina arrived in Hobart Town from London as passengers on board the barque *Calcutta*.[844] While the foursome very likely initially lived together, William was a shoemaker by trade having completed his apprenticeship with William Howitt in Dover, Kent.[845] He soon established himself in Hobart Town and in May 1847 formed a partnership with William Macbeth, Jacob Chandler's brother-in-law, to open a boot and shoe shop in Macquarie Street.[846]

Likewise, Mary Selina Chandler soon became part of Hobart society. In November 1847, for example, she presided over a stall as part of a bazaar held to raise funds for the local Baptist Chapel. Of note, two of Jacob Chandler's sisters-in-law, Eliza and Martha Macbeth, also attended the event, one of whom donated a music stool to the cause.[847]

Professionally, Jacob Chandler was also on the move. After several years spent building and repairing whaleboats at the Old Wharf, in July 1847 he established a boat yard at Battery Point next door to that of the Risby Brothers. It was at this location that Chandler went on to become one of the longest serving boat builders of Battery Point, operating his yard until 1899 where, in the process, at least 197 vessels were constructed (likely a very conservative estimate of the total number built).

Chandler's yard was located off Napoleon Street, next door to that of Risby's boat yard and along from John Watson's shipyard. It extended down to the River Derwent with a frontage of 120ft. The property had been purchased by James Peek Poynter in January 1846 from Sinclair Williamson (brother-in-law of William Williamson, refer to a previous chapter), and in the early 1840s was briefly used by the Derwent Ship Building Company. Though Chandler initially leased the land and a house from Poynter, by October 1853 he had purchased a portion of the property, with more land purchased in 1858 from Poynter's widow Sarah.[848]

Notice of Removal.

MR. J. B. CHANDLER,
BOAT BUILDER,

BEGS leave to acquaint his friends and the public, that he has removed from those premises on the Old Wharf, to more extensive and suitable premises, Battery Point, near Mr. J. Watson, Ship Builder, where he respectfully solicits a continuance of that support which has hitherto received.

Battery Point, 22nd July, 1847.   1714

Colonial Times, 23 July 1847.

Upon establishing his new business, Chandler continued to build and repair whaleboats for the numerous commercial vessels visiting and operating out of the Port of Hobart Town. He also continued to furnish boats for regattas. By way of illustration, he built at least two boats to compete at the 1847 Hobart Town Regatta, held on 1 December. These were the four-oared gig *Hippolyta* and the five-oared whaleboat *Lady Denison*.[849] The former, with Chandler as coxwain and a crew comprising Neil Lewis, Richard Westbrook, Walter Westbrook and Charles Lewis, won the Amateur

[842] *The Hobart Town Advertiser*, 26 December 1845; Libraries Tasmania (RGD37/1/5 no. 266).
[843] *The People's Horn Boy*, 13 December 1834.
[844] *The Hobart Town Advertiser*, 27 October 1846.
[845] 1841 England Census for William Chandler.
[846] *Colonial Times*, 21 May 1847.
[847] *The Courier*, 13 November 1847.
[848] *The Hobart Town Advertiser*, 22 April 1853; www.thelist.tas.gov.au (Historical Deed 03/1556 and 04/5710).
[849] *The Hobart Town Advertiser*, 30 November 1847; *Colonial Times*, 7 December 1847.

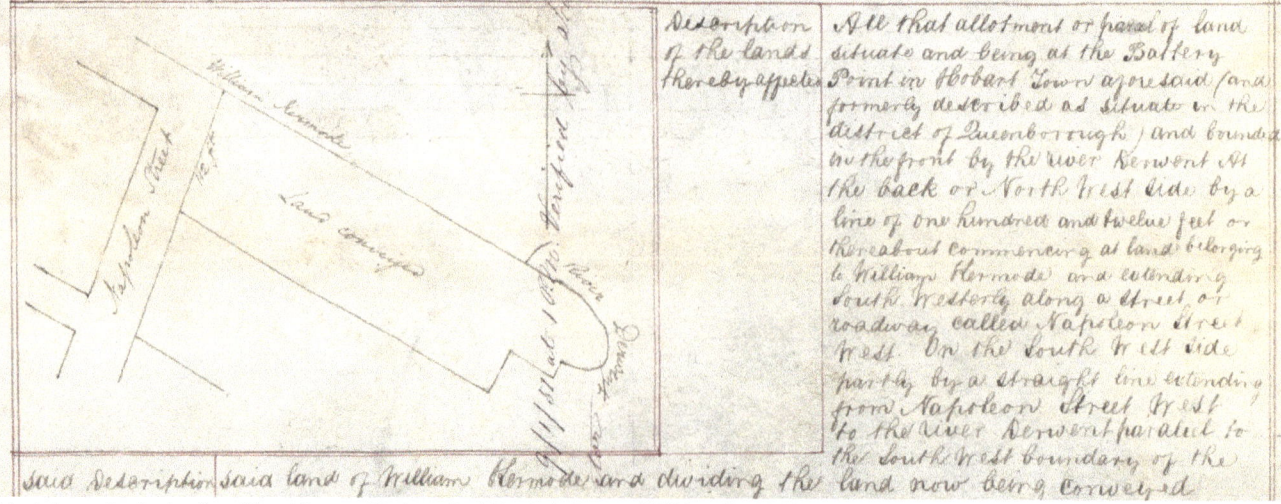

Adapted map showing location of '*Land Conveyed*' to James Peek Poynter in January 1846 from Sinclair Williamson (William Williamson's brother-in-law). Part of this property was leased to Jacob Chandler in July 1847 and purchased by him in the 1850s.
Courtesy www.thelist.tas.gov.au (Historical Deed 03/1556).

Gig Race receiving a Silver Cup valued at £15.[850] The latter won the Native Youths' Race though one report in the local press noted that, 'One or two of the Native Youths were as grey as badgers, the regulations say "not exceeding 18 years of age!!!" There is no accounting for these things, but more than one of the Native Youths were old enough to be our grandfather and we are no chicken'.[851] The *Lady Denison*, with a different crew, also finished second in the race for the Tasman Prize.[852]

As was becoming a regular occurrence, several challenges for private matches were issued in the days, weeks, and months following the Hobart Town Regatta. In particular, a race involving another whaleboat built by Chandler, the four-oared *Pearl*, took place in April 1848 with the craft winning the six-mile event by 100 yards.[853] Later that year a new four-oared whaleboat named the *Rose* won a race against Joseph Risby's *Odd Fellow*.[854]

In addition to repairing boats, 1848 saw Chandler build several smaller craft for the colonial government.[855] Statistics reveal that he was one of only 35 shipwrights and boat builders operating in Van Diemen's Land at the time; Chandler's expertise in building and repairing vessels likely filling a much-needed void for commercial, government and recreational clients.[856]

During this period Chandler also completed a wherry by the name of *Sea Gull* to compete at the Sandy Bay Regatta held on 1 January 1850. In an enterprising scheme, he raffled off the boat in the months prior to the event, with 16 subscribers paying £1 to enter.[857] It was the second time the Sandy Bay Regatta had been held. Of note, Chandler had been part of the committee that convened to organise the previous year's regatta and determine the program of races, as well as the rules and regulations.[858] He also built the four-oared whaleboat *Pirate*, launched in late 1849 to compete at that year's Hobart Town Regatta, where it finished second.[859]

Chandler spent the early 1850s continuing to build smaller boats at his Battery Point boat yard, and undertake repair work, including for the Government of Van Diemen's Land.[860] Of his new builds, Chandler launched the waterman's boat *Columbia* for Thomas Tandy in mid-1851; the four-oared whaleboat *Runnymede*, built to the order of James Weir specifically to compete in the native youths' race at the 1851 Hobart Town Regatta; a first-class whaleboat, complete with oars and sail, to be awarded to the winner of the licenced waterman's race held as part of the Williamstown Regatta in January 1854 that was shipped to Melbourne in late 1853 at the request of Lewis Michell of the Ship Inn; and three additional whaleboats, all completed in 1854, including the four-oared *Scottish Chief* that was used by O'May Brothers in the 1860s to help establish their trans-Derwent ferry business.[861]

Like his neighbours the Risby Brothers, Chandler also became involved in the timber trade, from 1851 supplying boards to the colonial government.[862] At the time, there was great demand for palings and shingles for use in the building and construction of commercial and residential buildings, particularly in mainland areas affected by the gold rush. In addition to meeting his own timber requirements and possibly some local demand, in the early to mid-1850s Chandler exported timber to the more lucrative Sydney and Melbourne markets. The timber was likely sourced from 500 acres of Crown land that Chandler leased at Taylors Bay, Bruny Island, up until early 1855.[863] To assist in these endeavours, he built the 35-ton schooner *Fairy* in 1853.[864] Described as a '*fast sailer and remarkably well adapted to the timber trade*', the craft represented Chandler's first attempt at building larger vessels.[865] It also appears that he built the *Fairy* for his own use, specifically to take advantage of the profitable timber trade. The craft was noted as sailing between Hobart Town, Recherche Bay and Macquarie Harbour in 1854.[866] It was then advertised for sale in January 1855 in conjunction with 20,000 square feet of Macquarie Harbour pine that was deemed fit for cabinet making or boat building purposes.[867]

Chandler's involvement in the timber trade no doubt explains why he built only a few boats in the 1850s. However, the profitability of the trade, and thereby his interest, was short-lived with timber prices and mainland demand suffering a dramatic decrease in the mid-1850s due to the arrival of timber from America. As such, Chandler sold the *Fairy* and returned to his niche of boat building. Other business enterprises he was involved with during this period, however, included becoming a shareholder in the Hobart Town & Sydney Steam Navigation Company, in 1854 purchasing five shares.[868]

On 26 February 1855, very likely using funds made available from the sale of the schooner *Fairy*, Chandler purchased part of an allotment of land at the New Wharf from Askin Morrison for the sum of £368.[869] Measuring 46 x 95ft, the property was in the vicinity of the ordinance store; today considered highly-lucrative real estate.[870] Showing his benevolence, in April 1855,

---

[850] *The Britannia and Trades' Advocate*, 2 December 1847; *The Hobart Town Advertiser*, 3 December 1847.
[851] *The Britannia and Trades' Advocate*, 2 December 1847; *The Hobart Town Advertiser*, 3 December 1847.
[852] *The Hobart Town Advertiser*, 3 December 1847; *The Courier*, 4 December 1847.
[853] *Hobarton Guardian, or, True Friend of Tasmania*, 26 April 1848.
[854] *The Hobart Town Advertiser*, 14 November 1848; *The Britannia and Trades' Advocate*, 16 November 1848.
[855] *The Hobart Town Advertiser*, 21 April, 7 July, 6 October 1848; *Hobarton Guardian, or, True Friend of Tasmania*, 9 May 1849.
[856] *The Hobart Town Advertiser*, 28 January 1851.
[857] *Colonial Times*, 23 October 1849.
[858] *Colonial Times*, 26 December 1848; *The Courier*, 30 December 1848.
[859] *Hobarton Guardian, or, True Friend of Tasmania*, 1 December 1849.
[860] *Launceston Examiner*, 15 June, 7 September 1850, 15 February 1851.
[861] *Colonial Times*, 8 August 1851, 2 August 1855; *The Tasmanian Colonist*, 29 December 1851; *The Argus*, 14 January 1854; *The Courier*, 4 May 1854; *The Mercury*, 15 November 1875, 15 August 1921, 23 September 1935.
[862] *The Hobart Town Advertiser*, 31 January 1851.
[863] *The Courier*, 6 February 1855.
[864] R. Parsons (1992). *Australian Shipowners and their Fleets. Book 12 (Hobart to 1859, A - L)*.
[865] *The Colonial Times*, 5 January 1855; R. Parsons (1992). *Australian Shipowners and their Fleets. Book 12 (Hobart to 1859, A - L)*.
[866] *The Hobart Town Advertiser*, 17 January 1854, 29 December 1854.
[867] *The Courier*, 1 January 1855.
[868] *The Courier*, 24 May 1854.
[869] www.thelist.tas.gov.au (Historical Deed 04/0913).
[870] www.thelist.tas.gov.au (Historical Deed 04/0913).

he also donated to the Patriotic fund, in support of servicemen involved in the Crimean War, on behalf of himself, his wife Hannah and his sister Mary Selina.[871] Sadly, Hannah died just over six months later, on 4 December 1855, after a short illness, officially noted as 'inflammation'.[872] She was 29 years of age. Chandler was left a widow and the sole carer of their three children: Emma Selina (born 1848), John Thomas (born 1851) and Marian Ellen (born 1854).[873]

Persevering, Chandler continued to build new craft and undertake repair work. Of the former, he is known to have built a square-sterned pleasure boat that was advertised for sale in January 1856, complete with oars and sails, and the four-oared gig *Star*, which finished third at the 1856 Tamar Regatta.[874] He also continued to be involved in the timber trade. On 28 March 1856, for example, the 281-ton schooner *Lion* sailed to Sydney with 25,000 feet of timber and 20 boxes of apples, both consigned to Chandler.[875] Expanding his property portfolio, a few days later Chandler purchased three allotments of land within the township of Bellerive, across the River Derwent. The first allotment, comprising two roods and thirty perches was located

[871] *Colonial Times*, 14 April 1855.
[872] *The Hobart Town Advertiser*, 6 December 1855; Libraries Tasmania (RGD35/1/5 no. 433).
[873] Libraries Tasmania (RGD33/1/3 no. 587, RGD33/1/4 no. 513, RGD 33/1/5 no. 551).
[874] *The Courier*, 5 January 1856; *The Cornwall Chronicle*, 12 January 1856.
[875] *The Courier*, 29 March 1856; *The Hobart Town Advertiser*, 29 March 1856.

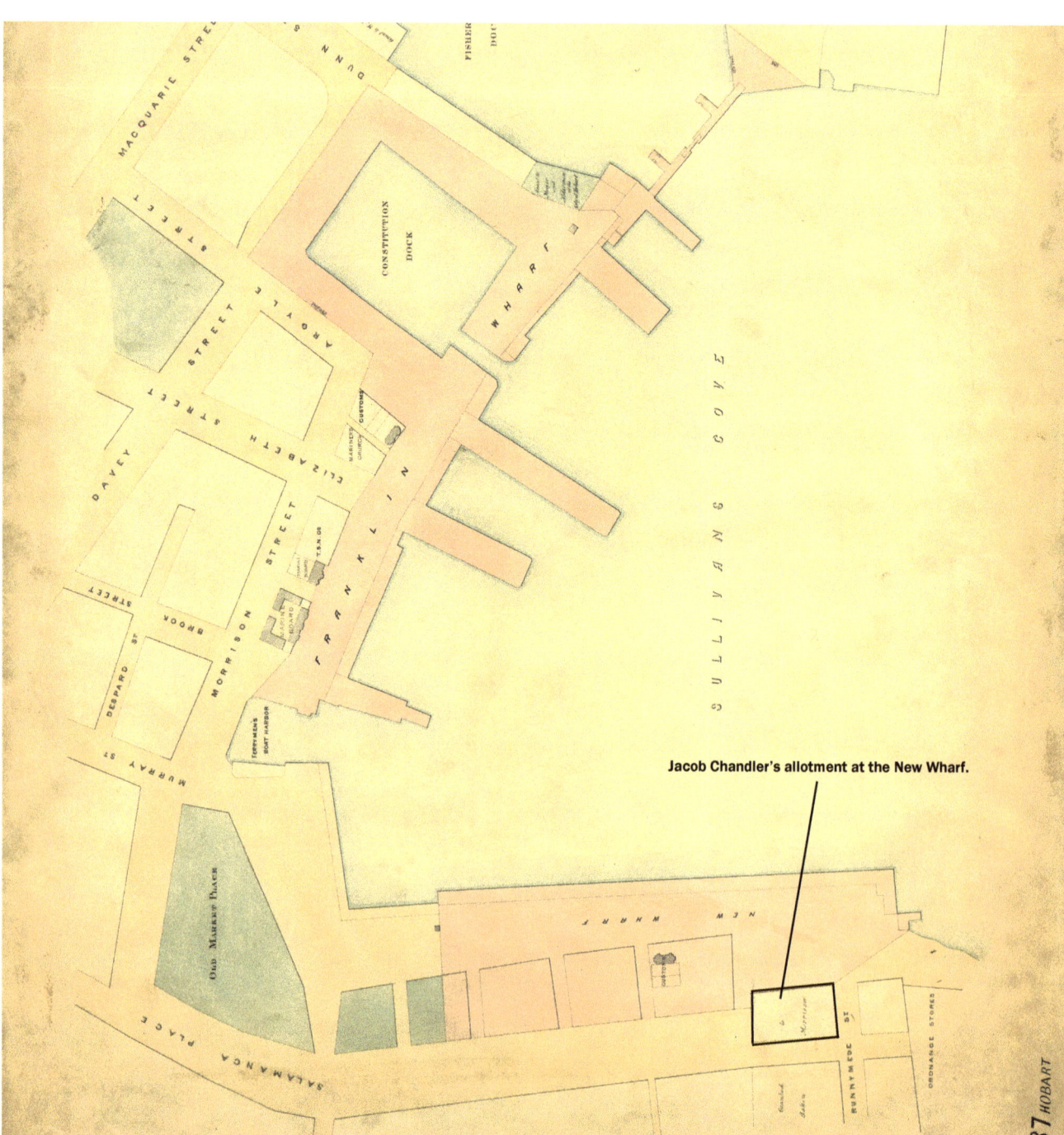

Adapted map of the Hobart Wharves (c1880s) showing location of land purchased by Jacob Chandler from Askin Morrison in 1855. Courtesy Tasmanian Archives (AF394/1/87).

at the current site of 17 South Street.[876] The second allotment was much larger, at over three acres, and was located between South Street and the Esplanade. It was sold to Georgina Featherstone in September 1886 for £80.[877] The third allotment, was much larger still, comprising more than six acres. Located on the Esplanade, Chandler only retained this property for a brief period; on-selling it to T. D. Chapman in March of the following year.[878] All three parcels of land were purchased from Charles Dillon, Hobart Town waterman, with whom Chandler would have an ongoing business and very likely social relationship for a number of decades.[879] Combined, the three properties amount to a staggering proportion of real estate from today's perspective, though at the time would have been considered of limited use, predominantly for farming or housing, considering their remote location on the other side of the River Derwent, away from the commercial activities of Hobart Town.

In addition to building more smaller craft, the end of the 1850s marked another turning point in Chandler's career. His involvement in private whaleboat races and regattas during the 1840s and 1850s evolved into a higher stakes game—that of yacht racing. Spurred by local efforts to form a 'Tasmanian Yacht Club', as well as the increasing popularity and competitiveness of private sailing matches, in early October 1859 Chandler attended the first general meeting of the Tasmanian Yacht Club at the Bird in Hand Hotel, Argyle Street. Here, discussion took place as to the *'best means of promoting the best competition for the prize, (as yet unannounced)'*.[880] Within days the Club announced its officers, flag, signals and schedule for monthly meetings, as well as confirmed that the Governor, S. H. Young, had agreed to be patron.[881] The creation of the organisation also inspired Hobart Town's budding yachtsmen, with four new vessels noted under construction, including one at Peppermint Bay by a boat builder named Norris (likely Joseph), while existing craft were being lengthened and overhauled in anticipation of the first race.[882]

In December 1859, only weeks before the staging of the Tasmanian Yacht Club's first race, Chandler launched his 16-ton cutter yacht *Secret*.[883] Earlier that year he may have also built the 18-ton cutter *Vindictive*, initially involved in the D'Entrecasteaux Channel trade.[884] This specific vessel was then purchased by Peter Oldham in early December 1859 and renamed *Sea Gull*.[885] Both vessels were registered in Hobart Town on 9 January 1860, though the builder of *Sea Gull* is unfortunately not stated.[886]

[876] www.thelist.tas.gov.au (Historical Deed 04/3039).
[877] www.thelist.tas.gov.au (Historical Deed 07/6930).
[878] www.thelist.tas.gov.au (Historical Deed 04/3039).
[879] www.thelist.tas.gov.au (Historical Deed 04/3039).
[880] *The Hobart Town Daily Mercury*, 5 October 1859.
[881] *The Hobart Town Daily Mercury*, 8 October 1859.
[882] *The Hobart Town Daily Mercury*, 1 November 1859; *The Hobart Town Advertiser*, 3 January 1860.
[883] *The Hobart Town Daily Mercury*, 1 November, 30 December 1859.
[884] *The Hobart Town Daily Mercury*, 25 July, 10 August, 26 August 1859; *Hobart Town Advertiser*, 10 December 1859; E. H. Webster & L. Norman (1936). *A Hundred Years of Yachting*.
[885] E. H. Webster & L. Norman (1936). *A Hundred Years of Yachting*.
[886] Appropriation Books, Official Numbers 32051 - 32100.

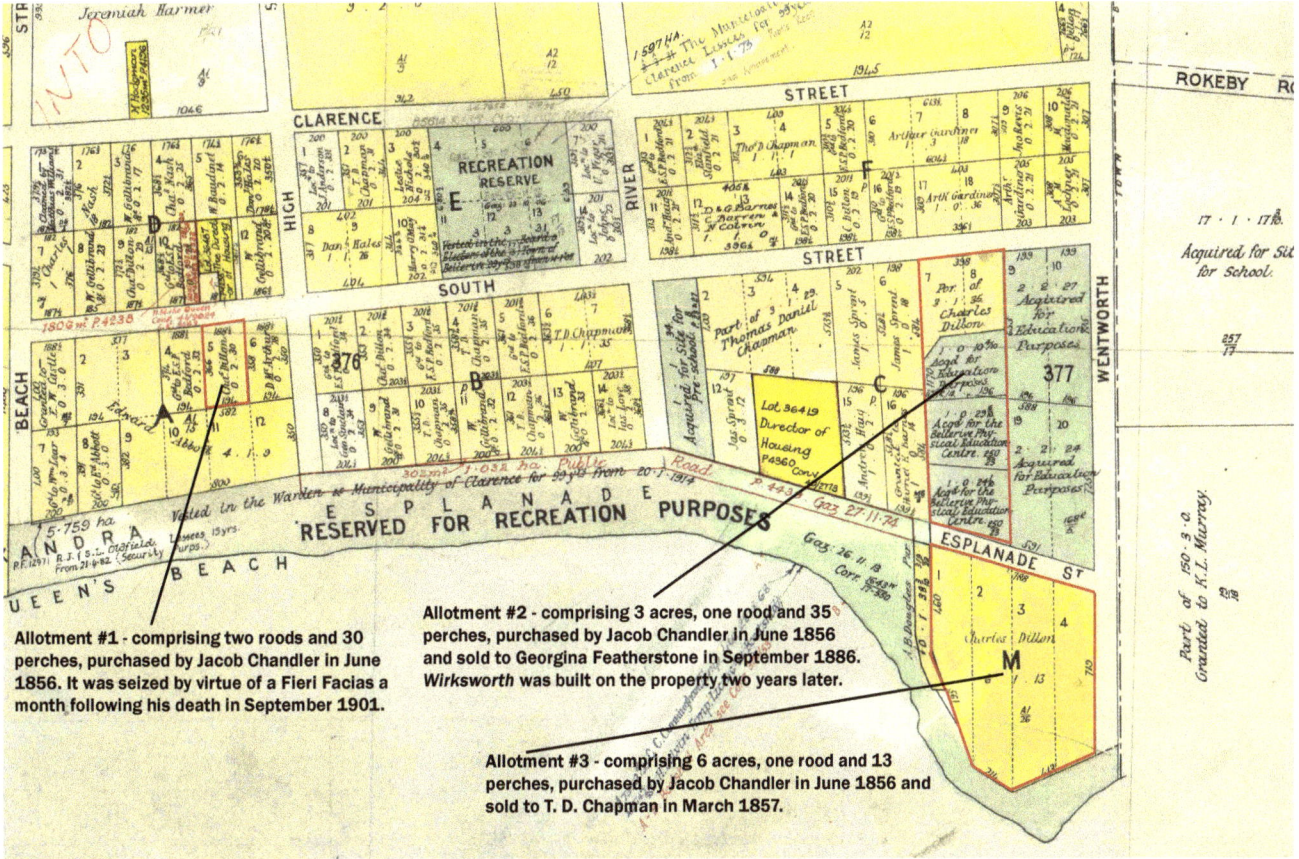

Adapted c1960s map of initial property owners at Bellerive overlaid with allotments purchased by Jacob Chandler from Charles Dillon in 1856. Courtesy Tasmanian Archives (AF819/1/18).

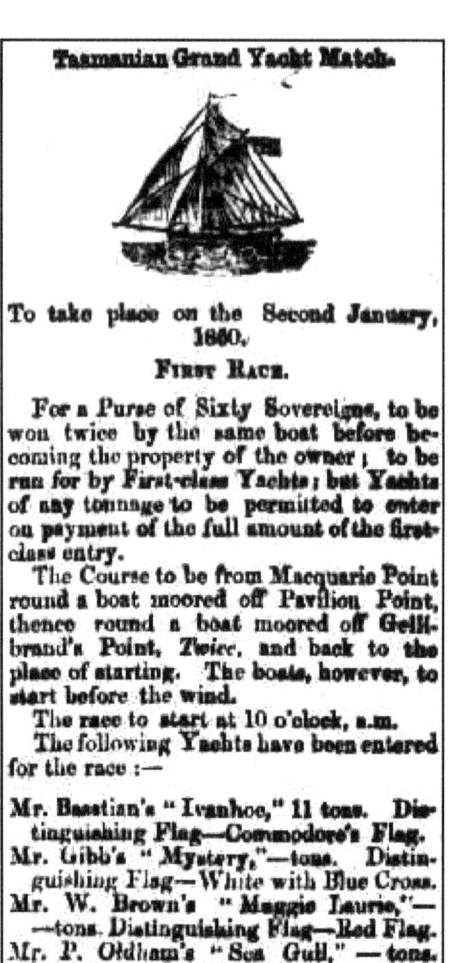

The Hobart Town Daily Mercury, 30 December 1859.

Competing against four other vessels, *Secret* and *Sea Gull* made their first appearance on the River Derwent on 2 January 1860 at the opening race of the newly-formed Tasmanian Yacht Club. Described as a *'very pretty vessel'* and considered a *'dangerous customer in any weather'*, the *Secret*, sailed by Ambrose Harrington, claimed victory by more than seven minutes from the *Maggie Laurie* with the *Phantom* in third.[887] The *Secret* continued its success by winning the yacht race at the Hobart Town Regatta, held on 11 January 1860. Second place went to D. T. Kilburn's cutter *Phantom* and third to the cutter *Mystery*, owned by A. Gibbs.[888] The first prize purse was £25.

Secret and *Sea Gull* went on to compete in two additional Tasmanian Yacht Club races that year for a total prize purse of £60; equivalent to nearly half the annual salary of a shipwright. The former finished runner-up in both races by narrow margins to the *Maggie Laurie* and was thus unable to claim the purse; awarded to the winner of two out of the three races.[889]

Showing his competitiveness and determination, less than one week following the third race, in November 1860, Chandler placed an advertisement in *The Mercury* challenging the owner of the *Maggie Laurie* (William Brown) to a race for £100 a-side.[890] It appears, however, that this challenge was not accepted. Instead, by November of the following year, Chandler lengthened the *Secret* and installed a new mast.[891] One month later, the vessel competed in the Champion Sailing Race at the Hobart Town Regatta for a prize of a whopping £230. Though the *Secret* won the race, the prize was ultimately awarded to the lighter *Maggie Laurie* on handicap, with a cutter from Sydney (the *Surprise*) finishing third.[892]

Forever the entrepreneur, however, Chandler gave up yacht racing and in July 1862 chartered the *Secret* to W. Luttrell, who employed it in the Channel timber trade.[893] Two years later, Chandler sold the craft to John Ellis, timber merchant of Launceston, for £275.[894] The *Secret* spent the next few years trading between Hobart Town and Launceston. In its place, Chandler purchased the cutter yacht *Ivanhoe*.[895]

In April 1865 John Ellis sold the *Secret* to two men connected with the South Australian pilot service (Messers Pickhaver and Woolnough) for £325.[896] In the succeeding years, the *Secret* changed ownership several more times, though remained in South Australian waters.[897] In July 1873, the vessel was wrecked five miles north of Point Boilingbrooke, all hands saved.[898] At the time of loss, the *Secret* was owned by John Watherstone of Port Lincoln[899]

Other vessels built by Chandler in the early to mid-1860s included the 7-ton fore and aft schooner *Emily Ellen* which first sailed out of Hobart Town on 2 March 1860 with its new owner John Austin of Port Albert, Victoria, at the helm.[900] Described as *'well adapted for the [Gippsland] Lakes or any of the adjacent waters'*, the vessel was advertised for sale in July 1861 for £60 and subsequently sold to George Evans of Lucknow to ply between Bairnsdale and Port Albert.[901] With navigating the shallow waters of the Gippsland Lakes proving a tricky task, the vessel sunk off French Island in October 1862 having sprung a leak on a previous voyage.[902]

[887] *The Hobart Town Advertiser*, 3 January 1860.
[888] *The Hobart Town Daily Mercury*, 12 January 1860.
[889] *The Hobart Town Daily Mercury*, 6 February 1860; *The Hobart Town Advertiser*, 6 February 1860.
[890] *The Mercury*, 15 November 1860.
[891] *The Hobart Town Advertiser*, 20 November 1861.
[892] *The Mercury*, 9, 23 December 1861.
[893] *The Mercury*, 23 December 1863, 2 June 1864.
[894] *The Mercury*, 2, 23 June 1864.
[895] *The Mercury*, 7 October 1864.
[896] *Launceston Examiner*, 20 April 1865.
[897] *Evening News*, 5 July 1869; *The Express and Telegraph*, 6 September 1870, 27 January 1871, 7 August 1872; *Evening Journal*, 13 August 1872; *The South Australian Register*, 5 August, 1873.
[898] *Evening Journal*, 5 August 1873.
[899] *Evening Journal*, 5 August 1873.
[900] *The Hobart Town Daily Mercury*, 3 March 1860; Graeme Broxam, pers. comm.
[901] *Gippsland Guardian*, 26 July 1861, 24 January 1862.
[902] *Gippsland Times*, 14 November 1862.

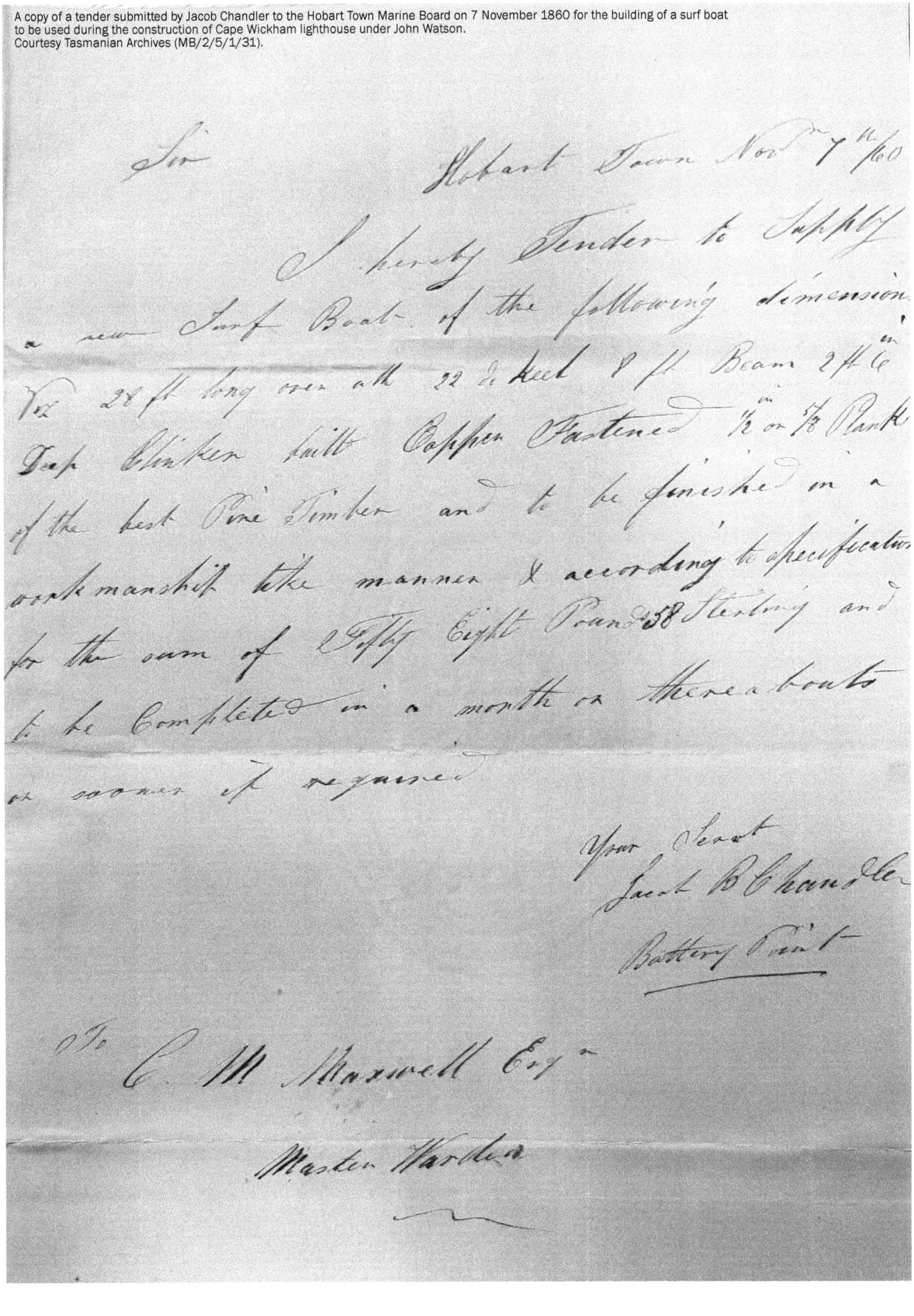

A copy of a tender submitted by Jacob Chandler to the Hobart Town Marine Board on 7 November 1860 for the building of a surf boat to be used during the construction of Cape Wickham lighthouse under John Watson.
Courtesy Tasmanian Archives (MB/2/5/1/31).

Sir

Hobart Town Nov'r 7th /60

I hereby Tender to Supply a new Surf Boat of the following dimensions Viz 28 ft long over all 22 d Keel 8 ft Beam 2 ft 6 in Deep Clinker built Copper Fastened ½ or ⅝ in Plank of the best Pine Timber and to be finished in a workmanship like manner & according to specification for the sum of Fifty Eight Pounds 58 Sterling and to be Completed in a month or thereabouts or sooner if required

Your Servt
Jacob B Chandler
Battery Point

To C. M. Maxwell Esqr

Master Warden

Chandler also built the passage boat *Peter and James* in 1861, most likely to the order of John Potter.[903] It traded between South Arm and Hobart Town until the late 1870s. More commercial craft were also completed, including whaleboats for use onboard international vessels, as well as the waterman's boats *Star of Tasmania* and *Perseverance* for O'May Brothers, and the *Picnic* for Charles Dillon.[904]

Chandler continued his involvement with the Hobart Town Regatta; between 1860 and at least 1873 he was a member of the event's organising committee.[905] In terms of vessels, he built a five-oared whaleboat, helmed by J. Hopwood, that finished first in the race for the Derwent Prize at the 1861 New Norfolk Regatta, held on 2 January of that year.[906] Later that year Chandler completed the *Shelahlah*, a four-oared whaleboat that competed in the native youths' race at the Hobart Town Regatta, while in 1862 he turned out a five-oared whaleboat named *Sir John Franklin* to compete at the Hobart Town Regatta, as well as the four-oared whaleboat *Morning Light* which competed at the Port Cygnet Regatta, held on 1 January 1863, winning the race for the Ladies' Purse.[907] In December 1863 Chandler launched the skiff *Prince of Wales* for J. Smart.[908] The vessel was pulled by C. Gaylor at the 1863 Hobart Town Regatta, finishing in second place.[909] Two new boats were noted on the stocks at Chandler's yard in preparation for the 1864 Hobart Town Regatta.[910]

On a personal level, Jacob Chandler remarried. On 29 March 1861 at his Battery Point residence, Chandler married Martha Macbeth, youngest sister of his late wife Hannah.[911] While marrying ones sister-in-law would be considered somewhat strange in today's society, it was apparently frowned upon though not illegal in Van Diemen's Land in the 1860s.

1861 additionally saw Chandler involved in a unique project. With an exhibition of worldwide products to be showcased in London at the International Exhibition of 1862, the Government of Tasmania moved to send a 'Tasmanian Timber and Whaling Trophy' illustrating the colony's timber and whaling resources to the event, along with mineral samples, agricultural and manufactured products. Built at a cost approaching £3,000, the trophy itself was a substantial piece of work, being octagonal with a 12ft base, reaching nearly 100ft in height, and constructed of multiple types of endemic timbers.[912] 'Two fine whaleboats built by Messrs Chandler and Miller of Hobart Town' were suspended on davits on opposite sides of the pedestal platform.[913] The boats were complete with masts, sails, oars, whaling gear, harpoons, lances, etc., and could be viewed from the floor with their fittings examined via a hand rail leading from the bottom of the pedestal.[914]

The International Exhibition was opened on 1 May 1862 and continued until November of that year, with components of the Tasmanian Timber and Whaling Trophy shipped to London a few months prior. All told more than 28,000 exhibitors were involved in the event, representing 36 counties, with over six million people attending.[915]

Continuing to be involved in international exhibitions, in December 1864 Chandler contributed boat building timbers to the Dunedin Industrial Exhibition in New Zealand.[916] In mid-1866 he built a four-oared whaleboat of Huon pine for display at the Intercolonial Exhibition of Australasia, held in Melbourne from 24 October 1866 to 23 February 1867.[917]

The exodus of thousands of Tasmanians to New Zealand in search of gold in the early 1860s resulted in another lucrative market opening up for Chandler. He took great advantage of the lack of boat builders in New Zealand at the time and built many boats specifically for export to this colony. These included a four-oared whaleboat forwarded to Lyttelton by the brig *Lady Denison* in November 1862 to participate in local races and regattas.[918] That same month Chandler's brother William, his wife Kezia (nee Cox) and their two sons sailed to New Zealand as passengers on board the barque *Eucalyptus*, intending to establish themselves in Invercargill.[919] William's relocation would prove fruitful for Chandler, opening up another pathway for business opportunities, though it was only short-term. William (by now widowed) and his two sons returned to Hobart Town in March 1866.[920]

Additional craft sent to New Zealand by Chandler comprised a four-oared whaleboat that was advertised for sale in Dunedin in late April 1863 by George Perriman who was agent for the brig *Pryde* that had sailed from Hobart Town the previous month with a large cargo.[921] In September 1863 Chandler shipped a '*splendid regatta boat*' to Dunedin on board the barque *Bella Vista*, built to the order of a Mr Fisher.[922] The 31ft craft was described as '*whale-boat built, gig style*' and a '*very beautiful model*'. A boat built to the order of the Akaroa Boating Club was ordered from Chandler

---

[903] *The Mercury*, 18 July, 3 October 1861, 24 April 1874; *The Advertiser*, 28 August 1865.
[904] *The Mercury*, 18 July, 3 October 1861, 15 November 1875, 15 August 1921, 23 September 1935; *The Advertiser*, 2 August, 3 October 1862.
[905] *The Mercury*, 12 November 1860, 20 August 1861, 28 October 1862, 4 November 1863, 6 October 1864, 11 October 1865, 12 October 1866, 21 September 1867, 13 October 1869, 28 November 1870, 12 September 1871, 19 December 1872, 2 December 1873; *The Tasmanian Times*, 9 October 1868.
[906] *The Hobart Town Advertiser*, 31 December 1860.
[907] *The Mercury*, 14 November 1861, 5 December 1862; *The Advertiser*, 3 January 1863.
[908] *Hobart Town Advertiser*, 12 December 1863; *The Mercury*, 23 December 1863.
[909] *Hobart Town Advertiser*, 12 December 1863; *The Mercury*, 23 December 1863.
[910] *The Mercury*, 10 October 1864.
[911] *The Mercury*, 4 April 1861.
[912] *The Mercury*, 23 November, 3 December 1861.
[913] *The Mercury*, 23 November, 3 December 1861.
[914] *The Mercury*, 23 November, 3 December 1861.
[915] en.wikipedia.org/wiki/1862_International_Exhibition.
[916] *The Mercury*, 23 December 1864.
[917] *The Mercury*, 11 April, 18 April 1866; guides.slv.vic.gov.au/interexhib/1866to67.
[918] *The Advertiser*, 3 November 1862.
[919] *The Advertiser*, 13 November 1862.
[920] *West Coast Times*, 2 March 1866; *The Argus*, 8 March 1866; *The Mercury*, 27 March 1866.
[921] *Otago Daily Times*, 20, 28 April 1863.
[922] *The Mercury*, 3 September 1863.

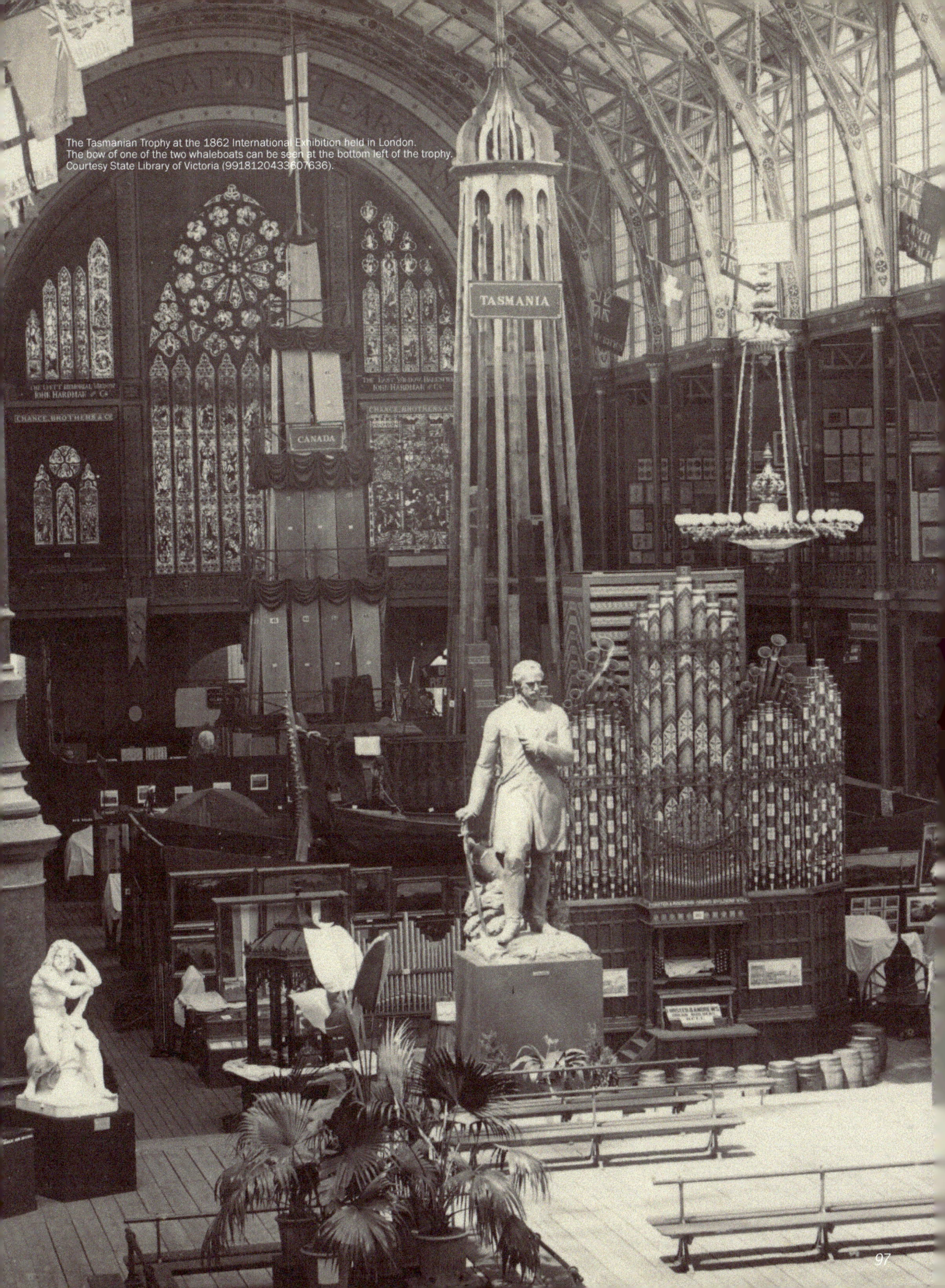

The Tasmanian Trophy at the 1862 International Exhibition held in London.
The bow of one of the two whaleboats can be seen at the bottom left of the trophy.
Courtesy State Library of Victoria (9918120433607636).

in May 1864.[923] A flat-bottomed 35ft lifeboat built of Macquarie pine and fitted with a water-tight locker for storing mail was sent to Nelson on board the *Annie* in October 1865.[924] The 12-ton cutter *Hope*, two whaleboats and a wherry, all built by Chandler in 1866; and two more whaleboats built in 1867, were additionally sent to New Zealand.[925] All of these craft appear to have been purpose-built for specific customers, indicating the extent of Chandler's reputation. His trade with New Zealand was also helped by the increasing regularity of vessels travelling between Hobart Town and several of New Zealand's coastal ports.

Other boats built by Chandler during the mid-to late-1860s included the waterman's boat *Commodore* for William Weir (1864); two whaleboats for Dr Crowther's whaling barque *Offley* for use as part of the Wreck Reef guano trade (1864); and a racing whaleboat built of Macquarie pine, a four-oared whaleboat built to the order of John Godfrey, a five-oared whaleboat built to the order of Messrs Willis and Perry, the four-oared whaleboat *Paul Pry*, and a four-oared whaleboat built to the order of William Weir, all five boats were built to compete at the 1864 Hobart Town Regatta.[926]

In 1865 Chandler completed a 25ft pleasure boat to the order of John Meredith of Swansea, and four boats to compete at the Hobart Town Regatta.[927] The following year his tender to the Government of Tasmania's was accepted for the construction of a four-oared whaleboat of Macquarie Harbour pine at a cost of £20.[928] 1866 also saw Chandler build at least four new boats specifically to compete at the Hobart Town Regatta, including one to the order of Charles Dillon.[929]

In 1867 Chandler built at least two whaleboats for use on board the barque *Planter* which was undergoing a refit at John Ross' Battery Point slip in June of that year.[930] A few months later he was noted as having a vessel of about 25 tons nearing completion on the stocks, built of Port Davey pine.[931] This was very likely the 55ft schooner *Louise* that he launched in 1869.[932] Later in 1867 Chandler completed at least seven vessels to compete at the upcoming Hobart Town Regatta.[933]

While Jacob Chandler's Battery Point boat yard was proving a success, having been in operation for 20 years, on a personal level there was more sadness. Chandler's wife Martha gave birth on 1 July 1864 to a son named James. The infant, born premature, sadly died the following day.[934] Less than three years later, on 18 April 1867 at their Battery Point home, Martha died of kidney disease after a long and painful illness.[935] She was 38 years of age.[936]

While Chandler privately mourned the loss of his wife, there was much excitement occurring in Hobart Town. The 1867 Hobart Town Regatta, scheduled to take place in early December of that year, had been delayed until 9 January 1868. The highly-anticipated arrival of His Royal Highness, Prince Alfred, the Duke of Edinburgh, whose expected patronage of Hobart Town's most favoured holiday had resulted in the delay. It was worth the wait.

Notably the first ever visit to Australia by a member of the Royal Family, the Duke had left England at the command of HMS *Galatea* in January 1867, first visiting the Mediterranean and South America. The vessel then reached Adelaide on 31 October to commence a royal tour of Australia. After spending several weeks in South Australia, the Duke's party sailed to Melbourne before arriving in Hobart Town on 6 January 1868. The population of Van Diemen's Land was buzzing. Numerous formal events and festivities, including receptions, tours, dinners and balls, had been organised to showcase the colony and its growing populace. Hobart Town had also been extensively decorated with flags and bunting to welcome the Prince and his contingent.

The official State Landing took place on 7 January 1868 starting at the New Wharf. Here a Royal Salute was fired and the Duke escorted to his carriage by the Governor and other dignitaries, thereupon travelling to the Landing Stage where formal speeches and addresses took place. From here, the Duke travelled via carriage to Franklin Square, on the way travelling through three decorative arches. The first arch, the 'Welcome to Tasmania' emblematic arch featured two whaleboats, manned by Tasmanian-born youths dressed in costume, amongst other colonial-produced items and products.[937] It is extremely likely that one or both of these whaleboats were built by Chandler.

Another event held in honour of the Duke of Edinburgh's visit to Hobart Town was a torchlight aquatic procession. Held on the River Derwent, approximately 40 boats of various types and sizes, containing about 600 people, began assembling at 7:30pm on 7 January.[938] Of note, several of the participating craft had been built by Chandler in the years prior. The procession proved a success, thanked in part to favourable weather conditions and clear skies.[939]

The years 1868 and 1869 saw Chandler continue to build smaller vessels, including waterman's boats and

---

[923] *Lyttelton Times*, 21 May 1864.
[924] *The Mercury*, 7 October 1865.
[925] *Otago Daily Times*, 19 November 1866, 23 May 1867; *The Mercury*, 10 October, 21 November 1866, 7 May 1867; *Tasmanian Morning Herald*, 5 November 1866.
[926] *The Mercury*, 11, 22 October, 14, 23 November, 1 December 1864; *The Advertiser*, 12 October, 7 November 1864.
[927] *The Mercury*, 7 October, 28 November 1865.
[928] *The Cornwall Chronicle*, 23 June 1866.
[929] *The Mercury*, 5 December 1866.
[930] *The Mercury*, 10 June 1867.
[931] *The Tasmanian Times*, 24 August.
[932] *The Mercury*, 24 August 1867.
[933] *The Tasmanian Times*, 24 October, 25 November 1867, 3 January 1868; *The Mercury*, 25 November 1867; HOBART, Register of ships, Volume 9, 1865-1877, [pages 1-173, continues on film roll 2], Folio 112.
[934] *The Advertiser*, 4 July 1864; Libraries Tasmania (RGD35/1/7 no. 4516).
[935] *The Mercury*, 18 April 1867; Libraries Tasmania (RGD35/1/7 no. 6713).
[936] *The Mercury*, 18 April 1867; Libraries Tasmania (RGD35/1/7 no. 6713).
[937] *The Mercury*, 15 July 1868.
[938] *The Mercury*, 31 January 1868.
[939] *The Mercury*, 31 January 1868.

Welcome to Tasmania emblematic arch at the Hobart Town wharf, showing two whaleboats and crew (January 1868).
Courtesy Tasmanian Archives (PH30/1/31).

Aquatic torchlight procession held on the River Derwent in January 1868 in honour of the Duke of Edinburgh's visit. Courtesy State Library of Victoria (9916525993607636).

whaleboats, for use commercially as well as in races.[940] He also branched further into the construction of larger craft. The deep-sea fishing boat *Eclipse* was built to the order of Henry Thompson of Hobart Town.[941] The craft, however, would be converted into a passage boat for the local river trade a few years later. The commercial fishing industry was still in its infancy, but in the coming decades would be established with many vessels built by Tasmania's boat builders to furnish the demand.

Another passage boat built by Chandler in 1868 was the *Eliza* for George Elwell of Oyster Cove.[942] The vessel arrived at Constitution Dock on 9 December of that year, having completed its first round trip between Hobart Town and the D'Entrecasteaux Channel.

The 1870s proved to be a monumental decade for Jacob Chandler. Early in 1870 he was commissioned to build what would be the first of four steam ferries for O'May Brothers.[943] Measuring 46ft overall, the hull of the *Enterprise* was launched from his Battery Point boat yard on 10 September 1870.[944] The press reported on the event and the vessel. '*On Saturday afternoon a boat was launched from Chandler's yard, intended to be used as a steam ferry vehicle between Hobart Town and Kangaroo Point. There were a large number of persons present besides those connected with the shipping interest of the port. The boat is built for the brothers O'May of Kangaroo Point, and she is without exception one of the finest that we have seen launched from a Tasmanian yard. She was built on no model, but her lines are faithful, showing a fine clear entrance, and considering the size of the boat, a very pretty run: the hull in general giving promise of good steaming qualities. The boat is appropriately named the "Enterprise," and we hope that the enterprise will prove a success. Her dimensions are as follows: overall 46ft, keel 38ft, beam 9ft, depth of hold 4ft 10 inches. The boat is more like a yacht than anything else, and is comfortably proportioned, the seats being laid down fore and aft, with plenty of room allowed for the passengers; she has sweeping bows and a round stern. The boat will be worked by a pair of inverted direct engines, non-condensing, which can be worked up to 30-horse power; the boiler is a vertical tubular one, and the top of it [is] almost flush with*

---

[940] *The Mercury*, 18 May, 28 November 1868, 1 December 1869; *The Cornwall Chronicle*, 18 November 1868, 2 December 1869; *The Tasmanian Times*, 30 June 1868, 16 June 1869, 11 December 1869.
[941] *The Mercury*, 20 August 1868.
[942] *The Mercury*, 10 December 1868.
[943] *The Tasmanian Times*, 22 April 1870.

[944] *The Tasmanian Times*, 12 September 1870.

the gunwale; it is placed for convenience amidships. It is expected that the Enterprise will carry about 60 passengers with a rate of speed of between 8 and 9 knots, so that she will be enabled to accomplish the distance between here and Kangaroo Point in a little over 10 minutes. The Enterprise, as we mentioned before in the columns of this journal, was laid down about three months ago, and great care has been taken in her construction; the frame is of blue gum, and the planking of Macquarie pine. ... In conclusion we can only say that the boat is a credit to the establishment where she was built, and we believe is likely to compete successfully with other boats of the same class which may be launched on Tasmanian waters. The Enterprise will be brought round to the wharf about Wednesday next for the purpose of having the machinery fitted, and she will then be open to inspection'.[945]

After having its engines and machinery, manufactured by John Clark of the New Wharf, fitted, from mid-October 1870 the *Enterprise* began making eight runs per day on weekdays across the River Derwent between Hobart Town and Kangaroo Point, with several trips scheduled for the weekends.[946] The vessel proved such a success that six years later Chandler completed a second steam ferry for O'May Brothers. Over 10ft larger than the *Enterprise*, the 57ft

[945] *The Tasmanian Times*, 12 September 1870.
[946] *The Mercury*, 15 September, 13, 14 October 1870; *The Tasmanian Times*, 14 October 1870.

Success was launched from his Battery Point yard on 26 October 1876 already fitted with 14 h.p. engines that had been manufactured by Messrs Appleby and Co. of London and imported to Hobart Town by the late Henry Hopkins who, before his death, had intended to build a steam yacht.[947] From December 1876 the *Success* joined the *Enterprise* in making multiple daily trips between Kangaroo Point and Hobart Town's Franklin Wharf.[948]

In mid-1877 Chandler lengthened the *Enterprise* by 10ft and gave the craft a new bow.[949] Its engines and boiler were also overhauled.[950] Following these alterations, the vessel was considered as commodious as the *Success*. The two ferries were still not enough to meet demand for O'May Brothers' river crossing services. On 7 November 1879 Chandler launched the 57ft *Result* — the third steam ferry he built for O'May Brothers' increasingly popular Hobart Town to Kangaroo Bay ferry service.[951] Of similar appearance to the *Success*, the craft joined both this vessel and the *Enterprise* on the Kangaroo Bay to Hobart ferry run, and was also used for pleasure trips and day tours. It was

[947] *The Mercury*, 27 October 1876; *Tribune*, 10 March 1877.
[948] *The Tasmanian Tribune*, 10 June 1876.
[949] *Tribune*, 29 June 1877.
[950] *Tribune*, 19 September 1877.
[951] *The Mercury*, 8 November 1879.

SS *Success* at Bellerive (c1880s). Courtesy Peter O'May.

SS *Victory* leaving the Hobart Wharf (c1900s). Courtesy Peter O'May.

fitted with 12 h.p. twin cylinder engine manufactured by Appleby Bros. of London, capable of attaining an average speed of 8 knots per hour.[952]

Finally, in early 1883, Jacob Chandler was commissioned to build his fourth steam ferry for O'May Brothers; a necessary addition to meet further demand for the River Derwent passenger trade.[953] With its keel procured from Garden Island Creek, the 86ft *Victory* took over a year to complete and was launched on 16 June 1884; notably being the largest vessel Chandler is known to have built.[954] The delay in construction was the result of a scarcity of ship carpenters. Once fitted with its Sydney-manufactured 25 h.p. non-condensing engines, from September 1884 the *Victory* began a regular run on the Derwent.[955] The vessel was capable of carrying 250 people and, like its three predecessors, was also used to convey passengers to regional events and regattas, and available for private charter.

Throughout the 1870s Jacob Chandler also continued to be heavily involved in whaleboat racing and built many boats specifically for competing in local, regional and intercolonial regattas.[956] Significantly, he built the string-test gig *Derwent Belle*, launched from his Battery Point yard on 1 October 1870.[957] The craft was built of Huon pine at a cost of £35 and in a time frame of six weeks specifically to race at the 1870 Intercolonial Balmain Regatta using money generated by subscription.[958] Described as *'one of the finest-looking racing boats ever built in the colony'*, the *Derwent Belle* measured 39ft overall with a beam of 3.2ft and a depth in midships of 1.2ft.[959] Weighing 180 pounds, it was intended to pull four sculls of 13ft in length and had five thwarts, double kneed.[960]

The *Derwent Belle* and its crew of amateurs, consisting of W. Abbott (stroke), I. Archer, H. E. Best, C. Gaylor, J. Hopwood (coxswain), and D. Lewis (emergency), arrived in Sydney from Hobart Town per the *City of Hobart* on 14 October 1870.[961] The vessel was then taken to the Sydney Rowing Club's boat house.[962] Notably, it was the only intercolonial contender to participate in the much-anticipated gig race. Though entrants from Victoria and Queensland had been expected to enter, neither colony sent a competitor.[963]

Held on 9 November 1870, the gig race at the Balmain Regatta generated much interest, the Tasmanian contingent in the *Derwent Belle* finishing a gallant second behind a team from the Sydney Rowing

---

[952] *The Mercury*, 8 November 1879.
[953] *The Mercury*, 28 May 1883.
[954] *The Mercury*, 28 May 1883; 16 June 1884; *Launceston Examiner*, 19 June 1884.
[955] *Tasmanian News*, 23 April 1884.
[956] *The Ballarat Star*, 23 November 1870; *The Cornwall Chronicle*, 25 January 1871; *The Mercury*, 4 November 1871, 9 November 1875.
[957] *The Mercury*, 1 October 1870.
[958] *The Mercury*, 16, 27 August 1870.
[959] *The Mercury*, 1 October 1870; *The Tasmanian Times*, 3 October 1870.
[960] *The Tasmanian Times*, 3 October 1870.
[961] *The Mercury*, 22 October 1870.
[962] *The Tasmanian Times*, 22 October 1870.
[963] *The Tasmanian Times*, 3 December 1870.

Club.[964] While the vessel had been highly credited by the Tasmanian press, the Sydney-based press reported otherwise, as well as publicly admonished the host organisation, the Sydney Rowing Club. *'That they have not obtained first place is certainly owing to no fault of theirs, for they had almost insurmountable obstacles to contend against. Comparative strangers to the water and the set of the currents, and practicing in a boat much too heavy and otherwise ill adapted - a boat which is described as "a nice thing to look at, but possessing certain peculiarities of construction, of which, though some may be advantageous, others are the reverse. In the first place she has rather a flat, as well as a great length of floor, which is a desideratum in carrying a heavy crew. In the next place she is very narrow, and the men have to row short oars, which accounts for their rapid rowing - thirty-eight to forty strokes per minute. She is high wooded forward and aft; her timbers are very thin. When looking into the midships she appears something like an elongated prawn-basket. Her worst fault, however, appears to be weakness, and when travelling through rough water her vibration is something alarming." After practicing for some time in this boat the crew found that she was too weak, and one day when the Dandenong steamer was steaming up to the harbour she passed close to the Derwent Belle, and her waves broke over the boat straining and otherwise damaging it. This rendered it necessary to place her in a boat builder's hands to be repaired and strengthened. This work, which was entrusted to Mr. Dunn, of Lavendar Bay, occupied a week, during which time several improvements were effected. A stringer was fitted in flush with the gunwale; also a bulkhead at each end of the box, and the craft otherwise strengthened with stays, and fitted with a new cover, the alterations adding, as a matter of course, to the weight of the boat. While the boat was under alteration, the crew were left without a suitable boat for practice, for, though they applied to the Sydney Rowing Club for the use of a boat, they only obtained the use of a tub gig, which the Town and Country Journal says, "was quite unsuited to the requirements of the men," and, as a consequence, they had to suspend their training till they regained possession of their own boat. Such is not the treatment that we should have anticipated from the oarsmen of New South Wales to stranger rivals whom they had "dared to the encounter," and to whom, one would have thought, they would have willingly accorded any favor that lay in their power, more especially as their acquaintance with the course, the water, and its currents, gave them a decided advantage of their rivals. ... The result of the contest has, however, been highly creditable to Tasmanian pluck under the circumstances; and it is a result of which Tasmanians may well be proud.'*[965] It is interesting to state that despite all of the criticism levelled at the *Derwent Belle*, it only lost by half a boat length to the winning team from the Sydney Rowing Club. A crew from the *Osprey* finished third, a crew from the *Adelphi* fourth, and a crew from Woolloomooloo fifth.[966]

The *Derwent Belle* and its crew returned back at Hobart Town a few weeks after the race.[967] Raffled off early in the following year and renamed *Fireflash*, the boat went on to enjoy great success on local and regional waters for a number of years, including winning the Ladies' Purse at the 1871 Hobart Town Regatta.[968] A few weeks later, it near-effortlessly won the Ladies' Purse Race at the Tamar Regatta.[969]

In January 1872 another intercolonial gig race was organised to be held on the River Derwent in conjunction with the Hobart Town Regatta. The event featured entrants from the Barwon Rowing Club in Geelong, Victoria; the Sydney Rowing Club; a crew from the Parramatta River (Sydney); and two local crews, pulling in the *Fireflash* and a new vessel, respectively.[970] Chandler was again tasked with building the new gig specifically for the event. His boat yard was additionally used to store the visiting boats.[971]

The New South Wales gigs were both built of Kauri pine by George Green of Sydney and measured 42.8ft in length. In comparison, Chandler's new gig, named *Satanella*, was similar to the *Fireflash* in design, though measured much longer, at 45ft, and was constructed of Macquarie pine.[972] The vessel was also more than 50lbs heavier than the visiting Sydney gigs, weighing 170lbs, though still 10lbs lighter than the *Fireflash*.[973]

Dubbed *'the most interesting race ever rowed in the Australias'*, and vying for a purse of £100, the Intercolonial Champion Gig Race was held on 20 January 1872. It generated a great deal of interest not only in Tasmania, but in New South Wales and Victoria, as well as from eager shore-side punters hoping to make a speculative profit.[974] The race, over a distance of five-miles, was competitive, with the crew from the Sydney Rowing Club finishing first, just under a minute from the Parramatta River crew.[975] The two local teams in the *Fireflash* and *Santanella* finished third and fourth, respectively.

During the 1870s Jacob Chandler also built many smaller boats for local, regional and mainland commercial customers, including for Hobart Town's watermen.[976] However, the potential profitability of the transport of goods, produce and timber from ports in the Huon, D'Entrecasteaux Channel, and Ralphs Bay to Hobart Town, saw him pivot to another lucrative market—the local river trade. Vessels he launched

---

[964] *The Mercury*, 11 November 1870.
[965] *The Mercury*, 11 November 1870.
[966] *The Mercury*, 11 November 1870; *Evening News*, 10 November 1870.
[967] *The Mercury*, 21 November 1870.
[968] *The Mercury*, 13 January 1871, 2 November 1871; *Launceston Examiner*, 7 February 1871.
[969] *The Mercury*, 3 February 1871; *Launceston Examiner*, 9 February 1871.
[970] *The Mercury*, 17 January 1872.
[971] *The Mercury*, 13 January 1872.
[972] *The Mercury*, 13 January 1872.
[973] *The Mercury*, 13 January 1872.
[974] *The Mercury*, 31 January 1872.
[975] *The Mercury*, 31 January 1872.
[976] *The Mercury*, 10 March, 17 November 1870, 20 April 1871, 20 April, 7 September, 11 October, 5 November 1872, 7 October, 14 November 1873, 1 February, 9 June, 11 September 1875, 5 September 1876, 17 October 1877, 1 April, 27 May, 23 October 1878; *The Tasmanian Times*, 20 April 1870; *The Cornwall Chronicle*, 10 March 1871; *The Tasmanian Tribune*, 20 April, 4 May 1875, 29 July 1876; *Tribune*, 1 April 1878; *The Ballarat Star*, 23 November 1870.

for this use included the *Edith Ellen*, built in 1871 for Thomas Young of Bruny Island; the *Pearl*, built in 1872 for Donald McKay of the D'Entrecasteaux Channel; the *Henrietta Elizabeth*, completed in 1874 to the order of Captain John Chamberlain; the *Emerald Isle*, built in 1874 for Thomas Doherty specifically for transporting timber from Port Davey to Hobart Town; the *Crystal Wave*, built in 1874 for William Hughes of Oyster Cove; the *Lurline*, built in 1874 for W. H. Yeoland of Long Bay (now Middleton); an un-named 60ft ketch first noted to be under construction in 1875 and slowly advancing towards completion the following year; the *Forget-Me-Not* (built in 1876) and the *Gertrude Lucy* (built in 1879), both to commissioned by the Calvert family of South Arm; and the *Annie Ward*, launched in 1879 for Robert Langdale of North West Bay.[977]

As well as the river trade, during the 1870s Tasmania's coastal and deep-sea fishing industries developed resulting in more orders for Chandler. The first fishing boat he built this decade was the *Edward and Joseph*, launched in 1871.[978] It was followed by the *Spray*, launched late in 1873 for Robert Sangwell of Sandy Bay; a 35ft partly-decked vessel built for a Mr King, and a 41ft Huon pine fishing smack built for Alfred Easther, both launched in 1874; and the *Grace Darling*, built for Thomas Atkins and launched early in 1875.[979] On 26 May 1877 Chandler launched the 47ft deep-sea ketch-rigged fishing smack *Rachel Thompson*, built to the order of Llewellyn (Louis) Jones, and intended to ply between the east coast of Tasmania and the Bass Strait fishing grounds.[980] The vessel was fitted with a well 13ft in length, capable of holding a large number of fish without crowding them.[981] It was also one of the first decked fishing boats built in Tasmania, going on to revolutionise not only the deep-sea fishing industry but also the how fishing boats were constructed. After 45 years of service, the *Rachel Thompson* was ultimately wrecked on Victoria Rocks, Eddystone Point, in Tasmania's north-east coast in July 1922, all hands saved.[982]

Continuing a family tradition, the mid-1870s saw Jacob Chandler's son John establish a boat yard in partnership with J. Doig at Hobart Town's New Wharf, very likely on the property that Chandler had purchased in 1855.

[977] *The Mercury*, 13 July 1871, 2 December 1873, 2 March, 27 April, 8 May, 23 July, 26 August, 11 September, 18 November 1874, 25 January, 20 August 1879; *The Tasmanian Tribune*, 8 May 1874, 4, 18 May, 29 July 1876.
[978] *The Mercury*, 18 August 1880.
[979] *The Mercury*, 7 October, 4 November, 2, 23 December 1873, 22 January, 4 May, 22 June, 11 July, 23 July 1874, 1 February 1875; *The Tasmanian Tribune*, 9 January 1875.
[980] *The Mercury*, 1 January 1877, 28 May 1877.
[981] *The Mercury*, 1 January 1877.
[982] *The Mercury*, 20 July 1922.

Rachel Thompson at Hobart.
Courtesy Tasmanian Archives (PH40/1/1684).

Waterman's boat *Orlando* at Watermans Dock, Hobart. Courtesy Tasmanian Archives (NS73/1/1/7).

Here the duo built a 26ft sailing boat, constructed of Huon pine, that was launched in early January 1875.[983] In describing the craft, the press noted that it had been built during evenings and weekends, perhaps indicating that John Chandler remained employed at his father's boat yard during the day.[984] Jacob Chandler also looked to further develop his Battery Point yard during this period. In April 1875 he was noted as extending his workshop further up the bank and making preparations for construction of a boat slip.[985]

Unfortunately the prosperous economic times of the 1870s did not last through the following decades. As such there were sharp decreases in the number of new vessels commissioned, and the downturn hit Jacob Chandler's business accordingly. Apart from the steam ferry *Victory* which he constructed for O'May Brothers, only 19 boats have been identified as being built by him in the 1880s. These included five whaleboats; four pleasure boats; three passage boats (i.e., the *Lenna* for Donald McKay and the *Seacroft* for Robert Calvert); the waterman's boat *Aquilla*; the dinghy *Royalist* for the O'May family; and the fishing boat *Maggie Read*, built to the order of Moses Barnett.[986] He is also stated to have built, towards the latter part of the decade, a ketch of around 20 tons, name unknown; a 15-ton passage boat measuring 42ft in length; and a small fishing boat.[987] Another vessel constructed at Chandler's yard in 1889 was the small steam launch *Sandfly*, built to the order of J. T. Read of Sandy Bay.[988] In addition, the yard continued to be active in repair, refit and overhaul work throughout this decade. To help augment a likely diminished income, however, Jacob Chandler sold off the remaining three acre parcel of land he owned at Bellerive in 1886 to Georgina Featherstone for £80 upon with Wirksworth House built a few years later.[989] He also mortgaged his boat yard at Battery Point to the Bank of Van Diemen's Land for £1,000, as well as sold his property located at the New Wharf, though by this time it too was also heavily mortgaged.[990]

---

[983] *The Tasmanian Tribune*, 19 January 1875; *The Mercury*, 28 January 1875.
[984] *The Tasmanian Tribune*, 19 January 1875; *The Mercury*, 28 January 1875.
[985] *The Tasmanian Tribune*, 20 April 1875.
[986] *The Mercury*, 26 June, 1 September, 5 October, 30 November 1880, 30 April, 1 June 1881, 21 December 1885, 18 May 1886;
Tasmanian News, 16 November 1885, 20 August 1887, 24 January, 1, 6 November 1888;
Daily Telegraph, 24 October 1889;
The Weekly Courier, 2 May 1903.
[987] *Tasmanian News*, 24 January, 6 November 1888.
[988] *Tasmanian News*, 26 February 1889; *The Mercury*, 21 October, 1 November 1890.
[989] www.thelist.tas.gov.au (Historical Deed 07/6930); www.easternshoresun.com.au/history-corner-wirksworth-house-howrah.
[990] www.thelist.tas.gov.au (Historical Deed 07/1722 and 08/5472).

Nellie.
Courtesy Maritime Museum of Tasmania (P_GSL305).

In the early 1890s at least one dinghy, one whaleboat and six pleasure boats were built by Chandler, as well as the waterman's boats *Orlando*, *Starling* and *Ringdove*.[991] Continuing to undertake repair work, in late 1893 he was also noted as altering the steam launch *Sandfly*, which he had built in 1889, for its new owner J. Cook of Glenorchy.[992] The vessel was cut in half with an additional 13ft added to its length. New engines by Tangye were also installed. It was subsequently renamed *Tasma*.[993] However, the depression of this decade affected Jacob Chandler greatly and several more mortgages were taken out on his boat yard, including one for £500 borrowed from Maud Montgomery, wife of Henry Montgomery, the fourth Anglican Bishop of Tasmania.[994] Now in his 70s, Chandler was also likely slowing down for health reasons.

In 1894 Chandler completed what would be one of his last vessels — the ketch *Nellie*. The 18-ton Huon pine craft was built to the order of Messrs Risby Bros. and launched on 8 September of that year.[995] Intended for the coastal trade, it was advertised for sale a week after launch and subsequently chartered by W. T. Grubb, secretary of the Derwent Sailing Club, for use as a yacht.[996] Advertised for sale less than a year later, the *Nellie* was later involved in the D'Entrecasteux Channel trade.[997] It was ultimately wrecked off Robbins Island with the drowning of 98 sheep in late August 1919.[998] At the time of loss, it was owned by Luke Williams of the Copper Reward Company's of Balfour and employed on Tasmania's north-west coast.[999]

Despite his increasing age, Jacob Chandler continued to build smaller boats, including by tender, in the mid-to-late 1890s.[1000] In April 1899, by now aged 77, he launched what is considered to be the last vessel he is known to have constructed.[1001] The 41ft Huon pine fishing boat *Ruby Louise* was built to the order of George Clarke.[1002] Shortly following, Chandler appears to have entered semi-retirement with his son, John, taking over some of the workload.[1003]

---

[991] *The Mercury*, 4 April, 13 May 1890, 20 January, 8 April 1891, 27 October 1892; *Tasmanian News*, 31 May 1890, 15 January 1891, 3 October 1891.
[992] *The Mercury*, 12 September 1893.
[993] *Tasmanian News*, 24 January 1894.
[994] www.thelist.tas.gov.au (Historical Deed 09197).
[995] *Tasmanian News*, 10 September 1894; *The Mercury*, 11 September 1894.
[996] *The Mercury*, 15 September 1894; *Tasmanian News*, 16 October 1894; *The Clipper*, 20 October 1894.
[997] *Launceston Examiner*, 2 August 1895; *The Mercury*, 2 August 1918.
[998] *World*, 28 August 1919.
[999] *The Mercury*, 2 August 1918.
[1000] *Tasmanian News*, 29 November 1895, 7 April 1898.
[1001] *Tasmanian News*, 23 March, 25 April 1899.
[1002] *Tasmanian News*, 23 March, 25 April 1899.
[1003] *Daily Post*, 22 July 1910.

Jacob Bayly Chandler died at the age of 79 on 17 September 1901 at the Charitable Institution, New Town.[1004] He was buried at Queenborough Cemetery, Sandy Bay.[1005] The Launceston press reported on the news and his life in detail. '*There passed away the other day a very old aquatic identity. Jacob B. Chandler first saw the light of day in an English seaport town, when George the Third was King. Fifty years ago he was one of the best known boat builders down south, and his yards at Battery Point was the chief resort of rowing men long before rowing clubs were established, or even thought of. Jacob 40 years since built the racing gigs of the time, and pulling one of Chandler's boats meant victory nine times out of ten for the crew that hired them. The gigs of the period one is speaking about, were not the racing shells now in use. They ranged from 40ft to 45ft in length, and were high-wooded and stoutly built enough to resist a sea, and to propel them over a four-mile course involved considerable labor, and a large expenditure of wind and muscle. When the Whitehouses and Macquarie entered the arena of gig building Jacob retired from the field of racing boat construction, and took up the work of laying down fishing boats. The subject of this notice was a shrewd business-like dapper little fellow, as tough as pin wire, and his frugality enabled him to acquire a decent amount of property. The decadence of the whaling trade and competition caused evil days to visit the house of Chandler, and Jacob's little bit of hard-earned real estate melted away under the influence of mortgagees and high rates of interest like snow before sunshine, and he topped his boom dependant almost on strangers for subsistence. A few kind souls who knew him in better days did their best to make his fading days bearable. At 85 [he was in fact 79] one outlives the friends of his young days. The was exactly the case of old Jacob Chandler.*'[1006]

Chandler was survived by his daughter Emma Selina and son John Thomas. His youngest daughter Marian Ellen had died on 18 September 1874 at the age of 20 years from consumption.[1007] Chandler died intestate, leaving assets worth £188 and debts of £500.[1008] His remaining property at Bellerive was seized by virtue of a writ of Fieri Facias a month later, as was a life insurance policy valued at £500.[1009]

In the years immediately following his death, Chandler's boat yard was leased, likely under direction of his children, with H. S. Kerr laying down a slip and erecting a jetty at the property in late 1901.[1010] Subsequent to the death of his daughter Emma Selina in late 1907 (John Thomas Chandler died three years later), Chandler's Battery Point boat yard was sold at auction in November 1908.[1011] The property was later purchased by Thomas Purdon (of Purdon and Featherstone) and used by him and members of his family as a boat yard for several decades.[1012]

A determined boat builder, risk-taker, ardent competitor, and entrepreneur, Jacob Chandler is remembered as one of Tasmania's premier boat builders, and also one of the longest serving at Battery Point.

[1004] Tasmanian Federation Index - Deaths 1900-1930; *The Mercury*, 18 September 1901.
[1005] *The Mercury*, 18 September 1901.
[1006] *Daily Telegraph*, 28 September 1901.
[1007] *The Mercury*, 19 September 1874.
[1008] Tasmanian Archives (SC389/1/211).
[1009] *The Mercury*, 21 October 1901.
[1010] *The Mercury*, 14 November 1901.
[1011] Tasmanian Federation Index - Deaths 1900-1930; *The Mercury*, 5 November 1908.
[1012] www.thelist.tas.gov.au (Historical Deed 13/1008).

The Mercury, 3 November 1908.

Jacob Chandler's Battery Point boat yard (c1890s). Courtesy Tasmanian Archives (PH30/1/2065).

Vessels built by Jacob Chandler and employees at Battery Point (1847 - 1899)

Year	Name	Type	Description
1847	Hippolyta	Gig	Four-oared gig built by Jacob Chandler to compete at the 1847 Hobart Town Regatta. Finished first in the amateur gig race with Chandler as coxswain.
1847	Lady Denison	Whaleboat	Five-oared whaleboat built by Jacob Chandler to compete at the 1847 Hobart Town Regatta. Finished first in the native youths' race and second in the race for the Tasman Prize.
1848	Pearl	Whaleboat	Four-oared whaleboat built by Jacob Chandler. Won a race on the River Derwent in April 1848.
1848	--	Boat	Built by Jacob Chandler to the order of the Government of Van Diemen's Land with payment provided in October 1838.
1848	--	Boat	Built by Jacob Chandler to the order of the Government of Van Diemen's Land with payment provided in October 1838.
1848	Rose	Whaleboat	Four-oared whaleboat built by Jacob Chandler that won a private race held on the River Derwent in November 1848 against Joseph Risby's *Odd Fellow*.
1849	Sea Gull	Wherry	Carvel constructed wherry built by Jacob Chandler to compete at the 1850 Sandy Bay Regatta, held on 1 January of that year. Raffled off a few months prior with Alexander Orr the winner.
1849	Pirate	Whaleboat	Four-oared whaleboat built by Jacob Chandler to compete at the 1849 Hobart Town Regatta.
1850s	--	Whaleboat	Five-oared whaleboat built by Jacob Chandler likely in the early 1850s and offered for sale at auction by W. A. Guesdon in May 1854 having 'recently undergone a thorough repair by Chandler, and is now in first-rate order, and nearly equal to a new boat'.
1851	Columbia	Waterman's boat	Built by Jacob Chandler to the order of Thomas Tandy, waterman of Hobart Town, and launched in August 1851. At the time of completion, noted to be the 183rd licenced boat plying at trade at the Hobart Town wharf. Transferred to Geelong, Victoria, by its owner and advertised for sale there in January 1852.
1851	Runnymede	Whaleboat	Four-oared whaleboat built by Jacob Chandler to the order of James Weir specifically to compete in the native youths race at the 1851 Hobart Town Regatta.
1853	--	Whaleboat	A 'first-class' whaleboat built by Jacob Chandler, complete with oars and sail, awarded to the winner of the licenced waterman's race held as part of the Williamstown Regatta in January 1854. Shipped to Melbourne in late 1853 at the request of Lewis Michell of the Ship Inn, Williamstown.
1853	Fairy	Schooner	52.6 x 12.0 x 16.1ft. ON 32089. 35 tons. Built by Jacob Chandler for his own use and initially involved in the Macquarie Harbour timber trade. Advertised for sale in January 1855 and sold to James Baynton of Hobart Town. First registered on 6 March 1855 and placed in the Tasmanian coastal trade. Sold to George Perriman of Hobart Town in November 1860. Just under two years later sold to William Spode of Brisbane and transferred to Queensland. Subsequent owners included Edward Saunder and Henry Lander Pethridge. Departed Mackay for Maryborough on 12 January 1874 and was not heard from again.
1854	--	Whaleboat	33ft. Four-oared, copper-fastened whaleboat built by Jacob Chandler in early 1854 and raffled off at the Victoria Tavern in November of that year with 25 subscribers paying £2 per ticket.
1854	Scottish Chief ex Breeze	Whaleboat	25ft. Four-oared whaleboat built by Jacob Chandler, originally named *Breeze* Later purchased by the O'May Brothers and renamed *Scottish Chief*. Part of the fleet that helped establish their trans-Derwent ferry company.
1854	--	Whaleboat	Built by Jacob Chandler and sold to Charles Manser late in 1854 for £40. He then became insolvent in mid-1855. Purchased by a Mr Wrathall just prior to bankruptcy proceedings.
1855	--	Pleasure boat	Square-sterned pleasure boat built by Jacob Chandler. Advertised for sale by auction in early January 1856, complete with oars and sails.
1855	Star	Gig	Four-oared gig built by Jacob Chandler to compete at the 1856 Tamar Regatta, held in January of that year. Owned by M. L. Goodwin and helmed by J. Taylor, finished third in the race for the Mayor & Aldermen's Purse.
1857	--	Whaleboat	Built by Jacob Chandler and advertised for sale at Hobart in November 1857. Fitted with a well for fishing.
1857	--	Whaleboat	Built by Jacob Chandler to compete at the 1857 Hobart Town Regatta, held on 3 December of that year.
1857	Tasman	Sailing boat	Built by Jacob Chandler and noted for sale by private contract at Geelong, Victoria, in February 1859. Stated to be 16 months old and for sale complete with oars, sails, etc.
1859	Sea Gull ex Vindictive	Cutter yacht	43.9 x 13.4 x 5ft. ON 32085. 19 tons. Possibly built by Jacob Chandler and involved in the D'Entrecasteaux Channel trade before advertised for sale in August 1859. By December 1859 purchased by Peter Oldham to compete with the Tasmanian Yacht Club and renamed *Sea Gull*. First registered in January 1860. Advertised for sale in February 1861 as part of Oldham's insolvent estate. Temporarily transferred to Charles Colvin and J. E. Risby (executors) and placed in the local timber and coal trade. Later involved in deep-sea fishing. In September 1867 sold to William Ferguson and a year later to Andrew Brown. In March 1871 sold to Francis Evans and transferred to Melbourne. Wrecked in July 1871 off the Yassawa Group, Fiji.

Year	Name	Type	Description
1859	Secret	Cutter yacht	37.3 x 12.1 x 7.6ft. ON 32084. 16 tons. Built by Jacob Chandler for his own use specifically to compete with the Tasmanian Yacht Club. Launched in December 1859 and won its first race, held in mid-January 1860, becoming a competitive sailing vessel on the Derwent. In July 1862 chartered to W. Luttrell and employed in the Channel timber trade. In June 1864 sold to John Ellis, timber merchant of Launceston, for £275. Spent the next few years trading between Hobart and Launceston. In April 1865 sold to Robert Woolnough and Thomas Pickhaver of the South Australian pilot service for £325. Several further changes of ownership, though remained in South Australian waters. Wrecked on 20 July 1873 five miles north of Point Boilingbrooke, all hands saved. At the time owned by John Watherstone of Port Lincoln.
1860	Emily Ellen	Schooner	35.4 x 8.8 x 4.0ft. ON 32086. 7 tons. Built by Jacob Chandler to the order of John Austin of Port Albert, Victoria, sailing out of Hobart Town for its new home port on 2 March 1860. Well-adapted to the Gippsland Lakes trade, it was advertised for sale in July 1861 for £60 and sold to George Evans of Lucknow to ply between Bairnsdale and Port Albert. Sunk off French Island in October 1862 having sprung a leak on a previous voyage.
1860	–	Whaleboat	Five-oared whaleboat built by Jacob Chandler and helmed by J. Hopwood. Finished first in the race for the Derwent Prize at the 1861 New Norfolk Regatta, held on 2 January of that year.
1861	–	Whaleboat	Five-oared whaleboat built by Jacob Chandler for the whaling barque Offley. Painted green with a white nose. Advertised as lost or stolen in October 1861 from Hobart Town, complete with oars, sail, boat hook, irons, lances and other gear.
1861	Peter and James	Passage boat	6 tons. Built by Jacob Chandler and first noted as carrying firewood between South Arm and Hobart Town in July of 1861. Advertised for sale by auction in August 1865, though failed to sell. Remained in the South Arm firewood trade, most likely owned by John Potter. Disappears from reports of coastal vessels after December 1879.
1861	Shelahlah	Whaleboat	Four-oared whaleboat built by Jacob Chandler to compete in the race for native youths at the 1861 Hobart Town Regatta.
1861	–	Whaleboat	Built by Jacob Chandler as part of the Tasmanian Timber and Whaling Trophy that was sent to London and exhibited at the 1862 International Exhibition.
1862	Picnic	Waterman's boat	25 x 6ft. Built by Jacob Chandler to the order of Charles Dillon, waterman of Hobart Town. Last licenced in 1890 to carry up to 13 people. Not renewed in 1894.
1860s	–	Loading boat	20ft. Four-oared loading boat built by Jacob Chandler. Advertised as lost or stolen from his Battery Point boat yard in October 1862.
1862	–	Whaleboat	Four-oared whaleboat built by Jacob Chandler for a customer located at Lyttelton, New Zealand, for use in local races and regattas. Sent to Lyttelton in November 1862 via the brig Lady Denison.
1862	Morning Light	Whaleboat	Four-oared whaleboat built by Jacob Chandler to compete in the race for the Ladies' Purse at the 1863 Port Cygnet Regatta where it finished first with George Whitehouse at the helm.
1863	–	Whaleboat	31ft. Four-oared, gig-style whaleboat built by Jacob Chandler for a Mr Fisher of Dunedin, New Zealand, for use in local races and regattas. Sent to New Zealand in September 1863 via the barque Bella Vista.
1863	–	Whaleboat	Four-oared whaleboat built by Jacob Chandler and advertised for sale at Dunedin, New Zealand, in late April 1863 by George Perriman who was agent for the brig Pryde that sailed from Hobart the previous month with a large cargo.
1863	Prince of Wales	Skiff	<18ft. Built by Jacob Chandler to the order of J. Smart compete in the race for the Alexandra Prize at the 1863 Hobart Town Regatta where it finished second, helmed by C. Gaylor.
1863	Perseverance	Waterman's boat	25 x 5ft. Built by Jacob Chandler to the order of the O'May Brothers, watermen of Hobart Town. Involved in a fatal accident in November 1875 whereby six persons were drowned in the River Derwent. Drifted ashore and broke up near South Arm.
1863	Star of Tasmania	Waterman's boat	24.6 x 5.0 x 1.7ft. Built by Jacob Chandler to the order of the O'May Brothers, watermen of Hobart Town. Utilised on the River Derwent as a licenced vessel up until at least 1882.
1864	–	Waterman's boat	Built by Jacob Chandler's apprentice George Whitehouse to the order of Charles Dillon, Hobart Town waterman.
1864	Commodore	Waterman's boat	27 x 6ft. Built by Jacob Chandler to the order of William Weir, waterman of Hobart Town. Fitted with a square stern and high gunwales with brass furniture throughout. Copper-fastened.
1864	–	Whaleboat	Built by Jacob Chandler for use on board Dr Crowther's whaling barque Offley as part of the Wreck Reef guano trade.
1864	–	Whaleboat	Built by Jacob Chandler for use on board Dr Crowther's whaling barque Offley as part of the Wreck Reef guano trade.
1864	–	Whaleboat	Built by Jacob Chandler of Macquarie pine to compete at the 1864 Hobart Town Regatta.
1864	–	Skiff	Single-handed skiff built by Jacob Chandler's foreman George Hubbard after hours for his father Thomas Hubbard, waterman of Hobart Town.
1864	Lady Bird (?)	Skiff	Single-handed skiff built by Jacob Chandler's foreman George Hubbard after hours specifically for racing.

Year	Name	Type	Description
1864	–	Whaleboat	Four-oared whaleboat built by Jacob Chandler of Macquarie pine to compete at the 1864 Hobart Town Regatta.
1864	–	Whaleboat	25ft. Four-oared whaleboat built by Jacob Chandler to the order of John Godfrey to compete at the 1864 Hobart Town Regatta.
1864	–	Whaleboat	33ft. Five-oared whaleboat built by Jacob Chandler to the order of Messrs Willis and Perry to compete at the 1864 Hobart Town Regatta.
1864	–	Whaleboat	25ft. Four-oared whaleboat built by Jacob Chandler to the order of William Weir to compete at the 1864 Hobart Town Regatta.
1864	*Paul Pry*	Whaleboat	Four-oared whaleboat built by Jacob Chandler to compete at the 1864 Hobart Town Regatta. Finished second in the race for the Ladies' Purse, helmed by A. Bock.
1865	–	Lifeboat	35 x 6 x 2.2ft. Flat-bottomed lifeboat built by Jacob Chandler of Macquarie pine and copper-fastened throughout. Fitted with a water-tight locker forward for holding mail. Pulled sever oars and carried two sails and a jib. Conveyed to Nelson, New Zealand, in October 1865 via the *Annie*.
1865	–	Pleasure boat	25 x 5.4 x 2ft. Square-sterned pleasure boat built by Jacob Chandler of Macquarie pine and copper-fastened throughout. Fitted with four oars and made to carry a sail and jib. Built to the order of John Meredith of Swansea.
1865	*Vision*	Skiff	18 x 2.2ft. Built by Jacob Chandler to compete for the Mayor's Cup and Amateur Scullers' Race at the 1865 Hobart Town Regatta. Won the skiff race, pulled by Abbott. Was pulled by Lynch in the 1866 Hobart Town Regatta, and then Abbott in the race for Alexandra Prize.
1865	–	Whaleboat	25 x 4ft. Four-oared whaleboat built by Jacob Chandler to compete for the Youths' Race and the amateurs pulling in four-oared whaleboats at the 1865 Hobart Town Regatta.
1865	–	Skiff	18 x 3.2ft. Two-oared skiff built by Jacob Chandler to compete at the 1865 Hobart Town Regatta in the race for two youths and a steerer all under 16 years of age.
1865	*Sir John Franklin* (?)	Whaleboat	Five-oared whaleboat built by Jacob Chandler to compete for the Tasman Prize at the 1865 Hobart Town Regatta, its crew being from the Huon region. Finished first in the event.
1866	–	Whaleboat	33ft. Built by Jacob Chandler and transferred to New Zealand by the captain of the *Glencoe* in November of 1866. Subsequently purchased by W. Goldie of Careys Bay.
1866	–	Whaleboat	Four-oared Huon pine whaleboat built by Jacob Chandler in mid-1866 for display at the Intercolonial Exhibition of Australasia, held in Melbourne 24 October 1866 to 23 February 1867.
1866	–	Whaleboat	Four-oared whaleboat built by Jacob Chandler by tender for the Government of Tasmania's Board of Stores. Constructed of Macquarie Harbour pine and built as a cost of £20.
1866	*Hope*	Cutter	39.0 x 12.5 x 5.2ft. ON 32153. 11 tons. Built by Jacob Chandler to the order of Captain James Black of Hokitika. Sailed to New Zealand to be involved in the coastal trade, leaving Hobart Town in October 1866. First registered in Auckland in November 1870 upon being sold to P. H. White. Supposedly lost on a voyage to Fiji a month later.
1866	–	Whaleboat	Five-oared whaleboat built by Jacob Chandler and transferred to New Zealand by the schooner *Isabella* in November 1866. Intended for regatta racing and afterwards to be used in the transfer passengers across the inside surf at Hokitika.
1866	–	Wherry	Built by Jacob Chandler and transferred to New Zealand by the schooner *Isabella* in November 1866. Intended for pleasure purposes at Hokitika.
1866	–	Whaleboat	32.5 x 5.1 x 2ft. Five-oared whaleboat built by Jacob Chandler to compete for the Tasman Prize at the 1866 Hobart Town Regatta, its crew being from the Huon region.
1866	–	Whaleboat	25 x 4ft x 20in. Four-oared whaleboat built by Jacob Chandler to compete in the native youths race, as well as the race for general amateurs at the 1866 Hobart Town Regatta.
1866	–	Skiff	18 x 3.5ft x 20in. Two-oared skiff built by Jacob Chandler to compete at the 1866 Hobart Town Regatta in the race for two youths and a steerer all under 16 years of age.
1866	–	Whaleboat	25 x 4.3ft x 20in. Four-oared whaleboat built by Jacob Chandler to the order of Charles Dillon specifically to compete in the native youths race, as well as the race for general amateurs at the 1866 Hobart Town Regatta.
1867	–	Whaleboat	One of two whaleboats built by Jacob Chandler and transferred to Lyttelton, New Zealand, on board the barque *Crishna* in May of 1867.
1867	–	Whaleboat	Second of two whaleboats built by Jacob Chandler and transferred to Lyttelton, New Zealand, on board the barque *Crishna* in May of 1867.
1867	–	Whaleboat	One of at least two whaleboats built by Jacob Chandler for use on board the barque *Planter* in June of 1867.
1867	–	Whaleboat	Second of at least two whaleboats built by Jacob Chandler for use on board the barque *Planter* in June of 1867.
1867	–	Whaleboat	25 x 4ft x 20in. First of two four-oared whaleboat built by Jacob Chandler specifically to compete in the native youths race at the 1867 Hobart Town Regatta, to be pulled by Jacob's son John Chandler.

Year	Name	Type	Description
1867	--	Whaleboat	25 x 4ft x 20in. Second of two four-oared whaleboat built by Jacob Chandler specifically to compete in the native youths race at the 1867 Hobart Town Regatta, to be pulled by a crew from the Huon.
1867	Galatea (?)	Whaleboat	33.7 x 4ft. Four-oared whaleboat built by Jacob Chandler of Huon pine for J. O'Boyle specifically to compete in the race for the Ladies' Purse at the 1867 Hobart Town Regatta.
1867	--	Whaleboat	First of two four-oared whaleboat built by Jacob Chandler specifically to compete in the race for general amateurs at the 1867 Hobart Town Regatta, manned by the Lynch brothers.
1867	--	Whaleboat	Second of two four-oared whaleboat built by Jacob Chandler specifically to in the race for general amateurs at the 1867 Hobart Town Regatta.
1867	--	Whaleboat	32 x 5.2 x 2ft. First of two five-oared whaleboat built by Jacob Chandler to compete for the Tasman Prize at the 1867 Hobart Town Regatta, to be pulled by a crew from the Huon region.
1867	--	Whaleboat	32 x 5.2 x 2ft. Second of two five-oared whaleboat built by Jacob Chandler to compete for the Tasman Prize at the 1867 Hobart Town Regatta, to be pulled by a crew from Sorell.
1868	--	Skiff	24 x 4.8 x 2.7ft. Four-oared skiff built by Jacob Chandler to the order of John Smart, waterman of Hobart Town. Intended for the local ferry trade.
1868	Eclipse	Fishing boat	40ft. Deep-sea fishing boat built by Jacob Chandler to the order of Henry Thompson of Hobart Town. Launched on 19 August 1868. Competed in the fishing boat race at the Hobart Town Regatta later that year. By mid-1873 very likely converted to a passage boat and owned by Tasman Young. On 30 April 1877 run down by the brig *Maid of Erin* and sunk off Crayfish Point on the River Derwent, all hands saved.
1868	Coquette	Whaleboat	33ft. Four-oared whaleboat built by Jacob Chandler specifically to compete in the race for the Ladies' Purse at the 1868 Hobart Town Regatta.
1868	Iris	Skiff	Skiff built by Jacob Chandler specifically to compete in the race for the Alexandra Prize at the 1868 Hobart Town Regatta.
1868	Fairy Queen	Dinghy	Built by Jacob Chandler specifically to compete in the race for dinghies at the 1868 Hobart Town Regatta.
1868	Earl of Kent	Whaleboat	Four-oared whaleboat built by Jacob Chandler specifically to compete in the native youths race at the 1868 Hobart Town Regatta, his son John one of the crew.
1868	Goodwill	Whaleboat	Four-oared whaleboat built by Jacob Chandler specifically to compete in the native youths race at the 1868 Hobart Town Regatta.
1868	Nil Desparandum	Skiff	Skiff built by Jacob Chandler specifically to compete at the 1868 Kangaroo Point Regatta. Competed for the Alexandra Prize at the 1869 Hobart Town Regatta, helmed by W. B. Jones.
1868	Eliza	Passage boat	36 x 7.2 x 3ft. 5 tons. Centreboard passage boat built by Jacob Chandler to the order of George Elwell of Oyster Cove. Launched on 3 December 1868. Involved in the Huon timber trade for a few years. Either then sold and renamed or possibly converted to a fishing smack.
1868	--	Whaleboat	Six-oared whaleboat built by Jacob Chandler for the whaling barque *Offley*. Constructed of Macquarie pine.
1869	--	Whaleboat	Built by Jacob Chandler for use on board the whaling barque *Velocity*.
1869	--	Whaleboat	Four-oared whaleboat built by Jacob Chandler for the ketch *Sea Gull*.
1869	--	Gig	35 x 3.5ft. Four-oared gig built by Jacob Chandler specifically to compete at the 1869 Hobart Town Regatta.
1869	Derwent Belle	Whaleboat	Four-oared whaleboat built by Jacob Chandler specifically to compete for the Ladies Purse at the 1869 Hobart Town Regatta. Finished first, crewed by W. Robinson, Richard Archer, Isaac Archer, Richard King and William Lucas.
1869	Louise	Schooner	55 x 13.5 x 5.8ft. ON 57523. 29 tons. Built by Jacob Chandler for his own use and employed in the Melbourne to Hobart trade, as well as conveying timber from Port Davey to Hobart Town. Sold in August 1874 to Captain James Carver and on-sold in January 1875 to his brother John Carver. Sold again in July 1875 to Joseph Coleman of Port Adelaide and its register transferred to South Australia. Employed in the 'gulf' trade. Stranded at Port Rickaby in November 1878 and subsequently wrecked during a gale, all hands saved.
1869	Faugh-a-Ballah	Skiff	Single-handed skiff built by Jacob Chandler's foreman George Hubbard. Raced by T. Shirley at the 1869 Hobart Town Regatta.
1870	--	Waterman's boat	Square-sterned skiff capable of accommodating 10 persons built by Jacob Chandler to the order of Mr Jacobs, waterman of Hobart Town.
1870	--	Whaleboat	First of two whaleboats built to the order of Messrs Fisher and Facy for use at their whaling station located at Wreck Reef, Bird Island, as part of efforts to collect and convey guano. Sent on board the brigantine *Annie* in April 1870.
1870	--	Whaleboat	Second of two whaleboats built to the order of Messrs Fisher and Facy for use at their whaling station located at Wreck Reef, Bird Island, as part of efforts to collect and convey guano. Sent on board the brigantine *Annie* in April 1870.

Year	Name	Type	Description
1870	Silver Queen ex Enterprise	Steam ferry	48.9 x 9.3 x 4.4ft. ON 119246. 8 tons. Screw launch built by Jacob Chandler to the order of O'May Brothers and launched on 10 September 1870. Fitted with 30 h.p. non-condensing engines. Became a pioneer of the trans-River Derwent ferry run, first entering service in October 1870. Advertised for sale in mid-1885 and again in early 1888. Sold to C. E. Featherstone in January 1890, extensively altered, converted to a steam yacht and renamed Silver Queen. Advertised for sale throughout 1893 and sold to Messrs Taylor and Stewart. Sold again in 1901 to James Paterson. Rebuilt in 1906 and first registered. Pre-1920 abandoned in New Town Bay where its wreck still lies.
1870	Fireflash ex Derwent Belle	Gig	39 x 3.2 x 1.2ft. Four-oared string-test gig built by Jacob Chandler specifically to compete at the 1870 Intercolonial Balmain Regatta where it finished second. Returned to Hobart Town, raffled off and renamed Fireflash. Won the Ladies' Purse at the 1871 Hobart Town Regatta. Continued to compete in local regattas in and around Hobart Town for many years.
1870	--	Whaleboat	First of two whaleboats noted under construction at Jacob Chandler's yard in November 1870.
1870	--	Whaleboat	Second of two whaleboats noted under construction at Jacob Chandler's yard in November 1870.
1870	--	Whaleboat	25ft. Four-oared Huon pine whaleboat built by Jacob Chandler and transferred to Melbourne in November 1870 on board the steamer Southern Cross. Built to the order of Messrs Gates and Sons of Ballarat. Intended for local regatta races on Lake Wendouree and fitted with a centreboard and fore-and-aft schooner rig.
1871	Violet	Whaleboat	Four-oared whaleboat built by Jacob Chandler specifically to compete for the Ladies' Purse at the 1871 Hobart Town Regatta, held in late January of that year.
1871	--	Whaleboat	26 x 4.2ft. Four-oared whaleboat built by Jacob Chandler to the order of Samuel Jacobs, Hobart Town waterman, and completed in March 1871. Intended for use as a pleasure boat.
1871	--	Whaleboat	First of two whaleboats noted to be under construction at Jacob Chandler's yard in April 1871.
1871	--	Whaleboat	Second of two whaleboats noted to be under construction at Jacob Chandler's yard in April 1871.
1871	Edith Ellen	Passage boat	40.5 x 8.5 x 3.5ft. 7 tons. Built by Jacob Chandler to the order of Thomas Young of Bruny Island for the local firewood trade. A regular competitor in the sailing races at the Hobart Town Regatta. By 1874 owned by Henry Denne, also of Bruny Island. Driven ashore near Kelly's Point during a gale in early May 1882 and broken up.
1871	Brisk	Waterman's boat	27 x 5.5ft. Built by Jacob Chandler to the order of Samuel Jacobs and launched in November 1871. Stated to seat 16 passengers comfortably.
1871	Satanella	Gig	45ft. Four-oared string-test gig built by Jacob Chandler specifically to compete in the Intercolonial Gig Race held at the 1871 Hobart Town Regatta in January of that year.
1871	Edward and Joseph	Fishing boat	Built by Jacob Chandler for an unknown client. In early 1877 temporarily involved in the local river trade, though returned to fishing a month or two later. Completely wrecked on 14 August 1880 at Schouten Passage, all hands saved. At the time of loss, owned by Joseph Barnett and rented to John Bolton.
1872	--	Whaleboat	Noted to be under construction at Jacob Chandler's yard in April 1872.
1872	Pearl	Passage boat	40 x 9 x 4ft. Built by Jacob Chandler to the order of Donald McKay of the D'Entrecasteaux Channel. First noted in May 1872 bringing firewood from Peppermint Bay to Hobart Town. Advertised for sale in March 1877 and sold to a Mr Peak of Davey Street. Completely wrecked on 12 August 1877 at Woodcutter's Point, Bruny Island, all hands saved.
1872	--	Whaleboat	Noted to be under construction at Jacob Chandler's yard in September 1872.
1872	Liffey	Waterman's boat	24 x 5ft x 20in. Built by Jacob Chandler to the order of Samuel Jacobs and launched in October 1872. Constructed of Huon pine.
1872	--	Whaleboat	Noted to be under construction at Jacob Chandler's yard in November 1872.
1873	Lady of the Lake	Waterman's boat	Four-oared centreboard waterman's boat built by Jacob Chandler to the order of James Weir and launched in October 1873. Constructed of Huon pine and intended for pleasure parties.
1873	Hero	Waterman's boat	Four-oared centreboard waterman's boat built by Jacob Chandler to the order of James Weir and launched in October 1873. Constructed of Huon pine and intended for pleasure parties.
1873	Renown	Skiff	Square-sterned skiff built by Jacob Chandler to the order of James Weir and launched in October 1873. Constructed of Huon pine and intended for pleasure parties.
1873	Spray	Fishing boat	42 x 10 x 4ft. Huon pine, deep-sea fishing boat fitted with a centreboard and well built by Jacob Chandler to the order of Robert Sangwell of Sandy Bay. Launched in December 1873. Used for deep-sea fishing vessel of the east coast until 1878 when contracted to transport mail between Hobart Town and Port Arthur. Returned to fishing in 1880. Sold to John Walsh of Lyttleton in April 1881. Forwarded to New Zealand as deck cargo on board the SS Rotomahana. Subsequent history not known.
1874	--	Fishing boat	33 x 7.5 x 3ft. Partly-decked deep-sea fishing boat built by Jacob Chandler to the order of a Mr King of Battery Point and launched in late January 1874. Constructed of Huon pine and capable of carrying 5 tons. No additional details known.

Year	Name	Type	Description
1874	--	Whaleboat	20 x 5ft x 21in. Four-oared whaleboat built by Jacob Chandler to the order of H. L. Crowther of Oyster Cove and completed in February 1874.
1874	*Evelyn* ex *Eveline* ex *Henrietta Elizabeth*	Passage boat	42 x 10 x 4ft. Built by Jacob Chandler to the order of Captain John Chamberlain and launched on 25 April 1874 (incorrectly named *Susan* in the press). Constructed of Huon pine and stated to have a carrying capacity of over 12 tons, as well as *'not unlike the Henrietta which sank a short time ago in the river'*. Sold in December 1874 to Messrs T. and J. Young of Battery Point to run between Barnes' Bay and Hobart Town, renamed *Eveline*. By the 1880s involved in the D'Entrecasteaux Channel trade, possibly owned by George Davis. From 1889 often referred to as *Evelyn* in the local press. Sold in September 1890 to Walter Leach. Possibly the fishing ketch *Evelyn* wrecked at Gabo Island in 1923.
1874	--	Fishing boat	41 x 8.5 x 3.2ft. Fishing boat built by Jacob Chandler to the order of Alfred Easther. Constructed of Huon pine and launched on 20 June 1874. No additional details known.
1874	*Emerald Isle*	Ketch	43 x 12 x 4ft. ON 57546. 13 tons. Clinker-constructed, Huon pine ketch built by Jacob Chandler to the order of Thomas Doherty of Port Davey specifically to transport timber to Hobart Town. Launched in August 1874. Many owners throughout its 32-year history, primarily involved in the local river trade: August 1878 - William Davies, April 1880 - George Gubbey, April 1880 - Charles Clark, January 1886 - John Turner, September 1890 - Francis Endsor, March 1901 - Moses Paling, April 1902 - Edward Conley, September 1902 - George Jackson. Wrecked off Dennes Point, Bruny Island, in early July 1906, all hands saved.
1874	*Crystal Wave*	Passage boat	42.6 x 10.6 x 4ft. Built by Jacob Chandler to the order of William Hughes of Oyster Cove. Constructed of Huon pine and launched on 10 September 1874. Involved in the D'Entrecasteaux timber trade for several years, also competed in local regatta races. Foundered during the sailing vessel race at the 1877 Hobart Town Regatta, held on 5 December 1877, Not recovered.
1874	--	Loading boat	30 x 7 x 2.3ft. Built by Jacob Chandler to the order of the Anglo-Australian Guano Company for use at Bird Island. Constructed of Huon pine.
1874	*Lurline*	Passage boat	43 x 12 x 4ft. Clinker-built ketch built by Jacob Chandler to the order of W. H. Yeoland of Long Bay. Constructed of Huon pine and launched on 17 November 1874. Involved in the D'Entrecasteaux Channel trade for 18 years. Converted to a fishing boat in 1892. Spent several decades fishing in waters off Tasmania's east and west coasts. Wrecked in June 1946 at Swansea after part of the jetty collapsed. At the time of loss, owned by the Whelan family.
1875	*Grace Darling*	Fishing boat	38 x 8.6 x 3ft. Fishing boat built by Jacob Chandler to the order of Thomas Atkins. Constructed of Huon pine and launched in early January 1875. By 1880 owned by J. Barnett. Wrecked on 10 September 1930 after dragging it anchor near Fluted Cape, Bruny Island, all hands saved. At the time of loss, owned by V. Jordan of Bellerive.
1875	--	Whaleboat	26 x 5.5 x 2.2ft. Four-oared whaleboat built by Jacob Chandler and noted to be under construction in February 1875.
1875	--	Whaleboat	30 x 5.2 x 2ft. Five-oared whaleboat built by Jacob Chandler for the whaling brig *Velocity*.
1875	--	Whaleboat	30 x 5.2 x 2ft. Five-oared whaleboat built by Jacob Chandler of Huon pine and noted under construction in April 1875.
1875	--	Waterman's boat	23 x 5 x 2ft. Huon pine boat built by Jacob Chandler and noted under construction in June 1875.
1875	--	Whaleboat	30 x 5.2 x 2ft. Four-oared Huon pine whaleboat built by Jacob Chandler and noted under construction in September 1875.
1875	--	Boat	15 x 5.5 x 2ft. Square-sterned Huon pine boat built by Jacob Chandler for the schooner *Kingston*.
1875	--	Pleasure boat	24 x 5.5 x 2ft. Huon pine boat built by Jacob Chandler. Under completion in September 1875.
1875	--	Waterman's boat	23 x 5.2ft x 20in. Waterman's boat built by Jacob Chandler. Constructed of Huon pine and noted to be under completion in September 1875.
1875	--	Racing boat	30 x 4ft x 16in. Four-oared racing boat built by Jacob Chandler for Messrs P. Cunningham and Co. of Christchurch, New Zealand. Constructed of Huon pine. Transported to New Zealand on board the barque *Italy*. Intended to compete at an intercolonial regatta to be held at Lyttelton.
1876	--	Passage boat	60 x 15 x 5.5ft. Ketch-rigged passage boat built by Jacob Chandler of Huon pine and first noted to be under construction in September 1875. Intended for the river trade and stated to register between 30 and 40 tons. Still under construction in May 1876, noted in advanced state a few months later. No additional details known.
1876	*Forget-Me-Not*	Passage boat	38 x 8 x 3.2ft. 6 tons. Passage boat built by Jacob Chandler for C. and D. Calvert of South Arm and launched on 13 May 1876. Involved in the South Arm produce and firewood trade until the early 1890s. Subsequently converted to a fishing boat. Wrecked in July 1907 at Bicheno, all hands saved.
1876	--	Whaleboat	30ft. Five-oared whaleboat built by Jacob Chandler and noted to be just completed in May 1876. Constructed of Port Davey pine.
1876	*Kathleen* ex *Success*	Steam ferry	57.0 x 9.6 x 5.6ft. Second steam ferry built by Jacob Chandler for the O'May Brothers. Launched on 26 October 1876 already fitted with 14 h.p. engines manufactured by Messrs Appleby and Co. of London. A stalwart of the Hobart to Kangaroo Bay ferry service. Sold in April 1899 to E. T. Miles and transferred to Strahan. Renamed *Kathleen*. Spent the next 35 years employed primarily as a day-tripper on Macquarie Harbour, its remains still lie.

Year	Name	Type	Description
1876	–	Whaleboat	31ft. Whaleboat built by Jacob Chandler and noted to be completed in July 1876. Constructed of Huon pine for use on board the barque *Islander*.
1876	–	Whaleboat	31ft. Whaleboat built by Jacob Chandler and noted to be completed in July 1876. Constructed of Huon pine for use on board the barque *Runnymede*.
1876	–	Gig	Pleasure gig built by Jacob Chandler for a customer based at George Town and sent to Launceston in September 1876 on board the schooner *Lillian*.
1877	Rachel Thompson	Fishing ketch	47.3 x 12.6 x 5.9ft. ON 57577. 16 tons. Built by Jacob Chandler to the order of Llewellyn (Louis) Jones and launched on 26 May 1877. Spent many years involved in the deep-sea fishing trade, primarily off Tasmania's east coast, transporting the catch to Hobart or Melbourne. Changed hands several times after Louis Jones' death on 21 August 1901, including to Daniel Jones (from 1901), James and Walter Rattenbury (from 1904), John Norling (from 1917) and John Burgess (from May 1922). Wrecked at Victoria Rocks, Eddystone Point, in July 1922, all hands saved.
1877	–	Whaleboat	Four-oared centreboard whaleboat built by Jacob Chandler to the order of Samuel Jacobs, Jr, waterman of Hobart Town, and launched in October 1877.
1878	Racquet	Sailing boat	24 x 7 x 2ft. Square-sterned clinker-built sailing boat fitted with a centerboard extending over three thwarts (on the American principle) built by Jacob Chandler to the order of S. S. Travers and Charles Dillon, watermen of Hobart Town and launched in March 1878. Designed by Joseph Munyard, fisherman, of Queenscliff, Victoria. Constructed of Huon pine.
1878	Young Dick	Pleasure boat	21 x 5.3ft. Pleasure boat built by Jacob Chandler to the order of John Smart, waterman of Hobart Town, and launched in May 1878. Constructed of Huon pine.
1878	–	Pleasure boat	26 x 5 x 1.5ft. Four-oared pleasure boat built by Jacob Chandler to the order of Samuel Jacobs, waterman of Hobart Town and launched in October 1878. Constructed of Huon pine.
1879	Gertrude Lucy	Passage boat	39 x 9.5 x 3.5ft. Centreboard passage boat built by Jacob Chandler for C. and D. Calvert of South Arm and launched on 24 January 1879. Carried produce and firewood between South Arm and Hobart Town for several decades, also competed in local regattas. By 1904 converted to a fishing smack and owned by J. Pretty. Subsequent history not known.
1879	Annie Ward	Passage boat	43 x 11 x 4.5ft. Huon pine centreboard passage boat built by Jacob Chandler for Robert Langdale of North West Bay and launched on 19 August 1879. A regular in the D'Entrecasteaux Channel and South Arm trades; owned by J. Davis from around 1882 and J. Haines from 1885. Sank off Half Moon Bay, South Arm, in November 1898 with the loss of three lives, including its owner.
1879	Result	Steam ferry	57 x 10.2 x 4.4ft. Third steam ferry built by Jacob Chandler for the O'May Brothers. Launched on 7 November 1879. Fitted with 12 h.p. double engines manufactured by Appleby Bros. of London. Employed on the Kangaroo Bay to Hobart ferry run, also used for pleasure trips and day tours. Semi-retired in 1900. Advertised for sale in 1921 and 1923. Gutted with the hulk abandoned on the west bank of the River Derwent near Bridgewater.
1880	–	Whaleboat	Five-oared whaleboat built by Jacob Chandler and noted to be under construction in July 1880.
1880	–	Whaleboat	35 x 5ft x 20in. Five-oared racing whaleboat built by Jacob Chandler to the order of the Belfast Rowing Club in Victoria. Shipped to Melbourne in August 1880 via the SS *Southern Cross*. Advertised for sale by the club in May 1884, stated to have won every race in which it competed.
1880	–	Whaleboat	Four-oared whaleboat built by Jacob Chandler for use in conjunction with the Swan Island lighthouse. Transferred to this location on behalf of the Marine Board by the ketch *Korunah* in October 1880.
1880	–	Whaleboat	First of two five-oared whaleboat built by Jacob Chandler on speculation and noted to be under construction in November 1880.
1880	–	Whaleboat	Second of two five-oared whaleboat built by Jacob Chandler on speculation and noted to be under construction in November 1880.
1881	–	Pleasure boat	22 x 5ft x 19in. Huon pine pleasure boat built by Jacob Chandler to the order of Samuel Jacobs, waterman of Hobart Town, and launched in April 1881. Copper-fastened with brass fittings.
1881	Progress	Pleasure boat	22 x 5.2ft x 18in. Huon pine pleasure boat built by Jacob Chandler to the order of Samuel Jacobs, waterman of Hobart Town, and launched in May 1881. Copper-fastened.
1884	Victory	Steam ferry	86 x 14.9 x 7.2ft. Fourth steam ferry built by Jacob Chandler to the order of O'May Brothers. Launched on 16 June 1884. Once fitted with its Sydney-manufactured 25 h.p. non-condensing engines, from September 1884 began a regular run on the Hobart to Kangaroo Bay ferry service. Also used for day trips and available for private charter. Joined the Hobart to Lindisfarne ferry service in 1905. Broken up in 1936.
1885	Aquilla	Waterman's boat	22ft. Copper-fastened Huon pine waterman's boat built by Jacob Chandler to the order of Thomas Smart and launched in November 1885.
1885	–	Long boat	Long boat built by Jacob Chandler for the barque *Pet*.

Year	Name	Type	Description
1886	*Lenna*	Passage boat	40 x 10 x 3.5ft. Passage boat built by Jacob Chandler to the order of Donald McKay of Peppermint Bay and launched in May 1886. Constructed of Huon pine and intended for the Channel trade though immediately swapped for Richard Musk's *Laura Louise*. Under the patronage of the Musk family, a regular in the Hobart to Ralphs Bay trade. Later converted to a fishing boat. Capsized and sank off Blackmans Bay in December 1941, all hands saved.
1886	*Seacroft*	Passage boat	41 x 11.2 x 4ft. Passage boat built by Jacob Chandler to the order of Robert Calvert of South Arm and launched in August 1887. Constructed of Huon pine and kauri. Employed in the South Arm to Hobart trade. Advertised for sale in mid-1894. Sold to a Mr Purcell and transferred to the Huon. Later converted to a fishing boat. Last noted in service on the east coast in 1920.
1888	--	Ketch	20 tons. Noted to be under construction in January 1888, built on speculation.
1888	--	Passage boat	42ft. 15 tons. Noted to be under construction in January 1888, built on speculation.
1888	*Bronco*	Pleasure boat	20ft. Copper-fastened Huon pine pleasure boat built by Jacob Chandler to the order of Henry Power, waterman of Hobart, and launched in October 1888.
1888	--	Pleasure boat	Pleasure boat built by Jacob Chandler and completed in November 1888.
1888	--	Fishing boat	Small fishing boat built by Jacob Chandler. Noted to be under construction in November 1888.
1889	*Maggie Read*	Fishing boat	42 x 12.5 x 5ft. Built by Jacob Chandler to the order of Moses Barnett and launched in late 1889. Constructed of Huon pine and fitted with an 11ft well. Engaged in deep-sea fishing for many years under several owners, including Messrs Cox and Longwood. Wrecked on 20 January 1908 at Sulphur Creek, during heavy fog, all hands saved.
1889	*Royalist*	Dinghy	Racing dinghy that competed out of Bellerive. Built by Jacob Chandler to the order of the O'May family, by 1903 owned and sailed by O. O'May.
1889	*Tasma ex Sandfly*	Steam launch	31ft. Steam launch built by Jacob Chandler to the order of J. T. Read of Sandy Bay and launched in 1889. Advertised for sale the following year. By mid-1893 owned by J. Cook of the New Town Tannery and undergoing substantial alteration at Chandler's yard, including being lengthened by 13ft and having new Tangye engines installed. Renamed *Tasmania*. Fate not known.
1890s	--	Sail boat	26ftt. Half-decked sailing boat built by Jacob Chandler and advertised for sale at Hobart in October 1892, complete with sails and gear.
1890	--	Dinghy	14 x 5ft. Copper-fastened Huon pine dinghy built by Jacob Chandler to the order of Henry Power, waterman of Hobart, and launched in April 1890.
1890	--	Pleasure boat	Square-sterned pleasure boat built by Jacob Chandler on speculation and noted to be under construction in May 1890.
1890	--	Dinghy	15 x 5ft. Copper-fastened Huon pine clinker-built dinghy constructed by Jacob Chandler to the order of Henry Power, waterman of Hobart, and launched in May 1890. Expected to be licenced to hold seven people.
1891	*Orlando*	Waterman's boat	21 x 7.2 x 2.8ft. Copper-fastened Huon pine waterman's boat built by Jacob Chandler to the order of George Hales of Hobart. Launched in January 1891. Licenced to carry 18 passengers.
1891	--	Whaleboat	27 x 5.2 x 2ft. Macquarie Harbour pine whaleboat constructed by Jacob Chandler for use on board HMS *Orlando* and completed in early 1891, coinciding with the vessel's visit to Hobart.
1891	--	Pleasure boat	One of two small pleasure boats built by Jacob Chandler on speculation and noted to be under construction in January 1891.
1891	--	Pleasure boat	Second of two small pleasure boats built by Jacob Chandler on speculation and noted to be under construction in January 1891.
1891	--	Pleasure boat	12 x 4.8ft by 20in. Huon pine pleasure boat built by Jacob Chandler and noted to be under construction in April 1891.
1891	*Ringdove*	Waterman's boat	16.5 x 5.5ft. Copper-fastened Macquarie pine waterman's boat built by Jacob Chandler to the order of George Carter, waterman of Hobart, and launched in October 1891.
1891	*Starling*	Waterman's boat	20 x 5.8ft. Copper-fastened Macquarie pine waterman's boat built by Jacob Chandler to the order of George Carter, waterman of Hobart, and launched in October 1891. Licenced to carry 12 passengers.
1894	*Nellie*	Ketch	49.1 x 13.4 x 5.4ft. ON 57636. 18 tons. Built by Jacob Chandler to the order of Messrs Risby Bros. and launched on 8 September 1894. Advertised for sale a week after launch and subsequently chartered by W. T. Grubb, secretary of the Derwent Sailing Club, for use as a yacht. Later involved in the D'Entrecasteux Channel. Wrecked off Robbins Island with the drowning of 98 sheep in late August 1919. At the time of loss, owned by Luke Williams of the Copper Reward Company's of Balfour and employed on Tasmania's north-west coast.
1898	--	Dinghy	11ft. Built by Jacob Chandler. Advertised for sale in April 1898, with rollicks and paddles.
1899	*Ruby Louise*	Fishing boat	41.4 x 12.3 x 5.0ft. ON 133500. 10 tons. Built by Jacob Chandler to the order of George Clarke. Launched on 8 May 1899 to be mastered by Edward Pretty who later became owner. Fitted with an engine in 1908, owned by W. Martin. Next owned by R. Gillam. Purchased by William and Frederick Thomas and first registered in 1921. Advertised again for sale in July 1931. Subsequent fate not known.

James Mackey (1890s).
Courtesy Tasmanian Archives (NS738/1/1743).

James Mackey

'Mr. Mackey will no doubt turn out such a vessel as will not only redound to his architectural skill and workmanship, but will tend to strengthen Tasmania's already well earned name for marine architecture.'

The Mercury, 21 June 1861.

James Doig Mackey (McKay, Mackay, Mackie) was a productive and enterprising shipwright of Battery Point, building or assisting in the construction of at least 22 vessels over a 53-year period. Having arrived in Hobart Town from Scotland in 1832 at the age of seven, Mackey learned the craft of shipbuilding from John Watson in the 1840s, and in the early 1850s established his own yard at Battery Point in partnership with Thomas Cullen and his brother David Mackey (Jr). Together the trio built many successful intercolonial and coastal schooners and ketches, and also furnished vessels for the New Zealand coastal trade. When his partners retired, James Mackey continued on with the firm, culminating in the launch of the steamer *Warrentinna* in 1883, eventually passing the reins to his nephew Henry Featherstone.

Born in 1825 in Burntisland, Fife, Scotland, Mackey was the third of eleven children born to David and Margaret Mackey, nee Doig.[1013] At the time of his birth, Burntisland was a small though important port town located 22 miles from Edinburgh and well-known for its shipbuilding, as well as trade in coal and herring. In 1809, at the age of 14, Mackey's father (David, Sr) had joined the Third Battalion of His Majesty's Royal Regiment of Artillery.[1014] A native of Dunfermline, a town located less than 10 miles inland from Burntisland and known for its textile manufacturing, David Mackey (Sr) met Margaret Doig while stationed at Burntisland as a gunnery and driver; the couple married in 1822.[1015]

Following 23 years of military service, including possibly seeing battle in the Napoleonic Wars, on 30 June 1832 David Mackey (Sr) retired from the Third Battalion with a pension.[1016] One week later he escorted his wife and young family (at the time consisting of six children, including six-year old James Doig), from Leith, Scotland, to Van Diemen's Land on board the *North Briton*.[1017] The family, accompanied by John Doig, Margaret Mackey's brother, arrived in Hobart Town on 12 November 1832.[1018]

David Mackey (Sr) appears to have near-immediately found work as a shipwright. Though there is no confirmation of where or who he was working for in Hobart Town, it is likely he found work with William Williamson at his Battery Point shipyard (refer to a previous chapter). The Mackey family also settled into a home in Murray Street, in October 1833 welcoming another child to their midst; a daughter named Helen.[1019]

With some capital, in 1836 David Mackey (Sr) partnered with William Williamson, John Eason and Samuel Kendall to purchase the schooner *Alligator*, trading as Williamson and Company.[1020] Though the partnership sold the vessel shortly thereafter, David Mackey (Sr) and his family's interest in the maritime industry were spawned.[1021] He remained employed as a ship carpenter throughout the late 1830s, with the family taking up residence in Elizabeth Street.[1022]

Continuing his association with William Williamson, in 1842 David Mackey (Sr) began a rope works at Williamson's Battery Point shipyard; the first operation of its kind in the colony.[1023] Unfortunately in October 1844 a weatherboard building used as a hackling loft and store room for the rope works was destroyed by fire and David Mackey (Sr) suffered serious loss of supplies, equipment and machinery.[1024] He was not insured.[1025] The fire was ignited by a spark from a cigar, *'which an idle and careless stranger who visited the works was recklessly smoking amongst the loose refuse*

[1013] www.scotlandspeople.gov.uk.
[1014] UK, Royal Hospital Chelsea Pensioner Soldier Service Records, 1760-1920.
[1015] www.scotlandspeople.gov.uk.
[1016] British Army Service Records (1760 – 1915).
[1017] *The Hobart Town Courier*, 16 November 1832.
[1018] *The Hobart Town Courier*, 16 November 1832.
[1019] Libraries Tasmania (RGD32/1/2/ no 4998, RGD34/1/1 no 3953).
[1020] R. Parsons (1992). *Australian Shipowners and their Fleet. Owners Registering in Hobart to 1859. Book 12.*
[1021] R. Parsons (1992). *Australian Shipowners and their Fleet. Owners Registering in Hobart to 1859. Book 12.*
[1022] Libraries Tasmania (RGD32/1/2/ no 7072, RGD32/1/2/ no 8649).
[1023] *Colonial Times*, 23 August 1842.
[1024] *Colonial Times*, 29 October 1844.
[1025] *Colonial Times*, 29 October 1844.

flax in the loft'.[1026] The Hobart Town press reported, 'We understand that the proprietor intends to bring an action against the person who has been the reckless cause of this destruction, and it is probable that, if he has the means, he will have to pay for the consequences of his folly'.[1027] It is not known if David Mackey (Sr) followed up with this legal action.

Persevering, David Mackey (Sr) remained in the shipbuilding industry until the early 1860s, working for many years with John Watson at his Battery Point shipyard.[1028] The large Mackey family lived close by at 9 Francis Street, Battery Point.[1029] It was only fitting that three of David Mackey's sons, including James, would follow his footsteps in the shipbuilding industry.

A model made by James Mackey during his apprenticeship.
Courtesy Maritime Museum of Tasmania (A_2019-060).

In the late 1840s, after learning the craft of shipbuilding through apprenticeship to John Watson, James Mackey partnered with his brother David, along with James Bailey (who had previously worked for both William Williamson, as his foreman, and John Watson) and Thomas Cullen to form a shipbuilding firm.[1030] Operating as Bailey and Company, the first vessel built by the firm was the *Aberdeen*, described as a 'Clipper Brig ... well adapted for the Cattle, New Zealand, or Colonial Trade' which they launched in late 1849, having built it on the banks of the Huon River.[1031] The 133-ton vessel was sold in February 1850 to John Watson who subsequently renamed it *Dart*.[1032] An intercolonial and trans-Tasman trader for many years, primarily under the ownership of Captain Henry Sansom, the vessel was wrecked on a reef in November 1865 near the mouth of the Anson River on Tasmania's east coast, all hands saved.[1033] At the time of loss, the *Dart* had been en route to Melbourne.[1034]

By January 1851 Bailey and Company had established a shipyard along Napoleon Street at Battery Point, primarily undertaking repair, refit and overhaul work.[1035] With frontage on the River Derwent of 89ft, the property was part of William Kermode's original land grant and also shared boundaries with the newly-created Marine Terrace and Derwent Road (branching towards the river off the northern end of Napoleon Street and forming part of the border of Jacob Chandler's boat yard). However, perhaps through lack of funds or uncertainty over the success of their enterprise, or even a combination of the two, the partnership appears to have initially leased the land. This may have been the right decision as just over a year later, in May 1852, James Mackey, David Mackey and Thomas Cullen announced the dissolution, by mutual consent, of their shipbuilding partnership as it related to James Bailey.[1036] Shortly thereafter, Bailey relocated to Victoria.[1037]

Notice.

THE PARTNERSHIP hitherto subsisting between Thomas Cullen, David Mackay, James Mackay, and James Bailey, carrying on business as Shipwrights at Battery Point, Hobart Town, has been DISSOLVED by mutual consent, as far as relates to the said James Bailey, who has ceased to be a partner in the said business, which will be carried on for the future by the said Thomas Cullen, David Mackay, and James Mackay; who will receive and pay all debts due to, and by the said Partnership.—Dated this eighth day of May, 1852.

THOMAS CULLEN,
DAVID MACKAY,
JAMES MACKAY,
JAMES BAILEY.

1152

Colonial Times, 11 May 1852.

It was a life-changing few months for James Mackey, both professionally and personally. On 8 April 1852 at the Holy Trinity Church in Warwick Street, Hobart Town, he married Scottish-born Marion McMillan, daughter of Archibald and Janet McMillan (nee Fenton).[1038] The couple moved into a house at 2 Mona Street, Battery Point, with their first and only child, a daughter named Janet 'Jessie', born on 3 October that same year.[1039]

Continuing their business under the new name of 'Cullen and Mackey', the remaining trio launched their first vessel at Battery Point late in 1852, a 50-ton barge named *Success*.[1040] It was purchased by George Wilson and placed in the Hobart Town to Melbourne

---

[1026] *The True Colonist Van Diemen's Land Political Despatch, and Agricultural and Commercial ...*, 31 October 1844.
[1027] *The True Colonist Van Diemen's Land Political Despatch, and Agricultural and Commercial ...*, 31 October 1844.
[1028] *The Courier*, 8 February 1856; *The Mercury*, 16 September 1863; *The Mercury*, 15 August 1879.
[1029] *Colonial Times*, 2 September 1851; *The Mercury*, 11 June 1872.
[1030] *The Courier*, 21 June 1848; *Colonial Times*, 27 November 1849; *Launceston Examiner*, 8 December 1849; *The Mercury*, 11 June 1872, 18 March 1887.
[1031] *Colonial Times*, 27 November 1849; R. Parsons (1992). *Australian Shipowners and their Fleets. Book 12 (Hobart to 1859, A - L)*.
[1032] *The Courier*, 27 February 1850; R. Parsons (1992). *Australian Shipowners and their Fleets. Book 12 (Hobart to 1859, A - L)*.
[1033] *Launceston Examiner*, 21, 23 November 1865.
[1034] *The Mercury*, 8, 27 November 1865.
[1035] *The Hobart Town Advertiser*, 14, 21 January 1851, 17 August 1852; *The Courier*, 27 September 1851.
[1036] *Colonial Times*, 11 May 1852.
[1037] Libraries Tasmania (RGD37/1/4 no 1840); *The Tasmanian Daily News*, 24 August 1855.
[1038] Libraries Tasmania (RGD37/1/11 no 537); McMillan family tree via ancestry.com.au.
[1039] Libraries Tasmania (RGD33/1/4 no 1813); *The Courier*, 7 May 1856.
[1040] R. Parsons (1992). *Australian Shipowners and their Fleets. Book 13 (Hobart to 1859, M - Z)*.

The *Jubilee* on the River Derwent.
Courtesy Maritime Museum of Tasmania (P_OM_Q_5d).

trade.[1041] A 50-ton schooner was launched on 10 August of the following year.[1042] Built to the order of Henry Marsh and Henry Chapman, timber traders of Hobart Town, this particular vessel's launch coincided with the ceasing of convict transportation to Van Diemen's Land such that it was aptly named *Jubilee*.[1043] The craft went on to become a regular in the river trade, transporting timber and produce to Hobart Town from the Huon until the late 1860s.[1044] Later, under Michael Reardon's ownership, it transported produce and hay from Ralphs Bay to Hobart Town.[1045] The *Jubilee* remained active on the River Derwent until at least 1920.[1046]

Shortly following completion of the *Jubilee*, Cullen and Mackey launched two more vessels. These were the *Uncle Tom* and *Eva*.[1047] The 46-ton schooner *Uncle Tom* was built late in 1853 to the order of the Geeves family of Geeveston and was employed in the Huon timber trade for 60 years, becoming another stalwart of the port of Hobart.[1048] The 56-ton schooner *Eva* was built to the order of Captain George Pryde of Battery Point and is first noted in the press as a *'new schooner'* when used as the flagship for the Sandy Bay Regatta held in late November 1854.[1049] The craft spent its career as an intercolonial trader under various owners before being wrecked at Whales Head Harbour, Tasmania, in May 1880 while en route from Macquarie Harbour to Port Adelaide, all hands saved.[1050]

On 28 April 1855, Mackey and his brother David, along with Thomas Cullen formally purchased their shipyard property from the estate of William Kermode, who died in August 1852, as executed by his son Robert Quayle Kermode.[1051] The land was formally conveyed to the Mackey brothers, along with Thomas Cullen, for the price of £1,350.[1052] It was one of at least 34 allotments, totalling over four acres, located in the vicinity of Marine Terrace, Mona Street and Colville Street that was sold by the Kermode family since its patriarch's death.[1053]

Following a two-year period in which no new vessels appear to have been built, the shipbuilding firm instead absorbed in repair, refit and overhaul work, 1857 proved to be a big year for Cullen and Mackey.[1054] First, they established a patent slip at their

---

[1041] R. Parsons (1992). *Australian Shipowners and their Fleets. Book 13 (Hobart to 1859, M - Z)*; *The Hobart Town Advertiser*, 23 December 1852.
[1042] *The Courier*, 11 August 1853.
[1043] *The Courier*, 11 August 1853.
[1044] *The Mercury*, 6 September 1867.
[1045] *The Mercury*, 5 September 1900; *Tasmanian News*, 25 October 1902.
[1046] HOBART, Continuation [Transactions] Register, Volume 7, 1855-1949, Folio Tr 134.
[1047] *The Mercury*, 21 August 1911.
[1048] R. Parsons (1992). *Australian Shipowners and their Fleets. Book 12 (Hobart to 1859, A - L)*; *The Hobart Town Daily Mercury*, 7 November 1859; *The Mercury*, 11 September 1883, 27 January 1886, 15, 21 August 1911, 25 June 1913.
[1049] R. Parsons (1992). *Australian Shipowners and their Fleets. Book 12 (Hobart to 1859, A - L)*; *The Courier*, 2 December 1854; *The Hobart Town Advertiser*, 16 November 1859.
[1050] R. Parsons (1992). *Australian Shipowners and their Fleets. Book 12 (Hobart to 1859, A - L)*; *Launceston Examiner*, 29 May, 2 June 1880.
[1051] www.thelist.tas.gov.au (Historical Deed 04/1405).
[1052] www.thelist.tas.gov.au (Historical Deed 04/1405).
[1053] *The Courier*, 15 March 1854.
[1054] *The Tasmanian Daily News*, 27 August 1856; *The Hobarton Mercury*, 3 November 1856.

Uncle Tom at Kermandie (c1890s).
Courtesy Tasmanian Archives (NS1013/1/1173).

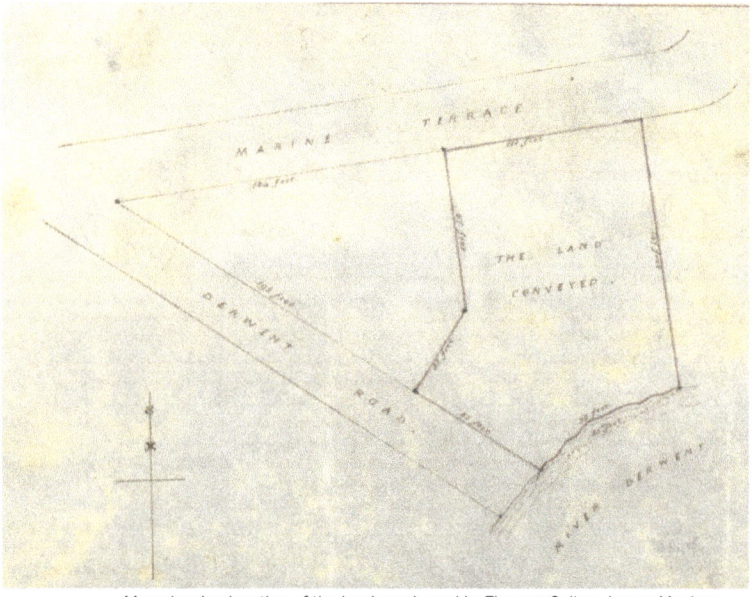

Map showing location of the land purchased by Thomas Cullen, James Mackey and David Mackey at Battery Point in 1855.
Courtesy www.thelist.tas.gov.au (Historical Deed 04/1405).

Battery Point shipyard. Measuring 300ft in length with a 100ft cradle, the slip was capable of accommodating vessels of up to 200 tons.[1055] Noted in the press as being entirely a colonial enterprise, the slip was constructed by the local foundry of Messrs Clark and Davidson and showed '*proof of what can be done in the colony if the people would encourage Tasmanian skill and ingenuity, instead of sending to England for the machinery they may require*'.[1056] Interestingly, the price of the slip was estimated to be significantly less than slips imported from England.[1057] It was the second such patent slip to be installed at Battery Point and the third in Hobart Town and was initially operated via manual labour before being converted to steam power.[1058]

Second, Cullen and Mackey launched the 21-ton sloop *Topsy*, built to the order of William Domeney for

[1055] *The Hobart Town Daily Mercury*, 1 January 1858.
[1056] *The Hobart Town Daily Mercury*, 1 January 1858.
[1057] *The Hobart Town Daily Mercury*, 1 January 1858.
[1058] *The Hobart Town Daily Mercury*, 13 January 1858.

the ever-increasing Huon River trade.[1059] Finally, on 29 December 1857, the 99ft screw steamer *Emu* (often referred to as *Emeu* in the press) was launched.[1060] Built to the order of Captain John Hanson, with blue gum supplied by John Watson from his land at Middleton in the D'Entrecasteaux Channel, the vessel was intended to run between Hobart Town, Richmond and Sorell.[1061] Continuing their preference for colonial manufacturing, the *Emu*'s 20 h.p. engines, capable of propelling it at one knot per hour, were built by Easby and Robertson of the Albion Foundry, Hobart Town.[1062] The craft undertook its trial trip in June 1858, going on to work on the River Derwent and its tributaries for several decades.[1063]

SS *Emu* at New Norfolk (c1880s).
Courtesy Tasmanian Archives (NS6904/1/81).

The installation of a patent slip at Cullen and Mackey's Battery Point yard proved to be a huge windfall for the firm, as well as the local economy.

The *Hobart Town Daily Mercury* of 18 January 1859, in summarising the previous years' shipping statistics, stated that in 1858 alone 46 vessels, varying from 35 to 150 tons register, were cleaned and repaired on the slip at a cost of £4,000.[1064] These figures combined with those from the two other patent slips meant that '*for the repairs of vessels the Port of Hobart offers accommodation scarcely to be surpassed by any port in the colonies*'.[1065] In 1859 the steamers *Monarch* and *Oberon* were noted in the press as undergoing repair on Cullen and Mackey's slip.[1066]

Diversifying their business interests further, in 1859 Cullen and Mackey submitted a tender to the Hobart Marine Board for erecting part of the New Wharf at Hobart Town.[1067] Unfortunately their bid was unsuccessful, Thomas Oldham being awarded the contract.[1068] However, it marked the first of many tenders submitted by the firm in the coming years.

The 1860s also proved an active decade for Cullen and Mackey. In 1860 the firm continued to overhaul and repair commercial vessels, including the schooner *Goldseeker* and the steamer *Monarch*.[1069] The following year Cullen and Mackey began building their largest vessel yet, a three-masted schooner for Captain William Pie, James and David Mackey's brother-in-law.[1070] Intended for the trans-Tasman trade, the 141-ton *David and Jessie*, built of blue gum sourced from the foothills of Mount Wellington, was launched on 20 September 1862.[1071] It left Hobart Town on its maiden voyage to Otago, New Zealand, with a full cargo on 15 January 1863.[1072] During the course of the *David and Jessie*'s construction, Cullen and Mackey also completed a fishing smack of 30 tons register, as well as a yacht intended to compete at the 1862 Hobart Town Regatta, and an unidentified small craft.[1073]

[1059] R. Parsons (1992). *Australian Shipowners and their Fleets. Book 12 (Hobart to 1859, A - L).*
[1060] *The Hobart Town Daily Mercury*, 1 January 1858.
[1061] *The Tasmanian Daily News*, 15 June 1857; *The Hobart Town Daily Mercury*, 1 January 1858; *The Courier*, 25 June 1858.
[1062] *The Hobart Town Daily Mercury*, 1 January 1858; *The Courier*, 19 July 1858.
[1063] *The Courier*, 25 June 1858.
[1064] *The Hobart Town Daily Mercury*, 18 January 1859.
[1065] *The Hobart Town Daily Mercury*, 18 January 1859.
[1066] *The Hobart Town Daily Mercury*, 21 October, 10 November 1859.
[1067] *The Courier*, 31 May 1859.
[1068] *The Courier*, 31 May 1859.
[1069] *The Hobart Town Daily Mercury*, 17 January 1860; *The Mercury*, 26 November 1860.
[1070] Libraries Tasmania (RGD37/1/15 no 363); *The Mercury*, 21 June 1861.
[1071] *The Mercury*, 9 January, 22 September 1862.
[1072] *The Advertiser*, 23 January 1863.
[1073] *The Hobart Town Advertiser*, 10 July 1861, 1 April 1862; *The Mercury*, 9 January 1862.

View from Sandy Bay of the Battery Point boat and ship yards (c1860s).
Courtesy Tasmanian Archives (PH1/1/24B).

In mid-1863 Cullen and Mackey laid down the keel of a barge for H. F. Armstrong of the Cardiff Coal Company in New South Wales.[1074] Registering at 79 tons, the *Tasman* was launched on 13 October 1863 and was the largest barge built in Tasmania for some time.[1075] Intended for use as a collier, the *Tasman* took only six months to complete, with its timber sourced from the back of Mount Wellington.[1076] During construction, however, the Cardiff Coal Company discovered that the craft was too large for their intended purpose and instead the vessel was purchased by a group of local shipowners before being on-sold to the Seymour Coal Company (also of New South Wales) just after launch for £1,650.[1077] After spending many years involved in intercolonial trade, mainly hauling timber, the *Tasman* was wrecked near Sandy Cape on Tasmania's west coast on 16 January 1891, all hands saved.[1078]

In April 1864 Cullen and Mackey launched the 56ft fore-and-aft schooner *Marie Louise*, built to the order of Dr William Crowther and intended for the D'Entrecasteaux Channel trade.[1079] Some years later the craft was converted into a sea-going yacht for its new owner Henry Hopkins (Jr).[1080] During the course of 1864 the firm was also noted as repairing the barge *Shannon*, coppering and painting the barge *Esther*, as well as overhauling the schooners *Twins*, *Independence* and *Blanche* and converting the yacht *Sea Gull* into a fishing smack.[1081]

On 11 March 1865 Cullen and Mackey launched a 36-ton schooner named *Falcon*.[1082] Built on speculation, the 66ft vessel was intended for the east coast trade.[1083] Failing to find an immediate local buyer, James Mackey and Thomas Cullen instead filled the vessel with flour, shingles and palings and sailed it to Nelson, New Zealand, in April 1865 with the intention of selling both the craft and its cargo.[1084] With Hans Aamodt at the helm, also on board as passengers were Mackey's brother-in-law Donald McMillan and either his uncle or cousin J. Doig.[1085] The *Falcon* arrived in Nelson on 2 May after a 12-day voyage.[1086]

At the time, demand for shallow draft vessels for the New Zealand coastal trade was high owing to the number of wrecks experienced on the west coast of the South Island.[1087] After spending a profitable few months employing the vessel in the New Zealand coastal trade under the continued management of Aamodt, the *Falcon* was sold to Captain Milo of Wellington in October 1865, the price being £1,000.[1088]

Returning to Hobart Town via Sydney as passengers on board the SS *City of Hobart* on 23 July 1865, Thomas Cullen and James Mackey did not stay in Tasmania very long.[1089] The duo returned to Nelson, New Zealand, on 1 November 1865 after a three-week voyage as passengers on board the brigantine *Annie*, perhaps to finalise the sale of the *Falcon*.[1090]

Back in Hobart Town by the following year, Cullen and Mackey repaired the schooner *Marie Louise* following its collision on the river with the *Windward*.[1091] They also lengthened the river barge *McEvoy*, owned by John Chandler and built by George and Neil Morris at Peppermint Bay some years prior.[1092] The Hobart Town City Council additionally contracted the pair to repair the drainage along Derwent Lane, i.e., the road leading to their shipyard.[1093] Repairs were also carried out on the *Huon Belle*.[1094] Meanwhile another vessel was taking shape at Cullen and Mackey's yard, a 50-ton schooner being built on speculation though designed specifically for the New Zealand bar harbour trade.[1095] Fitted with a large centreboard, the craft's completion was delayed until mid-1868, while a buyer could be found.[1096] In August 1868 the barge-rigged schooner was finally launched.[1097] Subsequently named *Kestrel*, the vessel was purchased by Captain Henry Williams in October of that year for use in the Tasmanian east coast trade.[1098] In 1874 it was sold to buyers from New Zealand with *Kestrel* employed in the coastal trade for many decades before being broken up in 1932.[1099]

More overhaul and repair work was carried out by the firm of Cullen and Mackey in 1867, including to the fishing smack *Sea Gull*, the schooner *Annie*, and the London trader *Oryx*.[1100] Also noted as being overhauled were the Huon River traders *Fleetwing*, *Happy Jack*, *Huon Belle* and *Petrel*, and the barge *Shannon* involved in the Tasman Peninsula trade.[1101] Cullen and Mackey's slip continued to be moderately busy into the late 1860s.

In early 1870 Cullen and Mackey tendered for completing certain stages of the Sorell Causeway, estimating the work to cost £18,920 and to take 23 months to complete.[1102] The tender was awarded to Thomas Oldham who offered to do the work at a significantly lower price of £13,205.[1103] Still, the firm was kept busy building the 61ft blue gum ketch *Osprey* (which would be launched in 1871) and, to a far greater extent, repairing, painting and overhauling vessels.[1104]

[1074] *The Hobart Town Advertiser*, 2 May 1863; *The Mercury*, 26 May, 23 June 1863.
[1075] *The Mercury*, 16, 23 October, 23 November 1863.
[1076] *The Mercury*, 23 November 1863.
[1077] *The Mercury*, 14, 16 October, 23 November 1863; *The Advertiser*, 19 November 1863.
[1078] *Launceston Examiner*, 20 January 1891.
[1079] *The Mercury*, 19, 22 April 1864; *The Advertiser*, 19 April 1864.
[1080] *Tasmanian Times*, 13 July 1869.
[1081] *The Advertiser*, 20 April 1864; *The Mercury*, 31 May, 5 July, 21 September, 11 October 1864, 10 November 1865.
[1082] *The Mercury*, 13 March, 21 April 1865.
[1083] *The Mercury*, 13 March, 21 April 1865.
[1084] *The Advertiser*, 21 April 1865; *The Mercury*, 21 April 1865.
[1085] *The Advertiser*, 21 April 1865.
[1086] *Nelson Examiner and New Zealand Chronicle*, 4 May 1865.
[1087] *The Mercury*, 1 November 1865.
[1088] *Nelson Examiner and New Zealand Chronicle*, 1, 6 July, 26 August 1865; *Evening Post*, 11 October 1865;
[1089] *The Mercury*, 1 November 1865.
[1089] *The Advertiser*, 24 July 1865.
[1090] *The Mercury*, 7 October 1865; *Nelson Examiner and New Zealand Chronicle*, 2 November 1865.
[1091] *The Mercury*, 6 January 1866.
[1092] *The Mercury*, 23 November 1864, 11 June 1866; *The Advertiser*, 24 July 1865.
[1093] *The Mercury*, 11, 26 June 1866.
[1094] *The Mercury*, 13 September 1866.
[1095] *Tasmanian Morning Herald*, 23 November 1866.
[1096] *The Tasmanian Times*, 24 August 1867; *The Tasmanian Times*, 1 February 1868.
[1097] *The Tasmanian Times*, 16 July, 3 August 1868.
[1098] *Launceston Examiner*, 8 October 1868; Register of British Ships: Main Register (with continuation entries), Port of Hobart [contains Volumes 7, 8, 9 (part)].
[1099] New Zealand, Registered Ships & Owners, 1840 – 1950.
[1100] *The Mercury*, 12 March, 15, 21 June 1867.
[1101] *The Mercury*, 22 March, 26 October, 13 November 1867.
[1102] *The Cornwall Chronicle*, 13 August 1870.
[1103] *The Cornwall Chronicle*, 13 August 1870.
[1104] *The Mercury*, 8 October 1870, 26 February 1871; *Tasmanian Times*, 22 April, 5 November 1870.

1870 also saw the partnership of Thomas Cullen and the two Mackey brothers dissolved by mutual consent. In late 1870 Cullen gave up shipbuilding to become licencee of McLaren's Hotel located at 41 Collins Street in Hobart Town.[1105] This change in vocation also coincided with his marriage to Mary Ann McCulloch (nee Bruce), a widower, on 28 November 1870.[1106] Sadly, she would die six years later after a short illness.[1107]

Cullen remained the publican of McLaren's Hotel up until 1880 after which time he moved back to his birth place of Glasgow, Scotland, where he died on 9 February 1897 at the age of 77.[1108] Interestingly, the executors of Cullen's substantial estate, worth nearly £2,000 and including properties at 34 Hampden Road and 12 Arthur Circus, Battery Point, were James Mackey and Donald McMillan.[1109]

Following Thomas Cullen's departure from the firm, James and David Mackey continued with their Battery Point shipbuilding enterprise under the new name of 'J. and D. Mackey'. The first vessel completed by the pair was the ketch *Osprey*, launched in January 1871 and advertised for sale the following month.[1110] The craft was subsequently purchased by William G. Cheverton and placed in the Huon timber trade, though ultimately spent most of its career operating in South Australian waters until foundering after leaving Port Julia on 11 September 1903.[1111]

In mid-1871 the firm of J. and D. Mackey began building a schooner yacht to the order of Henry Hopkins (Jr) of New Town with Hopkins' intention to sail the vessel around the world for the sake of his health.[1112] With a sense of grandeur and a pocketbook to support such a venture, Hobart Town's most esteemed citizen was proposing to build a ship near-equivalent to one of the larger vessels ever constructed in Tasmania The keel of the vessel, measuring 112ft in length, 16 inches deep and 12 inches in breadth, was bought up to Hobart Town in May 1871 from Port Cygnet where it had been sourced.[1113] During the course of construction, however, Hopkins' plans changed and he instead opted for the building of a barque with the intention of placing it in the whaling industry.[1114] The craft's subsequent early history is one worth relaying.

[1105] *The Mercury*, 2 December 1870.
[1106] *The Mercury*, 30 November 1870.
[1107] *Tribune*, 23 December 1876.
[1108] Libraries Tasmania (AD960-1-22 Will Number 5225).
[1109] *Tasmanian News*, 21 February 1898; *The Mercury*, 24 February, 23 March 1898; Libraries Tasmania (AD960-1-22 Will Number 5225).

[1110] *The Mercury*, 8 October 1870; *Launceston Examiner*, 11 February 1871.
[1111] *The Mercury*, 13 July, 28 August 1871; Register of British Ships: Main Register (with continuation entries), Port of Hobart [contains Volumes 7, 8, 9 (part)]; Register of British Ships: Main Register subsequent to Merchant Shipping Act 1854, Port Adelaide [Roll 1 of 5] [Volume 1 to Volume 2 folio 186]; *The Register*, 14 October 1903.
[1112] *The Mercury*, 18 May 1871.
[1113] *The Mercury*, 27 May 1871.
[1114] *The Mercury*, 26 July 1872.

Osprey operating in South Australian waters (c1890s).
Courtesy State Library of South Australia (PRG 1373/35/55).

The barque *Nautilus*.
Courtesy Maritime Museum of Tasmania (P_OM_G_18h).

Nearing midday on 25 July 1872 the *Nautilus*, designed by James Mackay, was launched from the Battery Point yard of J. and D. Mackey, the wife of Henry Hopkins (Jr), Catherine, dashing the customary bottle of champagne against the bow.[1115] Intended to be a private ceremony, around 400 people crowded the slips and nearby higher ground to witness the event. *The Mercury* reported that the barque was to be placed in the China trade under the command of Captain D. Cowen. Taking another four months to be fitted out, rigged and coppered, the 243-ton *Nautilus* left Hobart Town on its maiden voyage on 18 January 1873.[1116] The substantial craft was loaded with timber for Adelaide, with its next destination likely to be Guam. However, not relinquishing his dream of a global voyage, Henry Hopkins (Jr) and his wife were both on board when it set sail for South Australia.[1117]

After discharging its cargo, Henry Hopkins (Jr) made another somewhat spontaneous decision. Instead of heading for Guam or China as had been proposed, sensing further financial opportunity and a yearning to once more visit his motherland, he loaded the *Nautilus* with 2,292 bags of wheat and set sail for London.[1118] The vessel cleared out of Adelaide on 24 February 1873.[1119]

After a voyage via Cape Town, the *Nautilus* reached London on 28 June 1873.[1120] Thereupon being surveyed by Lloyds, the vessel was awarded the Maltese Cross for its superior build; a great honour for the firm of J. and D. Mackey.[1121] The *Nautilus* then departed London on 17 September 1873 with Henry Hopkins (Jr) and his wife Catherine once more on board.[1122]

The *Nautilus* made a splendid return run to Hobart Town of just over 90 days, calling in only at Madeira for water and provisions.[1123] The craft arrived back in the River Derwent on 24 December 1874, its cargo a veritable assortment of goods, most of which was intended for subsequent sale, including sherry, chocolate, confectionery, sugar, spices, sardines and herring, salt, medicine, boots, books, drapery, clothing and sewing machines.[1124] Also on board were a pure Alderney cow, six Lincoln sheep and several Dorking fowls; Henry Hopkins (Jr) intending to expand his farming stock.[1125]

The *Nautilus* remained in port for a month before clearing Hobart Town for Newcastle, New South Wales, on 30 January 1874 with 100 cases of jam on board.[1126] It next sailed for Hong Kong with a cargo of coal.[1127] The vessel returned to Hobart Town in November 1874 with tea from China, maintaining its role in the Australia to Asia trade for some time thereafter.[1128]

The *Nautilus* went on to have a fruitful career in intercolonial and international trade under various owners over several decades. It was ultimately destroyed by fire at Noumea in August 1891.[1129]

[1115] *The Mercury*, 26 July 1872.
[1116] *The Mercury*, 20 January 1873.
[1117] *The Mercury*, 3 December 1872; *The South Australian Advertiser*, 29 January 1873.
[1118] *The South Australian Advertiser*, 20 February 1873.
[1119] *South Australian Register*, 25 February 1873.
[1120] *Lloyd's List*, 30 June 1873.
[1121] *Australian and New Zealand Gazette*, 4 October 1873.
[1122] *Australian and New Zealand Gazette*, 4 October 1873.
[1123] *Australian and New Zealand Gazette*, 4 October 1873.
[1124] *The Mercury*, 25 December 1873.
[1125] *Weekly Examiner*, 3 January 1874.
[1126] *The Mercury*, 14, 29 January 1874; *The Tasmanian Tribune*, 30 January 1874; *The Newcastle Chronicle*, 7 February 1874.
[1127] *The Mercury*, 18 February 1874.
[1128] *The Mercury*, 28 November 1874.
[1129] *Australian Town and Country Journal*, 22 August 1891.

Less than two weeks following the launch of the *Nautilus*, J. and D. Mackey received an order from Captain John McLeod of Adelaide for the construction of a new trading vessel.[1130] The 65ft ketch *Alert* was subsequently launched on 6 May 1873.[1131] Intended for the South Australian coastal trade, where it spent nearly 70 years employed, the *Alert* was eventually beached and condemned in the late 1950s, and broken up at Port Adelaide in the 1960s.[1132]

Alert operating in South Australian waters (c1920s).
Courtesy State Library of South Australia (PRG 1373/35/52).

Immediately following the launch of the *Alert*, J. and D. Mackey began building another ketch intended for the coastal trade. Shortly after construction began, the 79ft vessel was purchased by Captain Joseph Davies with G. R. Sealth and Charles Heath of Adelaide subsequently entering into a partnership to take over its ownership prior to completion.[1133] The 58-ton *Lurline* was launched on 27 November 1873, taking only four months to complete, a month less than contracted.[1134] The vessel left Hobart Town on 18 December en route to Port Pirie, South Australia, with seven passengers on board and a cargo of timber and palings.[1135] Like the *Alert*, the *Lurline* spent its entire life operating mainly in South Australian waters until the vessel was driven ashore at Sellicks Beach in April 1946.[1136]

[1130] *The Mercury*, 5 August 1872.
[1131] *The Mercury*, 7 May 1873.
[1132] Register of British Ships: Main Register subsequent to Merchant Shipping Act 1854, Port Adelaide [Roll 3 of 5] [Volume 4 folio 184 to Volume 5].
[1133] *The Mercury*, 7 July, 7 October, 28 November 1873; Register of British Ships: Main Register subsequent to Merchant Shipping Act 1854, Port Adelaide [Roll 1 of 5] [Volume 1 to Volume 2 folio 186].
[1134] *The Mercury*, 28 November, 2 December 1873.
[1135] *The Mercury*, 19 December 1873.
[1136] *Recorder*, 17 April 1946; Register of British Ships: Main Register subsequent to Merchant Shipping Act 1854, Port Adelaide [Roll 3 of 5] [Volume 4 folio 184 to Volume 5].

Lurline sailing in South Australian waters (c1880s).
Courtesy State Library of South Australia (PRG 1373/35/46).

The ship building boom of the early to mid-1870s saw the Mackey brothers expand their business with the erection of a shed 90ft long, 32ft wide and 34ft high completed in May 1874.[1137] With sufficient room to construct a 300-ton vessel, the building was also of benefit to the firm's employees, providing protection from the cold and wet weather often experienced in the winter months. The shed consisted of a spacious ground floor, on which vessels were to be built, as well as a first floor moulding room and a second floor workshop to be used for light carpentry and cabinet-making.[1138]

Shortly thereafter, on 28 July 1874, J. and D. Mackey launched the ketch *Victor* having laid down its keel in January 1874.[1139] A near-replica of the *Lurline*, the craft was built of blue gum, kauri and Huon pine to the order of Captain McLeod of Port Adelaide and was the second such vessel built for him in as many years.[1140] Intended for the South Australian coastal trade, where it spent 50 years employed, the *Victor* was wrecked in January 1925 near Belgowan on the Yorke Peninsula, all hands saved.[1141]

Wreck of the *Victor* near Belgowan, South Australia (1925).
Courtesy State Library of South Australia (PRG 1373/35/87).

[1137] *The Mercury*, 5 May, 1874.
[1138] *The Mercury*, 5 May, 1874.
[1139] *The Mercury*, 10 January 1874.
[1140] *The Mercury*, 10 January, 29 July 1874.
[1141] *The Mail*, 3 January 1925.

In August 1874 the Tasmanian press reported, 'Messrs. J. and D. Mackey have received orders from Mr. Saunders, of Dunedin, to build an eighty ton barge for the New Zealand coasting trade', Saunders at the time being present in Hobart Town.[1142] The resulting craft was launched on 8 June 1875 as the topsail schooner *Martha Reid*.[1143] The 83ft by 22ft vessel was in fact built to the order of G. F. Reid of Dunedin, New Zealand, with the intention of placing it in the New Zealand coastal trade, Mr Saunders acting as an intermediary for its purchase.[1144] After departing Hobart Town a month after its launch, the *Martha Reid* was involved in trade off New Zealand's west coast until 1883 thereafter being sold to buyers from Queensland and employed in that region's coastal trade.[1145] Later it was used as a lighter by Walter Reid and Company of Rockhampton, Queensland, and was still in existence in 1913.[1146]

Sadly the day that the *Martha Reid* was launched from Battery Point coincided with the death of David Mackey's 39-year-old wife Jane (nee Gracie), after a long and painful illness involving heart disease and anasarca.[1147] Widowed, David was left with six children in his care.

In the weeks following the launch of the *Martha Reid*, while David Mackey obviously mourned the loss of his wife, the firm's workers remained busy, laying the keel of a centreboard topsail schooner, to be built off the same moulds as the *Martha Reid*.[1148] Built on speculation albeit slightly longer and deeper than its predecessor, it would be some years before the craft was completed, though it was noted as being planked, both inside and out by May 1876.[1149]

Also in 1875, a new ketch, built to nearly the same dimensions as the *Lurline* and *Victor*, was constructed on speculation, the yard's workers only attending to it when other work was not pressing.[1150] This particular vessel, the 58-ton *Starling*, was purchased by Captain James Carver for £1,600 just prior to launch with the intention of employing it in the Tasmanian coastal trade.[1151] The craft was released from the stays on 14 December 1875 and near-immediately placed on the Launceston to Hobart run.[1152] Completion of the *Starling* was not without mishap, however. A week prior to its launch James Mackey received a severe wound when he fell to the ground at the shipyard. He had been standing upon a stage suspended under the stern of the vessel that gave way. During the fall, a piece of timber struck the left side of his face, knocking out three of his teeth.[1153]

This period additionally coincided with the Mackey brothers busy with their usual slip work, as well as the repair and overhaul of vessels. Another shed was erected at their yard to provide shelter to workers in inclement weather.[1154] Perhaps looking to enter the river trade, the pair also purchased the river barge *Sisters* for £140 in November 1875.[1155]

In May 1876 J. and D. Mackey received an order from Captain Robert Austin Hall for a new vessel to be employed in the Tasmanian coastal trade and were also continuing to build the 98-ton topsail schooner noted below.[1156] Captain Hall's ketch, the *St. Helens*, was launched on 9 December 1876 and soon thereafter began trading between Hobart, Launceston and Georges Bay.[1157] Remaining in Hall's hands, the 74ft vessel was wrecked less than four years later, on 2 October 1880, after striking Black Reef en route from Launceston to Georges Bay with a cargo of sundries, all hands saved.[1158]

J. and D. Mackey finally completed the 98-ton topsail schooner which they named *Falcon* in early 1877, built on speculation, though did not launch the vessel until 14 August of that year.[1159] Under the direction of Captain J. Garth, the vessel sailed for Lacepede Bay, South Australia, on 14 November 1877 on its maiden voyage carrying 29,000ft of timber.[1160] From there the craft sailed to Adelaide where it was advertised for sale or charter.[1161] Failing to sell, the *Falcon* remained in James Mackey's hands until November 1880 upon which time it was purchased by Henry and Robert Castle of Little Swanport.[1162] During the intervening period it was mainly involved in the South Australian coastal trade, also making occasional trips to Victoria, New Zealand and New Caledonia, sometimes with James on board.[1163] The vessel was eventually sold to buyers from Wellington, New Zealand, in 1889 and subsequently wrecked in October 1915 at Raglan on the country's North Island.[1164]

The *Falcon* was the last vessel launched by the firm of J. and D. Mackey. On 1 January 1878 the partnership of James Mackey and his brother David was dissolved by mutual consent.[1165] Retiring from the firm and selling off part of his tools and equipment, David later moved to Victoria.[1166] He died at his residence, 153 Evans Street, Port Melbourne, on 29 July 1899 at the age of 72.[1167]

[1142] *Launceston Examiner*, 4 August 1874; *The Mercury*, 8 August 1874.
[1143] *The Mercury*, 9 June 1875.
[1144] *The Tasmanian Tribune*, 20 April 1875; *The Mercury*, 9 June 1875.
[1145] *The Tasmanian Tribune*, 8 July 1875; *Maryborough Chronicle, Wide Bay and Burnett Advertiser*, 13 March, 9 May 1883.
[1146] ROCKHAMPTON, QUEENSLAND, Main register, Volume 1, 1866-1953, Folio 26; *Cairns Post*, 25 September 1913.
[1147] *The Mercury*, 12 June 1875; Libraries Tasmania (RGD35/1/8 no 2806).
[1148] *The Mercury*, 9 June 1875.
[1149] *The Mercury*, 19 August 1875.
[1150] *The Tasmanian Tribune*, 20 April 1875; *The Mercury*, 5 September 1874.
[1151] *The Mercury*, 1 October 1875.
[1152] *The Mercury*, 12 January 1876.
[1153] *The Mercury*, 8 December 1875.
[1154] *The Mercury*, 26 June 1876.
[1155] *The Mercury*, 2 November 1875.
[1156] *The Tasmanian Tribune*, 4 May 1876; *The Mercury*, 8 May 1876.
[1157] *The Mercury*, 11 December 1876.
[1158] *The Mercury*, 4 October 1880.
[1159] *The Mercury*, 15 August 1877.
[1160] *The Mercury*, 15 November 1877.
[1161] *South Australian Register*, 13 December 1877.
[1162] Register of British Ships: Main Register (with continuation entries), Port of Hobart [contains Volumes 9 (part), 10, 11].
[1163] *The Mercury*, 11 June, 18 September, 1 November 1878; 1 August, 19 September, 23 October 1879.
[1164] *Evening Post*, 20 October 1915; New Zealand Registered Ships & Owners, 1840-1950.
[1165] *The Mercury*, 1 January 1878.
[1166] *Tribune*, 1 January 1878.
[1167] *The Age*, 31 July 1899.

The schooner *Falcon* (left) and *Jessie Nicoll* (right) racing at the Lyttleton Regatta (1 January 1905). Courtesy State Library of South Australia (PRG 1373/41/21).

Continuing operations at his Battery Point shipyard, James Mackey spent the ensuing years primarily involved in the slipping, repair, painting and overhaul of vessels, often helped by his younger brother John who acted as foreman.[1168] Though this area of business remained vigorous, in the 1880s demand for new vessels was at an all-time low.

In August 1882 Mackey was awarded a Hobart Marine Board tender for £426 to build a 48ft punt capable of holding a Priestman's dredge based on plans developed by John Watson, the work to start immediately.[1169] A few months later he received an order from Captain Robert Austin Hall, one of his most valued clients, for a steamer to trade between Hobart, Launceston and Georges Bay.[1170] Hall had travelled to Sydney with the intention of procuring a suitable vessel but had been deterred by all of the leading builders of that city having too much work on hand such that they were unable to accommodate his order.[1171] Instead, he contracted with James Mackey to have the craft built in Hobart.[1172] Obviously needing workers to help with the construction, Mackey then placed an advertisement in *The Mercury* calling for shipwrights specifically from the Huon region, '*accustomed to axe and adze*'.[1173] A few weeks later a separate advertisement called for '*two or three apprentices for shipwright business*'.[1174] The steamer's keel was laid on 15 December 1882.[1175]

Progress on the vessel continued with vigour, helped significantly by the installation of a new steam sawmill at Mackey's Battery Point yard; its engine could also be used for the slipping of vessels, up until this point in time served by windlass.[1176] Diversifying his business enterprises, Mackey was additionally looking to saw and ship timber for export and in April 1883 was also about to open a coal yard.[1177]

Captain Hall's demand for his new vessel became even greater when his east coast trader, the *Starling*, was wrecked during a heavy gale at Bicheno in July 1883.[1178] Built by James Mackey and his brother David in December 1875, the craft had been purchased by Hall in 1880 at a cost of £900 though he had since spent an additional £350 on new rigging, sails, chains and anchors.[1179] Sensing some parts of the craft could be salvaged, Captain Hall sent James Mackey to Bicheno to assess the situation. By the time of his arrival, however, the vessel had broken up and become a total loss; Hall received only £800 from the Derwent and Tamar Assurance Company for the wreck.[1180]

With a length of keel of 112ft, Captain Hall's new steamer, the largest steamer built in Tasmania at the time, was finally launched on 20 December 1883.[1181] Designed from a model by James Mackey, the *Warrentinna* was rigged as a fore-and-aft schooner, and capable of carrying between 30 and 40 passengers.[1182]

[1168] *Tribune*, 27 January 1879.
[1169] *Launceston Examiner*, 5 August 1882; *The Mercury*, 7 August 1882.
[1170] *The Mercury*, 18 October 1882.
[1171] *The Mercury*, 18 October 1882.
[1172] *The Mercury*, 18 October 1882.
[1173] *The Mercury*, 9 November 1882.
[1174] *The Mercury*, 9 November 1882.
[1175] *The Mercury*, 18 December 1882.
[1176] *The Mercury*, 19 April 1883.
[1177] *The Mercury*, 9 November 1882.
[1178] *The Mercury*, 14 July 1883.
[1179] *The Mercury*, 14 July 1883.
[1180] *Launceston Examiner*, 16 July 1883; *The Mercury*, 27 July 1883.
[1181] *The Mercury*, 21 December 1883.
[1182] *The Mercury*, 21 December 1883.

SS *Warrentinna* on James Mackey's Battery Point slip (1883).
Courtesy Tasmanian Archives (NS1013/1/22).

Built of blue gum and kauri pine at a cost of between £6,000 and £7,000, with its engines supplied by Messrs Plenty and Sons of England, the vessel went on to become a linchpin of the east coast trade and remained in Captain Hall's possession until December 1902 when it was sold to William Holyman and Sons and Hall retired from the trade.[1183] After 34 years of total service, in July 1918 the craft was taken off the east coast trade and sold to Captain P. W. Grierson of Sydney to be employed in the New South Wales coastal trade.[1184] The 102-ton *Warrentinna* was noted as being involved in the Hawkesbury River trade in 1922.[1185] It was subsequently advertised for sale at Rose Bay, Sydney, in October of that year.[1186] It is believed to have been broken up a decade later.[1187]

[1183] *The Mercury*, 26 March 1884, 11 December 1902.
[1184] *The Mercury*, 23 July 1918.
[1185] *The Sydney Morning Herald*, 2 February 1922.
[1186] *The Daily Telegraph*, 31 October 1922.
[1187] SYDNEY, NEW SOUTH WALES, Register of ships, single number series (II), Volume 24, 1914-1919, Folio 104.

Buoyed by his shipyard's activity related to the repair, overhaul and slipping of vessels, particularly the larger steamers, as well as the sawing of timber, helped by his new sawmill, Mackey's income was further supplemented by the sale of firewood to residents of Battery Point and Sandy Bay.[1188] The success of these enterprises saw James Mackey purchase the ketch *William and Susan* in July 1885 for use in transporting timber.[1189] Two years later Mackey began selling apple cases built at his yard.[1190] During this period he also purchased the river barge *Friendship* which Mackey owned for several years, employed in the river trade with G. Arnett (Jr) as its master.[1191]

At some point in the mid-to-late 1880s James Mackey employed his nephew Henry Inkerman Featherstone (born 1871) to work at his shipyard. Henry had lived with James and his family from at least 1873, following the death of his father Captain John Featherstone in 1873. It was likely that Featherstone was mentored by Mackey in an apprentice-to-successor type role, likely owing to the fact that Mackey had no sons of his own.[1192] In 1899 the pair received an order from Joseph Graves of Huon Island to build a 98ft steam scow for the timber trade.[1193] It was the first order Mackey had received since the SS *Warrentinna* some 15 years prior. Unfortunately Graves died at Mackey's Battery Point residence on 9 May 1900 while the vessel was part-way through construction, having likely come up to Hobart to view its progress.[1194] The twin screw single-masted scow was subsequently purchased by Bowser and Company of Queensland, contractors for the Alexandra Pier at the time being built at the Hobart Wharf, with the intention of using it to convey timber from the Huon and Channel.[1195] Named *Marie Corelli*, the vessel was launched on 31 July 1901.[1196] Following completion of the Alexandra Pier, in June 1902 the 64-ton craft was subsequently towed to Sydney by the *Whangape* whereupon it was advertised for sale.[1197]

In June 1902 James Mackey announced his retirement and *The Mercury* advertised the dissolution of the Mackey and Featherstone partnership.[1198] Mackey's firewood cutting establishment at his Battery Point yard was also offered for rent, along with a weighbridge.[1199] On 1 February 1904 Mackey sold his shipbuilding yard to Henry Featherstone, in partnership with Thomas Purdon, for the price of £800.[1200] He additionally advertised for sale several building allotments he owned along Marine Terrace at Battery Point.[1201]

James Mackey died at the age of 79 at his residence, 10 Marine Terrace, Battery Point, on 4 June 1905.[1202] He was buried two days later at Cornelian Bay Cemetery.[1203] His wife Marion had died at their home only five months prior, on 10 January 1905, at the age of 74.[1204] She was also buried at Cornelian Bay.[1205] For many years Marion had been involved with the Hobart City Mission.[1206] James Mackey left his entire estate, worth over £2,250 to their daughter and only child Janet 'Jessie' who had been living in Camberwell, Victoria, for several decades.[1207] In March 1879 Jessie had married Robert Alexander Rae of Melbourne, son of Captain R. G. Rae who had been connected with the Hobart-based barques *Eucalyptus* and *Juno*.[1208] The couple had thereupon moved to Melbourne and raised a family.

All told James Mackey was a successful and persevering shipwright over a 53-year period, building or assisting in the building of more than 20 commercial vessels, including the steamers *Emu* and *Warrentinna*, and the barque *Nautilus*, many of which played vital roles in the Tasmanian, South Australian and New Zealand coastal trades. In partnership with his brother David and Thomas Cullen, Mackey was also an entrepreneur, successfully building vessels on speculation and profiting from their trade and subsequent sale. When these two men retired, Mackey continued on with the firm, riding out the lean years of the 1880s and 1890s by supplementing his income with timber transport and sales. A firm believer in the use of local resources and companies, Mackey also stands out as an ambassador of Tasmanian-based private enterprises. Yet, perhaps his greatest achievement was securing the future of his craft through the mentoring of his apprentices, particularly his nephew Henry Featherstone, as well as E. A. Jack, who later went on to establish a successful boat building yard in Launceston.[1209]

[1188] *The Mercury*, 15 June 1885, 8 August 1892.
[1189] *The Mercury*, 23 July 1885.
[1190] *Tasmanian News*, 5 February 1887.
[1191] *The Mercury*, 6 June, 6 November 1889, 8 July 1891.
[1192] *The Tasmanian*, 27 December 1873; N. Mays (2018). *Industrious, Innovative, Altruistic: The 20th Century Boat Builders of Battery Point*.
[1193] Maritime Museum of Tasmania (object D_2010-154); *The Mercury*, 6 June 1900.
[1194] *The Mercury*, 10 May 1900.
[1195] *The Mercury*, 10 July 1901.
[1196] *The Mercury*, 1 August 1901.
[1197] *The Sydney Morning Herald*, 12 July 1902.
[1198] *The Mercury*, 20 June, 1902.
[1199] *The Mercury*, 12 June, 1902.

[1200] www.thelist.tas.gov.au (Historical Deeds 10/8844, 10/8845, 10/5546).
[1201] *The Mercury*, 19 September 1903.
[1202] *The Mercury*, 5 June 1905.
[1203] *The Mercury*, 5 June 1905.
[1204] *The Mercury*, 11 January 1905.
[1205] *The Mercury*, 11 January 1905.
[1206] *Tasmanian News*, 8 April 1893.
[1207] Libraries Tasmania (AD960-1-27 Will Number 6597).
[1208] *The Mercury*, 27 March 1879.
[1209] *Examiner*, 5 December 1946.

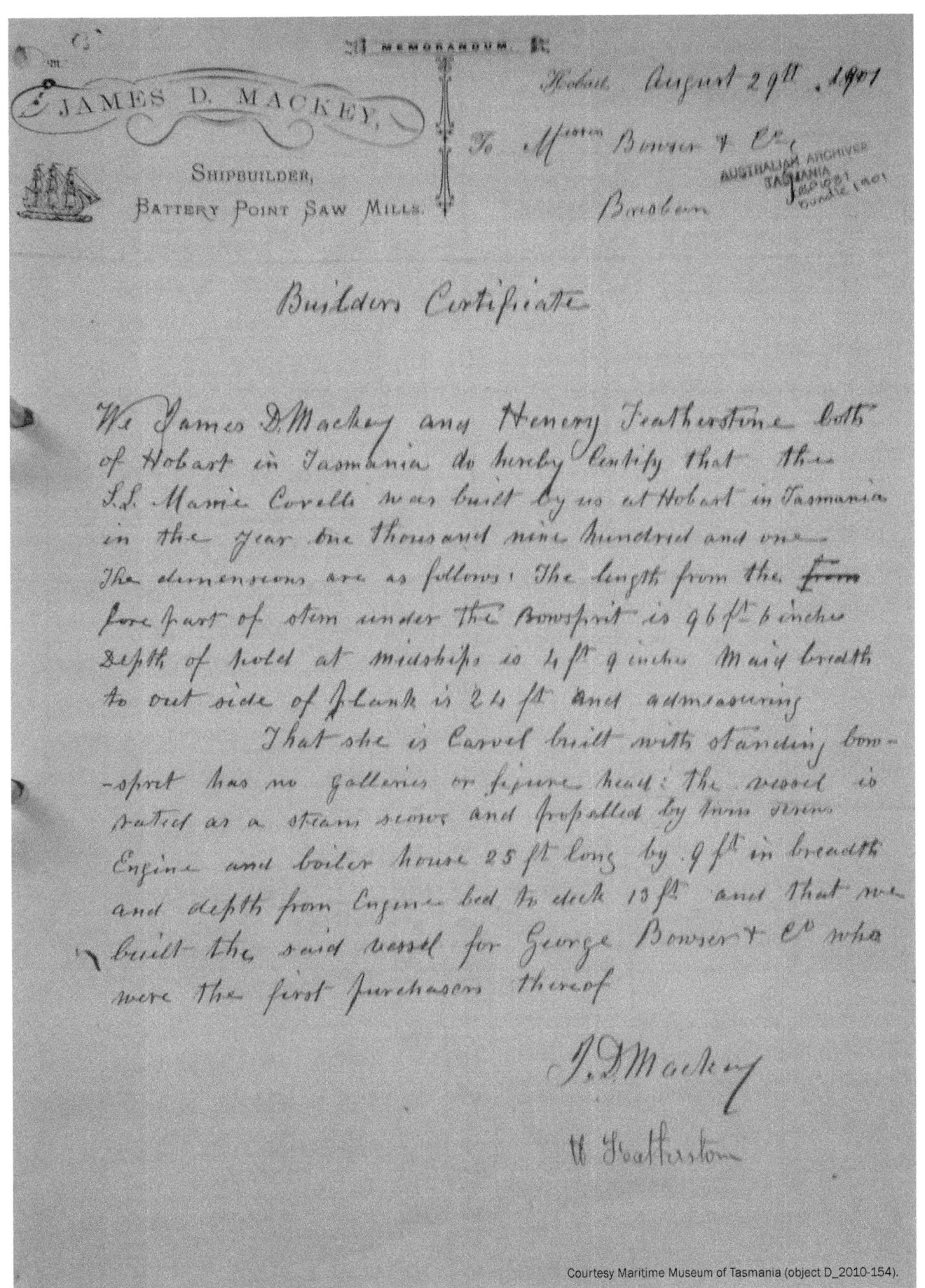

JAMES D. MACKEY,
SHIPBUILDER,
BATTERY POINT SAW MILLS.

Hobart, August 29th, 1901

To Messrs Bowser & Co,
Brisbane

Builders Certificate

We James D. Mackey and Henery Featherstone both of Hobart in Tasmania do hereby certify that the S.S. Marie Corelli was built by us at Hobart in Tasmania in the year one thousand nine hundred and one. The dimensions are as follows: The length from the fore part of stem under the Bowsprit is 96 ft 6 inches Depth of hold at midships is 4 ft 9 inches Main breadth to out side of plank is 24 ft and admeasuring

That she is Carvel built with standing bowsprit has no galleries or figure head: the vessel is rated as a steam scow and propelled by twin screw Engine and boiler house 25 ft long by 9 ft in breadth and depth from Engine bed to deck 13 ft and that we built the said vessel for George Bowser & Co who were the first purchasers thereof

J. D. Mackey

H. Featherstone

Vessels built by Thomas Cullen, James Mackey, David Mackey and/or Henry Featherstone and employees at Battery Point (1852 - 1901)

Year	Name	Type	Description
1852	Success	Schooner	63.6 x 15.7 x 6.4. ON 40908. 44 tons. Built by James Mackey (in association with Thomas Cullen and David Mackey) to the order of George Wilson. Involved in the Hobart Town to Melbourne trade. Transferred to Melbourne in December 1855 after being sold to William Poole of Port Melbourne and shortly thereafter to Arthur Devlin. Employed in coastal trade. In September 1856 sold to John Kerr, James Fowler and Edwin Fowler, all of Melbourne; in June 1858 to John Allbeury and Alfred Saunders; in 1859 to Thomas Hutchinson; and in 1861 to Captain Simon Saunders who employed it in various coastal trades. Wrecked at Palliser Bay, New Zealand, on 30 December 1863, with the loss of two lives. At the time, owned by Captain James Brownell of Lyttelton who had only just purchased the vessel.
1853	Jubilee	Schooner	47 x 11.3 x 4ft. ON 32162. 23 tons. Built by Thomas Cullen and James and David Mackey to the order of Henry Marsh and Henry Chapman, timber traders of Hobart Town, and launched on 'Jubilee Day', 10 August 1853. Employed in the Huon River timber trade. Sold to James Rimon of Mountain River in June 1867. By the 1890s owned by Michael Reardon and involved in the Ralphs Bay trade until July 1919 when purchased by J. H. Burton. Advertised for sale a year later. Subsequent fate unknown.
1853	Uncle Tom	Schooner	69.0 x 14.9 x 5.3ft. ON 32052. 46 tons. Built by Thomas Cullen and James and David Mackey to the order of Osborne and John Geeves and launched late in 1853. Involved in the Huon timber trade for many decades, from April 1857 owned by Henry Pearce. Sold back to Osborne Geeves in February 1888. In March 1911 sold to George Carlisle, though transferred to the liquidator of his estate, Ernest Tinning, a few months later and advertised for sale. Foundered in Frederick Henry Bay on 31 May 1913, all hands saved.
1854	Eva	Schooner	69.1 x 18.3 x 5.2ft. ON 31963. 56 tons. Centreboard fore-and-aft schooner built by Thomas Cullen and James and David Mackey to the order of Captain George Pryde and launched in late 1854. Advertised for sale in August 1858 by order of the mortgagee and again in November 1859. Sold to Edward Edwards of Launceston. Changed ownership several more times during the 1860s, though remained a regular in intercolonial trade. Wrecked at Whales Head Harbour, Tasmania, on 22 May 1880 en route from Macquarie Harbour to Port Adelaide, all hands saved. At the time of loss, owned by Robert Jones of Melbourne.
1857	Topsy	Sloop	45.9 x 13.0 x 5.4ft. ON 32058. 21 tons. Built by Thomas Cullen and James and David Mackey to the order of William Domeney and launched in 1857. Employed in the Huon River trade. Sold to Francis Canes in October 1860, though Domeney remained its master. Went ashore and was wrecked near Bruny Island Lighthouse on 14 March 1861, all hands saved.
1857	Emu	Steamer	99.6 x 10.4 x 6.1 ft. ON 32066. 28 tons. Built by Thomas Cullen and James and David Mackey for Captain John Hanson and intended for the Hobart Town, Richmond and Sorell trade. Launched in 29 December 1857. Fitted with 20 h.p. engines. In September 1859 sold to Edward Luttrell and Frederick Wise, remaining in the same trade. The latter later became sole owner. Abandoned around 1898 after it sank at its moorings at New Norfolk where its hulk still lies on the bottom of the River Derwent.
1861	--	Fishing boat	30 tons. Built by Thomas Cullen and James and David Mackey. Noted under construction in July 1861. No additional details known.
1862	--	Yacht	Built by Thomas Cullen and James and David Mackey and intended to compete at the 1862 Hobart Town Regatta.
1862	--	Boat	Built by Thomas Cullen and James and David Mackey. Under construction in April 1862.
1862	David and Jessie	Schooner	106 x 22 x 11ft. 141 tons. Built by Thomas Cullen and James and David Mackey to the order of Captain William Pie and launched on 20 September 1862. Intended for the New Zealand trade. Later traded between Ceylon, Singapore and various Australian ports. Stranded at Colombo Harbour on 12 September 1870 and sold as a wreck; all hands saved.
1863	Tasman	Ketch	82.6 x 22.4 x 6.2ft. ON 32114. 79 tons. Built by Thomas Cullen and James and David Mackey to the order of H. F. Armstrong for the Cardiff Coal Company, NSW. Launched on 13 October 1863 and a month later sold to William Waterhouse, James Harcourt and O. H. Hedberg of Hobart Town. Purchased on 3 December 1863 by the Seymour Coal Company, NSW. Sold to James Dunn of Hobart Town in June 1867. In March 1869 sold back to Messrs Waterhouse, Harcourt and Hedberg, along with H. S. Barrett. In September 1871 sold to Henry Dale of Port Adelaide and its register transferred to South Australia. Several additional short-term owners over the next two decades. Sold to Joseph Lee of Duck River, Tasmania, in June 1888 and involved in the local coastal trade. Wrecked off Sandy Cape on 16 January 1891, all hands saved.
1864	Marie Louise	Schooner	56.8 x 14.7 x 6.7ft. ON 32125. 22 tons. Fore-and-aft schooner built by Thomas Cullen and James and David Mackey to the order of Dr William Crowther and launched in early April 1864. Intended for the D'Entrecasteaux Channel timber trade in which it spent several years employed, also competing in local regattas. Advertised for sale in August 1866 though failed to sell. Sold in October 1868 to George Salier of Hobart Town and in March 1869 to Henry Hopkins (Jr). Converted to a sea-going yacht, re-launched in May 1869 and used as a pleasure craft. Sold to Edward Atkinson in June 1871 and sailed to Fiji. Wrecked there a few months later.

Year	Name	Type	Description
1865	Falcon	Schooner	66.5 x 17 x 5.4 ft. ON 32137. 36 tons. Built on speculation by Thomas Cullen and James and David Mackey specifically for the Tasmania east coast trade. Instead sailed to Nelson, New Zealand, by Thomas Cullen and James Mackey a month after launch where it was subsequently sold to Joseph Milo of Wellington. Foundered at Patea River on the North Island in February 1884, all hands saved. At the time of loss, owned by its master Captain P. Leslie.
1868	Kestrel	Schooner	71.2 x 17.2 x 6.6ft. ON 57499. 50 tons. Built by Thomas Cullen and James and David Mackey on speculation, though designed specifically for the New Zealand bar harbour trade. Launched in August 1868 and purchased by Captain Henry Williams and placed in the Tasmanian east coast trade. Sold to buyers from New Zealand in 1874 and employed in the coastal trade there for many decades. Ultimately broken up in 1932.
1871	Osprey	Schooner	65.5 x 17.5 x 5.3ft. ON 57524. 38 tons. Built by Thomas Cullen and James and David Mackey on speculation and launched in January 1871. Near-immediately sold to William G. Cheverton and placed in the Huon timber trade. By 1872 trading between Launceston and Hobart. Purchased by W. H. Binney of Adelaide in January 1873 for £740. Became a regular trader in South Australia. Foundered after leaving Port Julia on 11 September 1903, no survivors. At the time of loss, owned by Samuel Bishop of Port Adelaide.
1872	Nautilus	Barque	119.4 x 26.0 x 14.0ft. ON 57527. 243 tons. Built by James and David Mackey to the order of Henry Hopkins (Jr) with the intention of placing it in international trade. Launched on 25 July 1872. Left Hobart Town on its maiden voyage on 18 January 1873 sailing to Adelaide and then England with its owner on board. Then made several trips to Asia. Sold in October 1875 for £3,000, following Henry Hopkins' death, to H. F. Armstrong of Hobart and employed in intercolonial trade, mainly out of Sydney. Subsequently sold in 1887 to a syndicate from Sydney and placed in the South Seas trade. Destroyed by fire in Noumea in August 1891.
1873	Alert	Ketch	65.6 x 17.9 x 6.5ft. ON 57535. 44 tons. Built by James and David Mackey to the order of John McLeod of Adelaide and launched on 6 May 1873. Well-known coastal trader of South Australia, where it spent 70 years employed under many owners. Beached and condemned in the late 1950s and broken up at Port Adelaide in the 1960s.
1873	Lurline	Ketch	79 x 18.5 x 7.1 ft. ON 57541. 58 tons. Built by James and David Mackey. Purchased by G. R. Selth and Charles Heath of Adelaide, shortly after construction began. Launched on 27 November 1873. Involved in South Australia's coastal trade under several owners in the following decades. Driven ashore at Sellicks Beach in July 1946, all hands saved.
1874	Victor	Ketch	79 x 19.9 x 7.5ft. ON 57547. 67 tons. Built by James and David Mackey to the order of Captain McLeod of Adelaide. Well-known trading vessel of the South Australian gulf trade for many decades under several owners. Wrecked in January 1925 near Belgowan, all hands saved.
1875	Martha Reid	Schooner	83.0 x 22.0 x 6.7ft. ON 57556. 80 tons. Topsail centreboard schooner built by James and David Mackey to the order of G. F. Reid of Dunedin. Launched on 8 June 1875. Employed in coastal trade on New Zealand's west coast until 1883. Subsequently sold to August Cross of Townsville and employed in the Queensland coastal trade. Later used as a lighter by Walter Reid and Company of Rockhampton. Still in existence in 1913.
1875	Starling	Ketch	77.0 x 18.7 x 7.1ft. ON 57561. 58 tons. Built by James and David Mackey on speculation and purchased by Captain James Carver just prior to completion. Launched on 14 December 1875 and placed in the Tasmanian coastal trade. Sold to John Pearce of Hobart Town in July 1879. Wrecked in July 1883 at Bicheno, all hand saved.
1876	St. Helens	Ketch	74.8 x 20.4 x 8.1ft. ON 57575. 68 tons. Built by James and David Mackey to the order of Captain Robert Austin Hall. Launched on 9 December 1876 and employed in the Tasmanian coastal trade. Wrecked on 2 October 1880 at the entrance to the Tamar River, all hands saved.
1877	Falcon	Schooner	92.0 x 22.6 x 7.3ft. ON 57585. 98 tons. Top-sail centreboard schooner built by James and David Mackey on speculation. Launched on 14 August 1877. Remained in James Mackey's hands and employed in the Tasmanian and South Australian coastal trades, as well as sailing to New Caledonia. Sold to local buyers in June 1880 and buyers from Wellington in 1889. Transferred to New Zealand. Wrecked at Raglan Harbour in October 1915, all hands saved.
1882	--	Punt	48ft. Built by James Mackey to the order of the Hobart Marine Board based on plans developed by John Watson. Intended to hold a Priestman's steam dredge.
1883	Warrentinna	Steamer	111.9 x 19.6 x 10.2ft. ON 57608. 102 tons. Built by James Mackey to the order of Captain Robert Austin Hall for the Tasmanian east coast trade. Launched on 20 December 1883. Sold to W. Holyman and Sons in December 1902 but remained in the east coast trade. In July 1918 sold to Captain P. W. Grierson of Sydney to be employed in the NSW coastal trade. Last noted in the Hawkesbury River trade in 1922. Advertised for sale at Rose Bay in October 1922. Register states it was broken up in the 1930s.
1901	Marie Corelli	Steam scow	98.5 x 23.9 x 5.8ft. ON 105690. 64 tons. Built by James Mackey and Henry Featherstone to the order of Joseph Graves of Huon Island. Purchased by Bowser and Company following Graves' death part-way through construction. Launched on 31 July 1901 and used to transport timber from the Huon and D'Entrecasteaux Channel to build the Alexandra Pier. Chartered in March 1902 to E. A. Bruce for the Huon passenger trade. Subsequently towed to Sydney by the *Whangape* in June 1902 and advertised for sale.

Spirited, Skilled and Determined

John Ross.
Courtesy Tasmanian Archives (NS2511/1/233).

John Ross

'The health of Mr. Ross, under whose superintendence the vessel had been built, was given by Mr. Perry, who complimented him upon the handsome way in which she had been turned off the stocks. Mr. Ross said he was not much of an orator, but returned thanks for the honour conferred upon him.'

The Courier, 20 December 1848.

Born and formally trained in Canada, John Ross immigrated to Melbourne from England in 1842 with fellow shipwright John Dunn, who may have been a distant cousin. Together the pair built several schooners and barques at a yard located on the banks of the Yarra River. In 1848 Ross moved to Hobart Town where he supervised the building of vessels at the Degraves family's Battery Point shipyard, including the 403-ton *Derwent*. In 1851 Ross established his own shipyard at Battery Point where he installed Tasmania's first patent slip. Capable of accommodating vessels up to 1,500 tons, the slip was a boon for Hobart Town's maritime industry. Between 1852 and 1871 John Ross also built ten vessels. These included one ship, three barques, and four schooners.

Unfortunately documents confirming John Ross' early years are quite elusive. Descendants state he was born in Halifax, Nova Scotia, Canada, on 22 December 1814 and that he undertook his shipbuilding apprenticeship at the Halifax Royal Naval Dockyard.[1210] However, the accuracy of these claims requires further investigation as by 1818, i.e., when John Ross was just four years of age, the North American base for the Royal Naval Dockyard was formally moved from Halifax to Bermuda.[1211] What is more plausible is that Ross undertook his shipwright training at the Royal Navy Dockyard in Kingston, Ontario, which remained in operation until the early 1850s.[1212] If this is the case, it's very likely that Ross was descendant from Scottish-born Highlanders who served with one of several foot battalions during the American Revolutionary War, including with the King's Royal Regiment of New York.[1213] Following the war, the regiments were reduced, moving to the Canadian provinces, with some men continuing in service based in Halifax, while others were disbanded. Referred to as 'United Empire Loyalists', thousands of the soldiers discharged from these regiments remained in Canada where they were granted parcels of land to farm. They settled in Ontario, along the St Lawrence River, as well in Nova Scotia. Included amongst these men, for example, was one Thomas Taylor Ross (born in Glencalvie, Kincardine, Scotland in 1726) who along with his wife and four sons settled in the South Lancaster area of Glengarry county, Ontario, in the late 1780s, with many lineal descendants being produced from this branch of family, possibly including John Ross.[1214]

More family anecdotes state that following a period of apprenticeship John Ross moved to Boston, Massachusetts, in the United States, where he gained further experience as a shipwright.[1215] He is then stated to have travelled to Scotland, again likely his family's native place, where in Glasgow he sought passage to Australia on the recently launched 560-ton ship *Ocean*.[1216] The vessel sailed from Liverpool, England, on 12 May 1842 arriving in Melbourne, Victoria, on 27 September of that year.[1217] Travelling on board the vessel with John Ross was John Dunn, a fellow shipwright from Halifax.[1218] The pair apparently worked their passage to Australia, employed on board the vessel as carpenters.[1219]

> First Vessel warranted to sail in all April.
> **FOR PORT PHILIP & SYDNEY, N.S.W.**
> The splendid new frigate-built Ship OCEAN, JAMES WARD, Commander; A 1 at Lloyd's, 560 tons per register, thoroughly copper-fastened and coppered, and sails very fast. This noble ship has elegant and spacious accommodations for passengers in the cabin, second cabin, and steerage, and carries an experienced Surgeon.—For freight or passage apply to H FOX and GRICE, 2, King-street.

Liverpool Mercury, 22 April 1842.

[1210] W. Lawson and the Shiplovers' Society of Tasmania (1949). *Blue Gum Clippers and Whale Ships of Tasmania*.
[1211] http://en.wikipedia.org/wiki/Royal_Naval_Dockyard,_Halifax.
[1212] http://en.wikipedia.org/wiki/Kingston_Royal_Naval_Dockyard.
[1213] https://www.uelac.org/SirGuyCarleton/PDF/Kingnote.pdf.
[1214] https://freepages.rootsweb.com/~guppyross/genealogy/rosstt.html.
[1215] *The Mercury*, 6 May 1932.
[1216] *The Mercury*, 6 May 1932.
[1217] *Liverpool Mercury*, 13 May 1842; *The Sydney Morning Herald*, 10 October 1842.
[1218] *The Mercury*, 6 May 1932, 7 January 1936.
[1219] W. Lawson and the Shiplovers' Society of Tasmania (1949). *Blue Gum Clippers and Whale Ships of Tasmania*.

Ross and Dunn appear to only have stayed in Melbourne a few days before boarding a schooner to Hobart Town.[1220] They must have returned some months later as by October 1843 the pair petitioned the Melbourne Town Council for the *'indulgence of being allowed to occupy the land below Dobson's wharf'* without occurring the cost of a squatters licence.[1221] The purpose of occupying the property was to build a craft of 40 tons.[1222] While it is not known if their effort to thwart a licence was successful, the enterprising duo established a shipbuilding firm on the south bank of the Yarra River basin operating under the name of Messrs Dunn and Ross.[1223] Here they built several vessels in the succeeding years. These included the 75-ton schooner *Teazer*, launched in December 1844; as well as the 40-ton schooner *Henry*, launched in October 1845 to the order of Captain Lawler; and the *Jane Cain*, a barque of 290 tons built to the order of Captain Cain and launched on 27 January 1848.[1224] Throughout this period, Messrs Dunn and Ross also undertook overhaul and repair work.[1225] In mid-1845 Ross additionally traded in the *Teazer* between Adelaide, Portland and Melbourne.[1226]

At 120ft in length, the *Jane Cain* was the largest class of ship yet built in Victoria and was launched in front of 4,000 spectators, all eager to witness the event.[1227] In relaying the specifications of the *Jane Cain*, the press notably made reference to the 547-ton ship *Harpley* that only 12 months prior had been launched from the banks of the Tamar River north of Launceston in Van Diemen's Land.[1228] This particular vessel had proved a disaster, owing to the use of inadequately seasoned swamp gum in its construction. By comparison, the *Jane Cain* was noted to be *'strongly built, and of the best native materials, having none of the "cabbage stalk" about her'*.[1229] Significantly, the same press report stated that John Ross had been present at the launch of the *Harpley*, built by John Patterson to the order of John Raven.[1230]

While John Ross was enjoying professional success in the newly-developing colony of Victoria, he was also building a family. On 24 September 1846 in Melbourne Ross married Margaret Laurie Paterson, youngest daughter of the late James Paterson of Scotland.[1231] Margaret's father had been a surveyor of Montrose who published several books on the survey of roads and highways, as well as on the use of microscopes and telescopes.[1232] Paterson also undertook experiments on the use and storage of gas from coal for street lights in public places.[1233]

Margaret 'Maggie' Paterson had immigrated to Victoria in the mid-1840s following the death of her father many years prior. She followed in the path of several brothers and sisters, as well as her mother Grace.[1234] Of note, Margaret's older sister Jessie had departed England in late February 1836 as one of 10 cabin passengers on board the ship *Eveline*.[1235] The vessel arrived in Hobart Town on 12 July, with Jessie marrying Thomas Napier just three weeks later.[1236] The pair knew one another prior, as Napier was also from Montrose, Scotland, and had immigrated to Hobart Town in 1832, arriving per the barque *Lavinia* in November of that year.[1237] Thomas and Jessie Napier moved to Melbourne early in 1837 where they became established settlers of the Moonee Ponds area.[1238] Three years later Jessie and Margaret's brother William Paterson arrived in Melbourne from Scotland, going on to establish himself as a watchmaker.[1239] Soon followed another brother, James in 1843, who became secretary of the Melbourne Mechanics' Institution.[1240] James travelled with their mother Grace. All told, the Paterson's were an educated and enterprising family, taking advantage of the many opportunities afforded to them in the growing colony of Victoria.

In May 1848, a few months after the launch of the *Jane Cain*, John Ross and John Dunn ended their partnership. Ross then advertised the whole of his stock of timber, pitch, tar and tools for sale by auction, as well as the contents of the house he and his wife were living in. The decision to vacate the property and cease operation of his shipbuilding was detailed in the local press. *'Ship Building - We regret to hear that there existing no employment in this branch of business at present, Mr. Ross, the builder of the Jane Cain, is about to leave the colony, and proceed to follow the same line of business in Hobart Town.'*[1241] The article continued. *'The great objection to ship-building, upon an extensive scale, in this county is, that although the red gum is the most durable wood known for vessels, yet it is so difficult to work that the labour tells up so fast that ships cost 20 per cent. more than in Van Diemen's Land, and although they are more durable no person likes to pay so high for them. It will be an immense disadvantage to this colony to lose so excellent a builder as Mr. Ross, who is acquainted with naval architecture in all its branches'*.[1242]

[1220] *Port Phillip Patriot and Melbourne Advertiser*, 6 October 1842.
[1221] *Melbourne Times*, 27 October 1843.
[1222] *Melbourne Times*, 27 October 1843.
[1223] *Geelong Advertiser*, 19 December 1844; *The Port Phillip Patriot and Morning Advertiser*, 2 October 1845; *Port Phillip Gazette and Settler's Journal*, 24 June 1846.
[1224] *Geelong Advertiser*, 19 December 1844.; *Port Phillip Gazette*, 9 July 1845; *The Port Phillip Patriot and Morning Advocate*, 2 October 1845, 23 June 1846; *Port Phillip Gazette and Settler's Journal*, 4, 29 October 1845, 19, 29 January 1848; *Geelong Advertiser and Squatters' Advocate*, 11 June 1847.
[1225] *Port Phillip Gazette and Settler's Journal*, 29 October 1845, 24 March 1847.
[1226] *The Sydney Morning Herald*, 10 May 1845; *Adelaide Observer*, 21 June 1845; *Commercial Journal and General Advertiser*, 16 July 1845.
[1227] *Port Phillip Gazette and Settler's Journal*, 29 January 1848.
[1228] *The Port Phillip Patriot and Morning Advertiser*, 31 January 1848.
[1229] *Port Phillip Gazette and Settler's Journal*, 29 January 1848.
[1230] *The Port Phillip Patriot and Morning Advertiser*, 31 January 1848; Libraries Tasmania (CSO95/1/1 p373).
[1231] *The Melbourne Argus*, 25 September 1846.
[1232] *The Scots Magazine*, 1 April 1819; 1 May, 1 September 1822, 1 July 1823.
[1233] *Hereford Journal*, 16 December 1816.
[1234] *Melbourne Times*, 15 September 1843.
[1235] Libraries Tasmania (CSO92/1/2 p71).
[1236] Libraries Tasmania (RGD36/1/3 no 3343, CSO92/1/2 p71).
[1237] Libraries Tasmania (CUS30/1/1 p154).
[1238] *The Tasmanian*, 10 March 1837; *The Hobart Town Courier*, 8 September 1837; *The Argus*, 24 October 1848.
[1239] Public Records Office of Victoria, Register of Assisted Immigrants from the United Kingdom, VPRS 14/P0000, Book No.2; *Geelong Advertiser*, 17 May 1848.
[1240] *Melbourne Times*, 15 September 1843; *The Age*, 20 February 1855.
[1241] *Port Phillip Gazette and Settler's Journal*, 20 May 1848.
[1242] *Port Phillip Gazette and Settler's Journal*, 20 May 1848.

> **FRIDAY, MAY 26.**
>
> **To Ship-builders and Others**
>
> **G. S. BRODIE**
>
> Has received instructions from Mr. Ross (who is leaving the colony), to sell by auction, on the ground, South Yarra, on
>
> **FRIDAY, MAY 26,**
>
> at 12 o'clock.
>
> THE whole of his Stock of Timber, Pitch, Tar, Tools, &c.
>
> Immediately after which,
>
> The Materials of the House he is at present living in.
>
> ALSO,
>
> The Woolsheds, &c.
>
> The Auctioneer begs to call attention to this sale of Timber; the whole of it is well seasoned, and well adapted for ship or boat building.
>
> Terms cash.

The Port Phillip Patriot and Morning Advertiser, 22 May 1848.

John Ross and his wife Maggie travelled to Hobart Town on board the *Flying Fish*, departing Melbourne on 31 May 1848.[1243] Also on board was their first child, a son named John James who was born at South Yarra earlier that year.[1244] In addition, a shipwright named William Martin, who worked for Messrs Dunn and Ross relocated to Hobart Town with the Ross family.[1245] In November 1848 Martin married Jessie Anderson at Hobart Town, witnesses were John Ross and his wife Maggie.[1246] However, John Dunn, Ross' business partner, chose to remain in Melbourne where he died in 1862 at the age of 56 leaving a wife and one child.[1247]

Upon arrival in Hobart Town, John Ross immediately found work managing the Degraves family's newly established Battery Point shipyard, located off Hampden Road near the Prince of Wales' Battery (refer to map on page 37). Likely also providing employment to William Martin, his first major task was construction of the 230-ton barque *Lady Emma* for Peter and Henry Degraves. The vessel was launched at Battery Point on 16 December 1848, just six months after their arrival from Port Phillip Bay.[1248]

On 18 August 1849 the substantial 403-ton blue gum barque *Derwent* was launched from the Degraves' Battery Point shipyard, built to the order of Messrs Brown and Company under the superintendence of Ross.[1249] Less than six months later, on 29 November 1849, the 137-ton schooner *Jenny Lind* was launched from the Degraves' Battery Point shipyard, also likely under the superintendence of Ross.[1250] The craft was built to the order of Henry Degraves and intended for the Port Phillip Bay trade where it spent several years employed.[1251]

Some time after the launch of the *Jenny Lind*, Ross ended his employment with the Degraves family and moved with his wife and two children to the Huon region.[1252] It was here, at the Esperance Narrows, that Ross then built the 102-ton schooner *Albert Packet*, in conjunction with Anthony McMechan and Duncan McInnes.[1253] The craft was intended for the Port Albert cattle trade and, shortly after launch in August 1850, was purchased by Messrs Boys and Hall.[1254]

Back in Hobart Town, by May 1851 Ross had established his own shipyard at Battery Point. Located on the banks of the River Derwent near the present-day bottom of Finlay Street, it was situated on a portion of the Secheron property that Ross had leased from Mrs Perry and was next door to the Degraves family's shipyard where he had previously worked.[1255] The first vessel laid down at Ross' shipyard was a barque, built to order.[1256] He also began undertaking repair, refit and overhaul work.[1257]

On 4 March 1852 the 194-ton schooner (re-rigged as a barque) *Eucalyptus* was launched, built to the order of Messrs Maxwell and Smith and intended for the Port Phillip Bay trade.[1258] After spending two decades employed on this route, with occasional stints in the trans-Tasman trade, the craft was wrecked near Swan Island on Tasmania's east coast on 26 November 1870, all hands saved.[1259]

The next vessel off the stocks at Ross' Battery Point shipyard was the fore-and-aft schooner-rigged screw steamer *Fire Fly*. Launched in December 1852 and built to ply between Williamstown and Liardet's Beach on Port Phillip Bay, the 43ft craft was instead placed in the Huon trade under the management of Captain Andrew Haig.[1260] However, by August 1853 the *Fire Fly* was advertised for sale at Hobart Town after being found too small for the Huon route.[1261] Failing to sell Ross subsequently altered the vessel to a cutter-rigged

---

[1243] *The Port Phillip Patriot and Morning Advertiser*, 1 June 1848.
[1244] Australia, Birth Index, 1788-1922 (registration number 15694); *Colonial Times*, 9 June 1848.
[1245] *The Port Phillip Patriot and Morning Advertiser*, 1 June 1848.
[1246] *The Argus*, 20 December 1849; Libraries Tasmania (RGD37/1/8 no 455).
[1247] *The Argus*, 10 November 1862.
[1248] *The Courier*, 20 December 1848.
[1249] *The Courier*, 22 August 1849.
[1250] *The Hobart Town Advertiser*, 30 November 1849; *The Courier*, 29 December 1849.
[1251] *The Courier*, 29 December 1849, 31 May 1851.
[1252] Australia Cemetery Index, 1808-2007 for Grace Clark.
[1253] *Colonial Times*, 20 August 1850; R. Parsons (1992). *Australian Shipowners and their Fleets. Book 12 (Hobart to 1859, A - L)*.
[1254] *Colonial Times*, 20 August 1850.
[1255] *The Mercury*, 6 May 1832; *The Courier*, 31 May 1851.
[1256] *The Courier*, 31 May 1851.
[1257] *Colonial Times*, 18 November 1851.
[1258] *Launceston Examiner*, 6 March 1852.
[1259] *The Mercury*, 8 December 1870.
[1260] *The Courier*, 4 April, 26 August 1853.
[1261] *The Courier*, 20 August 1853.

The barque *Eucalyptus* at John Ross's Battery Point Shipyard in front of Secheron House.
Courtesy Maritime Museum of Tasmania (P_2023-051).

schooner and sold its engine to operators of a Huon sawmill for £300.[1262] Still for sale in January 1856, the *Fire Fly* was eventually purchased by Peter Oldham who sailed it recreationally on the Derwent for a number of years.[1263] Sold again in early 1859, the vessel was subsequently placed in the river trade.[1264] The *Fire Fly* was completely wrecked 18 months later, on 9 July 1860, after stranding off Betsey Island, all hands saved.[1265]

With business prospects good, particularly related to the repair, refit, alteration and overhaul of vessels, Ross looked at ways to expand his shipyard's operations. In July 1853 he sent to England for a patent slip.[1266] The slip arrived in Hobart Town on 30 March 1854 on board the *Cornhill*.[1267] The following month Ross successfully petitioned the government to lease the foreshore fronting his shipyard from the Crown.[1268] The lease was for a period of 11 years.[1269]

After many months spent excavating, constructing and installing the patent slip, it was operational by late March 1855 with the 120-ton brig *Cosmopolite* the first vessel hauled up on it.[1270] His Excellency, the Governor, Sir Henry Fox, the Colonial and Private Secretaries, and many of Hobart Town's principal merchants, along with hundreds of spectators, were on hand to witness the auspicious event.[1271]

With a cradle of 170ft by 40ft, the slip was operated by a 20 h.p. steam engine and was capable of receiving vessels up to 1,000 tons.[1272] It was the first of its kind in Tasmania and promised to be a significant asset for the port of Hobart Town. The *Hobarton Mercury* reported, '*The whole affair is admirably adapted for the purpose to which it is to be applied, and has been arranged and completed at a very great expense; its proximity to the harbour, however, will render it extremely convenient for those vessels, which need repairs, and we have no doubt, but that the great outlay of the enterprising proprietor will be profitably compensated*'.[1273] Stated to have cost £20,000, one-quarter of which was borrowed from the Commercial Bank, the slip was also a significant supposition on Ross' part.[1274]

[1262] *Colonial Times*, 20 October 1853.
[1263] *The Courier*, 22 January, 29 December 1856; G. Broxam & M. Nash (2020). *Tasmanian Shipwrecks (Volume 1), 1797 - 1899*.
[1264] *The Courier*, 24 May 1859; *The Hobart Town Daily Mercury*, 24 February 1859.
[1265] G. Broxam & M. Nash (2020). *Tasmanian Shipwrecks (Volume 1), 1797 - 1899*.
[1266] *Colonial Times*, 2 July 1853.
[1267] *Colonial Times*, 29 April 1854.
[1268] *Colonial Times*, 29 April 1854.
[1269] *The Mercury*, 6 May 1932.

[1270] *Colonial Times*, 26 September 1854; *The Courier*, 30 March 1855; *Colonial Times*, 30 March 1855.
[1271] *The Hobarton Mercury*, 30 March 1855; *The Courier*, 30 March 1855; *The Hobart Town Advertiser*, 30 March 1855.
[1272] *The Courier*, 30 March 1855; *Tasmanian Morning Herald*, 21 February 1866.
[1273] *The Hobarton Mercury*, 30 March 1855.
[1274] *Colonial Times*, 30 March 1855; *The Mercury*, 6 May 1932.

In the months that immediately followed its installation, the patent slip proved an extremely worthwhile investment for Ross, such that he repaid the money owed to the Commercial Bank within a year.[1275] It also drew the attention of ship owners in neighbouring colonies, with a lack of similar facilities elsewhere seeing vessels sent to Hobart Town specifically to go on the slip.[1276] Ross also travelled to Melbourne on several occasions to promote and make arrangements for bringing over specific craft to be taken up on the slip.[1277]

In April 1856 prominent members of Hobart Town's business community gave a complimentary dinner to Ross in gratitude for services rendered through the building of his slip.[1278] Appropriately, the dinner was held in the saloon of the locally-owned steamer *Tasmania* which had been hauled up on the patent slip that day.[1279] It was stated during the dinner that in its first year of operation, 40 vessels had used the slip.[1280] Ross was duly presented with a gold watch to mark the occasion, along with a small service plate for his wife.[1281]

The success of Ross' patent slip continued. In 1858 alone 11 steamers and 17 ships, barques, brigs, and schooners were surveyed, cleaned, painted, altered and/or and repaired on the slip, generating nearly £9,000 in income.[1282] There was also joy for Ross and his wife Maggie on a personal level with the birth of three more children, all boys, between 1854 and 1858: Hector, Horatio and Percy.[1283]

SS *City of Hobart* on John Ross' Patent Slip near Secheron (1856). Courtesy Maritime Museum of Tasmania (P_OM_Z_17b).

[1275] *The Mercury*, 6 May 1932.
[1276] *Colonial Times*, 4 March 1856.
[1277] *Colonial Times*, 25 July, 17 October 1856; *The Hobarton Mercury*, 25 July, 4 August 1856.
[1278] *The Hobarton Mercury*, 7 April 1856.
[1279] *The Hobarton Mercury*, 7 April 1856.
[1280] *The Hobarton Mercury*, 7 April 1856.
[1281] *The Hobarton Mercury*, 7 April 1856.
[1282] *The Hobart Town Daily Mercury*, 18 January 1859.
[1283] Libraries Tasmania (RGD33/1/5/ no 1048, RGD33/1/6/ no 619, RGD33/1/7 no 1422).

View of Hobart Town wharves looking over toward Battery Point (1857). Shows a craft under construction at John Ross' Shipyard near the Prince of Wales' Battery, as well as several large vessels moored in its vicinity, likely awaiting their turn on the patent slip.
Courtesy Tasmanian Archives (NS1013/1/991).

Launch of the *Isabella Brown* at Battery Point on 26 February 1859. Courtesy Maritime Museum of Tasmania.

Owing to the popularity of the patent slip, few vessels were built by Ross at his shipyard during the first five years of its operation. However, in October 1855 another, albeit smaller (capable of receiving vessels up to 500 tons), patent slip began operation at Hobart Town's Domain, under the proprietorship of Alexander McGregor.[1284] Less than 15 months later Cullen and Mackey installed a patent slip for vessels up to 200 tons at their Battery Point shipyard, while by May 1861 John Lucas and Robert Jeffrey had also installed a patent slip at their Battery Point shipyard.[1285] Though still considered the primary slip in Hobart Town, it was during the late 1850s that Ross returned to shipbuilding. The 359-ton blue gum clipper *Isabella Brown* and the 13-ton yacht *Maggie Laurie* were both completed in 1859.

Built to the order of Messrs Thomas Brown and Company of Hobart Town and measuring 132ft in length with a beam of 26ft, the *Isabella Brown* was launched on 26 February 1859.[1286] Of note, the vessel was fully rigged as a ship and fitted with an entirely new type of reefing topsail for which Ross, as the inventor, considered applying for a patent.[1287] Intended for the London trade, the craft spent its early years sailing between Australia and England, as well as to the sugar ports of Chile and Mauritius. In March 1865, following the death of its owner, the *Isabella Brown* was sold to Captain Lindsay for £3,500.[1288] Lindsay immediately set about converting the vessel to a barque.[1289] The craft then spent six years employed in various foreign trades, primarily sailing between Australia and California, Mauritius, China, India, Singapore and Guam. Sold again in early 1868 the *Isabella Brown* was ultimately wrecked, owing to negligence of the pilot, en route to Calcutta, India, on 16 April 1871, all hands saved.[1290]

In contrast, the 41ft yacht *Maggie Laurie* (likely named for Ross's wife Maggie Laurie, nee Paterson) was built to the order of William Brown and launched on 21 November 1859.[1291] Constructed specifically to compete in Tasmanian Yacht Club events, the craft which was stated to be of an American model, won the club's inaugural series, as well as the sailing race at the 1861 Hobart Town Regatta, second-place going to Jacob Chandler's *Secret*.[1292] *Maggie Laurie* was often helmed by Ross.

[1284] *Colonial Times*, 10 October 1855; *Tasmanian Morning Herald*, 21 February 1866.
[1285] *The Hobart Town Daily Mercury*, 1, 13 January 1858; *The Mercury*, 14 May 1861.
[1286] *The Hobart Town Daily Mercury*, 18 January 1859; *The Courier*, 28 February 1859.
[1287] *The Hobart Town Daily Mercury*, 18 January 1859.
[1288] *The Mercury*, 17 March 1865.
[1289] *The Mercury*, 24 March 1865.
[1290] *The Sydney Morning Herald*, 10 February 1868; *The Argus*, 7 June 1871.
[1291] *The Hobart Town Daily Mercury*, 11 August, 1 November 1859; *Bell's Life in Tasmania*, 29 November 1859.
[1292] *The Hobart Town Daily Mercury*, 1 November 1859; *The Mercury*, 9 November 1860, 9 December 1861.

By the mid-1860s the 13-ton *Maggie Laurie* was under new ownership and employed in the river trade, transporting fruit and palings from ports in the Huon and D'Entrecasteaux Channel to Hobart Town.[1293] With the exception of a stint as a recreational yacht under the ownership of Henry Hopkins (Jr) and a short period spent in the fishing industry, the vessel maintained its role in the river trade under various owners until 1878 when it was reportedly broken up at Browns River (now Kingston).[1294]

Like his peers, it was also during the late 1850s that Ross began supplementing his shipyard's operations by tendering for various public works projects. In March 1858, for example, he was successfully awarded the Marine Board of Hobart's tender to design and build a swing bridge over the mouth of Constitution Dock, estimating the work to cost £143.[1295] Measuring 40ft by 3ft, the bridge first became operational during May of that year.[1296]

In March 1859 Ross successfully tendered the Government of Tasmania to provide a wooden framed building and flag staff with flags and signal codes, to be delivered to the wharf at Launceston and subsequently forwarded to King Island, requesting £176 for the work.[1297] Later in 1859 Ross received the news that he was unsuccessful at gaining the tender to erect the New Wharf at Hobart Town over a two-year period.[1298]

Between 1861 and 1865 four more vessels were launched from Ross' Battery Point shipyard. These were the *Thomas Brown*, sister-ship to the *Isabella Brown*, and the schooners *Mary Williams*, *Hector* and *Gift*.

Launched on 13 April 1861 the 278-ton barque *Thomas Brown* was built and designed by Ross to the order of William Brown.[1299] An improved model of the *Isabella Brown*, it joined this particular vessel in the tea and sugar trade, also making occasional trips to America and New Zealand. Unfortunately the *Thomas Brown* disappears from the records in June 1879 after arriving in Shanghai, China, from Albany, Western Australia.[1300] It is reported to have been sold to buyers from Japan and subsequently renamed.[1301]

By 1861 Ross and his family were living close to his shipyard, in a house located along Hampden Road.[1302] Involved in the community and interested in its improvements, Ross built a bridge at the bottom of St Georges Hill across the Sandy Bay Rivulet to provide pedestrian access to the public baths. Though compensated for some of its construction, Ross was left with expenses of over £4 for the work.[1303] Education was also important to Ross and his family. In late 1861 his oldest son John (Jr) was awarded first prize for arithmetic at an end of year ceremony for students attending the City School located at 90 Macquarie Street.[1304] In 1866 his son Hector would receive a scholarship to this institution, with Hector and his younger brothers Horatio and Percy all receiving prizes at the end of year awards ceremony in subsequent years.[1305]

Bridge Built by John Ross connecting Battery Point to Sandy Bay (1860s). Courtesy Tasmanian Archives (PH1/1/17).

Christmas 1861 was celebrated with Ross' wife Maggie's sister Jessie and her husband Thomas Napier and two of their children; the family having travelled to Hobart Town from Melbourne.[1306] Several weeks latter Maggie gave birth to their seventh child, a daughter named Mabel.[1307] The Napier family returned to Victoria late in January 1862 taking John Ross (Jr) with them, perhaps in pursuit of further education opportunities.[1308] In June of that same year, Ross escorted two of his daughters (likely Grace, by now aged 12, and Jessie, aged 10) to Melbourne per the *Tasmania*.[1309] While the trio returned to Tasmania a few weeks later, another son (likely Hector) sailed to Melbourne on board the same vessel on 2 July 1862.[1310] Ross' children would continue to travel back and forth between Hobart Town and Melbourne over the coming months and years, very likely staying with their relations, the Napier family.[1311]

[1293] *The Mercury*, 18 November 1864, 29 January 1866.
[1294] *The Tasmanian Times*, 27 February 1869; *The Mercury*, 14 September 1871, 10 January 1872; *The Tasmanian Tribune*, 18 August 1873; HOBART, Register of ships, Volume 8, 1865-1877, Folio 179.
[1295] *The Hobart Town Daily Mercury*, 24 March 1858.
[1296] *The Hobart Town Daily Mercury*, 8 May 1858.
[1297] *The Hobart Town Daily Mercury*, 20 March 1859; *The Hobart Town Advertiser*, 30 March 1859; *The Tasmanian Telegraph*, 6 April 1859
[1298] *The Courier*, 31 May 1859.
[1299] *The Hobart Town Advertiser*, 15 April 1861; *The Mercury*, 15 April, 21 June 1861; HOBART, Register of ships, Volume 8, 1865-1877, Folio 108.
[1300] *The Mercury*, 15 July 1879.
[1301] LAUNCESTON, TASMANIA, Register of British ships, Volume 4, 1855-1885, Folio 102.
[1302] *The Mercury*, 30 May 1861; *The Advertiser*, 7 May 1862; www.thelist.tas.gov.au (Historical Deeds 04/7731 and 04/8819).
[1303] *The Mercury*, 23 November 1861.
[1304] *The Mercury*, 24 December 1861.
[1305] *The Mercury*, 29 September 1866, 18 December 1867, 18 December 1868; *The Tasmanian Times*, 17 December 1870.
[1306] *The Hobart Town Advertiser*, 24 December 1861.
[1307] Libraries Tasmania (RGD33/1/8 no 4983).
[1308] *The Mercury*, 29 January 1862.
[1309] *The Advertiser*, 4 June 1862.
[1310] *The Mercury*, 30 June, 3 July 1862; Libraries Tasmania (MB2/39/1/28 p. 145).
[1311] *The Advertiser*, 24 December 1862; *The Mercury*, 5 April 1864; *Hobart Town Advertiser*, 31 December 1864.

A lover of dogs, Ross imported a retriever and Scotch terrier from London, the pair arriving in Hobart Town as cargo on board the *Heather Bell* in September 1862.[1312] A few months later he entered both dogs in a canine exhibition.[1313] Ross also provided a sample of blue gum for exhibition as part of the Tasmanian showcase at the International Exhibition held in London in 1862.[1314]

With regards to new vessels, the 87ft ketch-rigged schooner *Mary Williams* was launched from Ross' Battery Point shipyard on 23 May 1863, his daughter Jessie doing the customary christening ceremony.[1315] Intended as a collier and purchased just prior to completion by the Cardiff Coal Company of Newcastle, New South Wales, for £2,100, the craft was initially put to use as a coal transport.[1316] However, the *Mary Williams* spent little time in this role. It was advertised for sale in conjunction with other assets of the Cardiff Coal Company throughout 1864.[1317] In January 1865 the vessel was purchased by Alexander Smail of Sydney for £1,226.[1318] Placed in the trans-Tasman trade, the *Mary Williams* sadly went missing off the west coast of New Zealand in late 1865 with the loss of all on board.[1319]

On 6 April 1865 the 115-ton schooner *Hector* was launched from Ross' Battery Point shipyard.[1320] Built on speculation, the vessel remained in Ross' hands for some months, sailing to Sydney on its first voyage with a cargo of timber in June 1865.[1321] Perhaps to broker a sale, Ross, his wife and two of their children also travelled to Sydney during this period, arriving back in Hobart Town per the steamer *City of Hobart* on 23 July 1865.[1322] However, the *Hector* was not sold until November of that year having been purchased by Messrs G. Fisher and Captain Bell of New Zealand with the intention of placing the craft in intercolonial and trans-Tasman trades.[1323] After several mishaps, including being abandoned by its crew in the west channel of Port Phillip Bay in June 1871, and several changes of ownership, the *Hector* went missing en route from Sydney to Ballina, New South Wales, in February 1875 with the loss of all passengers and crew.[1324]

Shortly after the launch of the *Hector*, Ross was engaged by the Venerable Archdeacon Thomas Reibey to build a mission boat for use in visiting the islands of Bass Strait.[1325] The resulting vessel, a schooner named the *Gift*, was launched on 18 October 1865.[1326] Paid for by donations to the Church of England, Ross was noted in the press as having supplied the labour *pro bono* such that the total cost of the vessel was only £600 instead of the market value of £1,000.[1327]

The *Gift* spent its infant years cruising the islands of Bass Strait, though by 1867 had been found too expensive to maintain.[1328] The craft was subsequently purchased by Messrs Robinson and Lilly and placed in the Tasmanian coastal trade.[1329] Yet again found to be unsuitable, by December 1868 the *Gift* had been transferred to Western Australia.[1330] After several years spent in the coastal trade, by 1872 the vessel was employed in the pearling industry off the north-west coast of Western Australia.[1331] Unfortunately in October of that same year some of the craft's Malaysian crew mutineered, killing the captain and capturing the vessel in brutal circumstances.[1332] The *Gift* and its rogue crew were subsequently captured by Dutch authorities in Indonesia, with the vessel handed back to its owners, Messrs Roe and Passey, in due course.[1333] Returning to Western Australia the *Gift* spent a decade successfully employed in the pearling industry before being lost during a cyclone off Timor in 1882.[1334]

Venerable Archdeacon Thomas Reibey.
Courtesy Tasmanian Archives (NS407/1/14)

With the lease of his shipyard property near Secheron drawing to a close and an agreement for an extension not reached, in April 1865 Ross purchased

---

[1312] *The Mercury*, 8 September 1862.
[1313] *The Mercury*, 7, 11 November 1862.
[1314] *The Advertiser*, 14 April 1863.
[1315] *The Mercury*, 25 May 1863; *The Advertiser*, 23 June 1863.
[1316] *The Mercury*, 25 May 1863.
[1317] *Newcastle Chronicle & Hunter River District News*, 7 May 1864; *The Sydney Morning Herald*, 22 December 1864.
[1318] *Empire*, 11 January 1865.
[1319] *Grey River Argus*, 6 January 1866; *Daily Southern Cross*, 23 March 1866.
[1320] *The Mercury*, 11 October 1864; 7 April 1865.
[1321] *The Mercury*, 9 June 1865.
[1322] *Hobart Town Advertiser*, 29 July 1865.
[1323] *The Mercury*, 6 November 1865.
[1324] *The Argus*, 12 July 1871; *The Sydney Morning Herald*, 18 July 1874; *The Maitland Mercury & Hunter River General Advertiser*, 27 February 1875.
[1325] *Launceston Examiner*, 13 April 1865.
[1326] *The Mercury*, 19 October 1865.
[1327] *The Mercury*, 19 October 1865.
[1328] *The Cornwall Chronicle*, 16 March 1867.
[1329] *The Cornwall Chronicle*, 11 May 1867; *The Mercury*, 14 May 1867.
[1330] *The Perth Gazette & West Australian Times*, 18 December 1868.
[1331] *The Daily News*, 18 November 1929.
[1332] *The Sydney Morning Herald*, 10 February 1873.
[1333] *The Inquirer and Commercial News*, 23 April 1873; *The Argus*, 21 May 1873; *The Daily News*, 18 November 1929.
[1334] R. Parsons (2008). *Shipping Losses and Casualties concerning Australia and New Zealand*; *The Daily News*, 18 November 1929.

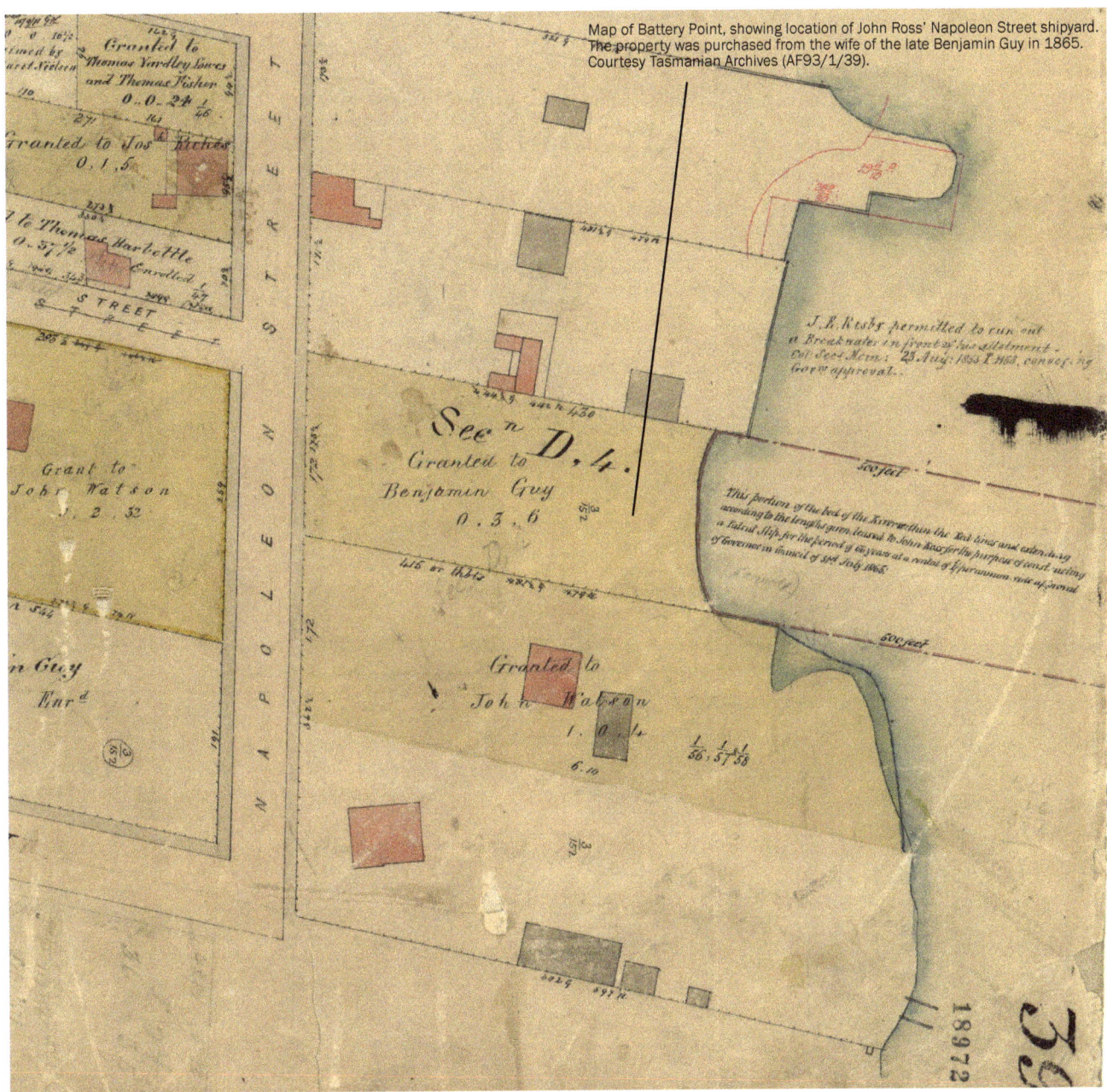

Map of Battery Point, showing location of John Ross' Napoleon Street shipyard. The property was purchased from the wife of the late Benjamin Guy in 1865. Courtesy Tasmanian Archives (AF93/1/39).

an allotment of land at Battery Point between the River Derwent and Napoleon Street for £800.[1335] Previously in the possession of the late Benjamin Guy, and used primarily to house livestock, the nearly one-acre parcel was situated between the shipyard operated by John Lucas and Robert Jeffrey (the duo had taken over the site from John Watson) and the boat yard operated by Charles Miller (formerly operated by the Risby family).[1336] Purchased from Guy's widow Jane, it was the first instance the property had been used as a shipyard and also marked a significant improvement from Ross' existing shipyard in terms of it being sheltered from prevailing winds, tides and currents.[1337] Coinciding with the purchase of the Napoleon Street property, Ross was also granted a 66-year lease from the Government of Tasmania for 500ft of sea bed leading into the River Derwent.[1338] The land occupied by his old shipyard near Secheron was instead leased to the Pyrolignite Company who also owned the neighbouring property which they had purchased from the Degraves family.[1339]

Beginning in December 1865 Ross began establishing his shipyard at the new location, including excavating the site for installation of his patent slip. During the interim, he continued to operate out of his existing yard. The Napoleon Street site was completed in August 1866.[1340] The move was substantial, both in terms of infrastructure and finances, all told estimated to have cost Ross £16,000.[1341]

[1335] *The Mercury*, 22 April 1865; 7 January 1936.
[1336] *The Hobart Town Daily Mercury*, 21 February 1859; *The Mercury*, 22 April 1865.
[1337] *The Advertiser*, 27 July 1865; *The Mercury*, 27 November 1866.
[1338] https://stors.tas.gov.au/RD1-1-58$init=RD1-1-58P064JPG.
[1339] *The Mercury*, 10 January 1867.
[1340] *The Mercury*, 5 December 1865, 25 June, 10 August 1866.
[1341] *The Mercury*, 6 May 1932.

The entire operation may have been why Ross stated that he 'forgot' to pay his carriage licence, as required for vehicles with four wheels under the Carriage Duties Act, when it came for renewal in October 1865. For this misdemeanor, he was summoned by the Hobart Town Police to appear in court in February of the following year.[1342] Upon receiving the summons, Ross sent his son, John (Jr), to pay the licence fee and any costs incurred.[1343] This resolution was, however, flatly refused by the clerk of the bench, stating that Ross must instead appear in court upon which he failed to do. An article published in *The Mercury* discussed the matter, offering much sympathy to '*Mr. Ross [who] has long, as is well known been in an infirm state of health, and he had moreover, to attend on the following day to some over-hauling of the Tasmania and Derwent steamers, which did not admit of delay*'.[1344] The article continued. '*He could not, therefore, appear in court himself, and under the pressure of business of the deepest urgency, unfortunately forgot to desire any one to appear for him. He was, therefore, fined five pounds for contempt of court. This Mr. Ross distinctly affirms not to have been his intention, and he complains, as we think justly of the fine imposed upon him as being far too heavy*'.[1345] The issue was resolved shortly thereafter, however, it was not the last experience the Ross family had with the court system. Maggie Ross was summoned to appear in court a few months later, charged with assaulting Eliza Walker, the 10-year-old daughter of George Walker, a cow keeper.[1346] Not in attendance, due to her own health issues, she pled not guilty. The details of the case were soon revealed, the incident apparently initiated by Eliza's brother fighting with one of Ross' sons.[1347] Both Eliza and Maggie Ross had then intervened in the scuffle with the latter physically assaulting the young girl in the process. With the evidence corroborated by witnesses, Maggie was found guilty and fined 10s and costs.[1348] A second court case immediately followed with Maggie Ross charging George Walker with assaulting her, including breaking one of her teeth.[1349] He too was found guilty by witnesses corroboration and fined 60s and costs.[1350] Considering the cases were all reported in detail in the Hobart Town press, it was likely an embarrassing series of events for the Ross family.

Following the long and arduous task of relocating of his shipyard, not helped by Ross' declining health nor that of his wife, business remained steady, particularly in terms of repairing, refitting and overhauling steamers and larger vessels. For example, in October 1866 the steamers *Black Swan*, *City of Hobart* and *Tasmania* were all cleaned and painted on his slip.[1351] However, perhaps in an attempt encourage new clients, and thereby pay off debt, Ross began advertising for slip yard work in the local press, the first time he had ever done so.

PORT OF HOBART TOWN.

ROSS'S PATENT SLIP

AT BATTERY POINT, IN THIS HARBOR,

Having been removed to a most eligible site, southward of Perry's Point, where it is out of the influence of the tides, currents, &c., and sheltered from the prevailing winds, is now in thorough working order, and offers a safe and convenient place for the repairs and equipment of vessels resorting to this port, particularly those which being disabled by stress of weather, bear up for this excellent haven of refuge.

This slip is capable of taking up with the greatest ease and safety vessels of 1000 tons register. The machinery is in perfect order, having been recently tested, by placing on the slip in succession three large steamers, one of them, the Southern Cross, being the heaviest of her class in these colonies.

Every description of timber, of excellent quality, fit for ship work in particular, is abundant, and labor and materials generally at moderate rates, shipwrights at 10s. per day, and other labor in proportion, being much cheaper than in any of the other colonies.

The charges for slipping for vessels of 1000 tons down to 200 tons, are 1s. per register ton, and 3d. per ton for lay days, Sundays excepted. All vessels below 200 tons and steamers, as may be agreed upon.

N.B.—Vessels touching here for repairs, or supplies, that do not break bulk, "except to pay expenses," are exempt from port charges

JOHN ROSS,

SHIPBUILDER,

HOBART TOWN.

2nd November, 1866.

The Mercury, 13 November 1866.

While Ross was finally settled in to his new shipyard premises and reinvigorating his professional activities, his main focus during 1867 continued to centre around family. On 11 January his sister-in-law Jessie Napier, her husband Thomas and their daughter Eleanor arrived from Melbourne.[1352] Sadly, while they were in Hobart Town, Jessie and Thomas' 18-year-old son, Thomas (Jr), committed suicide by shooting himself in a paddock in Kew, a suburb of Melbourne, the result of, '*suffering from disease of the brain, brought on by fatigue*

[1342] *Tasmanian Morning Herald*, 9 February 1866.
[1343] *The Mercury*, 16 February 1866.
[1344] *The Mercury*, 12 February 1866.
[1345] *The Mercury*, 12 February 1866.
[1346] *The Mercury*, 28 April 1866.
[1347] *The Mercury*, 28 April 1866.
[1348] *The Mercury*, 28 April 1866.
[1349] *Tasmanian Morning Herald*, 28 April 1866.
[1350] *The Mercury*, 28 April 1866.
[1351] *The Mercury*, 25 October 1866.
[1352] *Launceston Examiner*, 12 January, 1867; *Telegraph*, 12 January 1867; en.wikipedia.org/wiki/Thomas_Napier_(builder).

and exposure to the sun, when in Queensland'.[1353] It was a despairing state of affairs that added to prolonged grief as the couple had previously endured the loss of six infants, as well as the death of their 19-year-old son Hector in 1858.[1354]

Ironically, it was very likely that Ross' wife Maggie, who was also quite ill at the time, was the chief reason for her sister's visit. Jessie, Thomas and Eleanor Napier sailed back to Melbourne per the SS *Southern Cross* on 13 February, taking at least one of Ross's daughters with them.[1355]

The melancholy continued. Maggie Ross died at the couple's home, Rosebank, 11 Hampden Road, Battery Point, on 9 May 1867.[1356] She was 44 years of age. Cause of death was '*degeneration of the kidneys and anaemia*'.[1357] Two days later the flags of vessels in the harbour were lowered to half-mast as a mark of respect to her memory.[1358] Ross was left with eight children in his care, ranging in age from 20 months to 19 years. The couple's youngest child, a son named Ernest Sydney, had only been born in August 1865.[1359] Help soon arrived with Jessie Napier sailing back from Melbourne on board the *Southern Cross*, arriving in Hobart Town on 17 May.[1360]

She appears to have stayed several weeks, returning to Melbourne on 8 June.[1361] Jessie and her husband Thomas were again in Hobart Town early in 1868, returning to Melbourne in February, taking Ross' youngest daughter Mabel, then aged 6 years, with them.[1362]

Despite the loss, Ross persisted, needing to support his family. While the patent slip continued to be actively involved in the overhaul, cleaning, painting, repair and refit of large vessels, on the whole there were less vessels visiting Hobart Town.[1363] Likely in an effort to keep his workers busy, in August 1867 Ross began construction of a new vessel.[1364] Built on speculation and intended for coastal trade, the 40-ton cutter *Duke of Edinburgh* was advertised for sale in April 1868 and subsequently purchased by Isaac Wright, local merchant.[1365] It was named for His Royal Highness, Prince Alfred, the Duke of Edinburgh, who visited Hobart Town in early January of that year, with Ross and his foreman John Bradley both participating in the torchlight aquatic procession in honour of the visit.[1366]

Sadly, the relocation of Ross' patent slip and shipyard to Napoleon Street, combined with a decline in revenue, stretched him financially. Ross still owed £8,000 to the Commercial Bank for a mortgage associated

[1353] *The Mercury*, 7 February 1867.
[1354] www.findagrave.com/memorial/193051051/thomas-napier.
[1355] *Launceston Examiner*, 14 February 1867.
[1356] *The Mercury*, 10 May 1867.
[1357] Libraries Tasmania (RGD35/1/7 no 6754).
[1358] *The Mercury*, 11 May 1867.
[1359] Libraries Tasmania (RGD33/1/9 Image 119 no 7982).
[1360] *The Mercury*, 18 May 1867.

[1361] *The Mercury*, 10 June 1867.
[1362] *The Mercury*, 1 February 1868.
[1363] *The Tasmanian Times*, 23 November 1867.
[1364] *The Mercury*, 24 August 1867.
[1365] *The Mercury*, 16 April, 25 April, 30 June 1868.
[1366] *The Mercury*, 31 January 1868.

Rosebank, Hampden Road, Battery Point.
Courtesy University of Tasmania Special and Rare Materials Collection.

with his Napoleon Street shipyard.[1367] Also plagued by ill health, Ross' financial and physical resources were exhausted such that he relinquished his shipyard in the early 1870s. Ross had also been forced to mortgage his home, Rosebank, as well as an adjoining property. Thankfully help came from his brother-in-law, Thomas Napier, who loaned him the money.[1368] The Napier family also continued to provide for Ross' children, with several of the girls travelling to Melbourne to stay with the couple for extended periods of time.[1369]

The last vessel built by Ross was the clipper barque *Acacia*, likely another attempt to keep his workers employed since slip yard business was generally rather slack.[1370] Measuring 118ft, the 232-ton blue gum craft was again built on speculation.[1371] Nearing completion the *Acacia* was sold at public auction on 31 January 1871 to Messrs Belbin and Dowdell for £2,550.[1372] Formally launched on 22 February 1871 in front of 800 spectators, the absence of John Ross, owing to illness, from this most significant of occasions was duly noted in the local press.[1373]

Placed in intercolonial trade, where it spent three decades employed, the *Acacia* went missing en route to South Australia from Port Esperance, Tasmania, on 20 June 1904 with a cargo of timber.[1374] No trace of the craft was found until March of the following year when pieces of wreckage and human remains were identified near Mainwaring Inlet on the west coast of Tasmania.[1375] At the time of loss, the vessel was owned by Robert Richmond Rex and Thomas Charles Herbert of Hobart.[1376]

Of note, while the *Acacia* was under construction, a smaller commercial vessel was also being built at Ross' yard by four shipwrights, including John Bradley, who had formed a company.[1377] Built using their own resources and in their spare time, the 121-ton schooner named *Gleaner* was launched on 7 September 1870.[1378]

[1367] www.thelist.tas.gov.au (Historical Deed 05/5089).
[1368] www.thelist.tas.gov.au (Historical Deed 05/5056).
[1369] *The Mercury*, 22 January 1870; *The Tasmanian Times*, 7 March 1870.
[1370] *The Tasmanian Times*, 16 June 1870; *The Mercury*, 28 January 1871.
[1371] *The Mercury*, 3 December 1870, 19 May 1871.
[1372] *The Mercury*, 1 February 1871.
[1373] *The Mercury*, 25 February 1871.
[1374] *Daily Telegraph*, 21 June 1904.
[1375] *Examiner*, 15 March 1905.
[1376] HOBART, Register of ships (with continuation entries), Volume 10, 1877-1898, Folio 197.
[1377] *The Mercury*, 8 September 1870.
[1378] *The Mercury*, 8 September 1870.

Acacia.
Courtesy State Library of Victoria (H99.220/939).

On 22 November 1871 Ross' Battery Point shipyard was advertised for sale or lease with immediate possession.[1379] The property, comprising nearly an acre of land, also included the patent slip, a drafting loft, a blacksmith's shop and other buildings.[1380] By January of the following year the Commercial Bank had leased the shipyard to John Lucas, shipbuilder of Battery Point.[1381]

With an inability to earn an income due to his health, Ross very likely relied on his children to provide for him, both in terms of care and financial resources. Help likely also came via donations or loans from the Napier family. With Ross' eldest son having previously worked for his father, being mentored for a role that he would never achieve, manager of his father's shipyard, the demise of the yard was multi-generational.[1382] John (Jr) left Tasmania sometime in mid-1870, likely in search of more prosperous work opportunities, possibly heading to Victoria or New Zealand.[1383] Ross' second-eldest son Hector appears to have become the primary provider for the family. In mid-1872 he became second master of St. John's Grammar School in Macquarie Street.[1384] The family remained living at Rosebank, Hampden Road, during this period, with an adjoining block of vacant land, rented out.[1385]

In mid-1874 Hector left his position at St. John's Grammar School and relocated to Melbourne where he successfully completed his matriculation at the Melbourne University, including passing examinations for the civil service.[1386] He returned to Hobart Town to take up a position at Hutchins School as Assistant Master where his brother Ernest was soon enrolled.[1387] By this time Ross' third son, Horatio, had become second mate of the barque *Grasmere*.[1388]

John Ross died of rheumatic arthritis at the General Hospital, Hobart Town, on 17 November 1876, aged 62.[1389] It was likely a severe and protracted death as he had been admitted to the hospital on 23 May 1874, i.e., over two years prior and appears not to have been discharged during this time.[1390] Newspaper reports state that he suffered from paralysis for some years such that death *'mercifully removed him from our midst'*.[1391] Ross was buried in the Church of Scotland section of Cornelian Bay Cemetery.[1392] The flags of the shipping in the Port of Hobart Town were lowered to half-mast as a mark of respect.[1393]

Several of Ross' children remained living at Rosebank with Thomas Napier handing the property over to Ross' three daughters, Grace, Jessie and Mabel in 1878. It was subsequently purchased by Grace and her husband Andrew Inglis Clark and became the home where they raised a large family.[1394] Inglis Clark went on to become a prominent lawyer, politician and judge, as well as vice-chancellor of the University of Tasmania.[1395] Of note, he was also a founding father and co-author of the Australian Constitution, in addition to introducing the Hare-Clark voting system to Tasmania.[1396]

Meanwhile Hector Ross married Hannah Facy at Hobart in 1883, the fifth daughter of the late Joseph Facy.[1397] Hector went on to become a member of the Tasmanian Public Service employed as Sheriff and Registrar of the Supreme Court for several decades.[1398] He died in 1937 at Hobart, aged 82.

Several of John Ross' other children moved to Victoria, Queensland and New Zealand. His second-eldest daughter Jessie married William Pirie of Melbourne in 1883.[1399] She died at Invercargill, New Zealand, in 1923 at the age of 71.[1400]

Ross' youngest daughter Mabel did not marry and died in her sleep at Moonee Ponds, Victoria, on 10 May 1915 at the age of 53.[1401] She had remained in Melbourne in close contact with the Napier family. Upon her aunt Jessie Napier's death in Melbourne in 1890, Mabel was bequeathed part of her substantial estate.[1402]

Ross' sons Horatio and Percy died in Nelson, New Zealand, in 1911, and Ingham, Queensland, in 1927, respectively.[1403] Ross' youngest child, Ernest Sydney, died at Camberwell, Victoria, on 24 October 1943.[1404] For many years he was Inspector of Machinery for the Government of Tasmania.[1405] It it not known what happened to his eldest son John (Jr).

All told, John Ross was an energetic and enterprising shipbuilder who took a calculated risk with the building of Tasmania's first patent slip at his Battery Point shipyard in 1855. The slip proved a windfall, not only for him personally but also for Hobart Town's maritime community and associated commercial enterprises. Though much of his shipyard's more than 20 years of operation comprised overhaul and repair work, particularly of larger vessels and steamers, Ross also notably built several large barques and ships, as well as four schooners during this period, many of which were prominent in international and intercolonial trades.

[1379] *The Mercury*, 22 November 1871.
[1380] *The Mercury*, 22 November 1871.
[1381] *The Mercury*, 30 January, 20 April 1872.
[1382] *The Tasmanian*, 6 May 1871.
[1383] *The Mercury*, 5 May 1871; *The Tasmanian*, 6 May 1871.
[1384] *The Mercury*, 22 June 1872, 22 January, 1 July 1873.
[1385] *The Mercury*, 26 September 1874.
[1386] *The Mercury*, 18 December 1874, 23 January 1875; *The Tasmanian Tribune*, 22 January 1875.
[1387] *Tribune*, 7 July, 22 December 1876; *The Mercury*, 22 December 1876.
[1388] *The Cornwall Chronicle*, 1 November 1876.
[1389] *The Mercury*, 18 November 1876; Libraries Tasmania (RGD35/1/9 no 93).
[1390] Libraries Tasmania (HSD145/1/1 Oct-Nov 1876).
[1391] *Tribune*, 18 November 1876.
[1392] Libraries Tasmania (AF35-1-1 (BU 1322)).
[1393] *The Mercury*, 20 November 1876.
[1394] *The Mercury*, 18 January 1878.
[1395] adb.anu.edu.au/biography/clark-andrew-inglis-3211.
[1396] hen.wikipedia.org/wiki/Andrew_Inglis_Clark.
[1397] *The Mercury*, 13 January 1883.
[1398] *Advocate*, 12 October 1937.
[1399] *The Mercury*, 19 January 1883.
[1400] www.findagrave.com/memorial/191754840.
[1401] *The Argus*, 13 May 1915.
[1402] *Table Talk*, 19 September 1890.
[1403] www.findagrave.com/memorial/145322098; Australia, Death Index, 1787-1985 (Registration Number 003943).
[1404] *The Mercury*, 26 October 1943.
[1405] *The Mercury*, 26 October 1943.

Vessels built by John Ross and employees at Battery Point (1852 - 1871)

Year	Name	Type	Description
1852	*Eucalyptus*	Barque	101.0 x 22.4 x 9.7ft. ON 32009. 194 tons. Built by John Ross to the order of Messrs Maxwell and Smith and launched on 4 March 1852. Intended for the Port Phillip Bay trade where it spent nearly two decades employed under several owners, with occasional stints in the trans-Tasman trade. Wrecked near Swan Island on Tasmania's east coast on 26 November 1870, all hands saved. At the time of loss, owned by William Belbin and Charles Dowdell.
1852	*Fire Fly*	Steamer (Schooner)	43.4 x 10.0 x 5.0ft. ON 32036. 13 tons. Fore-and-aft schooner-rigged screw steamer built by John Ross and launched in December 1852. Built to ply between Williamstown and Liardet's Beach on Port Phillip Bay, instead placed in the Huon trade though advertised for sale shortly thereafter. Engine removed and converted to a schooner in mid-1853. Used to sail recreationally on the River Derwent by owner Peter Oldham for a number of years until sold and placed in the river trade. Wrecked after stranding on Betsey Island, Tasmania, on 9 July 1860.
1859	*Isabella Brown*	Ship (Barque)	132.0 x 26.5 x 16.6ft. ON 32073. 359 tons. Built by John Ross to the order of Thomas Brown and Company of Hobart Town and launched on 26 February 1859. Intended for the London trade where it spent its early years, as well as trading to the sugar ports of Chile and Mauritius. Sold to Captain Samuel Lindsay in March 1865 and converted to a barque. Spent six years employed in various foreign trades, primarily sailing between Australia and California, Mauritius, China, India, Singapore and Guam. Sold to Victorian buyers in January 1868 and transferred to Melbourne. Ultimately wrecked, owing to negligence of the pilot, en route to Calcutta, India, on 16 April 1871, all hands saved.
1859	*Maggie Laurie*	Yacht	41.3 x 10.5 x 5.6ft. ON 32132. 13 tons. Built by John Ross to the order of William Brown to compete in Tasmanian Yacht Club events. Won the club's inaugural series, as well as several local regatta races in its infant years. By the mid-1860s employed in the river trade. With the exception of a stint as a recreational yacht under the ownership of Henry Hopkins (Jr) and a short period spent in the fishing industry, maintained its role in the river trade under various owners until 1878 when it was reportedly broken up at Browns River (now Kingston).
1861	*Thomas Brown*	Barque	144.0 x 24.7 x 13.2ft. ON 32093. 278 tons. Built and designed by John Ross to the order of William Brown. Sister-ship to the *Isabella Brown*. Launched on 13 April 1861 and involved in the tea and sugar trade, also making occasional trips to America and New Zealand for nearly two decades. Disappears from the records in June 1879 after arriving in Shanghai, China, from Albany, Western Australia. Reportedly sold to Japanese buyers and subsequently renamed.
1863	*Mary Williams*	Schooner	87.0 x 20.0 x 6.3ft. ON 32110. 81 tons. Built by John Ross and launched on 23 May 1863. Purchased by the Cardiff Coal Company of NSW shortly before launch. Sold in April 1865 to Alexander Smail of Sydney and placed in the trans-Tasman trade. Went missing off New Zealand's west coast in late 1865 with the loss of all on board.
1865	*Hector*	Schooner	93.5 x 19.9 x 8.4ft. ON 32139. 115 tons. Launched on 6 April 1865, built by John Ross on speculation, remaining in his hands for some months and employed in intercolonial trade. Purchased by G. Fisher and Captain Bell of New Zealand in November 1865 with the intention of placing it in intercolonial and trans-Tasman trades. After several mishaps, including being abandoned by its crew in the west channel of Port Phillip Bay in June 1871, and several changes of ownership, went missing en route from Sydney to Ballina, New South Wales, in February 1875 with the loss of all passengers and crew.
1865	*Gift*	Schooner	53.0 x 13.0 x 7.0ft. ON 32146. 30 tons. Built by John Ross to the order of Venerable Archdeacon Thomas Reibey for use visiting the islands of Bass Strait. Paid for by donations to the Church of England and launched on 18 October 1865. Spent its infant years cruising the islands of Bass Strait, though by 1867 was found too expensive to maintain. Purchased by Messrs Robinson and Lilly and placed in the Tasmanian coastal trade. By December 1868 transferred to Western Australia. After several years spent in the coastal trade, by 1872 employed in the pearling industry off the north-west coast of Western Australia. In October 1872 some of its Malaysian crew mutineered, killing the captain and capturing the vessel in brutal circumstances. Subsequently recaptured by Dutch authorities in Indonesia and handed back to its owners, Messrs Roe and Passey. Spent a decade successfully employed in the pearling industry before being lost during a cyclone off Timor in 1882.
1868	*Duke of Edinburgh*	Schooner	44.5 x 14.1 x 7.4ft. ON 57492. 26 tons. Built by John Ross on speculation. Advertised for sale in April 1868 and subsequently purchased by Isaac Wright, local merchant. A regular in the Hobart Town to Launceston trade for several years, in early 1873 re-rigged and lengthened by John Bradley at Battery Point. Wrecked the following year, on 1 August 1874, shortly after leaving the Tamar Heads, all hands saved.

Year	Name	Type	Description
1870	Gleaner	Schooner	89.8 x 21.2 x 8.3ft. ON 57511. 121 tons. Built by Charles Bradley, John Bradley, John Downie and Alick Harley at John Ross' Battery Point shipyard and launched on 7 September 1870. Built over a two year period during spare time, For many years involved in intercolonial and trans-Tasman trades. First registered in Melbourne in 1871. Register transferred to New Zealand (Auckland owners) in 1889 and Sydney owners in 1898. Wrecked at Borley Point, NSW, on 19 May 1900 while loading timber for Sydney, At the time owned by F. H. Guy.
1871	Acacia	Barque	118.0 x 24.0 x 12.0ft. ON 57515. 232 tons. Built by John Ross on speculation. Purchased by Messrs Belbin and Dowdell for £2,550 just prior to completion. Launched on 22 February 1871. Placed in intercolonial trade where it spent three decades employed. Went missing en route to Adelaide from Port Esperance on 20 June 1904 with a cargo of timber. No trace of it was found until March of the following year when pieces of wreckage and human remains were identified near Mainwaring Inlet on the west coast of Tasmania. At the time of loss, owned by Robert Richmond Rex and Thomas Charles Herbert of Hobart.

The wooden barque *Wagoola* docked at Hobart Town with the PS *Kangaroo* in the background (c1870s).
Courtesy State Library of South Australia (PRG 1373/20/27).

John Lucas.
Courtesy Maritime Museum of Tasmania (P_GSL259).

John Lucas

'The workmanship throughout reflects credit on the builder, Mr Lucas, and on the shipwrights, joiners, blacksmiths, and other artizans employed in the construction of the vessel, which has a smart sprightly—looking appearance, and will evidently prove a quick sailer, as she is thoroughly modelled.'

The Cornwall Chronicle, 14 June 1872.

Born and raised at Browns River, Van Diemen's Land, south of Hobart Town, John Lucas served his apprenticeship with John Watson at his Battery Point shipyard, eventually becoming foreman. In 1856 he partnered with Robert Jeffrey to lease Watson's shipyard and for the next 10 years the pair were primarily involved in the repair, painting, cleaning, refit and/or alteration of vessels, with the building of new vessels supplementing their income. Following Jeffrey's exit from the partnership, Lucas continued on at the shipyard for 17 years before moving to the Domain. Towards the end of his career he returned to Battery Point, where he built and/or designed several of Hobart's more successful racing yachts.

Lucas was born on 11 June 1826, the second of twelve children born to John (Sr) and Sophia Lucas (nee Sherburd).[1406] His parents had both arrived in Van Diemen's Land as children per the *City of Edinburgh* in 1808 as part of Norfolk Island's resettlement program.[1407] A short time later, the Lucas and Sherburd families received land grants in the Browns River area and went on to establish themselves as the region's first farmers.[1408]

The Lucas family, particularly John (Sr) and his three brothers Thomas, Richard and Nathaniel, were respected and resourceful early settlers. Given the immaturity of the colony, particularly its outer communities, the Lucas' lived relatively well at Browns River. In addition to farming over 1,000 acres of land, John (Sr) for several years served as constable of both the Kingborough and Queenborough districts, and was noted for his service in apprehending bushrangers.[1409] He was also instrumental in the founding of the Kingston parsonage and church.[1410] Obviously an enterprising family, in 1822 Thomas Lucas built a 30-ton schooner named *Governor Brisbane* at Browns River.[1411] The vessel was described in the press as *'the handsomest vessel of her size that has been yet built at this Settlement'*.[1412]

Following in his uncle Thomas' footsteps, in October 1840 at the age of 14, Lucas was apprenticed to John Watson, shipwright of Battery Point. The position was for a period of six years with Watson responsible for providing Lucas with *'sufficient Meat, Drink, Apparel and Lodging and all other necessaries during the said term'*.[1413] He was to be paid on an increasing scale, in his sixth and final year earning 11 shillings per week. In this role Lucas was likely involved in the building of the *Native Youth*, *Flying Fish*, *Miranda* and *Flying Childers*, among other vessels. During this period Lucas was also a regular participant in local regattas. For example, he crewed in the *Rose* (built by Jacob Chandler, boat builder of Battery Point) in the amateur gig race at the 1846 Hobart Town Regatta, finishing third.[1414]

After completing his apprenticeship in 1846 Lucas remained at Watson's Battery Point shipyard, eventually becoming foreman.[1415] There was also personal growth. On 9 March 1848, at St. David's Church in Hobart Town with his parents as witnesses, Lucas married 20-year-old Sophia Strang.[1416] Born in France, her background was rather unique and worth re-telling.[1417]

In February 1836 Sophia had arrived in Hobart Town from Gravesend, England, as a passenger on board the *Boadicea* along with her widowed mother Sophia (nee Henderson), 15-year-old sister Jane, 10-year-old brother Joseph, and 57-year-old grandmother Martha Wilkins (nee Henderson, nee Lacoste).[1418] Sophia (Sr) had been born in Honfleur, France, in 1798 to an English-born

---

[1406] Libraries Tasmania (RGD32/1/1/ no 2034); *Tasmanian News*, 28 April 1908; www.geni.com/people/Sophia-Lucas/6000000004327594978.
[1407] peopleaustralia.anu.edu.au/biography/lucas-thomas-silas-31415.
[1408] P. Macfie (2013). *A History of North West Bay and Margate, Tasmania 1792-2000*.
[1409] *Hobart Town Gazette and Van Diemen's Land Advertiser*, 4 May 1822; *Colonial Times and Tasmanian Advertiser*, 25 August 1826.
[1410] *The Hobart Town Mercury*, 12 October 1857.
[1411] *Hobart Town Gazette and Van Diemen's Land Advertiser*, 27 April 1822.
[1412] *Hobart Town Gazette and Van Diemen's Land Advertiser*, 27 April 1822.
[1413] Maritime Museum of Tasmania (object number D_2010-125).
[1414] *The Courier*, 5 December 1846.
[1415] *The Examiner*, April 29 1908.
[1416] Libraries Tasmania (RGD37/1/7 no 1522).
[1417] Libraries Tasmania (RGD35/1/9 no 3191).
[1418] Libraries Tasmania (CSO1/1/848 file 17942, RGD37/1/1 no 66); *Hertford Mercury and Reformer*, 6 October 1835.

This Indenture witnesseth that John Lucas the son of George Lucas — of Browns River Van Diemens Land Hereby and with the consent of his said Father doth put himself apprentice to John Watson of Hobart Town aforesaid Shipwright to learn his art and with him after the manner of an apprentice to serve from the day [date] one thousand eight hundred [and forty] until the full end and term of Five Years from thence next ensuing and fully to be complete and ended, during which time the said apprentice his said master faithfully shall serve his secrets keep, his lawful commands every where gladly do, he shall do no damage to his said master nor see it done by others but to the best of his power shall let or forthwith give notice to his said master of the same, The goods of his said master he shall not waste nor give or lend unlawfully to any. He shall neither buy nor sell without his masters leave Taverns Inns or Alehouses he shall not haunt At Cards dice Tables or any other unlawful games he shall not play, Matrimony he shall not contract nor from the service of his said master day or usual working hours absent himself But in all things as a faithful apprentice he shall behave himself towards his said master during the said term And the said John Watson in consideration of the services of the said apprentice and of the sum of five shillings in hand well and truly paid by the said John Lucas (the receipt whereof is hereby acknowledged) the said apprentice in the art of a Shipwright which he now useth shall and will teach and instruct or cause to be taught and instructed in the best way and manner that he can. And shall and will pay unto the said John Lucas — for and towards the maintenance and support of his said son the following sums of money that is to say the sum of Six shillings per week During the first year the sum of Seven shillings per week During the second year the sum of Eight shillings per week During the third year the sum of Nine shillings per week During the fourth year the sum of Ten shillings per week During the fifth year

John Lucas' Indenture Papers for his Apprenticeship to John Watson (October 1840). Courtesy Maritime Museum of Tasmania (D_2010-125).

the Sum of Eleven Shillings per Week during the Fifth & last
Year   And the said — John Lucas — doth hereby agree that
he will find and provide for the said apprentice sufficient
Meat Drink Apparel and Lodging and all other necessaries
during the said term And for the true performance of all and every
the said covenants and agreements each of the said parties bindeth
himself the one to the other firmly by these presents In Witness
whereof the said parties to these presents have hereunto set their hands
and seals the ………………………………………………………………………………

…… year of the Reign of Sovereign Lady Queen Victoria of the United Kingdom of
Great Britain and Ireland Defender of the faith and so forth
and in the year of our Lord one thousand eight hundred and Forty

Signed Sealed and delivered }   John Lucas
by all the above named   }
Parties in Presence of   }

                                     John Watson

I hereby certify that the above named John
Lucas has duly and faithfully performed the
time specified in the above indenture

                                     John Watson
                                     Battery Point

father, Thomas Henderson, and French-born mother.[1419] The couple then moved to London where more children were born, including a daughter Jane in 1804, and a son Thomas (Jr) in 1806, with Thomas supporting the family through employment as a master mariner.[1420] He had also very likely served in the Royal Navy during the war years, the reason for his presence in France.

By the 1810s, Martha, the widowed mother of Sophia (Sr), had returned to France where she was operating the London Tavern in Le Havre.[1421] From December 1814 Martha managed the establishment in partnership with her second husband Henry Wilkins.[1422] Previously a master mariner and originally from Wales, Henry died in June 1830 at the age of 79 and was buried at Le Havre.[1423]

Continuing a pattern of regularly crossing the English Channel, in July 1814, at the age of 15, Sophia (Sr) married Robert Strang in London. While they appear to have remained in England for a number of years, by the mid-to-late 1820s the couple had removed themselves to France where their son Joseph and daughter Sophia (Jr) were born; the coastal French town of Le Havre growing rapidly in the years since the end of the Napoleonic Wars.

By the mid-1830s, however, with the death of her husband Robert, Sophia (Sr) and her three children, along with her mother Martha, had returned to England and were living at Brighton.[1424] A few years later the group boarded the *Boadicea* for Van Diemen's Land.

Chartered by the Emigration Committee at a cost estimated to be around £7,000, in addition to several families the *Boadicea* carried some 220 single or widowed young girls and women primarily between the ages of 12 and 35, and 30 of their children.[1425] Near immediately upon stepping foot in Van Diemen's Land, Sophia's mother and grandmother lost their entire savings, a purse containing 50 sovereigns.[1426] Hard on their luck, Joseph was admitted to the Queens Orphan School, with Sophia following a few months later.[1427] Their mother Sophia (Sr) then set about establishing herself as a milliner and dressmaker in Liverpool Street, being able to discharge the pair from the orphanage the following year.[1428] It is likely that more settled childhood and teenage years eluded Sophia. Her mother died in March 1842 in Hobart Town only a few years after re-marrying (to James Strong).[1429] To date no death record has been found for her grandmother. Instead Sophia likely lived with her older sister Jane leading up to her marriage to John Lucas in 1848.

Lucas and his new bride Sophia settled in Battery Point, by the mid-1850s building a home in Mona Street.[1430] Between the years 1849 and 1871, nine children were born to the couple: Elizabeth Sophia (1849-1914), Robert John (1851-1853), William Joseph (1855-1917), Clara (1858-1920), Herbert Edwin (1860-1910), Emily Frances (1862-1933), Marian Elizabeth (1865-1924), Ethel Jessie (1868-1952), and John Arthur (1871-1943).[1431] All but one of their children would survive childhood; the couple's oldest son Robert John Lucas died in July 1853 just shy of his second birthday. Cause of death was scarlet fever.[1432]

In terms of his professional activities, Lucas continued to work for John Watson up until Watson's bankruptcy in late 1855.[1433] The latter's Napoleon Street shipyard was subsequently purchased by Duncan McPherson for £4,000. He subdivided the property, leasing the allotments to various commercial and residential tenants, including shipbuilder Lucas in partnership with Robert Alexander Jeffrey.[1434] Born in Hobart Town in 1828, Jeffrey was the son of James Jeffrey, a cabinetmaker, and his wife Isabella (nee Maclean).[1435] The couple had arrived in Van Diemen's Land in September 1824 from Leith, Scotland, via the Australian Company's ship *Portland*.[1436] Newlyweds, James and Isabella went on to have a handful of children in Hobart Town between 1826 and the mid-1830s, with James establishing himself as a cabinetmaker at 76 Elizabeth Street.[1437] As the oldest surviving son, it appears that Jeffrey initially followed in his father's footsteps, learning the trade of cabinetmaking. However, by the late 1840s he had taken up shipbuilding.[1438] The mid-1850s saw Jeffrey living in Macquarie Street with his wife Catherine (nee Grady) and several young children.[1439] It is highly likely that he was an employee of John Watson with his professional partnership with John Lucas evolving through this pathway.

Lucas and Jeffrey's shipyard was located on the shore of the River Derwent just off Napoleon Street, the pair seem to have taken over the yard early in 1856. One of the first vessels they were noted as working on was the whaling barque *Offley* which was offered for sale, along with a list of stores, in April 1856.[1440]

[1419] France, Calvados, Etat-Civil, 1792-1942," database, FamilySearch (https://familysearch.org/ark:/61903/1:1:QPPZ-D1KB : 12 October 2018), Thomas Henderson in entry for Sophie Henderson, 15 Jul 1798; citing Birth, Calvados, Normandie, France, Archive.
[1420] London, England, Church of England Baptisms, Marriages and Burials, 1538-1812 for Jane Neale Henderson; London, England, Church of England Baptisms, Marriages and Burials, 1538-1812 for Thomas Young Henderson.
[1421] *Salisbury and Winchester Journal*, 12 December 1814; *Hampshire Chronicle*, 19 August 1816.
[1422] *Salisbury and Winchester Journal*, 12 December 1814; *Hampshire Chronicle*, 19 August 1816.
[1423] UK, Foreign and Overseas Registers of British Subjects, 1628-1969 for Henry Wilkins. RG 33: Foreign Registers and Returns, 1627-1960, Piece 056: Le Havre: Baptisms, Marriage, Burials, 1817-1843.
[1424] *Hertford Mercury and Reformer*, 6 October 1835.
[1425] *Morning Post*, 2 October 1835.
[1426] *The Hobart Town Courier*, 12 February 1836; *Bent's News and Tasmanian Three-Penny Register*, 5 March 1836.
[1427] www.orphanschool.org.au/showorphan.php?orphan_ID=5178; www.orphanschool.org.au/showorphan.php?orphan_ID=5179.
[1428] *Colonial Times*, 10 May 1836.
[1429] Libraries Tasmania (RGD35/1/1 no 970).
[1430] www.thelist.tas.gov.au (Historical Deed 03/9680); *The Cornwall Chronicle*, 7 March 1866; *The Mercury*, 6 June 1870, 15 March 1877, 29 April 1879, 7 March 1882.
[1431] Family tree for John Lucas created by the author on www.ancestry.com.au.
[1432] Libraries Tasmania (RGD35/1/4 no 220).
[1433] *The Courier*, 12 December 1855.
[1434] *The Courier*, 30 January 1856; *The Hobart Town Gazette*, 8 February 1861.
[1435] Old Parish Registers Marriages 692/2 220 115 Leith South, page 115 of 167, National Records of Scotland.
[1436] *Hobart Town Gazette and Van Diemen's Land Advertiser*, 10 September 1824.
[1437] Libraries Tasmania (CEN1/1/10).
[1438] *The Courier*, 26 April 1844; Libraries Tasmania (RGD33/1/2/ no 621, RGD33/1/3/ no 42, RGD33/1/3/ no 2012, RGD33/1/4/ no 1834); Tasmania, Australia, Police Gazettes, 1884-1933 for Robert A Jeffrey.
[1439] Family tree for Robert Alexander Jeffrey created by the author on www.ancestry.com.au; *Launceston Examiner*, 20 November 1852.
[1440] *Colonial Times*, 29 April 1856.

Painting of the Schooner *Kingston* (c1875). Courtesy Tasmanian Archives (NS2511/1/184).

The first vessel built by Lucas and Jeffrey was the 37-ton clipper schooner *Kingston*, launched two years later, built to the order of Henry Hopwood.[1441] A regular in the Tasmanian coastal trade for more than a decade, in April 1869 it was transferred to the intercolonial trade after being purchased by George James and sailed by Nathaniel Lucas, brother of its builder John Lucas.[1442] In January 1871 the *Kingston* returned to the Tasmanian coastal trade, again under Hopwood's ownership.[1443]

> FOR SANDSPIT, SPRING BAY, LITTLE AND GREAT SWANPORT. — The Schooner
> "KINGSTON,"
> H. HOPWOOD, Master, will sail for the above port, THIS DAY, 14th instant.
> For freight or passage apply on board, or to
> A. G. WEBSTER.

The Mercury, 14 March 1871.

In November 1872, Hopwood sold the *Kingston* to brothers James and John Carver though the vessel remained in the coastal trade.[1444] Sadly its ultimate fate somewhat echoes that of the schooner *Gift* built in 1865 by John Ross at Battery Point. In September 1875 the *Kingston* was purchased by George William Robinson of Hobart Town and fitted out for the pearl trade off the north-west coast of Australia.[1445] Leaving Hobart Town soon after, it then spent a few years cruising the pearling grounds before disaster struck.[1446] In November 1878 a mutiny broke out on board the vessel while it was anchored near Warrior Reef in the Torres Strait, resulting in the tragic death of Captain Robinson and his brother Charles.[1447] Taken by its captives, no trace of the *Kingston* was ever found.

On 30 April 1859 Lucas and Jeffrey launched their second vessel, the fore-and-aft schooner *Star of Tasmania* built

[1441] HOBART, Register of ships, Volume 8, 1865-1877, Folio 48; *The Hobart Town Advertiser*, 17 March 1859.
[1442] *The Mercury*, 7 April, 26 April 1869.
[1443] *The Mercury*, 23 January 1871.
[1444] *Launceston Examiner*, 28 November 1872; HOBART, Register of ships, Volume 8, 1865-1877, Folio 48.
[1445] *The Mercury*, 2 September 1875; HOBART, Register of ships, Volume 8, 1865-1877, Folio 48.
[1446] *The Mercury*, 29 June 1876; 13 January 1877.
[1447] *Evening News*, 24 January 1878; *Morning Bulletin*, 1 February 1878; *The Mercury*, 21 May 1878.

to the order of Thomas Patterson, corn dealer of Hobart Town, and intended for the Pittwater trade in which it was initially employed.[1448] By October 1861 the *Star of Tasmania* was trading between Hobart Town and New Zealand, taking advantage of a lucrative trade market recently made popular by New Zealand's gold rush.[1449] While undergoing several changes of ownership in the intervening years, the craft maintained this route until October 1867 when it disappeared in Storm Bay en route to Hobart Town, presumed sunk with the loss of all on board.[1450]

Another vessel constructed by Lucas and Jeffrey and launched on 26 November 1859 was the barge *Wild Wave*, built to the order of Alexander Bruce Smith of Long Bay.[1451] Fitted with a centreboard, the craft was expressly built for the river trade.[1452] It was initially employed to bring up piles and timber from Long Bay for completion of the New Wharf under contract to a Mr Oldham.[1453] A few months later *Wild Wave* began transporting timber from Hobart Town to Melbourne for use in construction of a wharf at Williamstown.[1454] On 24 October 1861 it sailed to Otago on New Zealand's South Island with a cargo of timber.[1455] On arrival, the craft was near-immediately sold to John Jones of Dunedin.[1456] Involved in New Zealand's coastal trade, *Wild Wave* was wrecked on 21 June 1866 after capsizing at the entrance to Pelorus Sound with the unfortunate loss of five of its complement of seven.[1457] At the time of loss, it was owned by Messrs Brownell and Co. of Christchurch, though based out of Lyttelton.[1458]

Following the success of John Ross' Battery Point patent slip, in May 1861 John Lucas and Robert Jeffrey installed a patent slip at their shipyard, with the schooner *Kingston* the first vessel to undergo repairs on the new slip.[1459] A few months later the whaling barque *Isabella* was hauled up on the slip for overhaul, the first of this type of vessel to utilise the equipment with the slip noted to be working '*admirably*' during the process.[1460] Since the majority of work they were involved with to date, and for many years to come, comprised the cleaning, painting, repair, refit and alteration of vessels, the slip proved an extremely worthwhile investment for the pair.

The slip was laid down under the direct supervision of Lucas and though not as large as other slips located in Hobart Town, its incline was not as great such that it was considered to be an improvement in its utility.[1461] A small engine of around 8 h.p. was employed to haul vessels of up to 300 tons burthen upon the cradle.[1462]

While slip work took up the bulk of their time, in November 1862 Lucas and Jeffrey completed construction of a new punt for Christina Herbertson, licencee of the Ferry Inn at Risdon.[1463] Following installation of its gear, the Restdown ferry punt began traversing the River Derwent, leaving from the hotel.[1464]

In April 1864 Lucas and Jeffrey laid down the keel of a schooner, built to the order of the Government of Britain.[1465] Named *Harriet*, the vessel was launched on 28 July of that year under the superintendence of John Watson.[1466] It entered service a few months later, following fit-out and installation of sails and rigging, going on to become a regular on the Hobart Town to Port Arthur route.[1467] Following the closure of the Port Arthur penal settlement, the 49-ton vessel was sold in late December 1877 to William Snell Verren of Hobart Town for £500.[1468] Two years later Verren had the *Harriet* overhauled on Lucas and Jeffrey's slip with the intention of sailing it to New South Wales.[1469] It arrived at this location in March 1880 with a cargo of iron and timber and was advertised for sale two days later.[1470]

Though remaining in Verren's ownership, the *Harriet* was laid on to carry cargo to Fiji in June of that year.[1471] It then appears to have been chartered by the London Missionary Society for use in visiting newly-established stations in New Guinea.[1472] Back in Sydney, the *Harriet* was sold to William Walton in April 1882 and placed in the pearlshelling trade off the coast of Western Australia.[1473] It was, however, advertised for sale seven years later while lying at Cossack in Western Australia, this time the result of Walton's insolvency.[1474] The craft was sold by auction for £60.[1475] Remaining in the pearling industry under several different owners, the *Harriet*'s register was ultimately closed in 1919.[1476]

In August 1864 Lucas and Jeffrey were noted as having another vessel in the course of construction and advertised for sale.[1477] Though originally laid down for the Invercargill trade, the contract appears to have fallen through as the craft was purchased

---

[1448] *The Courier*, 2 May 1859.
[1449] *The Mercury*, 3 October 1861.
[1450] *The Tasmanian Times*, 10 December 1867.
[1451] *The Hobart Town Daily Mercury*, 1, 29 November 1859.
[1452] *The Hobart Town Daily Mercury*, 29 November 1859.
[1453] *The Hobart Town Daily Mercury*, 29 November 1859; *The Mercury*, 28 August 1860.
[1454] *The Mercury*, 28 August 1860.
[1455] *The Hobart Town Advertiser*, 22 October 1861; *The Mercury*, 23 November 1861; *Otago Witness*, 9 November 1861.
[1456] *The Hobart Town Advertiser*, 3 December 1861; HOBART, Register of ships, Volume 8, 1865-1877, Folio 88.
[1457] *Press*, 27 June 1866; *Marlborough Press*, 27 June 1866.
[1458] *Press*, 27 June 1866; *Otago Daily Times*, 29 June 1866.
[1459] *The Mercury*, 14 May 1861.
[1460] *The Hobart Town Advertiser*, 16 August 1861; *The Mercury*, 17 August 1861.
[1461] *The Advertiser*, 1 April 1862.
[1462] *The Advertiser*, 1 April 1862.
[1463] *The Mercury*, 26 November 1862; *The Advertiser*, 18 December 1862, 2 March 1863.
[1464] *The Mercury*, 25 November 1862.
[1465] *The Mercury*, 11 April 1864.
[1466] *The Mercury*, 29 July 1864; *Tribune*, 27 December 1877.
[1467] *The Advertiser*, 10 August, 20 October 1864; *The Mercury*, 22 October 1864.
[1468] HOBART, Register of ships (with continuation entries), Volume 10, 1877-1898, Folio 8; *The Mercury*, 29 December 1877.
[1469] *The Mercury*, 24 December 1879.
[1470] *The Sydney Daily Telegraph*, 8 March 1880; *The Sydney Morning Herald*, 10 March 1880.
[1471] *The Sydney Morning Herald*, 9 June 1880.
[1472] *The Sydney Mail and New South Wales Advertiser*, 28 May 1881.
[1473] *Goulburn Herald*, 3 May 1887; SYDNEY, NEW SOUTH WALES, Register of ships, single number series (II), Volume 10, 1881-1882, Folio 63.
[1474] *The Sydney Morning Herald*, 5 October 1887.
[1475] *The Sydney Morning Herald*, 18 April 1888.
[1476] SYDNEY, NEW SOUTH WALES, Register of ships, single number series (II), Volume 10, 1881-1882, Folio 63.
[1477] *The Mercury*, 23 August 1864.

Schooner *Harriet* at Port Arthur (c1870s).
Courtesy Tasmanian Archives (NS1013/1/623).

part-way through completion by Thomas Paterson of the Old Wharf for the sum of £1,300.[1478] The resulting top-sail schooner was launched on 5 April 1865 and named *Storm Bird*.[1479] Described as resembling more of a *'gentlemen's yacht than a trading vessel'*, the craft was fitted with a centreboard that could be hoisted and lowered by machinery worked by a winch.[1480] It was placed in the coastal trade under the command of Captain John Featherstone (father of future Battery Point shipwright Henry Featherstone), mainly sailing between Hobart Town and Launceston.[1481]

In November 1866 the *Storm Bird* was sold to A. G. Fisher of Melbourne for £2,000 and placed in intercolonial trade.[1482] It stranded near Green Cape, New South Wales, on 28 March 1870 after being dismasted in foul weather; Captain Featherstone and his crew managing to make it to land safely.[1483] Sold as a wreck by A. G. Fisher's insurance company, *Storm Bird* was refloated in June 1870 and found to be relatively unscathed from its misadventure.[1484] Repaired and re-registered in Sydney, the vessel was eventually sold to the Government of Hawaii in October 1877 and wrecked at Bonham Island in the Marshall Islands in August 1881.[1485]

Diversifying their skills and expertise, and likely in an effort to generate more revenue, in November 1865 Lucas and Jeffery tendered for undertaking alterations and repairs to Constitution Dock.[1486] A few months later they tendered for building a new pier extending from the Franklin Wharf.[1487] Neither application was successful. The pair were, however, awarded the contract to build a jetty at Rosny for use by passengers, stock and cargo of the steamer *Kangaroo*, on behalf of its proprietor Captain James Taylor.[1488] Construction of the jetty began immediately and was completed by March 1866.[1489]

Steamer *Kangaroo* at Bellerive (c1860s).
Courtesy Tasmanian Archives (LPIC54/1/47/012).

[1478] *The Mercury*, 1 December 1864.
[1479] *The Mercury*, 6 April 1865.
[1480] *The Advertiser*, 27 April, 4, 23 May 1865.
[1481] *The Mercury*, 21 April 1865; *The Advertiser*, 27 April, 4 May 1865; *Launceston Examiner*, 3 June 1865.
[1482] *The Mercury*, 9 October 1866; HOBART, Register of ships, Volume 9, 1865-1877, [pages 1-173, continues on film roll 2], Folio 39.
[1483] *The Argus*, Monday 28 March 1870; MELBOURNE, Main Register subsequent to Merchant Shipping Act 1854, Volume 4, 1867-1872, Folio 204.
[1484] *The Argus*, 1 April 1870; *The Sydney Morning Herald*, 8 June 1870.
[1485] SYDNEY, NEW SOUTH WALES, Register of ships, A series, Folio 105.
[1486] *The Mercury*, 3 November 1865.
[1487] *The Mercury*, 2 February 1866.
[1488] *The Mercury*, 3, 27 February 1866.
[1489] *The Mercury*, 27 February 1866.

On 12 May 1866 the partnership of Lucas and Jeffrey was dissolved by mutual consent; Lucas remaining at their Battery Point shipyard.[1490] Continuing operations, his business principally involved the repair, refit and maintenance of existing vessels. For example, in 1868 nearly 20 vessels were noted as being on his slip. These included the barges *Seymour*, *Shannon* and *Alabama*; the brig *Daniel Watson*; the schooners *Harriet*, *Robert Burns*, *Dancing Wave*, *Twinkling Star* and *Maria Louise*; the barques *Isabella*, *Australian Packet* and *Free Trader*; the brigantines *Zephyr* and *Macquarie*; the whaling brigs *Maid of Erin* and *Louisa*; the steamers *City of Hobart* and *Cobre*; and the yacht *Phantom*.[1491]

DISSOLUTION OF PARTNERSHIP

Notice is hereby given, that the Partnership hitherto subsisting between the undersigned JOHN LUCAS and ROBERT ALEXANDER JEFFREY, carrying on business as Ship Builders under the firm of "Lucas & Jeffrey," has been this day dissolved by mutual consent. All debts due to the late firm will be received by the said JOHN LUCAS, who will pay all liabilities.

Dated this 12th day of May, 1866.
    ROBT. ALEX. JEFFREY.
    JOHN LUCAS.
Witness—JOHN ROBERTS, Solicitor, Hobart Town.   19m

The Mercury, 19 May 1866.

Meanwhile Jeffrey became licencee of the Denison Hotel in Macquarie Street.[1492] By the early 1870s he had returned to work as a shipwright, in the employ of John MacGregor at Hobart Town's Domain shipyard.[1493] He was also noted as providing the design of a vessel built by James MacLaren at Kermandie on the Huon River in 1874: the schooner *Annie Hill*.[1494] Later Jeffrey undertook tendered work, including to repair the various piers and docks at the Hobart Town wharf.[1495] He died at his home, 9 Victoria Street, Hobart, on 6 December 1902 at the age of 74.[1496]

The late 1860s and early 1870s proved busy years for John Lucas, particularly in terms of new builds. On 3 April 1869, the *Grace Darling*, a schooner designed and built to the order of Captain Henry Hopwood (late owner of the schooner *Kingston*) was launched.[1497] Construction of this 83ft craft had began in June of the previous year.[1498] While initially intended for the east coast trade, the vessel having been fitted with a centreboard in lieu of a deeper keel, after undertaking a handful of trips between Hobart Town, Orford, Spring Bay, Little Swanport, Great Swanport and Swansea, it became apparent that there was sufficient support for the route.[1499] Instead, Captain Hopwood began trading the *Grace Darling* between New Zealand and Hobart Town, the vessel for sailing for Auckland on 18 August 1869 with a cargo of fruit, palings, cart shafts, jam and rails.[1500] It returned in ballast on 1 December with seven passengers on board.[1501] Becoming somewhat of a journeyman, the *Grace Darling* was sailed to Port Davey a few weeks later to procure a cargo of Macquarie pine.[1502] It was then laid on to transport timber and palings to Melbourne.[1503]

On 28 December 1870, the *Grace Darling* was sold to Thomas Edward Seal of Melbourne, and Alexander Bishop and John Hills Callacombe of Hamilton (Victoria).[1504] It was subsequently placed in the coastal trade, sailing between Port Phillip Bay and Belfast (now Port Fairy).[1505] This route also proved not as profitable as expected such that the vessel was sent on occasional jaunts to various ports in search of cargo, including Shoalhaven, the Clarence River, and Sydney in New South Wales; Timaru in New Zealand; Adelaide and Wallaroo in South Australia; and even a return to Hobart Town.[1506]

On 8 September 1873, the *Grace Darling* was sold to William Tullock of Adelaide with its registry transferred to Port Adelaide. Operating out of this port, the craft then became involved in the South Australian coastal trade, including plying to the ports of Venus Bay, Fowlers Bay, Streaky Bay and Port MacDonnell, spending nearly two decades in this service.[1507] Some 20 years later it embarked on a career in the Western Australian coastal trade having been purchased by Captain Frederick Douglas of Albany.[1508] Sold again in September 1910 to R. J. Lynn and Company, the *Grace Darling* next conveyed cargo between Geraldton and Fremantle.[1509] It was ultimately wrecked four years later, on 4 February 1914, on a reef some 70 miles north of Fremantle, the crew of five fortunate to escape the ordeal with their lives.[1510]

[1490] *The Mercury*, 19 May 1866.
[1491] *The Mercury*, 3, 29, 31 January, 21, 26 February, 12, 17 March, 7 April, 5 June, 9 October, 2, 7, 26 November 1868; *The Tasmanian Times*, 7, 24 August, 10 September, 16, 20, 30 October, 28 November, 30 December 1868.
[1492] *The Mercury*, 6 February 1866; *Tasmanian Morning Herald*, 3 December 1866; *The Mercury*, 2 October 1876.
[1493] *The Mercury*, 18 May 1872.
[1494] *The Mercury*, 6 February 1866; *Tasmanian Morning Herald*, 3 December 1866; *The Mercury*, 2 October 1876.
[1495] *The Mercury*, 16 March 1871, 21 November 1896.
[1496] Libraries Tasmania (NAME_INDEXES:1980708).
[1497] *The Mercury*, 27 March, 1 April 1869; *The Tasmanian Times*, 5 April 1869.
[1498] *The Tasmanian Times*, 18 June 1868.
[1499] *The Mercury*, 27 March, 7 April, 7, 11, 24 May, 7, 17, 26 June, 9, 15, 24, 30 July 1869.
[1500] *The Mercury*, 11, 19 August 1869.
[1501] *The Mercury*, 2 December 1869.
[1502] *The Tasmanian Times*, 30 December 1869.
[1503] *The Mercury*, 27 January 1870.
[1504] HOBART, Register of ships, Volume 9, 1865-1877, [pages 1-173, continues on film roll 2], Folio 76; PORT FAIRY, VICTORIA, Register of ships, 1854-1895, Folio 8; *The Tasmanian Times*, 30 December 1870; *Hamilton Spectator*, 14 January 1871.
[1505] *The Ballarat Star*, 13 January 1871.
[1506] *The Argus*, 16 January, 25 November 1872, 6 June, 9 July 1873; *Mount Alexander Mail*, 1 October 1872; *The Age*, 8 October 1872, 3 June 1873.
[1507] ADELAIDE, Register of ships subsequent to Merchant Shipping Act 1854, Volume 2, 1873-1878, Folio 19; *South Australian Register*, 2 September, 12 December 1873; *Evening Journal*, 5 February 1892.
[1508] FREMANTLE, Main Register, Volume 2, 1884-1897, [for additions - see barcode 32825060], Folio 66; *Evening Journal*, 13 May 1892; *The Inquirer & Commercial News*, 15 June 1892.
[1509] FREMANTLE, Main Register, Volume 2, 1884-1897, [for additions - see barcode 32825060], Folio 66; *The West Australian*, 5 September 1910.
[1510] FREMANTLE, Main Register, Volume 2, 1884-1897, [for additions - see barcode 32825060], Folio 66; *The West Australian*, 5 February 1914.

Grace Darling in South Australia (c1880s).
Courtesy State Library of South Australia (PRG 1373/35/7).

In addition to the *Grace Darling*, in 1869 Lucas' yard launched the schooner *Dawn*, the blue gum frame of which had been constructed at Barnes Bay on Bruny Island by Messrs Barrett and towed up to Hobart Town in May of that year.[1511] Built to the order of Captain J. R. Gourlay, the 72ft vessel was launched on 23 August 1869 and immediately advertised for sale.[1512] Failing to find a local buyer, Gourlay sent the craft to Newcastle, New South Wales, with a cargo of timber and produce.[1513] It returned to Hobart Town and soon thereafter made several more trips to the mainland with various cargoes. *Dawn* was then sailed to Sydney where it was advertised for sale in April 1870.[1514] Again failing to sell, *Dawn* began carrying machinery from Brisbane to Bustard Bay in Queensland for use in construction of a sawmill.[1515] It was while working this route on 14 July of 1870, carrying two boilers of both nearly four tons in weight, that the craft was reportedly deemed a complete wreck near Double Island Point, all hands saved.[1516] A few days later it was revealed that the vessel had been intentionally beached during a fierce storm such that the *Dawn* was lying '*about high-water mark, and is said to be deeply embedded in the sand*'.[1517] Salvaged from its misadventure after 14 days stuck in the sand, the *Dawn* returned to Brisbane and a month later was advertised for sale on behalf of the National Marine Insurance Company of South Australia.[1518] It was purchased by William Collin for £400 and, after undergoing repairs, was employed in the North Queensland coastal trade.[1519]

Under several additional owners, the *Dawn* remained in the Queensland coastal trade until 1883 whereupon its register was transferred to Darwin.[1520] It then became involved in the pearling industry.[1521] In 1891 the craft was reportedly broken up.[1522]

In October 1870 Lucas began construction of a '*centreboard schooner of large dimensions*' to the order of William Fisher and Peter Facy of Messrs Fisher and Facy.[1523] However, it would be nearly two years before this particular vessel, now a barque, was completed. Still, business remained brisk. In October 1871, for example, approximately 30 men were employed at Lucas' yard working on the new barque, as well as repairing the whaling barque *Sapphire*.[1524] The work carried out on the latter vessel was substantial, estimated to cost nearly £2,000.[1525]

[1511] *The Mercury*, 20 November 1868; *The Tasmanian Times*, 20 May, 24 August 1869.
[1512] *The Mercury*, 14 May 1869; *The Tasmanian Times*, 24 August 1869.
[1513] *The Tasmanian Times*, 30 August 1869.
[1514] *The Sydney Morning Herald*, 9 April 1870.
[1515] *The Brisbane Courier*, 2 July, 15 September 1870.
[1516] *The Brisbane Courier*, 25, 28 July, 19 August 1870.
[1517] *The Brisbane Courier*, 28 July 1870.
[1518] *Maryborough Chronicle, Wide Bay and Burnett Advertiser*, 4 August 1870; *The Brisbane Courier*, 15 September, 12 October 1870.
[1519] *The Brisbane Courier*, 24, 27 October 1870.
[1520] BRISBANE, Main register, Volume 2, 1868-1887, Folio 7.
[1521] *Northern Territory Times and Gazette*, 19 April 1884.
[1522] R. Parsons (2008). *Shipping Losses and Casualties concerning Australia and New Zealand*.
[1523] *The Tasmanian Times*, 8 October 1870; *The Mercury*, 12 October 1871
[1524] *The Mercury*, 12 October 1871.
[1525] *The Mercury*, 27 February 1872.

Waratah at Hobart Town (c1870s).
Courtesy Maritime Museum of Tasmania (P_2020-172).

Messrs Fisher and Facy's three-masted barque was finally launched on 10 June 1872.[1526] Named *Waratah*, the 123ft blue gum vessel glided into the water without a hiccup in the presence of 800 spectators.[1527] Immediately following, approximately 90 workers and their wives were treated to a celebratory dinner hosted by the new vessel's owners and held at the Odd Fellows' Hall.[1528] Though intended for the China trade, the *Waratah* was ultimately placed in the intercolonial and trans-Tasman trades, sailing from Hobart Town to various ports including Launceston, Geelong, Newcastle, Lyttelton, and Dunedin, as well as Rockhampton in Queensland.[1529] In July 1882 the vessel was sold to the River Don Trading Company Limited of Tasmania to trade between the island's north-west coast and the mainland.[1530] Less than two years later it was sold to a buyer from Sydney and near immediately on-sold to Anton Schlenk of Adelaide, ultimately becoming involved in the northern guano trade.[1531] The 201-ton *Waratah* was wrecked at Rocky Island, Queensland, on 20 January 1894 with fortunately no loss of life.[1532]

In January 1872 Lucas leased the shipyard property next door to his that had previously been owned and operated by John Ross.[1533] Included on site was Ross' famous patent slip capable of accommodating vessels of up to 1,500 tons.[1534] While Lucas appears to have operated out of both sites for a number of months, in July 1872, shortly after launching the *Waratah*, he gave up the lease of his existing shipyard with the property subsequently advertised to let by its owner Duncan McPherson.[1535] At the time the site consisted of an acre of land with a large frontage on the River Derwent upon which was installed a patent slip capable of taking vessels up to 300 tons by steam. Several buildings, including three brick cottages, sheds, blacksmith shops and other amenities, were also installed on the property.[1536] In October 1872 the site was leased to John Bradley, previous in the employ of John Ross as his foreman.[1537]

Upon re-establishing his yard, business remained active for Lucas, particularly with regards to the repair, overhaul and maintenance of existing vessels. In December 1872, for example, his workers were employed in fitting out the new ketch *Clematis* which had been built by Thomas Inches and Sons at Shipwrights Point to the order of Captain Bendall of Hawkes Bay, New Zealand.[1538] They also overhauled

---

[1526] *The Tasmanian Tribune*, 10 June 1872.
[1527] *The Mercury*, 11 June 1872.
[1528] *The Mercury*, 11 June 1872.
[1529] *The Mercury*, 2 July, 17 August, 25 September, 22 October 1872, 18 February, 28 March, 12 June 1873, 13 February 1874; *Rockhampton Bulletin*, 22 July 1873; *The Tasmanian Tribune*, 3 October 1873.
[1530] HOBART, Register of ships, Volume 9, 1865-1877, [pages 1-173, continues on film roll 2], Folio 114; *The Mercury*, 1 July 1883.
[1531] ADELAIDE, Register of ships subsequent to Merchant Shipping Act 1854, Volume 3, 1878-1896, Folio 139; *Queensland Times*, 3 February 1894.
[1532] *The Week*, 2 March 1894.
[1533] *The Mercury*, 30 January, 20 April 1872.
[1534] *The Mercury*, 7 August 1875.
[1535] *The Mercury*, 12 February, 27 July 1872.
[1536] *The Mercury*, 27 July 1872.
[1537] *Cornwall Advertiser*, 29 October 1872.
[1538] *The Mercury*, 29 November, 3 December 1872.

the Government schooner *Harriet* and brigantine *Sword Fish*, as well as undertook repair and alterations to the schooner *Guiding Star*.[1539]

> TO SHIPBUILDERS AND OTHERS.
>
> TO BE LET BY TENDER,
>
> With possession on the 15th August,
>
> THE SHIP YARD AT BATTERY POINT,
>
> HOBART TOWN,
>
> Belonging to D. McPherson, Esq., and now in the occupation of MR. JOHN LUCAS.
>
> The property consists of an acre of land, which has a large frontage on the River Derwent. On the property is a powerful PATENT SLIP, capable of taking up, by steam, vessels up to 300 tons, and which is supplied with ways, rollers, chains, rods, and all necessaries for immediate work.
>
> The business premises comprise building sheds, large blacksmiths' shops, and other requisites.
>
> In addition to the Slip, there are the ways worked by winches, upon which the small craft plying on the river are safely and economically drawn up and repaired.
>
> The large Punt moored off the yard will be let with the slip.
>
> On part of the property are three well-built Brick Cottages, which are let for 9s. per week, and these will be let with the yard and slip.
>
> Each Tenderer is requested to send in two Tenders, one stating a fixed rental for Yard, Slip, and Cottages, and the other stating a fixed rental for the three Cottages, and what proportion of slip dues the Tenderer is prepared to pay in lieu of rent for the yard and slip.
>
> Full inventories of the winches, punts, blocks, stages, &c., used with the slip and premises, together with terms and all other particulars, can be obtained on application to the Undersigned, by whom Tenders will be received until twelve o'clock on the third day of August next.
>
> HENRY DOBSON,
>
> 4569   69, Macquarie-street.

The Mercury, 23 July 1872.

1873 proved yet another busy year for John Lucas, though business may have been hindered by local ship carpenters being on strike during March of that year.[1540] There was also bad weather to contend with in August, reducing the amount of time available for outdoor work at the slip yards. Further, the Hobart Town press reported that same month that '*many of the shipwrights have gone to work on the railway, as skilled artisans have been required for some considerable viaducts and bridges on the line, which are being constructed of our hard wood timber*'.[1541] Still vessels noted on his slip included the brigs *Maid of Erin*, *Clematis*, *Fairy Rock* and *Chanticleer*; the schooner yacht *Linda* (of the Royal Yacht Squadron); the barques *Natal Queen*, *Waratah*, *Sapphire*, *Southern Cross*, *Marie Laure* and *Addison*; the steamers *Kangaroo*, *Southern Cross*, *Tasman* and *City of Hobart*; the schooners *Swansea Packet* and *Robert Burns*; and the barges *Annie*, *Cape Pigeon*, *Hero*, *Victoria* and *Shannon*.[1542]

In August 1873 the keel of a large centreboard craft was laid down at Lucas' yard, though a lack of timber delayed the build from progressing.[1543] This vessel was likely the 82ft fore-and-aft schooner *Lily* that was launched on 19 October 1874.[1544] In February 1874 the keel of another vessel, this time a barque, built to the order of Captain Robert Firth of Melbourne, was also laid down at the same yard.[1545] It would be another two years before this specific craft was completed; launched as the 320-ton *Oceania* on 13 May 1876.[1546]

Though built to the order of Messrs Facy and Fisher, the schooner *Lily* was sold to Alex Russell in early December 1874, without making a single voyage with the exception of trial to test out its sea qualities.[1547] It immediately sailed for South Australia carrying a cargo of timber and was subsequently placed in the South Australian coastal trade, sailing between Port Adelaide and Port MacDonnell, occasionally also sailing between South Australia, Victoria and Tasmania.[1548] Tragedy, however, struck the vessel when its chief officer was knocked overboard and drowned in late May 1876 a few hours after leaving Port MacDonnell en route to Victoria.[1549] The drama associated with the craft continued when two months later it went ashore on Tipara Reef on a voyage between Wallaroo and Port Adelaide, though appears to have been relatively unscathed by the incident.[1550] A similar episode occurred in February 1879 when the *Lily* grounded in Fanny's Cove.[1551]

Remaining in the South Australian coastal trade, the bad luck of those associated with the *Lily* continued. On 15 March 1880 the vessel's master, Captain McIntosh, was drowned while proceeding to shore at Port MacDonnell in a small boat.[1552] Then on 5 April the *Lily* collided with the schooner *Annie Taylor* in the Port River, though only received minor damage. It was very soon thereafter that the *Lily* was sold to Captain Henry Hopwood of Hobart Town for service in Tasmania's east coast trade; Hopwood having an immediate need to replace his recently wrecked schooner *Guiding Star*.[1553]

In August 1882 the *Lily* was purchased by James Cowle of Tasmania's north-west coast (mentioned in further detail in the coming pages), again finding employment in intercolonial trade, the price being

---

[1539] *The Mercury*, 30 November, 14, 28 December 1872.
[1540] *The Mercury*, 25 March 1873.
[1541] *The Mercury*, 9 August 1873.
[1542] *The Mercury*, 7, 10, 17 January, 21 February, 24 April, 21, 30 May, 30 June, 1 July, 9 August, 26 September, 28 November, 23, 31 December 1873; *The Tasmanian Tribune*, 4, 17 April, 26 August, 4, 22 October, 4 November 1873.
[1543] *The Mercury*, 9 August 1873.
[1544] *The Tasmanian Tribune*, 19 October 1874.
[1545] *The Mercury*, 20 February 1874.
[1546] *The Mercury*, 20 October 1874, 15 May 1876.
[1547] *The Mercury*, 16 November, 3 December 1874; ADELAIDE, Register of ships subsequent to Merchant Shipping Act 1854, Volume 2, 1873-1878, Folio 77.
[1548] *The Mercury*, 29 December 1874, 24 August 1875; *South Australian Register*, 27 February 1875; *The Argus*, 25 December 1875.
[1549] *The Argus*, 5 June 1876.
[1550] *South Australian Register*, 14 July 1876.
[1551] *Evening Journal*, 12 February 1879.
[1552] *Evening Journal*, 16 March 1880.
[1553] *The Mercury*, 30 April, 24 May 1880; HOBART, Register of ships (with continuation entries), Volume 10, 1877-1898, Folio 34.

£1,750.[1554] Though the vessel was advertised for sale six months later, it is not clear who next purchased the craft.[1555] However, just under four years later, in December 1886, the *Lily* was sold to William and Colin Cook of Lyttelton, New Zealand, where, finally finding its niche, the craft spent over 30 years employed in the coastal trade.[1556] The *Lily* was wrecked at Kapiti Island on 2 November 1920, all hands saved.[1557] At the time of loss, it was owned by Messrs A. and D. Campbell of Wellington.[1558]

In contrast to the history of the *Lily*, Captain Firth's barque, the 142ft *Oceania* launched in May 1876, was the largest vessel built by John Lucas and likely the crowning achievement of his career.[1559] During the 'Shipwright's Soiree', held the evening of the launch, Captain Firth toasted Lucas stating that *'the Oceania was one of the finest built vessels in the colonies, he having for the last twenty-five years seen most of those build, and none were in his estimation equal to her'*.[1560] The vessel was also the largest vessel built in Hobart Town for some time and considered one of the finest barques ever built in Tasmania.

With its owner at the helm, the *Oceania* sailed for Adelaide on its maiden voyage on 7 July 1876 with a cargo of timber, palings, laths, staves, cart shafts, jam, fruit, hops and leather.[1561] It then spent several years engaged in intercolonial trade, also making supplemental trips to Mauritius, China, Japan, Guam, Java, South Africa and New Zealand.[1562] However, its life was cut dramatically short when on 4 May 1885 the vessel was wrecked on Karori Rock near Terawhit Station, in Cook Strait, New Zealand, while en route from Adelaide to Wellington, its crew of 10, including Captain Firth, managing to make it safely to land via the craft's boats.[1563]

WRECK OF THE OCEANIA.

[By Wire.—From Our Correspondent.]
AUCKLAND, Monday.

The barque Oceania, bound from South Australia to Wellington with a cargo of bark, wheat, and salt, struck on Terawhiti, and after hanging for some time on the rocks, slipped off. The captain, finding that the vessel was making water, got the boats out, and the crew reached Wellington with a few articles of clothing. The captain lost everything. The vessel is valued at £4000, and was insured in Sydney for £1000.

The Age, 5 May 1885.

A large number of vessels were placed on Lucas' patent slip during the mid-to-late 1870s, receiving various degrees of work, including minor and major refit, overhaul, repairs, and painting, etc. One such craft that was cause for great celebration was the Tasmanian Steam Navigation (T.S.N.) Company's new vessel *Mangana* which first arrived in Hobart Town on 18 October 1876.[1564] A large number of people assembled at the wharf to admire the *'fine lines'* of the *'nice-looking ship'* that had been constructed of iron at the shipyards of Messrs D. and W. Henderson on the Clyde in Scotland.[1565]

Founded in Tasmania in 1852 with a capital of £40,000 divided into £10 shares, in the decades since the T.S.N. Company had played a major role in the development of coastal and intercolonial steam passenger and cargo trade, particularly between Hobart Town and Melbourne.[1566] The company's new screw steamer, *Mangana*, was expected to broaden its service offerings, becoming a doyen of the Launceston-Melbourne route.[1567] The 208ft vessel had departed Scotland on 21 June with Captain Andrew E. Berry Brown at the helm.[1568] Its subsequent arrival in Hobart Town had been much anticipated; the vessel being one of only a handful of purpose-built steamers commissioned by the Tasmanian owned and operated company. Following several days spent unloading its cargo of coal, the *Mangana* was placed on Lucas' patent slip for cleaning, painting (inside and out) and general overhaul where it presented *'an imposing appearance'* and was subsequently viewed by many onlookers and interested residents of the greater Hobart Town area.[1569] The steamer entered service a few weeks later, leaving Launceston for Melbourne, under the command of Captain J. R. Young.[1570]

The *Mangana* was soon followed by the arrival in Hobart Town from Scotland of the nearly-new steamer *Vampire* in July 1878.[1571] Renamed *Esk* by the T.S.N. Company, the vessel was intended to service the Launceston to Sydney route which at the time was experiencing a substantial increase in demand for trade. At 190ft, the Glasgow-built vessel was slightly smaller than the *Mangana* and capable of accommodating 30 passengers. Soon after its arrival, the craft was placed on Lucas' slip for general overhaul and painting.[1572] The *Esk* commenced service in late August 1878 though would be wrecked less than a decade later, on 24 April 1886, on Hebe Reef near Low Head, Tasmania, all hands saved.[1573]

[1554] *The Mercury*, 24 August, 10 October 1882; *Launceston Examiner*, 15 August 1882; HOBART, Register of ships (with continuation entries), Volume 10, 1877-1898, Folio 34.
[1555] *Telegraph*, 26 February 1883.
[1556] *The Mercury*, 16 July 1886; HOBART, Register of ships (with continuation entries), Volume 10, 1877-1898, Folio 34.
[1557] *Auckland Star*, 5 November 1920.
[1558] *Auckland Star*, 5 November 1920.
[1559] *The Mercury*, 15 May 1876.
[1560] *The Mercury*, 24 May 1876.
[1561] *The Mercury*, 7 July 1876; *The Express and Telegraph*, 17 July 1876.
[1562] *The Mercury*, 9 December 1876, 30 April 1877, 5 February 1878, 7 April 1881; *The Argus*, 6 January 1879, 7 May 1884; *South Australian Register*, 12 July 1879, 7 June 1884; *The Sydney Morning Herald*, 6 December 1879, 20 July, 5 October 1880; *The Express and Telegraph*, 31 May 1884.
[1563] *The Age*, 5 May 1885; *Evening Post* (NZ), 4 May 1885.
[1564] *The Mercury*, 19 October 1876.
[1565] *The Mercury*, 19 October 1876.
[1566] D. O'May (1976). *Song of Steam: A Chronicle of Paddle Steamers and Screw Steamers in Tasmanian Waters 1832-1939*.
[1567] D. O'May (1976). *Song of Steam: A Chronicle of Paddle Steamers and Screw Steamers in Tasmanian Waters 1832-1939*.
[1568] *The Mercury*, 19 October 1876.
[1569] *Tribune*, 19 October, 8 November 1876; *The Mercury*, 31 October, 2, 10 November 1876.
[1570] *Launceston Examiner*, 28 November, 5 December 1876.
[1571] *Tribune*, 26 July 1878.
[1572] *The Mercury*, 7 August 1878.
[1573] *The Mercury*, 26 April 1878.

Mangana on John Lucas' Patent Slip (1876).
Courtesy W L Crowther Library, State Library of Tasmania
(AUTAS001125641019w800).

The 1880s dawned and with steamers becoming more and more prevalent in local, intra- and intercolonial cargo and passenger trades, there were few new commercial sailing vessels being built. In late 1880, *The Mercury* reported, '*The construction of sailing vessels in the colonies, and especially at Hobart Town, is becoming rare, steam communication, which is making such rapid strides, gradually forcing sailing vessels out of date. It is now nearly three years ago since the last vessels was built at Hobart Town, and beyond occasional repairs having been effected to different craft, the shipwrights have had scarcely anything to do*'.[1574] The article continued. '*Mr. Lucas, Battery Point, will, however, now be enabled to give a little employment, as he has received an order to build a small vessel, which it is to be hoped will be the forerunner of something else in this line. The craft in questions is to be constructed for Mr. James Cowle, who intends making a tour to foreign ports in her. Her dimensions are to be as follows: Length of keel, 71ft.; beam, 18ft.; and depth of hold, 9ft. 3in.; and these are expected to give her a register of 60 tons. She is to be built on the deep keel principle, and to be rigged as a fore-and-aft schooner. Blue gum will be used for the frame of the vessel, whilst the other principal parts of her will be made of kauri and Huon pine. Mr. Lucas intends laying the keel of the new vessel on Monday next, and expects to have her launched in about eight or nine months.*'[1575]

Cowle was an interesting client for Lucas to engage with. An accomplished surveyor, he had made his fortune in the survey of lands for mining in both Western Australia and Tasmania. He had also invested heavily in the industry, including in tin mining ventures at Mount Bischoff on Tasmania's north-west coast, as well as in the mining of slate.[1576] Cowle was from an esteemed local family. His parents had established a school at Pressland House in Melville Street, Hobart

[1574] *The Mercury*, 20 November 1880.
[1575] *The Mercury*, 20 November 1880.
[1576] *Launceston Examiner*, 31 July 1873; *The Cornwall Chronicle*, 22 October, 8 December 1873; *The Mercury*, 11 November 1873, 3 December 1877.

Spirited, Skilled and Determined

Esk on John Lucas' Patent Slip (1878).
Courtesy Tasmanian Archives (NS1013/1/1228).

John Lucas

Town, operating the Commercial Academy for several decades beginnings in the early 1840s; his older brother Thomas was a prominent Tasmanian farmer and businessman of Braxholm in Tasmania's north-east region.[1577] With Cowle's involvement in tin mining at Mount Bischoff becoming more and more permanent, in the mid-1870s he had moved his family to Ellenton (now Cuprona) on the River Blythe.[1578] In March 1877 Cowle was appointed a Justice of the Peace for nearby Emu Bay.[1579] However, it was in the Penguin magistrate's court in November of that same year that Cowle was sensationally charged by his 15-year-old servant Eliza Jane Brown, an indentured apprentice from the Queen's Orphan School at New Town, with *'carrying on with her'*; Brown stating that she would not have received a fair trial had she made the charges at Emu Bay.[1580] Cowle, in turn, charged Brown with gross misconduct and absconding, while Cowle was subsequently charged with horsewhipping Brown and otherwise ill-treating her, in particular *'rubbing her face in human dirt'*.[1581]

The court cases were played out in the press across Tasmania, the details of which were altogether quite shocking. While Cowle pled guilty to the horsewhipping and ill-treatment charges, he argued that he was *'provoked by the girl's filthy habits to chastise her in the manner stated'*.[1582] The Bench gave judgment for Brown stating that Cowle had *'forgot his position as a magistrate and his sense of decency'*.[1583] As such, he was fined £10 and costs.

Of the charge by Brown that Cowle had been *'carrying on with her'* since *'the third day of her arrival'* at his home, he was found not guilty, despite numerous witness testimony to the contrary.[1584] Instead, Brown was ridiculed for making the charge up, with the *'usual amount of precocious cleverness and cunning of Orphan School children'*. The Bench further clarified that given *'the character and position'* of the defendant, i.e., Cowle, that it had no alternative but to dismiss the case.[1585]

While Brown was sent back to the Orphan School in Hobart Town, Cowle's reputation appears to have remained relatively intact. He continued to enjoy the spoils of a middle to upper class existence, also retaining his position as a Justice of the Peace for the district of Emu Bay, as well as being appointed to the same position for the district of Glenorchy following his return to Hobart Town in 1878.[1586] In April of the following year Cowle was elected a councillor of this district with the Hobart Town *Tribune* publishing the following statement, *'We congratulate the inhabitants of Glenorchy in having secured the services of Mr. Cowle in the Council, as that gentleman has ever been known as the possessor of straitforward and honest principles'*.[1587] However, just over a year later, in August 1880, Cowle was being reprimanded for his lack of appearance at numerous Council meetings with his conduct deemed *'somewhat discourteous'*.[1588] Though Cowle claimed that his lack of attendance was due to the fact that he had recently moved to Hobart Town, his fellow councillors were not convinced.

Buoyed by the success of his tin mining ventures and investments and an ever-expanding pocketbook, it was at this stage of Cowle's life that he commissioned John Lucas to build him a pleasure schooner.[1589] He also sought to learn navigation, receiving instruction from J. B. Waller of Hobart Town. Unfortunately the lessons proved too onerous for Cowle such that he refused to pay and was thus sued for £3, a case in which he lost.[1590] Still, this did not preclude Cowle from calling himself 'Captain' with his new vessel, still under construction, now stated to be for the pearling trade.[1591]

Despite not being able to navigate his vessel, Cowle's substantial 79ft schooner yacht, the *Erne* was launched from Lucas' Battery Point shipyard on 18 October 1881.[1592] It was described as a *'very pretty model, designed by Mr. Lucas himself'*, though since it was originally planned as a pleasure yacht, *'she has not much cargo room, the greater part of the space being taken up with the cabin and forecastle'*.[1593]

While Cowle was likely a demanding and obstinate customer that Lucas did not perhaps enjoy interacting with, during the latter stages of the *Erne*'s build, he likely had other things on his mind. His beloved wife Sophia died at their home in Mona Street, Battery Point, on 21 June 1881.[1594] She was 52 years of age. Cause of death was morbus cordis, i.e., heart disease, combined with edema of the lungs and kidney disease.[1595] A day after Sophia's death, ships in the Port of Hobart lowered their flags to half-mast out of respect.[1596]

And just what become of the *Erne*? The vessel took its trial trip, taking a party of ladies and gentlemen to Port Arthur in January 1882 and soon thereafter was placed at the disposal of the organising committee of the Hobart Town Regatta.[1597] The *Erne* was then sailed to Melbourne on a pleasure trip, arriving in Port Phillip Bay early in March 1882 before heading to George Town, in Tasmania's north.[1598] A few months later it was noted to be in Sydney.[1599]

[1577] *Tasmanian Weekly Dispatch*, 25 September 1840; *The Hobart Town Advertiser*, 7 July 1860; *The Cornwall Chronicle*, 2 August 1876; *The Tasmanian*, 19 May 1894.
[1578] *The Cornwall Chronicle*, 14 May 1875, 1 October 1877.
[1579] *The Mercury*, 20 March 1877.
[1580] *Weekly Examiner*, 17 November 1877; *Launceston Examiner*, 1, 4 December 1877; www.orphanschool.org.au/showorphan.php?orphan_ID=529.
[1581] *Launceston Examiner*, 1 December 1877.
[1582] *Launceston Examiner*, 1 December 1877.
[1583] *Launceston Examiner*, 1 December 1877.
[1584] *Launceston Examiner*, 4 December 1877.
[1585] *Launceston Examiner*, 4 December 1877.
[1586] *The Mercury*, 25 April 1878; *Tribune*, 3 May 1878.
[1587] *Tribune*, 28 April 1879.
[1588] *The Mercury*, 9 August 1880.
[1589] *The Mercury*, 20 November 1880.
[1590] *The Mercury*, 3 December 1880.
[1591] *The Mercury*, 16 September 1881.
[1592] *The Mercury*, 19 October 1881, 14 February 1882.
[1593] *The Mercury*, 19 October 1881.
[1594] *The Mercury*, 22 June 1881.
[1595] Libraries Tasmania (RGD35/1/9 no 3191).
[1596] *The Mercury*, 22 June 1881.
[1597] *The Mercury*, 11 January 1882.
[1598] *Launceston Examiner*, 10, 13 March 1882; *The Mercury*, 11 March 1882.
[1599] *Launceston Examiner*, 2 June 1882.

With Captain James Simm at the helm, the *Erne* returned to Hobart Town, its arrival coinciding with Cowle and his family's relocation to Emu Bay.[1600] The vessel was then engaged to transfer 400 packages of luggage and household effects, as well as a four-wheeled carriage, to Penguin.[1601] The *Erne* then commenced its voyage to Hobart Town and had only sailed a short distance from Penguin when disaster struck. John Frith, a passenger on board the craft, fell overboard.[1602] He was thankfully rescued by a sailor, Henry Hall, who had jumped in the water to save him.[1603] Both men were a short time later delivered back on board. However, Frith was apparently '*insensible*' and though '*every means were tried to bring him to consciousness, efforts were unavailing. He remained in an insensible state for about two hours and a half and expired half an hour before midnight*'.[1604] Upon arrival in Hobart Town, Frith's body was conveyed to the General Hospital.

An inquest was held into the death of Frith at Hobart Town's Carlton Hotel on 25 July 1882. Interviewed were Cowle, Captain Simm and Henry Hall, among others. It soon became evident that facts surrounding Frith's apparent drowning were being relayed differently, including by Simm who, in contrast to Cowle, stated that Frith had remained alive until 4 am, i.e., a duration of some six hours after the accident.[1605] In addition, given the accident had occurred two miles from shore and only six miles from Frith's home in Penguin, questions began to be asked as to why the *Erne* had not been turned around so as to transfer Frith off the craft such that he could receive medical attention.[1606] Alternatively, given the graveness of Frith's state as the vessel sailed further along the north-west coast, why didn't they enter in to Leven or the Tamar? Instead, the vessel had maintained its course for Hobart Town.

While the inquest resolved that Frith's death was by accidental drowning, and that the bravery of Henry Hall should be acknowledged, Frith's family was adamant that he had died of '*cold and neglect*', his father stating '*that if a man lives for six hours after being in the water only fifteen minutes, and most of that time his head held above water, you cannot say he was drowned*'.[1607] The Frith family also admonished the '*inhumane act of taking him on instead of putting back*'.[1608] The response from Cowle to this statement was outrageous; that the family should be grateful they had a body to bury at all since '*he could have thrown the body overboard had he liked*'.[1609] The criticism continued. At a meeting of the Farmer's Club held at Leven shortly after the inquest, '*Much indignation was expressed at the conduct on the part of the owner, who refused to positively allow the vessel to put in at the Leven, although medical aid could have been obtained there; for it appears the man continued to breath several hours after being extricated from the water*'.[1610]

With allegations of his behaviour again swirling in the press, Cowle purchased the schooner *Lily*, that John Lucas had launched in October 1874, with an eye to establishing it in the coastal trade, operating along the north-west coast; a role which it would have been more suited to in comparison to the *Erne*.[1611] However, the longevity of this venture was shirt-lived with Cowle advertising the *Lily* for sale six months later.[1612]

On 3 August 1883 Cowle was admitted to the New Norfolk Hospital for the Insane. Signing the admittance form was his older brother, Thomas Pressland Cowle, who stated that Cowle suffered from '*gradual mental decline which commenced about two years ago*' and that he was '*reported dangerous by* [his] *wife, family and attendant*'.[1613] Cowle remained a patient of this institution until his death in August 1887 at the age of 47.[1614]

While the schooner yacht *Erne* was involved in the Tasmanian coastal trade, sailing between Hobart Town, Launceston and various ports along the north-west coast, for the latter half of 1882, in June of the follow year it was sailed to Sydney and subsequently advertised for sale.[1615] A few weeks later the vessel was sailed to Tonga under the name *Upolu*.[1616] Its subsequent history is not confirmed.

> FOR Immediate SALE, the Schooner Yacht ERNE, 65 tons register, nearly new. Splendid vessel for pearling, trading, sealing, or pilot boat. Built regardless of cost. Fastest sailer in the Australian waters. Particulars, &c., inquire on board at Market Wharf.

The Sydney Morning Herald, 10 July 1883.

Throughout the early 1880s slip work continued to be the primary focus of John Lucas' yard. In 1883, for example, the yard was noted as fitting out and finishing Messrs Facy and Fisher's new steamer *Huon*, the hull of which had been built at Port Cygnet by John Wilson; and undertaking overhauls of the steamers *Amy*, *Wakefield* and *Southern Cross*; the barques *Wild Wave*, *Pet*, *Planter*, *Natal Queen* and *Acacia*; the yacht *Neva*; the barquentines *Guiding Star*, *Sword Fish*, and *Sedwell Jane*; the ketch *Enchantress*; and the brig *Fairy Rock*.[1617]

The last vessel Lucas built at his Battery Point shipyard was the centreboard ketch *Vesta* which is first noted in the press in February 1883 bringing a load of firewood from Barnes Bay, Bruny Island, to

---

[1600] *The Mercury*, 8 June 1882.
[1601] *The Mercury*, 24 June 1882.
[1602] *The Mercury*, 24 July 1882.
[1603] *The Mercury*, 24 July 1882.
[1604] *The Mercury*, 24 July 1882.
[1605] *The Mercury*, 27 July 1882.
[1606] *The Mercury*, 27 July 1882.
[1607] *The Mercury*, 2 August 1882.
[1608] *Launceston Examiner*, 2 August 1882.
[1609] *Launceston Examiner*, 2 August 1882.
[1610] *The Tasmanian*, 2 September 1882.
[1611] *Launceston Examiner*, 15 August 1882; *The Mercury*, 18 August 1882.
[1612] *Telegraph*, 26 February 1883.
[1613] Libraries Tasmania (HSD285/1/532).
[1614] Libraries Tasmania (RGD35/1/56 no 979).
[1615] *The Mercury*, 29 August, 25 September, 14 November 1882, 22 June 1883; *The Sydney Morning Herald*, 10 July 1883.
[1616] *The Sydney Morning Herald*, 30 July 1883.
[1617] *The Mercury*, 20 January, 6, 16 February, 3, 22 March, 2, 7 June, 7, 26 July, 3 August, 28 September 1883; *Tasmanian News*, 29 November, 31 December 1883.

Hobart Town.[1618] Built to the order of Henry Denne of Bruny Island, the Huon pine craft soon became a success in sailing boat races at local regattas such that in early 1888 it was lengthened to 55ft, in addition to other improvements to its sailing abilities.[1619] Later that year Denne sailed *Vesta* to Victoria to compete in the Melbourne Centennial Aquatic Carnival, held on 23-24 November 1888. Significantly, the event marked the first time that representatives from multiple colonies, encompassing Victoria, New South Wales, South Australia, Tasmania and New Zealand, competed against one another across a broad spectrum of sailing races. Competing in the race for keel or centre plate yachts between 10 and 20 tons, the *Vesta* finished a respectable third behind the *Tasma* (also of Tasmania) and the *Coolana* (of Victoria).[1620]

The *Vesta* returned to Hobart Town where it appears to have been primarily used as a yacht. In 1894 the craft was purchased by A. James of Hobart with the intention of sailing it to New Caledonia on a pleasure cruise.[1621] Upon reaching Newcastle, New South Wales, in December 1894, however, the vessel was sold to Evan Evans.[1622] Sold again shortly thereafter, the *Vesta* was first registered in Sydney in 1901 when purchased by Holmes Samuel Chipman.[1623] In October of that same year, *Vesta* was sold to Thomas Thomson, master mariner of Queensland.[1624] Its register was closed on 22 September 1902 after having been purchased by Robert Wilson of British New Guinea where it had been transferred.[1625]

In September 1884, at the age of 58, John Lucas relinquished his Battery Point shipyard to the Derwent Iron Works and Engineering Company; the company having recently been purchased by J. W. Syme from the Clark family.[1626] Since November 1871 the shipyard had

[1618] *The Mercury*, 10 February 1883, 24 November 1888.
[1619] *The Mercury*, 26 March, 24 November 1888.
[1620] *The Mercury*, 26 November 1888.
[1621] *The Mercury*, 21 August 1894.
[1622] *Newcastle Morning Herald & Miners' Advocate*, 6 December 1894.
[1623] *Newcastle Morning Herald and Miners' Advocate*, 19 January 1895; SYDNEY, NEW SOUTH WALES, Register of ships, single number series (II), Volume 18, 1899-1902, Folio 36.
[1624] SYDNEY, NEW SOUTH WALES, Register of ships, single number series (II), Volume 18, 1899-1902, Folio 36.
[1625] SYDNEY, NEW SOUTH WALES, Register of ships, single number series (II), Volume 18, 1899-1902, Folio 36.
[1626] *The Mercury*, 2 September 1884.

Vesta (early 1890s).
Courtesy Maritime Museum of Tasmania (P_OM_H_45c).

been owned by Crawford Mayne Maxwell of Hobart Town; he having paid £2,500 to the Commercial Bank for the property and then leased it back to Lucas.[1627]

An enterprising businessman, J. W. Syme purchased the Napoleon Street shipyard from Maxwell for £1,500 with the goal of using the patent slip to undertake repair work of local steamers to complement the Derwent Iron Works' existing foundry work.[1628] By January of the following year, however, the Derwent Iron Works and Engineering Company had been taken over by Robert Kennedy and Sons, with the latter paying a substantial £2,379 for the property.[1629] Not yet ready to retire, Lucas remained at the shipyard managing its operations.[1630] For example, in May 1885 Robert Kennedy and Sons was awarded the contract to undertake repairs on the ship *Irby* with Lucas responsible for repairs to the vessel's woodwork.[1631] Lucas was also involved in the survey of various vessels that visited the Port of Hobart having been appointed Master Shipwright by the Marine Board of Hobart in July 1884.[1632]

During this period Lucas was additionally involved in converting the barques *Aladdin* and *Emily Downing* into coal hulks for the Tasmanian Government.[1633] His partnership with Kennedy and Sons also saw the successful overhaul of the SS *Esk* in November 1885; Lucas being responsible for the shipwright's work, including installing new decking, and Kennedy and Sons being responsible for the machinery.[1634]

By September 1886 Lucas had moved his slip yard operation to Hobart's Domain, taking over the lease from the McGregor family.[1635] Here, in addition to general overhaul and repair work, he was noted as having launched, on 3 May 1887, the 38ft yacht *Hesione* for W. J. Lindsay of Bruny Island.[1636] Lucas also made extensive additions to the newly-launched steamer *Koonya*, and the steamer *Huon* (he lengthened this craft by cutting it in two forward of the bridge), as well as the barques *Kassa* and *Phoenix* and ketch *Belle Brandon*.[1637] The following year Lucas' Domain slip yard undertook overhauls of the brig *Prospero*, the barques *Natal Queen* and *Wild Wave*, the barquentine *Guiding Star*, the schooners *Falcon*, *Mary Wadley* and *Wanganui*, and the steamers *Warrentinna*, *Koonya* and *Myall*.[1638]

On 1 January 1889 Lucas relinquished the lease of the Domain slip yard to the partnership of John Dalgleish and Robert Taylor, the former having served his apprenticeship with Lucas.[1639] Still not ready to retire, on 13 December 1888, at the age of 62, Lucas notified the public that he was returning to work at Robert Kennedy and Sons patent slip, Battery Point.[1640] Here, up until his retirement, Lucas was primarily involved with the repair, modification and survey of vessels.[1641]

The start of the 1890s saw Lucas building two more yachts. The first, *Volant*, was constructed at Bruny Island to the order of Henry Denne, based on Denne's own model, with Lucas personally supervising its build.[1642] It was launched in November of 1890 and went on to become one of the more successful and noteworthy 28ft yachts of its time.[1643] Later converted to a fishing boat, *Volant* was wrecked on 1 May 1978 near the entrance to Port Davey, Tasmania, all hands saved.[1644]

The second yacht, built at Sandy Bay to the order of Douglas Brothers, was advertised for sale in an incomplete state in August 1890.[1645] The 28-footer was subsequently advertised for sale by auction in April 1891 where it was noted to still require a deck and fittings, though the timber for these items would be sold with the yacht.[1646] Failing to sell, it remained in the hands of Douglas Brothers and was launched by November 1891, just in time for the start of the Derwent Sailing Club's 1891 season.[1647] Named *Gitana*, the vessel spent the next four years participating in local yacht races and regattas until it was sold to J. W. Moffat of the Royal Brighton Yacht Club, Victoria, in January 1896.[1648] Prior to its transfer to Melbourne, the craft was, '*as both a racer and a cruiser*', stated to be '*far away the best boat of her class in the colony*'.[1649]

Expanding his skill-set even further Lucas' next endeavour saw him design several yachts, including the *Kaa-Ana*, *Thelma* and *Alice*. The *Kaa-Ana* was a steam yacht built by Joseph Clinch at Battery Point to the order of Messrs H. Nicholls and W. P. Gibson.[1650] The 21ft yacht *Thelma* was built at Robert Inches' Battery Point shipyard to the order of Messrs Oldmeadow.[1651] Finally, the *Alice* was a steam yacht built by George Miller at the soap works in Macquarie Street, Hobart, and launched in July 1895.[1652]

By the end of the 1890s and into the early 1900s Lucas had reduced his workload, though was yet to enter full retirement. For example, in early 1898 he was jointly appointed with Robert Inches to supervise the repair of E. H. Webster's yacht *Ella*; the work undertaken by James Mackey and Henry Featherstone at Battery Point.[1653] In July of that same year he was noted as having surveyed the ketch *King Billy* following

---

[1627] www.thelist.tas.gov.au (Historical Deed 05/8129).
[1628] *The Mercury*, 6 September 1884; www.thelist.tas.gov.au (Historical Deed 07/3566).
[1629] *The Mercury*, 17 January, 28 March 1885; www.thelist.tas.gov.au (Historical Deed 07/9576).
[1630] *The Mercury*, 6 September 1884.
[1631] *The Mercury*, 13 May 1885.
[1632] *Tasmanian News*, 26 July 1884.
[1633] *The Mercury*, 22 May 1885.
[1634] *The Mercury*, 17 November 1885, 26 April 1886.
[1635] *The Mercury*, 4 September 1886.
[1636] *Tasmanian News*, 4 May 1887; *The Mercury*, 5 May 1887.
[1637] *The Mercury*, 13 January, 5 August, 11 November, 23, 30 December 1887; *Tasmanian News*, 28 December 1886.
[1638] *Tasmanian News*, 10, 25 February, 8 October, 7, 21 November, 8 December 1888; *The Mercury*, 24 April, 5 June, 11 August, 29 October 1888.
[1639] *The Mercury*, 11 December 1888, 1 May 1916; *Tasmanian News*, 26 June 1889.
[1640] *The Mercury*, 13 December 1888.
[1641] *The Mercury*, 11 June 1895, 5 February 1900.
[1642] *Tasmanian News*, 24 September 1890; *The Mercury*, 10 October 1895.
[1643] *The Mercury*, 1 November 1890, 29 October 1926.
[1644] G. Broxam & M. Nash (2013). *Tasmanian Shipwrecks: Volume 2. 1900-2012*.
[1645] *The Mercury*, 18 August 1890.
[1646] *The Mercury*, 17 April 1891.
[1647] *The Mercury*, 2 November 1891.
[1648] *The Mercury*, 3 January 1896; *The Argus*, 10 June 1935.
[1649] *The Mercury*, 3 January 1896.
[1650] *The Mercury*, 21 December 1892, 14 March 1893.
[1651] *The Mercury*, 25 October 1893.
[1652] *The Mercury*, 28 February, 23 May 1894, 22 July 1895.
[1653] *The Mercury*, 8 March 1898.

a collision with the ketch *Huon Chief*.[1654] In September 1901, at the age of 75, he was appointed Shipwright Surveyor of the Hobart Marine Board to temporarily replace Donald McMillan who had been granted a one month leave of absence due to illness.[1655]

John Lucas remained active in the local maritime community up until his death and was noted in the press for his remarkable memory in relation to vessels associated with the Port of Hobart, the press stating *'that he could recall to mind without the slightest effort, the length, breadth, depth, beam and rig, etc., of any vessel for the last fifty years'*.[1656] He died at Regent Street, Sandy Bay, on April 27 1908 at the age of 82 and was buried at Cornelian Bay Cemetery.[1657]

In his will Lucas left all of his tools, implements, drawings and models to his son William J. Lucas who, by that time, was carrying on the family tradition at his own Battery Point shipyard. The property had previously been in the possession of Robert Inches.[1658]

On reflection, having learned the craft of shipbuilding from John Watson, Lucas was a resolute and well-respected shipwright who spent much of his career successfully involved in the slipping and repair of the larger intercolonial and international trading vessels that visited the Port of Hobart. He was also involved in the outfitting of local steamers and whaling vessels. Unlike demand for the building of new vessels, which fluctuated with changes in local economic conditions and trade patterns, demand for the slipping of existing vessels remained consistent

[1654] *The Mercury*, 29 July 1898.
[1655] *The Mercury*, 4 September 1901.
[1656] *The Examiner*, 29 April 1908.
[1657] *The Mercury*, 29 April 1908; www.findagrave.com/memorial/175777697.

[1658] *Tasmanian News*, 3 September 1904; Libraries Tasmania (AD960-1-31 Will Number 7507).

Volant at Battery Point (1890s).
Courtesy Maritime Museum of Tasmania (P_Y_389).

over his multi-decade career. Still, between 1858 and 1883 Lucas built at least 13 vessels at Battery Point, including nine schooners and two barques, many of which furnished international and intercolonial trades.

Later on in his career Lucas diversified his expertise with the designing and building of several of Hobart's more prominent and successful racing yachts.

Vessels built by John Lucas, Robert Jeffrey and employees at Battery Point (1858 - 1883)

Year	Name	Type	Description
1858	Kingston	Schooner	63.0 x 16.3 x 6.7ft. ON 32063. 37 tons. Built by John Lucas and Robert Jeffrey to the order of Henry Hopwood. A regular in the Tasmanian coastal trade for more than a decade, in April 1869 transferred to the intercolonial trade after being purchased by George James and sailed by Nathaniel Lucas. Returned to Hopwood's ownership in January 1871. Sold a year later to James and John Carver. Purchased by George Robinson in September 1875 and placed in the pearl trade off the north-west coast of Western Australia. In late 1878 a mutiny broke out on board in Torres Strait resulting in the death of Captain Robinson, his brother Charles and other crew members. Taken by it captives, no trace of the Kingston was ever found.
1859	Star of Tasmania	Schooner	60.4 x 16.1 x 5.2ft. ON 32077. 31 tons. Built by John Lucas and Robert Jeffrey for Thomas Patterson of Hobart Town. Launched on 30 April 1859, intended for the Pittwater trade, though by October 1861 was trading between Hobart and New Zealand. Disappeared, presumed sunk, in Storm Bay, Tasmania, in October 1867 with the loss of all on board.
1859	Wild Wave	Schooner	78.7 x 20.8 x 7.0ft. ON 32083. 70 tons. Built by John Lucas and Robert Jeffrey to the order of Alexander Bruce Smith of Long Bay. Launched on 26 November 1859 and involved in local then intercolonial trade. Sailed to New Zealand in October 1861 and sold to John Jones of Dunedin. Wrecked on 21 June 1866 in Pelorus Sound with the unfortunate loss of five lives. At the time, owned by Messrs Brownell and Co. of Christchurch, though based out of Lyttelton.
1862	--	Punt	Built by John Lucas and Robert Jeffrey and completed in November 1862 to the order of Christina Herbertson, licencee of the Ferry Inn at Risdon. Used to transport goods and passengers across the River Derwent, leaving from the hotel.
1864	Harriet	Schooner	66.0 x 16.7 x 7.7ft. ON 57586. 49 tons. Built by John Lucas and Robert Jeffrey to the order of the Government of Britain. Launched on 28 July 1864, intended to sail between Port Arthur and Hobart Town. Sold in December 1877 to William Snell Verren of Hobart Town. Sailed to New South Wales two years later. Sold to William Walton in April 1882 and placed in the pearlshelling trade off the coast of Western Australia. Advertised for sale seven years later while lying at Cossack and sold by auction. Remaining in the pearling industry under several different owners, it was ultimately wrecked at Cossack Creek on 2 April 1899.
1865	Storm Bird	Schooner	86.0 x 21.1 x 8.1ft. ON 32138. 96 tons. Built by John Lucas and Robert Jeffrey. Purchased by Thomas Patterson of Hobart Town part-way through construction. Launched on 5 April 1865 and employed in coastal trade, primarily between Hobart Town and Launceston. Sold in November 1866 to A. G. Fisher of Melbourne and placed in intercolonial trade. Ashore near Green Cape, NSW, on 28 1870, all hands saved. Salvaged, repaired and in October 1877 sold to the Government of Hawaii. Wrecked at Bonham Island, Marshall Islands, in August 1881.
1869	Grace Darling	Schooner	83.2 x 20.3 x 8.1ft. ON 57502. 81 tons. Built by John Lucas to the order Captain Henry Hopwood. Launched on 3 April 1869, intended for the east coast trade though, after only a few trips, placed in the trans-Tasman, intercolonial and Tasmanian coastal trades. Sold to Thomas Seal, Alexander Bishop and John Callcombe of Victoria in December 1870. Sold to William Tullock of Adelaide in September 1873 and used in the South Australian coastal trade. Registered in Port Adelaide, SA, in 1873. Sold to Frederick Douglas of Albany in 1892 and employed in the Western Australian coastal trade, Sold again in September 1910 to R. J. Lynn and Company, conveying cargo between Geraldton and Fremantle. Wrecked four years later, on 4 February 1914, on a reef 70 miles north of Fremantle, all hands saved.
1869	Dawn	Schooner	72.0 x 18.3 x 6.0ft. ON 57505. 51 tons. Built by John Lucas to the order of J. R. Gourlay, launched on 23 August 1869 and immediately advertised for sale though failed to find a buyer. Placed in various coastal trades. Sold by the National Marine Insurance Company to William Collin for £400 after being beached during a storm near Double Island Point, Queensland. Employed in the North Queensland coastal trade. Under several additional owners, remained in the Queensland coastal trade until 1883 and then transferred to Darwin becoming involved in the pearling industry. Later broken up; register closed in January 1891.
1872	Waratah	Barque	123.0 x 25.0 x 11.0ft. ON 57525. 201 tons. Built by John Lucas for Messrs Facy and Fisher and launched on 10 June 1872. Spent many years employed in intercolonial and trans-Tasman trades. Sold to the River Don Trading Company Ltd in July 1882 to trade between Tasmania's north-west coast and the mainland. Sold two years later to a buyer from Sydney and near immediately on-sold to Anton Schlenk of Adelaide, ultimately becoming involved in the northern guano trade. Wrecked at Rocky Island, Queensland, on 20 January 1894, all hands saved.

Year	Name	Type	Description
1874	*Lily*	Schooner	82.6 x 20.8 x 7.6ft. ON 57552. 84 tons. Built by John Lucas to the order of Messrs Facy and Fisher and launched on 19 October 1874. Sold to Alex Russell in early December 1874 and sailed to South Australia to join the coastal trade, suffering several mishaps. Sold to Captain Henry Hopwood of Hobart Town in June 1880 for service in Tasmania's east coast trade. In August 1882 purchased by James Cowle of Tasmania's north-west coast, finding employment in intercolonial trade. In December 1886 sold to William and Colin Cook of Lyttelton, New Zealand, spending over 30 years employed in the coastal trade. Wrecked at Kapiti Island on 2 November 1920, all hands saved. At the time, owned by A. and D. Campbell of Wellington.
1876	*Oceania*	Barque	142.2 x 26.1 x 12.9ft. ON 57567. 320 tons. Built by John Lucas to the order of Captain Firth, Melbourne. Launched in May 1876, intended for the China trade but spent several years engaged in intercolonial trade, also making supplemental trips to Mauritius, China, Japan, Guam, Java, South Africa and New Zealand. Wrecked on 4 May 1885 on Karori Rock near Terawhit Station, in Cook Strait, New Zealand, while en route from Adelaide to Wellington, its crew of 10, including Captain Firth, managing to make it safely to land via the craft's boats.
1881	*Upolu ex Erne*	Schooner	79.2 x 18.0 x 9.3 ft. ON 57604. 65 tons. Built and designed by John Lucas to the order of James Cowle. Intended as a pleasure vessel but initially employed in the Tasmanian coastal trade. In June 1883 sailed to Sydney and advertised for sale. A few weeks later, sailed to Tonga under the name *Upolu*. Subsequent history not confirmed.
1883	*Vesta*	Yacht	51.2 x 10.4 x 4.4ft. ON 112493. 15 tons. Built by John Lucas to the order of Henry T. Denne of Bruny Island and first noted in February 1883. Competed in local yacht races and regattas. Lengthened in 1888 and sailed to Victoria to compete in the Melbourne Centennial Aquatic Carnival. Purchased by A. James of Hobart in 1894 with the intention of sailing to New Caledonia. Sold to Evan Evans of Newcastle, NSW, in December 1894. First registered in Sydney in 1901 when purchased by Holmes Samuel Chipman. Sold later that year to Thomas Thomson of Queensland. Register closed on 22 September 1902 after having been purchased by Robert Wilson of British New Guinea.

Waterman's Dock and New Wharf, Hobart Town (1860s).
Courtesy Tasmanian Archives (PH1/1/31).

Charles Miller

> 'Although the Messrs. Risby are no longer in the boat-building trade, the business is still carried on by one of their oldest apprentices, Mr. C. H. Miller, who maintains the high character for good workmanship the Messrs. Risby secured during the many years they were in business.'
>
> The Tasmanian Times, 9 October 1868.

Born 1830 in Greenwich, England, Charles Miller immigrated to Hobart Town as a young child where in his teens he was apprenticed to a local boat builder. By the mid-1850s Miller had been promoted to foreman of Joseph Risby's Battery Point boat yard. Here, in 1858, he established his own yard which he operated until 1889. During this period Miller was one of Tasmania's more successful boat builders, building at least 120 boats, including whaleboats, passage boats, yachts, fishing boats, and ship's boats. Of these, the passage boat *Fancy* and yacht *Maggie* (ex *Edith*) remain in existence.

Charles Henry Miller was born on 7 May 1830 at his parent's residence in Blackheath Road, Greenwich, England, and baptised at Greenwich St Alphege on 27 June of that year.[1659] He was the second surviving child and only son born to Charles Joseph and Harriet Ann Elizabeth Miller, nee Martin.[1660]

Though the Miller family lived in the maritime community of Greenwich, Charles Miller (Sr) was a miller by trade. Unfortunately in July 1832 he was convicted at the Essex Assizes, by voluntary confession, of stealing two separate quantities of flour from his employer, Charles Welstead of the Chingford Mill, and sentenced to 14 years transportation.[1661] He was one of 13 prisoners involved in the '*extensive robbery*', either as principal or receiver, though only five of the group were found guilty.[1662] A petition to Lord Melbourne, then Secretary of State for the Home Department, signed by 15 prominent members of his community, including the vicar, local church wardens, and overseers, indicated that Charles (Sr) was anticipating to become a witness to the Crown based on his testimony and had '*done everything in his power since his apprehension to make atonement for it, by giving such ample information as to discover a most extensive conspiracy against the property of the said Mr Welstead*'.[1663] Disappointingly, the petition failed to alter the decision of the authorities. Charles Miller (Sr) departed England two months later with 183 other convicts on board the *Georgiana*, including the four men he had been convicted with.[1664] The vessel arrived in Hobart Town on 28 May 1833.[1665]

Charles Henry Miller.
The Tasmanian Mail, 15 September 1906.

[1659] London, England, Church of England Births and Baptisms, 1813-1923 for Charles Henry Miller.
[1660] London, England, Church of England Births and Baptisms, 1813-1923 for Sarah Harriet Miller.
[1661] *Morning Chronicle*, 27 July 1832; *Essex Standard*, 4 August 1832.
[1662] *Essex Standard*, 4 August 1832; *Chelmsford Chronicle*, 3 August 1832.
[1663] UK, Criminal Records, 1780-1871 for Charles Joseph Miller (HO 17/032).
[1664] *The Colonist and Van Diemen's Land Commercial and Agricultural Advertiser*, 8 February 1833; Libraries Tasmania (CON31-1-30 Image 111).
[1665] *The Colonist and Van Diemen's Land Commercial and Agricultural Advertiser*, 8 February 1833; Libraries Tasmania (CON31-1-30 Image 111).

A resourceful woman, Harriet Ann Miller, the wife of Charles (Sr) departed England for Van Diemen's Land with her two children (daughter Sarah and son Charles) in search of her husband. The trio arrived in Hobart Town per the *Ellen* in September 1834. Also on board were a '*Mrs Martin*' and '*Miss Martin*', i.e., Harriet's mother Ann and her sister Sarah Ann.[1666]

Charles Miller (Sr) served out his sentence in various parts of Van Diemen's Land, including being initially assigned to W. Bryan who established the first flour mill on the Liffey River at Carrick, 10 miles west of Launceston.[1667] He was next assigned to James Houghton at Norfolk Plains (now Longford) though upon disobeying orders and insolence was placed in a road chain gang where he served many months.

In January 1836 Charles Miller (Sr) was assigned to William McRobie, a miller of Hobart Town, though 12 months later was transferred to Thomas Buxton of Mayfield at Little Swanport on Van Diemen's Land's east coast; Buxton had only the year prior built a flour mill on his substantial farming property.[1668] Charles (Sr) appears not to have remained at Mayfield for more than 10 months as late in 1837 he was noted to be at Oatlands. He finally received his Ticket of Leave in June 1839, meaning Charles Miller (Sr) could finally work for himself and enjoy other freedoms.[1669] His Conditional Pardon was approved in January 1845 and his full pardon in February of the following year.[1670]

During the period that Charles Miller (Sr) served out his term, his wife and two children were supported by Harriet's mother Ann Martin who likely received a pension as an Army widow; her late husband Thomas had served as lieutenant and adjutant with the 60th Regiment of Foot under King George III, very plausibly during the Napoleon Wars.[1671] It is assumed that the family unit remained in Hobart Town as there were limited opportunities for convicts under sentence to provide food, accommodation and monetary resources to family members. The 1842 Census for Hobart Town lists the Miller family as living in Goulburn Street with Ann Martin noted as the head of the household.[1672]

While it is not known where Charles Miller (Jr) received his early education, in 1845 he began an apprenticeship with Joseph Risby, boat builder of Battery Point.[1673] It was during this period that Miller also began competing in local regatta races. In January 1850, for example, he competed in a race for native youths and apprentices under 20 years of age pulling in four-oared whaleboats at the second annual Sandy Bay Regatta finishing fifth in the *Creeping Jane*.[1674] Just under two years later, on 20 December 1851, Miller married 21-year-old Mary Ann Chaplin at St Georges Church, Battery Point. Witnesses to the event were Mary Ann's father Edward, her sister Eliza, along with Sarah Ann Danby and John Herbert Woodward.[1675] Mary Ann had been born at New Norfolk in 1830, the eldest child of Edward Chaplin, an ex-convict turned successful farmer of the Black Brush area, and his first wife Sarah nee Campbell.[1676]

Miller and his new bride moved into a home in Battery Point's Arthur Circus where in the years immediately following two events of note took place. First, the couple's residence was the location where Eliza Chaplin, Mary Ann's sister, married John Herbert Woodward on 27 November 1852.[1677] Second, the couple expanded their family. A daughter named Harriet Sarah was born on 27 September 1853.[1678] Another daughter, Mary Caroline, was born at Battery Point on 13 February 1855, while a son named Charles Orlando Chaplin was born on 6 February 1857.[1679]

In terms of his professional activities, by 1855 Miller had been promoted to foreman of Joseph Risby's boat yard.[1680] Diversifying his income stream, in December 1856 Miller was granted a licence for a new hotel located in Hampden Road, Battery Point. Named the Duke of York, it was one of several new public houses granted licences in the Battery Point area that year.[1681] While Charles Miller (Jr) was the applicant and initial licensee, the Duke of York Hotel was very likely operated by his wife, possibly in conjunction with his parents. Miller did have some involvement, however, including raffling the '*Fast sailing Yacht Zephyr*' at the premises on 12 March 1857.[1682] Though he initially planned on naming the pub The Patent Slip, owing to the name already being used, it was coined as the Duke of York, very likely after Prince Frederick, second son of King George III, whom Miller's grandfather Thomas Martin likely served under.[1683]

In early November 1857 the licence for the Duke of York was transferred to Edward Prentis who had previously been licensee of the nearby Prince of Wales Hotel.[1684] Remarkably, the building remains in existence, used as self-contained accommodation under the name The Grand Old Duke.[1685] During this period Miller also took up the licence of the Royal Oak Hotel in Macquarie Street, though for only a few months.[1686] With his brother-in-law William Bales, he additionally became a brethren of the Masonic Lodge, remaining involved with this organisation for several decades.[1687]

[1666] *Colonial Times*, 23 September 1834, 4 March 1854; *The Hobart Town Advertiser*, 2 March 1854, 23 February 1858; *The Tasmanian Tribune*, 13 November 1875.
[1667] Libraries Tasmania (CON27-1-6 Image 15); *The Hobart Town Gazette*, 15 February 1833.
[1668] *The Hobart Town Courier*, 18 March 1836, 6 January 1837; *Former Times*, Glamorgan Spring Bay Historical Society Inc., Issue 6 (June 2014); Libraries Tasmania (CON31-1-30 Image 111).
[1669] *The Hobart Town Courier*, 7 June 1839.
[1670] *The Hobart Town Advertiser*, 28 November 1843, 17 January 1845, 27 February 1846.
[1671] *The Hobart Town Advertiser*, 22 February 1858; *The Hobart Town Daily Mercury*, 22 February 1858.
[1672] Libraries Tasmania (CEN1/1/19).
[1673] *The Tasmanian Telegraph*, 23 October 1858.
[1674] *Colonial Times*, 4 January 1850; *The Courier*, 5 January 1850.
[1675] Libraries Tasmania (RGD37/1/10 no 353).
[1676] micktopfer.com/familyhistory/1494.html.
[1677] Libraries Tasmania (RGD37/1/11 no 784).
[1678] Libraries Tasmania (RGD33/1/5/ no 181).
[1679] Libraries Tasmania (RGD33/1/5/ no 1854, RGD33/1/6/ no 170).
[1680] *The Courier*, 29 March 1855; *The Hobart Town Daily Mercury*, 12 October 1858.
[1681] *The Tasmanian Daily News*, 9 December 1856; *The Hobarton Mercury*, 10 December 1856.
[1682] *The Hobart Town Advertiser*, 11 March 1857.
[1683] *The Hobarton Mercury*, 10 December 1856.
[1684] *The Courier*, 2 November 1857; *The Tasmanian Daily News*, 5 November 1857.
[1685] www.grandoldduke.com.au.
[1686] *The Courier*, 4 May 1857; *Colonial Times*, 4 August 1857.
[1687] *The Courier*, 20 June 1857; *The Mercury*, 20 September 1869, 1 March 1877.

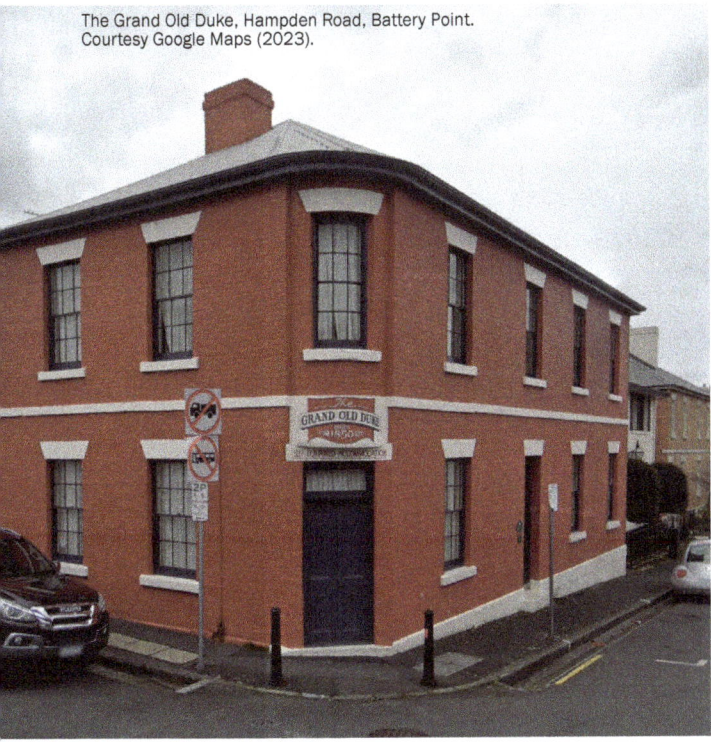

The Grand Old Duke, Hampden Road, Battery Point. Courtesy Google Maps (2023).

On 23 October 1858 *The Tasmanian Telegraph* announced that Charles Miller (Jr) had succeeded Joseph Risby at his Battery Point boat yard. In handing over management of his business, Risby noted that his yard had been transferred in its entirety to his former general manager and superintendent and that he had complete confidence in his successor's ability to execute all orders.[1688] The corresponding advertisement published in this and several other local newspapers gave a glowing reference to Risby's replacement, in all likelihood adding to Miller's already esteemed reputation. In consequence of taking over control of the business, Miller moved his family to a home in Napoleon Street.[1689]

The first boats Charles Miller (Jr) is known to have built at his newly-established Battery Point boat yard were two wherries that he raffled off in November 1858.[1690] Shortly thereafter, on 4 January 1859, the yacht *Phantom* was launched from his yard, built to the order of Douglas T. Kilburn to compete in local sailing races, including Tasmanian Yacht Club events.[1691] Rounding out the decade, in May 1859 a boat complete with oars built by Miller was sent to Launceston on board the *Circassian*, while the following month he built at boat for the Government of Tasmania.[1692] Miller also attended the first meeting of the Tasmanian Yacht Club held at the Bird in Hand Hotel in Argyle Street on 4 October 1859.[1693]

[1688] *The Tasmanian Telegraph*, 23 October 1858.
[1689] *The Mercury*, 31 July 1861.
[1690] *The Courier*, 8 November 1858.
[1691] *The Hobart Town Daily Mercury*, 6, 8 January 1859.
[1692] *The Hobart Town Daily Mercury*, 24 May 1859; *The Hobart Town Advertiser*, 5 July 1859.
[1693] *The Hobart Town Daily Mercury*, 5 October 1859.

J. E. RISBY,

IN RELINQUISHING the buisiness of Boat Builder, and whilst sincerely thanking his many friends for the encouraging patronage accorded to himself as well as to the old established firm of 'Risby and Sons,' for the past thirty years, has much pleasure in recommending for their future favors.

MR CHARLES HENRY MILLER,

so long known, as his general Manager and Superintendent, and to whom he has transferred the entire business of the Yard, so well known as "Risby's" situate at Battery Point, and in doing so, he feels assured that nothing will be wanting on the part of his Successor, to give that entire satisfaction in the execution of all orders entrusted to him for which he has always been so proverbial, and for whom J. E. R. solicits a continuance of the support and encouragement which it has been his good fortune for so many years especially to enjoy.

CHARLES HENRY MILLER

in taking over the above business from Mr. J. E. Risby desires to assure all who may be pleased to favor him with their support that his untiring energies and best exertions shall at all times be used to afford them satisfaction, and the fact of his having now been in the employ of the Messrs Risby for the past thirteen years will, he trusts be accepted as some guarantee that all orders entrusted to him will be punctually and faithfully executed. And he therefore looks forward to the hope of enjoying a fair share of the patronage of those requiring services, which he must now publicly and respectively tenders.

Hobart Town.
Battery Point, 8th October 1858.

The Tasmanian Telegraph, 23 October 1858.

Professionally, the 1860s proved a busy period for Miller and his boat yard. Like his predecessor Joseph Risby, he undertook boat repair work, including for the colonial government.[1694] During the early part of this decade Miller also built many boats. These included a two-ton passage boat advertised for sale in Hobart Town in August 1860; a 20ft square-sterned boat built for Christina Herbertson of the Risdon Ferry Inn; a 30ft six-oared man-of-war galley boat completed by October 1861 for use in coastal survey work under the supervision of Lieutenant Brooker; a whaleboat that

[1694] *The Hobart Town Advertiser*, 5 March 1861.

formed part of the Tasmanian Timber Trophy exhibited at the International Exhibition of 1862, a world's fair held in London, England; and the whaleboat *Sydney* which won the Tasmanian Champion Prize at the 1861 Hobart Town Regatta.[1695]

Unfortunately the year 1861 proved to be a personal disaster for Miller and his wife, the couple enduring multiple tragedies over a four-month period. First, on 27 May their youngest daughter Eleanor Annie died of measles, she was just shy of 14 months of age.[1696] Eleanor had been born at Battery Point on 12 April 1860.[1697] The next tragedy came on 29 July when the couple's son, Charles Orlando Chaplin Miller died of diphtheria.[1698] He was four years of age.[1699] Just over a week later, on 7 August, Miller and his wife's eldest child Harriet Sarah also died of diphtheria, aged eight years.[1700] Of the couple's four children, only their seven year old daughter Mary Caroline remained living.

While dealing with this grief, Miller continued to operate his boat yard. Of note, in August 1862 he built a boat of which there is very little additional information known.[1701] He also constructed two boats that were shipped to Melbourne on board the steamer *Tasmania* in September and November 1862, as well as a four-oared whaleboat that was shipped to Dunedin, New Zealand, in November of that same year, along with a four-oared gig built to the order of the Christchurch Rowing Club.[1702] The 3-ton cutter *Maggie* was also constructed late in 1862.[1703] With Miller at the helm, the craft first competed at the 1862 Hobart Town Regatta where it finished third in the sailing race for vessels under four tons.[1704]

In 1863 Miller completed another four-oared whaleboat that was shipped to Melbourne via the *Tasmania* in April of that year.[1705] Later in 1863 he shipped to Adelaide on board the brig *Wild Wave* 'one of the finest boats ever turned out of our yards'.[1706] It was a 40ft seven-oared whaleboat commissioned by the Government of South Australia and intended to carry mail ashore from steamers arriving in Holdfast Bay, i.e., Glenelg, from King Georges Sound, i.e., Albany in Western Australia.[1707] Unfortunately the vessel was destroyed en route to South Australia after being smashed during a heavy sea.[1708] Miller was thus instructed to build a second vessel of the same type, though with slightly more beam, that was shipped to Adelaide in October of that year.[1709] In addition, he completed the *Forget-me-not*, an 18ft skiff weighing just 47 pounds that was pulled by J. W. Perry in the race for the Alexandra Prize at the 1863 Hobart Town Regatta, finishing third.[1710] The race for sailing boats under four tons notably saw Miller competing in the 3½-ton schooner *White Squall*, a vessel he likely built.[1711]

Continuing to furnish craft for customers based in Victoria and New Zealand, in March 1864 Miller completed a whaleboat that was sent to Melbourne per the *Tasmania*.[1712] This month was not without controversy, however. On 18 March Miller was assaulted by James Bailey with the latter offering a public apology for the *'assault I committed upon him ... in the heat of passion, and likewise sincerely regret any expression I used hurtful to his feelings on that occasion'*.[1713]

In July 1864 the barque *Bella Mary* conveyed to Auckland a *'very beautiful boat, which has been built to the order of the New Zealand Government by Mr Miller, the well-known boatbuilder of this city'*.[1714] A month later he supplied two boats for use on board the intercolonial barque *Countess of Seafield*.[1715] Next, to the order of a gentleman from Lyttelton, New Zealand, in October 1864 Miller built a 30ft whaleboat.[1716] He also built a five-oared whaleboat of Macquarie Harbour pine on speculation that was subsequently purchased by a gentleman from Picton, New Zealand, for local regatta racing and transferred to its new home by the *Lady Emma* in early November 1864.[1717] Finally, for the annual Hobart Town Regatta, an event that took place on 1 December 1864 for which Miller was a member of the organising committee, he built the *Silver Crest* (later named *Iris*), a four-oared whaleboat commissioned by a Mr Russell.[1718] Miller additionally competed in the event, finishing second in the sailing boat race in a 1-ton cutter named *Mystery*, a craft he may very well have constructed specifically for the race.[1719]

While only a few vessels are reported to have been constructed by Miller in 1865, including a boat for use on board the whaling barque *Flying Childers* and a four-oared whaleboat to compete for the Ladies' Purse at the Hobart Town Regatta, it is likely that he built many more and also continued to be involved in repair work.[1720] On a personal level, Miller and his wife Mary Ann welcomed their fifth child, a daughter named Emma Louise born sometime in 1861/62. A son named Edward Henry was born on 2 July 1863.[1721] The arrival of these children likely coincided with a happier period for the couple given the loss of three of their four children in 1861. Their son's birth also came several

---

[1695] *The Hobart Town Advertiser*, 24 May, 4 December 1861; *The Mercury*, 21 August 1860, 2 August, 28 October, 9 December 1861.
[1696] Libraries Tasmania (RGD35/1/6 no 2773).
[1697] Libraries Tasmania (RGD33/1/7 no 3359).
[1698] Libraries Tasmania (RGD35/1/6 no 2889).
[1699] *The Mercury*, 31 July 1861.
[1700] Libraries Tasmania (RGD35/1/6 no 2915); *The Mercury*, 8 August 1861.
[1701] *The Advertiser*, 23 August 1862.
[1702] *The Advertiser*, 27 September, 3 November 1862; *The Mercury*, 27 September, 7, 8 November 1862.
[1703] *The Advertiser*, 5 December 1862.
[1704] *The Mercury*, 2 December 1862; *The Advertiser*, 5 December 1862.
[1705] *The Advertiser*, 21 April 1863.
[1706] *The Advertiser*, 2 September 1863.
[1707] *The Advertiser*, 2 September 1863.
[1708] *The Advertiser*, 23 October 1863.
[1709] *The Advertiser*, 23 October 1863.
[1710] *The Advertiser*, 24 November, 23 December 1863.
[1711] *The Advertiser*, 23 December 1863.
[1712] *The Advertiser*, 10 March 1864.
[1713] *The Advertiser*, 31 March 1864.
[1714] *The Advertiser*, 4 July 1864.
[1715] *The Advertiser*, 4 August 1864.
[1716] *The Mercury*, 22 October 1864.
[1717] *The Mercury*, 7 November 1864.
[1718] *The Advertiser*, 4 October 1864; *The Mercury*, 24 November, 1 December 1864, 28 November 1868.
[1719] *The Mercury*, 1 December 1864; *The Advertiser*, 2 December 1864.
[1720] *The Mercury*, 23 February, 28 November 1865.
[1721] Libraries Tasmania (RGD33/1/9 Image 105 no 7857).

months after a court case widely reported in the press whereby Miller had been charged with not supporting his illegitimate child, a son born on 31 January 1865 to his servant Rosa Sarah Harless (nee Miles).[1722] The bulk of the case's defense, rather than denying the affair, charged that since the child was born after Rosa married George Harless, a mariner, in the months prior to his birth then George was not *per se* 'illegitimate'. However, after days of testimony, including from Miller's pregnant wife, the case was dismissed.[1723] The five-week-old baby, named George Harless, sadly died just days before the verdict was to be announced.[1724]

While the previous year had been rather tumultuous for Miller on a personal level, professionally he continued to build his business. In early 1866 he was acknowledged for providing boat planks of Macquarie Harbour pine, as well as boat ribs, knees and other timbers, as part of Tasmania's complement of products sent to New Zealand for an intercolonial exhibition held in Dunedin.[1725] For the Melbourne International Exhibition of 1866 he also contributed a varnished four-oared whaleboat.[1726] Additionally, Miller furnished at least four boats for the Hobart Town Regatta. These were a four-oared whaleboat for the Ladies' Purse, a dinghy built to compete in the youth's race, a five-oared whaleboat built to compete for the Tasman Prize, and a four-ton yacht built to compete in the sailing race.[1727] Earlier in 1866 Miller had also built a dinghy specifically for competing at the New Norfolk Regatta.[1728] Racing craft he constructed were certainly proving popular with newspapers reporting on their build and prospects, a stark contrast to Miller's commercial craft which received little to no publicity.

In 1867 Miller built a whaleboat that was sent to Melbourne on board the *Southern Cross*.[1729] He was also noted as building a '*new craft of 40 feet keel, 11 feet beam, and 5 feet hold, ... of Macquarie Harbor pine, copper fastened, &c., and is intended for the trade between the islands in the Straits and Launceston*'.[1730] In November 1867 the craft was stated to be on the stocks, half-finished and '*from her model promises to be a fast and handy vessel*'.[1731] Supposedly built to the order of J. T. Clarke, the schooner-rigged vessel was also intended to compete in the race for sailing vessels at the 1867 Hobart Town Regatta, though would not have been ready in time.[1732] Despite being one of the largest craft Miller had built to date, there is little additional information known about it, other than it was clinker built and completed by mid-1868.[1733]

Personally, the year 1867 also saw Miller and his wife Mary Ann continue to expand their family. A son named Alfred Ernest was born at Battery Point on 25 March.[1734] Another son, Charles Stuart Campbell,

[1722] Libraries Tasmania (RGD37/1/23 no 337, RGD33/1/9 Image 62 no 7473); *The Advertiser*, 1, 4, 8 March 1865.
[1723] Libraries Tasmania (RGD37/1/23 no 337, RGD33/1/9 Image 62 no 7473); *The Advertiser*, 1, 4, 8 March 1865.
[1724] *The Advertiser*, 17 March 1865.
[1725] *The Mercury*, 2 April 1866.
[1726] *Tasmanian Morning Herald*, 11 April 1866; *The Mercury*, 2 May, 13 September 1866.
[1727] *The Mercury*, 28 November, 5 December 1866.
[1728] *The Mercury*, 21 February 1866.
[1729] *The Mercury*, 3 October 1867.
[1730] *The Tasmanian Times*, 23 November 1867.
[1731] *The Tasmanian Times*, 23 November 1867.
[1732] *The Mercury*, 25 November 1867.
[1733] *The Tasmanian Times*, 18 June 1868.
[1734] Libraries Tasmania (RGD33/1/9 Image 253 no 9174); *The Mercury*, 26 March 1867.

A whaleboat in Southern Tasmania (late 1860s).
Courtesy Tasmanian Archives (NS1013/1/1740).

was born on 1 May 1869 at Battery Point, while the couple's eight child, another son, was stillborn on 16 December 1870.[1735] Their last child, a daughter named Edith Isabel was born six years later, on 25 July 1875, at their home in Napoleon Street.[1736]

At least four whaleboats were built by Miller during 1868 for service in the gulfs of South Australia.[1737] Built to order, one of these was shipped to Adelaide on board the *Malcolm* in March 1868.[1738] Another was shipped by the *Fairy Rock* in June 1868.[1739] Continuing to export boats to the mainland, a four-oared whaleboat built by Miller was shipped to Sydney on board the *City of Hobart* in November 1868.[1740] That same month he completed a *'fine new pleasure boat for the officers of the garrison'*, measuring 28ft long and fitted with a centreboard.[1741]

In February 1869 Miller built a whaleboat for Dr William Crowther's whaling brig *Velocity*.[1742] Six months later, in August 1869, he completed a 7-ton yacht built to the order of T. Fisher for his son (J. M. Fisher) residing in Otago, New Zealand.[1743] The yacht was shipped to Otago as cargo on board the *Free Trader*.[1744] Named *Belle*, it competed in local sailing races under the auspices of the Otago Yacht Club.[1745] Also in August 1869 Miller sent two boats to Launceston per the schooner *Hally Bayley*.[1746] Finally, in December 1869 Miller completed a skiff for a Mr Symons specifically to compete at the Hobart Town Regatta.[1747]

Like fellow Battery Point boat builder Jacob Chandler, the 1870s proved a climactic decade for Charles Miller (Jr) with the building of several passage boats and fishing boats to supply developing industries. Miller also continued to build whaleboats and other smaller boats for use on board ships involved in intercolonial trade.

One of the first boats known to have been built by Miller during this decade was a 40ft barge constructed of blue gum and Huon pine.[1748] Likely built on speculation, the vessel took more than a year to complete and was launched in mid-1871.[1749] Also in 1870 Miller resumed his role as a publican, taking on the licence of the Star of Tasmania hotel located at 7 Napoleon Street, Battery Point (now 1 Sloane Street, see page 54 for photo).[1750] He would remain licensee of the premises until at least late in 1874, coinciding with a productive period at his boat yard and the death of his parents, Charles (Sr) in November 1874 and Harriet Miller, a year later.[1751]

In early 1871 Miller built several more whaleboats.[1752] He also completed the *Hope*, a 40ft open centreboard boat built to the order of Angus McKay in the style of a whaleboat.[1753] Intended for the D'Entrecasteaux Channel trade, the vessel was later converted to a pleasure yacht and renamed *The Dream*.[1754] In addition, 1871 saw Miller construct a passage boat to the order of Thomas Wright of the Huon, a five-oared whaleboat, as well as two fishing boats.[1755] The last mentioned craft were the 43ft *Colleen Bawn*, built to the order of David Wilson, and the *Tasman*, built to the order of Messrs Scott and Jones.[1756]

The *Colleen Bawn* remained in David Wilson's possession for several years before being rented and then purchased by William Holyman.[1757] A regular trader between ports on Tasmania's north-west coast for many decades, the *Colleen Bawn* helped solidify the Holyman family's standing as prosperous local master mariners and shipowners.[1758] The craft was ultimately wrecked at Ninety Mile Beach, Victoria, in 1913.[1759] At the time of loss, it was owned by Thomas William Barrett of Flinders Island.[1760]

The 37ft fishing boat *Tasman*, with co-owner Louis Jones at the helm, was a regular competitor in local fishing boat races for many years.[1761] It was likely sold in 1877 and may have been placed in the local river trade.[1762]

In addition to several whaleboats, another fishing boat built by Miller was completed in 1872.[1763] Named *Pride* and launched on 9 December, the 35ft Huon pine vessel was built to the order of William Brown of Hobart Town.[1764] December 1872 also coincided with the launch of a 28ft pleasure boat built by Miller to the order of Daniel Stanfield of Clarence Plains under the supervision of his late employer Joseph Risby, as well as several boats built for the new barque *Nautilus*.[1765]

A boat built to the order of the Hon. J. R. Scott was completed by Miller early in 1873.[1766] Of note, the craft was transported to Lake St Clair on a dray whereupon

---

[1735] Libraries Tasmania (RGD33/1/10/ no 310); *The Mercury*, 19 December 1870.
[1736] Libraries Tasmania (RGD33/1/11/ no 1375); *The Mercury*, 28 July 1875.
[1737] *Launceston Examiner*, 23 July 1868.
[1738] *The Tasmanian Times*, 30 March 1868; *The Mercury*, 30 March 1868.
[1739] *The Mercury*, 24 June 1868.
[1740] *The Mercury*, 14 November 1868.
[1741] *The Tasmanian Times*, 7 November 1868.
[1742] *The Tasmanian Times*, 30 January 1869; *The Mercury*, 22 February 1869.
[1743] *The Mercury*, 30 August 1869.
[1744] *The Mercury*, 30 August 1869.
[1745] *Otago Daily Times*, 21 December 1869.
[1746] *The Mercury*, 9 August 1869.
[1747] *The Mercury*, 1 December 1869.
[1748] *The Mercury*, 8 October, 5 November 1870.
[1749] *The Mercury*, 3 July 1871.
[1750] *The Mercury*, 4 December 1860; *The Mercury*, 2 December 1870; *The Tasmanian Tribune*, 1 December 1873.
[1751] *The Mercury*, 4 December 1872, 3 December 1874; *The Tasmanian Tribune*, 14 November 1874, 13 November 1875; Libraries Tasmania (RGD35/1/8 no 2342 and RGD35/1/8 no 3087).
[1752] *The Mercury*, 20 April 1871.
[1753] *The Mercury*, 13 July 1871.
[1754] *The Mercury*, 13 July, 30 October 1871, 26 August, 1 November 1875.
[1755] *The Mercury*, 30 October, 4 November 1871.
[1756] *The Mercury*, 30 October, 4 November 1871, 17 August 1874; *The Cornwall Chronicle*, 26 January, 16 September 1872.
[1757] *Weekly Examiner*, 16 May 1874; HOBART, Register of ships, Volume 9, 1865-1877, [pages 1-173, continues on film roll 2], Folio 111.
[1758] adb.anu.edu.au/biography/holyman-william-7067.
[1759] vhd.heritagecouncil.vic.gov.au/shipwrecks/155.
[1760] LAUNCESTON, TASMANIA, Register of British ships, Volume 5, 1870-1930, Folio 279.
[1761] *Weekly Examiner*, 15 February 1873; *The Tasmanian Tribune*, 28 January 1874, 29 January, 1 November 1875, 26 January 1876; *The Mercury*, 1 December 1874, 11 December 1876.
[1762] *The Mercury*, 3 January 1878.
[1763] *The Mercury*, 7 September, 10 December 1872.
[1764] *The Mercury*, 10 December 1872; *The Cornwall Chronicle*, 7 February 1873.
[1765] *The Mercury*, 27 December 1872, 18 January 1873.
[1766] *The Tasmanian Tribune*, 19 March 1873.

it was left padlocked and chained to a purpose-built log cabin to deter kangaroo hunters and others from stealing it.[1767] For recreationalists visiting the area however, the key to the padlock could be obtained from the municipal offices in Hamilton.[1768]

The keel of another passage boat was laid down by Miller in August 1873.[1769] Built to the order of Walter Ward of Three Hut Point, the *Excelsior* was launched in early November of that year and intended to carry passengers and cargo from Three Hut Point to Hobart Town.[1770] A regular in the D'Entrecasteaux Channel trade, Ward's ownership of the vessel proved disastrous. He sadly drowned, along with three others, including a mother and her small child, in February 1875 when the *Excelsior* was upset during a squall off Peppermint Bay.[1771] The craft was subsequently advertised for sale.[1772] *Excelsior* was ultimately wrecked in Swan Basin, Macquarie Harbour, in late April 1882 after parting from its cables, all hands saved.[1773] At the time of loss, the vessel was owned by a Mr Lawson who had only purchased it a few days prior.[1774]

Next off Miller's stocks late in 1873, following construction of the *Excelsior*, were a 36ft deep-sea fishing boat built to the order of W. Sherwood of Hobart Town and a long boat built to the order of H. B. Evans and intended for the barque *Glencoe*.[1775] Two jolly boats were also completed, one for the barge *Lurline* and one for the ketch *Spindrift*.[1776]

Early in 1874 Charles Miller built a 19ft long boat for the brigantine *Malcolm*, as well as a 30ft whaleboat and a ship's jolly boat of 18ft.[1777] He also completed a loading boat for the schooner *Victor*, recently built by J. and D. Mackey at Battery Point; a four-oared whaleboat to the order of John Smith of Havelock, New Zealand; a loading boat to the order of Joseph Risby for the ketch *Alabama*; a 16ft loading boat for Captain Saunders' new ketch the *Edith Reid*; a boat for the schooner *Guiding Star*; and a boat for the schooner *Louise*.[1778] Rounding off a busy year, four more boats were completed towards the end of 1874. These were a 23ft lifeboat for the steamer *Tasman*; a whaleboat to the order of Captain Carver; and two jolly boats, one for the ketch *Edith Reid* and one for the schooner *Lily*.[1779]

[1767] *The Tasmanian Tribune*, 19 March 1873.
[1768] *The Tasmanian Tribune*, 19 March 1873.
[1769] *The Mercury*, 28 August 1873.
[1770] *The Mercury*, 14 November 1873.
[1771] *The Mercury*, 2 February 1875; *The Tasmanian Tribune*, 2 February 1875.
[1772] *The Tasmanian Tribune*, 10 February 1875.
[1773] *The Mercury*, 12 May 1882.
[1774] *The Mercury*, 12 May 1882.
[1775] *The Mercury*, 4 November, 24 December 1873.
[1776] *The Mercury*, 30 December 1873.
[1777] *The Mercury*, 23 February, 4 May 1874.
[1778] *The Mercury*, 13, 29 July, 5 September 1874.
[1779] *The Mercury*, 20 October 1874.

Schooner *Guiding Star* at the New Wharf, Hobart Town (1870s).
Courtesy Maritime Museum of Tasmania (P_OM_D_128a).

1875 was another demanding year for Miller. The beginning of the year saw him complete a 25ft whaleboat for a customer based on Tasmania's east coast, intended for pleasure purposes.[1780] In June he completed a boat for the newly-launched schooner *Martha Reid*.[1781] He was also noted as building a square-sterned boat for a customer based in Launceston, a long boat for Messrs Belbin and Dowdell, and a small surf boat for the ketch *Three Sisters*.[1782] In September 1875 Miller finished a 13ft centreboard dinghy for the schooner *Kingston*.[1783] He was also commissioned to build a dinghy for the schooner *Guiding Star*, and a small coble of 16ft.[1784]

At least six boats were built by Miller in 1876, though this is likely a gross underestimate of the output from his boat yard. These included a five-oared Huon pine whaleboat; a 22ft gig commissioned by the Marine Board of Hobart for use by the lighthouse keeper of the Iron Pot; a 22ft long boat for Captain Firth's new vessel, the barque *Oceania*, then being built at Battery Point by John Lucas; a boat for the new schooner *Annie Hill*; a two-pair 18ft Huon pine wherry built to the order of His Excellency the Governor, Sir Frederick Weld; and a long boat for the new ketch *St. Helens*.[1785] Conversely, while only one boat has been identified to date as having been built by Miller in 1877, an artefact of the Tasmanian press reducing their reporting on boat and shipbuilding activities and no requirements for smaller craft to be registered, this is obviously not the case.[1786] His yard would have continued to build and repair smaller craft, for commercial and recreational uses alike in 1877 and the years to come.

In 1878 Miller is known to have built a fore-and-aft rigged centreboard boat to the order of Isaac Wright of Hobart Town.[1787] The 36ft Huon pine craft was built for his son, T. S. Wright, who resided in Fiji, with the intention of employing it for cotton plantation work associated with the island of Ono.[1788] The vessel was transshipped to the Pacific Islands via the SS *Tasman*, leaving Hobart Town in December 1878.[1789]

Continuing to build boats for export, in 1879 Miller completed a 26ft waterman's whaleboat for Messrs Godsiff, Newton and Company of Wellington, New Zealand.[1790] The boat was sent on board the steamer *Ringarooma* in January of that year.[1791] He also built a square-sterned boat for William Verrin intended for use in association with the schooner *Harriet*.[1792]

Though not as busy as the previous decade, the 1880s were still brisk for Miller. For example, in 1880 he built a four-oared whaleboat for use at the Currie Harbour Lighthouse, a large whaleboat for use as a loading boat in conjunction with the schooner *Lily*, and a ship's jolly boat.[1793] In 1881 he completed a four-oared loading boat, as well as two boats for James Cowle's new schooner *Erne*, while in April 1882 a whaleboat built by Miller was sent to Sydney on board the steamer *Southern Cross*.[1794] Also in 1882 he is noted as constructing a 16ft long boat for the brig *Prospero*, a four-oared jolly boat for the barque *Free Trader*, a dinghy for the schooner *Erne*, and a 20ft square-sterned waterman's boat to the order of a Mr Chapman of Devonport.[1795] A whaleboat, built to the order of the Hobart Marine Board for use at the Low Head Pilot Station was launched from Miller's yard the following year, as was a 14ft boat with a flat floor for the Government of Tasmania's 'torpedo service'.[1796]

In 1884 Miller completed another boat for the Marine Board of Hobart, this particular vessel for use by the harbourmaster.[1797] In April of that year he completed *'one of the largest fishing smacks ever built in Hobart'*, built to the order of Messrs Veal and Gower, well-known local fishermen.[1798] Intended for the coastal fishing industry, the 38ft *Lady Brassey* was estimated to hold 100-dozen fish in its wells.[1799] Later that year Miller completed a yacht for a Mr Ritchie specifically to compete in Derwent Sailing Club events.[1800] This was likely A. M. Ritchie's 28-footer *Tara* that competed in the sailing boat race at the 1886 Hobart Regatta.[1801]

The year 1885 saw Miller launch the Huon pine passage boat *Fancy*, built to the order of W. Gellibrand of South Arm, as well as a 12ft dinghy for the vessel.[1802] Intended for the South Arm to Hobart trade, where it spent many years employed, the 38ft *Fancy* was later converted to a cruising boat and subsequent to that a fishing boat.[1803] Still in existence, the *Fancy* is currently being restored south of Hobart.[1804]

Two months following the launch of *Fancy*, in December 1885, Miller completed the *Mabel*, a second-class yacht built to the order of George Cheverton to compete in Derwent Sailing Club events.[1805] The 28ft craft was a regular on the River Derwent for many years. It ultimately became a total loss in February 1902 after developing a leak while competing in the 100-mile Bruny Island race; *Mabel*'s crew having little choice but to beach the vessel at Cloudy Bay where it subsequently went to pieces.[1806]

[1780] *The Mercury*, 1 February 1875.
[1781] *The Mercury*, 9 June 1875.
[1782] *The Mercury*, 9 June 1875.
[1783] *The Mercury*, 11 September 1875.
[1784] *The Mercury*, 11 September 1875.
[1785] *The Tasmanian Tribune*, 4 May 1876; *Tribune*, 29 July 1876; *The Mercury*, 30 November 1876.
[1786] *Tribune*, 28 December 1877.
[1787] *The Mercury*, 18 December 1878.
[1788] *The Mercury*, 18 December 1878.
[1789] *The Mercury*, 18 December 1878.
[1790] *The Mercury*, 10 January 1879.
[1791] *The Mercury*, 10 January 1879.
[1792] *The Mercury*, 24 December 1879.
[1793] *The Mercury*, 26 June, 26 July 1880.
[1794] *The Mercury*, 23 February, 16 September 1881, 28 April 1882.
[1795] *The Mercury*, 8 September, 27 October, 7 November 1882.
[1796] *Launceston Examiner*, 7 March 1883; *The Mercury*, 15 October 1883.
[1797] *Tasmanian News*, 26 January 1884.
[1798] *Tasmanian News*, 24 April 1884; *The Mercury*, 25 April 1884.
[1799] *The Mercury*, 25 April 1884; *Launceston Examiner*, 26 April 1884.
[1800] *The Mercury*, 17 November 1884.
[1801] *The Mercury*, 17 February 1886.
[1802] *The Mercury*, 23 July, 13 October 1885.
[1803] *The Mercury*, 13 October 1885; G. Broxam & N. Mays (2022). *Those That Survive: Tasmania's Vintage and Veteran Commercial and Government Vessels*.
[1804] G. Broxam & N. Mays (2022). *Those That Survive: Tasmania's Vintage and Veteran Commercial and Government Vessels*.
[1805] *The Mercury*, 15 December 1885.
[1806] G. Broxam & M. Nash (2021). *Tasmanian Shipwrecks Volume II (1900-2020)*.

Fancy during a cruise in 1905.
Weekly Courier, 12 August 1905.

Fancy under restoration (2022).
Courtesy Graeme Broxam.

Mabel (circa 1890s).
Courtesy Maritime Museum of Tasmania (P_2023-072).

While little is known about activities at Miller's Battery Point boat yard in the first half of 1886, in August of that year he turned out a 16ft boat to be used in conjunction with the Hobart Marine Board's steam dredge.[1807] Later that year Miller completed a 21ft boat, capable of accommodating a dozen people, built to the order of the Hobart Police Department.[1808] December of 1887 saw Miller complete two more vessels: a 28ft yacht named *Edith* to the order of Messrs Gregory Bros. and a boat for Messrs R. Kennedy and Sons for use in conjunction with their iron dredge.[1809]

The late 1880s coincided with a series of devastating events for Miller. The first occurred in January 1887 when a runaway cow crashed through the gate of his boat yard tragically trampling and killing a two-year-old boy, Charlie McClymont, who happened to be swinging on it at the time while playing with an older girl.[1810] The child's father worked next door for Robert Kennedy's shipyard.[1811] Six months later Miller's eldest daughter Mary Caroline died from complications associated with childbirth at her home in Heathcote Valley, New Zealand, aged 33.[1812] She was survived by her husband William Henry Griffin, late of Hobart Town, whom she married at Lyttelton in September 1877, as well as their five children.[1813] On 15 May 1889 Miller's second oldest surviving son Alfred Ernest died

[1807] *The Mercury*, 12 August 1886.
[1808] *The Mercury*, 29 November 1886.
[1809] *The Mercury*, 11 December 1886, 28 March 1887, 16 April 1888.
[1810] *The Mercury*, 14 January 1887.
[1811] *The Mercury*, 14 January 1887.
[1812] *The Mercury*, 23 July 1887.
[1813] *Tribune*, 26 September 1877.

The Colonial Mutual Life Assurance Society

HOBART STREET DIRECTORY.

NAPOLEON-STREET.

Right-hand Side.
5 Baynton, J.
7 Miller, C. A., boatbuilder
9 Morse, F. W.
11 Pitt, Mrs.
23 Robinson, ——, mariner
25 Viney, C., clerk
27 Murdoch, Mrs.
31 M'Cance, J.

Left-hand Side.
2 Chandler, J. B., boatbuilder

6 Lynch, J., shipwright
8 Horne, T., shipwright
10 Cracknell, W., mariner
12 Downie, J., shipwright
14 Risby, J., timber merchant
16 M'Clemont, J., labourer
18 Roland, W. J., storeman
26 Kennedy's Ship Yard
28 Smith, W., stonemason
30 Nettle, W., bootcloser
32 Williams, E., shipwright
34 Eckford, A., clerk
36 Inches, R., shipbuilder
40 Horne, T., manager, Tennis Club
42 Wright, A., chemical manufacturer
44 Miller, R., soapmaker
46 Schott, J. A., professor of music
54 Kent, S., fisheries inspector

1887 Hobart Street Directory for Napoleon Street, Battery Point.
Courtesy Findmypast.com.au.

of enteric fever, i.e., typhoid fever, at Battery Point.[1814] He was 22 years of age. Two months later Miller attempted suicide by cutting his throat with a razor in the backyard of his home.[1815] He was fortunately found by his wife and son and conveyed to the General Hospital where his injuries were successfully attended to. The press noted that Miller had been in a state of *'general melancholy'* for some time.[1816]

In October 1889, at the age of 59, Charles Miller retired from boat building. His Battery Point boat yard was taken over by Messrs Clinch and Luckman.[1817] Fittingly, both men had learned the trade from him.[1818]

The last vessels attributed to being built by Miller were the 40ft fishing boat *Caroline and John*, commissioned by George Cookney and launched in November 1888, and the yacht *Phryne*, built around this period to the order of J. C. Macmichael of Georges Bay.[1819]

It is not known how Charles Miller supported himself and his family during the 1890s, though by 1894 the couple and their remaining children had moved from their home at 7 Napoleon Street, Battery Point, and were living with Miller's aunt at 12 Antill Street.[1820] A few years later the couple were operating a private boarding house at 287 Macquarie Street.[1821]

Charles Miller died at his residence, 25 St Georges Terrace, Battery Point, on 30 August 1906 aged 76.[1822] The press reported, *'Mr. C. H. Miller, who some years ago was well known throughout Southern Tasmania as a boat builder, died suddenly on Thursday. He had been a cripple for some time, and the cold snap experienced last week seemed to have a severe effect on him'*.[1823] He was buried at Queenborough Cemetery, Sandy Bay.[1824] Miller was survived by his wife Mary Ann, who died in January 1922, and four of their ten children.[1825]

Charles Henry Miller left quite a legacy, most notably at least two of the craft he built, the passage boat *Fancy* (of 1885, still based in Southern Tasmania) and the yacht *Maggie* (ex *Edith* of 1886, based in Perth, Western Australia), remain in existence approaching 140 years since they were launched into the River Derwent. Further, despite suffering much personal adversity, after learning the trade of boat building from the Risby family, Miller became a prolific and well-respected boat builder of Battery Point, operating his own yard between 1858 and 1889. During this period Miller built at least 120 vessels, including over 30 whaleboats and many ship's boats. However, this number likely grossly underestimates the output of his yard given the fact that smaller craft built for recreational, commercial and government clients were rarely mentioned in the press.

Maggie (ex Edith) sailing on the River Derwent (circa 1990s). Courtesy Graeme Broxam.

Like Jacob Chandler who owned the boat building yard next door, Miller also took great advantage of developing export corridors and growing industries, building numerous craft that were shipped to New Zealand and the mainland, as well as passage boats and fishing boats employed in local trades during his career. Also like Chandler, Miller has been relatively lost by history to date, receiving little recognition for his three-decade tenure at Battery Point, their input being overshadowed by shipbuilders operating nearby.

25 St Georges Terrace, Battery Point. Courtesy Google Maps (2024).

[1814] Libraries Tasmania (RGD35/1/12 no 566).
[1815] *The Mercury*, 13 July 1889.
[1816] *The Mercury*, 13 July 1889.
[1817] *The Mercury*, 10 October 1889.
[1818] *The Mercury*, 10 October 1889.
[1819] *Tasmanian News*, 7 November 1888; *Launceston Examiner* 25 January 1896.
[1820] *The Mercury*, 22 September 1894; Libraries Tasmania (RGD37/1/53 no 236).
[1821] *The Mercury*, 16 October 1897.
[1822] *The Mercury*, 21 August 1906.
[1823] *Examiner*, 3 September 1906.
[1824] *The Mercury*, 21 August 1906.
[1825] *The Mercury*, 20 January 1922.

Vessels built by Charles Miller and employees at Battery Point (1858 - 1888)

Year	Name	Type	Description
1858	--	Wherry	The first of two first-class wherries built by Charles Miller and advertised for sale via a raffle in November 1858.
1858	--	Wherry	The second of two first-class wherries built by Charles Miller and advertised for sale via a raffle in November 1858.
1859	Phantom	Yacht	26.5 x 7.7ft. 8 tons. Cutter yacht built by Charles Miller to the order of Douglas Thomas Kilburn to compete in Tasmanian Yacht Club events. Advertised for sale in 1861 and in early 1863 sold to Peter Oldham. Advertised for sale at Miller's yard in October 1863 though appears to have remained in Oldham's possession until 1868. Advertised for sale in January 1888.
1859	--	Boat	Built by Charles Miller and sent to Launceston on board the *Circassian* in May 1859.
1859	--	Boat	Built by Charles Miller for the Government of Tasmania.
1860	--	Passage boat	Two-ton passage boat built by Charles Miller and advertised for sale at Hobart Town by auction in August 1860.
1860	--	Boat	20ft. Square-sterned boat built by Charles Miller to the order of Christina Herbertson of the Risdon Ferry Inn. Advertised as lost or stolen in May 1861.
1861	--	Galley boat	30 x 6ft. Six-oared man-of-war's galley boat built by Charles Miller to the order of the Government of Tasmania for use in coastal survey work under the supervision of Lieutenant Brooker.
1862	--	Boat	Built by Charles Miller in August 1862. No additional information known.
1862	--	Boat	25ft. Built by Charles Miller to the order of a tradesman of Sandridge, Victoria, and shipped to Melbourne on board the *Tasmania* in September 1862.
1862	--	Whaleboat	Four-oared whaleboat built by Charles Miller and shipped to Dunedin, New Zealand, per the *Isabella* in November 1862.
1862	--	Boat	Built by Charles Miller and shipped to Melbourne on board the *Tasmania* in November 1862.
1862	--	Gig	Four-oared gig built by Charles Miller and shipped to Christchurch, New Zealand, per the *Lady Denison* in November 1862. Built to the order of the Christchurch Rowing Club.
1862	Maggie	Yacht	3 tons. Built by Charles Miller and first competed in the sailing boat race at the 1862 Hobart Town Regatta held in December of that year, finishing third.
1863	--	Whaleboat	Four-oared whaleboat built by Charles Miller and shipped to Melbourne via the *Tasmania* in April 1863.
1863	--	Whaleboat	40 x 6ft. Seven-oared whaleboat built by Charles Miller to the order of the Government of South Australia and shipped to Adelaide, South Australia, per the *Wild Wave* in September 1863. Intended for use in conveying mail from steamers arriving at Glenelg (Holdfast Bay) from King Georges Sound, Western Australia. Smashed to pieces during a heavy set while en route to its destination and completely destroyed.
1863	--	Whaleboat	40 x 6.5ft. Second of two seven-oared whaleboats built by Charles Miller to the order of the Government of South Australia and shipped to Adelaide, South Australia, in October 1863. For use in conveying mail from steamers arriving at Glenelg (Holdfast Bay) from King Georges Sound, Western Australia.
1863	Forget-me-not	Skiff	18ft. Built by Charles Miller. Pulled by J. W. Perry, an amateur, for the Alexandra Prize at the 1863 Hobart Town Regatta, finishing third. Weighed 47 pounds.
1863	White Squall	Schooner	3½ tons. Likely built by Charles Miller. Helmed by him in the sailing boat race for vessels under 4 tons at the 1863 Hobart Town Regatta, finishing second.
1864	--	Whaleboat	Whaleboat built by Charles Miller and shipped to Melbourne via the *Tasmania* in March 1864.
1864	--	Boat	Boat built by Charles Miller to the order of the Government of New Zealand and shipped to Auckland via the *Bella Mary* in July 1864.
1864	--	Boat	First of two boats built by Charles Miller in August 1864 for use on board the intercolonial barque *Countess of Seafield*.
1864	--	Boat	Second of two boats built by Charles Miller in August 1864 for use on board the intercolonial barque *Countess of Seafield*.
1864	--	Whaleboat	Five-oared whaleboat built by Charles Miller on speculation and purchased by a gentleman from Picton, New Zealand, for use in local regattas. Shipped to New Zealand via the *Lady Emma* in November 1864.
1864	Iris ex Silver Crest	Whaleboat	32 x 4ft x 18in. Four-oared whaleboat built by Charles Miller to compete at the 1864 Hobart Town Regatta, commissioned by a Mr Russell. Also competed in the same event in 1865. Renamed *Iris* in 1868.
1864	Mystery	Cutter	1 ton. Likely built by Charles Miller. Helmed by him in the third class sailing boat race for vessels under 4 tons at the 1863 Hobart Town Regatta, finishing second.

Year	Name	Type	Description
1865	--	Whaleboat	Built by Charles Miller for use on board the whaling barque *Flying Childers*.
1865	--	Whaleboat	Four-oared whaleboat built by Charles Miller to compete for the Ladies' Purse at the 1865 Hobart Town Regatta.
1866	--	Dinghy	Built by Charles Miller to compete at the 1866 New Norfolk Regatta.
1866	--	Whaleboat	Built by Charles Miller as part of the Melbourne International Exhibition of 1866.
1866	--	Dinghy	18 x 3.5ft x 15in. Built by Charles Miller to compete at the 1866 Hobart Town Regatta in the race for youths under 16 years of age.
1866	--	Whaleboat	31 x 5.3 x 2ft. Five-oared whaleboat built by Charles Miller to compete at the 1865 Hobart Town Regatta for the Tasman Prize.
1866	--	Yacht	4 tons. Built by Charles Miller to compete in the yacht race at the 1865 Hobart Town Regatta.
1867	--	Whaleboat	Four-oared whaleboat built by Charles Miller and shipped to Melbourne via the *Southern Cross* in October 1867.
1868	--	Schooner	40 (keel) x 11 x 5ft. Built by Charles Miller of Macquarie Harbour pine and intended to trade between the Bass Strait islands and Launceston. Launched in mid-1868. Clinker-built, supposedly to the order of J. T. Clarke.
1868	--	Whaleboat	Four-oared whaleboat built by Charles Miller and shipped to Adelaide via the *Malcolm* in March 1868.
1868	--	Whaleboat	Second of four whaleboats built by Charles Miller and shipped to Adelaide in 1868.
1868	--	Whaleboat	Third of four whaleboats built by Charles Miller and shipped to Adelaide in 1868.
1868	--	Whaleboat	Five-oared whaleboat built by Charles Miller and shipped to Adelaide via the *Fairy Rock* in June 1868.
1868	--	Pleasure boat	28 x 5.7 x 2ft. Built by Charles Miller for officers of the garrison and launched in November 1868. Fitted with a centreboard and rigged with a large sprit sail and jib.
1868	--	Whaleboat	Four-oared whaleboat built by Charles Miller and shipped to Sydney via the *City of Hobart* in November 1868.
1869	--	Whaleboat	Built by Charles Miller for Dr William Crowther's whaling brig *Velocity* in February 1869.
1869	Belle	Yacht	30 x 6.7 x 4ft. 7 tons. Centreboard yacht built by Charles Miller of blue gum and Huon pine to the order of J. M. Fisher of Otago, New Zealand, as a present from his father T. Fisher of Hobart. Transported to New Zealand on board the barque *Free Trader* in August 1869. Competed in yacht races with the Otago Yacht Club, as well as used for fishing and pleasure purposes.
1869	--	Boat	First of two boats built by Charles Miller and shipped to Launceston per the *Hally Bayley* in August 1869.
1869	--	Boat	Second of two boats built by Charles Miller and shipped to Launceston per the *Hally Bayley* in August 1869.
1869	--	Skiff	18ft. Built by Charles Miller to the order of a Mr Symons specifically to compete at the 1869 Hobart Town Regatta.
1871	--	Schooner	40 (keel) x 11 x 5ft. Built by Charles Miller likely on speculation, constructed of blue gum and Huon pine.
1871	--	Whaleboat	First of at least two whaleboats built by Charles Miller in April 1871.
1871	--	Whaleboat	Second of at least two whaleboats built by Charles Miller in April 1871.
1871	The Dream ex Hope	Passage boat	41 (keel) x 9.5ft. Centreboard open boat built by Charles Miller of Macquarie Harbour pine in the style of a whaleboat for Angus Mckay and intended for the D'Entrecasteaux Channel trade. Sold in August 1875 to G. and W. Whitehouse and then on-sold to A. T. Stewart. Converted to a pleasure yacht and renamed *The Dream*. Advertised for sale in early 1878. Disappears from the records thereafter.
1871	Colleen Bawn	Fishing ketch	43ft, Built by Charles Miller to the order of David Wilson, remaining in his possession for several years before being rented to and then purchased by William Holyman. A regular trader between ports on Tasmania's north-west coast for many decades, helping solidify the Holyman family's standing as prosperous local master mariners and shipowners. Ultimately wrecked at Ninety Mile Beach, Victoria, in 1913. At the time of loss, it was owned by Thomas William Barrett of Flinders Island.
1871	Tasman	Ketch	37ft. Built by Charles Miller to the order of Messrs Scott and Jones. With co-owner Louis Jones at the helm, was a regular competitor in local fishing boat races for many years. Was likely sold in 1877 and may have been placed in the local river trade.
1871	George and Thomas (?)	Passage boat	40 x 8 x 3ft. Centreboard passage boat built by Charles Miller to the order of Thomas Wright of the Huon. Intended for the river trade.
1871	--	Whaleboat	Five-oared whaleboat built by Charles Miller in November 1871.

Year	Name	Type	Description
1872	–	Whaleboat	First of at least two whaleboats built by Charles Miller in September 1871.
1872	–	Whaleboat	Second of at least two whaleboats built by Charles Miller in September 1871.
1872	Pride	Fishing boat	35.8 x 7.3 x 2.6ft. 5 tons. Huon pine fishing boat built by Charles Miller to the order of William Brown and launched on 9 December 1872. Operated out of Hobart Town, also successfully competed in fishing boat races on the River Derwent for more than a decade. Last noted in the press in October 1882 after having undertaken a search for the missing fishing boat *Panic*.
1872	–	Pleasure boat	28 x 5ft. Built by Charles Miller and launched in December 1872 to the order of Daniel Stanfield of Clarence Plains under the personal supervision of J. E. Risby.
1873	–	Boat	Built by Charles Miller and launched in early 1873 to the order of Hon. J. R. Scott. Conveyed to Lake St Clair via a dray where it was left for use by visitors to the area.
1873	*Excelsior*	Passage boat	41 x 9 x 2.8ft. Built by Charles Miller to the order of Walter W. Ward of Three Hut Point and launched in early November 1873, and intended to carry passengers and cargo from Three Hut Point to Hobart Town. A regular in the D'Entrecasteaux Channel trade, Ward sadly drowned, along with three others, including a mother and her small child, in February 1875 when the vessel was upset during a squall off Peppermint Bay. Subsequently advertised for sale, it was ultimately wrecked in Swan Basin, Macquarie Harbour, in late April 1882 after parting from its cables, all hands saved. At the time, owned by a Mr Lawson. Possibly refloated.
1873	–	Fishing boat	36 x 7.5 x 2.8ft. Deep-sea fishing boat built by Charles Miller to the order of W. Sherwood of Church Street, Hobart.
1873	–	Long boat	Built by Charles Miller to the order of H. B. Evans for the barque *Glencoe* in late 1873.
1873	–	Jolly boat	First of two long boats built by Charles Miller in late 1873. For use on board the barge *Lurline*.
1873	–	Jolly boat	Second of two long boats built by Charles Miller in late 1873. For use on board the ketch *Spindrift*.
1873	–	Whaleboat	30 x 5ft x 20in. Built by Charles Miller in early 1874.
1873	–	Jolly boat	18 x 4.5ft x 18in. Built by Charles Miller in early 1874.
1874	–	Long boat	19 x 6.5 x 2.5ft. Built by Charles Miller to the order of H. B. Evans for the brigantine *Malcolm* in May 1874.
1874	–	Loading boat	Built by Charles Miller for the schooner *Victor* in mid-1874.
1874	–	Whaleboat	27.5 x 5ft x 22in. Built by Charles Miller in mid-1874 ofr John Smith of Havelock, New Zealand.
1874	–	Loading boat	20 x 6 x 2ft. Built by Charles Miller for Joseph Risby's ketch *Alabama* in mid-1874.
1874	–	Loading boat	16 x 5.5 x 2ft. Built by Charles Miller for the Captain Saunders' new ketch *Edith Reid* in August 1874.
1874	–	Boat	Built by Charles Miller for the schooner *Guiding Star* in late 1874.
1874	–	Boat	Built by Charles Miller for the schooner *Louise* in late 1874.
1874	–	Lifeboat	23 x 6 x 2.5ft. Built by Charles Miller of Huon pine for the steamer *Tasman* in late 1874.
1874	–	Whaleboat	Built by Charles Miller to the order of Captain Carver in late 1874.
1874	–	Jolly boat	Built by Charles Miller for the Captain Saunders' new ketch *Edith Reid* in late 1874.
1874	–	Jolly boat	Built by Charles Miller for the schooner *Lily* in late 1874.
1875	–	Whaleboat	25 x 5.2 x 2ft. Built by Charles Miller in January 1875 for a customer based on Tasmania's east coast. Intended for pleasure purposes.
1875	–	Boat	17 x 5.5 x 2ft. Built by Charles Miller for the schooner *Martha Reid* in mid-1875.
1875	–	Ship's boat	20 x 5.7 x 2.2ft. Square-sterned ship's boat built by Charles Miller for a customer based in Launceston in mid-1875.
1875	–	Long boat	20 x 6 x 2.5ft. Built by Charles Miller to the order of Messrs Belbin and Dowdell in mid-1875.
1875	–	Surf boat	19 x 5 x 2ft. Built by Charles Miller for the ketch *Three Sisters* in mid-1875.
1875	–	Dinghy	13 x 5ft x 18in. Centreboard dinghy built by Charles Miller for the schooner *Kingston* in September 1875.
1875	–	Dinghy	Built by Charles Miller for the schooner *Guiding Star* in September 1875.
1875	–	Coble	16ft. Built by Charles Miller in September 1875.
1876	–	Whaleboat	Five-oared Huon pine whaleboat built by Charles Miller in May 1876.
1876	–	Gig	22ft. Built by Charles Miller in May 1876 to the order of the Marine Board of Hobart for use by the lighthouse keeper of the Iron Pot.

Year	Name	Type	Description
1876	–	Long boat	22ft. Built by Charles Miller in May 1876 to the order of Captain Firth for use on board the new barque *Oceania*.
1876	–	Boat	Built by Charles Miller in July 1876 for use on board the new schooner *Annie Hill*.
1876	–	Wherry	18 x 4.5ft x 18in. Two-paired wherry built by Charles Miller in November 1876 to the order of His Excellency the Governor of Tasmania, Sir Frederick Weld.
1876	–	Long boat	24 x 5.5 x 2ft. Built by Charles Miller in November 1876 to the order of Captain Hall for use on board the new ketch *St. Helens*.
1877	–	Boat	Built by Charles Miller and shipped to New Zealand via the *Tararua* in December 1877.
1878	–	Boat	36 x 8.5 x 3.5ft. Huon pine boat built by Charles Miller to the order of Isaac Wright of Hobart for his son, T. S. Wright, based in Fiji. Intended to be used in conjunction with the latter's cotton plantations on the island of Ono and Levuka. Transshipped to Sydney in December 1878 via the SS *Tasman*.
1879	–	Whaleboat	26 x 5ft x 21in. Waterman's whaleboat built by Charles Miller to the order of Messrs Godsiff, Newton and Co. or Wellington, New Zealand. Shipped to New Zealand via the *Ringarooma* in January 1879.
1879	–	Boat	Square-sterned boat built by Charles Miller to the order of William Verrin for the schooner *Harriet* in December 1879.
1880	–	Whaleboat	28 x 5.5 x 2ft. Huon pine, four-oared whaleboat built by Charles Miller for use at the Currie Harbour Lighthouse. Transferred to the station by the ketch *Starling* in June 1880.
1880	–	Whaleboat	Built by Charles Miller for use as a loading boat for the schooner *Lily* in July 1880.
1880	–	Jolly boat	Built by Charles Miller in July 1880.
1881	–	Loading boat	20 x 5.5 x 2ft. Built by Charles Miller in March 1881.
1881	–	Boat	First of two boats built by Charles Miller in late 1881 for James Cowle's schooner *Erne*.
1881	–	Boat	Second of two boats built by Charles Miller in late 1881 for James Cowle's schooner *Erne*.
1882	–	Whaleboat	Built by Charles Miller and sent to Sydney per the SS *Southern Cross* in April 1882.
1882	–	Long boat	16 x 6ft. Built by Charles Miller in September 1882 for the brig *Prospero*.
1882	–	Jolly boat	20 x 5ft. Four-oared jolly boat built by Charles Miller in September 1882 for the barque *Freetrader*.
1882	–	Dinghy	14 x 5ft. Built by Charles Miller in September 1882 for James Cowle's schooner *Erne*.
1882	–	Waterman's boat	20 x 5ft x 23in. Built by Charles Miller in November 1882 for William Chapman of Devonport.
1883	–	Whaleboat	34 x 6.5 x 2.5ft. Built by Charles Miller in March 1883 under the superintendence of John Watson to the order of the Hobart Marine Board for use at the Low Head Pilot Station.
1883	–	Boat	14 x 5ft. Square-sterned, flat-bottom boat built by Charles Miller in November 1883 to the order of the Government of Tasmania for use in the 'torpedo service'.
1884	–	Boat	Built by Charles Miller in early 1884 to the order of the Hobart Marine Board for use by the harbourmaster.
1884	*Lady Brassey*	Fishing boat	38.3 x 9.5 x 4ft. Huon pine fishing boat built by Charles Miller in April 1884 to the order of Messrs Veal and Gower, intended for the coastal fishing industry.
1884	*Tara?*	Yacht	28ft. Built by Charles Miller in November 1884 to the order of a Mr Ritchie to compete with the Derwent Sailing Club. Possibly the 28-footer *Tara* that competed in the sailing boat race at the 1886 Hobart Regatta.
1885	*Fancy*	Passage boat	38 x 10.0 x 4.5ft. Built by Charles Miller and launched on 12 October 1885 to the order of W. Gellibrand of South Arm. Intended for the South Arm to Hobart trade, where it spent many years employed. Later converted to a cruising boat and subsequent to that a fishing boat. Still in existence, currently being restored south of Hobart.
1885	–	Dinghy	12ft. Built by Charles Miller in mid-1885 for use in association with the passage boat *Fancy*.
1885	*Mabel*	Yacht	28 x 8 x 3ft. Built by Charles Miller and launched in December 1885 to the order of George Cheverton to compete with the Derwent Sailing Club. A regular on the River Derwent for many years. Ultimately became a total loss in February 1902 after developing a leak while competing in the 100-mile Bruny Island race; its crew having little choice but to beach the vessel at Cloudy Bay where it subsequently went to pieces.
1886	–	Boat	16 x 5.5 x 2ft. Built by Charles Miller in mid-1886 for use in conjunction with the Hobart Marine Board's steam dredge.

Year	Name	Type	Description
1886	--	Boat	21 x 5.2 x 2ft. Built by Charles Miller and launched in late November 1886 to the order of the Hobart Police Department. Capable of holding a dozen people.
1886	Maggie ex Margaret ex Edith	Yacht	28 x 8.5 x 3ft. Kauri pine yacht built by Charles Miller in December 1886 to the order of the Gregory Bros. Raced for several seasons on the River Derwent then dormant until sold in September 1893 to P. M. Windeatt of Launceston. Raced on the Tamar, as well as made occasional cruises. Sent back to Hobart in 1898 following its owner's relocation. Advertised for sale in 1901 and again in 1904. By the late 1940s owned by Max Hanson and briefly named *Margaret*. Named *Maggie* when sold to Allister and Jill Martin who had it rebuilt at Woodbridge. Sold to a Mr Hillyard in the late 1980s and owned by Peter Ward of Snug in the mid-1990s. Moved to Perth, WA, by later owner Dr Colin Sherrington. In the early 2010s restored at Fremantle, without making any major changes to its configuration.
1886	--	Boat	Built by Charles Miller and launched in December 1886 to the order of R. Kennedy and Sons for use in conjunction with their iron dredge.
1888	Caroline and John	Fishing boat	40 x 11.3 x 3.8ft. Cutter-rigged, carver-built fishing boat completed by Charles Miller in November 1888 to the order of George Cookney, intended for the coastal fishing industry. Advertised for sale at Jacob Chandler's yard in August 1890 following the tragic drowning of its owner. Subsequent fate not known.
1888	Phyrne	Yacht	23ft. Yacht built by Charles Miller in 1888 to the order J. C. Macmichael of Georges Bay. Successfully raced with the Georges Bay Sailing Club for a number of years.

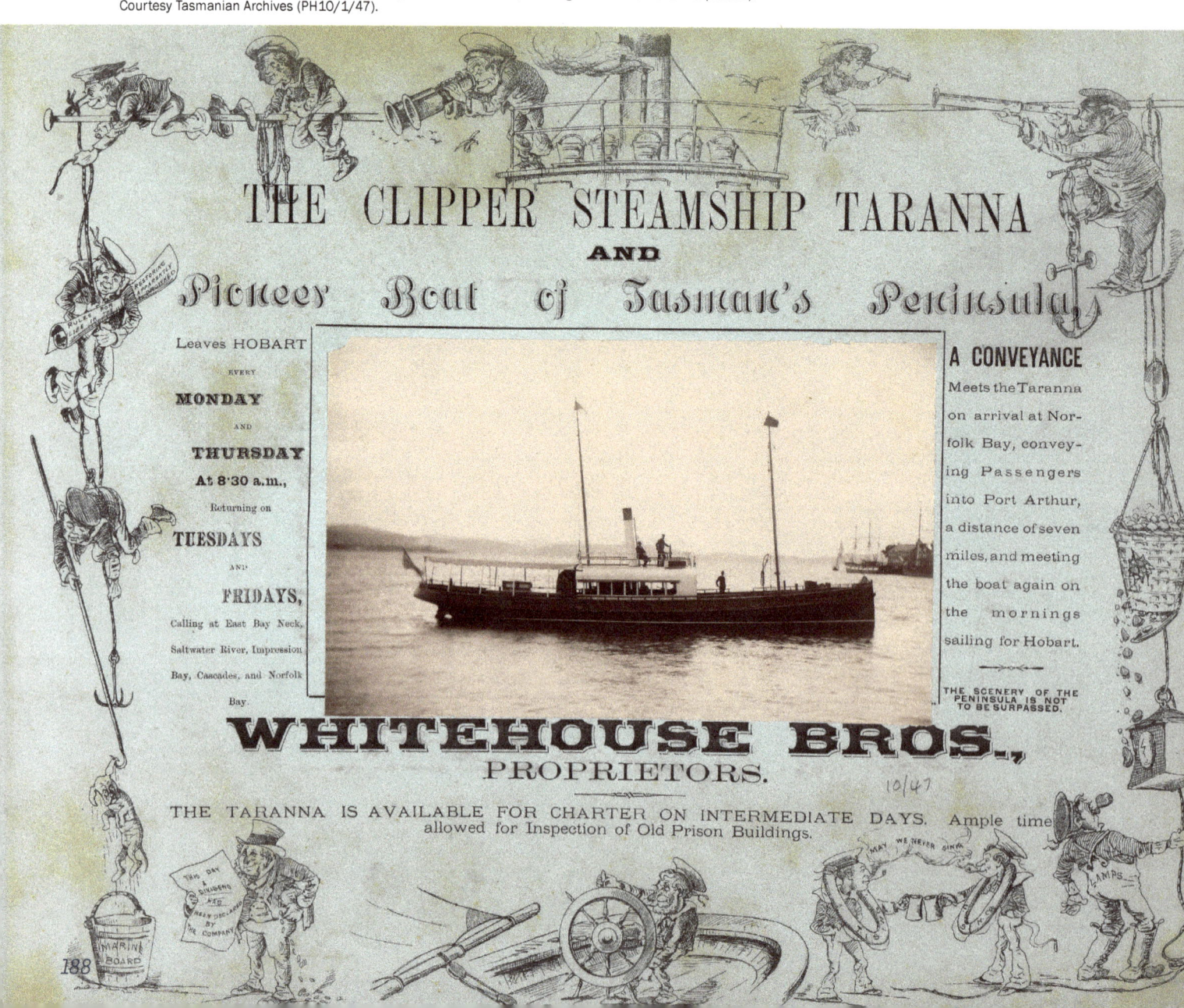

An advertisement for Whitehouse Brothers' ferry service to Taranna, showing the steamer *Taranna* (1880s).
Courtesy Tasmanian Archives (PH10/1/47).

George Whitehouse

'In the seventies there was no more popular boatbuilder in the yachting and rowing world than George Whitehouse.'

Tasmanian News, 9 July 1896.

Born in Hobart Town, George Whitehouse grew up around the Old Wharf area, entrenched in the local maritime community. In his teens he was apprenticed to Jacob Chandler, boat builder of Battery Point, with regatta races and private pulling matches also forming an integral part of his early adult years. Whitehouse later became a well-respected waterman, owning a large fleet of vessels. In 1874 he partnered with his brother William to establish a boat yard at Battery Point. Here the pair built at least 73 vessels, predominantly smaller racing boats and skiffs. They also built the steamers *Express* and *Pinafore* which helped propel the duo into their next mode of business — the regional steamer trade.

George Whitehouse was born on 14 December 1842 in Hobart Town, the third of ten children and eldest surviving son of William and Eliza Whitehouse, nee Pegg.[1826] His father's life story was somewhat unique and is itself worthy of a few paragraphs. With his birth in December 1813 likely taking place at a women's prison in Birmingham, England, William Whitehouse had arrived in Sydney, New South Wales, as a three-year-old child with his convict mother Sarah on board the *Mary Ann*. She had been convicted of '*stealing goods privately in a shop*' at Warwick Assizes in July 1813 with her initial sentence recorded as death.[1827] Following appeals for clemency, in December 1814 this drastic measure was subsequently reduced to 14 years transportation.[1828] Six months later Sarah Whitehouse and her son William found themselves transferred to London and then on board the convict ship *Mary Ann* en route to Sydney. The vessel arrived in Port Jackson on 19 January 1816.[1829]

Fortunately for Sarah, her husband Edward and their 12-year-old son Edward (Jr) had also departed England en route to Australia, arriving in Sydney as free settlers per the male convict ship *Fanny* only the day prior to the *Mary Ann*'s arrival.[1830] It is likely that Sarah was near-immediately assigned to her husband such that the Whitehouse family unit was once more reunited, albeit on the other side of the globe.

A brass founder and candlestick maker by trade, a month after his arrival Edward Whitehouse notified the public of Sydney that he was also able to furnish them with '*axle sash pulleys*' for windows of the '*best construction and most elegant appearance*' and '*on the lowest terms*'.[1831] The family based themselves in Phillip Street

George Whitehouse.
Tasmanian Mail, 9 December 1899.

[1826] Libraries Tasmania (RGD32/1/3/ no 2083); Whitehouse family tree via ancestry.com.au.
[1827] England & Wales, Criminal Registers, 1791-1892 for Mary Whitehouse.
[1828] England & Wales, Criminal Registers, 1791-1892 for Mary Whitehouse; UK, Criminal Records, 1780-1871 for Mary Whitehouse, Criminal Entry Books 1814-1815, HO 13/26.
[1829] *The Sydney Gazette and New South Wales Advertiser*, 20 January 1816.
[1830] freesettlerorfelon.com/convict_ship_fanny_1816.htm; freesettlerorfelon.com/convict_ship_mary_anne_1816.htm; *The Sydney Gazette and New South Wales Advertiser*, 17 February 1816.
[1831] *The Sydney Gazette and New South Wales Advertiser*, 17 February 1816;

with Edward stating his workshop was able to provide *'every description of Compositions of Metal in the fancy line, and all sorts of Brass Foundry Work done in the neatest manner'*.[1832] In addition he offered cleaning and repair of quadrants, sextants, compasses and telescopes.[1833]

Edward and Sarah expanded their family in the intervening years, with two more sons born in 1816 and 1819.[1834] They also moved to new premises on the corner of Castlereagh and Park streets, fronting the Sydney race course.[1835] However, perhaps to alleviate the stain of Sarah's convict status in April 1821 the couple and their four children (Edward, Jr; William; John; and Robert) sailed to Hobart Town as passengers on board the government brig *Prince Leopold* where they intended to settle.[1836] Here Edward resumed his brass foundry business, establishing a workshop in Liverpool, then Argyle and finally Murray Street; his sons spent the remaining part of their childhood in Hobart Town before beginning their own careers.[1837]

> E. WHITEHOUSE, Brass and Iron Founder, returns his sincere Thanks to the Inhabitants of the Colony, for the very liberal Encouragement he has experienced since his arrival from Port Jackson, and begs leave to inform his Customers and the Settlers, that he has removed to his own Residence, at the further end of Murray-street, facing the New-town Road, where he carries on the Brass Foundery Business of every description in the solid way.—Brass coach or gig springs, patent brass cocks and candlesticks, brass weights from 1 ounce to 200 lb. weight, mill work of every description either in brass, cast iron, copper, or composition, made to order ; also, bells cast from 1 to 200 lbs. by gentlemen finding their own paterns, and cast iron boxes of all sizes; together with every other article of brass or iron work.
> ☞ Old Brass, Iron, and Copper purchased.

Hobart Town Gazette and Van Diemen's Land Advertiser, 7 December 1822.

While Edward Whitehouse (Jr) successfully petitioned Lieutenant-Governor George Arthur for grants of land, by the early 1830s having the bulk of his 55-acre property grubbed, stumped and under cultivation and also running sheep and cattle on a property bordering the Jordan River in the Broadmarsh area, his younger brother William Whitehouse, took to the sea.[1838] In 1833, at the age of 20, he was noted as being employed by Captain James Kelly as part of his bay whaling operations based out of Recherche Bay.[1839]

At the time of William's marriage six years later to Eliza Pegg, his occupation was still noted as a whaler.[1840] With a growing family to provide for, however, this risky and nomadic occupation was given up by the early 1850s for work closer to home with various public records noting William's employment as an oysterman, boatman, mariner, fisherman or labourer throughout the decades that followed.[1841] In 1882 he was granted a waterman's licence.[1842] During the late 1840s and into the early 1850s William Whitehouse also competed in fishing boat races at local regattas.[1843]

As a child, George Whitehouse would have been ensconced in Hobart Town's maritime community, living with his family at the Old Wharf.[1844] Sticking with this theme, as a teenager he was apprenticed to Jacob Chandler, boat builder of Battery Point. It was during this period that he also began competing in local regatta races. George Whitehouse's first race appears to have been at the 1859 Hobart Town Regatta where he won the dinghy race for youths under 16 years of age in a boat named *Cygnet*.[1845] The following year he competed in the Youth's Race for Lads and Apprentices at the Hobart Town Regatta, claiming victory in the four-oared whaleboat *Caroline*.[1846] In January and December 1861 he won the same race in the four-oared whaleboat *Flying Buck*, receiving £15 and £20 in prize money, respectively.[1847]

Whitehouse's initial success at the Hobart Town Regatta, and the potential to supplement his boat building income with race winnings, saw him travel to regional regattas. For example, at the 1861 New Norfolk Regatta he finished second in the race for the Ladies Purse, once more competing in the *Flying Buck*.[1848] He also finished second in the race for four-oared whaleboats at the 1862 Port Esperance Regatta, this time competing in the *Tasman*.[1849] A few weeks later Whitehouse won the Tasman Champion Race at the Huon Regatta in the *Who'd Have Thought It* claiming the £20 prize purse.[1850] In January of the following year he won £20 in the race for general amateurs at the Huon Regatta competing in the whaleboat *Morning Light*.[1851] On 26 December 1864 he won the Ladies' Purse at the New Norfolk Regatta in the four-oared whaleboat *Eclipse* earning £15.[1852] It is plausible that Whitehouse may have built one or more of these craft.

By the mid-1860s George Whitehouse had become one of Southern Tasmania's more successful helmsmen. During this period he also added private

---

[1832] *Trumpeter General*, 28 November 1834.
[1833] *The Sydney Gazette and New South Wales Advertiser*, 7 September 1816.
[1834] *The Sydney Gazette and New South Wales Advertiser*, 7 September 1816.
[1834] Australia, Births and Baptisms, 1792-1981 for John George Whitehouse (1816) and Robert Whitehouse (1819).
[1835] *The Sydney Gazette and New South Wales Advertiser*, 23 October 1819, 4 November 1820.
[1836] *The Sydney Gazette and New South Wales Advertiser*, 25 November, 2 December 1820, 24 February 1821; *Hobart Town Gazette and Van Diemen's Land Advertiser*, 14 April 1821; stors.tas.gov.au/CSO1-1-92-2106.
[1837] *Hobart Town Gazette and Van Diemen's Land Advertiser*, 3 November 1821, 30 March 1822.
[1838] *The Hobart Town Courier*, 3 September 1831, 29 June 1832, 29 March 1833, 17 October 1834; stors.tas.gov.au/CSO1-1-92-2106.
[1839] *The Tasmanian*, 20 December 1833.
[1840] Libraries Tasmania (RGD37/1/1 no 434).
[1841] Libraries Tasmania (RGD33/1/4/ no 647, RGD33/1/5/ no 1112, RGD33/1/6/ no 1549, RGD33/1/7 no 1001, RGD35/1/5 no 224, RGD33/1/8 no 5551); *The Mercury*, 19 July 1862, 29 June 1867, 17 September 1880.
[1842] *The Mercury*, 21 January 1882.
[1843] *The Hobart Town Advertiser* 3 December 1847; *Colonial Times*, 6 December 1850.
[1844] *Colonial Times*, 2 September 1851; *The Courier*, 15 December 1855.
[1845] *The Courier*, 5 January 1859.
[1846] *The Hobart Town Daily Mercury*, 12 January 1860.
[1847] *The Hobart Town Advertiser*, 10 January 1861; *The Mercury*, 7 December 1861.
[1848] *The Hobart Town Advertiser*, 27 December 1861.
[1849] *The Advertiser*, 2 January 1862.
[1850] *The Mercury*, 6 February 1862.
[1851] *The Mercury*, 2 January 1863.
[1852] *The Mercury*, 27 December 1864.

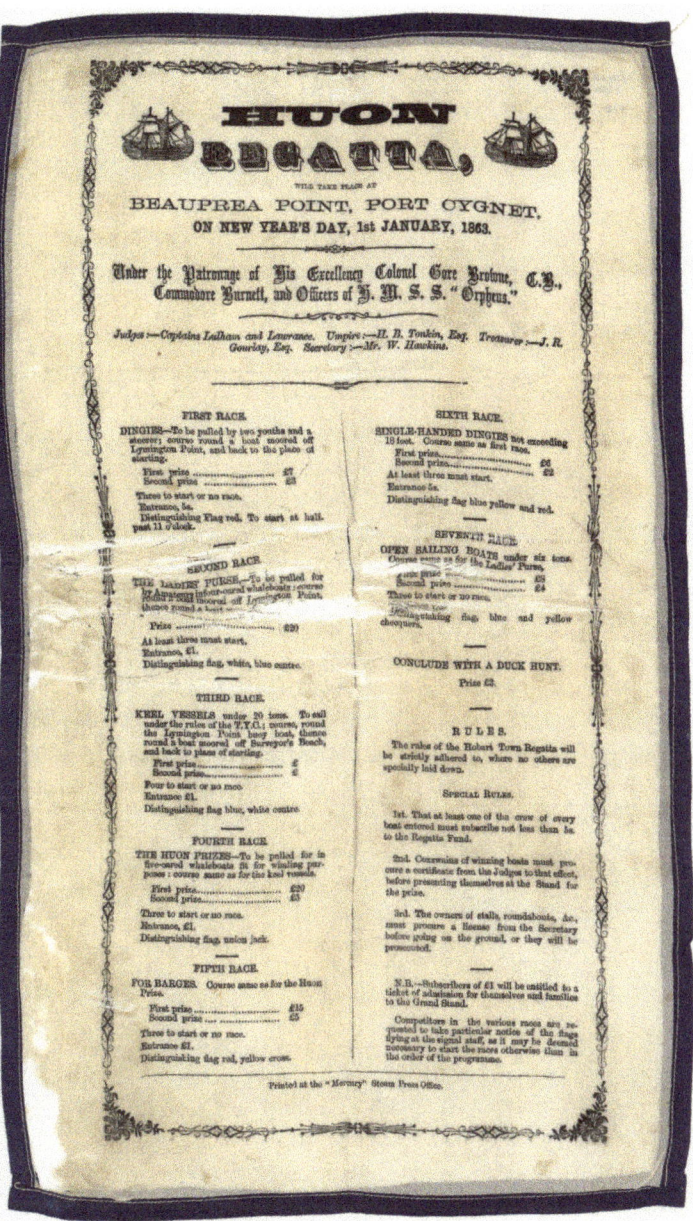

1863 Huon Regatta Program.
Courtesy State Library of New South Wales (74VMb5rlWjOM).

pulling matches to his repertoire, regularly challenging local crews to races and accepting challenges from others.[1853] Some of these races were for up to £25 aside, likely the equivalent of half his annual salary.[1854]

Having completed his apprenticeship, though still employed at Jacob Chandler's Battery Point yard, in September 1863 Whitehouse launched the first vessel he is known to have built. The racing dinghy *Princess Alexandra* was commissioned by Charles Dillon, local waterman, with the intention of competing in private pulling matches and at local regattas.[1855] A few months later Whitehouse launched an 18ft cedar racing skiff built to the order of James Reid specifically to compete at the upcoming Hobart Town Regatta.[1856]

[1853] *The Mercury*, 8 January 1863, 19 October 1865.
[1854] *The Mercury*, 8 January 1863; www.measuringworth.com/datasets/auswages/result.php.
[1855] *The Advertiser*, 29 September, 8 October 1863.
[1856] *The Advertiser*, 8 December 1863.

In April 1864 George Whitehouse completed an excursion boat built to the order of Charles Dillon.[1857] Combining his passion for boat racing with boat building, the next vessel Whitehouse launched was a skiff built to compete for the Alexandra Prize at the New Norfolk Regatta, held on 26 December 1864.[1858] In late 1865 Whitehouse completed two more racing skiffs, the *Paragon* and *Violet*.[1859] Both were built to compete in the Amateur Scullers' and Mayor's Cup races at the 1865 Hobart Town Regatta, with the *Paragon* built to the order of T. Turner, while the *Violet* was built for his own use.[1860] By this period of time George Whitehouse's younger brother William was also involved in local regatta racing, first competing in events for lads and apprentices under 18 years of age.[1861]

Two years later, in October 1867, Whitehouse launched a four-oared Huon pine whaleboat built in conjunction with Henry Hobbs Grubb, boat builder of Battery Point, to the order of the Reverend J. Wilkes Simmons.[1862] The 21ft Huon pine craft was intended for mission service in the D'Entrecasteaux Channel.[1863]

More racing boats soon followed. An 18ft King Billy pine skiff weighing just 32 pounds, also built by Whitehouse in partnership with Grubb, was launched in November 1867 specifically to compete at the 1867 Hobart Town Regatta.[1864] This particular craft was very likely named *Midge*.[1865] For the same event Whitehouse built a lightweight dinghy for a crew of juveniles nicknamed the 'Snuffs'.[1866] A few weeks later Whitehouse completed a 18ft outrigger skiff built on the '*tubular principle*' to the order of Charles Dillon and intended to compete in the Amateur Sculler's Race at the 1867 Hobart Town Regatta.[1867] The widely anticipated event, however, by now Hobart Town's most favoured holiday, was delayed until 9 January 1868 owing to the late arrival of His Royal Highness, Prince Alfred, the Duke of Edinburgh, in Hobart Town.

In late 1868 Whitehouse completed the Macquarie pine four-oared whaleboat *Cherry Picker*, built to compete for the Ladies' Purse at the Hobart Town Regatta.[1868] He also completed, for the same event, the 18ft racing dinghy *Secret*.[1869]

In April 1869 George Whitehouse and his younger brother William were awarded licences to plant, harvest and sell oysters, likely taking over the business that

[1857] *The Mercury*, 4 April 1864.
[1858] *The Mercury*, 24, 26 December 1864.
[1859] *The Mercury*, 28 November, 6 December 1865.
[1860] *The Mercury*, 28 November, 6 December 1865.
[1861] *The Mercury*, 6 December 1865.
[1862] *The Mercury*, 15 October 1867.
[1863] *The Mercury*, 15 October 1867.
[1864] *The Mercury*, 25 November 1867.
[1865] *The Tasmanian Times*, 28 December 1867, 6 January 1868.
[1866] *The Tasmanian Times* 24 October 1867.
[1867] *The Mercury*, 2 January 1868.
[1868] *The Mercury*, 13 October, 28 November 1868; *The Tasmanian Times*, 20 October 1868.
[1869] *The Tasmanian Times*, 13 November 1868; *The Mercury*, 28 November 1868.

their father had spent several decades developing.[1870] A few months later William received a licence to '*form and plant an oyster bed in the vicinity of the Royal Society's Gardens*'.[1871] Situated on the banks of the River Derwent near the Domain, the area was likely in the vicinity of the Royal Tasmanian Botanical Gardens.

It was an interesting period for George Whitehouse, both professionally and personally. Just over a month after receiving his oyster fishing licence, on 20 May 1869 at the age of 25, he married 21-year-old Martha Bayes.[1872] The ceremony took place at 187 Elizabeth Street, Hobart Town, the residence of the Reverend J. Wilkes Simmons with George's sister Louisa and his brother William acting as witnesses.[1873] A few months prior, on 16 January 1869, the couple had welcomed their first child, a son named William George Whitehouse.[1874] George and Martha would go on to have four more children during the 1870s, all of whom would live to adulthood: Frederick John (1872), Linda Louise (1874), Herbert Edward (1877), and Ernest Edward (1879).[1875]

With a growing family to support, George Whitehouse looked to expand his income streams. In addition to oyster fishing, late 1869 coincided with him successfully being awarded a waterman's licence, allowing him to augment his living through the transport of passengers and cargo to various reaches of the River Derwent, as well as visiting vessels, and through the hiring out of small boats to picnickers, fishing and pleasure parties.[1876] Though still operating as a waterman into the early 1870s, Whitehouse continued to compete in and build racing craft for local regattas. Having left Jacob Chandler's employ, George and his brother William established their own boat building business under the name of 'Whitehouse Brothers'.[1877] Working out of the upper floor of an old stone building on the east side of Victoria Dock at the Old Wharf, George Whitehouse built the skiff *Galatea* for J. H. Burn, as well as a skiff named *Eva* to be pulled by William Martin at the upcoming 1869 Hobart Town Regatta.[1878] At that same event, held on 9 December of that year, Whitehouse won the Tasman Prize in the five-oared whaleboat *Runnymede*.[1879] A few weeks later he competed in several races at the 1870 Huon Regatta.[1880] George Whitehouse next competed in the sailing boat race at the 1870 Kangaroo Point Regatta, competing in the *Fleur-de-Lis*, a cutter he may well have built.[1881]

At the 1871 Hobart Town Regatta, held on 24 January of that year, Whitehouse debuted a new craft which he had built, the 23ft skiff *Sylph*.[1882] From a commercial standpoint, he was also awarded the tender to lay buoys for the event.[1883]

While he continued to operate as a licenced waterman, 1871 saw George Whitehouse build a 21ft waterman's boat for Charles Dillon named *Fly*.[1884] Later in the year he completed a centreboard whaleboat of 26ft and fitted with sails, commissioned by William Tarleton.[1885] For the upcoming New Norfolk and Hobart Town regattas, Whitehouse furnished an 18ft skiff named *Fireflash*, a four-oared whaleboat named *Rose of Castile*, and an 18ft skiff and four-oared whaleboat, both named *Vision*.[1886]

The following year Whitehouse built another waterman's boat; the *Osprey* was launched in August 1872 for his younger brother William who by now was also operating as a licenced waterman.[1887] That same year George Whitehouse completed a four-oared whaleboat, *Bashful*, to compete for the Ladies' Purse at 1872 New Norfolk Regatta, held on 26 December of that year.[1888]

1873 was another busy year for George Whitehouse and his brother William, who had joined forces to form 'Whitehouse Brothers', watermen and boat builders of the Old Wharf.[1889] In terms of the latter occupation, they built a four-oared whaleboat, the *Star of the Sea*, for use by William as part of his waterman activities, as well as a small centreboard ferry boat intended for hire.[1890] In early October 1873 the pair built the *Derwent Belle*, a 22ft square-sterned centreboard pleasure boat also intended for their ferry boat business, and purchased the sailing boat *Annie* to add to their commercial fleet.[1891] In December 1873 George and William Whitehouse completed a four-oared whaleboat to compete at upcoming local regattas.[1892]

Two more boats built by Whitehouse Brothers were completed in early 1874. These included a pair-oared gig built to compete at the Launceston Regatta.[1893] The 24ft boat, fitted with sliding seats, was notably the first of its kind constructed in Hobart Town.[1894] The second vessel was a four-oared whaleboat, also built to compete at the upcoming Launceston Regatta.[1895] Unfortunately this particular vessel was trans-shipped to Launceston on board the *Wynaud* which was subsequently wrecked en route near Eddystone Point.[1896] The loss of the boat was a significant financial blow for George Whitehouse such that local watermen established a subscription to help recoup the cost of the vessel, estimated at £30.[1897]

[1870] *Launceston Examiner*, 8 April 1869; *The Mercury*, 16 April 1870.
[1871] *The Mercury*, 26 May 1869.
[1872] Libraries Tasmania (RGD37/1/28 no 249).
[1873] Libraries Tasmania (RGD37/1/28 no 249).
[1874] Libraries Tasmania (RGD33/1/10/ no 113).
[1875] Whitehouse family tree via ancestry.com.au.
[1876] G. Broxam (2009). *Pride of the Port: The Watermen of Hobart Town*.
[1877] *The Tasmanian Times*, 22 May 1869; *The Mercury*, 1 December 1869, 2 February 1871.
[1878] *The Mercury*, 2, 10 December 1869, 21 August 1873; *Tasmanian News*, 9 July 1896.
[1879] *The Tasmanian Times*, 11 December 1869.
[1880] *The Mercury*, 25 January 1870.
[1881] *The Mercury*, 23 April 1870.
[1882] *The Mercury*, 24 January 1871.
[1883] *The Mercury*, 21 January 1871.
[1884] *The Mercury*, 2 February, 12 October 1871.
[1885] *The Mercury*, 10 November 1871.
[1886] *The Mercury*, 2, 28 December 1871, 17, 25 January 1872.
[1887] *The Mercury*, 7 September 1872.
[1888] *The Tasmanian Tribune*, 16 December 1872; *The Mercury*, 27 December 1872.
[1889] *The Mercury*, 6 October 1873.
[1890] *The Mercury*, 21 August, 9 September 1873.
[1891] *The Tasmanian Tribune*, 4 October 1873; *The Mercury*, 6 October, 12 November 1873.
[1892] *The Mercury*, 13 December 1873.
[1893] *The Mercury*, 18 February 1874; *Launceston Examiner*, 5 March 1874.
[1894] *The Mercury*, 18 February 1874.
[1895] *The Tasmanian Tribune*, 20 February 1874.
[1896] *The Tasmanian Tribune*, 20 February 1874.
[1897] *The Tasmanian Tribune*, 20 February 1874.

Indicative of his persistence, George Whitehouse arranged to transport a second vessel to Launceston for the approaching regatta on the Tamar River, this time opting to send it overland by coach. Unfortunately the craft, along with another owned by a Mr Williams, was also damaged in transit, rendering it incapable for being used.[1898] *The Mercury* reported, '*These boats were two skiffs, the property of Messrs. Whitehouse and Williams, and were sent by Burbury's coach, leaving Hobart Town on Saturday afternoon. They arrived at Campbell Town safely, secured on the top of the coach lengthways. Here however, contrary to agreement, as the owners of the boats assert, the coaches were changed, and it was found necessary to place the boats across the top of the coach the ends projecting on either side. On the way from Campbell Town, the night being dark, the projecting ends of the boats came in contact with a telegraph post, the coach having been driven too near the side of the road. The result was, one of the boats was completely broken across, and the side of the other stove in and shattered*'.[1899] The article continued. '*This unfortunate accident will shut down the Hobart Town oarsmen out of two races, in addition to the gig race, in which the gig of the Messrs. Whitehouse was to have competed, and much sympathy is felt for their misfortune*'.[1900]

Despite the loss of two of their racing vessels and the expected winnings from their potential success at the Launceston Regatta, George and his brother William persevered. They would continue to patronise and enter vessels to compete in local, regional and Launceston-based regattas for many years to come, often winning handsomely in boats they had built.

With demand for boats built by Whitehouse Brothers high, by June 1874 the pair returned to premises at Battery Point to establish their own boat yard, employing others to operate their waterman's boats.[1901] Located along the shore of the River Derwent near the present-day bottom of Finlay Street, the yard was situated on a portion of the Secheron property that John Ross had leased from the Perry family up until 1865 and where he had initially installed his patent slip.[1902]

The first vessel launched from this new enterprise was the *Iris*, a 27ft centreboard sailing boat built to the order of Messrs Hayle and Wilson and intended to compete in events of the newly-formed Derwent Sailing Boat Club.[1903] Shortly thereafter Whitehouse Brothers completed the sailing boat *Spray*, nearly identical to the *Iris* in terms of lines and rigging, though slightly larger, built to the order of W. A. Guesdon (Jr) and E. J. Freeman also to compete with the Derwent Sailing Boat Club.[1904] The establishment of this club, within a few months numbering upwards of 80 members, was

[1898] *The Mercury*, 3 March 1874; *The Cornwall Chronicle*, 4 March 1874.
[1899] *The Mercury*, 3 March 1874.
[1900] *The Mercury*, 3 March 1874.
[1901] *The Mercury*, 17 June, 16 October 1874.
[1902] *The Mercury*, 20 November 1876; *The Courier*, 4 October 1883.
[1903] *The Mercury*, 8, 15 July 1874.
[1904] *The Mercury*, 15 July, 10 August, 5, 14 September 1874.

A glance over at Secheron House and its extensive property. Whitehouse Brothers likely leased the area of shore now the bottom of Finlay Street, between the buildings shown in the image and the Secheron Estate's fence (late 1880s). The chimney was part of the Pyrolignite factory. In 1873 it was re-purposed into a blast furnace for iron smelting works. Courtesy Tasmanian Archives (NS3121/1/65).

certainly proving profitable for Whitehouse Brothers in terms of new commissions. The pair also became members of the organisation, regularly attending meetings and sailing their vessels *Star of the Sea* and *Derwent Belle* in some of the early races.[1905]

Another sailing craft, this one built to the order of A. G. Webster to compete with the same club, was launched by Whitehouse Brothers in October 1874.[1906] The Huon pine vessel measured 25ft in length with a beam of 5ft and depth of 2ft.[1907] Shortly following, the pair completed a carver-built four-oared whaleboat, also 25ft long, built specifically for regatta racing, and a one-plank outrigger skiff named *Linda* that was pulled by Thomas Bell at the 1875 Huon Regatta held on New Year's Day.[1908] They also converted George Elwin's fishing smack *Kent* into a passage boat, and took on other painting, repair and overhaul work.[1909]

> G. AND W. WHITEHOUSE,
> BOAT BUILDERS AND WATERMEN.
>
> Boats of all descriptions can be ordered from the Ferry, and the Boat Yard, Battery Point.
> TERMS MODERATE. 1162

The Tasmanian Tribune, 29 October 1874.

George and William Whitehouse entered the second year of their boat yard's operation in good spirits. Demand for new commercial, recreational and racing craft in Hobart Town continued to be high and, with a good reputation, the pair received many orders. In 1875 alone they were noted as building at least 12 vessels, including three ferry boats; three racing skiffs and two four-oared racing boats; one dinghy; one waterman's boat; one loading boat; and one pleasure boat.[1910] During this year the pair also expanded their fleet of boats available for hire with the purchase of the passage boat *Blue Jacket* from George Elwin in August 1875.[1911] That same month they purchased the passage boat *Hope* from Angus McKay (built by Charles Miller at Battery Point).[1912] The *Blue Jacket* was altered to a pleasure boat for use in the summer season.[1913] The *Hope* was on-sold to A. T. Stuart with the intention of converting the craft into a pleasure yacht.[1914] The Whitehouse Brothers were fittingly entrusted with the work and the renamed vessel, *The Dream*, ketch-rigged and measuring 42ft on the keel, was launched from their Battery Point yard in October 1875.[1915]

In 1876 Whitehouse Brothers built at least five vessels. These were a 26ft Huon pine ketch-rigged sailing boat commissioned by W. Ritchie of Launceston; two boats for use on the River Derwent measuring 26ft and 27ft, respectively; a 22ft Huon pine boat to the order of a Mr Pettow of Launceston; and the *Good Templar*, a 26ft four-oared racing boat which finished second in the Champion Race at the 1876 Hobart Town Regatta.[1916]

Another outrigger skiff of 22ft was completed by George and William Whitehouse in January 1877.[1917] Constructed of cedar, the boat competed at that years' Tamar Regatta and was likely named *Young Australia*.[1918] In September 1877 Whitehouse Brothers also completed two more outrigger skiffs, both to the order of A. G. Scott of Launceston.[1919] While one suffered considerable damage en route to its destination, the other, named *Young Tasmania*, finished third in the Alexandra Race at the 1877 Tamar Regatta.[1920]

Late in 1877 Whitehouse Brothers began building a yacht on speculation.[1921] Stated to be '*the largest yet constructed in Hobart Town since the introduction of the present style*', the 31ft vessel was auctioned off a few months later.[1922] Purchased by H. W. Bailey, the 7-ton craft was subsequently named *Haidee*.[1923] The same time period additionally involved Whitehouse Brothers converting the passage boat *Kent* into a yacht for Major-General Hodgson, as well as making improvements to the yacht *Wanderer*.[1924]

Haidee (circa 1880s).
Courtesy Maritime Museum of Tasmania (P_Y_581).

[1905] *The Mercury*, 18 July, 6, 17 October 1874, 11 January, 15 February, 18 October 1875.
[1906] *The Mercury*, 10 August, 26 October 1874.
[1907] *The Mercury*, 26 October 1874.
[1908] *The Mercury*, 26 October, 2 November, 14 December 1874; *Launceston Examiner*, 3 November 1874; *The Tasmanian Tribune*, 2 January 1875.
[1909] *The Mercury*, 26 October, 21 November 1874, 2 January 1875.
[1910] *The Mercury*, 11, 28 January, 22 February, 1 March, 19 April, 28 June, 10, 16 August, 10 December 1875; *The Tasmanian Tribune*, 9 February 1875.
[1911] *The Mercury*, 6 August 1875.
[1912] *The Mercury*, 6, 26 August 1875.
[1913] *The Mercury*, 6 August 1875.
[1914] *The Mercury*, 4 September 1875.
[1915] *The Mercury*, 4 September, 1 November 1875.
[1916] *Tribune*, 30 October 1876; *The Mercury*, 20, 30 November, 4, 13 December 1876.
[1917] *The Mercury*, 10 January 1877.
[1918] *The Mercury*, 10 January 1877; *Cornwall Chronicle*, 2 February 1877.
[1919] *The Mercury*, 26 September 1877.
[1920] *Weekly Examiner*, 8 December 1877; *The Tasmanian*, 8 December 1877.
[1921] *The Mercury*, 26 September 1877.
[1922] *Weekly Examiner*, 29 September 1877; *The Mercury*, 21 November 1877; *The Cornwall Chronicle*, 25 January 1878.
[1923] *The Cornwall Chronicle*, 25 January 1877; *The Mercury*, 6 December 1877.
[1924] *Weekly Examiner*, 29 September 1877.

The start of 1878 saw George and William Whitehouse complete a 22ft waterman's boat built to the order of a Mr Setton of Launceston.[1925] During this period they also continued to actively participate in and furnish boats for local and regional regattas, as well as the Derwent Rowing Club. However, the pair's perceived dominance saw them excluded from entering a race at the 1878 Port Esperance Regatta, possibly to allow those less successful competitors a chance to claim part of the prize pool.

> **THIRD RACE,**
> FOUR-OARED RACE. – Open to all (provided that Bayes and Whitehouse shall not be included in any crew), for whaleboats not over 26 feet.
> First Prize £10 0 0
> Second ,, ... 5 0 0
> Entrance. 20s. Three to start.
>
> *The Mercury*, 26 February 1878.

Not all were impressed by the outputs of Whitehouse Brothers' premises at Battery Point. In March 1878 a discussion of typhoid in the Hobart Town press noted the presence of '*terror of nuisances*' with the attention of readers then drawn to the condition of '*a stagnant pool situated in Whitehouse's boat yard, being the receptacle of the drainage of Hampden Road and surroundings*'.[1926] The hole in question '*was excavated originally for a slip steam engine, by Ross, now abandoned*' and was deemed to be '*in the most filthy condition imaginable*', the writer claiming that '*When a sea breeze is blowing, the residents of Battery Point are treated to a mouthful of foul air for which they are truly thankful - ugh! See this hole; stir it, and die!*'.[1927] While the stated outrage was a legitimate public health concern, the question of who was responsible for fixing the drainage issue was squarely laid on the council with Hobart Town's mayor and aldermen charged with needing to provide the authority and resources to make the necessary improvements.[1928] It would be some decades, however, before Battery Point was provided with better drainage of its streets. In the meantime, typhoid remained a justifiable cause for concern, resulting in around ten deaths per year in Hobart Town alone.[1929] In the decade to come, however, this mortality rate would only rise until better drainage and sanitation systems were introduced.[1930]

While working conditions at their yard may have been far from ideal, Whitehouse Brothers continued its operation. Next off the stocks in 1878 was the 28ft pleasure boat *Ada*, built to the order of a '*number of young gentlemen*'.[1931] The Huon pine craft, fitted with a centreboard and fishing well, was stated to be '*admirably adapted*' for the purpose for which it was designed.[1932] A few months later the pair completed a 19ft pleasure boat named *Millewa*, this time built to the order of James Warrington of Echuca, Victoria.

Switching focus to their ferry operations, Whitehouse Brothers next built four boats to add to their existing fleet of vessels available for hire. These were the pleasure boats *Calamia* and *Haidee*, completed in December 1878, and the pleasure boat *The Lily* and a whaleboat, both completed in mid-to-late 1879.[1933] Also in 1879 the duo completed a ferry punt of 25ft to the order of the Public Works Department for use conveying passengers and cargo across the Henty River; a square-sterned boat to the order of P. Butler; two dinghies for the ketch *Enchantress;* and the second class yacht *Pacific*, built to the order of R. Lewis.[1934] With a view to increasing their repair and overhaul operations, a new patent slip was additionally installed at their Battery Point yard.[1935] Extending 180ft into the water, the slip was capable of taking up vessels between 40 to 60 tons in burden.[1936]

1879 certainly ushered in a period of expansion of Whitehouse Brothers' Battery Point boat yard, as well as their business interests more generally. While they had plenty of work on hand, including building boats and yachts, and repairing small craft and boats, the pair were also looking to the future and investigating new opportunities. Likely capitalising on a perceived gap they saw in the market associated with the conveyance of passengers and goods between the Tasman Peninsula and Hobart Town, in October 1879 William Whitehouse purchased just over an acre of land from the Crown at Taranna on the Tasman Peninsula.[1937] However, it would be some years before this land became a useful part of their business. Still, it was the first step in a new direction.

Another step in the establishment of a steam ferry business came in July 1880 when they began building a small steam launch.[1938] Motivated by the success of the O'May Brothers' steam ferry business, the vessel was intended for pleasure purposes during the summer season, as well as for private excursions and for use in conveying passengers to visiting ships moored in the River Derwent.[1939] The resulting craft, the 42ft *Express*, was launched at Battery Point on 18 December 1880, its machinery and boiler were supplied by John Gellie of Barrack Street, Hobart Town.[1940]

[1925] *Tribune*, 26 February 1878.
[1926] *The Mercury*, 16 March 1878.
[1927] *The Mercury*, 16 March 1878.
[1928] *The Mercury*, 16 March 1878.
[1929] R. G. Kellaway (1989). *The Hobart Typhoid Epidemic of 1887-88*.
[1930] R. G. Kellaway (1989). *The Hobart Typhoid Epidemic of 1887-88*.
[1931] *Tribune*, 8 June 1878.
[1932] *Tribune*, 8 June 1878.
[1933] *Tribune*, 9 November 1878; *The Mercury*, 9 November 1878, 6 August, 15, 29 October 1879.
[1934] *The Mercury*, 7 May, 15, 29 October, 29 December 1879; *Tribune*, 9 October 1879; *Launceston Examiner*, 28 January 1880.
[1935] *The Mercury*, 6 August 1879.
[1936] *The Mercury*, 6 August 1879.
[1937] *The Mercury*, 22 October 1879.
[1938] *The Mercury*, 26 July 1880.
[1939] *The Mercury*, 20 December 1880.
[1940] *The Mercury*, 20 December 1880.

1880 was a busy period for Whitehouse Brothers. In addition to construction of the *Express*, in March of that year the pair completed a 15ft pleasure boat to the order of W. S. Sharland of New Norfolk.[1941] That same year they also produced a 14ft half-decked yacht to the order of H. Calder; a 21ft pleasure boat to add to their existing fleet of vessels based out of the Hobart Town wharf; two outrigger skiffs for the Tamar Rowing Club; a pleasure boat to the order of a Mr Gaffin of Barnes Bay, Bruny Island; two racing boats for customers based at New Norfolk; and a second-class yacht to the order of F. Turner.[1942]

With the *Express* added to their existing fleet of vessels, William Whitehouse took the helm of the craft while George managed operations of their ferry business and boat yard.[1943] In January 1881 two boats for use on board HMS *Wolverine* were completed.[1944] The following month they launched a 28ft whaleboat and a skiff for use on board HMS *Beagle*.[1945] In March 1881 they completed a whaleboat for use on board HMS *Renard*, and in April of that year, an 18ft pleasure boat for R. Lewis of Kangaroo Point.[1946] A few months later Whitehouse Brothers completed a 28ft ketch-rigged half-decked boat to the order of W. Tarleton of Wellington, New Zealand.[1947] During this period, George's brother-in-law William Bayes also began building vessels at their Battery Point boat yard.[1948]

Though in regular use, the steamer *Express* appears not to have been a long-term endeavour. The vessel was advertised for sale by Whitehouse Brothers less than five months after its launch.[1949] Failing to find a purchaser, it was laid up until May 1882 when sold to Facy and Company for use at Southport down the Huon in conjunction with the loading of barges.[1950]

It was likely that the *Express* was found too small for the local passenger trade and its engines too heavy, as in July 1881 Whitehouse Brothers began building a larger steamer.[1951] Launched on 11 October 1881, at 57ft in length, the *Pinafore* was 15ft longer than the *Express* and stated to be slightly faster and better fitted out for passenger traffic.[1952] Fitted with engines from the *Express*, this particular vessel was also intended to run between Hobart and Kangaroo Point on a regular schedule, as well as be made available for occasional excursions, private charter and fishing trips.[1953]

While the *Pinafore* successfully commenced service, George and William Whitehouse continued operations at their boat yard. Still favoured for their expertise in building racing craft, in January 1882 they completed a boat to vie in the All-Comers Race at the upcoming Hobart Regatta.[1954] However, bigger business decisions were on the horizon, with Whitehouse Brothers opting to forego the local passenger service for a more regional route. In April 1882 the pair placed the *Pinafore* on a weekly schedule between the Tasman Peninsula and Hobart, including '*calling in at intermediate ports, and touching at East Bay Neck*'.[1955] Two months later the vessel was also tasked with delivering the mail to Saltwater River and other settlements, and by December 1882 the *Pinafore* was making bi-weekly trips to the Peninsula, indicative of high demand.[1956]

[1941] *The Mercury*, 5 March 1880.
[1942] *The Mercury*, 24 April, 26 July, 6, 19 October, 30 November 1880.
[1943] *The Mercury*, 20 December 1880.
[1944] *The Mercury*, 17 January 1881.
[1945] *The Mercury*, 3 February 1881.
[1946] *The Mercury*, 3 February, 5 March, 15 April 1881.
[1947] *The Mercury*, 21 July, 26 August 1881.
[1948] *The Mercury*, 14 March 1881.
[1949] *Launceston Examiner*, 8, 14 April 1881; *The Mercury*, 11 May 1881.
[1950] *The Mercury*, 2 May 1882.
[1951] *The Mercury*, 21 July 1881.
[1952] *The Mercury*, 21 July, 12, 29 October 1881.
[1953] *The Mercury*, 29 October, 18 November 1881; *The Hobart Herald*, 5 November 1881.
[1954] *The Mercury*, 24 January 1882.
[1955] *The Mercury*, 19, 22 April 1882.
[1956] *The Mercury*, 15 July, 19 December 1882.

Pinafore (circa 1880s).
Courtesy Maritime Museum of Tasmania (P_GSL338).

Tasman's Hotel, Taranna (late 1880s).
Courtesy Tasmanian Archives (PH30/1/3015).

Realising the need not only for a regular and more frequent passenger and cargo service between Norfolk Bay and Hobart but also more facilities for their customers, during this period Whitehouse Brothers purchased additional property at Taranna with the intention of establishing a hotel and other conveniences in the township.[1957] There was definitely a niche to be filled, *The Mercury* on 29 November 1882 reporting, *'Accommodation is urgently wanted at Norfolk Bay for passengers arriving late during the winter months, who may be proceeding to Port Arthur or Eagle Hawk Neck. It is also central for all travellers arriving at or leaving the Peninsula overland. The nearest inn is East Bay Neck, and there have been several instances where passengers arriving late at Norfolk Bay have had to make their abode for the night in the old prisoners' dormitory with a leaky roof sooner than proceed over several broken bridges and culverts after sunset'*. Capitalising on this demand, in March 1883 George Whitehouse was successfully granted a licence to operate a 12-room hotel at Taranna with Tasman's Hotel officially opened to the public on 21 March 1883.[1958]

With their focus more and more centred on the regional steamer trade, there were very few boats built by Whitehouse Brothers in 1882. In addition to the racing craft mentioned previously, the only other boat that they are known to have produced this year was the ferry boat *Miranda* which was launched in December of that year for their own use.[1959] A month later, the *Huon Belle*, a four-oared boat built to compete in the 1883 Hobart Regatta was launched and in April 1883 they completed the ketch *Lady Franklin*.[1960] The latter was built to the order of E. T. Miles with the 36ft vessel near immediately on-sold to A. F. Smith who used it for police work in Bass Strait.[1961] *Lady Franklin* was the last vessel built by George and William Whitehouse at their Battery Point boat yard. In October 1883, after nearly a decade of operation, they advertised their boat yard, based near Secheron, for lease; the brothers opting to focus their attention on expanding their business operations at Taranna.[1962] However, a tenant proved not immediately available such that Whitehouse Brothers were still using a boat shed located on the property in April of the following year for storage when it was completely demolished by a squall, in the process damaging six racing boats valued at £60.[1963]

TO LET.—The BOATYARD at SECHERON, Battery Point, lately occupied by the Messrs. Whitehouse, together with the Slip constructed by them. Possession immediate. Apply to DOBSON & MITCHELL, Solicitors.
j213

The Mercury, 6 October 1883.

[1957] *The Mercury*, 29 November, 15 December 1882, 7 February 1883; Libraries Tasmania (AF721-1-701 and AF819-1-340).
[1958] *The Mercury*, 7 February, 5 March, 2 April, 29 October 1883.
[1959] *The Mercury*, 22 December 1882.
[1960] *The Mercury*, 20, 24, 30 January, 2 April 1883.
[1961] *The Mercury*, 1 May 1883; *Daily Telegraph*, 6 September 1883.
[1962] *The Mercury*, 4 October 1883.
[1963] *The Mercury*, 17 April 1884.

With a regular steamer service to the Tasman Peninsula proving popular for tourists, a hotel in which to accommodate passengers upon arrival at Taranna, by now itself a growing township, in operation, as well as managing a well-established and respected boat hiring enterprise at the Hobart wharf, business for George and William Whitehouse was thriving. In May 1883, due to increased demand for their Tasman Peninsula steam service, the pair began building a new steamer to take the place of the *Pinafore*.[1964] Constructed from a model made by their brother-in-law William Bayes, and built under his direct supervision, the 85ft *Taranna* was substantially larger than the *Pinafore* and also much faster.[1965] Notably built at Taranna and launched on 22 July 1884, by mid-December it commenced a regular service between the Tasman Peninsula and Hobart.[1966] Complete with a liquor licence, the *Taranna* proved a resounding success for George and William Whitehouse.[1967] While the *Pinafore* was initially retained as a back-up vessel, and also made available for private charter, fishing and pleasure trips, in March 1885 it was sold to Messrs Facy and Fisher and placed in the Huon and Channel fruit trade.[1968]

Though now a commercial fleet owner and operator, and hotelier, from January 1884 George Whitehouse was appointed postmaster of Taranna. He and his brother, likely in conjunction with other family members, also began cultivating oysters in the shallows of Norfolk Bay, using spat collected locally.[1969] It was during this period, however, that George relinquished the licence of Tasman's Hotel and the position of postmaster. Both roles were taken over by his sister-in-law Susannah, wife of his brother William.[1970] Perhaps because of illness or personal reasons, George and his family appear to have returned to Hobart where he retained his position at the helm of *Taranna*.[1971] Still, George was not yet ready to give up his original vocation of boat building.[1972] In the mid to late 1880s he completed several boats, often by request. For example, in November 1886 he constructed a 26ft racing boat to compete at the Norfolk Bay Regatta, an event Whitehouse Brothers helped to establish in 1883.[1973] It was soon followed by a boat of similar dimensions to compete at the New Town Regatta.[1974] The Mercantile Rowing Club also requested that George build a practise boat for them in late 1886.[1975] In January 1889 he built a 26ft four-oared outrigger to race at the upcoming Hobart Regatta.[1976] Most, if not all, of these vessels were constructed at the Franklin Wharf in Hobart.[1977]

With the resounding success of the *Taranna* on the Tasman Peninsula run, in February 1889 Whitehouse Brothers announced the construction of a larger steamer intended to accommodate increasing numbers of passengers and cargo.[1978] Once again their brother-in-law, William Bayes, was charged with building the vessel.[1979]

With its keel sourced from Koonya, the 110ft steamer *Nubeena* was launched from one of the Battery Point yards situated along the Napoleon Street corridor on 24 September 1890.[1980] Though intended to take the place of the *Taranna*, Whitehouse Brothers instead initiated a new west coast service, operating the vessel between Trial Harbour and Hobart.[1981] The utility of this service, however, was short-lived and by October 1891 Whitehouse Brothers had cancelled the route, and also an associated contract with the Hobart Marine Board to convey stores to Maatsuyker Island.[1982] Instead, the *Nubeena* was placed in the Tasman Peninsula trade, with the smaller steamer *Taranna* employed in the New Norfolk trade, and also made available for excursions and private charters.

Nubeena (circa 1890s).
Courtesy Maritime Museum of Tasmania (P_OM_L_42b).

In May 1894, following more than 20 years of operation, Whitehouse Brothers announced the dissolution of their partnership.[1983] In dividing their assets, George Whitehouse retained possession of the steamer

---

[1964] *The Mercury*, 28 May 1883.
[1965] *The Mercury*, 28 May, 25 July 1883.
[1966] *The Mercury*, Friday 25 July, 18 December 1884.
[1967] *Launceston Examiner*, 2 December 1884.
[1968] *The Mercury*, 17 December 1884, 10 March, 9 December 1885.
[1969] *The Mercury*, 14 June 1884.
[1970] *The Mercury*, 25 May 1884, 12 May 1885.
[1971] *The Mercury*, 2 December 1885, 23 February, 3 March, 16 June 1886; *Tasmanian News*, 27 May 1887.
[1972] *Tasmanian News*, 23 January 1884.
[1973] *The Mercury*, 2, 16, 27 August 1883, 12 September 1884, 5 November 1886; *Tasmanian News*, 3 November 1886.
[1974] *Tasmanian News*, 6 December 1886.
[1975] *The Mercury*, 10 December 1886.

[1976] *Launceston Examiner*, 14 January 1889.
[1977] *Tasmanian News*, 3 November 1886.
[1978] *Launceston Examiner*, 8 February 1889.
[1979] *The Mercury*, 28 October 1889, 21 January 1890.
[1980] *The Mercury*, 25 September 1890.
[1981] *Zeehan and Dundas Herald*, 3 July 1891.
[1982] *The Mercury*, 1 September, 17 October 1891; *Launceston Examiner*, 8 October 1891.
[1983] *The Mercury*, 24 May 1894.

Taranna with the intention of continuing it in the New Norfolk trade, as well as making the vessel available for pleasure trips, excursions and private charters.[1984] William Whitehouse, partnering with William Pitfield, an engineer who had worked for Whitehouse Brothers for many years, retained possession of the *Nubeena* with the intention of continuing this particular craft in the Tasman and Channel trades.[1985]

In the ensuing months both parties set about expanding their respective customer bases with George Whitehouse having the *Taranna* widened by 3ft, a 'large and commodious deck cabin' built, and a new steel steam boiler installed.[1986] Messrs Whitehouse and Pitfield in turn placed an order for a new steamer with the Wilson family of Port Cygnet.[1987] The 67ft *Lottah* was launched from Wilson's shipyard on 14 January 1895.[1988] It was built to join the *Nubeena* in the Tasman and Channel trades.[1989] Messrs Whitehouse and Pitfield amalgamated with others to form the very successful Huon, Channel and Peninsula Steamship Company in 1900.

George Whitehouse died at his residence, 7 Montpelier Street, Battery Point, on 8 July 1896 of '*dilatation of stomach*'.[1990] He was 53 years old. He was survived by his wife Martha and their five children, by now all adults. His eldest son William George Whitehouse, master mariner, carried on the family business, continuing to run the *Taranna* between Hobart and New Norfolk for many years in conjunction with another son, Herbert Edward Whitehouse.

All told, George Whitehouse was a hard working and persevering entrepreneur. Beginning work as an apprenticed boat builder at Battery Point in the early 1860s, he became one of the Derwent's more successful helmsmen and was extremely prominent in local and regional rowing and sailing circles for several decades. With his younger brother William he also became a well-respected licensed waterman owning a large fleet of vessels, and thereafter a master mariner of several steamers. Added to this list of achievements are the more than 70 boats that George built at Battery Point between 1863 and 1883; many of these at a Battery Point boat yard established near Secheron House in conjunction with William Whitehouse.

Yet George Whitehouse's greatest achievement likely lies in his involvement with the local steamer trade. It was precipitous that George and William Whitehouse built a steamer specifically for the Tasman Peninsula trade at a time when regional steam communication and passenger services to this locale were in their infancy. Their service proved a boon, not only for the increasing number of residents of the Tasman Peninsula, but also for those wishing to take excursions and short holidays to the area. Together George and William Whitehouse were also instrumental in the development of the Tasman Peninsula township of Taranna, including establishing the township's first hotel and guest accommodation, its post office, and helping establish the Norfolk Bay Regatta.

Unfortunately George Whitehouse's career was cut short by his premature death at the age of 53. Still his New Norfolk steamer service was carried on for several more decades by two of his sons (coincidentally operating as Whitehouse Brothers), culminating in the launch of the *Mongana*, *Marana* and *Maweena* in 1905, 1908 and 1913, respectively.[1991] Fittingly all three vessels were built (by Purdon and Featherstone) at Battery Point.

[1984] *The Mercury*, 24 May 1894.
[1985] *The Mercury*, 29 December 1890, 24 May 1894.
[1986] *The Mercury*, 1 September 1894, 30 December 1885.
[1987] *The Mercury*, 1 September 1894.
[1988] *The Mercury*, 16 January 1895.
[1989] *The Mercury*, 16 January 1895.
[1990] *Tasmanian News*, 9 July 1896; *The Mercury*, 10 July 1896; Libraries Tasmania (RGD35/1/15 no 770).
[1991] *The Mercury*, 3 July 1905, 10 July 1908, 11 August, 24 October 1913.

Taranna.
Courtesy Tasmanian Archives (NS869/1/178).

Vessels built by George Whitehouse and employees at Battery Point (1863 - 1883)

Year	Name	Type	Description
1863	*Princess Alexandra*	Dinghy	Racing dinghy built by George Whitehouse to the order of Charles Dillon, local waterman, to compete in regattas and private pulling matches.
1863	--	Skiff	18ft. Cedar racing skiff built by George Whitehouse to the order of James Reid to compete in sculling races.
1864	--	Excursion boat	Built by George Whitehouse to the order of Charles Dillon, local waterman, for use as an excursion boat.
1864	--	Skiff	18ft. Racing skiff built by George Whitehouse to compete for the Alexandra Prize at the 1864 New Norfolk Regatta, held on 26 December that year.
1865	*Paragon*	Skiff	18ft. Racing skiff built by George Whitehouse to the order of T. Turner specifically to compete at the 1865 Hobart Town Regatta.
1865	*Violet*	Skiff	18ft. Racing skiff built by George Whitehouse for himself to compete at the 1865 Hobart Town Regatta.
1867	--	Whaleboat	21 x 4.5ft. Four-oared Huon pine whaleboat built by George Whitehouse in conjunction with Henry Grubb to the order of T. Westbrock for use by Rev. Wilkes Simmons and intended for the D'Entrecasteaux Channel mission service.
1867	--	Dinghy	Lightweight racing dinghy built by George Whitehouse to compete at the 1867 Hobart Town Regatta to be crewed by a team of juveniles nicknamed the 'Snuffs'.
1867	--	Skiff	18ft x 22 x 8in. Racing skiff weighing 32 lbs. built of King Billy pine by George Whitehouse and Henry Grubb to compete at the 1867 Hobart Town Regatta. Possibly named *Midge*.
1867	--	Skiff	18ft x 23 x 8in. Outrigger racing skiff weighing 30 lbs. built on the '*tubular principle*' by George Whitehouse to the order of Charles Dillon specifically to compete in the Amateur Scullers' Race at the 1867 Hobart Town Regatta.
1868	*Cherry Picker*	Whaleboat	31.5 x 3.9ft x 7in. Four-oared Macquarie pine whaleboat built by George Whitehouse to compete in the race for the Ladies' Purse at the 1868 Hobart Town Regatta. Pulled by a crew comprising Messrs. Ledwell, Archer, Spurling (Jr), Welsh and Goulding.
1868	*Secret*	Dinghy	18 x 3.2ft. Racing dinghy built by George Whitehouse to compete at the 1868 Hobart Town Regatta to be crewed by two men from the Huon.
1874	*Iris*	Sail boat	27 x 5.8 x 2ft. Centreboard sailing boat built by Whitehouse Brothers of Macquarie pine to the order of Messrs Hayle and Wilson specifically to compete in Derwent Sailing Boat Club events.
1874	*Spray*	Sail boat	28 x 6.5 x 2ft. Centreboard sailing boat built by Whitehouse Brothers to the order of W. A. Guesdon (Jr) and E. J. Freeman specifically to compete in Derwent Sailing Boat Club events. Identical to the *Iris*, see above. Wrecked off Sandy Bay during a squall on 11 December 1874 with the loss of one crew member, George Dear.
1874	--	Sail boat	25 x 5 x 2ft. Sailing boat built by Whitehouse Brothers to the order of A. G. Webster specifically to compete in Derwent Sailing Boat Club events.
1874	--	Whaleboat	25 x 4ft x 16in. Carver constructed four-oared whaleboat built by Whitehouse Brothers for racing in local regattas.
1874	*Linda*	Skiff	18 x 2ft x 8in. One plank outrigger skiff built of King William pine by Whitehouse Brothers and pulled by Thomas Bell at the 1875 Huon Regatta.
1875	--	Ferry boat	22 x 5ft x 18in. Square-sterned Huon pine boat built by Whitehouse Brothers in early 1875.
1875	--	Skiff	18ft x 22 x 9.5in. One-plank cedar skiff built by Whitehouse Brothers for competing in local regattas.
1875	*Comet*	Boat	25 x 4ft x 15in. Four-oared, single-planked, oval-bottomed Huon pine boat built by Whitehouse Brothers for racing in local regattas. Fitted with sliding seats.
1875	--	Ferry boat	22 x 5.1ft x 22in. Built by Whitehouse Brothers in early 1875 and intended for their fleet of commercial waterman's craft.
1875	--	Skiff	25 x 4ft x 10in. Huon pine, copper-fastened racing skiff built by Whitehouse Brothers for competing in local regattas. Pulled on the gunwale.
1875	--	Dinghy	11 x 5.2 x 2ft. Dinghy built by Whitehouse Brothers in April 1875 for use on board the steamer *Monarch*.
1875	--	Waterman's boat	21 x 5.1ft x 14in. Huon pine, copper-fastened waterman's boat built by Whitehouse Brothers in mid 1875 and intended for their commercial fleet.
1875	*Leisure Hour*	Ferry boat	21 x 4.8ft x 19in. Huon pine, copper-fastened, centreboard ferry boat built by George Whitehouse in August 1875 and intended for their commercial fleet.
1875	*Smiling Morn*	Whaleboat	28.5 x 5.5 x 2ft. Built by Whitehouse Brothers from the wreck of Pilot Bleach's whaleboat that was run down by the steamer *Monarch*. Intended for pleasure purposes.

Year	Name	Type	Description
1875	–	Loading boat	15ft. Built by Whitehouse Brothers in August 1875 for use by the ketch *May Queen*.
1875	Aphrodite?	Skiff	20 x 2ft x 7.5in. Cedar, copper-fastened skiff built by Whitehouse Brothers for W. Terry of New Norfolk to compete in local regattas. Possibly named *Aphrodite*.
1875	–	Boat	25 x 4ft x 13in. Four-oared, oval-bottomed boat built by Whitehouse Brothers for competing in local regattas.
1876	–	Sail boat	26 x 5.5 x 2ft. Huon pine, ketch-rigged boat built by Whitehouse Brothers built to the order of W. Ritchie of Launceston.
1876	–	Boat	26ft. Boat built by Whitehouse Brothers for use on the River Derwent.
1876	–	Boat	27ft. Boat built by Whitehouse Brothers for use on the River Derwent.
1876	–	Boat	22 x 5.5ft x 20in. Huon pine, copper-fastened boat built by Whitehouse Brothers to the order of a Mr Pettow of Launceston.
1876	Good Templar	Boat	26ft. Four-oared boat built by Whitehouse Brothers for racing in local regattas. Finished second in the Champion Race at the 1876 Hobart Town Regatta.
1877	Young Australia?	Skiff	22ft x 20 x 8in. Cedar, outrigger skiff built by Whitehouse Brothers for competing at the 1877 Launceston Regatta. Possibly named *Young Australia*.
1877	–	Skiff	One of two outrigger skiffs built by Whitehouse Brothers to the order of A. G. Scott of Launceston. Sent via train to northern Tasmania and suffered considerable damage en route.
1877	Young Tasmania	Skiff	Second of two outrigger skiffs built by Whitehouse Brothers to the order of A. G. Scott of Launceston. Finished third in the Alexandra Race at the 1877 Tamar Regatta.
1877	Haidee	Yacht	31 x 9.6 x 3.4ft. 7 tons. Cutter-rigged yacht built by Whitehouse Brothers on speculation. Purchased at auction by H. H. Baily and successfully sailed with the Derwent Yacht Club. Also competed in regatta races, including on the Tamar River. Sold to W. J. Cleary in November 1881. Advertised for sale many times throughout 1884 into 1885. Purchased by John Cross. Advertised for sale in 1886 though failed to sell. Foundered and not recovered after colliding with the ketch *Margaret* during the sailing race for first-class yachts at the 1887 Hobart Regatta, all hands saved.
1878	–	Waterman's boat	22 x 5.1ft x 22in. Built by Whitehouse Brothers in early 1878 to the order of a Mr Setton of Launceston.
1878	Ada	Pleasure boat	28 x 6.5 x 2ft. Huon pine pleasure boat built by Whitehouse Brothers and completed in mid-1878, built to the order of a number of young gentlemen from Hobart Town. Fitted with a centreboard and fishing well.
1878	Millewa	Pleasure boat	19 x 4.8ft x 22in. Huon pine and copper-fastened boat built by Whitehouse Brothers to the order of James Warrington of Echuca, Victoria.
1878	Calamia	Pleasure boat	20 x 5ft x 21in. Huon pine, copper-fasted boat built by Whitehouse Brothers in late 1878 and intended for their fleet of pleasure craft available for hire. Fitted with a centreboard and water-tight locker.
1878	Haidee	Pleasure boat	22 x 5.1ft x 22in. Huon pine, copper-fastened boat built by Whitehouse Brothers in late 1878 and intended for their fleet of pleasure craft available for hire. Fitted with a centreboard and water-tight locker.
1879	–	Ferry punt	25 x 8 x 2.5ft. Built by Whitehouse Brothers in May 1878 to the order of the Public Works Department for use transporting passengers and cargo across the Henty River. Stated to be capable of carrying a horse and cart or up to 5 tons dead weight.
1879	The Lily	Pleasure boat	18 x 4.6ft x 18in. Huon pine, copper-fasted boat built by Whitehouse Brothers and intended for their fleet of pleasure craft available for hire.
1879	–	Whaleboat	26 x 5.6ft x 21in. Four-oared American red pine whaleboat built by Whitehouse Brothers and intended for their fleet of pleasure craft available for hire. Fitted with a centreboard.
1879	–	Dinghy	First of two dinghies built by Whitehouse Brothers for use by the fishing smack *Enchantress*.
1879	–	Dinghy	Second of two dinghies built by Whitehouse Brothers for use by the fishing smack *Enchantress*.
1879	–	Boat	Square-sterned, centreboard boat built by Whitehouse Brothers to the order of P. Butler.
1879	Pacific	Yacht	27 x 6.5 x 2ft. 3 tons. Second class cutter-rigged yacht built by Whitehouse Brothers to the order of R. Lewis of Kangaroo Point. Constructed of Huon pine and copper-fastenend. First competed in the sailing boat race at the 1880 Hobart Town Regatta. Advertised for sale in September 1884, by Alfred Mitchell. Last noted when advertised for sale in October 1886 by L. Rapp.
1880	–	Pleasure boat	15 x 4.7ft x 18in. Huon pine and copper-fastened boat built by Whitehouse Brothers to the order of W. S. Sharland of New Norfolk.
1880	Syren?	Yacht	14 x 5 x 2ft. Small, half-decked, cutter-rigged yacht built by Whitehouse Brothers to the order of H. Calder. Built of Huon pine and copper-fastenend.

Year	Name	Type	Description
1880	–	Pleasure boat	21 x 5.3 x 2ft. Square-sterned boat built by Whitehouse Brothers in mid-1880 and intended for their fleet of pleasure craft available for hire. Fitted with a centreboard and water-tight locker.
1880	–	Skiff	First of two outrigger skiffs built by Whitehouse Brothers to the order of the Tamar Rowing Club.
1880	–	Skiff	Second of two outrigger skiffs built by Whitehouse Brothers to the order of the Tamar Rowing Club.
1880	–	Pleasure boat	Built by Whitehouse Brothers to the order of a Mr Gaffin of Barnes Bay, Bruny Island.
1880	–	Skiff	Racing skiff built by Whitehouse Brothers to the order of a customer from New Norfolk.
1880	–	Skiff	Racing skiff built by Whitehouse Brothers to the order of a customer from New Norfolk.
1880	*Express*	Steam launch	42.0 x 10.5 x 3.5ft. ON 79288. 6 tons. Built by Whitehouse Brothers for their own steam ferry business. Launched on 18 December 1880, its machinery and boiler supplied by John Gellie of Barrack Street, Hobart Town. Found too small for service and its engines too heavy. In May 1882 sold to Facy and Company for use at Southport loading barges Transferred to Launceston in late 1883 after being purchased by Alex Evans for use as a pleasure vessel. Sold in May 1889 to E. Devlin of Leven. Advertised for sale in August 1893 and returned to Launceston where it was laid up for some time. Advertised for sale in October 1900 by the Bank of Australasia. Returned to Hobart a year later. Owned by W. Burnett and employed in the local fishing industry. Sunk in Victoria Dock in early 1913. Subsequently recovered and broken up on Charlie Lucas' Battery Point slip.
1880	–	Yacht	20 x 5.2 x 2ft. Second class yacht built by Whitehouse Brothers to the order of F. Turner. Built of Huon pine and copper-fastened. Competed with the Derwent Yacht Club.
1881	–	Whaleboat	27 x 5.5 x 2.1ft. First of two small boats built by Whitehouse Brothers for use by HMS *Wolverine*.
1881	–	Boat	16 x 4.8ft x 20 in. Second of two small boats built by Whitehouse Brothers for use by HMS *Wolverine*.
1881	–	Whaleboat	28ft. Huon pine and copper-fastened whaleboat built by Whitehouse Brothers for use by HMS *Beagle*.
1881	–	Skiff	Skiff built by Whitehouse Brothers for use by HMS *Beagle*.
1881	–	Whaleboat	25 x 5.5 x 2.1ft. Huon pine, copper-fastened, centreboard whaleboat built by Whitehouse Brothers for use by HMS *Renard*.
1881	–	Pleasure boat	18 x 5ft x 22 in. Built by Whitehouse Brothers to the order of R. Lewis of Kangaroo Point.
1881	–	Sail boat	28 x 6.5 x 2.5ft. Built by Whitehouse Brothers to the order of W. Tarleton of Wellington, New Zealand. Half-decked and fitted with a centreboard and side lockers. Constructed of Huon pine. Shipped to New Zealand in late August 1881.
1881	*Pinafore*	Steam launch	57.0 x 12.1 x 5.7ft. ON 57611. 13 tons. Built by Whitehouse Brothers for their own use and launched on 11 October 1881. Fitted with enginers from the *Express*, initially employed between Hobart and Kangaroo Point on a regular schedule then transferred to the Tasman Peninsula run. Sold to Messrs Facy and Fisher in March 1885 and placed in the Huon and Channel fruit trade. Later sold to Edward Kenny and employed on the River Derwent. In 1919 sold to the Electrolytic Zinc Company for use as a tender but driven ashore at Hobart's Domain in March of that year and subsequently deemed a total loss. Sold to the Rosny Estates & Ferry Company, its engines and other items were removed and its hull towed to Bridgewater and abandoned.
1882	–	Boat	Boat built by Whitehouse Brothers to compete in the All-Comers Race at the 1882 Hobart Regatta.
1882	*Miranda*	Ferry boat	20 x 4.5ft. Built by Whitehouse Brothers in late 1882 and intended for their fleet of vessels available for hire. Constructed of Huon pine and copper-fastened.
1883	*Huon Belle*	Boat	Four-oared boat built by Whitehouse Brothers to compete in the All-Comers Race at the 1883 Hobart Regatta where it finished second.
1883	*Lady Franklin*	Ketch	36 x 12.5 x 4ft. 12 tons. Ketch built by Whitehouse Brothers to the order of E. T. Miles though quickly sold to A. F. Smith. Used as a police boat in Bass Strait. By the early 1900s converted to a fishing smack and employed in waters off the north-west coast operated by E. Dalley. In March 1905 caught fire and destroyed at East Devonport, all hands saved. At the time of loss, owned either by Savage Bros. or F. H. Furner.

Partial map of the west coast of Scotland, showing the islands of Mull and Ulva (c1850s).
Courtesy National Library of Australia (nla.obj-773055325).

Lachlan Macquarie

'The Hobartonians will row in a new boat built by Mr Macquarie to order and I feel assured that a better boat could not be turned out in Melbourne or Sydney.'

Tribune, 23 January 1877.

Born on the island of Ulva off the west coast of Scotland, Lachlan 'Lark' Macquarie arrived in Hobart Town with his parents in 1853 at the age of seven. Here he later undertook a boat building apprenticeship with Thomas Morland at the Domain, and by 1875 had established his own boat yard at Battery Point. Macquarie's niche was in the building of smaller racing boats, particularly gigs and skiffs, many of which were successful at local regattas and in rowing club races. Following ten years of operation, Macquarie closed his Battery Point boat yard opting to travel the colony building new vessels to order and undertaking repair work. Still, between 1876 and 1885 at least 72 boats were built at his Battery Point boat yard located near Castray Esplanade in the shipyard previously operated by the Degraves family, including 28 racing boats and four yachts.

Lachlan 'Lark' Macquarie was born on the small island of Ulva, 500 metres from the island of Mull, off the west coast of Scotland, in 1845.[1992] He was the second of at least three children born to Allan and Catherine Macquarie, nee Mackey.[1993] Lark's family were descendants of the Macquarie clan who possessed the island of Ulva, measuring 12 kilometres in length by 4 kilometres wide, from at least the thirteenth century and were likely distant relatives of one of Ulva's more celebrated subjects, Lachlan Macquarie, who was notably Governor of New South Wales between 1810 and 1821 and is often colloquially referred to as the 'Father of Australia'.[1994] Governor Macquarie was buried on the island of Ulva following his death in London in 1824, his body travelling by boat to be interred in a mausoleum on the island.[1995] Unfortunately that same year coincided with the entire island of Mull being advertised for sale, together with several neighbouring properties.[1996] Later purchased by Francis William Clark, a wealthy lawyer from Stirling, he soon set about systematically evicting his tenants, the approximately 900 residents of the island, often in harsh circumstances.[1997] Others, including members of the Scottish Free Church, left Ulva voluntarily due to religious persecution.[1998]

By the late 1840s, a few years after Lark Macquarie's birth, the population of Ulva had declined to less than 200 people.[1999] Adding to their destitution was the Highland potato famine, a diet staple of those living in the Scottish Hebrides, including residents on the islands of Mull and Ulva.[2000]

While Lark Macquarie's father Allan was a boat builder by trade who would have also supported his family by collecting kelp and shellfish, by the late 1840s all avenues of work for him on the island of Ulva had dissipated.[2001] Likely forced from Ulva, the Macquarie family moved to nearby Mull with the 1851 Census noting Catherine and her three children living at Argyll Terrace in Tobermory, along with two of Catherine's sister-in-laws.[2002] Indicative of the state of the local economy and lack of opportunities, the same census noted Allan Macquarie as working as a fisherman in Acharacle, Inverness, around 40 miles by sea from Tobermory.[2003]

Struggling to make ends meet, Allan Macquarie approached the Highland and Island Emigration Society who provided support in the form of emigration

---

[1992] 1851 Scotland Census for Lachlan Macquarie.
[1993] Scotland, Select Marriages, 1561-1910 for Allan McQuarie and Catherine McKay; 1851 Scotland Census for Catherine Mcquarrie.
[1994] en.wikipedia.org/wiki/Ulva; en.wikipedia.org/wiki/Lachlan_Macquarie.
[1995] en.wikipedia.org/wiki/Lachlan_Macquarie; *Caledonia Mercury*, 24 July 1824.
[1996] *Caledonian Mercury*, 9 September 1824, 17 February 1834.
[1997] *Inverness Courier*, 10 August 1825, 26 August 1845; *Caledonia Mercury*, 13 January 1838.
[1998] *Inverness Courier*, 10 August 1825, 26 August 1845; *Caledonia Mercury*, 13 January 1838.
[1999] en.wikipedia.org/wiki/Ulva.
[2000] *Elgin Courier*, 25 December 1846.
[2001] Tasmania, Australia, Immigrant Lists, 1841-1884 for Lachlan McQuarrie; 1851 Scotland Census for Catherine Macquarrie.
[2002] 1851 Scotland Census for Catherine Mcquarrie.
[2003] 1851 Scotland Census for Allan Macquarrie.

to Australia. Allan, his wife Catherine and their three children, Effy, Lark and Hugh, arrived in Hobart Town from Scotland on 27 April 1853 on board the ship *Panama*.[2004] They were amongst many working-class families provided passage to Van Diemen's Land, several of whom were from Ulva including Hector Macquarie and his family who were relatives.[2005] Described as poor, the Macquarie family's luggage included a clock, a set of bagpipes and a copy of Henry Mackenzie's book *Man of Feeling*.[2006]

Upon arrival in Hobart Town, Allan Macquarie was immediately hired by T. G. Gregson, Esq, MLC, likely undertaking general labouring work at Gregson's property at Restdown on the River Derwent just outside of Hobart Town.[2007] He later gained employment as a carpenter and the Macquarie family found housing in Goulburn Street.[2008] Sadly, Allan died on 1 December 1858 of a fistula, possibly connected to bowel cancer, just five years after the family's arrival.[2009] He was 63 years of age. As the oldest son, yet only 13 years of age, Lark Macquarie was next in line to support his family.

While his younger brother Hugh was apprenticed to Charles Greig, a tailor and clothier of Hobart Town, Lark opted to follow in his father's professional footsteps and, late in his teens, was apprenticed to Thomas Morland, at the time a boat builder of Hobart Town's Domain.[2010] While he would have been involved in the construction of many vessels during this period, the first vessel Lark Macquarie is noted as solely building was a dinghy named *Polyphemus* that raced at the 1868 Hobart Town Regatta.[2011]

Following completion of his apprenticeship, likely a period of six years, Macquarie remained employed at the Domain boat yards until 1874; the latter part of this period spent working for Thomas Williams.[2012] During this time he was noted as building several vessels. For example, in 1871 he began construction of a Huon pine steam launch in conjunction with Messrs Gellie and Edwards at No. 3 Goulburn Street, Hobart Town.[2013] Built during the trio's leisure hours and holidays and likely in the backyard of Macquarie's house, the 40ft vessel was named *Resolute* and launched into Fishermen's Dock at the Hobart Town wharf on 14 December 1872.[2014] Purchased by James Herrington Brown in October 1873, the craft was renamed *Little Nell* and placed in the Tamar River passenger trade.[2015] Sadly it was wrecked in February 1874 following a boiler explosion which resulted in the death of nine of *Little Nell*'s complement of eleven.[2016] The vessel's remains were subsequently used to construct a ketch that was later named *Rescue*, launched in 1876 by Henry Plummer of West Tamar.[2017]

By February 1873 Lark Macquarie, employed at Thomas William's Domain shipyard, helped in the construction of several vessels to compete in that years' Hobart Town Regatta.[2018] A year later, based at the same yard, he was noted as building the racing cutter *Swift*, which owned by S. Moriarty competed in events of the newly-formed Derwent Sailing Boat Club; a 20ft racing skiff likely named *Minnehaha*; and the *Comet*, a one-plank cedar four-board boat of 25ft that finished first in the All-Comers' Race at the 1875 New Norfolk Regatta.[2019] It was during this period, however, that Macquarie narrowly missed serious injury after cutting his leg with an adze whilst framing a spar and having to be taken to hospital.[2020] Returning to work, another four-oared racing boat, the *Lurline*, was completed by Macquarie

---

[2004] Tasmania, Australia, Immigrant Lists, 1841-1884 for Lachlan McQuarrie; R. W. Munro & Alan Macquarie (1996). *Clan MacQuarrie: A History*; *The Courier*, 28 April 1853; *The Hobart Town Advertiser*, 9 May 1853.
[2005] Tasmania, Australia, Immigrant Lists, 1841-1884 for Lachlan McQuarrie; R. W. Munro & Alan Macquarie (1996). *Clan MacQuarrie: A History*; *The Courier*, 28 April 1853; *The Hobart Town Advertiser*, 9 May 1853.
[2006] R. W. Munro & Alan Macquarie (1996). *Clan MacQuarrie: A History*.
[2007] Libraries Tasmania (CB7/13/1/1 p71); R. W. Munro (1996). *Clan MacQuarrie: A History*; *Colonial Times*, 23 June 1854.
[2008] Libraries Tasmania (RGD35/1/5 no 1219).
[2009] Libraries Tasmania (RGD35/1/5 no 1219).
[2010] Libraries Tasmania (RGD33/1/9 Image 207 no 8767); *The Advertiser*, 19 January 1865; *The Mercury*, 27 November 1868.
[2011] *The Mercury*, 27, 28 November 1868.
[2012] *The Mercury*, 23 June, 1874.
[2013] *The Mercury*, 4 November 1871, 16 December 1872.
[2014] *The Tasmanian Tribune*, 16 December 1872; *The Tasmanian*, 21 December 1872.
[2015] *The Tasmanian*, 18 October 1873; *The Mercury*, 4 March 1874.
[2016] *Cornwall Chronicle*, 20 February 1874.
[2017] *The Mercury*, 23 February 1874.
[2018] *The Mercury*, 1 February 1873.
[2019] *The Mercury*, 11 June, 21, 26 November, 28 December 1874; *The Tasmanian Tribune*, 2 January 1875.
[2020] *The Mercury*, 23 June 1875.

Hobart Town's Domain ship and boat yards, also showing the Derwent Rowing Club's Clubhouse under construction (c1873). Courtesy Tasmanian Archives (NS6351/1/62).

A view towards Hobart Town's Glebe, showing Domain House (then known as High School of Hobart Town), in the vicinity of which Lark Macquarie established a boat yard in his backyard (c1860s).
Courtesy Tasmanian Archives (NS6904/1/84).

in early 1875, while several skiffs and gigs, including *Nemesis and Transit*, were launched by Macquarie in April 1875, built to race in Derwent Rowing Club events.[2021]

While a popular sport and pastime for several decades on the River Derwent, rowing in Tasmania was enjoying a period of more organised expansion and greater patronage during the mid-1870s, helped by the establishment of several rowing clubs, particularly the Derwent Rowing Club, as well as the introduction of school-based regattas, and the staging of specific events and races for rowers on local, regional and intercolonial waterways. The sport was also being aided by the introduction of new technologies, including sliding seats and outriggers, as well as lighter materials, all producing faster craft. Of course, spectator numbers also benefited from the wagers and shore-side bets that had always been a part of the races, in turn adding more appeal to the sport. It was certainly a pivotal time for Macquarie to be involved in the building and development of rowing gigs, skiffs and sculls and an area which he would soon capitalise, quickly becoming a local expert, leading to increased demand for his services.

Perhaps wanting to concentrate more on the construction of rowing, racing and smaller boats, as opposed to larger fishing and sailing craft, in early 1875 Macquarie established his own boat yard, operating out of his backyard, likely in the vicinity of Aberdeen and Edward streets, Glebe.

The Mercury reported, '*Mr. L. Macquarie, boatbuilder, who carries on operations in a yard attached to his house at the rear of the High School, has, during the past few months been very busily engaged on several species of racing boats. He recently forwarded to Launceston, for Messrs. Allan and Atkins, a pair-oared gig, measuring 28 feet in length, 3 feet 6 inches beam, and 9 inches deep. To the order of Mr. Westbrook, he has just completed a skiff constructed of cedar, in plans extending from stem to stern. This boat is very nicely finished inside. It measures 20 feet in length, 18 inches beam, 8 inches deep. He has also finished a four-oared boat similar to the Comet, built last year by Mr. Macquarie, but with a little more rise, which it is believed will improve her speed. Its length is 25 feet, depth 15 inches, beam 4 feet 1 inch. The interior of this boat is like a piece of joiner's work. A skiff measuring 20 feet in length, 8 inches deep, with a beam of 20 in., just requires the finishing touches. A pair-oared boat, outrigger, to be pulled at the next Derwent Rowing Club Regatta is also under-way. It measured 30ft. long, 9 in. deep, 2ft,*

[2021] *The Mercury*, 29 January, 26 April 1875; *The Tasmanian Tribune*, 1, 3 May 1875.

4 in. beam. The foregoing boats are built on the curved keel principle, which was introduced here by Mr. Macquarie. The Material used is cedar, copper-fastened. By the end of the current week Mr. Macquarie is expected to launch a centerboard sailing boat, built to the order of Messrs. Harold and Howard Wright. It measures 30ft. on the keel, 6ft. beam, 2ft. 2in. deep. It has a straight floor. The wood used is Huon pine, copper-fastened.'[2022] The latter mentioned vessel was the second-class sailing boat *Corsair*, which along with a handful of other racing craft, was completed in late 1875.[2023] A keen participant in the sport of rowing that was by now supporting his livelihood, Macquarie then travelled to Launceston where he and several of his boats successfully competed at the 1876 Tamar Regatta.[2024]

Perhaps needing more room and a site closer to the River Derwent, by May 1876 Lark Macquarie had relocated his boat yard to Battery Point where he was noted to be widening Messrs Wright's sailing boat *Corsair*.[2025] The yard was located on edge of the River Derwent near the Prince of Wales' Battery and was previously in the possession of the Derwent Iron Smelting Works, the Tasmanian Pyrolignite Company Ltd. and the Degraves family.[2026] The first craft he completed at the property was the 7-ton cutter yacht *Whirlwind*, built to the order of Harold and Howard Wright (repeat customers), as well as a four-oared gig and corresponding sculls shipped to New Zealand via the *Otago* in October 1876.[2027]

The *Whirlwind* was a successful yacht on the Derwent for many years, competing under the auspices of the Derwent Yacht Club. It was later owned by Messrs Davidson and Clark who in 1889 converted the vessel to a steam launch. The *Whirlwind* was sold again in 1896 and transferred to Launceston.[2028]

The next boat out of Macquarie's new premises at Battery Point was the *Chance*, built specifically to compete in the Champion Race for four-oared gigs at the Hobart Town Regatta of which it won handsomely, pulled by a crew from the Huon consisting of T. Bell, J. Bell, W. McLean and T. Bayes.[2029] For the same occasion, Macquarie built a one-plank gig of 43.5ft in length, aptly named *Macquarie*, that finished third in the race for the Ladies' Purse, pulled by J. Hibbard, G. Lloyd, J. Lloyd and H. Owen, as well as a 23ft skiff for E. Hely of Launceston that was intended to compete in the race for the Alexandra Prize, though was likely not ready in time.[2030] Named *Alabama*, the vessel first competed for the South Esk Purse at the Perth Regatta held in late December 1876, finishing a commendable third.[2031]

With his reputation for building prize-winning racing boats now firmly established, Lark Macquarie furnished more boats for local and regional regattas in the succeeding years. These included a 42ft four-oared gig constructed of American pine and built specifically to compete at the 1877 Tamar Regatta pulled by a representative crew from the Derwent Rowing Club.[2032] However, for reasons unknown, the crew appears to have instead raced in the *Chance*.[2033] At least four craft built by Macquarie did feature at this event: the skiffs *Chance*, *Cupid* and *Atalanta*, and the four-oared gig *Venus*.[2034] While the *Chance* and *Cupid* raced for the Tradesmen's Purse and the *Atalanta* for the Youth's Race, the *Venus* vied for the Miners' Purse.[2035] The boats were all freighted between Hobart Town and Launceston via train.[2036] These vessels were soon followed by a cedar racing skiff built for a Mr McEwan of Launceston and the yacht, *Mischief*, launched on 14 April 1877 to the order of Messrs Risby and Watchorn.[2037] The *Mischief* soon joined the Derwent Sailing Club's complement as did another yacht, the 34.5ft *Neva*, built by Macquarie and completed toward the end of November 1877.[2038]

While Macquarie built the *Neva* for his own use, successfully racing it with the Derwent Sailing Club and in local and regional regattas, by November 1878 it was

Whirlwind.
Weekly Courier, 23 January 1908.

[2022] *The Mercury*, 9 August 1875.
[2023] *The Mercury*, 14, 18 October, 6 November, 10 December 1875; *The Cornwall Chronicle*, 20 October 1875.
[2024] *Weekly Examiner*, 26 February, 4 March 1876; *The Cornwall Chronicle*, 1 March 1876; *Launceston Examiner*, 2 March 1876; *The Tasmanian*, 4 March 1876.
[2025] *The Tasmanian Tribune*, 11 May 1876.
[2026] *The Mercury*, 5 July 1873, 30 November 1875, 13 February 1877, 1 January 1886.
[2027] *The Tasmanian Tribune*, 11 May 1876; *The Mercury*, 28 October, 3 November 1876; *Tribune*, 7 November 1876.
[2028] *The Mercury*, 26 September 1887; *Launceston Examiner*, 19 March 1889, 10 November 1896.
[2029] *The Mercury*, 30 November 1876; *Launceston Examiner*, 14 December 1872.
[2030] *The Mercury*, 30 November, 13 December 1876.
[2031] *The Cornwall Chronicle*, 27 December 1876.
[2032] *The Mercury*, 10 January 1877.
[2033] *The Cornwall Chronicle*, 2 February 1877.
[2034] *Tribune*, 23 January, 2 February 1877; *Cornwall Advertiser*, 2 February 1877; *Launceston Examiner*, 3 February 1877.
[2035] *Tribune*, 2 February 1877; *Launceston Examiner*, 3 February 1877.
[2036] *Tribune*, 3 February 1877.
[2037] *Launceston Examiner*, 8 March 1877; *Tribune*, 17 April 1877.
[2038] *The Mercury*, 26 September, 27 November 1877; *Launceston Examiner*, 6 December 1877.

owned by William Lucas (later shipbuilder of Battery Point) in partnership with R. R. Rex.[2039] The yacht was sold five years later to a Mr Olson of Cooktown, Queensland, with the intention of employing it in the pearling industry.[2040] In a sensational turn of events, however, its new owner turned out to be the Weiberg brothers, notorious gold robbers from Avoca, Victoria.[2041] The pair sailed the craft from Hobart to Melbourne and shortly thereafter one of the brothers disappeared.[2042] The *Neva* was subsequently advertised for sale, remaining active in Victorian yachting circles for several years.[2043]

Notably also built by Macquarie late in 1877 was a 42ft four-oared gig built at a cost of £30 to the order of the Derwent Rowing Club.[2044] It was shipped to Sydney per the *Tasman*, along with its crew, and raced at the Balmain Regatta held in Sydney in November 1877.[2045] The intercolonial race for the Gardiner Challenge Cup, featuring two representative boats from the Sydney Rowing Club, as well as the Tasmanians, was a highlight of the New South Wales rowing calendar, indicative of the fact that the Tasmania crew were met on their arrival in Sydney by '*some fifty or sixty of the Sydney oarsmen in the most cordial manner*'.[2046] The Tasmanians finished a commendable third in the event, only half a length behind the winner, returning to Hobart Town with much fanfare and congratulations.[2047] The gig was shortly thereafter raffled off with tickets costing 10 shillings, it being won by the Mayor of Hobart Town, the Hon. John Perkins who subsequently donated it to the Hobart Town Regatta Committee who then sold it back to Macquarie for £20.[2048]

The year 1877 also coincided with completion by Macquarie of the four-oared gig *Phoenix*, raced by a crew from Hobart Town for the Ladies' Purse at the 1878 Tamar Regatta, a similar craft (named *Alabama No. 2*) for a Launceston-based crew to compete in the same race; and several racing skiffs, including one for a Mr Horne from Launceston, one for a Mr Clark of New Norfolk, and others named *Northern Light*, *Vixen*, and *Princess*; as well as the skiff *Fleetwing* which competed at the Perth Regatta held in late December 1877.[2049]

In April 1878 Macquarie launched a 17ft Huon pine pleasure boat to the order of W. C. Prentis of Battery Point.[2050] Except for two pair-oared racing skiffs sent to Launceston and a 23ft pleasure boat built on speculation, there are no known vessels built by Macquarie between this time and early 1879, perhaps owing to the fact that his 30-year-old younger brother Hugh was seriously ill.[2051] Though he had been living in Launceston for a number of years, he died on 1 December 1878 at Macquarie's home, situated on the corner of Hampden Road and Castray Esplanade.[2052] Cause of death was bowel cancer.[2053] Hugh left behind his wife Annie and four children.[2054]

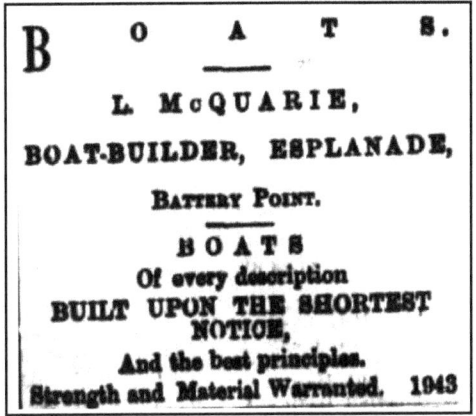

Tribune, 19 April 1878.

Returning to work, Macquarie built two four-oared gigs to compete for the Ladies' Purse at the 1879 Hobart Town Regatta. These were the *Laura*, pulled by D. Lewis, E. Creswell, R. Wing and E. Buchanan, and the *Vivandiere*, pulled by G. Lloyd, J. Lloyd, A. Cane and E. Pearce.[2055] The highly popular race was won by the latter.[2056] A 30ft wager boat named *Isabel* was then built by Macquarie to the order of G. Lloyd specifically to compete for the Weld Purse at the 1879 Tamar Regatta, the first of its type reportedly built in colony.[2057] The craft was fitted with steel outriggers and reportedly weighed just 30 pounds.[2058] Next came two four-oared Huon pine training gigs of 32ft built to the order of the Tamar Rowing Club; the *Countess* and *Empress*, a pair of skiffs built for two members of the Derwent Rowing Club (F. Shanley and W. J. Dobbie); and two four-oared gigs built to the order of this same organisation.[2059] Disappointingly, the second of the Tamar Rowing Club's training gigs was all but smashed to pieces after falling from the roof of the train carriage it was secured to while en route to Launceston.[2060] Upon receiving the vessel back in Hobart Town, Macquarie soon set about repairing the boat, producing a nearly-new gig.[2061] Fortunately, the press reported a few months later that the '*two gigs built by Mr Macquarie of Hobart Town, at a cost of £58, were a decided success, and answered the requirements of the Club most satisfactorily, and had a good deal to do with the largely increased list of members*'.[2062] In

---

[2039] *The Mercury*, 11 November 1878, 20 February 1883.
[2040] *Launceston Examiner*, 5 October 1883.
[2041] *Launceston Examiner*, 1 December 1883; *The Mercury*, 12 December 1883.
[2042] *Launceston Examiner*, 1 December 1883.
[2043] *The Mercury*, 12 December 1883, 1 May 1886.
[2044] *Tribune*, 3 September 1877; *The Mercury*, 26 September, 1 October 1877.
[2045] *The Mercury*, 9 November 1877.
[2046] *The Mercury*, 9 November 1877.
[2047] *Launceston Examiner*, 13 November 1877; *The Mercury*, 13 November 1877.
[2048] *The Mercury*, 23, 26, 27 November 1877.
[2049] *Tribune*, 1 October 1877; *The Mercury*, 26, 27 November 1877, 24 January 1878.
[2050] *Tribune*, 30 April 1878.
[2051] *Launceston Examiner*, 31 August 1878; *Tribune*, 19 November 1878.
[2052] *The Mercury*, 2 December 1878.
[2053] Libraries Tasmania (RGD35/1/9 no 1525).
[2054] Macquarie family tree via ancestry.com.au.
[2055] *The Mercury*, 28, 31 January 1879.
[2056] *The Mercury*, 5 February 1879.
[2057] *The Tasmanian*, 22 February 1879; *The Mercury*, 19, 26 February 1879.
[2058] *The Tasmanian*, 22 February 1879.
[2059] *The Mercury*, 15 October, 18, 26 November 1879, 28 January, 14 August 1880; *The Tasmanian*, 8 November 1879.
[2060] *The Mercury*, 25 December 1879.
[2061] *The Cornwall Chronicle*, 24 December 1879.
[2062] *Launceston Examiner*, 9 September 1880.

consequence, Macquarie received another large order from the Tamar Rowing Club, this time for two 26ft pair-oared string test practice boats and two open clinker outrigger skiffs.[2063] Shortly thereafter he built two 42ft gigs (*Tamar* and *Fireflash*) specifically for racing in the Ladies' Purse at the 1881 Hobart Regatta, a 33ft pair-oared gig to race at the 1881 Tamar Regatta, and two skiffs for the Derwent Rowing Club.[2064] Two additional practice skiffs for the Derwent Rowing Club, as well as four cedar wager boats were also completed by Macquarie in July 1881.[2065] The following year Macquarie completed a cedar batswing skiff of 33ft named *Derwent* that was rowed by Sharland and Stuart at the 1882 Tamar Regatta, as well as a cedar wager skiff for the same event; and an 18ft practice skiff built for the Bellerive Rowing Club.[2066]

Macquarie was certainly capitalising on the growing sport of rowing and the increasing membership of rowing clubs around Tasmania. He was also noted as regularly overhauling and repairing these craft, in addition to building new ones.[2067] By the early 1880s, Macquarie was definitely the most high-profile builder of this type of craft in Tasmania.

Non-racing boats were also built by Lark Macquarie at Battery Point during the late 1870s and into the early 1880s. These included a small 14ft Huon pine pleasure boat built to the order of a Mr Hume in April 1879; a 16ft Huon pine pleasure boat completed in June 1879; a 33ft five-oared whaleboat built of Tasmanian endemic timbers for display at the Sydney International Exposition, held between September 1879 and April 1880; a 15ft Huon pine pleasure boat, referred to as a *'whaleboat dinghy'*, built to the order of a *'gentleman well-known in aquatic circles'*; a 23ft Huon pine ferry boat built commissioned by Samuel Jacobs, waterman of Hobart Town; a 16ft Huon pine gig built to the order of a gentleman from Glenelg, South Australia, for recreational purposes; a 33ft five-oared whaleboat built for display at the Melbourne International Exhibition held in 1880; a 16ft sailing boat to the order of a Mr Morris of Hobart Town; a pleasure boat for a client based at Bicheno; a dinghy built to the order of a Mr Castray; and a 33ft fishing boat launched in September 1881 to the order of Martin Brothers.[2068]

Lark Macquarie's whaleboats built on behalf of the Government of Tasmania for display at the Sydney and Melbourne International Exhibitions earned him much praise and admiration both locally and interstate. At the Sydney Exhibition his workmanship was noted by the judges such that he was awarded the very prestigious prize of a First Class Medal.[2069] Similarly, Macquarie received a First Class Award and a silver medal for the five-oared whaleboat he exhibited at the Melbourne International Exhibition.[2070] Ironically, the boat built for the Sydney Exhibition nearly didn't make it out of Macquarie's boat yard when an attempt was made in mid-August 1879 to burn down the shed in which it was being readied. Fortunately Macquarie's mother noticed the fire and it was quickly extinguished before much damage could be done.[2071]

In September 1882 Lark Macquarie left Hobart as a passenger on board the steamer *Amy*, headed for Tasmania's west coast.[2072] He was one of a number of prospectors that disembarked at Trial Harbour with the hope of finding tin in and around the Mount Bischoff and Corinna regions.[2073] It is not known whether Macquarie found what he was looking for, though he returned to Hobart via the ketch *Coral* in early November having boarded this particular vessel at Port Davey, indicating that he had managed to walk and/or find sea transport to traverse the 100-mile distance between the two remote locations.[2074]

Macquarie resumed work at his Battery Point boat yard a few months later. Vessels that he built between September 1882 and early 1883 included an 18ft square-sterned pleasure boat intended for river excursions; a gig for the Derwent Rowing Club specifically to race for the Ladies' Purse at the 1883 Hobart Regatta; and a string test gig built to the order of the Tamar Rowing Club to compete for the Ladies' Purse at the 1883 Tamar Regatta.[2075]

In April 1884 Lark Macquarie completed the 35ft Huon pine fishing boat *Chance*, built to the order of John Martin.[2076] Later that year he built two four-oared boats for the newly-formed Mercantile Rowing Club who were using a shed at his boat yard as a temporary club room. These were likely some of the last vessels built by Macquarie at Battery Point. In May of the following year he auctioned off his household furniture and effects and most of the racing boats in his possession, including a four-oared boat recently built.[2077] All up, at least seven boats were sold, many for prices well below expectation, indicating a decrease in local demand for this type of vessel.[2078]

It was likely that Macquarie opted to vacate his boat yard owing to executors of John Degraves' estate looking to end the lease and sell the property, along with two adjoining allotments.[2079] The fact that the Hobart City Council's newly appointed Building Surveyor condemned a residence within the bounds of

---

[2063] *The Mercury*, 19 October 1880.
[2064] *The Mercury*, 5, 9, 23 February, 4 June 1881.
[2065] *The Mercury*, 15 April, 21 July 1881, 15 July 1882.
[2066] *The Mercury*, 15 July, 8 September 1882; *Launceston Examiner*, 10 March 1882, 24, 28 February 1883.
[2067] *The Mercury*, 22 February 1877, 14 August 1880; *The Tasmanian*, 20 January 1883.
[2068] *The Mercury*, 12, 17 April, 7, 10 June, 1 September, 15 October 1879, 24 April, 1, 26 July, 4 August 1880, 15 April, 4 June, 16 September 1881; *Launceston Examiner*, 21 July 1880; en.wikipedia.org/wiki/Sydney_International_Exhibition.
[2069] *Launceston Examiner*, 30 June 1880.
[2070] *Launceston Examiner*, 12 February, 17 May 1881.
[2071] *Devon Herald*, 16 August 1879; *The Mercury*, 1 September 1879.
[2072] *Launceston Examiner*, 23 September 1881.
[2073] *Launceston Examiner*, 23 September 1881.
[2074] *The Mercury*, 3 November 1881.
[2075] *The Mercury*, 2 March, 8 September 1882; *Launceston Examiner*, 10 March 1882, 23 January 24, 28 February 1883.
[2076] *Launceston Examiner*, 28 April 1884.
[2077] *The Mercury*, 12, 15 May 1885.
[2078] *The Mercury*, 15 May 1885.
[2079] *The Mercury*, 24 April 1888; www.thelist.tas.gov.au (Historical Deeds 08/0705, 08/0706 and 08/0707).

The Tasmanian Court at the 1881 Melbourne International Exhibition showing Lachlan Macquarie's whaleboat. Courtesy Robert Dowling (Artist), Ludovico Hart (Photographer), Museums Victoria (collections.museumsvictoria.com.au/items/1563121).

the boat yard during this year may have also influenced the decision of the lawyers.[2080] While the stone house containing two rooms had been tenanted by *'four or five inmates'*, it was in a serious state of decay such that it was fortunately vacated only weeks before its was partially destroyed during a wind storm.[2081]

The Mercury, 12 May 1885.

While Macquarie was certainly in the process of selling his tools and effects, he managed to turn out a few more vessels. These included a short-four completed in December 1885 for one of the local rowing clubs to compete in the forthcoming regatta.[2082] He very likely vacated his Battery Point boat yard a few weeks later.

Without a yard of his own and with limited family to support, perhaps only his mother, Lark Macquarie spent the next two decades travelling Tasmania building various vessels and undertaking repair work for numerous rowing clubs.[2083] For example, in April 1886 he was noted as 'caretaker' of the Derwent Rowing Club, operating out of the organisation's sheds at Hobart's Domain where he was involved in the repair, overhaul, maintenance and fine-tuning of racing boats.[2084] Later that year Macquarie was tasked with repairing the Mercantile Rowing Club's suite of boats.[2085] In 1888 he assisted Richard Stone with the *Lil* (later named *Mistral*), a 28ft yacht built at Long Bay near Port Arthur.[2086] In 1889 and 1890 he built two rowing boats to the order of George Nation, a renowned sculler from the Huon, the latter to compete in the Tasmanian Sculling Championships.[2087] 1889 also coincided with Macquarie building a cedar racing boat at Nubeena for competing in forthcoming regattas, pulled by a crew from the Tasman Peninsula, while the following year Macquarie was noted as building several new racing boats for the Mercantile Rowing Club.[2088]

In 1892 Lark Macquarie was operating out of a boat yard in Campbell Street, Hobart.[2089] Here he completed a fishing boat to the order of Louis Smith that had been designed and partly laid down by the late J. Mazey.[2090] The 37ft vessel named *Glenloth* was wrecked in January 1901 at Maria Island.[2091]

By 1894 Macquarie had temporarily moved back to the Tasman Peninsula where he helped build a fishing boat to the order of Edward Noye.[2092] Another fishing boat, the *Ethel May*, was built by Macquarie at Nubeena in 1896, also to the order of Edward Noye.[2093] In addition, four first class boats were constructed by Macquarie towards the end of the nineteenth century, all to the order of the Nubeena Rowing Club.[2094] 1896 additionally coincided with Macquarie travelling to Tasmania's far south-west to prospect.[2095] It may have been during this adventure or a subsequent one that he was credited as first finding tin near Point Eric in the vicinity of Cox Bight.[2096]

Several more boats were built by Macquarie in and around Hobart in the intervening years. These included a racing four for the Hobart Rowing Club and a boat for the Derwent Rowing Club, both constructed in 1898.[2097]

Macquarie likely led somewhat of a nomadic existence into the early years of the twentieth century, prospecting in various regions of Tasmania's south-west and crewing on board local fishing craft. One such experience he became well known for. On 9 February 1905 Lark Macquarie joined Edward Noye and T. Pretty on the fishing boat *Britannia* for a voyage to Tasmania's west coast in search of the ill-fated iron barque *Brier Holme* which had been lost en route from London several months earlier.[2098] The trio miraculously succeeded in locating the only survivor of the wreck, a 29-year-old seaman named Oscar Larsen, who had spent more than three months stranded near Port Davey.[2099] Returning to Hobart with Larsen on board the *Britannia*, the three men were celebrated in the Tasmanian press for not only having found Larsen, but subsequently, the wreck of the *Brier Holme*, when several previous searches of the area had failed.[2100]

[2080] *The Mercury*, 18 March, 9 December 1885.
[2081] *The Mercury*, 18, 25 March 1885.
[2082] *The Mercury*, 15 December 1885.
[2083] *The Mercury*, 7 October 1886.
[2084] *The Mercury*, 7, 12 April 1886.
[2085] *The Mercury*, 7 October 1886.
[2086] *Tasmanian News*, 23 January 1888; *The Mercury*, 15 November 1892.
[2087] *Launceston Examiner*, 16 May 1889, 5, 10 April 1890.
[2088] *The Mercury*, 28 October 1889; *The Colonist*, 16 August 1890.
[2089] *The Mercury*, 11 October 1892.
[2090] *Tasmanian News*, 7 November 1892; *The Mercury*, 10, 11 October 1892.
[2091] *The Mercury*, 23 January 1901.
[2092] *The Mercury*, 24 May 1894, 13 March 1909.
[2093] G. Broxam & M. Nash (2013). *Tasmanian Shipwrecks. Volume 2: 1900 - 2012*.
[2094] *The Mercury*, 27 October 1892.
[2095] *Tasmanian News*, 6 November 1896.
[2096] *Examiner*, 14 January 1907.
[2097] *The Mercury*, 28 October 1898; *Tasmanian News*, 4 November 1898.
[2098] *The Mercury*, 21 February 1905; G. Broxam & M. Nash (2013). *Tasmanian Shipwrecks. Volume 2: 1900 - 2012*.
[2099] *The Mercury*, 21 February 1905; G. Broxam & M. Nash (2013). *Tasmanian Shipwrecks. Volume 2: 1900 - 2012*.
[2100] *The Mercury*, 21 February 1905; G. Broxam & M. Nash (2013). *Tasmanian Shipwrecks. Volume 2: 1900 - 2012*.

The fishing boat *Britannia* sailing up the River Derwent in February 1905 with Oscar Larsen, the sole survivor of the wreck of the *Brier Holme* on board. Also on board were Edward Noye, T. Pretty and Lark Macquarie.
Courtesy Tasmanian Archives (PH30/1/5701).
Inset: Likely a photo of Lark Macquarie on board the *Britannia* after docking at Hobart.
Weekly Courier, 25 February 1905.

Lark Macquarie died on 20 August 1907 at Melton Mowbray in the Tasmanian midlands at the age of 62.[2101] He is supposed to have disappeared while prospecting for gold, with his niece Alice Newall (nee Macquarie) contacting the police when he failed to return.[2102] Macquarie was buried, along with other members of his family, at Queenborough Cemetery, Sandy Bay.[2103] He never married and had no children.

PERSONS ENQUIRED FOR.

SOUTHERN DISTRICT (HOBART).—Enquiry is requested as to the whereabouts of *Lachlan Macquarie*, a retired boatbuilder, who has been missing from his home, No. 4 Hamilton-street, since the 29th ultimo. Description: Age about 60 years, height about 5 feet 7 inches, very active and erect, grey hair and full grey beard, ruddy complexion; dressed in grey tweed suit and brown cap; has a serious impediment in his speech; has a mania for collecting curios in the shape of natural walking-sticks. Enquiry at the instance of his niece, Mrs. Alice Newall.

Tasmanian Police Gazette, 5 July 1907.

Born on the tiny island of Ulva, Scotland, and emigrating to Tasmania as a young child, Lachlan 'Lark' Macquarie spent most of his career concentrating on the building of gigs, skiffs and other racing boats and was one of only a few builders in the colony to excel at this type of craft. His involvement with rowing clubs and regatta racing was propitious as it came at a time when scull races and formal rowing clubs were being established and demand for vessels was high. Macquarie was also a leader of his trade, being the first to build certain types of vessels in Tasmania and, in some cases, introduce new components and design improvements, such as reduced weight. His skill and craftsmanship also saw him achieve success nationally. He was awarded several coveted prizes at international exhibitions held in Sydney and Melbourne. He operated a boat yard near Castray Esplanade, Battery Point, leased from the estate of the Degraves family, between the years 1876 and 1885.

[2101] Libraries Tasmania (NAME_INDEXES:1990027).
[2102] *Tasmanian News*, 1 July 1907; *Tasmanian Police Gazette*, 5 July 1907.
[2103] Australian Cemetery Index, 1808-2007.

Vessels built by Lachlan Macquarie and employees at Battery Point (1876 - 1885)

Year	Name	Type	Description
1876	Whirlwind	Yacht	32 x 9 x 2.8ft. 7 tons. Cutter-rigged yacht built by Lachlan Macquarie to the order of Harold and Howard Wright specifically to compete with the Derwent Yacht Club. A successful yacht on the Derwent for many years. Later owned by Messrs Davidson and Clark who in 1889 converted it to a steam launch. Advertised for sale in July 1896 and transferred to Launceston. Subsequent fate not known.
1876	--	Gig	Four-oared racing gig and sculls built by Lachlan Macquarie and shipped to New Zealand per the *Otago* in October 1876.
1876	Chance	Gig	Four-oared racing gig built by Lachlan Macquarie. Won the Champion Race for four-oared boats at the 1876 Hobart Town Regatta, pulled by a crew from the Huon consisting of J. Bell, W. McLaren, T. Bayes and T. Bell.
1876	Macquarie	Gig	43.6ft. One-plank gig built by Lachlan Macquarie to compete for the Ladies' Purse at the 1876 Hobart Town Regatta. Finished third in the event, pulled by a crew consisting of J. Hibbard, G. Lloyd, J. Lloyd and H. Owen.
1876	Alabama	Skiff	23ft. Built to the order of E. Hely of Launceston to compete for the Alexandra Prize at the 1876 Hobart Town Regatta, though withdrew from the race. Competed in the race for the South Esk Purse, finishing third, at the Perth Regatta held in late December 1876.
1877	--	Gig	42 x 4ft x 9in. Four-oared racing gig built by Lachlan Macquarie to compete at the 1877 Tamar Regatta pulled by a representative crew from the Derwent Rowing Club. Appears not to have been used in the race, the crew instead pulling in the *Chance*.
1877	Chance	Skiff	Racing skiff built by Lachlan Macquarie that first competed for the Tradesmen's Purse at the 1877 Tamar Regatta.
1877	Cupid	Skiff	Racing skiff built by Lachlan Macquarie that first competed for the Tradesmen's Purse at the 1877 Tamar Regatta.
1877	Atalanta	Skiff	Racing skiff built by Lachlan Macquarie that first competed in the Youth's Race at the 1877 Tamar Regatta.
1877	Venus	Gig	Four-oared racing gig built by Lachlan Macquarie that first competed in the race for the Miners' Purse at the 1877 Tamar Regatta.
1877	--	Skiff	Cedar racing skiff built by Lachlan Macquarie to the order of a Mr McEwan of Launceston.
1877	Mischief	Yacht	24ft. 4 tons. Cutter-rigged yacht built by Lachlan Macquarie to the order of Messrs Risby and Watchorn specifically to compete with the Derwent Yacht Club. Launched on 14 April 1877. Sunk during a race in October 1877 after being struck by a squall, all hands saved. Recovered after several attempts and repaired. Raced on the Derwent for several more seasons.
1877	Sea Queen ex Neva	Yacht	34.5 x 9.1 x 3.2ft. 8 tons. Huon pine yacht built by Lachlan Macquarie for his own use specifically to compete in Derwent Yacht Club events and in local and regional regattas. Launched in late November 1877. By November 1878 owned by William Lucas in partnership with R. R. Rex. Sold five years later to a Mr Olson of Cooktown, Queensland, with the intention of employing it in the pearling industry. In a sensational turn of events, its new owner turned out to be the Weiberg brothers, notorious gold robbers from Avoca, Victoria. The pair sailed the craft from Hobart to Melbourne and shortly thereafter one of the brothers disappeared. The *Neva* was subsequently advertised for sale, remaining active in Victorian yachting circles for several years under the name of *Sea Queen*. Last noted when advertised for sale in April 1892.
1877	--	Gig	42ft. Racing gig built by Lachlan Macquarie to be crewed by a representative crew from Hobart Town and compete at the 1877 Intercolonial Regatta, held in Balmain, New South Wales, where it finished third. Returned to Hobart Town and raffled off with tickets costing 10 shillings, it being won by the Mayor Hobart Town, the Hon. John Perkins who subsequently donated it to the Hobart Town Regatta Committee. It was then sold back to Macquarie for £20.
1877	Phoenix	Gig	Four-oared racing gig built by Lachlan Macquarie to be pulled by a crew from Hobart Town to compete at the 1878 Tamar Regatta.
1877	--	Skiff	Racing skiff built by Lachlan Macquarie to the order of a Mr Horne of Launceston.
1877	--	Skiff	Racing skiff built by Lachlan Macquarie to the order of a Mr Clark of New Norfolk.
1877	Fleetwing	Skiff	Racing skiff built by Lachlan Macquarie that is first noted competing at the Perth Regatta held in late December 1877.
1877	Alabama No. 2	Gig	Racing gig built by Lachlan Macquarie to be pulled by a crew from Launceston to compete for the Ladies' Purse at the 1878 Tamar Regatta.
1877	Northern Light	Skiff	Racing skiff built by Lachlan Macquarie that first competed at the 1878 Tamar Regatta.
1877	Vixen	Skiff	Racing skiff built by Lachlan Macquarie that first competed at the 1878 Tamar Regatta.
1877	Princess	Skiff	Racing skiff built by Lachlan Macquarie that first competed at the 1878 Tamar Regatta.

Year	Name	Type	Description
1878	–	Boat	17ft. Huon pine pleasure boat built by Lachlan Macquarie to the order of W. C. Prentis of Battery Point and launched in April 1878. Fitted with a centreboard with sails made by Messers Bain and Dale.
1878	–	Skiff	Pair-oared cedar racing skiff built by Lachlan Macquarie to the order of C. Bain and T. Thompson of Launceston. Shipped to the Tamar region in August 1878.
1878	–	Skiff	Pair-oared cedar racing skiff built by Lachlan Macquarie to the order of a Mr Lambert of Launceston. Shipped to the Tamar region in August 1878.
1878	–	Pleasure boat	23 x 5.5ft. Built by Lachlan Macquarie of Pieman River pine on speculation. Completed in November 1878.
1879	Laura	Gig	Four-oared racing gig built by Lachlan Macquarie and pulled by a crew comprising D. Lewis, E. Creswell, R. Wing and E. Buchanan in the race for the Ladies' Purse at the 1879 Hobart Town Regatta.
1879	Vivandiere	Gig	Four-oared racing gig built by Lachlan Macquarie and pulled by a crew comprising G. Lloyd, J. Lloyd, A. Cane and E. Pearce in the race for the Ladies' Purse at the 1879 Hobart Town Regatta.
1879	Isabel	Wager skiff	30ft wager skiff built by Lachlan Macquarie to the order of G. Lloyd specifically to compete for the Weld Purse at the 1879 Tamar Regatta. Fitted with steel outriggers and reportedly weighed only 30 pounds.
1879	–	Pleasure boat	14 x 5ft x 18in. Built by Lachlan Macquarie to the order of a Mr Hume. Huon pine construction, cutter-rigged.
1879	–	Pleasure boat	16 x 5.6ft x 21in. Huon pine, copper-fastened pleasure boat built by Lachlan Macquarie and completed in June 1879.
1879	–	Whaleboat	33 x 5.4ft x 23.5in. Five-oared whaleboat built by Lachlan Macquarie of Tasmanian endemic timbers to the order of the Government of Tasmania for display at the Sydney International Exposition held between September 1879 and April 1880. Clear varnished and copper-fastened.
1879	–	Whaleboat	15 x 4.2ft x 21in. Centreboard pleasure boat known as a 'whaleboat dinghy' built by Lachlan Macquarie to the order of a *gentleman well-known in aquatic circles*. Huon pine with cedar mouldings and copper-fastened.
1879	–	Gig	32 x 3.6ft x 16in. First of two four-oared training gigs built by Lachlan Macquarie to the order of the Tamar Rowing Club. Fitted with swivel rowlocks, shifting stretchers and sliding steel seats. Built of Huon pine and copper-fastened.
1879	–	Gig	32 x 3.6ft x 16in. Second of two four-oared training gigs built by Lachlan Macquarie to the order of the Tamar Rowing Club. Fitted with swivel rowlocks, shifting stretchers and sliding steel seats. Built of Huon pine and copper-fastened. Nearly destroyed after being blown from the top of the carriage of the train it was secured to while en route to Launceston. Returned to Macquarie with repairs effected, resulting in a nearly-new boat.
1879	Empress	Skiff	Built by Lachlan Macquarie to the order of W. J. Dobbie, a member of the Derwent Rowing Club to compete at the 1880 Hobart Town Regatta.
1879	Countess	Skiff	Built by Lachlan Macquarie to the order of F. Shanley, a member of the Derwent Rowing Club to compete at the 1880 Hobart Town Regatta.
1880	–	Ferry boat	23 x 4.8ft x 19in. Huon pine ferry boat built by Lachlan Macquarie to the order of Samuel Jacobs, waterman of Hobart Town.
1880	–	Whaleboat	33ft. Five-oared whaleboat built by Lachlan Macquarie of Tasmanian endemic timbers to the order of the Government of Tasmania for display at the Melbourne International Exposition held between October 1880 and April 1881.
1880	–	Gig	16 x 5.1 x 2ft. Huon pine gig built for pleasure purposes by Lachlan Macquarie to the order of a Mr Chapman of Glenelg, South Australia.
1880	–	Gig	20 x 3.8ft x 16in. First of two four-oared gigs built by Lachlan Macquarie to the order of the Derwent Rowing Club. Fitted with swivel rowlocks, shifting stretchers and sliding steel seats. Built of Huon pine and copper-fastened.
1880	–	Gig	20 x 3.8ft x 16in. Second of two four-oared gigs built by Lachlan Macquarie to the order of the Derwent Rowing Club. Fitted with swivel rowlocks, shifting stretchers and sliding steel seats. Built of Huon pine and copper-fastened.
1880	–	Gig	26 x 3.2ft x 13in. First of two pair-oared string test practice gigs built by Lachlan Macquarie to the order of the Tamar Rowing Club.
1880	–	Gig	26 x 3.2ft x 13in. Second of two pair-oared string test practice gigs built by Lachlan Macquarie to the order of the Tamar Rowing Club.
1880	–	Skiff	First of two open clinker outrigger skiffs built by Lachlan Macquarie to the order of the Tamar Rowing Club.

Year	Name	Type	Description
1880	--	Skiff	Second of two open clinker outrigger skiffs built by Lachlan Macquarie to the order of the Tamar Rowing Club.
1881	*Fireflash*	Gig	42 x 3ft x 16in. Built by Lachlan Macquarie and raced by A. Stuart for the Ladies Purse at the 1881 Hobart Town Regatta. Fitted with swivel rowlocks and sliding steel seats. Built of Huon pine and copper-fastened.
1881	*Tamar*	Gig	42 x 3ft x 16in. Built by Lachlan Macquarie and raced by a crew from Launceston for the Ladies Purse at the 1881 Hobart Town Regatta. Fitted with swivel rowlocks and sliding steel seats. Built of Huon pine and copper-fastened.
1881	--	Gig	33ft. Cedar pair-oared gig built by Lachlan Macquarie to compete at the 1881 Tamar Regatta. Fitted with swivel rowlocks and sliding seats.
1881	--	Sailing boat	16 x 5ft x 21.5in. Huon pine sailing boat built by Lachlan Macquarie to the order of a Mr Morris of Hobart Town. Fitted with a centreboard, lockers and benches. Copper-fastened.
1881	--	Skiff	First of two lightweight skiffs built by Lachlan Macquarie to the order of the Derwent Rowing Club.
1881	--	Skiff	Second of two lightweight skiffs built by Lachlan Macquarie to the order of the Derwent Rowing Club.
1881	--	Skiff	First of two practice skiffs built by Lachlan Macquarie to the order of the Derwent Rowing Club.
1881	--	Skiff	Second of two practice skiffs built by Lachlan Macquarie to the order of the Derwent Rowing Club.
1881	--	Dinghy	Built by Lachlan Macquarie to the order of a Mr Castray.
1881	--	Pleasure boat	Pleasure boat built by Lachlan Macquarie to the order of a client based at Bicheno.
1881	--	Fishing boat	33.7 x 7 x 2.8ft. 'Deep-heeled' fishing boat built by Lachlan Macquarie to the order of Martin Brothers and launched in September 1881.
1881	--	Wager skiff	First of four wager skiffs built by Lachlan Macquarie in mid-1881.
1881	--	Wager skiff	Second of four wager skiffs built by Lachlan Macquarie in mid-1881.
1881	--	Wager skiff	Third of four wager skiffs built by Lachlan Macquarie in mid-1881.
1881	--	Wager skiff	Fourth of four wager skiffs built by Lachlan Macquarie in mid-1881.
1882	*Derwent*	Wager skiff	33ft. Cedar batswing skiff built by Lachlan Macquarie to compete at the 1882 Tamar Regatta, rowed by Sharland and Stuart.
1882	--	Wager skiff	Cedar wager skiff built by Lachlan Macquarie to compete at the 1882 Tamar Regatta, rowed by Sharland.
1882	--	Skiff	Practice skiff built by Lachlan Macquarie to the order of the Bellerive Rowing Club.
1882	--	Pleasure boat	18 x 4.5ft x 19in. Cedar square-sterned pleasure boat built by Lachlan Macquarie and intended for river excursions. Likely built for the local waterman.
1883	--	Gig	Gig built by Lachlan Macquarie to the order of the Derwent Rowing Club. Competed for the Ladies' Purse at the 1883 Hobart Regatta.
1883	--	Gig	String test gig built by Lachlan Macquarie to the order of the Tamar Rowing Club. Competed for the Ladies' Purse at the 1883 Tamar Regatta.
1884	*Chance*	Fishing boat	35 x 8 x 2.8ft. Huon pine fishing boat built by Lachlan Macquarie to the order of John Martin. Launched on 20 April 1884, estimated to hold 40 5- 50 dozen fish. Finished second in the fishing boat race at the 1890 Hobart Regatta. Still owned by John Martin when a dinghy was stolen from the craft in June 1902. Advertised for sale in Hobart in August 1918. By 1927 owned by C. Chambers. By 1947 owned by John Coleman. Possibly the boat that went missing with all crew off the west coast of Tasmania in August 1958.
1884	--	Boat	First of two four-oared boats built by Lachlan Macquarie to the order of the Mercantile Rowing Club.
1884	--	Boat	Second of two four-oared boats built by Lachlan Macquarie to the order of the Mercantile Rowing Club.
1885	--	Boat	Four-oared boat built by Lachlan Macquarie. Advertised for sale in May 1885.
1885	--	Boat	Short-four boat built by Lachlan Macquarie for a local rowing club. Intended to be rowed in the upcoming regatta.

Robert Inches

> 'To Mr. Robert Inches, of Battery Point, the building of the new racer was entrusted, and right well has he carried out the work — the unanimous opinion being that she is a masterpiece in the art of yacht building, being well finished to the slightest detail — in fact, it is impossible to conceive better workmanship.'
>
> The Mercury, 5 November 1898.

Hailing from Tasmania's Huon region and the eldest son of Thomas Inches, celebrated shipbuilder of Shipwrights Point, Robert Inches learned the craft of shipbuilding from his father and in 1878 established his own yard at Battery Point. Considered one of the finest builders of his era, between 1882 and his death in 1904 Inches built at least 19 vessels, including nine yachts and five ketches. Of these, the five yachts he built to the order of F. N. Clarke of nearby Secheron House, the *Fairlie*, *Ailsa*, *Clutha*, *Fairlie II* and *Fairlie III*, were particularly noteworthy. Designed by William Fife (Jr) of Scotland, these craft were pioneers of the Tasmanian yachting landscape during the late 1890s and into the twentieth century. Remarkably at least three vessels built by Inches, the yachts *Fairlie II* and *Fairlie III*, and the steam yacht *Preana*, likely remain in existence.

Robert Inches was born on 4 March 1849 at Shipwrights Point on the Huon River, Van Diemen's Land, the second eldest and first son born to Thomas and Mary Inches, nee Garth.[2104] His father, Thomas, was born in the small rural village of Balbeggie on the outskirts of Perth, Scotland, in 1819, the fourth child of Robert Inches, a shoemaker, and his wife Ann, nee Reech.[2105] After learning the trade of shipbuilding through apprenticeship, Thomas Inches and his younger brother Robert successfully applied for free passage to Australia as bounty immigrants. The pair left Greenock in November 1841 per the *Marquis of Bute*, a relatively new vessel, along with 230 other bounty immigrants.[2106] Thomas was listed as 22 years of age while Robert was 19. Both were protestant and they could read and write.

While initially securing work in New South Wales, on 31 March 1843 Thomas Inches, along with fellow Scottish shipwright James McLaren, arrived in Hobart Town via the *City of Sydney*. The industrious duo were on a quest to find *'a river with an outlet to the sea for shipbuilding facilities'*.[2107] The pair, along with fellow Scottish shipbuilder Alexander Harley, soon established a yard at what would become known as Shipwrights Point on the Huon River, going on to become pioneers of shipbuilding in the region. The location was ideal for their operation, the nearby forests of Huon pine and blue gum offering much needed timber for the construction of vessels. The Huon River itself provided a suitable waterway with minimal tidal and extreme weather events thus allowing Thomas Inches and his colleagues to build craft on its banks. Though settlement of the region by Europeans was then in its infancy, and communication with Hobart Town was sporadic, they were pioneers of not only shipbuilding on the Huon but the region and its services more generally. Many

Robert Inches.
Weekly Courier, 4 June 1904.

[2104] Libraries Tasmania (RGD33/1/3/ no 1741); Inches family tree via ancestry.com.au.
[2105] Scotland, Select Births and Baptisms, 1564-1950 for Thomas Inches, son of Robert Inches and Ann Reech.
[2106] New South Wales, Australia, Assisted Immigrant Passenger Lists, 1828-1896 for Thomas and Robert Inches.
[2107] Libraries Tasmania (CB7/10/1/1 P23); *The Courier*, 31 March 1843; *The Mercury*, 6 April 1942.

of the schooners, ketches and barges they built over the following decades became the backbone of the local Huon River and D'Entrecasteaux Channel trade, as well as New Zealand's domestic trade. Vessels built by Thomas Inches and James McLaren, and to a lesser extent Alexander Harley, included the *Aeolus* (1843), *Caledonia* (1844), *Thistle* (1846), *Sarah Ann* (1850), *Huon* (1851) and *Rebecca* (1853).[2108]

On 29 July 1845, in Hobart Town, Thomas Inches married Mary Garth, the 18-year-old daughter of James Garth, who farmed and also operated a sawmill at the Huon.[2109] Two years later James McLaren married 16-year-old Eliza Adelaide Garth, another daughter of James Garth, thus Thomas Inches and James McLaren became related by marriage, as well as business partners.[2110] While their first vessel, the *Aeolus*, had been built on Crown land on the edge of the Huon River, somewhere between Little Flights Bay and Hospital Bay, within a few years of establishing themselves in the Huon, Inches and McLaren moved further up the river to the northern peninsula of Hospital Bay where it meets the Huon River.[2111] The area soon became known as Shipwrights Point, with Thomas Inches officially receiving a 50-acre land grant from the Government of Van Diemen's Land in 1848, though he had likely been established at the site for some time.[2112] A few years later, Thomas Inches sold 25 acres of this property to James McLaren, the two families thus becoming neighbours.[2113]

For Robert Inches, growing up in the Huon River region was likely rudimentary yet adventurous. Though Shipwrights Point was a buzz of activity with regards to the sourcing of timber and the building of vessels, there were few neighbours and it would be some years before a school was established. At the time of Robert Inches' birth in 1849, the only school was located at Franklin, some 10 kilometres up the Huon River. It is likely due to a lack of a school in the area that Thomas Inches held a meeting at his house at Shipwrights Point in June 1854 with the goal of '*taking the necessary steps to establish a Public School*' for children residing in Hospital Bay, Shipwrights Point and Castle Forbes Bay.[2114] With attendees initially subscribing £60 a year to the cause, to go towards wages for a schoolmaster, as well as offering a school room and residence at moderate rental, it was estimated that between 20 and 30 children would attend the school, each paying additional fees for tuition.[2115] However, it would be some years before the school became established.[2116] In the meantime, it is not known if Robert Inches and his brothers and sisters, as well as their cousins on the McLaren side, ventured daily to school in Franklin or were educated by their parents, all of whom could read and write.

While shipbuilding constituted one avenue of employment for Thomas Inches, to support his growing family he also established a farm at Shipwrights Point, helped in part by further land grants of 200 and 400 acres received in 1852 and 1856, respectively.[2117] He was also noted as leasing 500 acres of land in the Huon from 1853 specifically for grazing purposes.[2118] Over the coming years and decades Thomas Inches would sell off parts of these grants, as well as purchase additional properties, primarily in the Huon region.[2119] He also leased off portions. In April 1858, for example, it was noted that in reference to his farms at the Huon, '*Three years ago it was a dense forest. There are now upon it more than 20 families; and, after a careful personal inspection of the now nearly matured crops, we cannot estimate the supply of potatoes to our market from that farm alone, for the present season, at less than 900 tons of the finest sample of this precious vegetable we have ever seen. On many of these little farms the produce per acres will be at least 12 to 14 tons*'.[2120]

However, the need to provide an education for his family may have been why Thomas Inches advertised his Shipwrights Point homestead situated on 25 acres of land for rent in March 1857, and ultimately for sale in November of that year.[2121] Likely gaining income through the sublet of his farming property to multiple small farming tenants, he subsequently moved his family to the very respectable location of Holbrook Place (now Upper Davey Street) in Hobart Town.[2122] Originally granted to Robert McCracken and situated on the corner of Davey and Anglesea streets, Thomas paid £450 for the parcel of land, comprising 3 roods and 15 perches.[2123] While later having built on it a very fine stone residence, that is still in existence today at 313 Davey Street, a photograph from the period during which Thomas Inches purchased the property shows a small cottage and several outbuildings on the site.

While Robert Inches, by now 8 years of age, and his siblings likely relished being near the excitement and bustle of Hobart Town, the move closer to medical care proved to be prophetic. It was in their home at Upper Davey Street that Mary Inches gave birth to twin boys in July 1859.[2124] These were the last two children born to Thomas Inches and his wife. Mary died just under three years later at their home of '*Continued fever*'.[2125] She was 35 years of age and described as a '*Gentleman's wife*'.[2126]

[2108] R. Parsons (1992). *Australian Shipowners and Their Fleets: Book Twelve* (Hobart to 1859 A - L); R. Parsons (1992). *Australian Shipowners and Their Fleets: Book Thirteen* (Hobart to 1859 M - Z); *The Hobart Town Advertiser*, 30 August 1844; *The Mercury*, 27 December 1865; *The Tasmanian Times*, 30 September 1869.
[2109] Libraries Tasmania (RGD37/1/4 no 1834, CEN1/1/43); www.thelist.tas.gov.au (Historical Deed 04/6588); *The Mercury*, 5 May 1921.
[2110] Libraries Tasmania (RGD37/1/6 no 957).
[2111] R. Woolley and W. Smith (2004). *A History of the Huon and Far South: Before the Orchards Grew*.
[2112] Libraries Tasmania (RD1/1 Book 23, page 88); www.thelist.tas.gov.au (Historical Deed 03/5873).
[2113] www.thelist.tas.gov.au (Historical Deed 03/5873).
[2114] *The Hobart Town Advertiser*, 22 June 1854.
[2115] *Colonial Times*, 19 July 1854.
[2116] *The Hobart Town Advertiser*, 20 June, 4 July 1855.
[2117] Libraries Tasmania (RD1/1 Book 33, page 30); www.thelist.tas.gov.au (Historical Deed 03/6830).
[2118] *Colonial Times*, 6 August 1863.
[2119] www.thelist.tas.gov.au/app/content/the-list/historic-deeds/index-files/1827-1926_IMS-INN.pdf.
[2120] *The Hobart Town Daily Mercury*, 9 April 1858.
[2121] *The Tasmanian Daily News*, 20 March 1857; *The Courier*, 16 November 1857.
[2122] *The Tasmanian Daily News*, 20 March 1857.
[2123] *The Courier*, 9 April 1858; www.thelist.tas.gov.au (Historical Deed 04/5695).
[2124] Libraries Tasmania (RGD33/1/7 no 2685 and RGD33/1/7 no 2684).
[2125] Libraries Tasmania (RGD35/1/6 no 3389).
[2126] Libraries Tasmania (RGD35/1/6 no 3389).

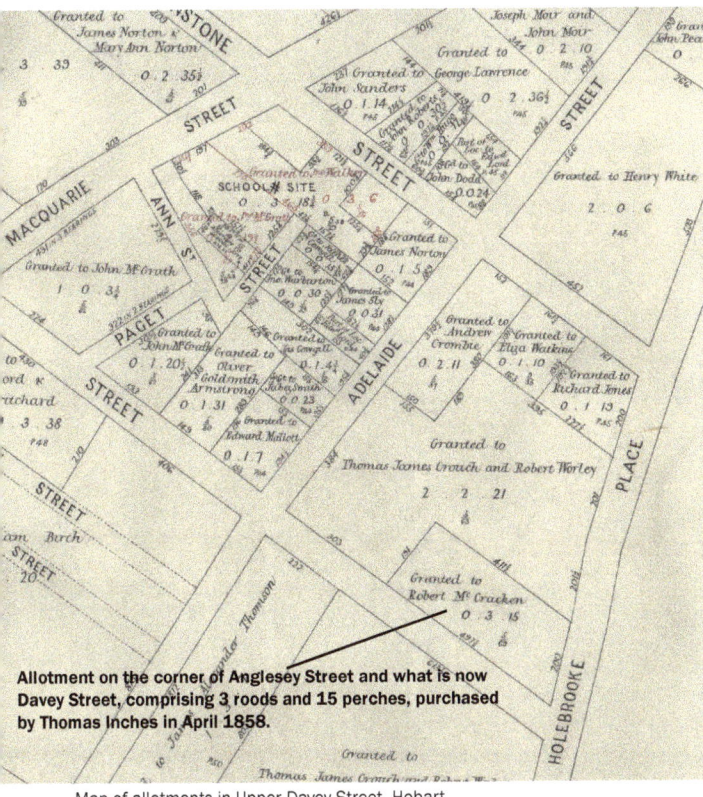

Allotment on the corner of Anglesey Street and what is now Davey Street, comprising 3 roods and 15 perches, purchased by Thomas Inches in April 1858.

Map of allotments in Upper Davey Street, Hobart.
Courtesy Tasmanian Archives (AF394/1/109).

Sadly, the couple had also lost a daughter during the interim. Their five-year-old daughter Clara had died of '*cancer in the mouth*' at Upper Davey Street in October 1860.[2127]

Widowed with seven children to care for between the ages of two and 15 years, Thomas Inches advertised his Upper Davey Street cottage for let and returned with his family to Shipwrights Point.[2128] Two years later, at the age of 45, he married 35-year-old Rebecca Blofield, the local school mistress.[2129] A daughter was born to the couple in April 1866, and another in September of the following year.[2130]

For Robert Inches, by now approaching his late teens, the move back to Shipwrights Point proved fortuitous in terms of his future career track. In addition to taking up management of his farm and various properties, Thomas Inches resumed shipbuilding in the Huon. Once more partnering with James McLaren, the pair built the 72ft barge *Crest of the Wave* for Messrs Armstrong and Gourlay, launched in June 1864.[2131] Next came the 56ft barge *Dashing Wave*, completed in December 1865 to the order of H. F. Armstrong.[2132] The

[2127] Libraries Tasmania (RGD35/1/6 no 2421).
[2128] *The Mercury*, 13 November, 15 December 1862.
[2129] *The Mercury*, 17 October 1862, 12 August 1864.
[2130] Libraries Tasmania (RGD33/1/44 no 471); *The Tasmanian Times*, 24 September 1867.
[2131] *The Mercury*, 3 June 1864.
[2132] *The Mercury*, 27 December 186.

Views of Upper Davey Street, Hobart, showing location of Thomas Inches' property.
The substantial stone residence, named Hillcrest, was built by James H. B. Walch in the 1870s.
Courtesy Tasmanian Archives (NS1013/1/535, inset: NS6904/1/61).

Shipwrights Point on the Huon River.
Courtesy Tasmanian Archives (PH40/1/1822).

following year saw Thomas Inches collaborate with another part-time shipbuilder of the Huon region, William Hawkins, who was also proprietor of the local store. The duo launched the 70ft barge *Fleetwing* from Shipwrights Point in February 1867.[2133] In November 1869 Thomas Inches completed the 67ft barge *Edith Alice*, built on speculation.[2134] Fifteen months later he launched the 90ft barge *Strathmore* intended for the South Australian coastal trade.[2135]

Following in his father's professional footsteps, Robert Inches learned the craft of shipbuilding at Shipwrights Point during this period. By the early 1870s he was working alongside his father and younger brother Thomas as 'Messrs Inches and Sons'.[2136] In October 1872 the trio launched the 80ft ketch *Clematis*, again built on speculation though soon sold to Captain Bendall of Hawkes Bay, New Zealand.[2137] By this time, the small settlement of Shipwrights Point had certainly grown in the nearly 30 years since Thomas Inches first established himself in the area. With a population approaching 150 residents, it now boasted a post office, jam factory, a hotel, two small shipyards (one of which belonged to the Inches family), a chapel, a graveyard, a dozen houses and a regatta ground.[2138]

While Robert Inches was gaining further experience building vessels with his father, he was also building relationships. On 4 October 1873 at the age of 24 Robert married 24-year-old Alice Mary Joseph, the second eldest daughter of Benjamin and his wife Margaret.[2139] Alice was the sister-in-law of Hannah Wilkinson who in turn was the sister-in-law of Robert Inches' oldest sister Mary Anne. It may be through this connection that the pair met, considering Robert was living in the Huon at the time while Alice was living at Clarence Plains on her family's farm called Riversdale.[2140]

With Robert and his new bride settling at Shipwrights Point, the shipbuilding continued apace. A few weeks after his marriage, on 29 October 1873, Messers Inches and Sons launched the 75ft double centreboard ketch *Spindrift*, built to the order of W. H. Bundy of Adelaide at a sea-ready cost of £1,550.[2141] Soon a new vessel was on the stocks, purchased while under construction by Captain Saunders of Dunedin, New Zealand, for £1,300 for hull and spars.[2142] Named *Edith Reid* and intended for the coastal trade, the 90ft craft was launched in late September 1874.[2143]

Early 1875 saw Robert Inches and his wife Alice welcome their first child, a son named Arthur Robert

[2133] *The Mercury*, 6 February 1867.
[2134] *The Tasmanian Times*, 1 November 1869.
[2135] *The Mercury*, 11 February 1871; *The Cornwall Chronicle*, 26 June 1871.
[2136] *The Mercury*, 24 October 1872.
[2137] *The Mercury*, 24 October, 19 November 1872.
[2138] *The Tasmanian Tribune*, 5 March 1873; *The Mercury*, 15 July 1875.
[2139] Libraries Tasmania (RGD37/1/32 no 380 and RGD32/1/3/ no 3632).
[2140] *The Mercury*, 6 October 1873.
[2141] *The Mercury*, 1 November 1873.
[2142] *The Tasmanian Tribune*, 10 July 1874; *The Mercury*, 11 July 1874.
[2143] *The Mercury*, 29 September 1874.

born at Shipwrights Point on 21 March.[2144] Several months later, on 15 July 1875, Messrs Inches and Sons launched the ketch *Venus*, the naming ceremony performed by Alice Inches.[2145] The 75ft craft was soon purchased by Robert and Henry Castle of Little Swanport for £1,700, intended for the east coast trade.[2146]

In June 1876 the 75ft centreboard top-sail schooner *Laurel* was launched from Inches' slip at Shipwrights Point, built on speculation for the South Australian barge trade.[2147] However, by this point in time demand for new coastal vessels in this mainland colony, principally to carry wheat, was waning, precipitated largely by the introduction of steam launches.[2148] Instead, the *Laurel* remained in the Inches family's hands (two-thirds owned by Thomas, Sr, and one-third by Robert), initially under charter by Messrs Fisher and Facy for employment in intercolonial trade.[2149] Upon its return to Hobart Town, the vessel was advertised for sale or charter.[2150] Again failing to find a buyer, it made more charter trips, including to Melbourne in October 1877 with Robert Inches on board as a passenger.[2151] Disastrously, it was on the return leg of a subsequent voyage between Hobart Town and Melbourne that the *Laurel* grounded off Portsea near Port Phillip Heads and was reportedly wrecked, all hands saved.[2152] An inquiry into the incident attributed the mishap to the recklessness of the captain (Benjamin Bettsworth) with his pilot certificate suspended for three months.[2153] During the interim, the *Laurel* was pulled off the sand by the steam tug *Resolute* and towed to Williamstown. Despite the misadventure, the only major damage proved to be the loss of the craft's rudder.[2154] The *Laurel* was repaired and returned to Hobart Town on 24 November, a few weeks later returning to the mainland with a cargo of timber and pailings.[2155]

Despite the on-going drama associated with the *Laurel*, which they still maintained ownership of, Messrs Inches and Sons persevered, constructing a river ketch to the order of John Drysdale, a sawmill owner of nearby Port Esperance.[2156] It was coincidentally a family affair. Drysdale was Thomas Inches' son-in-law via marriage to his second eldest daughter Jane, and thus the brother-in-law of Robert and Thomas Inches (Jr). The resulting craft, the 43-ton *Dauntless*, was launched on 24 November 1877.[2157] It has the distinction of being the last vessel built by Messrs Inches and Sons at Shipwrights Point.

By this point in time the Tasmanian economy was in a state of downturn. Shipbuilding in the Huon region was being supplanted by other industries. Specifically, apple orchards and the growing of fruit for jam, primarily raspberries and black currants, were beginning to dominate, providing a much needed source of income for its residents, in addition to the sourcing and sawing of timber. Both industries were helped significantly by more reliable and cheaper transport of produce to markets in Hobart Town, notably by the river barges which the Inches family had helped to pioneer and build. However, the shipping industry itself was not as brisk as it once was, with significantly less demand for new vessels. Soon would come the river steamers, providing an even faster and more convenient service to and from the Huon River and D'Entrecasteaux Channel region to Hobart Town, for both commercial operations and passengers.

For Robert Inches, the decline in the Huon's shipbuilding industry saw him seek new opportunities in Hobart Town. The move was reminiscent of his own family's relocation to the colony's capital when he was a child, in search of better education and medical resources. On 23 April 1878 he purchased property along the Napoleon Street corridor with the goal of establishing his own shipyard on the edge of the River Derwent. The parcel of land, comprising three roods and 27 perches, with a frontage along the water, was purchased from the executors of the estate of the late Robert Quayle Kermode for a price of £500.[2158] It was the first time the site had been used as a commercial shipyard. A decade earlier it had been suggested that sea water baths be built on the property, though this venture never materialised.[2159]

Likely needing capital, it was on 12 June 1878 that Robert Inches sold his one-third share in the schooner *Laurel* back to his father Thomas.[2160] Sadly this period of new beginnings was also one of tragedy. It was at No. 8 Francis Street, Battery Point, where Robert had initially established himself and his family, that his only child Arthur died on 8 May 1878, aged three.[2161] Cause of death was enteric fever, i.e., typhoid.[2162]

While Robert Inches was establishing his shipyard, he also built a house on the property. With the address of 36 Napoleon Street, it was here that Robert and his wife Alice welcomed a son named Percy Roland, born on 12 March 1879.[2163] Four more children would be born to the couple in the succeeding years including a daughter, Amy Mary Malvina, born in 1881; twin daughters, Olive Blanche and Lillian May, born in 1884; and a son named

[2144] Libraries Tasmania (RGD33/1/53 no 526); *The Mercury*, 24 March 1875.
[2145] *The Mercury*, 19 July 1875.
[2146] *The Mercury*, 1 September 1875.
[2147] *The Mercury*, 9 June 1876; *Tribune*, 10 August 1876.
[2148] *Tribune*, 9 August 1876.
[2149] *The Mercury*, 9 June, 9 September 1876; *Tribune*, 31 March 1877; HOBART, Register of ships, Volume 9, 1865-1877, [pages 1-173, continues on film roll 2], Folio 185.
[2150] *The Mercury*, 5 April, 16 October 1877.
[2151] *The Mercury*, 24 September, 16 October 1877; *The Argus*, 6 October 1877.
[2152] *The Mercury*, 18 October 1877; *Tribune*, 29 October, 5 November 1877; *The Age*, 3 November 1877; *The Argus*, 5 November 1877.
[2153] *The Sydney Morning Herald*, 8 November 1877; *The Argus*, 8 November 1877.
[2154] *The Mercury*, 9 November 1877.
[2155] *The Mercury*, 21, 26 November, 21 December 1877.
[2156] *The Mercury*, 18 August 1877.
[2157] *The Mercury*, 30 November 1877.
[2158] www.thelist.tas.gov.au (Historical Deed 06/4189).
[2159] *The Mercury*, 5 March 1868.
[2160] HOBART, Register of ships, Volume 9, 1865-1877, [pages 1-173, continues on film roll 2], Folio 185.
[2161] *The Mercury*, 9 May 1878.
[2162] Libraries Tasmania (RGD35/1/9 no 1198).
[2163] Libraries Tasmania (RGD33/1/12/ no 670); *The Mercury*, 13 March 1879.

Allotment bordering Napoleon Street, comprising 3 roods and 27 perches, purchased by Robert Inches in April 1878 that became his home and shipyard.

Location of houses on St Georges Terrace likely built by Robert Inches and his younger brother Adolphus in the early 1880s.

Map of various allotments in Battery Point.
Courtesy Tasmanian Archives (AF394/1/97).

Robert Horace, born in 1889.[2164] Sadly, their second son Percy died in October 1883 at the age of four of scarlet fever, while one of their twin daughters, Lillian May, passed away in September of the following year, aged just four weeks.[2165]

On a professional level, there is much to write about regarding Robert Inches. Though he initially spent several years overhauling and repairing vessels at his newly established Battery Point shipyard, he would soon become a successful and celebrated shipwright in his own right, over a 25-year period fruitfully oscillating between the building of commercial ketches and steamers to racing yachts designed by internationally acclaimed designers. Significantly, he was also one of a only handful of shipbuilders who bridged the gap between the old colonial pioneer builders and the more modern twentieth-century builders, particularly through the introduction of racing yachts based on international designs.

While his shipyard was first noted in 1880 as undertaking overhaul and repair work, as well as offering craft for sale second hand, it was not until mid-1882 that Robert Inches received his first order for a new vessel.[2166] During the interim he had supplemented his income by building houses for residents of Battery Point, including what appears to be numbers 4, 10 and 42 St Georges Terrace.[2167] All three residences were likely built in conjunction with Robert's younger brother Adolphus, a carpenter and builder by trade, who had also moved to Battery Point by this time.[2168]

Inches' first Battery Point-built vessel was a significant divergence from the river barges, commercial schooners and ketches he had built on the banks of the Huon River alongside his father and younger brother. Built to the order of Fleetwood P. Wilson and modelled by Alick Harley based off a Dixon Kemp design, the 28-footer racing yacht *Lughretta* was launched in January 1883, intended to race under auspices of the Derwent Yacht Club.[2169] The vessel was a consistent performer in local yacht races for a few years until its owner's death in late 1886.[2170] After several years of absence, *Lughretta* returned to racing on the Derwent under new ownership in the early 1890s, going on to successfully compete with its cohort until it disappears from the records in early 1899.

[2164] Libraries Tasmania (RGD33/1/12/ no 2681; RGD33/1/13/ no 2219; RGD33/1/13/ no 2220; RGD33/1/16/ no 1338).
[2165] Libraries Tasmania (RGD35/1/10 no 1217); *The Mercury*, 26 September 1884.
[2166] *The Mercury*, 14 December 1880.
[2167] *The Mercury*, 16 April 1883; Libraries Tasmania (RGD33/1/12/ no 2681).
[2168] www.thelist.tas.gov.au (Historical Deed 06/6210); *Tasmanian News*, 17 April 1886.
[2169] *Launceston Examiner*, 28 October 1882.
[2170] *Launceston Examiner*, 9 November 1886.

Lughretta sailing on the River Derwent (1890s). Courtesy Graeme Broxam.

A steam paddle punt, to be used for loading purposes, was the next vessel built by Robert Inches at Battery Point.[2171] Taking over a year to complete and launched in March 1884, it was the first of its kind constructed in Tasmania and was built to the order of David Chapman of Port Esperance and intended to carry logs to his Hopetoun sawmill.[2172] Named *Esperance*, the 57ft craft was considered a novelty on the River Derwent in that it was propelled by steam and also had a paddle wheel installed abaft of the rudder.[2173] Useful for several years, by the early 1890s the vessel was laid up on the beach near the Hopetoun sawmill.[2174] The *Esperance* was eventually purchased by T. A. Reynolds and Company, with the intention of placing it in the King River trade on Tasmania's west coast.[2175]

While he had started his shipbuilding business off slowly, likely distracted by house building work, the mid-1880s were busy years for Robert Inches. Looking to expand his shipyard, in June 1884 he wrote to the Hobart Marine Board requesting permission to construct a 150ft slip extending from his Napoleon Street property into the River Derwent.[2176] His request was approved the following month, though its installation was delayed owing to bad weather.[2177] Capable of accommodating vessels up to 60 tons register, the slip was operational by late 1884.[2178] It was a busy period as he was also noted as repairing and overhauling the yachts *Ella*, *Lughretta* and *Myrine*, and the river craft *Irazu*.[2179] In reporting these facts, the local press stated that, '*Mr. Inches is most obliging, and is an excellent tradesman, and we hope his venture will be both successful and profitable, at the same time bringing him that amount of patronage to which his enterprise entitles him*'.[2180]

The early part of 1886 was spent lengthening and altering the river trader *Mary Anne*, which had been built at Port Esperance in 1864, as well as undertaking extensive repairs of the yacht *Surprise* and overhauling the ketches *Gift* and *Foam*.[2181] A few months later Robert Inches began building a 46ft blue gum ketch to the order of E. H. Purdon. Intended for the river trade and based on a model by Tom Purdon (E. H. Purdon's brother), the aptly named *E. H. Purden* was launched on 24 December 1886.[2182] It was noted to present '*the appearance of a good model, and ought to prove a profitable boat to the owner*'.[2183] These words echoed true, with the *E. H. Purden* going on to become a doyen of both the local river and coastal trades and later the fishing industry over several decades. It was eventually wrecked on 13 December 1938 while sheltering off Flinders Island.[2184]

Continuing to undertake repair and overhaul work during the interim, the next vessel built by Robert Inches at Battery Point was the 32ft yacht *Vendetta*, completed in November 1888 to the order of George Clarke.[2185] Of note, Clarke was the second son of Thomas Biggs Clarke, a wealthy pastoralist and sheep grazier of the 10,000+ acre Quorn Hall estate near Campbell Town in Tasmania's Midlands district, and his wife Hannah.[2186] Upon the former's death in 1878, his widow had purchased the Secheron estate at Battery Point, taking up

---

[2171] *The Mercury*, 22 January 1883.
[2172] *The Mercury*, 22 January 1883, 20 March 1884, 5 June 1895; *Tasmanian News*, 12 December 1883.
[2173] *The Mercury*, 20 March 1884, 5 June 1895.
[2174] *The Mercury*, 5 June 1895.
[2175] *The Mercury*, 5 June 1895.
[2176] *The Mercury*, 5 July 1884.
[2177] *The Mercury*, Saturday 5 July 1884; *Tasmanian News*, 24 October 1884.
[2178] *The Mercury*, Saturday 5 July 1884; *Tasmanian News*, 24 October 1884.
[2179] *Tasmanian News*, 24, 30 October 1884.
[2180] *Tasmanian News*, 24 October 1884.
[2181] *The Mercury*, 22 January 1886; *Tasmanian News*, 11 February 1886.
[2182] *The Mercury*, 23 June, 25 December 1886.
[2183] *The Mercury*, 25 December 1886.
[2184] G. Broxam & M. Nash (2013). *Tasmanian Shipwrecks. Volume 2: 1900-2012*.
[2185] *Tasmanian News*, 9 February, 20 May 1887, 23 January, 21 November 1888; *The Mercury*, 28 February, 10 May, 21 November 1888.
[2186] *The Mercury*, 21 October 1899.

E. H. Purden by unknown artist, Turner Henderson Studio, Sydney. Courtesy Maritime Museum of Tasmania (P_2004-104).

residence there with several of her children, including her sons Thomas (Jr), George, Alfred and Frederick.[2187] Enthusiastic supporters of yachting, and with a pocket book to match their exuberance, the Clarke brothers would commission Inches to build several high-profile vessels over the coming years, beginning with *Vendetta*.

While intended for yacht racing on the River Derwent as part of the Derwent Sailing Club and later the Sandy Bay Sailing Club, in the craft's early years George Clarke also took *Vendetta* on pleasure cruises around the islands of Bass Strait.[2188] Described as *'one of the handsomest and most elaborately fitted up pleasure boats'*, the vessel was purchased by E. A. Bennison in December 1897 who, a few months later, took it on a cruise to Victoria.[2189] Back in Hobart, the *Vendetta* continued to feature in local yacht races, from November 1899 owned by Messrs McCormick and O'May.[2190] It then disappears from the record.

Returning to the construction of commercial craft, the 67ft ketch *Lillie May* was next launched by Robert Inches on 26 September 1889, built to the order of Michael Driscoll.[2191] Intended to trade between Hobart and Recherche Bay, the vessel spent most of its first decade involved in coastal trade (owned by H. A. Johnston) before being sold to buyers from Adelaide in 1902.[2192] After nearly 20 years trading in South Australian waters the *Lillie May* was wrecked in early June 1921 off Cape Elizabeth in the Spencer Gulf with the unfortunate loss of all on board.[2193]

With his Battery Point shipyard entering its second decade of operation, the early 1890s continued to be a busy period for Robert Inches. In 1890 he converted the cutter *Spray* into a fishing smack and built a loading punt to the order of a W. Gellibrand for his passage boat *Fancy*.[2194] In addition he was tasked with building a new steamer for Risby Brothers, with the requirements that the vessel not be a *'cockle-shell'* and that there was no need to *'spare the timber in her'*.[2195] The 82ft *Yolla* was launched on 28 August 1890, intended for the west

---

[2187] *The Mercury*, 14 December 1878, 4 April 1881, 18 December 1895, 22 September 1923.
[2188] *Daily Telegraph*, 4 January 1890.
[2189] *Tasmanian News*, 10 December 1897; *The Mercury*, 1 March, 26 April 1898.
[2190] *The Mercury*, 27 November 1899.
[2191] *Tasmanian News*, 26 February, 24 June, 26 September 1889; *The Mercury*, 27 September 1889, 7 May 1890.
[2192] *Launceston Examiner*, 13 August 1892.
[2193] *Recorder*, 8 June 1921.
[2194] *The Mercury*, 21 January 1890.
[2195] *The Mercury*, 10 April 1890; *Tasmanian News*, 29 August 1890.

coast trade where it spent its entire life employed.[2196] On 10 December 1898 the SS *Yolla* was purchased by the Union Steamship Company of New Zealand.[2197] Less than two weeks later, however, the vessel was wrecked in heavy fog at Sandy Cape en route from King Island, all hands saved.[2198]

Yolla on the Huon River.
Courtesy Tasmanian Archives (NS2511/1/244).

Also in 1890 Robert Inches completed a yacht named *Hebe* for Arthur James of Battery Point.[2199] Designed by Alfred Blore, the vessel was intended for the 21ft size class and launched on 24 October 1890.[2200] A popular racing craft for several decades under various owners, including Tucker Abel, R. R. Rex, and Messrs Walker and Gilham, by 1914 *Hebe* had been converted to a fishing boat.[2201] The vessel went on to spend several more decades involved in the local fishing trade under the ownership of E. A. Brooks.[2202]

Though no vessels are known to have been built in 1891 or 1892, indicative of the state of the industry as a whole, this period did involve Robert Inches overhauling the barges *Gift, Lily, Laurel* and *Oddfellow*; fitting a new centre case to the yacht *Sunbeam*; and overhauling a steam launch.[2203] In addition he received orders to ready the yachts *Imp, Daphne, Hebe, Olga, Gleam* and *Ionthe*, and the passage boat *Seacroft*, for racing at the 1891 Hobart Regatta.[2204] A few months later he was noted as overhauling the passage boats *Thames, Rosebud* and *Lurline*, as well as the keel yacht *Seabird*.[2205] Late in 1892 Inches and several of his workers, including Charles Lucas and J. Ludgrove, were noted as repairing O. H. Hedberg's new yacht *Viking*, which had been almost destroyed by fire while under construction at premises in Brisbane Street, Hobart.[2206] This particular craft was finally launched on 17 January 1893.[2207]

The next vessel off the stocks at Robert Inches' shipyard was the yacht *Thelma*, intended for the 21ft class.[2208] Designed by John Lucas, the vessel was built to the order of brothers Alfred and Arthur Oldmeadow and launched on 25 October 1893.[2209] It went on to very successfully compete in Derwent Sailing Club events and at local and regional regattas for many years, winning several major championships and titles.[2210]

Thelma at Barnes Bay.
Courtesy Maritime Museum of Tasmania (P_Y_309).

[2196] *The Mercury*, 7 July, 29 August 1890.
[2197] G. Broxam & M. Nash (2020). *Tasmanian Shipwrecks. Volume 1: 1797-1899*.
[2198] *Zeehan and Dundas Herald*, 26 December 1898.
[2199] *The Mercury*, 12 May, 7 July, 28 October 1890.
[2200] *The Mercury*, 12 May, 28 October 1890.
[2201] *Tasmanian News*, 22 June 1894, 2 June 1910; *The Mercury*, 26 July 1895, 10 April 1905, 13 January 1914; *The Clipper*, 14 February 1903.
[2202] *The Mercury*, 13 June 1942.
[2203] *The Mercury*, 20 January 1891.
[2204] *The Mercury*, 20 January 1891.
[2205] *The Mercury*, 8 April, 31 July 1891.
[2206] *The Mercury*, 6 December 1892; *Tasmanian News*, 17 January 1893.
[2207] *Tasmanian News*, 17 January 1893.
[2208] *Launceston Examiner*, 5 July 1893; *The Mercury*, 24 August 1893.
[2209] *Tasmanian News*, 15 September 1893; *The Mercury*, 25 October 1893.
[2210] *The Mercury*, 29 September 1894, 29 January 1902.

Around 1905 *Thelma* was sold to W. B. Townley and, following his untimely death in 1911, next passed to C. Chambers and then C. H. Richardson.[2211] The vessel changed owners several more times and, like many of its peers, was later converted to a fishing boat and subsequently lengthened.[2212] In mid-1931 *Thelma* was purchased by the Port Adelaide Central Methodist Mission, South Australia, to provide training to unemployed youths.[2213] Unfortunately the training scheme failed shortly after its establishment and it is possible that the vessel subsequently returned to Tasmanian waters where it was wrecked near Stanley in early 1939.[2214]

Robert Inches' next commission marked another highlight of his career. In early 1894, owing to the shock defeat of the Derwent-based 21ft yachts by the Launceston craft *Ventura* in the handicap race at that year's Hobart Regatta, Frederick Norman (F. N.) Clarke of Secheron, and his younger brother George who several years prior had commissioned Inches to build the yacht *Vendetta*, contracted with William Fife (Jr), the celebrated Scottish yacht designer, for a new racing yacht design fitted with a centreboard.[2215] Tasked with the vessel's construction, *Fairlie*, named for Fife's home town, was launched on 17 November 1894 at 6 am from Robert Inches' Battery Point shipyard, completed just hours prior to its first race.[2216] Built nearly entirely of Huon pine, with Alfred Blore employed to ensure Fife's plans were faithfully executed, the 21-footer *Fairlie* was one of the most anticipated builds of its time.[2217] Of note, it was stated to be '*almost a copy on a small scale of the American Cup holder*' *Vigilant*, designed by Nathaneal Greene Herreshoff and launched in 1893, the same year it won the coveted international trophy.[2218]

While there was much to celebrate with regards to the launch of the yacht *Fairlie*, after the festivities were over Robert Inches and his employees returned to work, primarily overhaul and repair projects. A few weeks later, on 14 December 1894, disaster struck, however. A 50-year-old worker named John Smith fell while altering the rigging of the yacht *Nellie*.[2219] He suffered a broken neck and died near instantly. It was a period of highs and lows for Inches.

Living up to expectations, *Fairlie* not only finished first in its maiden race, a long way ahead of the rest of the fleet, but also went on to dominate the Tasmanian yachting landscape, including winning the inaugural North vs South Challenge Cup held on the Tamar River against the new local yacht *America* (built by E. A. Jack) in March 1896.[2220] The yacht's success, however, appears not to have been up to its owner's high expectations, such that in early 1896 F. N. Clarke approached William Fife (Jr) for a second yacht design.[2221] The *Fairlie* was advertised for sale beginning in October 1896 and subsequently purchased by E. A. Bennison.[2222] Two years later, in December 1898, the vessel was trans-shipped via the steamer *Mararoa* to Sydney, having been purchased by T. W. Bremmer to race under the auspices of the Royal Sydney Yacht Squadron.[2223] By November 1900 *Fairlie* had been sold to E. H. Crossland and J. E. Joubert and presented as a gift to S. H. Fairland, secretary of the Sydney Cricket Ground, whose yacht *Pixie* had recently foundered.[2224] The *Fairlie* remained in Fairland's hands until at least 1919.[2225]

Fairlie on the River Derwent (c.1895).
Courtesy Maritime Museum of Tasmania (P_Y_061).

F. N. Clarke's second 21ft Fife-designed yacht, built by Robert Inches, was launched on 3 December 1896.[2226] Christened *Ailsa*, it was designed specifically to vie for the North vs South Challenge Cup, though the press noted that there was very little difference between this vessel and its predecessor, with the exception of a more graceful bow and larger counter.[2227] Still, *Ailsa* met expectations, successfully winning the 1897 Cup against the northern yacht *America*, the contest held on the Derwent in January of that year.[2228]

[2211] *The Mercury*, 26 March 1906, 1 January, 23 November 1912, 2 February 1914, 17 November 1919.
[2212] *The Mercury*, 6 December 1930, 13 March, 10 July 1931.
[2213] *Advertiser and Register*, 29 August 1931; *The Advertiser*, 10 October 1931.
[2214] G. Broxam & M. Nash (2013). *Tasmanian Shipwrecks. Volume 2: 1900-2012*.
[2215] *The Mercury*, 25 January, 2 August, 17 November 1894; *The Clipper*, 27 January 1894.
[2216] *The Mercury*, 17 November 1894.
[2217] *The Mercury*, 2 August, 17 November 1894.
[2218] *The Mercury*, 2 August 1894.
[2219] *Launceston Examiner*, 14 December 1894; *Zeehan and Dundas Herald*, 14 December 1894.
[2220] *The Mercury*, 19 November 1894; *Daily Telegraph*, 6 March 1896.
[2221] *The Mercury*, 4 December 1896, 15 August 1929.
[2222] *The Mercury*, 27 October 1896; *The Clipper*, 23 January 1897.
[2223] *The Sydney Morning Herald*, 23 December 1898.
[2224] *Evening News*, 12 November 1900.
[2225] *The Daily Telegraph*, 8 February 1919.
[2226] *The Mercury*, 4 December 1896.
[2227] *The Mercury*, 7 December 1896.
[2228] *The Mercury*, 22, 28 January 1897.

Ailsa on the River Derwent (c1895).
Courtesy Maritime Museum of Tasmania (P_OM_E_4c).

Though F. N. Clarke had been one of the founders and instigators of the North vs South Challenge Cup, the 1898 race, held on the Tamar River, saw Percy Lovett's new yacht *Caress* selected to represent the south.[2229] Disappointingly the craft, which had been built by Charlie Lucas at Battery Point, an ex-employee of Robert Inches, to a design by Alfred Blore, was outclassed by the northern-based yacht *America*.[2230] It was a mighty blow to Hobart's yachting fraternity. Vexed that the south failed to retain the trophy,

F. N. Clarke immediately contacted William Fife (Jr) for a new racing yacht design.[2231] Though it was to be framed in Scotland, Inches was once more commissioned with the build, though this time the yacht was constructed in an enclosed shed that had been specifically built to keep the craft out of the public's eye.[2232] Of note, in providing the design, Fife is stated to have '*deplored the necessity*' for solely a racing boat, believing that craft should have the dual purpose of racing and cruising.[2233] Still, he produced the design for F. N. Clarke with the singular purpose of regaining the reputation of Southern Tasmania's yachtsmen.

Considered the most up-to-date 21ft racing yacht in the country, the eagerly-anticipated *Clutha* was launched on 9 November 1898.[2234] Sadly, for Robert Inches, the weeks spent preparing the craft for launch were also associated with the death of his wife. Alice Mary Inches, aged 48 years, died at their home, 36 Napoleon Street on 20 October 1898.[2235] Cause of the death was apoplexy, i.e., a stroke, as well as heart failure.[2236] In consequence, proceedings for the launch of *Clutha* were of a reserved nature.[2237]

While he mourned the loss of his wife, *Clutha* became an immediate success such that in early January 1899 it was fittingly nominated by members of the Derwent Sailing Club to be the southern participant in the 1899 North vs South Challenge Cup, a race to be

[2229] *Launceston Examiner*, 31 July 1897; *Tasmanian News*, 7 September 1897.
[2230] *Launceston Examiner*, 31 July 1897, 25 February 1898; *Tasmanian News*, 7 September 1897.
[2231] *The Mercury*, 14 June 1898; *Tasmanian News*, 16 June 1898.
[2232] *The Mercury*, 14 June, 12 November 1898; *Tasmanian News*, 16 June 1898.
[2233] *The Mercury*, 5 November 1898.
[2234] *The Mercury*, 14 June, 5, 10 November 1898.
[2235] *The Mercury*, 21 October 1898.
[2236] Libraries Tasmania (RGD35/1/68 no 622).
[2237] *The Mercury*, 10 November 1898.

The Tasmanian Mail, 28 January 1899.

held on the Derwent later that month.²²³⁸ In a dramatic turn of events, however, the Tamar Yacht Club opted not to submit an entrant, the owners of the club's fastest yacht *America* declining to participate for private reasons.²²³⁹ Though the Cup was subsequently awarded to F. N. Clarke by default, there were hints in the press of animosity and unsportsman-like behaviour from both sides in the ensuing months.²²⁴⁰ This unpleasantness ultimately led to the Tamar Yacht Club failing to nominate a representative to vie for the Challenge Cup in the years immediately following *Clutha*'s launch, with the race ultimately stalled until 1909.²²⁴¹

Though the *Clutha* went on to enjoy further success, winning its respective races at the 1899 Port Esperance, Huon and Hobart regattas, a disgruntled F. N. Clarke sold the vessel to Scott and Company, a syndicate from Hobart, in September of that year, less than 12 months after its auspicious launch.²²⁴² *Clutha* was again listed for sale in December 1902, likely a direct result of the 21ft class of yachts losing its lustre.²²⁴³ By October 1904 it was owned by T. McPhie.²²⁴⁴ However, several years later, '*probably the fastest yacht ever seen in Tasmania*' was noted as being hauled up on the shore near Secheron, Battery Point, and out of commission; a sad demise for a yacht with such a prestigious introduction and an unbeaten record, with a regret that '*she never met anything able to give her a fair trial*'.²²⁴⁵ In a transformation entirely unfitting of its original design and intended use, it spent its final days as a scallop-splitting punt at the Hobart wharf.²²⁴⁶

Following completion of the first iteration of the *Fairlie*, and prior to the launch of the *Ailsa*, in February 1896 Robert Inches began construction of a 52ft steam yacht to the order of the Hon. W. G. Gibson, MLC, prominent Hobart miller and grain merchant.²²⁴⁷ With an engine and parts furnished by the English firm of Simpson and Strickland, the *Preana* was launched by November of that year and was noted to '*contain everything that is new in the construction of a steam launch*'.²²⁴⁸

Under the Gibson family's tenure, *Preana* was an eminent feature of the river, used regularly to convey family members across the Derwent and also made available to assist with local yachting races and aquatic events. Sold out of the Gibson family in 1912, the vessel passed to a series of owners in the succeeding decades.²²⁴⁹ Remaining on the Derwent, by the 1990s it had fallen into a dilapidated state. It was then taken in hand and extensively restored by a group of passionate and skilled volunteers, by the 2010s having the honour of being the only commercially-operated steam yacht in Tasmania, providing luxury river cruises out of Hobart's Franklin Wharf. These cruises continued until its owner, Jim Butterworth, died in February 2019.²²⁵⁰ *Preana* was later advertised for sale by tenders over $225,000, and ultimately purchased by a Melbourne syndicate where it now resides.²²⁵¹

Following construction of the *Fairlie, Ailsa, Clutha* and *Preana*, Robert Inches was certainly at the top of his craft as the twentieth century approached. More vessels soon followed. On 23 January 1900 *Fairlie II* was launched, the fourth yacht built to the order of F. N. Clarke.²²⁵²

---

²²³⁸ *Launceston Examiner*, 9 January 1899.
²²³⁹ *The Mercury*, 9 January 1899.
²²⁴⁰ *The Clipper*, 14 January, 25 March 1899; *The Mercury*, 2, 20 March 1899.
²²⁴¹ *The Mercury*, 11 January 1908; *Tasmanian News*, 27 January 1909
²²⁴² *The Mercury*, 28 September, 18 November 1899, 20 January 1900.
²²⁴³ *The Mercury*, 13 December 1902.
²²⁴⁴ *The Examiner*, 31 October 1904.
²²⁴⁵ *The Mercury*, 19 November 1906, 11 January 1908, 16 January, 21 August 1909.
²²⁴⁶ *The Mercury*, 3 May 1929.

²²⁴⁷ *The Clipper*, 29 February 1896.
²²⁴⁸ *The Mercury*, 9 November 1896.
²²⁴⁹ G. Broxam and N. Mays (2023). *Those That Survive: Tasmania's Vintage and Veteran Recreational Vessels*.
²²⁵⁰ G. Broxam and N. Mays (2023). *Those That Survive: Tasmania's Vintage and Veteran Recreational Vessels*.
²²⁵¹ G. Broxam and N. Mays (2023). *Those That Survive: Tasmania's Vintage and Veteran Recreational Vessels*.
²²⁵² *The Mercury*, 24 January 1900.

Clutha as a scallop-splitting punt, Hobart (late 1920s).
Courtesy Tasmanian Archives (NS1013/1/1674).

Preana at the Hobart Wharf (2013).
Courtesy author's collection.

Fairlie II on the River Derwent.
Courtesy Tasmanian Archives (NS4023/1/214).

Though having given up competitive intrastate yacht racing in the years immediately following the launch of the *Clutha*, F. N. Clarke had not given up on his love for yachting and, as such, commissioned William Fife (Jr) to design an up-to-date 31ft cruising yacht.[2253]

However, as with his previous builds, *Fairlie II* remained in Clarke's hands for only a short period of time before he disposed of it to make way for a larger yacht capable of coastal cruising.[2254] Purchased in late 1902 by a local syndicate (J. Sharp and Company), the craft then evolved into a popular and successful local racing yacht.[2255] Several years later, still on the Derwent, it was owned by Messrs Young, Dart and Mason, though by 1912 had been purchased by a Mr Jameson of Westernport and transferred to Victoria.[2256]

Beginning in the early 1920s *Fairlie II* was sailing out of the St Kilda Yacht Club. More changes of ownership and locations ensued and by 1947 it was transferred from Victoria to New South Wales. Fortunately, *Fairlie II* remains in existence and, after another stint in Melbourne, returned to Tasmania in 2023 to undergo restoration at Cygnet.[2257]

Following the launch of *Fairlie II* Robert Inches returned to the construction of commercial trading ketches with completion of the *Swift* and *Olive*. The former was launched from his yard on 30 July 1900, built to the order of T. and J. Underwood of North West Bay.[2258] Designed by Tom Purdon, the 48ft vessel was intended for the Huon and Channel river trade where it spent more than three decades employed.[2259] The *Swift* was wrecked off Cape Frederick Henry, Bruny Island, on 12 November 1935, all hands saved.[2260] At the time of loss, and for many years prior, it was owned by Herbert Sward.[2261]

Swift on the slip at Battery Point.
Courtesy Maritime Museum of Tasmania (P_OM_L_44a).

[2253] *The Mercury*, 4 September 1899.
[2254] G. Broxam and N. Mays (2023). *Those That Survive: Tasmania's Vintage and Veteran Recreational Vessels.*
[2255] G. Broxam and N. Mays (2023). *Those That Survive: Tasmania's Vintage and Veteran Recreational Vessels.*
[2256] G. Broxam and N. Mays (2023). *Those That Survive: Tasmania's Vintage and Veteran Recreational Vessels.*
[2257] G. Broxam and N. Mays (2023). *Those That Survive: Tasmania's Vintage and Veteran Recreational Vessels.*
[2258] *The Mercury*, 31 July 1900.
[2259] *The Mercury*, 31 July 1900.
[2260] *The Mercury*, 15 November 1935.
[2261] G. Broxam & M. Nash (2013). *Tasmanian Shipwrecks. Volume 2: 1900-2012.*

Slightly smaller than the *Swift*, the 49ft *Olive* was built by Robert Inches to the order of Auguste Nickel of the D'Entrecasteaux Channel and launched in June 1901.[2262] Like the *Swift*, the craft was intended for the Huon and Channel river trade.[2263] Tragically, however, Nickel's tenure of the vessel was brief. On 21 June 1902 he was found dead in the *Olive*'s cabin, the cause of death subsequently deemed accidental suffocation by coke fumes.[2264] Afterwards, the craft passed to the Pybus, then Sward, then Heatley families, remaining in the river trade for some years.[2265] In 1922 the *Olive* was transferred to New South Wales and converted to a pleasure yacht.[2266]

Launch of *Oceana*.
The Tasmanian Mail, 28 December 1901.

Olive on the River Derwent (c1910s).
Courtesy Tasmanian Archives (NS2511/1/172).

Continuing to receive orders for commercial vessels, in June 1901 Robert Inches was commissioned by the Tasmanian Timber Corporation to build a 48ft oil launch for use in association with the company's Port Esperance mill.[2267] The resulting vessel, the 13-ton *Oceana*, was launched on 14 December 1901, built to the order of company manager J. C. Kemsley.[2268] In January 1912 the *Oceana* was renamed *Makira* having been purchased by Francis Rigby of Hobart.[2269] A few weeks later the craft was transferred to Sydney to be readied for employment in the Solomon Island trade, a destination to which *Makira* made its way in March 1912.[2270]

In May 1902 Robert Inches was noted as building his fifth yacht to the order of F. N. Clarke, the 36ft blue gum keel of which had been sourced from Clement's mill at Port Esperance.[2271] Based on a design by William Fife (Jr), the yacht was aptly named *Fairlie III* and launched from Inches' shipyard on 8 November that year.[2272]

After enjoying success in local regatta and yacht races, F. N. Clarke once more tired of his new vessel and in mid-1905 *Fairlie III* passed to Thomas Marshall of Sydney.[2273] After arriving in Sydney on 31 August 1905 the vessel was dramatically driven ashore at Manly the following day.[2274] Successfully refloated and found relatively unscathed, the craft was renamed *Nanoya* and spent several decades operating out of the Prince Alfred Yacht Club, of which Thomas Marshall was commodore between 1907 and 1909.[2275] Several changes of owners and locations followed, and by the mid-1960s *Nanoya* was en route to Europe where it remained. The vessel was noted as undergoing a major restoration in Italy in the early 2000s and was last cited when advertised for sale in 2012.[2276]

Fairlie III just prior to launch).
Weekly Courier, 13 December 1902.

[2262] *Tasmanian News*, 29 June 1901; *The Mercury*, 31 July, 4 August 1900; HOBART, Main Register (with continuation entries), Volume 11, 1899-1911, Folio 47.
[2263] *The Mercury*, 28 December 1901.
[2264] *The North Western Advocate & the Emu Bay Times*, 24 June 1902; Libraries Tasmania (SC195-1-75-11463).
[2265] HOBART, Main Register (with continuation entries), Volume 11, 1899-1911, Folio 47; HOBART, Main Register (with continuation entries), Volume 12, 1911-1930, Folio 90.
[2266] HOBART, Main Register (with continuation entries), Volume 12, 1911-1930, Folio 90.
[2267] *The Mercury*, 8 June 1901.
[2268] *Tasmanian News*, 6 August 1901; *The Mercury*, 16 December 1901.
[2269] *The Mercury*, 2 March 1912; HOBART, Main Register (with continuation entries), Volume 12, 1911-1930, Folio 7.
[2270] *The Mercury*, 2 March 1912; HOBART, Main Register (with continuation entries), Volume 12, 1911-1930, Folio 7;

The Daily Telegraph, 27 February, 16 March 1912.
[2271] *The Mercury*, 27 May 1902.
[2272] *The Mercury*, 12 November 1902.
[2273] HOBART, Main Register (with continuation entries), Volume 11, 1899-1911, Folio 89.
[2274] *The Mercury*, 1 September 1905.
[2275] *The Mercury*, 2 September 1905; *The Sydney Morning Herald*, 25 October 1934.
[2276] G. Broxam and N. Mays (2023). *Those That Survive: Tasmania's Vintage and Veteran Recreational Vessels*.

On 9 December 1903 Robert Inches launched what would be his final vessel.[2277] Built to the order of Alex McKay of Peppermint Bay, the 47ft cutter *Dauntless* was also designed by Inches.[2278] Intended for the river trade, where it spent many years employed, in 1911 it was transferred to William Sward of Hobart. By the 1920s the *Dauntless* had been converted to a fishing vessel and its ownership transferred to the Rattenbury family.[2279] After two decades of employment in the coastal fishing industry, the vessel was wrecked at the entrance to Port Arthur on 27 April 1949, all hands saved.[2280] At the time of loss, it was owned by W. Spaulding of Dunalley.[2281]

Less than six months following the launch of the *Dauntless*, Robert Inches died at the General Hospital, Hobart, on May 29 1904 at the age of 55.[2282] Cause of death is not known. He was buried at Queenborough Cemetery, Sandy Bay.[2283]

On 30 June 1904 Robert Inches' Battery Point shipyard, comprising two roods and 27 perches of property and 92ft of frontage on the River Derwent, was advertised for sale.[2284] The yard also included a weatherboard house, two patent slips and three small jetties.[2285] The property was purchased by William Lucas in July 1904, son of John Lucas, the shipbuilder of Battery Point profiled in a previous chapter.[2286]

Robert Inches left his estate to his three surviving children: Amy, Olive and Robert Horace, who moved to 50 Napoleon Street.[2287] None of them married thus Inches was left with no descendants, a stark contrast to the many members of the Inches family that descended from Thomas Inches, quite a few who remained in the Huon Valley region. The last to die of Robert Inches' children was his son Robert Horace, a retired law clerk, who passed away at 50 Napoleon Street in 1961. He gave his personal estate to his cousins.[2288]

Still, Robert Inches left a lasting legacy, building at least 19 vessels, including nine yachts and five ketches, at his Battery Point shipyard between 1883 and 1903. Remarkably, at least three of these vessels (the *Fairlie II*, *Fairlie III* and *Preana*) likely remain in existence.

Yet Inches, like several of his peers, also left a legacy associated with those that he taught the trade of shipbuilding to, including Charlie Lucas and Percy Coverdale, who both undertook their apprenticeships with him and went on to establish their own successful boat yards at Battery Point. Moreover, Robert Inches was involved in the local yachting community. Associations of which he donated time and resources to were the Derwent Yacht Club, the Derwent Model Yacht Club and Derwent Dinghy Sailing Club, with events for the latter two organisations regularly taking place off his shipyard.[2289]

[2277] *Tasmanian News*, 9 December 1903.
[2278] *Tasmanian News*, 9 December 1903.
[2279] *The Mercury*, 11 December 1923.
[2280] G. Broxam & M. Nash (2013). *Tasmanian Shipwrecks. Volume 2: 1900-2012.*
[2281] *The Mercury*, 19 May 1949.
[2282] *The Mercury*, 30 May 1904.
[2283] *The Mercury*, 30 May 1904.
[2284] *The Mercury*, 30 June 1904.
[2285] *The Mercury*, 30 June 1904.
[2286] *The Mercury*, 17 November 1904.
[2287] Libraries Tasmania (AD960-1-26 Will Number 6402); *The Mercury*, 11 June 1910, 23 June, 26 November 1952.
[2288] Libraries Tasmania (AD960-1-93 Will Number 42429).
[2289] *Tasmanian News*, 18 June 1900, *The Mercury*, 12 May, 21 October 1902, 8 October, 16 November 1903.

Vessels built by Robert Inches and employees at Battery Point (1883 - 1903)

Year	Name	Type	Description
1883	*Lughretta*	Yacht	25 x 6 x 5.5ft. Built by Robert Inches to the order of Fleetwood P. Wilson, modelled by Alick Harley based off a Dixon Kemp design. Launched in January 1883, intended to race under auspices of the Derwent Yacht Club. A consistent performer in local yacht races until its owner's death in late 1886. After several years of absence, returned to racing on the Derwent, by 1896 owned by the Webster family. Disappears from the records in early 1899.
1884	*Esperance*	Steam launch	57 x 16 x 4ft. Built by Robert Inches to the order of David Chapman of Port Esperance to carry logs to his Hopetoun sawmill. Launched in March 1884. Propelled by steam and also had a paddle wheel installed abaft of the rudder. Useful for several years, by the early 1890s laid up. In 1895 purchased by T. A. Reynolds and Company with the intention of placing it in the King River trade on Tasmania's west coast. Believed later abandoned at Macquarie Heads.
1886	*E. H. Purden*	Ketch	46.0 x 13.4 x 4.7ft. ON 57618. 17 tons. Built by Robert Inches to the order of E. H. Purdon and intended for the river trade, based on a model by Tom Purdon (E. H. Purdon's brother). Launched on 24 December 1886. A doyen of the local river and coastal trades and later the fishing industry for several decades under various owners, including Richard Washbourne, John Norling and lastly Margharita Talbot. Wrecked on 13 December 1938 while sheltering off Flinders Island.
1888	*Vendetta*	Yacht	32ft. Built by Robert Inches to the order of George Clarke. Launched in November 1888, intended for yacht racing on the River Derwent. Purchased by E. A. Bennison in December 1897, from November 1899 owned by Messrs McCormick and O'May. Subsequent fate not known.
1889	*Lillie May*	Ketch	67.8 x 18.6 x 5.8ft. ON 57620. 42 tons. Built by Robert Inches to the order of Michael Driscoll. Launched on 26 September 1889. Spent most of its first decade involved in coastal trade (owned by H. A. Johnston) before being sold to buyers from Adelaide in 1902. After nearly 20 years trading in South Australian waters, wrecked in early June 1921 off Cape Elizabeth in the Spencer Gulf with the unfortunate loss of all on board.
1890	–	Punt	Loading punt built by Robert Inches to the order of a W. Gellibrand for his passage boat *Fancy*.

Year	Name	Type	Description
1890	Yolla	Steamer	82.8 x 19.7 x 7.3ft. ON 57628. 80 tons. Built by Robert Inches to the order of Risby Bros. and launched on 28 August 1890, intended for the west coast trade where it spent its entire life employed. On 10 December 1898 purchased by the Union Steamship Company of New Zealand. Wrecked less than two weeks later in heavy fog at Sandy Cape, all hands saved.
1890	Hebe	Yacht	21ft. Built by Robert Inches for Arthur James of Battery Point to a design by Alfred Blore. Launched on 24 October 1890. A popular racing craft for several decades under various owners, including Tucker Abel, R. R. Rex, and Messrs Walker and Gilham. By 1914 converted to a fishing boat and operated by E. A. Brooks. Later converted to a motor launched. Wrecked in 1971.
1893	Thelma	Yacht	21ft. Built by Robert Inches to a design by John Lucas to the order of Alfred and Arthur Oldmeadow. Intended for the 21ft class. Launched on 25 October 1893. A successful yacht for many years. Around 1905 sold to W. B. Townley and in 1911, to C. Chambers and then C. H. Richardson. Several more changes of owner. Later converted to a fishing boat and lengthened. In mid-1931 purchased by the Port Adelaide Central Methodist Mission. Possibly next returned to Tasmania where it was wrecked near Stanley in early 1939.
1894	Fairlie	Yacht	21ft. Built by Robert Inches to the order of F. N. Clarke to a design by William Fife (Jr). Launched on 17 November 1894. Dominated the Tasmanian yachting landscape. Advertised for sale in October 1896 and purchased by E. A. Bennison. In December 1898, trans-shipped to Sydney, having been purchased by T. W. Bremmer to race with the Royal Sydney Yacht Squadron. By November 1900 sold to E. H. Crossland and J. E. Joubert and presented as a gift to S. H. Fairland, secretary of the Sydney Cricket Ground, whose yacht had recently foundered. Remained in Fairland's hands until at least 1919. Subsequent fate not known.
1896	Preana	Steam launch	52.4 x 8.4 x 4.6ft. ON 105695. 8 tons. Built by Robert Inches to the order of the Hon. W. G. Gibson, MLC, and launched by November 1896, its engine furnished by Simpson and Strickland. Sold in 1912 with a series of owners in the succeeding decades. By the 1990s in a dilapidated state. Extensively restored by a group of volunteers. By the 2010s the only commercially-operated steam yacht in Tasmania. Later advertised for sale following the death of its owner, Jim Butterworth. Purchased by a Melbourne syndicate where it now resides.
1896	Ailsa	Yacht	21ft. Built by Robert Inches to the order of F. N. Clarke to a design by William Fife (Jr). Launched on 3 December 1896. Sold to Russell Ritchie in early 1899 and transferred to Launceston where it remained until lost in the disastrous floods of 1929, at the time owned by W. Burke.
1899	Clutha	Yacht	21ft. Built by Robert Inches to the order of F. N. Clarke to a design by William Fife (Jr). Launched on 9 November 1898. Sold to Scott and Company in September 1899. By October 1904 owned by T. McPhie. Several years later hauled up on the shore near Secheron, Battery Point, and out of commission. Then spent its days as a scallop-splitting punt at the Hobart wharf.
1900	Fairlie II	Yacht	31.7 x 8.6 x 5.7ft. ON 105691. 6 tons. Built by Robert Inches to the order of F. N. Clarke to a design by William Fife (Jr). Launched on 23 January 1900. Sold in 1902 to J. Sharp and Company. Later owned by Messrs Young, Dart and Mason, though by 1912 purchased by a Mr Jameson of Westernport and transferred to Victoria. In the early 1920s sailing out of the St Kilda Yacht Club. By 1947 transferred to New South Wales. Remains in existence and, after another stint in Melbourne, returned to Tasmania in 2023 to undergo restoration at Cygnet.
1900	Swift	Ketch	53.4 x 15.4 x 4.4ft. ON 105686. 23 tons. Built by Robert Inches to the order of John and Thomas Underwood of North West Bay and launched on 30 July 1900. Designed by Tom Purdon, intended for the Huon and Channel river trade where it spent more than three decades employed; from 1909 owned by Herbert Sward, from 1918 by Frederick Newell; from 1921 by Arthur Knott; from 1924 by W. G. Gorringe and D. W. Pearsall. Wrecked off Cape Frederick Henry, Bruny Island, on 12 November 1935, all hands saved. At the time, owned by Herbert Sward.
1901	Olive	Ketch	49.2 x 14.1 x 4.1ft. ON 105689. 15 tons. Built by Robert Inches to the order of Auguste Nickel and launched in June 1901. Intended for the Huon and Channel river trade. Sadly Nickel died on 21 June 1902 of suffocation by coke fumes in the vessel's cabin. It then passed to the Pybus, Sward, and Heatley families, remaining in the river trade. In 1922 transferred to Sydney and converted to a pleasure yacht by owner Roy Adams. Subsequent history not confirmed.
1901	Makira ex Oceana	Oil launch	48.5 x 10.7 x 5.1ft. ON 124550. 13 tons. Built by Robert Inches to the order of J. C. Kemsley, manager of the Tasmanian Timber Corporation for use in association with the company's Port Esperance mill. Launched on 14 December 1901. In January 1912 purchased by Francis Rigby of Hobart and renamed Makira. Transferred to Sydney a few weeks later for employment in the the Solomon Island trade. Departed Sydney in March 1912 for Tulagi. Register transferred to Fairley, Rigby and Company Limited of Brisbane in September 1919. Later derelict.
1902	Nanoya ex Fairlie III	Yacht	36.4 x 11.5 x 5.3ftft. ON 119231. Fifth yacht built by Robert Inches to the order of F. N. Clarke to a design by William Fife (Jr). Launched on 8 November 1902. Successful in local regatta and yacht races, in mid-1905 sold to Thomas Marshall of Sydney and renamed Nanoya. Spent several decades operating out of the Prince Alfred Yacht Club before several changes of owners and locations. By the mid-1960s en route to Europe where it remained. Last noted as undergoing a major restoration in Italy in the early 2000s and advertised for sale in 2012.
1903	Dauntless	Cutter	47.0 x 16.6 x 5.8ft. ON 105699. 21 tons. Built by Robert Inches to the order Alex McKay and launched on 9 December 1903, intended for the river trade. By the 1920s converted to a fishing vessel and owned by the Rattenbury family. Wrecked at the entrance to Port Arthur on 27 April 1949, all hands saved. At the time of loss, owned by W. Spaulding of Dunalley.

Other Builders

'He hoped that the name of Messrs. Kennedy and Sons would occupy the same place as that of the large shipbuilding firms on the Clyde.'

Daily Telegraph, 28 March 1887.

The previous chapters have concentrated on the men who were renowned and/or long-standing boat and ship builders of Battery Point during the nineteenth century. There were, however, others who operated yards at Battery Point during this period. Some of these men and the vessels they built are summarised in this chapter, profiled in alphabetical order.

William Bayes

The son of two English convicts, William Alfred Bayes was born in Hobart Town in August 1851.[2290] While his early years were spent around the New Wharf area; his family lived at the ordnance store where his father worked as a storekeeper, at the age of four, Bayes' life changed in tragic circumstances.[2291] His mother, Sarah, died on 2 February 1856, one day after giving birth to a daughter.[2292] Less than two weeks later, the infant also died.[2293] Perhaps owing to the grief, Bayes' father Thomas died less than a month later.[2294] Bayes was left in the care of several of his older sisters, themselves still only teenagers. While it is not known how Bayes and his siblings survived, it must have been tough. Indicative of these struggles, on 20 July 1857 Bayes was admitted to the Queen's Orphanage at New Town, along with his older sister Agnes.[2295] Fortunately both were released to an older sister on 8 January of the following year, thereby alleviating them from the chronic care and welfare issues associated with this institution.[2296] By late 1859 Bayes and his siblings, of which the oldest, Sarah, was by now 22 years of age, were noted as living at Hampden Road, Battery Point.[2297]

[2290] Libraries Tasmania (CON52/1/1 Page 13, RGD36/1/3 no 3259, RGD33/1/4/ no 684).
[2291] *The Tasmanian Daily News*, 8 March 1856.
[2292] Libraries Tasmania (RGD33/1/6/ no 928 RGD35/1/5 no 596).
[2293] Libraries Tasmania (RGD35/1/5 no 620).
[2294] Libraries Tasmania (RGD35/1/5 no 652).
[2295] Libraries Tasmania (SWD28-1-1 pages 36 and 46); www.orphanschool.org.au/searchorphans.php.
[2296] Libraries Tasmania (SWD28-1-1 pages 36 and 46); www.orphanschool.org.au/searchorphans.php.
[2297] Libraries Tasmania (RGD32/1/2/ no 7718); *The Hobart Town Advertiser*, 2 December 1859.

St John's Church and the Queen's Orphanage, New Town (c1870s).
Courtesy Tasmanian Archives (PH1/1/15).

On 5 January 1860 another of Bayes' older sisters, Lydia, married Thomas Abel, a shipwright of Battery Point.[2298] It was likely through this connection that Bayes became involved in the local maritime community. Though only 11 years old at the time, he is first noted in the records when he competed in the dinghy race for youths under 16 years of age at the 1862 Hobart Town Regatta.[2299] Bayes followed up a few weeks later by finishing first in the same race at the Huon Regatta, competing in the dinghy *Morning Light*.[2300] He would continue to participate in local and regional regattas, as well as private pulling matches, into the early 1870s.[2301] Bayes' older brother Thomas was also very heavily and successfully involved in the pastime during this period.[2302]

Needing employment at an early age, and despite the low pay, Bayes was apprenticed to John Lucas, shipbuilder of Battery Point, very likely providing much-needed funds to help support himself and his siblings.[2303] His brother was also employed there as a shipwright, though may have also moonlighted as a waterman.[2304] While Bayes was quickly recognised for his skill constructing models, being encouraged in this pursuit by his employer, it was at Lucas' shipyard that he accidentally jammed his fingers between two heavy pieces of wood while working on a new vessel, likely the barque *Waratah*, such that one had to be amputated.[2305] Undeterred Bayes persisted with the profession. He also got married, on 25 June 1876 to 16-year-old Ellen Elizabeth Burrows at All Saints Church in South Hobart.[2306] The couple then moved to the Huon where Bayes built the 35-ton ketch *Gertrude* in conjunction with James Heron to the order of William Hawkins of Shipwrights Point.[2307] The vessel was launched in January 1877. Just over two months later, back in Hobart Town, Bayes' wife Ellen gave birth to the couple's only child, a son named William Alfred Bayes (Jr).[2308] Over Christmas of 1878, however, Bayes' wife left him.[2309] Their son appears to have been placed initially in the care of his maternal grandparents with Bayes playing maintenance.[2310] The marriage was officially dissolved some years later.[2311]

While there was much going on personally for Bayes during this time, professionally he was doing well. Along with his brother Thomas, Bayes was still working for John Lucas in 1874.[2312] However, by the late 1870s, Bayes was working alongside his brother-in-law George Whitehouse and George's brother William at the pair's Battery Point boat yard, located near the Secheron property.[2313] Here Bayes built models and helped with construction of the small passenger steamers *Express* and *Pinafore*.[2314] These vessels were launched in December 1880 and October 1881, respectively.[2315]

The first boat Bayes is known to have constructed was a large open 35ft fishing boat which he built for himself in 1880 at the Whitehouse Brothers' Battery Point yard.[2316] This particular boat was sold to F. Hinsby shortly after completion and named *Mermaid*.[2317] It was soon followed by a 28ft second-class centreboard yacht built by Bayes on speculation. Launched on 14 March 1881 the craft was purchased by Messrs Barnard and Castray just prior to completion.[2318] Named *Scylla*, the vessel successfully competed in Derwent Sailing Boat Club and Derwent Yacht Club events over several years and was later converted to a fishing boat.[2319] Next came *Clara*, a 24ft second-class yacht built to the order of H. Calder and completed in May 1881.[2320] The vessel competed in Derwent Sailing Boat Club events from late 1881.[2321]

Sometime in mid-1881 Bayes relocated to Launceston, perhaps in search of more work.[2322] Here he completed at least two vessels: a 25ft pleasure boat of Huon pine and a 18ft waterman's boat built to the order of George Tetlow, both were launched in late 1882.[2323] Bayes then returned to Hobart, where his application for the dissolution of his marriage was granted in May 1883, very soon after making his way to Taranna on the Tasman Peninsula.[2324] It was in this remote location, on the edge of Norfolk Bay, that Bayes resumed his partnership with George and William Whitehouse, building their new passenger steamer to his own model.[2325] The 85ft *Taranna* was launched on 22 July 1884.[2326]

Following, Bayes returned to Battery Point where in April 1885 he completed a 26ft Huon pine pleasure boat to the order of a gentlemen from Adelaide.[2327] The following month he was noted as building a whaleboat.[2328] In June 1886, also at Battery Point, Bayes launched another yacht; a 21ft 'Una' type yacht built

---

[2298] Libraries Tasmania (RGD37/1/19 no 308).
[2299] *The Austral-Asiatic Review, Tasmanian and Australian Advertiser*, 12 April 1844; Libraries Tasmania (RGD35/1/5 no 652); *The Mercury*, 16 December 1862.
[2300] *Hobart Town Advertiser*, 3 January 1863.
[2301] *The Mercury*, 27 December 1866, 23 April 1867, 28 November, 2 December 1868, 29 December 1869, 24 January 1871, 21 January, 15 April 1873, 18 December 1876; *Tasmanian Times*, 6 January 1868, 25 May 1869; *Tasmanian Tribune*, 3 January 1874.
[2302] *The Mercury*, 8 January 1863, 13 August 1864, 11 May, 4 December 1865, 18 May 1866, 23 April 1867, 2 December 1868, 25 January 1871, 15 April 1873, 30 November, 18 December 1876; *Tasmanian Times*, 6 January 1868, 25 May 1869; *Tasmanian Tribune*, 3 January 1874.
[2303] *Tasmanian News*, 10 August 1896.
[2304] *Tasmanian Morning Herald*, 1 January 1866; *The Mercury*, 3 September 1867; *The Tasmanian Times*, 16 November 1868; Libraries Tasmania (RGD33/1/10/ no 1097, RGD33/1/10/ no 2382).
[2305] *The Mercury*, 12 December 1870; *Tasmanian News*, 10 August 1895.
[2306] Libraries Tasmania (RGD37/1/35 no 221); *The Mercury*, 25 July 1876.
[2307] *The Mercury*, 12 January 1877; *Telegraph*, 14 May 1883.
[2308] Libraries Tasmania (RGD33/1/11/ no 2668).
[2309] www.thelist.tas.gov.au (Historical Deed 09/8853); *Tribune*, 10 January 1878; *The Mercury*, 18 February 1879.
[2310] *The Mercury*, 3 June 1881.
[2311] Libraries Tasmania (SC89/1/3).
[2312] *The Mercury*, 12 December 1874.
[2313] *The Mercury*, 20 November 1876, 5 November 1878; *Tribune*, 9 November 1878.
[2314] *The Mercury*, 28 May 1883; *Launceston Examiner*, 10 February 1887.
[2315] *The Mercury*, 20 December 1880, 21 July, 12, 29 October 1881.
[2316] *The Mercury*, 26 July 1880.
[2317] *The Mercury*, 30 November 1880.
[2318] *The Mercury*, 14 March 1881.
[2319] *The Mercury*, 19 December 1881, 3 May 1882, 6 January, 1 December 1883, 9 February, 24 November 1884, 23 September 1886, 28 September 1895.
[2320] *The Mercury*, 5 May 1881.
[2321] *The Mercury*, 21 November 1881.
[2322] *The Mercury*, 3 June 1881.
[2323] *Launceston Examiner*, 25 October 1882; *Telegraph*, 6 November 1882.
[2324] *Telegraph*, 14 May 1883; *The Mercury*, 28 May 1883.
[2325] *The Mercury*, 28 May 1883.
[2326] *The Mercury*, 25 July 1884.
[2327] *The Mercury*, 3 September 1884, 20 April 1885.
[2328] *The Mercury*, 2 May 1885.

to the order of George Allwright.[2329] Named *Marie*, this vessel competed in Derwent Sailing Club events for several years.[2330]

In late 1886 Bayes began construction of the steamer *Koonya* on a small plot of land along Napoleon Street, that was between the shipbuilding yards then operated by William Tilley and Robert Inches, respectively.[2331] Intended to trade between Hobart, the Tasman Peninsula and Lewisham and built to the order of Risby Bros., the 107ft vessel was launched on 10 May 1887.[2332] However, it did not remain in its original trade for long, soon being transferred to the west coast and Launceston route. Just over a year after launch, in November 1888, Risby Bros. sold the *Koonya* to Captain Miles for £4,500 who immediately on-sold it to the United Steamship Company of Launceston with the intention of running the craft between Hobart and Macquarie Harbour on a weekly basis.[2333] In 1896 the *Koonya* was sent to Sydney and advertised for sale. Failing to find a buyer, it was chartered to the Moruya Steam Navigation Company who ultimately purchased the vessel a month later.[2334] The *Koonya* was wrecked on Cronulla Beach near Sydney on 25 January 1898 in heavy fog, its passengers and crew managing to make it safely to shore.[2335]

Certainly gaining a reputation for the modelling and construction of passenger steamers for local and regional trades, Bayes soon negotiated a new commission. Built to the order of O'May Bros. for their passenger service across the Derwent, the 83ft vessel was launched from Battery Point on 12 September 1889.[2336] For more than 40 years, the *Silver Crown* was a stalwart of the local steamer trade. Laid up in 1930, owing to a fault with its boiler, the vessel was broken up at Bellerive five years later.[2337]

Silver Crown entering Hobart Wharf.
Courtesy Maritime Museum of Tasmania (P_OM_L_40b).

[2329] *The Mercury*, 11 June 1886.
[2330] *The Mercury*, 21 June 1886; *Tasmanian News*, 16 November 1888.
[2331] *Tasmanian News*, 9 February 1887, 24 June 1889; *The Mercury*, 7 May, 5 August 1887.
[2332] *The Mercury*, 7 May 1887; *Tasmanian News*, 11 May, 1 August 1887.
[2333] *The Mercury*, 8 November 1888.
[2334] *The Daily Telegraph*, 14 May 1896; *Evening News*, 15 August 1896; *Daily Commercial News and Shipping List*, 25 September 1896.
[2335] *The Australian Star*, 25 January 1898.

[2336] *Tasmanian News*, 26 February 1889; *The Mercury*, 13 September 1889.
[2337] *The Mercury*, 20 June 1930, 11 February 1936.

Koonya.
Courtesy National Library of Australia (nla.obj-148980088).

Nubeena.
Courtesy Maritime Museum of Tasmania (P_OM_N_16a).

Just over a year after launching the *Silver Crown*, the substantial 110ft *Nubeena* was completed, another steamer modelled and built by Bayes.[2338] Launched from Battery Point on 24 September 1890, it was commissioned by George and William Whitehouse for employment in the regional passenger trade.[2339] A regular of the Tasman and Channel routes for two decades, the 138-ton *Nubeena* was wrecked on 7 October 1910 after running ashore at Pipeclay Lagoon, en route from the Tasman Peninsula to Hobart, all hands saved.[2340] At the time of loss it was owned by the Huon, Channel and Peninsula Steamship Company Ltd.[2341]

While also taking on repair and overhaul work, including at Tilley's Battery Point slip, Bayes continued to construct new craft on an adjoining piece of land.[2342] In a divergence from steamers, less than one year following the launch of the *Nubeena*, Bayes completed the Huon pine 36ft half-decked fishing boat *Lucy Adelaide*. The craft, constructed in conjunction with Bayes' older brother Thomas, was launched from Battery Point in August 1891, built to the order of Messrs Herrington and Son of Georges Bay.[2343] A decade later, purchased by William Gates, it was one of the first of its industry to be fitted with an oil engine.[2344] The *Lucy Adelaide* was wrecked in July 1905 near Wineglass Bay on Tasmania's east coast, all hands saved.[2345]

Continuing to combine requests for larger commercial craft with smaller vessels, Bayes built a loading punt to the order of W. H. Cheverton.[2346] It was launched early in 1892.[2347] Next came a 24ft Huon pine pleasure boat commissioned by James Young.[2348] It was launched in March 1893 and fitted with a spacious well.[2349] The final vessel Bayes is known to have built at Battery Point was a waterman's boat commissioned by George Jacobs.[2350] The 21ft Huon craft was completed in November 1893 and named *Tarcoola*.[2351] With demand

Nubeena beached at Pipeclay Lagoon (1910).
Courtesy Maritime Museum of Tasmania (P_OM_B_15d).

[2338] *Tasmanian News*, 26 November 1889; *The Mercury*, 25 September 1890.
[2339] *The Mercury*, 25 September 1890.
[2340] *The Mercury*, 10 October 1910.
[2341] *The Mercury*, 10 October 1910.
[2342] *Tasmanian News*, 27 June 1888, 13 March, 24 June 1889; *The Mercury*, 25 December 1889.
[2343] *The Mercury*, 21 August 1891; *Launceston Examiner*, 26 September 1891; *Daily Telegraph*, 9 November 1891.
[2344] *The Mercury*, 25 January 1895, 15 July 1902, 19 January 1904.
[2345] *The Mercury*, 15 July 1905.
[2346] *Tasmanian News*, 5 December 1891.
[2347] *Tasmanian News*, 5 December 1891.
[2348] *Tasmanian News*, 2 March 1893.
[2349] *Tasmanian News*, 2 March 1893.
[2350] *Tasmanian News*, 21 November 1893; *The Mercury*, 30 November 1893.
[2351] *Tasmanian News*, 21 November 1893; *The Mercury*, 30 November 1893.

for new vessels waning, owing to the depressed state of the Tasmanian economy, Bayes continued to undertake repair and overhaul work for several more years.[2352]

In April 1896 The Mercury reported that a small syndicate had formed to initiate a steamer service for employment in the Huon and Channel trade.[2353] Fittingly, Bayes was entrusted to build the steamer for the group though he died a few months later, on 8 August 1896 at his Napoleon Street home.[2354] Cause of death was typhoid fever and cardiac failure.[2355] Bayes was buried at Queenborough Cemetery, Sandy Bay.[2356] His untimely death, at the age of 44, cut short his career. Sadly, for his wider family, Bayes' death came only a few months after that of his brother-in-law George Whitehouse and only four days following his older sister Sarah's passing.[2357] Bayes' estate, valued at £1,411 was held in trust until his son William, by now employed as a law clerk and a popular local footballer, reached the age of 21.[2358] His properties, including two weatherboard cottages he had built on his Napoleon Street parcel and extending to the river, as well as 20 and 22 South Street, Battery Point, were advertised for sale in August 1898.[2359]

John Bradley

Born in Dundee, Scotland, in 1844, John Bradley was the second of at least seven children born to Charles and Helen Bradley, nee Fleming.[2360] Though his father was employed as a shipwright in Dundee, it was likely in search of new opportunities that the family immigrated to Australia.[2361] While it is not known which vessel Charles, Helen and their five children, including John, sailed on from Europe, the Bradley family arrived in Hobart Town on 22 January 1855 per the schooner *Scotia* from Port Phillip Bay.[2362] Charles near-immediately found work at the Battery Point shipyards with the family settling close by in Colville Street.[2363]

Following in his father's footsteps, as well as those of his older brother James, in his early teens Bradley was apprenticed to John Ross, shipbuilder of Battery Point.[2364] Obviously a proficient tradesman, by the late 1860s he had attained the position of foreman.[2365] As well as assisting with the slipping, repair and alteration of many vessels on Ross' patent slip and with the building of several schooners and barques, during this period Bradley also built the 35-ton barge *Eliza* to the order of Samuel Purdon on the banks of the Jordan River at Old Beach, Purdon also assisting with the vessel's construction which took two years to complete.[2366] The *Eliza* was launched from Old Beach in August 1868.[2367] Continuing his association with the Purdon family, two years later Bradley, along with Samuel Purdon and his 11-year-old son Tom Purdon (later of the firm Purdon and Featherstone, shipbuilders of Battery Point), were all nearly drowned while competing in the sailing race at the Kangaroo Point Regatta.[2368] Bradley's brother James was also competing that day in a separate boat and soon became involved in the rescue with all three crew members on board Bradley's boat *Sunny South* very fortunate not to lose their lives that day.[2369]

On 7 September 1870 Bradley launched the 121-ton schooner *Gleaner*, built by him and his younger brother Charles as well as two other shipwrights by the name of Alick Harley and John Downie.[2370] This particular vessel was launched from Ross' Napoleon Street shipyard taking two years to complete.[2371] It soon joined the intercolonial trade, with Bradley on board as it took its maiden voyage to Adelaide, Newcastle, Rockhampton and then back to Hobart Town.[2372] Bradley then took the helm of *Gleaner* on its second voyage, from Hobart Town to Dunedin, New Zealand.[2373] After many attempts, the vessel was sold in Hobart Town in August 1871.[2374]

Returning to Tasmania and likely in need of a more stable home base, in mid-1872 Bradley took over the lease of John Lucas' former shipyard at Battery Point.[2375] Here, one of his first projects was to fit a cabin to the Port Davey-built schooner *Guiding Star*.[2376] A few months later, on 16 November 1872, Bradley married Elizabeth Purdy at his parents' residence, 5 Colville Street, Battery Point.[2377]

TO MERCHANTS, SHIPOWNERS, AND OTHERS.

The undersigned begs to notify to Merchants, Shipowners, and others, that he has commenced business at Battery Point as SHIPWRIGHT, SPARMAKER, &c., and being for many years in the employ of Mr. John Ross, Shipbuilder, has gained considerable experience in the trade, trusts by attention to business to merit a fair share of patronage. Work will be done with despatch, and at terms to meet the times.

JOHN BRADLEY,
Battery Point.
October 14th, 1872.   6431

The Mercury, 14 October 1872.

With his shipyard's patent slip in operation and primarily involved in repair and overhaul work, Bradley's next endeavour was to lengthen by 20ft cutter *Duke of Edinburgh* which he had helped build in 1868.[2378] Another commission came when he was tasked with fitting out the schooner *Twins* for a pearling cruise, a vessel in which he became a part-owner.[2379]

Following less than three years of operation of his Battery Point shipyard, Bradley gave up the lease on the property. He next moved to Latrobe, in Tasmania's north, where in April 1875 he was noted as building a centreboard barge with his brother-in-law Arthur Purdy.[2380]

Taking nearly a year to complete, the ketch-rigged *Vivid* was launched at Latrobe jetty on 27 December 1875 with Bradley's wife Elizabeth breaking the customary bottle of champagne on its bow.[2381] The 49-ton vessel was sold to Edward W. Russell of Adelaide, soon making its way to South Australian waters where it remained in operation until April 1932 when it disappeared with the loss of three crew while en route from Tumby Bay to Port Lincoln.[2382]

Vivid in South Australian waters.
Courtesy State Library of South Australia (PRG 1373/35/72).

In the months following the launch of the *Vivid*, Bradley soon began preparing timber for another vessel, also built at Latrobe.[2383] Named *Berean* and built on speculation, the 76ft ketch was launched on 20 March 1877.[2384] It was purchased by Captain T. H. Urquhart of Launceston for employment in intercolonial trade.[2385]

By mid-1878 Bradley had returned to Hobart Town, securing employment by tendering for substantial local and regional public work projects, including repairing and building wharves, building bridges across rivers and creeks, laying telephone lines and erecting breakwaters.[2386] Of note, in 1880 he completed a new bridge over the River Derwent at New Norfolk.[2387] These works, carried out in conjunction with his older brother James, ultimately led to Bradley's appointment as Inspector for the Public Works Department in 1883.[2388]

With an interest in civic responsibility and local politics likely gained during this period, Bradley began regularly writing letters to the editors of local newspapers on a wide variety of topics covering whaling, shipbuilding, crime, unemployment, liquor licences, hospitals and nurses, education and trades, wages, mining, tourism and visitors to Tasmania, river pollution, and transport, etc.[2389] He also took up parliamentary debating, as part of the Hobart Parliamentary Debating Association becoming well versed in the intricacies and protocols of his future career.[2390] As well, Bradley invested in several west coast mining companies and became a vocal participant in local associations and clubs, particularly the Battery Point Ratepayers' Association and the Hobart Sanitary Association.[2391]

In early December 1892 Bradley was nominated for the Hobart Municipal Council.[2392] By now a popular and well-recognised member of the Hobart community, he was elected alderman upon receiving the most votes out of all eleven candidates on the night of 9 December.[2393] Several weeks later Bradley was appointed a Justice of the Peace.[2394] After only serving in the role of alderman for four months, in April 1893 Bradley announced his candidacy for the seat of Sorell in the House of Assembly.[2395] However, owing to an inadequate amount of time to fully address his political views to potential voters, he soon withdrew from the contest.[2396] In November of that same year Bradley announced himself as a candidate for South Hobart, encompassing Battery Point (where he lived at De Witt Street) in the upcoming Parliamentary election.[2397] On 21 December 1893 he was duly elected to the Tasmanian Parliament, receiving the highest number of votes out of four candidates.[2398] A few days later Bradley was elected a warden of the Hobart Marine Board.[2399] He subsequently resigned from the Hobart City Council, though was re-elected almost immediately owing to a lack of other nominees.[2400]

Continually re-elected, Bradley remained an alderman and member of the Tasmanian House of Assembly until his sudden death while chairing a meeting of the Hobart Stock Exchange on 14 November

---

[2378] *Tasmanian Tribune*, 25 October 1872.
[2379] *Tasmanian Tribune*, 7 April, 25 July 1873; *The Mercury*, 7 June 1873.
[2380] *Weekly Examiner*, 10 April, 26 June 1875; *The Cornwall Chronicle*, 27 August 1875; *The Mercury*, 23 November 1875.
[2381] *Cornwall Advertiser*, 31 December 1875.
[2382] *Cornwall Advertiser*, 31 December 1875; *Launceston Examiner*, 29 January 1876; *News*, 26 April 1932.
[2383] *Weekly Examiner*, 18 March 1876; *The Mercury*, 10 July, 2 October 1876.
[2384] *The Cornwall Chronicle*, 28 March 1877.
[2385] *The Cornwall Chronicle*, 2 March 1877.
[2386] *The Mercury*, 9 July 1878, 12 April, 7 June, 1, 12, 23 July, 22 August 1879, 30 January, 16 December 1882; *The Cornwall Chronicle*, 25 June 1879; *Tribune*, 5 August 1879.
[2387] *The Mercury*, 4 June 1880.
[2388] *The Mercury*, 24 February 1880, 7 March 1881, 19 April 1886; *The Tasmanian*, 16 June 1883, 3 October 1884.
[2389] *The Mercury*, 24 December 1886, 4, 6, 8 January, 21 February, 7 May, 30 June, 17 October 1887, 15 February 1888; *The Tasmanian*, 15 January 1887; *Tasmanian News*, 12, 17, 19 February 1887, 20 February 1889, 7 March 1892.
[2390] *The Mercury*, 24 September, 9 December 1890, 14 May 1892.
[2391] *Tasmanian News*, 17 May, 19 September, 20 December 1890; *The Mercury*, 24 September, 9 December 1890, 19 December 1891, 9, 26 April 1892.
[2392] *The Mercury*, 1, 6 December 1892.
[2393] *The Mercury*, 9 December 1892.
[2394] *Launceston Examiner*, 20 December 1892.
[2395] *The Mercury*, 12 April 1893.
[2396] *The Mercury*, 13 April 1893.
[2397] *The Mercury*, 6 November 1893, 16 November 1900.
[2398] *The Mercury*, 21 December 1893.
[2399] *The Mercury*, 22 December 1893.
[2400] *The Mercury*, 2, 12 February 1894.

1900.²⁴⁰¹ He was 56 years of age. Bradley was buried at Cornelian Bay Cemetery.²⁴⁰² He was survived by his wife Elizabeth. The couple did not have any children.

John Bradley, MHA.
The Tasmanian Mail, 24 November 1900.

Joseph Clinch and George Luckman

In October 1889 *The Mercury* announced that Joseph Clinch and George Dunkley Luckman had taken over the Battery Point boat yard of Charles Miller from whom both men had received their training.²⁴⁰³ The first vessel built by the pair was a 38ft Huon pine fishing boat, the *Gannet*, built to the order of H. Burston.²⁴⁰⁴ Looking to the future, Messrs Clinch and Luckman were also contemplating laying down a slip to accommodate yachts.²⁴⁰⁵

Born in Hobart Town on 20 December 1836, Joseph John Charles Clinch was the son of Captain John Clinch and his wife Esther, nee Camp.²⁴⁰⁶ His parents had married in London in October 1829 with his father's occupation noted to be a mariner.²⁴⁰⁷ In 1833 John, his wife and their infant son and daughter departed England for Australia where John was to have a long and prosperous career as a captain of various international and intercolonial trading vessels operating out of the port of Hobart Town.²⁴⁰⁸ These included the *Friendship*, *Britomart*, *Merope*, *Flying Squirrel*, *Flying Fish*, *Sword Fish* and the steamers *Tasmania*, *City of Hobart* and *Southern Cross*.²⁴⁰⁹ He sadly died on the bridge of the latter-named vessel in June 1875 while the *Southern Cross* was leaving the wharf at Sydney en route to Hobart.²⁴¹⁰ Ironically, it was to be his final voyage before retirement.²⁴¹¹

Growing up in Hobart Town, Joseph Clinch lived with his family at 79 Argyle Street where, sadly, his mother died in March 1846 at the age of 37.²⁴¹² His father remarried some years later and the family moved to a residence in Collins Street before finally settling at 55 Davey Street.²⁴¹³ Joseph Clinch attended Hutchins School and then, following in his father's professional footsteps, began working as a mariner in his teens.²⁴¹⁴ By 1862 he was second mate of the *Isabella Brown*.²⁴¹⁵

On 23 December 1863, Joseph Clinch married Annie Wright at St George's Church, Battery Point.²⁴¹⁶ The couple had six children between 1864 and 1883, with the family living in Colville Street, Battery Point.²⁴¹⁷ Professionally, he continued his employment at sea such that in the early years of his marriage Joseph Clinch was chief officer of the SS *Derwent*, though in 1866 he was transferred to the SS *Southern Cross*.²⁴¹⁸ By 1875 Joseph Clinch was second officer of the *Tasman*.²⁴¹⁹ The following year saw him appointed chief officer of the newly-built Tasmanian coastal vessel *St. Helens*.²⁴²⁰ In the mid-1880s, however, Joseph Clinch gave up the sea for a land-based career. It was during this period that he learned the craft of boat building from Charles Miller at his Battery Point yard.²⁴²¹ He also joined the Derwent Sailing Club.²⁴²²

A generation younger than Joseph Clinch, George Dunkley Luckman also learned the craft of boat building from Charles Miller during the mid-to-late 1880s.²⁴²³ Luckman had been born in Hobart Town on 16 February 1857, the son of George Luckman and his wife Esther, nee Dunkley.²⁴²⁴ His father was a printer and the growing Luckman family lived at Sandy Bay.²⁴²⁵

---

²⁴⁰¹ *Tasmanian News*, 14 November 1900.
²⁴⁰² *The Mercury*, 15 November 1900.
²⁴⁰³ *The Mercury*, 10 October 1889.
²⁴⁰⁴ *The Mercury*, 10 October 1889; *Tasmanian News*, 22 October 1889.
²⁴⁰⁵ *The Mercury*, 10 October 1889.
²⁴⁰⁶ Libraries Tasmania (RGD32/1/2/ no 7680).
²⁴⁰⁷ London, England, Church of England Marriages and Banns, 1754-1938; *Morning Post*, 30 July 1831; London, England, Church of England Births and Baptisms, 1813-1923 for John Richd Clinch; London, England, Church of England Births and Baptisms, 1813-1923 for Lucy Elizabeth Clench.
²⁴⁰⁸ *The Tasmanian Tribune*, 10 June 1875; *The Mercury*, 10 June 1875.
²⁴⁰⁹ *Trumpeter General*, 3 October 1834; *Colonial Times*, 8 December 1835; *The Hobart Town Courier*, 5 February 1836; *Tasmanian Weekly Dispatch*, 28 August 1840; *The Courier*, 8 March 1843, 2 June 1864; *The Mercury*, 12 June 1865, 21 April 1875.
²⁴¹⁰ *Launceston Examiner*, 10 June 1875; *The Tasmanian Tribune*, 10 June 1875.
²⁴¹¹ *Launceston Examiner*, 10 June 1875; *The Tasmanian Tribune*, 10 June 1875.
²⁴¹² *Colonial Times*, 6 March 1846.
²⁴¹³ *The Courier*, 3 November 1852; *The Mercury*, 25 January 1864, 31 March 1870.
²⁴¹⁴ Libraries Tasmania (NS36-1-1 Page 14).
²⁴¹⁵ New South Wales, Australia, Unassisted Immigrant Passenger Lists, 1826-1922 for Joseph Clinch.
²⁴¹⁶ *The Mercury*, 26 December 1863.
²⁴¹⁷ Libraries Tasmania (RGD33/1/9 Image 54 no 7408, RGD33/1/44 no 372, RGD33/1/10/ no 1480, RGD33/1/11/ no 2078, RGD33/1/12/ no 1395, RGD33/1/13/ no 818).
²⁴¹⁸ *Launceston Examiner*, 24 October 1866; *The Mercury*, 13 August 1870.
²⁴¹⁹ *Australian Town and Country Journal*, 3 July 1875.
²⁴²⁰ *The Mercury*, 11 December 1876.
²⁴²¹ *The Mercury*, 10 October 1889.
²⁴²² *Tasmanian News*, 5 November 1884.
²⁴²³ *The Mercury*, 10 October 1889.
²⁴²⁴ Libraries Tasmania (RGD33/1/6/ no 701).
²⁴²⁵ Libraries Tasmania (RGD33/1/6/ no 701, RGD33/1/7 no 3379).

After establishing their Battery Point yard in mid-to-late 1889, work for Messrs Clinch and Luckman was promising, particularly in terms of repair and overhaul work. In November 1889 they were noted as repairing the barge *Victoria*.[2426] A few months later they repaired two steam launches belonging to HMS *Rambler*.[2427] Clinch and Luckman were additionally noted as painting several yachts, and completing a dinghy for Mr Watchorn's yacht *Surprise*.[2428] Also in 1890, the duo completed two 13ft whaleboat skiffs for HMS *Rambler* and undertook repairs to the yachts *Mabel, Storm Bird Marie, Mayflower, Myrine, Zephyr, Syrene, Tiennah* and *Pacific*.[2429]

In November 1890 Messrs Clinch and Luckman completed two small Huon pine boats built to the order of Risby Brothers for the steamer *Yolla*, one of which was fitted with an air-tight tank while the other was of a whaleboat shape.[2430] The close of 1890, their first year of operation, saw the pair repairing the yacht *Myrine*.[2431]

In 1891 work continued apace. Messrs Clinch and Luckman built a 22ft Huon pine lifeboat for the steamer *Devon*, overhauled the yacht *Mayflower*, built a four-oared whaleboat to order of the Deputy Harbourmaster at Trial Harbour, and fitted out the new fishing smack *Hope*.[2432] Next came two waterman's boats built to the order of H. Sheen of Battery Point.[2433] With dimensions of 21ft and 19ft, respectively, they were named *Rachel* and *Rubina* with both constructed of Huon pine.[2434] Another lifeboat was completed in April 1892, this time for the barque *Doon*.[2435] After a promising start, however, in May 1892 George Luckman and Joseph Clinch announced the dissolution of their partnership.[2436] The former later moved to Sydney where he married in 1903.[2437]

Opting to continue operation of the Battery Point boat yard, in 1892 Joseph Clinch built two boats for the barque *Laira*, a pilot boat for Captain Anderson of the Pearsons Point Pilot Station, and the 16ft waterman's boat *Myrtle*.[2438] An unfinished 28ft yacht (21ft waterline) designed by Tom Purdon and likely built by Joseph Clinch was also advertised for sale as part of the estate of the late J. Stone in September 1892.[2439]

In December 1892 Joseph Clinch launched the steam yacht *Kaa-Ana* from his Battery Point boat yard.[2440] The vessel was built to the order of Messrs H. Nicholls and W. P. Gibson based on a design by John Lucas, previously a shipbuilder of Battery Point.[2441] Measuring 40ft with a beam of 7.8ft, the Huon pine craft was stated to accommodate up to 40 passengers and travel at a speed of 9 knots.[2442]

1893 was another busy year for Joseph Clinch. He was noted as overhauling the yacht *Ripple*; overhauling, cleaning and painting the *Kaa-Ana*; overhauling the yachts *Syrene, Myrene* and *Livadia*; and repairing and altering the yacht *Mayflower*.[2443]

In 1894 Joseph Clinch overhauled the yacht *Loyteah*, repaired and altered the yacht *Tiennah* and also built a whaleboat to the order of Alexander McGregor and Company for the *Waterwitch*.[2444] Shortly thereafter operations at his Battery Point boat yard ceased, with the property advertised for lease.[2445] The last record of him being actively employed in the boat building business was in 1895 when he was noted as building a 28ft whaleboat for a New Zealand firm, to be used in the Macquarie Island sealing trade.[2446] This craft was likely built at the Domain slip yards, along with another whaleboat built by him to the order of Alexander McGregor and Company for the *Waterwitch*.[2447] In November of that year Joseph Clinch unsuccessfully tendered to build two boats for the Hobart Marine Board.[2448]

By now in his mid-60s and a recent widower, Joseph Clinch moved to Bruny Island, where one of his daughters had settled.[2449] Continuing to be involved with the maritime industry, in 1910 he was noted to be the wharfinger at Lunawanna.[2450] He also established an orchard on property nearby.[2451] In 1917 Joseph Clinch attended the Hobart Regatta, significantly marking the 65th consecutive regatta he had attended.[2452]

Joseph Clinch died at his daughter's residence, South Bruny Island, on 3 August 1919, aged 82.[2453] He was buried at Queenborough Cemetery.[2454]

Solomon Cook

On 26 June 1851 Solomon Cook, his wife Elizabeth and their 16-year old daughter Elizabeth Ann departed Launceston per the *Algerine* for Sydney.[2455] The trio had arrived in Van Diemen's Land less than three years earlier, as steerage passengers by the barque *Ratler* from London.[2456] However, in this short space of time Cook had established a boat yard at Battery Point, operating out of the backyard of his home at 24 Kelly Street.

[2426] *The Mercury*, 16 November 1889.
[2427] *The Mercury*, 21 January 1890.
[2428] *The Mercury*, 21 January 1890.
[2429] *The Mercury*, 14 March, 10 April, 21 August 1890.
[2430] *The Mercury*, 4 November 1890.
[2431] *The Mercury*, 18 November 1890.
[2432] *The Mercury*, 20 January 1891; *Tasmanian News*, 2 June 1891.
[2433] *Tasmanian News*, 28 September 1891.
[2434] *Tasmanian News*, 28 September 1891.
[2435] *Tasmanian News*, 21 April 1892.
[2436] *The Mercury*, 11 May 1892.
[2437] George D Luckman n the Australia, Marriage Index, 1788-1950.
[2438] *The Mercury*, 13 July, 25 August 1892; G. Broxam (2009). *Pride of the Port: The Watermen of Hobart Town*.
[2439] *The Mercury*, 7 September 1892.
[2440] *The Mercury*, 21 December 1892.
[2441] *The Mercury*, 21 December 1892.
[2442] *The Mercury*, 21 December 1892.
[2443] *The Mercury*, 17 January, 14, 18 March, 19 August 1893.
[2444] *The Mercury*, 17 March, 26 April, 18 July 1894.
[2445] *The Mercury*, 1 January 1894.
[2446] *Tasmanian News*, 12 February 1895.
[2447] *Tasmanian News*, 1 May 1895.
[2448] *The Mercury*, 30 November 1895.
[2449] *The Mercury*, 3 September 1894; 1914 Tasmanian Electoral Roll.
[2450] *The Mercury*, 18 January 1910.
[2451] *The Mercury*, 2 January 1913.
[2452] *The Mercury*, 24 January 1917.
[2453] *The Mercury*, 4 August 1919.
[2454] *The Mercury*, 4 August 1919.
[2455] *The Hobart Town Advertiser*, 27 June 1851; London, England, Church of England Births and Baptisms for Elizabeth Ann Cook.
[2456] Libraries Tasmania (POL220/1/1 p390); *Launceston Examiner*, 6 December 1848; *Hobarton Guardian, or, True Friend of Tasmania*, 6 December 1848.

Seemingly keen to market himself, his qualifications and skills, he initially advertised himself as available to make business arrangements with merchants or companies. The incessant publicity in the local press began just 12 days after his arrival in Hobart Town whereby Cook announced himself as a naval architect and shipbuilder, providing several impressive testimonials.

> **MR. S. COOK,**
> NAVAL ARCHITECT AND SHIP-BUILDER,
>
> HAVING just arrived from England, where he has been in business for many years, is ready to enter into arrangement either with Merchants or Companies for the BUILDING of VESSELS.
>
> S. C. has such testimonials from several of the principal Companies and Merchants in England as will be sufficient guarantee of his abilities and character. The following are two out of many:—
>
> Commercial Steam Packet Company,
> Fish-street Hill, London, Nov. 30, 1840.
>
> I hereby certify that Mr. Solomon Cook has superintended the building of the following vessels, and that in every respect he has discharged his duty to the entire satisfaction of the Directors of the Company. Names of vessels:—Duchess of Kent, Prince George, City of Boulogne, and a vessel at Glasgow intended to have been purchased by the Company.
>
> JOHN BLEADEN, Secretary.
>
> Hanseatic Steam Navigation Company,
> Hamburg, June 29, 1842.
>
> I hereby certify that Mr. Solomon Cook has designed, constructed, draughted, laid down, and also had the whole superintendence of the building of the steam ship Leeds, now launched and nearly finished. She is a very handsome ship, upwards of five hundred tons, and he has acquitted himself therein to our entire satisfaction by his extraordinary exertions, talents, and honourable conduct, and we consider him perfectly competent for business of this kind.
>
> JOHN AMSINCK, Chairman of the Board of Directors of the Hanseatic Steam Navigation Company.
>
> Address—S. Cook, 24, Kelly-street, Battery Point, Hobart Town, where Testimonials, Models, and Drawings may be seen. 2612

The Courier, 16 December 1848.

Born in Tynemouth, Northumberland, England in May 1800, Cook was a widowed shipwright when he married Elizabeth Field in London in 1831.[2457] Five years later, in details of a criminal case whereby he was robbed of his watch-key, Cook was described as a '*modeller of ships*' of 29 Brunswick Street in Blackwall, East London.[2458] He and his family were living at the same address in 1839 when Cook was listed in a trade directory with his occupation noted to be a '*Surveyor of shipping*'.[2459] Given these credentials, it is no surprise that Cook travelled throughout England and Germany superintending the construction of large sea-going vessels, including for the Commercial Steam Packet Company, the Hanseatic Steam Navigation Company, the Elbe-Humber Steam Navigation Company and the Austrian Steam Navigation Company.[2460] Of note, in addition to those vessels mentioned in the above advertisement, he oversaw construction of the 400-ton paddle steamer *Manchester*, launched in 1841, as well as the screw steamers *Archduke John, Archduke Lewis, Hammonia, Archimedes,* and *Marshall,* launched in the late 1830s and early 1840s.[2461]

With such an impressive resume, it is strange that Solomon Cook did not find supervisory-level work with one of Hobart Town's shipbuilders upon his arrival in Van Diemen's Land or establish his own shipyard. Instead, he seems to have sauntered into the backdrop of the local maritime industry, only showing up in the Hobart Town press for crime-related incidents. First, in June 1850, he was the victim of a robbery via a ruffian equipped with a pistol.[2462] A few months later a whaleboat was stolen from his premises.[2463]

While Cook appears to have competently built smaller craft at his Battery Point yard, including several that were sent to California, there is no known detail of these vessels.[2464] The only inventory of boats of which there is information comes from a list of boats advertised for sale at Cook's yard by private contract in late December 1850. These included four long boats, three whaleboats and one jolly boat.[2465] As stated, six months later, Cook and his family left Hobart Town for Sydney, via Launceston. Their household furniture and kitchen utensils along with tools, timber and '*four valuable pictures of Steamships built for the Emperor of Russia and the Elbe and Humber Company*', were sold at public auction a few months prior.[2466]

Cook appears to have found shipwright work in Sydney, initially in partnership with William West.[2467] He then designed and helped build the *Star*, a 74ft steamer commissioned by James Entwisle that was launched from Balmain in September 1852.[2468] Shortly following, he established a boat yard between the Dove Inn and the Phoenix Wharf at Darling Harbor, though its long-term success is doubtful.[2469]

In early 1855 Cook's daughter Elizabeth Ann married a shipwright by the name of John Harrap with several of their children eventually taking up the trade.[2470] Solomon Cook died '*after a long and painful illness*' at his home of 18 Erskine Street, Sydney, on 25 June 1877.[2471] He was buried at Rookwood Cemetery.[2472] His wife Elizabeth died in September 1882 and was also buried at Rookwood.[2473]

[2457] Solomon Cook in the England & Wales, Christening Index, 1530-1980; London, England, Church of England Marriages and Banns, 1754-1938 for Solomon Cook; *Evening News*, 25 June 1877.
[2458] www.oldbaileyonline.org/record/t18360104-359.
[2459] UK, Midlands and Various UK Trade Directories, 1770-1941.
[2460] *The Courier*, 16 December 1848; *Shipping and Mercantile Gazette*, 17 May 1843; *The Britannia and Trades' Advocate*, 5 September 1850.
[2461] *Shipping and Mercantile Gazette*, 17 May 1843; *Sun*, 11 July 1844; *The Britannia and Trades' Advocate*, 5 September 1850; www.wrecksite.eu/wreck.aspx?313521.
[2462] *The Britannia and Trades' Advocate*, 13 June 1850.
[2463] *The Britannia and Trades' Advocate*, 26 December 1850; *Hobarton Guardian, or, True Friend of Tasmania*, 28 December 1850.
[2464] *The Britannia and Trades' Advocate*, 5 September 1850.
[2465] *The Britannia and Trades' Advocate*, 26 December 1850.
[2466] *The Hobart Town Advertiser*, 21 March 1851.
[2467] *The Sydney Morning Herald*, 24 March 1852.
[2468] *The Sydney Morning Herald*, 18 September 1852; *The Shipping Gazette and Sydney General Trade List*, 25 September 1852.
[2469] *Empire*, 29 November 1853.
[2470] *The Sydney Morning Herald*, 8 January 1855.
[2471] *Evening News*, 25 June 1877; *The Sydney Morning Herald*, 26 June 1877.
[2472] *The Sydney Morning Herald*, 26 June 1877.
[2473] *Evening News*, 26 September 1882; *The Sydney Morning Herald*, 28 September 1882.

Benjamin Dyer

In the months leading up to the staging of the 1865 Launceston Regatta, held in January of that year, Benjamin Dyer announced that he could make sculls to order at his Battery Point yard located at 29 Colville Street.[2474] Clearly seeking to broaden his customer base, this marketing ploy appears to have worked, with several orders for sculls and oars being placed by parties intending to pull in the ensuing regatta.[2475] Dyer also received orders from competitors based in New Zealand.[2476] Continuing with this niche trade, in August 1866 he notably furnished sculls and oars for the upcoming Intercolonial Exhibition to be held in Melbourne.[2477] Later that year Dyer sent a skiff and skulls he had built to Launceston per the *Tasman*.[2478]

In November 1868 a skiff built by Dyer to compete for the Alexandra Prize at the upcoming Hobart Town Regatta was launched. The 18ft craft, fitted with outriggers and built of Macquarie Harbour pine, was constructed of two planks, one forming each side.[2479] Given the somewhat roughness of the River Derwent, the craft was considered an anomaly in design with pundits eager to see how it managed the local conditions.[2480] Unfortunately the name of this particular vessel is not known so it is not possible to ascertain its success, or lack thereof.

By June 1869 Dyer had established his boat building yard at the property along from Castray Esplanade formerly operated by the Degraves family, though still in their possession.[2481] The site had been used for various applications since the Degraves family had closed their shipbuilding operations in the mid-1850s, including for the production of acid by the Tasmanian Pyrolignite Company Ltd up until late 1867.[2482] Sadly, this time period coincided with the death of Dyer's wife Elizabeth from anaemia at the age of 28.[2483]

Continuing to construct racing craft, in September 1869 a sculling match was held on the Derwent between John Ross, pulling in an 18ft skiff built by Dyer, and S. A. Hammett, pulling in the *Vision* built by Thomas Morland.[2484] The contest, for £2 a-side, was won by Ross, surpassing his rival by a considerable distance.[2485]

While Dyer's Battery Point boat yard remained in operation past 1872, there are no known records of him building any further vessels, though this is likely not the reality.[2486] He did, however, continue to produce sculls of high quality.[2487]

By 1876 Dyer was employed as a carpenter and in the years and decades that followed began undertaking contract work.[2488] In September 1879, for example, he was successfully awarded the contract to build a bridge '*over Russell's Falls River*' at a cost of £446 and 2 2s. per chain.[2489] In October 1887 he was awarded the contract for '*Removing Aquarium from Battery Point to the Museum Ground*' at a cost of £34 10.[2490] By the 1900s and now in his 60s, Dyer appears to have resumed boat building in the vicinity of the New Wharf.[2491] Several years later he was operating a yard at Princes Wharf.[2492]

With regards to genealogy, Benjamin Reay Dyer was born in Argyle Street, Hobart Town, on 4 December 1837 to parents Benjamin Bissell Dyer and Ann, nee Reay.[2493] Born in England and immigrating to Van Diemen's Land in the mid-1830s, Dyer's father initially advertised himself as a '*Professor of Dancing*', operating a studio out of 64 Liverpool Street, Hobart Town. However, lack of long-term success with this occupation saw him later transition to farming in the Brighton area, where he also became the postmaster.[2494]

On 14 March 1861 Benjamin Dyer married Elizabeth Ann Stewart, a minor.[2495] The couple had at least four children: two sons born in 1861 and 1869, and two daughters born in 1864 and 1867, respectively, though one child appears not to have survived infancy.[2496] Following Elizabeth's death in 1869, Dyer married Janet Munro in 1874.[2497] Three sons and two daughters were born to this couple between the years 1875 and 1884, with the family ultimately residing at numbers 40 and then 95 Hampden Road, Battery Point.[2498]

Benjamin Reay Dyer died on 21 September 1924 at the age of 86.[2499] His last place of residence was listed as 95 Hampden Road, Battery Point, with his occupation noted to be a miner.[2500] Dyer was buried at Cornelian Bay Cemetery. He was survived by his wife and several of his adult children.

John Gray and Sons

Born in 1796 in the Monkwearmouth parish of Durham, England, John Gray undertook his shipbuilding apprenticeship in nearby Sunderland on the banks of the River Wear, at the time described as '*the leading shipbuilding port for wooden trading vessels'*.[2501] On 15 November 1820, at the age of 24, Gray married Margaret Harper in Monkwearmouth.[2502] Two years later the couple sailed per the brig *Avon* to Van Diemen's Land, arriving at Hobart Town on 7 July 1823.[2503]

Continuing his trade as a shipbuilder, Gray built a 39-ton schooner at the Old Wharf in Hobart Town for Thomas Lucas that was launched in April 1828.[2504] Named *Contest*, the craft was intended for the whaling industry.[2505] A year later he completed the schooner *Industry*, built at the Old Wharf for Thomas Young and Bernard Walford and also intended for the whale fishery.[2506] Just over 12 months following Gray launched a similar vessel, the 47ft sloop *Tasmanian Lass*, built at the Old Wharf for the same customers and the same purpose.[2507] Soon thereafter came the 38ft schooner *Maria* likely built on speculation though later employed in the whaling industry.[2508] In 1831 the 36ft sloop *Richmond Packet* was completed, built by Gray at the Old Wharf to the order of George Wray and Francis Smith.[2509] This particular vessel was initially used to convey passengers, goods and produce between Hobart Town and Richmond, the Coal River and Pittwater.[2510]

John Gray maintained his ship building yard at the Old Wharf for several more years, constructing a handful of vessels. These included the 35ft schooner *Alert*, launched in 1832 for Charles Watts, and the 35ft cutter *Water Witch*, built in 1835 for the partnership of George Watson and James Smith, as well as several smaller craft that were advertised for sale.[2511] In early July 1835 the 36ft sloop *Mary Ann* was completed, commissioned by Thomas Lucas and intended for the whaling industry.[2512]

By July 1837, however, John Gray was suffering financially such that his yard with an 85ft frontage by 200ft deep extending to the creek, along with a neighbouring property featuring a stone edifice '*most substantially built, comprising 13 apartments*' was advertised for sale by auction.[2513] The purchaser was George Watson.[2514] Though no longer a landowner, Gray persisted at the Old Wharf, likely renting his old premises from Watson. Here, on Christmas Day 1839, he launched the 44-ton schooner *Mary*, built in collaboration with James Callaghan and intended for bay whaling.[2515] The vessel was commissioned by a Mr Witton of Hobart Town.[2516] A few months later Gray was declared insolvent.[2517] Still, he persisted, launching a schooner named *Cascade* from the Old Wharf in April 1841 and the 16-ton cutter *Prince of Wales* from the same location in 1842.[2518]

In May 1843 John Gray was officially declared insolvent.[2519] A large vessel, not yet finished, was subsequently advertised for sale by the assignee of his estate, Andrew Crombie, in an effort to recoup some of the losses.[2520] Gray was discharged from bankruptcy a few months later with an admonition from the court stating that he '*follow an honest livelihood, and avoid getting into debt'*.[2521] Taking this advice, he soon found work as foreman of the Degraves family's shipyard at Battery Point.[2522] Of note, he superintended the construction of the 562-ton ship *Tasman*, launched on 12 March 1847, the largest vessel ever built in Australia to date, and the 380-ton barque *Emu*, launched on 2 March 1848.[2523]

By late 1848 Gray had relocated with his ever-increasing family to Bruny Island where he began constructing vessels at Little Taylors Bay in collaboration with at least two of his sons, Benjamin and William.[2524] One of the first craft launched by the trio was the 260-ton barque *David & Elizabeth* launched in April 1850 and advertised for sale as a hull in Hobart Town a few months later.[2525] Estimated to be around 370 tons burthen, the vessel was likely renamed after being sold to new owners.[2526] Next came a blue gum schooner of 85 tons burthen, possibly the *Zephyr*, that was launched from Little Taylors Bay in August 1851 and advertised for sale at Hobart Town two months later.[2527]

By 1853 John Gray had moved to a house in James Street, Battery Point, with his family.[2528] With some of his children now adults, or approaching adulthood, several weddings soon took place.[2529] Continuing the family tradition of shipbuilding, his sons William and Benjamin also established a shipyard at Battery Point in conjunction with Thomas Horne, operating as 'Gray and Company'. The trio operated out of the Degraves family's shipyard along from Castray Esplanade and next to John Ross' patent slip. However it was only in operation for a year or two, ending with insolvency in July 1856 and there is no evidence of any new vessels being built, perhaps indicating that they focused on repair, overhaul and outfitting work.[2530] Sadly this

---

[2501] en.wikipedia.org/wiki/Sunderland; *The Mercury*, 31 July 1884.
[2502] England, Durham Diocese, Marriage Bonds & Allegations, 1692-1900.
[2503] *Hobart Town Gazette and Van Diemen's Land Advertiser*, 12 July 1823.
[2504] *The Tasmanian*, 18 April 1828.
[2505] *The Tasmanian*, 9 May 1828.
[2506] *The Hobart Town Courier*, 25 April 1829.
[2507] *The Tasmanian*, 20 May 1830; *Colonial Times*, 20 May 1830; R. Parsons (1992). *Australian Shipowners and their Fleets. Book 13 (Hobart to 1859, M - Z)*.
[2508] R. Parsons (1992). *Australian Shipowners and their Fleets. Book 13 (Hobart to 1859, M - Z)*; G. Broxam & M. Nash (2012). *Tasmanian Shipwrecks. Volume 1. 1797-1899*.
[2509] R. Parsons (1992). *Australian Shipowners and their Fleets. Book 12 (Hobart to 1859, A - L)*.
[2510] *The Hobart Town Courier*, 25 June 1831.
[2511] *The Tasmanian*, 2 November 1832; R. Parsons (1992). *Australian Shipowners and their Fleets. Book 12 (Hobart to 1859, A - L)*; R. Parsons (1992). *Australian Shipowners and their Fleets. Book 13 (Hobart to 1859, M - Z)*.
[2512] R. Parsons (1992). *Australian Shipowners and their Fleets. Book 12 (Hobart to 1859, A - L)*.
[2513] *The Hobart Town Courier*, 21 July 1837.
[2514] *Colonial Times*, 5 September 1837.
[2515] *Tasmanian Weekly Dispatch*, 10 January 1840.
[2516] *Tasmanian Weekly Dispatch*, 10 January 1840.
[2517] *The Hobart Town Advertiser*, 10 April 1840.
[2518] *The Austral-Asiatic Review, Tasmanian and Australian Advertiser*, 20 April 1841; R. Parsons (1992). *Australian Shipowners and their Fleets. Book 12 (Hobart to 1859, A - L)*.
[2519] *The Hobart Town Advertiser*, 19 May 1843.
[2520] *The Courier*, 9 June 1843.
[2521] *The Hobart Town Advertiser*, 7 July 1843.
[2522] *The Hobart Town Advertiser*, 20 October 1846.
[2523] *The Hobart Town Advertiser*, 5 March 1847; *The Courier*, 6, 17 March 1847; *Colonial Times*, 12 March 1847, 3 March 1847.
[2524] *The Courier*, 4 November 1848; *The Britannia and Trades' Advocate*, 18 April 1850; Libraries Tasmania (RGD35/1/5 no 398, RGD37/1/9 no 563).
[2525] *The Britannia and Trades' Advocate*, 18 April 1850; *Colonial Times*, 10 September 1850.
[2526] *The Hobart Town Advertiser*, 4 July 1851.
[2527] *Colonial Times*, 31 October 1851.
[2528] *The Hobart Town Advertiser*, 18 March 1853; *The Tasmanian Colonist*, 21 March 1853.
[2529] *The Tasmanian Colonist*, 22 June 1854; Libraries Tasmania (RGD37/1/9 no 563, RGD37/1/12 no 856).
[2530] *The Hobart Town Advertiser*, 20 September 1854, 12 January 1856; *The Courier*, 4 October 1855, 11 February 1856; *Colonial Times*, 24 July 1856; *The Advertiser*, 24 April 1863.

period also coincided with multiple deaths, including his son Benjamin at the age of 25 in November 1855 and his son Joseph at the age of 20 in April 1856.[2531] Both died of heart disease perhaps indicating some kind of genetic issue passed down through the family. Notably, Joseph had been master mariner of the schooner *Zephyr* plying between Hobart Town and Victoria at the time of his death.[2532]

With six of the at least 13 children born to John Gray and his wife Margaret between the years 1823 and 1851 now deceased, this period was likely one of melancholy for the family. Seeking new opportunities Gray, by now in his early 60s, his wife and their remaining dependent children relocated to Port Esperance on the Huon River in 1857.[2533] Here, over a period of nearly 15 years, several fine vessels were built by Gray. These included the 60ft barge *Esperance Belle*, built to the order of William Davis of Hobart Town and launched in June 1867; the 52ft barge *King Billy*, built to the order of John Judd for the coastal trade and launched in March 1869; and the 52ft barge *John and Margaret* which was launched in March 1871 and built for his own employment in the local river trade.[2534] He retained possession of the latter-named vessel until 1877, in conjunction with his son Robert.[2535]

Port Esperance (c1880s).
Courtesy Tasmanian Archives (PH30/1/844).

John Gray died at Port Esperance on 23 July 1884 at the age of 89.[2536] Sadly, only four of his children remained living by this point in time. His wife Margaret died six years later, on 5 February 1890, at the Port Esperance residence of her son Robert.[2537] Both John and Margaret were buried at Dover Cemetery.

Henry Hobbs Grubb

The 1842 Census for Hobart Town lists Henry Hobbs Grubb's parents, Henry (Sr) and Elizabeth, as living in rented premises at 104 Bathurst Street; W. Henry being the landlord.[2538] Though Henry (Sr) grew up in the seaport town of Poole, Dorset, England, where his father worked as a plumber, he sought the sea and a life of adventure for his own trade.[2539] By the time of his marriage to Elizabeth Thompson Hobbs on 6 March 1838 at St James' Church, Bermondsey, London, Henry noted his occupation as '*mariner*'.[2540] Apparently not wanting to waste time, just over three weeks later the couple departed England, arriving in Van Diemen's Land as free immigrants per the barque *Wave* on 17 July 1838.[2541] Given his occupation, it is very likely that Henry (Sr) worked his passage on board the vessel whereas Elizabeth travelled in steerage.[2542]

Settling in Hobart Town, Henry (Sr) and Elizabeth soon welcomed their first child, a daughter named Mary Elizabeth born in April 1840, though she sadly died of bowel complaints ten months later.[2543] In May 1842 their second child was born, a daughter named Anne Maria, with the birth register listing the occupation of Henry (Sr) as a '*Timber merchant*'.[2544] Four more children soon followed. These were Elizabeth (born 19 April 1844), Henry Hobbs (born 23 November 1846), Susan Priscilla (born 25 August 1849) and Eliza (born 12 October 1851), with the family by now living in a home in Murray Street.[2545] Returning to his original trade as a mariner, by 1845 Henry (Sr) was helming the 18-ton cutter *Victoria* in the local river trade, bringing timber to Hobart Town from the Huon and D'Entrecasteaux Channel, and also using the vessel to compete in local regattas.[2546]

While the growing Grubb family likely enjoyed over a decade of being firmly entrenched in Hobart Town's lower-to-middle class, sadly its patriarch Henry (Sr) died on 23 January 1854 at the age of 45. Cause of death was '*Tumour in the chest*'.[2547] His will was quite detailed with the personal estate of Henry (Sr) left to his wife Elizabeth, while his real estate interests were jointly bequeathed to Thomas Morland, boat builder of Recherche Bay, and James Chandler, house carpenter of Hobart Town, in trust with a stipulation that the '*rents and profits thereof* [be used] *to maintain, educate and bring up my children then living in such manner as they may think proper until the youngest of them shall arrive at the age of twenty one years*'.[2548] Following, the real estate assets were to be sold with the proceeds divided up equally amongst the surviving children of Henry (Sr) and Elizabeth Grubb. If no children remained living by this point in time, the estate was to be left to his younger sister Eliza Hole (nee Grubb) then living in Woolwich, England, though she immigrated to Australia in 1855 with her husband and four children, going on to settle in Melbourne.[2549]

With regards to the real estate portfolio left by Henry (Sr), it was not as substantial as his will implied. At the time of his death in 1854 he owned two parcels of property: an allotment comprising 39 perches with frontage on Murray Street, where the family lived, and which he purchased in 1843 (likely 204 Murray Street near the corner of Brisbane Street), and a small allotment at Battery Point along South Street near the intersection of Hampden Road which he purchased in 1848.[2550]

While the provisions of the will were honourable, it is likely that there was not enough money to support his widow and young children. Less than eight months after the death of Henry (Sr), a then pregnant Elizabeth Grubb remarried. On 19 August 1854 she wed John Martin, a 32-year-old draper who was also widowed.[2551] Three children were born to the couple between late 1854 and 1859 of whom two survived: a son named William Adam and a daughter named Eva Minnie.[2552]

As the only son of Henry (Sr) and Elizabeth Grubb, Henry Hobbs Grubb was seven years of age when his father passed away. Still, in this short period of time, he had already been immersed in the waterfront activities of Hobart Town and the workload of a mariner. He soon followed a similar pathway to that of his deceased father. Given his mother was quick to re-marry a tradesman, it is also likely that he benefitted from a more stable upbringing than may have otherwise been the case.

From December 1865, at the age of 19, Henry Hobbs Grubb began competing at local regattas in races featuring four-oared whaleboats.[2553] The following year saw him pulling in skiff races against the likes of George Whitehouse and Thomas Bayes.[2554] A keen sportsman, Grubb also began playing football for the Hobart Town Foot Ball Club for which he was nominated team captain.[2555] It was also likely that during this period Grubb was completing the last years of his boat building apprenticeship at Battery Point, possibly with Jacob Chandler where George Whitehouse had also been apprenticed. Here, in collaboration with Whitehouse, Grubb built several working and racing vessels. These included a 21ft four-oared Huon pine whaleboat commissioned by the Reverend J. Wilkes Simmons for the DÉntrecasteaux Channel mission service and completed in October 1867 and an 18ft racing skiff built to compete at the 1867 Hobart Town Regatta.[2556] Grubb also continued racing in local regattas, possibly in vessels he had built.[2557]

The year 1867 ended with some personal news for Henry Hobbs Grubb. On 11 November at the residence of the Reverend J. Wilkes Simmons, 187 Elizabeth Street, he married 20-year-old Jane Mcleod, daughter of Hugh Mcleod, a Scottish-born carpenter and builder, and his wife Elizabeth (nee Cooper).[2558] Witnesses to the ceremony were his brother-in-law Joseph Winch and his older sister Elizabeth.[2559]

Settling into a home in Murray Street, likely the residence his father mentioned in his will, Henry Hobbs Grubb continued to earn a living as a boat builder and build his family. The couple's first child, a daughter named Elizabeth Annie was born on 16 June 1869.[2560] Just over two years later, on 9 September 1871, a second daughter was born in Liverpool Street (Eliza Jane).[2561]

At some point between the birth of these two daughters, Henry Hobbs Grubb and his family relocated to Little Oyster Cove (now Kettering) on the shore of the D'Entrecasteaux Channel. In April 1870 Grubb purchased the cutter *Australasia Packet* (ex *Australian*, built at Hobart in 1824) for employment in the Huon and Channel firewood trade.[2562] The craft was advertised for sale late in 1873 and sold soon thereafter.[2563]

Continuing to build boats, Grubb was commissioned by a Mr Bridges to construct a barge. Named *Joseph and Mary*, the 47ft blue gum craft measured 40 tons register and was considered '*well adapted for the coasting trade*'.[2564] It was launched at Kettering in November 1872.

During this period Grubb and his wife Jane also welcomed their third child. A daughter named Mabel Florence Victoria was born on 27 May 1875 with Henry's occupation stated to be a '*boat builder*'.[2565] Sadly the infant died less than three months later of convulsions.[2566]

Persisting and looking to make the DÉntrecasteaux Channel region his family's permanent home, on 13 July 1876 Grubb purchased property at Kettering. For the price of £7 he received a parcel of two acres, 1 rood and 35 perches bordering the main road.[2567] Just a few weeks later he launched the ketch *Helena Jane*.[2568] Built at Kettering and intended for the river trade, the 44ft Huon pine vessel was constructed to the order of a Mr Torphey (likely of Snug) and launched on 1 August

---

[2549] 1851 England Census for James and Eliza Hole; Victoria, Australia, Assisted and Unassisted Passenger Lists, 1839-1923.
[2550] www.thelist.tas.gov.au (Historical Deeds 02/6174 and 03/4082); Libraries Tasmania (RGD33/1/7 no 2535); *Tasmanian Morning Herald*, 19 December 1865.
[2551] Libraries Tasmania (RGD37/1/13 no 597).
[2552] Libraries Tasmania (RGD32/1/3/ no 5108, RGD33/1/7 no 737, RGD35/1/5 no 1233, RGD33/1/7 no 2535).
[2553] *The Mercury*, 4 December 1865.
[2554] *The Mercury*, 24 May 1866.
[2555] *The Mercury*, 26 May 1866; *Tasmanian Morning Herald*, 28 May 1866.
[2556] *The Mercury*, 15 October, 25 November 1867.
[2557] *The Tasmanian Times*, 6 January 1868.
[2558] Libraries Tasmania (RGD37/1/26 no 240, RGD33/1/2/ no 1964, RGD35/1/7 no 6181).
[2559] Libraries Tasmania (RGD37/1/26 no 240).
[2560] Libraries Tasmania (RGD33/1/10/ no 462).
[2561] Libraries Tasmania (RGD33/1/10/ no 2134).
[2562] *The Mercury*, 16 May 1870; Shipping registers, National Archives of Australia,: HOBART, Continuation [Transactions] Register, Volume 7 , 1855-1949, Folio Tr 99.
[2563] *The Mercury*, 19 December 1873.
[2564] *The Mercury*, 11 November, 3 December 1872.
[2565] Libraries Tasmania (RGD33/1/11/ no 1275).
[2566] Libraries Tasmania (RGD35/1/44 no 348); *The Tasmanian Tribune*, 20 August 1875.
[2567] Libraries Tasmania (RD1/1 Book 81, page 135; AF819-1-152).
[2568] *The Mercury*, 16 August 1876.

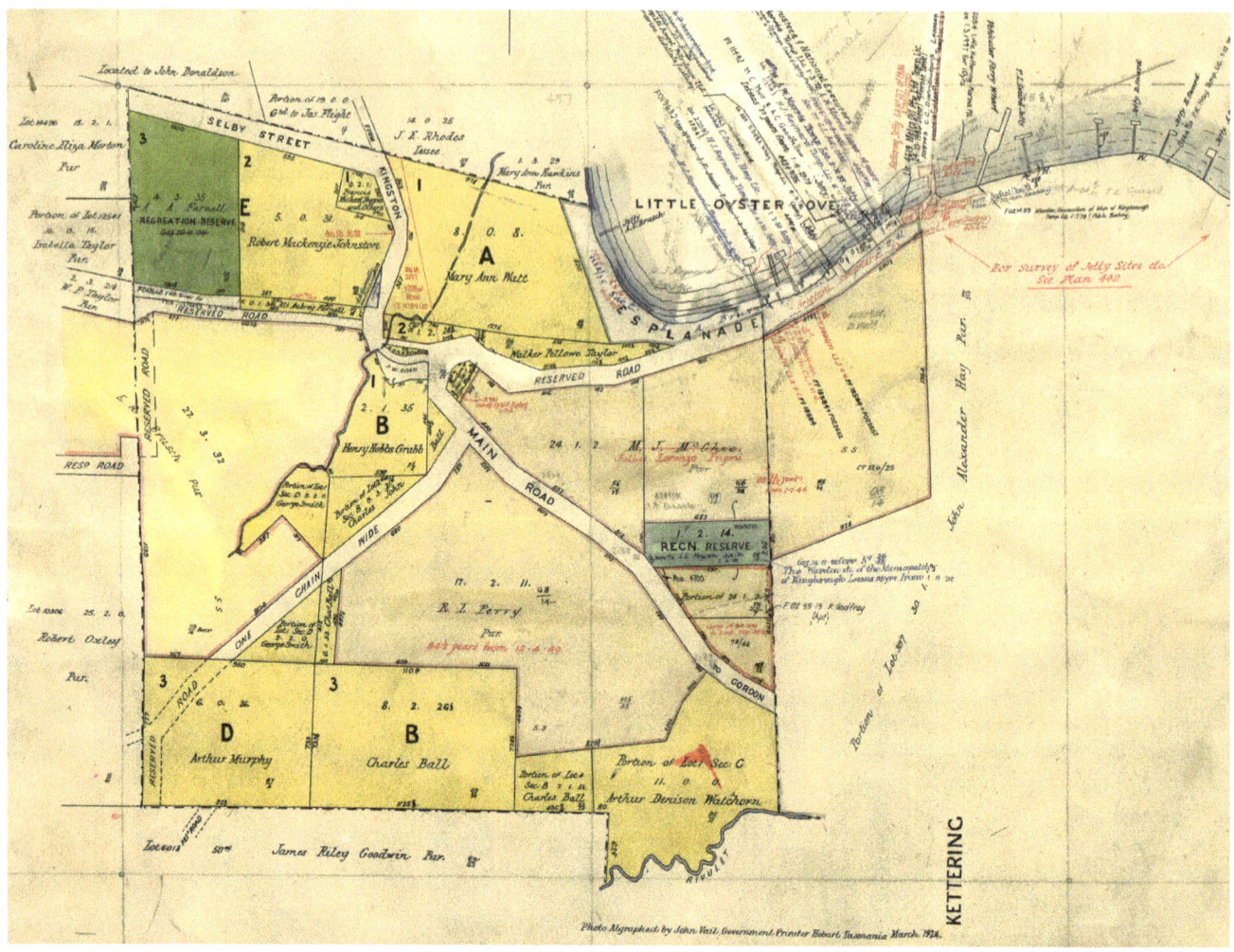

Map showing the location of Henry Hobbs Grubb's Kettering property at the intersection of the main road, reserved road and one chain wide road (marked 'B').
Courtesy Tasmanian Archives (AF819/1/152).

1876.[2569] A few months later another daughter was welcomed into the Grubb family with Henrietta Clara Isabel born at Kettering on 10 October 1876.[2570]

On 15 June 1878 the first son born to Grubb and his wife Jane was born at Peppermint Bay, less than three miles south of Kettering. Named Henry Joseph, the infant's birth register notes Grubb's professional as a publican indicating that he had given up boat building, at least for the time being, and had taken over as licencee of the Royal Hotel.[2571] Grubb was still listed as a publican when his second son, Hugh Benjamin John, was born on 29 June 1880.[2572] He was also elected a trustee of the Gordon Road Trust, signifying his standing within the local community.[2573] It was likely a pivotal time to open a hotel operation in the Channel region. Both Kettering and nearby Snug, Oyster Cove and Peppermint Bay were slowly manifesting into small villages with post offices, schools, roads, police, communication and other infrastructure and services being built. With this development came the construction of jetties and marine terminals to accommodate increasing passenger and cargo traffic.

By the time Grubb and his wife welcomed their seventh child and fifth daughter, Mary Jennet, on 19 August 1882, he was listed as a farmer of Trial Bay, i.e., the next small inlet south of Kettering.[2574] Here he had purchased a 100-acre allotment with the intention of clearing it to establish a farm with orchards.[2575] Grubb appears to have sold his property at Kettering by this time. The same occupation and Trial Bay location was noted on the birth register of the couple's eighth child, a son named Alfred Ernest, born on 23 September 1884.[2576] Diversifying his interests and showing support for his local community, that same year Grubb was noted as a builder of the St Simon and St Jude Anglican Church at Woodbridge with the foundation stone laid on 27 October 1884.[2577] Working in conjunction with two other builders, B. R. W. Mason and J. B. Edwards, the trio having jointly tendered for the project, the Church

[2569] *The Mercury*, 4 August 1876.
[2570] Libraries Tasmania (RGD33/1/11/ no 2304).
[2571] Libraries Tasmania (RGD33/1/56 no 790); *The Mercury*, 4 March 1878.
[2572] Libraries Tasmania (RGD33/1/58 no 1311).
[2573] *The Mercury*, 4 March 1878, 4 November 1879.
[2574] Libraries Tasmania (RGD33/1/60 no 1524).
[2575] *Tasmanian News*, 28 August 1885.
[2576] Libraries Tasmania (RGD33/1/13/ no 2280); *Tasmanian News*, 25 September 1884.
[2577] *Tasmanian News*, 31 October 1884.

was consecrated in April 1885.[2578] Still in existence, the original building was enlarged in the late 1890s.[2579]

St Simon and St Jude Anglican Church, Woodbridge.
Courtesy Tasmanian Archives (NS1029/1/184).

In mid-1885 Grubb announced the sale of his Trial Bay property, by now comprising five acres of orchard.[2580] The asking price was £550 cash.[2581] Upon its sale he and his family moved to Hobart with Grubb returning to his trade as a boat builder. Settling into the local community, in December 1885 he purchased 'Netherly Cottage' at 21 Colville Street, North Hobart, for £550.[2582] The street was later renamed Federal Street.[2583] It was here, on 26 August 1887, that Grubb's wife Jane gave birth to their ninth child, a daughter named Vida Marion.[2584] Education also became a priority for Grubb, with his sons Henry and Hugh sent to the King Street School attached to the King Street Church in what is now Pitt Street, North Hobart, with the building still in existence near the intersection with Andrew Street.[2585] Grubb also became active in the Church, participating in its Gospel Temperance meetings.[2586]

Though he remained in the boat building trade, it is not known where Grubb was working, whether at the Domain slip yards or along the Napoleon Street corridor of Battery Point. By 1890 the family had moved to 12 Napoleon Street, Battery Point, living in a house that backed on to Kennedy's slip yard and the patent slip, where the couple's last child, a son named Allan Mcleod was born on 12 December.[2587] This location indicates that Grubb was extremely likely to have found work at one of the yards in operation nearby, or perhaps had leased space from another boat builder. However, there is also a reference to Grubb fitting new planking and garboard streaks to the yacht *Austral* in November 1890 with the work carried out at Bruny Island.[2588] Perhaps he had turned into a journeyman boat builder, undertaking work whereever it was offered. Into the 1890s the state of the Tasmanian economy was generally trending in a downward trajectory with very few new builds being commissioned in terms of both larger recreational and commercial vessels. Still, it is known that Grubb built a 12ft Huon pine tender to the order of Henry Denne for his new yacht *Volant*.[2589] Completed at Battery Point in October 1891 it was stated, '*by those who have seen her, to be one of, if not, the handsomest boats of her class in Hobart*'.[2590] A few weeks later Grubb launched a 16.5ft Huon pine half-decked yacht for Messrs Davie Bros., members of the Sandy Bay Sailing Club.[2591] This specific craft was named *Lucretia* and became a successful racing yacht on the River Derwent over successive years and under several different owners.[2592] Another vessel was completed by Grubb in May 1892, a 22ft Huon pine boat built to the order of T. J. Chaplin, pilot of Macquarie Harbour.[2593]

It appears that Grubb then moved his boat building operation to the Sandy Bay Esplanade, though still maintained his residence at 12 Napoloen Street. In September 1893 he was noted as building a 30ft (20ft waterline) Huon pine yacht to the order of George Gregory of Sandy Bay to a design by Joe Mason.[2594] Described as a '*really good specimen of naval architecture*', the keel lugger was named *Atlanta* and launched in November 1892.[2595] It competed with the Sandy Bay Sailing Club over several seasons and is last noted when advertised for sale in November 1903.[2596]

Grubb next completed a fishing boat for D. Roberts of Battery Point, intended for cruising on the east coast.[2597] Built at Sandy Bay, the 35.6ft craft was fitted with a centreboard and well.[2598] It was named *Rubina* and launched on 19 January 1893.[2599] Another vessel built by Grubb at the Sandy Bay Esplanade was a 24ft (16.5ft waterline) Huon pine yacht commissioned by J. W. Tarleton (Jr) that was launched in November 1893.[2600] Designed by its new owner, the *Wyuna* was notably the first bulb fin yacht built in Tasmania.[2601] It went on to compete with the Sandy Bay Sailing Club, being recognised for its success, and later sailed with the Derwent Sailing Club.[2602] In 1908 *Wyuna* was sold to Launceston-based buyers.[2603]

While also undertaking repair work, January 1894 saw another 16.5ft yacht built by Grubb at Sandy Bay

---

[2578] *The Mercury*, 9 May 1884, 8 April 1885; *Tasmanian News*, 31 October 1884.
[2579] *The Mercury*, 15 August 1899.
[2580] *Tasmanian News*, 28 August 1885.
[2581] *Tasmanian News*, 28 August 1885.
[2582] *The Mercury*, 1, 4 December 1885.
[2583] Tasmanian Archives (AF394-1-107).
[2584] Libraries Tasmania (RGD33/1/15/ no 777).
[2585] *Tasmanian News*, 23 December 1886; *The Mercury*, 21 December 1887.
[2586] *Tasmanian News*, 1 June 1888.
[2587] Libraries Tasmania (RGD33/1/17/ no 1084).
[2588] *The Mercury*, 6 November 1890.
[2589] *Tasmanian News*, 29 October 1891.
[2590] *Tasmanian News*, 29 October 1891.
[2591] *Tasmanian News*, 29 October 1891.
[2592] *The Mercury*, 16 November 1891, 25 April, 24 October 1892.
[2593] *Tasmanian News*, 9 May 1892.
[2594] *The Mercury*, 10 September, 29 November 1892; *The Tasmanian*, 24 September 1892.
[2595] *The Tasmanian*, 24 September 1892.
[2596] *The Mercury*, 27 November 1903.
[2597] *Tasmanian News*, 23 January 1893.
[2598] *Tasmanian News*, 23 January 1893.
[2599] *Tasmanian News*, 23 January 1893.
[2600] *The Mercury*, 25 November 1893.
[2601] *The Clipper*, 25 November 1893.
[2602] *Tasmanian News*, 9 July 1894; *The Mercury*, 2 December 1895.
[2603] *The Mercury*, 12 December 1908.

Wyuna (front) and *Fairlie* (back) on the slip at Battery Point.
Courtesy Maritime Museum of Tasmania (P_Y_471).

to compete with the Sandy Bay Sailing Club.[2604] The 16.5ft Huon pine vessel was commissioned by Percy Willing.[2605] Unfortunately its name is not confirmed though may have been *Crugana*. Significantly, however, it represents the last vessel known to have been built by Grubb. Sadly he drowned, along with his 13-year-old son Hugh in the River Derwent off Blackmans Bay on 2 March 1894.[2606] The pair had been sailing to the Channel region to collect boat knees when a gale developed such that they put in to Blackmans Bay to add stone ballast to their hired waterman's craft *Racquet*.[2607] About 150 yards out from the beach, disastrously their vessel was struck by a heavy squall, causing the ballast to move and their craft to sink.[2608] Grubb, aged 47, and his son drowned near immediately. While *Racquet* was recovered a few days later, their bodies were never found.[2609]

Henry Hobbs Grubb was survived by his wife Jane and eight of their ten children aged between three and 24 years, only one of whom was married. Supported by a life insurance payment of £250 and the sale of four properties in South Street, Battery Point, and several properties in Murray Street, Hobart, undoubtedly some of the real estate assets initially left to Grubb and his siblings as part of their father's will in 1854, the remaining Grubb family members initially moved to 224 Murray Street.[2610] Jane Grubb died in Hobart on 30 June 1924 at the age of 77.[2611]

George Hubbard

On 27 March 1820 at the Surrey Lent Assizes just outside of London, Thomas Hubbard, along with '*twenty-five unhappy beings*', was charged with uttering forged notes from the Bank of England.[2612] Realising the seriousness of the situation sixteen members of the group chose to plead guilty to a minor offence of '*knowingly possessing*' a forged note as opposed to enduring a trial for the capital offence.[2613] While Hubbard was one of the group that initially pled '*not guilty*', upon being brought to the bar he retracted his earlier plea and was near immediately sentenced to 14 years' transportation.[2614] It was the better of two possible outcomes; the alternative being death.

Hubbard soon found himself among 149 other male convicts, as well as several passengers and a military guard on board the transport vessel *Shipley*.[2615] The ship

---

[2604] *Tasmanian News*, 6 January 1894; *The Mercury*, 12 February 1894.
[2605] *Tasmanian News*, 6 January 1894.
[2606] *Tasmanian News*, 3 March 1894.
[2607] *Tasmanian News*, 3 March 1894.
[2608] *Tasmanian News*, 3 March 1894.
[2609] *Daily Telegraph*, 5 March 1894.
[2610] *Launceston Examiner*, 6 March 1894; *The Mercury*, 15 May 1899; Libraries Tasmania (RGD37/1/55 no 353, RGD37/1/57 no 360).
[2611] *The Mercury*, 2 July 1894.
[2612] *Cobbett's Evening Post*, 29 March 1820.
[2613] *Cobbett's Evening Post*, 29 March 1820.
[2614] *Cobbett's Evening Post*, 29 March 1820.
[2615] Libraries Tasmania (CON13/1/2 Pages 114-115);

departed England for Australia on 5 June 1820 reaching Sydney on 26 September, just under four months later.[2616] While many of the convicts were disembarked in Sydney, Hubbard was one of 61 convicts from the *Shipley* that sailed for Van Diemen's Land per the ship *Guildford* on 19 October 1820 arriving in Hobart Town nine days later.[2617]

Upon disembarking in Hobart Town, Hubbard and his fellow convicts were inspected with their details recorded. With his occupation listed as '*water & lighterman*', Hubbard was described as 5 foot 1½ inches tall with hazel eyes, brown hair and a florid complexion.[2618] He was also noted to be '*well behaved*'.[2619] Hubbard appears to have lived up to this expectation throughout his sentence only being reprimanded on one occasion, in November 1823, whereby he absconded from the premises of J. Gordon, his master, and made his way to Hobart Town; a misadventure for which he received 50 lashes.[2620] Hubbard was granted his ticket of leave in August 1827 and his conditional pardon in March 1834.[2621]

It is very likely that Thomas Hubbard was the infant of the same name baptised in the parish of St John Horsleydown in Bermondsey on the banks of the River Thames just south of London on 10 September 1800.[2622] His parents were noted as John and Ann and he was apparently the fourth of at least six children born to the couple between 1795 and 1805.[2623] John's occupation was listed either as lighterman or waterman on the baptism records of his children. Thus it is plausible that Hubbard gained an apprenticeship in this trade through his father's connection and was definitely employed in the occupation on the River Thames at the time of his sentence in Surrey in 1820 at the age of 20.[2624] Given Hobart Town's location on the edge of the River Derwent, his skills and services would have been in demand.

Thomas Hubbard married fellow London-born convict Elizabeth Reed in Hobart Town on 2 January 1828.[2625] Just over two years later the couple welcomed their first child, a son named John Joseph. His birth register notes Thomas' occupation as a waterman.[2626] The family then moved into premises close to the Hobart Town wharf area where two more children were born: George (26 May 1833) and Henry (15 September 1837, died on 5 March 1840).[2627] Around this time Thomas Hubbard also began competing in local regatta races specifically for licenced waterman. In 1839 and 1840, for example, he competed in the boat *Trial* at the Hobart Town Regatta.[2628]

The 1842 Census for Hobart Town notes Thomas Hubbard and his family as living in Collins Street in a rented house made of brick.[2629] Just two years later, however, his wife was severely injured after her clothes accidentally caught alight while she was lying in front of the fire in the home. She succumbed a few weeks later.[2630] Thomas Hubbard appears to have quickly formed a relationship with Mary Ann Martin. A daughter named Eliza was born to the couple just under a year following his wife's death.[2631] Thomas and Mary eventually married in Hobart Town in January 1853.[2632]

For Thomas Hubbard's second son George little is known about his childhood though, considering the family by now lived in Macquarie Street, he likely had free reign over the Hobart Town wharf area, then a hive of activity due to the many whaling and international and intercolonial trading ships that visited and sailed out of the port.[2633] With his father's occupation as a waterman, he was likely also involved in helping to maintain and operate these smaller craft that were primarily used for conveying passengers and small cargo on the River Derwent, as well as by pleasure parties.

While George Hubbard's older brother John continued the family tradition of becoming a licensed waterman, George instead took advantage of an associated industry then in great demand in Hobart Town by entering the realm of boat building and repair.[2634] Though it is not known if he undertook an apprenticeship nor who he was working for, George's marriage certificate to 18-year-old Catherine Burgoyne on 4 May 1854 at St Joseph's Church, Hobart Town, notes his occupation as a boat builder.[2635] He was 20 years of age at the time.

George Hubbard and his new bride settled into a home in South Street, Battery Point, where their first child, a son named George Thomas was born on 24 February 1855.[2636] George also began competing in local and regional regattas.[2637] In 1860 he and his wife welcomed their second child, a son named James Edward.[2638] It was another six years, however, before the couple's third child was born, a daughter named Rosa Louisa.[2639] In 1868 another daughter was born, Fanny Catherine.[2640] In June 1871 George and Catherine

---

[2615] *The Sydney Gazette and New South Wales Advertiser*, 30 September 1820.
[2616] *The Sydney Gazette and New South Wales Advertiser*, 30 September 1820.
[2617] *The Sydney Gazette and New South Wales Advertiser*, 7, 21 October 1820; *The Hobart Town Gazette and Southern Reporter*, 28 October 1820.
[2618] Libraries Tasmania (CON13/1/2 Pages 114-115).
[2619] Libraries Tasmania (CON13/1/2 Pages 114-115).
[2620] Libraries Tasmania (CON31/1/18 Page 74).
[2621] *The Hobart Town Gazette*, 1 September 1827; *The Hobart Town Courier*, 21 March 1834.
[2622] London, England, Church of England Baptisms, Marriages and Burials, 1538-1812 for Thomas Hubbard.
[2623] Hubbard family tree via ancestry.com.au.
[2624] Thames Watermen & Lightermen 1688-2010; New South Wales, Australia, Convict Indents, 1788-1842 for Thomas Hubbard.
[2625] Libraries Tasmania (RGD36/1/1 no 1096).
[2626] Libraries Tasmania (RGD32/1/1/ no 3817).
[2627] *The Hobart Town Courier*, 11 July 1834; Libraries Tasmania (RGD32/1/2/ no 4769 RGD32/1/2/ no 8436, RGD35/1/1 no 378).
[2628] *Colonial Times*, 3 December 1839; *The Courier*, 1 December 1840.
[2629] Libraries Tasmania (CEN1/1/13).
[2630] Libraries Tasmania (SC195/1/14 Inquest 1115).
[2631] Libraries Tasmania (RGD33/1/2/ no 1029).
[2632] Libraries Tasmania (RGD37/1/12 no 238).
[2633] Libraries Tasmania (CEN1/1/84).
[2634] Libraries Tasmania (RGD37/1/10 no 560); *The Courier*, 3 January 1854; *The Hobart Town Advertiser*, 25 July 1855.
[2635] Libraries Tasmania (RGD37/1/13 no 698).
[2636] Libraries Tasmania (RGD33/1/5/ no 1818).
[2637] *The Courier*, 27 December 1856; *The Mercury*, 23 December 1863.
[2638] Libraries Tasmania (RGD33/1/8 no 3760).
[2639] Libraries Tasmania (RGD33/1/9 Image 158 no 8348).
[2640] Libraries Tasmania (RGD33/1/9 Image 368 no 10198).

Hubbard welcomed a son named William Henry.[2641] Their last child, a daughter named Catherine Louisa, arrived in June 1874.[2642]

During the decades that George Hubbard and his wife Catherine were building and raising their family, George maintained his trade as a boat builder and by the early 1860s, and possibly well beforehand, was working for Jacob Chandler as foreman of his Napoleon Street boat yard.[2643] The Hubbard family lived close by in Kelly Street.[2644]

Coinciding with this period, George built several vessels at Chandler's yard during spare hours. These included a single-handed skiff launched in October 1864 that he built for his father Thomas.[2645] Another skiff, this time intended purely for racing, soon followed and may have been named *Lady Bird*.[2646] In late 1869 George built a single-handed skiff to compete in the Hobart Town Regatta.[2647] Raced by T. Shirley, the craft was named *Faugh-a-Ballah*.[2648]

From 1872 George Hubbard began building boats in the backyard of his home at 16 Kelly Street. Craft he completed included a 20ft Huon pine pleasure boat named *Lydia* that was built to the order of Samuel Jacobs, licensed waterman and launched in August 1872; the 40ft passage boat *Alice Maud* that was built to the order of George Spaulding to trade between Hobart Town and Peppermint Bay that was launched at the New Wharf on 6 August 1873; the 22ft centreboard sailing boat *Coquette* that was built to the order of Samuel Jacobs, licensed waterman, and launched in September 1873; a 41.5ft partially-decked Huon pine passage boat to the order of Michael O'Brien to be employed between Snug and Hobart Town that was launched in October 1873 and named *Henrietta*; and the 40ft passage boat *Agnes* that was built to the order of Robert Meredith and launched at the Hobart Town wharf on 4 April 1874.[2649]

Less than five months after completing the *Agnes*, Hubbard launched the 42ft centreboard ketch *Caroline*, built to the order of a Mr Denehey of Snug and intended to trade between that location and Hobart Town.[2650] The vessel was advertised for sale in August 1875 and subsequently sold to Robert Meredith of North West Bay for £150.[2651] Undergoing various upgrades and alterations, it remained in existence up until the late 1920s.

[2641] Libraries Tasmania (RGD33/1/10/ no 1898).
[2642] Libraries Tasmania (RGD33/1/11/ no 516).
[2643] *The Mercury*, 8 June 1864; *The Advertiser*, 8 June, 24 October 1864.
[2644] Libraries Tasmania (RGD33/1/10/ no 1898, RGD33/1/11/ no 516); *The Tasmanian Tribune*, 28 June 1872.
[2645] *The Advertiser*, 24 October 1864.
[2646] *The Advertiser*, 24 October, 30 November 1864.
[2647] *The Mercury*, 2 December 1869.
[2648] *The Mercury*, 2, 10 December 1869.
[2649] *The Mercury*, 17 August 1872, 27 October, 4 November 1873, 6 April 1874; *The Tasmanian Tribune*, 19 August 1872, 6 August, 15 September, 25 October, 5 November 1873.
[2650] *The Mercury*, 11 August, 16 September 1875, 13 November 1886; *The Tasmanian*, 23 October 1875.
[2651] *The Mercury*, 11 August, 16 September 1875; *The Tasmanian*, 23 October 1875.

Caroline May ex *Caroline* at Battery Point after spending seven months submerged in the River Derwent off Sandy Bay. *Illustrated Tasmanian Mail*, 29 June 1916.

In April 1875 George Hubbard completed the passage boat *Annie Stubbs*, a Huon pine vessel built to the order of William Stubbs and intended to run between Port Esperance and Hobart Town.[2652] He then transitioned into the construction of competitive sailing craft, in October 1876 noted as building a yacht to compete with the Derwent Sailing Boat Club.[2653] Taking several more months to complete, the 31ft cutter-rigged vessel was launched on 29 January 1877.[2654] Named *Secret*, the craft was built by Hubbard for his own enjoyment, though he advertised it for sale a few months later.[2655]

In October 1877 Hubbard completed the 21ft square-sterned waterman's boat *Rescue*, commissioned by Samuel Jacobs (Jr).[2656] He then appears to have taken a hiatus from boat building out of his backyard, perhaps due to other work commitments, travel and/or illness. The next vessel known to have been built by George Hubbard was a 20ft pleasure boat built to the order of Edward Griffin and completed in September 1879.[2657] It was soon followed by another waterman's boat built to the order of Samuel Jacobs (Jr) and launched in December 1879.[2658] These are the last vessels built by George Hubbard at Battery Point.

In January 1881 Hubbard's father Thomas died at the family's home, 16 Kelly Street, Battery Point.[2659] He was 80 years of age. One of the first waterman to commence operations in the Port of Hobart Town, he had only retired the year prior due to ill health.[2660] Shortly thereafter George Hubbard, his wife Catherine and their children, most by now approaching adulthood, moved to Sydney where George continued to work as a boat builder into the early 1900s.[2661] His two sons, George Thomas and James Edward, also took up the trade, operating a boat yard at 18 Leichhardt Street, Glebe.[2662]

George Hubbard's wife Catherine died at their Glebe Point residence of 61 Wigram Road, on 21 January 1905 at the age of 70.[2663] George Hubbard died on 8 May 1913 at his residence, 253 Glebe Point Road, Glebe.[2664] He was 79 years of age.

Robert Kennedy

Born and raised on the remote Isle of Islay, off the west coast of Scotland, where his father worked as a weaver, Robert Kennedy emigrated to Australia at the age of 25 with his wife Florinda and their one-year-old son Malcolm.[2665] The trio sailed from Liverpool, England, on 5 December 1858 on board the *Ocean Chief*, arriving in Melbourne, Victoria, on 23 February of the following year after a voyage of 78 days.[2666] While Kennedy had initially undertaken an apprenticeship in weaving in the small town of Bowmore on the Isle of Islay, by the early-to-mid 1850s he had moved to Glasgow to undertake employment as a ship's carpenter.[2667] This move was very likely precipitated by the death of both his father and mother in 1848 and 1853, respectively.[2668] Glasgow was also the location of his wife's birth, though she had undertaken most of her childhood and schooling on the Isle of Islay, staying with her maternal grandmother Flora Currie.[2669] Kennedy and Florinda (nee Aitken), a dressmaker by trade, had married in June 1857 in the wharf and warehousing district of Tradeston in Glasgow.[2670]

Upon arrival in Australia, Kennedy found work as second engineer on board the iron paddle steamer *Thistle* which traded between Melbourne and Port Albert. On 23 December 1859 the vessel was wrecked on the Port Albert bar while attempting to enter the port during low tide.[2671] All 36 passengers and 21 crew members were fortunate to make it safely to shore with the *Thistle* breaking up several days later.[2672] Kennedy gave detailed testimony in the ensuing maritime inquiry which found the captain negligent on several faults, including being short of coal and entering the port during low tide.[2673]

An enterprising tradesman, Kennedy opted for a shore-based living, undertaking repair and overhaul work of larger vessels by contract and tender, including those pulled up on Gibbon's floating dock in Footscray.[2674] Certainly building a steadfast reputation, Kennedy by the early 1860s had taken out a lease on property in the vicinity of Lorimer Street, on the south bank of the Yarra River in Melbourne, opposite the Victorian Railway's goods shed.[2675] Here, on Crown land with a frontage of only 30ft to the Yarra, he established a shipyard, capitalising on the post-gold rush boom then fuelling expanding maritime trade routes and the need for increased resources and services.[2676]

By 1870 Kennedy was stated to be a '*noted shipwright*', with his family taking up residence in Evans Street, Sandridge, i.e., the area that became eventually known as Port Melbourne.[2677] At some point, his mother-in-law Ann Currie had also arrived from Scotland to live with the growing family, which between the years 1860 and

1879 would expand to encompass 10 more children: Ann Currie (1860), John (1862), Robert (1864), Catherine McAlister (1866), Colin (1868), Alexander Donald (1871), Angus (1872), Duncan William (1874), Florinda Marion Aitken (1876) and Clavey (1879).[2678]

Over the course of 25 years, in addition to repair, overhaul and alteration work, as well as the construction of pontoons and port infrastructure, Kennedy was noted as building several vessels.[2679] These included the 27-ton fore-and-aft schooner *Marten* that was launched on 29 December 1871.[2680] Kennedy built this particular craft for his own use, employing it between the north-west coast of Tasmania and Melbourne for several years before it was sold to a buyer from Fremantle, Western Australia.[2681] Additional vessels built by Kennedy during the 1870s included the 60ft by 30ft steam punt *Connecting Link*, commissioned by the Williamstown Borough Council at a cost of £1,740 and launched in May 1873 for use as a ferry at the mouth of the Yarra, connecting Williamstown and Port Melbourne, and the 90ft schooner *Florinda* launched in October 1873 and initially employed by Kennedy to trade between Victoria and Tasmanian ports.[2682]

In March 1876 the 104ft schooner *Wollomai* was launched from Kennedy's shipyard, built to the order of Frederick Chapman and Frederick Snewin, both of Melbourne, for employment in intercolonial trade.[2683] After nearly 50 years of service, the vessel was wrecked in Apollo Bay, Victoria, in June 1923.[2684]

Schooner *Wollomai*.
Courtesy Brodie Collection, La Trobe Picture Collection, State Library of Victoria (9917298103607636).

In November 1876 another fore-and-aft schooner was completed, this time for the Gippsland Lakes trade. Named *Maffra*, the 46-ton craft was built by Kennedy to the order of the Gippsland Lakes Shipping Company.[2685] For the same organisation, in September 1877 Kennedy successfully tendered to construct a 120ft wooden paddle steamer built at a cost of £4,290.[2686] With a guaranteed speed of 12 knots per hour and accommodation for 40 passengers, the *Tanjil* was launched three months later, on 15 December.[2687]

Paddle Steamer *Tanjil*.
Courtesy State Library of Victoria (9918012813607636).

With his oldest sons Malcolm and John now approaching adulthood, Kennedy reorganised his business as 'Robert Kennedy and Sons', keen to recognise and ensure their involvement in his shipyard's operations and management. Continuing to undertake contract and tender work, in December 1878 the firm successfully tendered the Melbourne Harbour Trust to build 20 punts of 40 tons each, at a cost of £4,469.[2688] In November 1879 they were awarded a second contract from the Melbourne Harbour Trust to construct three punts of 140 tons each, at a cost of £2,398.[2689] Several months later Robert Kennedy and Sons were noted as constructing a stern ladder dredge to the order of Captain W. H. Smith, intended to lift 40 tons of silt per hour.[2690]

Diversifying their business offerings, in May 1881 Robert Kennedy and Sons were contracted by the Victorian Railway Department to build 100 '*medium open goods wagons*' at a cost of £7,845.[2691] Later that year the firm was awarded the tender to build and supply 500 open goods wagons at a cost of £39,225, quite a substantial figure and undertaking, with the work to be completed by 20 October 1883.[2692]

Unfortunately, despite the increasing success of their business operations, the ongoing viability of the

---

[2678] Kennedy family tree via ancestry.com.au; *The Herald*, 19 June 1878; *The Argus*, 20, 21 June 1878.
[2679] *The Herald*, 10 July 1872; *The Record and Emerald Hill and Sandridge Advertiser*, 22 October 1875.
[2680] National Archives of Australia, Shipping Registers: MELBOURNE, Main Register subsequent to Merchant Shipping Act 1854, Volume 4, 1867-1872, Folio 175.
[2681] National Archives of Australia, Shipping Registers: MELBOURNE, Main Register subsequent to Merchant Shipping Act 1854, Volume 4, 1867-1872, Folio 175.
[2682] *The Herald*, 23 May 1873; *The Age*, 18 November 1873; MELBOURNE, Main Register subsequent to Merchant Shipping Act 1854, Volume 5, 1872-1878, Folio 41A.
[2683] *The Argus*, 23 March 1876; MELBOURNE, Main Register subsequent to Merchant Shipping Act 1854, Volume 5, 1872-1878, Folio 151.
[2684] *Geelong Advertiser*, 13 June 1923.
[2685] *The Age*, 16 November 1876.
[2686] *The Argus*, 11 September 1877.
[2687] *Gippsland Mercury*, 11 September 1877; *The Age*, 17 December 1877.
[2688] *The Argus*, 5 December 1878.
[2689] *The Argus*, 20 November 1879.
[2690] *The Herald*, 7 January 1880; *Weekly Times*, 10 January 1880.
[2691] *The Argus*, 28 May 1881.
[2692] *The Argus*, 8 October 1881; *The Age*, 18 April 1882.

Yarra River shipyard leased from the Crown by Robert Kennedy and Sons was threatened by development. In January 1883 the patriarch wrote a letter to the Melbourne Harbour Trust requesting provision for launching of any vessels he might build during the term of his current lease with regard to a proposed extension of the south wharf. After careful consideration, the resident engineer and harbourmaster determined that it was *'inexpedient for the commissioners to make any more launching slips in the prolongation of the south wharf'*.[2693] Several facts were then relayed, including that *'such a course would create vested rights along the south bank of the river, which is already too much hampered and circumscribed by Crown leasees ... That there is a launching slip near Johnson's foundry, which can be used by any person desiring to launch a vessel ... That in view of the rapid increase of tonnage at this port, and the necessity for building sheds and warehouse on the south side of the river, it is absolutely necessary that all graving docks, building yards, foundries or works, should be removed and erected at Coode Island, as the whole of the land contiguous to the river, from the falls to Sir John Coode's cutting on the south side is, or will be immediately required for the extension of the port and its proper working'*.[2694] It was a massive blow to the ongoing operation of Robert Kennedy and Sons.

Preservering, the same month they received news of the Harbour Trust's proposed wharf development impinging on their slip yard, Robert Kennedy and Sons finished construction of a 42ft steam launch to the order of the P. and O. Company for use in Albany, Western Australia.[2695] It was reportedly the second steam launch turned out by the firm for a customer based in Albany.[2696] Robert Kennedy and Sons also continued their involvement with government railway contracts. In July 1883, for example, they were contracted to supply fishbolts at a cost of £3,053.[2697]

Continuing to lobby for access to the Yarra River from his shipyard, in February 1884 Robert Kennedy and Sons made a formal complaint to the commissioner of the South Melbourne Council stating that the erection of a wharf by the Melbourne Harbour Trust in front of their property had obstructed operations such that their business had been all but destroyed.[2698] The following month the Trust met to discuss the possibility of creating an opening in the wharf to allow for the launching of vessels from Robert Kennedy and Sons' shipyard.[2699] After months of debate and some opposition, in April 1884 the Melbourne Harbour Trust approved the request for the moveable opening, with some stipulations, including that launchings be restricted to night time hours and that public and thoroughfare disruptions be kept to a minimum.[2700]

However, despite gaining regulatory approval, Robert Kennedy and Sons did not make the alterations to their shipyard, of which they were tasked with financing. Instead they looked for suitable locations further afield where they could grow their business in the comfort of less governmental interference. The last Victorian-based project the company was involved with appears to be a tender awarded to them in June 1884 to construct a pontoon for harbour improvement work.[2701]

In early January 1885 Kennedy's oldest son Malcolm began advertising his various real estate assets for sale, including his family's home.[2702] That same month he relocated to Tasmania, purchasing the Derwent Iron Works and Engineering Company from J. W. Syme (who retained a quarter share of the business until November 1887).[2703] Located in Hobart at the New Wharf the firm, operating as 'R. Kennedy and Sons', immediately set about establishing their customer base, advertising the various facets of their operations.

R. KENNEDY & SONS, Shipbuilders, Engineers, and Shipsmiths, Manufacturers of land and marine engines, boilers of all types, hoisting engines and cranes, bridges, girders, tanks and vats, and sawmill machinery, castings of every description in brass and iron; contractors' and iron work supplied with despatch; repairs executed at lowest rates. Address Derwent Ironworks and Engineering Co., New Wharf.

The Mercury, 24 January 1885.

Of note, part of the Derwent Iron Works and Engineering Company's assets included the Battery Point shipyard and patent slip located off Napoleon Street with R. Kennedy and Sons paying a substantial £2,379 for the property.[2704] The shipyard and slip had previously been operated by John Lucas (see a previous chapter), who remained at the site managing its operations for a number of years.[2705]

Meanwhile, during this period, Robert Kennedy remained in Melbourne seeking to renew the lease with the Crown on his existing shipyard property. The terms, however, were far from ideal. Kennedy and other leasees in similar positions instead proposed to surrender their sites upon receipt of a *'fair compensation for improvements'* they had made during the many decades they had all been commercial tenants of properties on the south bank of the Yarra River.[2706] Despite a lot of back and forth, it was clear they were

---

[2693] *The Argus*, 11 January 1883.
[2694] *The Argus*, 11 January 1883.
[2695] *The Argus*, 12 January 1883.
[2696] *The Argus*, 12 January 1883.
[2697] *The Herald*, 26 July 1883.
[2698] *Record*, 22 February 1884.
[2699] *The Argus*, 5 March 1884.
[2700] *The Argus*, 6, 20 March 1884; *Record*, 18 April 1884.
[2701] *The Herald*, 12 June 1884.
[2702] *The Age*, 3 January 1885.
[2703] *The Mercury*, 17, 24 January, 19 September 1885, 17 January 1888.
[2704] *The Mercury*, 17 January, 28 March 1885; www.thelist.tas.gov.au (Historical Deed 07/9576).
[2705] *The Mercury*, 2, 6 September 1884, 13, 22 May, 17 November 1885, 26 April 1886.
[2706] *The Herald*, 19 March 1885.

being pushed out. During the final months of 1885 Kennedy sold the entire complement of his shipyard's machinery, plant and tools, without reserve.[2707] The lease of the property was taken over by the Australasian Steam Navigation Company in January 1886 for use as a coal depot.[2708] Kennedy then relocated with his family to Hobart, joining his older son. He was 52 years of age and about to start a new enterprise in a new colony. He and his family established their home at 305 Macquarie Street.[2709]

Upon resuming their business operations in Hobart, one of the Kennedy family's first projects was to supply ironwork for railway bridges being constructed across the River Derwent near New Norfolk.[2710] In the years to come their foundry and engineering work would be heavily associated with Tasmania's mining industry. They also supplied components for the construction and maintenance of buildings, bridges, railways, churches and lighthouses.

In terms of their shipbuilding and slipyard business, specifically, in April 1885 R. Kennedy and Sons were tasked with building a new multi-tubular boiler, shaft and fly-wheel for the steamer *Minx*, as well as overhauling and renewing the vessel's machinery.[2711] Afterwards, R. Kennedy and Sons were awarded the contract to undertake repairs of the ship *Irby*; John Lucas being tasked with the woodwork component of the repairs, as well as the steamer *Esk*.[2712] A new boiler was next constructed for the ship *Emily Downing*.[2713]

The firm also secured various contracts, including with the Mersey Marine Board for the building of an iron steam dredge fitted with a Priestman crane for use at the Mersey Bar in Devonport (at a cost of £11,690).[2714] This particular vessel, the 112ft *Agnew*, was launched on 26 March 1887, with the event noted in detail in the local press, particularly because it was the first iron vessel built in Tasmania, and the fact that the whole of its machinery had been entirely manufactured in the colony.[2715] The auspicious occasion was further supplemented by the launch of the 69ft *Tarrina*, on the same day, a blue gum steam launch built by R. Kennedy and Sons to the order of the Launceston Marine Board.[2716] These two projects, as well as regular slip work, coincided with nearly 300 men being employed at the yard during the latter months of 1886 and up until the completion of both craft.[2717]

Steam launch *Tarrina*.
Weekly Courier, 15 November 1923.

[2707] *The Argus*, 28 November, 30 December 1885.
[2708] *The Age*, 9 January 1886.
[2709] Libraries Tasmania (NS36-1-1 Page 116).
[2710] *The Mercury*, 12 February 1885.
[2711] *The Mercury*, 18 April, 5 August, 26 October 1885.
[2712] *The Mercury*, 12, 13 May, 17 November 1885.
[2713] *The Mercury*, 31 July 1885.

[2714] *The Mercury*, 20 February 1886; *Launceston Examiner*, 20 February, 9 March 1886.
[2715] *The Mercury*, 26, 28 March 1887.
[2716] *The Mercury*, 26, 28 March 1887.
[2717] *The Mercury*, 11 December 1886, 26 March 1887; *Tasmanian*, 26 March 1887.

Steam dredge *Agnew*.
Weekly Courier, 2 July 1904.

Genevie M. Tucker on the patent slip at R. Kennedy and Sons' shipyard (February 1890). Courtesy Tasmanian Archives (NS1013/1/372).

For many years the Kennedy family's Battery Point shipyard was also busy with overhaul, alteration and repair work, particularly of steamships and larger vessels involved in intercolonial and international trade. From October 1890, adjacent to the patent slip, a silver lead ore smelter was fully established on the site.[2718] It was capable of smelting 15 tons over a 24-hour period, though was only operational for a few years.[2719] Continuing the mixed-use of the property, R. Kennedy and Sons built one more vessel. The 78ft wooden ketch *Aristides* was launched on 19 August 1902 and built for their own employment in interstate trade.[2720] It joined at least one other vessel that the Kennedy family owned that was then operating in the same trade, the brigantine *Carin*.[2721]

Robert Kennedy died on 15 May 1903 at his residence, Ardmore, 51 Davey Street, Hobart, and was buried at Cornelian Bay Cemetery.[2722] He was 69 years of age. Kennedy was survived by his wife Florinda and all eleven of their children. The business of R. Kennedy and Sons was subsequently transferred to his sons Malcolm, John and Colin who increasingly became more and more involved in investing in and providing engineering services, machinery and equipment to the local, interstate and overseas mining industries.[2723]

Though R. Kennedy and Sons maintained possession of their Battery Point shipyard for many decades; the patent slip originally purchased from England by John Ross and installed there in 1866 was removed from the site in 1911 to be relaid in Devonport.[2724] In the years that followed, the property was leased to various parties, including H. Jones and Company for construction of their three-masted schooner *Amelia J.* in 1919 (built by Henry Moore of Launceston).[2725] The steamers *Excella* (built by John Dalgleish and launched in 1912) and *Rosny* (built by Fred Moore, brother of Henry Moore, and launched in 1913) were also built on the property.[2726]

On 14 November 1947 the entire parcel of land was conveyed by R. Kennedy and Sons to the Marine Board of Hobart, with various tenants using part of it over the following decades.[2727] It is now an asset of the Hobart City Council.

After over 60 years of operation in Tasmania, the firm of R. Kennedy and Sons Pty. Ltd. was wound up in 1947, with its assets sold.[2728] This process took place several years after the death of its managing director, Malcolm Kennedy.[2729]

Robert Kennedy.
Courtesy Tasmanian Archives (NS2511/1/219).

William Tilley

William James Tilley was born on 31 August 1829 in Hobart Town, the son of Edward and Elizabeth Ann Tilley (nee Norman).[2730] His was the couple's sixth child with their five older children all born in England.[2731] On 27 July 1824 Tilley's father Edward had arrived in Van Diemen's Land as one of 180 convicts on board the transport ship *Chapman*.[2732] Also on board was Edward's older brother John.[2733] Both had been employed as sawyers in the small rural village of Lodsworth, West Sussex, known for its agriculture and forestry.[2734] At the age of 31 and 37 years, respectively, Edward and John Tilley were sentenced to seven years' transportation for the crime of being found at night on land belonging to the Duke of Richmond, some 10 miles from Lodsworth in the neighbouring parish of Boxglove.[2735] The pair were in possession of a gun with the intent to illegally destroy game.[2736] Both were married with children.

The two brothers were not the first of their siblings to be confined to Van Diemen's Land. Their older brother William had been transported to Hobart Town several years prior after being sentenced to life for stealing a mare.[2737] Given the fact that all three were

---

[2718] *The Mercury*, 25 October 1890.
[2719] *The Mercury*, 25 October 1890; *Tasmanian News*, 19 June 1897.
[2720] *The Mercury*, 20 August 1902.
[2721] *The Mercury*, 3 November 1900, 3 September 1901; *Tasmanian News*, 23 September 1902.
[2722] *The Mercury*, 16 May 1903.
[2723] *The Mercury*, 29 July 1944.
[2724] *The Mercury*, 21 August 1911, 5 September 1923; *Tasmanian Government Gazette*, 2 June 1919.
[2725] *The Mercury*, 4 March, 27 June 1918, 1 August 1919; *Tasmanian Government Gazette*, 2 June 1919.
[2726] *Huon Times*, 9 November 1912; *The Mercury*, 27 June, 1918.
[2727] *The Mercury*, 9 July 1948, 20 September 1950, 4 July 1953; www.thelist.tas.gov.au (Historical Deed 23/3023).
[2728] *The Mercury*, 2 March 1946.
[2729] *Examiner*, 31 July 1944.

[2730] Libraries Tasmania (RGD32/1/1/ no 3040).
[2731] Libraries Tasmania (CSO1/1/344 file 7875 pp48 & 57).
[2732] *Hobart Town Gazette and Van Diemen's Land Advertiser*, 30 July 1824; Libraries Tasmania (CON31/1/42).
[2733] Libraries Tasmania (CON31/1/42).
[2734] Libraries Tasmania (CON23/1/3 no 282).
[2735] *Sussex Advertiser*, 19 January 1824.
[2736] *Sussex Advertiser*, 19 January 1824.
[2737] London, England, Newgate Calendar of Prisoners, 1785-1853 for William Tilley;

under sentence, any meeting, if one at all took place, would have been very short-lived.

Edward and John Tilly were soon sent to work as sawyers at Birchs Bay in the D'Entrecasteaux Channel where they appear to have largely avoided trouble. In contrast, their brother William was noted for absconding and stealing, adding increasingly more years to his long-term sentence.[2738]

With her primary income earner transported to Van Diemen's Land, Edward Tilley's wife Elizabeth Ann and the couple's five children became paupers, applying to the vestry of the parish of Lodsworth for relief. Her plea was thankfully answered with the parish agreeing to pay for the passage of Elizabeth Ann and their children to Van Diemen's Land.[2739] The group arrived in Hobart Town per the ship *Borneo* on 1 November 1828.[2740]

With the arrival of Edward Tilley's wife Elizabeth and their five children, the family unit was once more restored with the couple's son William James Tilley, as stated in a previous paragraph, born in Hobart Town on 31 August 1829.[2741] Sadly, the reunification did not last long. On 12 May 1831 Edward Tilley, by now a sawyer and timber merchant living with his family in Bathurst Street, was drowned along with five others when the small schooner they were sailing in to fetch timber from Three Hut Point in the D'Entrecasteaux Channel was upset off Tinderbox during a sudden squall.[2742] His wife Elizabeth Ann gave birth to the couple last child six months later, a son named Edward James.[2743] In the years ahead Elizabeth Ann and her children received support from her brother-in-law John Tilley who in 1837 became licensee of the Sawyers Arms Hotel in Murray Street which he operated until 1850.[2744] Several children were born to the couple during the 1830s.[2745]

After a somewhat muddled childhood, given his family's situation, William Tilley likely found an apprenticeship in shipbuilding at one of the many yards then in operation in Hobart Town. By 1849, at the age of 20, he also began competing in local regatta races.[2746]

With a spark for adventure and the opportunity for handsome returns, in early 1852 William Tilley sailed for Port Phillip Bay as one of many young, single men in search of gold.[2747] He returned to Van Diemen's Land some months later though sailed back to Victoria in October of that same year.[2748] His two older brothers, George and Charles, and his younger brother Edward were also in Victoria during this period.[2749] While Edward sadly died, aged only 21, George and Charles returned to Hobart Town in November 1852 bringing with them 60lbs weight of gold which they on-sold at £3 10s. 6d per ounce.[2750]

It is not known how William fared, though he too had returned to Hobart Town by late 1873. On 7 December at Trinity Church he married 19-year-old Anne Abigail Martin.[2751] The couple then moved to Melbourne, returning to Tasmania in 1857. They had at least 15 children between the years 1855 and 1883 of whom 10 survived infancy.[2752]

Needing to support an increasingly growing family, William Tilley settled in to work as a shipwright, though by 1861 was operating as a grocer in Murray Street.[2753] He returned to shipwright work two years later.[2754] This trade appears to have been a more opportune income source for Tilley such that in May 1880 he took out a lease on John Lucas' former Battery Point shipyard off Napoleon Street.[2755]

Tilley maintained operation of this Battery Point yard for nearly 14 years, primarily undertaking overhaul, repair and fit-out work.[2756] From 1883 he operated the site in partnership with Edward Williams, who had undertaken his shipbuilding apprenticeship with John Ross at Battery Point.[2757] During this period only one vessel is known to have been built at the yard: the 21ft yacht *Venus*, launched on 31 July 1886 and built by Tilley's son Alfred for his own personal use.[2758] The steamer *Koonya*, built by William Bayes to the order of Risby Brothers, was also launched from Tilley and Williams' Battery Point slip yard on 10 May 1887, as was the ferry boat *Tarcoola*, built by Bayes in November 1893.[2759]

Having relinquished operation of his Battery Point shipyard in early 1894, William Tilley entered retirement.[2760] His wife, Anne Abigail, had died of breast cancer a decade prior, on 2 October 1883.[2761] She was 49 years of age and only seven months earlier had given birth to the couple's last child, a daughter named Ruby Grace.[2762] William Tilley died at his residence, 195 Murray Street, Hobart, on 2 February 1902 aged 72.[2763] He was buried at Queenborough Cemetery, Sandy Bay.[2764]

Libraries Tasmania (CON23/1/3 no 225).
[2738] Libraries Tasmania (SC32-1-1 Image 147); *The Hobart Town Gazette*, 3 May 1828; *The Hobart Town Courier*, 13 November 1830.
[2739] West Sussex Record Office (Par128/12/2: Paupers' relief and vestry minute book (1825-1840).
[2740] Libraries Tasmania (CSO1/1/344 file 7875 pp48 & 57).
[2741] Libraries Tasmania (RGD32/1/1/ no 3040).
[2742] *Colonial Times*, 11 May 1831; *The Hobart Town Courier*, 14 May 1831.
[2743] Libraries Tasmania (RGD32/1/1/ no 4192).
[2744] *The Hobart Town Courier*, 6 October 1837; *The True Colonist Van Diemen's Land Political Despatch, and Agricultural and Commercial ...*, 7 September 1838; *Colonial Times*, 12 December 1848; *The Hobart Town Advertiser*, 12 December 1848, 8 February 1850.
[2745] *The True Colonist Van Diemen's Land Political Despatch, and Agricultural and Commercial ...*, 7 September 1838; Libraries Tasmania (RGD34/1/1 no 3388).
[2746] *The Courier*, 5 December 1849.
[2747] Libraries Tasmania (POL220/1/1 p533).
[2748] Libraries Tasmania (CUS36/1/217).
[2749] Libraries Tasmania (POL220/1/2 p283); Edward Tilley in the Victoria, Australia, Wills and Probate Records, 1841-2009.
[2750] *Hobarton Guardian, or, True Friend of Tasmania*, 13 November 1852; *Geelong Advertiser and Intelligencer*, 4 September 1852.
[2751] Libraries Tasmania (RGD37/1/12 no 576).
[2752] Tilley family tree via ancestry.com.au.
[2753] Libraries Tasmania (RGD33/1/8 no 4142).
[2754] Libraries Tasmania (RGD33/1/8 no 5915).
[2755] *The Mercury*, 28 June 1880, 23 June 1882.
[2756] *The Mercury*, 17 May, 3 September 1890, 28 June 1892, 30 June, 9 August 1893; *Tasmanian News*, 2 March 1891, 20 December 1893.
[2757] *The Mercury*, 31 March 1883, 17 May 1890; Maritime Museum of Tasmania (D_1997-005).
[2758] *Tasmanian News*, 2 August 1886.
[2759] *The Mercury*, 7 May 1887; *Tasmanian News*, 21 November 1893, 22 January 1894.
[2760] *The Mercury*, 30 June, 9 August 1893; *Tasmanian News*, 20 December 1893.
[2761] Libraries Tasmania (RGD35/1/10 no 1192).
[2762] *The Mercury*, 3 October 1883; Libraries Tasmania (RGD37/1/13/ no 638).
[2763] *The Mercury*, 3 February 1902.
[2764] *The Mercury*, 3 February 1902.

Vessels built by various builders and their employees, as well as amateurs at Battery Point (1850 - 1895)

Year	Name	Type	Description
1850	--	Long boat	20ft. Copper-fastened. Built by Solomon Cook at his Kelly Street home and advertised for sale in December 1850.
1850	--	Whaleboat	29.5ft. Built by Solomon Cook at his Kelly Street home and advertised for sale in December 1850.
1850	--	Whaleboat	25.5ft. Built by Solomon Cook at his Kelly Street home and advertised for sale in December 1850.
1850	--	Whaleboat	22ft. Built by Solomon Cook at his Kelly Street home and advertised for sale in December 1850.
1850	--	Long boat	14ft. Clinker-built. Constructed by Solomon Cook at his Kelly Street home and advertised for sale in December 1850.
1850	--	Jolly boat	16ft. Built by Solomon Cook at his Kelly Street home and advertised for sale in December 1850.
1850	--	Long boat	17ft. Built by Solomon Cook at his Kelly Street home and advertised for sale in December 1850.
1850	--	Long boat	25ft. Built by Solomon Cook at his Kelly Street home and advertised for sale in December 1850.
1850	--	Whaleboat	30ft. Built by Solomon Cook at his Kelly Street home to the order of Charles Wilson.
1866	--	Skiff	Built by Benjamin Dyer at his Colville Street home and shipped to Launceston per the *Tasman* in December 1866, along with a pair of sculls.
1868	--	Skiff	18ft x 24in. Built by Benjamin Dyer at his Colville Street home in November 1868 to compete for the Alexandra Prize at the Hobart Town Regatta. Constructed of two planks of Macquarie Pine.
1868	--	Skiff	18ft. Built by Benjamin Dyer at his Colville Street home by September 1869 and raced by John Ross in a £2 a-side sculling match held on the River Derwent against S. A. Hammett in the *Vision* (built by Morland). Won the race by a considerable margin.
1872	Lydia	Pleasure boat	20 x 4ft x 20in. Huon pine boat built by George Hubbard at his Kelly Street home to the order of Samuel Jacobs, licensed waterman. Launched in August 1872. Used as part of Jacobs' hire boat business. In December 1876 recovered from Ralphs Bay after being overturned and nearly lost when five lads, who hired it, attempted to board the whaling barque *Aladdin*.
1872	Star of the South	Whaleboat	25 x 4.5ft. Racing whaleboat built by Peter Sullivan of Battery Point, a self-taught boat builder, to compete in two events at the 1872 Hobart Town Regatta.
1873	Alice Maud	Passage boat	40 x 8ft. Passage boat built by George Hubbard at his Kelly Street home to the order of George Spaulding and launched on 6 August 1873 at the New Wharf. Employed carrying firewood and fruit from Peppermint Bay to Hobart Town for many decades. Competed in the sailing race at the 1874 Hobart Town Regatta. By 1878 owned by W. Edwards. By 1882 owned by B. Mason. Capsized off Blackmans Bay in December 1883 though recovered. At the time owned by Frank Nickolls of Long Bay and sailed by his teenage sons, August and Frank (Jr). By 1890 owned by Alex McKay. By 1897 owned by E. Tolman of Flowerpot. By 1918 converted to a fishing boat owned by Moses Barnett and leased to the Bennett family to whom it was transferred following Barnett's death in 1920. Remained in the Bennett family's hands and later used as a scallop boat. Collided with the police patrol vessel *Allara* in 1944 in the D'Entrecasteaux Channel though sustained little damage. Believed broken up in mid-to-late 1958 by order of the Marine Board of Hobart after sinking at Kangaroo Point and becoming a navigation hazard.
1873	Coquette	Pleasure boat	22 x 4.8 x 1.5ft. Centreboard, clinker, copper-fastened boat built by George Hubbard at his Kelly Street home to the order of Samuel Jacobs, licensed waterman. Launched in September 1873.
1873	Henrietta	Passage boat	41.5 (oa) x 9 x 4ft. Partially decked carvel planked Huon pine passage boat built by George Hubbard at his Kelly Street home to the order of Michael O'Brien and launched on 25 October 1873. Began carting firewood, palings and fruit between Snug, Long Bay and North West Bay and Hobart Town from early November 1873. Finished second in the sailing boat race at the 1874 Hobart Town Regatta. Sunk off Crayfish Point, River Derwent, on 23 April 1874 with the loss of its owner Michael O'Brien and a young crew member named Thomas Driscoll. The two bodies and the vessel were never recovered.
1874	Agnes	Passage boat	40 (oa) x 8 x 3ft. Huon pine passage boat built by George Hubbard at his Kelly Street home to the order of Robert Meredith and launched on 4 April 1874 at the Hobart Town wharf. Intended for the river trade in which it was initially employed. Advertised for sale in Hobart Town in March 1876 though failed to sell. Advertised again in March 1879. Sunk at its moorings in North West Bay on 20 April 1879, though recovered. Advertised for sale in June 1880, sold to John Cross of the Old Wharf and converted to a fishing boat. Advertised for sale in Hobart in June/July 1882 and January 1883. Sailed to Launceston in April 1883 and advertised for sale. Sold in July 1883 to Messrs G. T. Glenwright, J. Smith, Dunning and Porter of Launceston for £80. Advertised for sale at Launceston in November/December 1883 and January 1884. Likely sold to Henry Parkes who advertised *Agnes* for sale in June 1884 at Launceston though it failed to sell. Wrecked off Badger Island in February 1885 after dragging its anchor during rough weather. Its captain (George Spiers) and a crew member ('Yankee Bill') were both drowned. At the time of loss, employed in supplying wood to the Goose Island Lighthouse.

Year	Name	Type	Description
1874	Caroline May ex Caroline	Passage boat	42 x 10ft. ON 133488. Built by George Hubbard at his Kelly Street home to the order of a Mr Denehey of Snug and launched by mid-September 1874. Advertised for sale in August 1875 and sold to Robert Meredith of North West Bay for £150. Traded between the Huon, D'Entrecasteaux Channel and Hobart Town for many years. With H. Meredith at the helm, won the race for passage boats at the 1881 Hobart Regatta. Advertised for sale in November 1886 though failed to sell. By 1889 owned by Charles Chipman. By 1893 owned by J. Langford. Advertised for sale in December 1902. Between 1909-14 noted in the South Arm firewood and produce trade, owned by Walter Barrett Richardson and sailed by his brother Joseph. Fitted with a 5 h.p. Bolinder engine in August 1912. Seized as part of Richardson's bankrupt estate and in August 1915 first registered (as Caroline May). Sold to Robert Crawford (of Websters and Sons) and on-sold to Robert Harvey. Foundered in the River Derwent on 3 December 1915 and due to legalities not raised until seven months later. Repaired and returned to the river trade. By 1918 operating as a fishing smack owned and helmed by Walter Barrett Richardson. By 1924 owned by William Bloom. Advertised for sale in October 1926. Sunk near Catamaran Creek on 16 December 1928 after springing a leak at Port Davey several days earlier, all crew saved. At the time of loss owned by Erle Young of Rokeby.
1875	Iowa ex Annie Stubbs	Passage boat	43 x 11.5 x 4ft. Huon pine copper-fastened passage boat built by George Hubbard at his Kelly Street home to the order of William Stubbs and launched in April 1875. Traded between Port Esperance and Hobart Town from May 1875. Sold to William Pulfer in July 1875 for £196 though remained in the Huon and D'Entrecasteaux Channel trade. Collided with the barge Gertrude while racing at the 1879 Hobart Town Regatta, at the time owned by W. P. Lindsay. Repaired and returned to service. Overturned and foundered at Bruny Island in February 1886, at the time owned by a Mr Davis. Resumed service a few months later. In 1890 sold to the Pybus family of Bruny Island. By 1899 renamed Iowa. Noted beached at Barnes Bay, Bruny Island, in 1938 and likely broken up.
1877	Secret	Yacht	31 x 7.5 x 2.8ft. Huon pine centreboard cutter-rigged yacht built by George Hubbard at his Kelly Street home for his own use to compete with the Derwent Sailing Boat Club. Launched on 29 January 1877. Advertised for sale in March 1877 and again in July 1879. Refitted as a fishing vessel and advertised for sale June 1884 etc. Possibly sunk in collision with SS Devon off Recherche Bay in 1891.
1877	Rescue	Waterman's boat	21 x 5 x 2ft. Square-sterned Huon pine waterman's boat built by George Hubbard at his Kelly Street home to the order of Samuel Jacobs (Jr), licensed waterman. Launched in October 1877.
1879	–	Pleasure boat	20 x 5ft x 20in. Copper-fastened, Huon pine centreboard pleasure boat built by George Hubbard at his Kelly Street home to the order of Edward Griffin. Launched in September 1879.
1879	–	Waterman's boat	21 x 5.5 x 1.3ft. Square-sterned Huon pine centerboard pleasure boat built by George Hubbard at his Kelly Street home to the order of Samuel Jacobs (Jr), licensed waterman. Launched in December 1879.
1880	Emma Louise (?) ex Mermaid	Fishing boat	35 x 8 x 3.6ft. Open fishing boat built by William Bayes for himself though just prior to completion purchased by F. Hinsby. Competed in the fishing boat race at the 1882 Hobart Regatta. Advertised for sale in March 1882 and sold to Joseph Barnett a month later. Possibly renamed Emma Louise.
1881	Alice Maud ex Fairy ex Scylla	Yacht	28 x 6.6 x 2.5ft. Huon pine centreboard second-class yacht built by William Bayes for himself though purchased by Messrs Barnard and Castray just after completion. Launched on 14 March 1881. Successfully competed in Derwent Sailing Boat Club and Derwent Yacht Club events over several years, as well as at local regattas. Renamed Fairy in late 1884 when purchased by A. J. Mitchell. Advertised for sale in September 1886 and again in October 1889. Subsequently converted to a fishing boat and renamed Alice Maud. Wrecked off Southport during a storm in September 1895, at the time owned by Anthony Matthews.
1881	Tas (?) ex Clara	Yacht	24 x 5.8 x 2.7ft. Huon pine centreboard second-class yacht built by William Bayes to the order of H. Calder. Launched in May 1881. Competed with the Derwent Sailing Boat Club and at various Hobart regattas over a number of years, by March 1882 owned by H. D. Hull, by 1884 owned by A. H. Luckman. By 1886 possibly renamed Tas and sailed by P. Luckman. Last noted by that name in 1887.
1885	–	Pleasure boat	26 x 5.8 x 2.1ft. Huon pine pleasure boat built by William Bayes to the order of a gentleman from Adelaide, South Australia. Fitted with a well and copper-fastened. Completed in April 1885.
1885	–	Whaleboat	Built by William Bayes in May 1885.
1885	–	Yacht	16 x 6.7 x 2.2ft. Half-decked, Huon pine 'Una' type yacht built by an amateur named William Boon of Battery Point, likely in the backyard of his home.
1885	Clytie	Yacht	23.7 x 7.2 x 3ft. Second class Huon pine yacht built by Alfred Mason at Battery Point for his personal use and launched in September 1885. Competed in inaugural events of the Derwent Sailing Club during the 1889/90 season. Purchased by George Clarke in 1891 remaining in his hands for several years. Lengthened to 40ft (oa) during this period and cruised extensively around the Tasmanian coast. Advertised for sale as part of Clarke's estate in February 1900. Purchased by McGregor Brothers. Post-1910 sold and converted to a fishing vessel. Wrecked on 16 November 1914 near Cape Pillar, Tasmania, all hands saved.

Year	Name	Type	Description
1886	*Marie*	Yacht	21ft. Kauri and Huon pine 'Una' type yacht built by William Bayes to the order of George Allwright. Launched in June 1886. Advertised for sale several times throughout its career as both a yacht and then fishing boat, including in November 1889, in December 1902 and February 1904. Subsequent fate not known.
1886	*Venus*	Yacht	21 x 7 x 2.3ft. Huon pine, copper-fastened yacht built by Alfred Tilley, the 18-year-old son of William Tilly at Tilly and Williams' slip and launched on 31 July 1886. Sailed by Alfred Tilley in Derwent Sailing Club events. Sunk off Sandy Bay during a squall on 27 October 1887 with its six occupants swimming to shore. Uncertain if recovered.
1886	*Imp ex Claretta*	Yacht	21 x 8.5 x 3.2ft. Kauri and Huon pine cutter yacht built by James Davey to the order of Alfred Mitchell and launched in November 1886. Raced with the Derwent Sailing Club and competed in local and regional regattas. Sold to E. H. Webster in late 1888 and renamed *Imp*, becoming one of the River Derwent's more successful racing craft. In mid-1899 purchased by Arthur Timbs and transferred to Strahan. Converted to a motor launch several years later. Remained in Strahan under various owners, in ever-deteriorating condition, until 2011 when sold to Andrew Denman. Still in existence and in storage at Kettering awaiting restoration.
1887	*Agnew*	Steam dredge	112.2 x 26.2 x 9.5ft. ON 57613. 203 tons (grt). Iron steamship, the first of its kind in built in Tasmania, built by R. Kennedy and Sons to the order of the Marine Board of the Mersey and launched on 26 March 1887. Remained in their possession for many decades, employed in various works, until holed and subsequently wrecked off the Mersey Heads during thick fog on 13 February 1939, all hands saved.
1887	*Tarrina*	Steam launch	69.5 x 14.8 x 5.3ft. ON 79286. 35 tons (grt). Screw steam launch built by R. Kennedy and Sons to the order of the Marine Board of Launceston and launched on 26 March 1887. Employed in various uses on the River Tamar for more than 50 years, undergoing alterations and improvements. Sold to private owners in July 1940 and likely converted to a houseboat.
1887	*Koonya*	Steam ferry	107.2 x 19.4 x 9.6ft. ON 57614. 180 tons (grt). Steam screw ferry built by William Bayes to the order of Risby Bros., intended to trade between Hobart, the Tasman Peninsula and Lewisham. Launched on 10 May 1887. Sold in November 1888 to Captain Miles for £4,500 and immediately on-sold to the United Steamship Company of Launceston to run between Hobart and Macquarie Harbour on a weekly basis. In 1896 sent to Sydney and advertised for sale. Failing to find a buyer, chartered to the Moruya Steam Navigation Company who ultimately purchased the vessel a month later. Wrecked off Cronulla Beach near Sydney on 25 January 1898 in heavy fog, its passengers and crew managing to make it safely to shore.
1889	*Silver Crown*	Steam ferry	84 x 17.3 x 6.6ft. ON 57622. 26 tons (net). Steam screw ferry built by William Bayes to the order of O'May Bros. for their River Derwent passenger service. Launched on 12 September 1889. A stalwart of the local steamer trade for many decades. Laid up in June 1930, owing to a fault with its boiler. Broken up at Bellerive in 1935.
1889	*Gannet*	Fishing boat	38 x 10.5 x 3.6ft. Huon pine, copper-fastened fishing boat built by Joseph Clinch and George Luckman to the order of H. Burston. Launched in mid-October 1889. Sold in February 1890 to F. Pender. Advertised for sale in Launceston in September 1893, purchased by J. M. Clarke of Penguin for use as a pleasure yacht. Advertised for sale by tender in May 1894. Returned to commercial fishing. Last noted when advertised for sale in Hobart in December 1904.
1889	*Lydia*	Yacht	21 (lwl) x 8.3 x 3.5ft. Built by Fred Shea of the Flagstaff, Battery Point, to a design by James Davey. Launched in mid-1889. Competed with the Derwent Sailing Club until in June 1894.
1890	*Inez*	Yacht	26 (oa) x 21 (lwl) x 9 x 3.5ft. Huon pine centreboard yacht built by William Creese in the backyard of his brother Joseph's house, Kelly Street, Battery Point, to the order of another brother, Mark Creese. Launched in March 1890 at Waterman's Dock. Competed with the Derwent Sailing Club for a number of seasons.
1890	*Mildura*	Fishing boat	40 (oa) x 11 x 4.2ft. Huon pine, copper-fastened fishing boat built by William Creese in the backyard of his brother Joseph's house, Kelly Street, Battery Point. Launched in May 1890 at Fisherman's Dock. Operated by its owner/builder for several years before being lost off Penguin Island, Adventure Bay, late in 1894.
1890	–	Dinghy	Huon pine dinghy built by Joseph Clinch and George Luckman to the order of Mr Watchorn for use in conjunction with his yacht *Surprise*.
1890	–	Whaleboat skiff	13 x 4.5ft. First of two Huon pine whaleboat skiffs built by Joseph Clinch and George Luckman for HMS *Rambler*.
1890	–	Whaleboat skiff	13 x 4.5ft. Second of two Huon pine whaleboat skiffs built by Joseph Clinch and George Luckman for HMS *Rambler*.
1890	–	Lifeboat	15 x 5.3 x 2.1ft. Huon pine, copper-fastened lifeboat fitted with an airtight tank built by Joseph Clinch and George Luckman for Messrs Risby Bros.' steamer *Yolla*. Capable of carrying 20 people.
1890	–	Whaleboat	18 x 6 x 2ft. Huon pine, copper-fastened whaleboat built by Joseph Clinch and George Luckman for Messrs Risby Bros.' steamer *Yolla*.

Year	Name	Type	Description
1890	Nubeena	Steam ferry	106.6 x 21 x 9.6ft. ON 57630. 138 tons (grt). Steam screw ferry built by William Bayes to the order of Whitehouse Bros., for their Tasman Peninsula passenger service. Wrecked at Roaring Beach, South Arm, on 7 October 1910, all hands saved.
1890	–	Lifeboat	22 x 6.5 x 2.2ft. Huon pine, copper-fastened lifeboat fitted with an airtight tank built by Joseph Clinch and George Luckman for the steamer Devon.
1890	Kobold	Yacht	Huon pine, copper-fastened yacht built by Messrs Dunstan and Boulby (two amateurs) and launched in September 1890.
1891	–	Whaleboat	20 x 5.5 x 2ft. Four-oared Huon pine, copper-fastened whaleboat built by Joseph Clinch and George Luckman to the order of the Government of Tasmania for use by the Deputy Harbourmaster at Trial Bay.
1891	Lucy Adelaide	Fishing boat	36 x 10.5 x 3ft. Half-decked Huon pine fishing boat built by William Bayes in conjunction with his older brother Thomas to the order of Messrs Herrington and Son of Georges Bay. Launched in August 1891. Advertised for sale in August 1894 and purchased by William Gates. In 1904 one of the first of its industry to be fitted with an oil engine. Wrecked in July 1905 near Wineglass Bay on Tasmania's east coast, all hands saved.
1891	Rachel	Waterman's boat	21 x 5ft. Huon pine, copper-fastened waterman's boat by Joseph Clinch and George Luckman for H. Sheen of Battery Point. Capable of carrying 13 people.
1891	Rubina	Waterman's boat	19 x 5ft. Huon pine, copper-fastened waterman's boat by Joseph Clinch and George Luckman for H. Sheen of Battery Point. Capable of carrying 11 people.
1891	–	Tender	12 x 5.5ft x 18in. Huon pine tender fitted with a centreboard and sails built by Henry Hobbs Grubb to the order of Henry Denne. To be used in conjunction with Denne's new yacht Volant.
1891	Lucretia	Yacht	16.5 x 6 x 2ft. Huon pine, copper-fastened, half-decked yacht built by Henry Hobbs Grubb to the order of Messrs Davie Bros. to sail with the Sandy Bay Sailing Club. By late 1892 owned by David West, by 1894 jointly owned by A. E. Chancellor and Ethelbert Hull, by 1895 owned by B. Bennett. Several further changes of ownership over successive years, though remained a successful racing yacht on the River Derwent.
1892	–	Lifeboat	26 x 7.5ft. Huon pine, copper-fastened lifeboat by Joseph Clinch and George Luckman for the barque Doon.
1892	–	Boat	First of two boats built by Joseph Clinch for the barque Laira.
1892	–	Boat	Second of two boats built by Joseph Clinch for the barque Laira.
1892	–	Boat	Boat built by Joseph Clinch to the order of Captain Anderson of the Pearsons Point Pilot Station.
1891	–	Boat	22 x 6 x 2ft. Huon pine, copper-fastened boat built by Henry Hobbs Grubb to the order of T. J. Chaplin, pilot of Macquarie Harbour.
1892	–	Yacht	28 x 21 (lwl)ft. Unfinished yacht designed by Tom Purdon and presumed to have been built by Joseph Clinch advertised for sale in September 1892 as part of the late J. Stone's estate.
1892	Myrtle	Waterman's boat	16 x 5 x 1.6ft. Waterman's boat built by Joseph Clinch to the order of Thomas Smart. Remained in the Smart family's possession until at least the early 1940s. Noted to be one of the last traditional waterman's boats operating out of the Hobart wharf.
1892	Kaa-Ana	Steam yacht	40 x 7.8 x 3.8ft. Huon pine steam yacht built by Joseph Clinch to the order of Messrs H. Nicholls and W. P. Gibson to a design by John Lucas. Launched in December 1892. Sold to T. A. Reynolds and Company in October 1894 and transferred to Strahan for employment on the King River. Advertised for sale by the Union Steamship Company in June 1900. Later transferred to Sydney where it was advertised for sale in late 1910/early 1911.
1892	–	Loading punt	Large loading punt built by William Bayes to the order of W. H. Cheverton.
1893	–	Pleasure boat	24 x 6.5 x 3ft. Huon pine pleasure boat built by William Bayes to the order of James Young. Fitted with a spacious well. Completed in March 1893.
1893	Tarcoola	Ferry boat	21 x 5.8 x 2.3ft. Huon pine ferry boat built by William Bayes to the order of George Jacobs. Fitted Copper-fastened and launched in September 1893.
1894	–	Whaleboat	Huon pine, copper-fastened whaleboat built by Joseph Clinch to the order of Alexander McGregor and Company.
1894	Pinega	Yacht	16 x 5ft. Half-decked, Huon pine, copper-fastened 'Bouncer" yacht built by Messrs J. A. Roberts and J. A. Douglas (two amateurs) and launched in October 1894. Last noted in December 1900 competing at the New Norfolk Regatta with C. O'May at the helm.
1895	Venture	Fishing boat	42 (oa) x 10.5 x 4.5ft. Macquarie Harbour pine, copper-fastened fishing boat built by William Creese in the backyard of his brother Joseph's house, Kelly Street, Battery Point. Launched in May 1895. Operated by its owner/builder for several years. Last noted when advertised for sale by G. Thompson in Hobart in 1918.

Demolition of the patent slip at Battery Point, off Napoleon Street in August 1911.
Tasmanian Mail, 24 August 1911.

Synopsis

'Tasmanian-built vessels shoved their long flying jibbooms into many ports of the world, and were admired by men who understood the sea and ships. Indeed, they played an important part in making Tasmania known in the Old World.

Examiner, 12 March 1946.

The Builders

During the nineteenth century there were upwards of 24 boat and ship builders who operated commercial yards at Battery Point. The earliest of this cohort was Irish immigrant Daniel Callaghan who established a boat yard near the Mulgrave Battery, almost certainly on property then owned by Thomas Smith, in late 1830. It was operational for only a few years before Callaghan sailed to New South Wales in search of new opportunities. However, he was soon followed by Scottish immigrant William Williamson and English-born John Watson. The former established a shipyard in 1834 on the same site previously occupied by Daniel Callaghan. The latter established a shipyard along the Napoleon Street corridor in 1839. Both men had immigrated to Hobart Town in the early 1830s with their families and both were experienced shipwrights in their native places. In the 14 and 16 years, respectively, that William Williamson and John Watson spent at Battery Point, they launched at least 20 schooners, eight barques and three brigs. Many of these vessels played important roles in the development of intercolonial and trans-Tasman trades, while others became pioneers of international trade and were among the first Tasmanian-built vessels to arrive in Asia, Europe and South America. Yet others were the first locally-built vessels to be employed in the whaling industry.

In 1846 Peter Degraves established a shipyard at Battery Point on land he initially leased though quickly purchased from Thomas Smith. The property was sandwiched between William Williamson's shipyard and the Secheron estate. One of Tasmania's wealthiest and more powerful businessmen, Degraves[1] determination and resolve culminated in the building of the largest vessel yet built in Australia, the 562-ton *Tasman* launched in March 1847. Together with his son Henry, Peter Degraves continued to oversee the building of larger vessels at Battery Point up until his death in 1853, primarily barques and schooners destined for intercolonial and international trades and/or the whaling grounds.

Also in the late 1840s Joseph Risby (and his brothers) and Jacob Chandler both established boat yards between the River Derwent and Napoleon Street, in close proximity to John Watson's shipyard. The Risby family's yard was the first commercial boat yard in operation at Battery Point and in the succeeding years at least 67 vessels were built here, many of which were prominent in local races and regattas, while others were exported to the mainland. By 1858, however, Joseph Risby opted to forgo boat building in lieu of his rapidly expanding timber milling and export business; the enterprise made lucrative by the mainland gold rush. Significantly, the company he created would remain in operation for more than 135 years, eventually closing its doors in 1995.

Like the Risby family, Jacob Chandler was a prolific builder of whaleboats, particularly those used for racing, as well as boats for local watermen. Yet the evolution of his craft in the 52 years he spent at his Battery Point boat yard saw him transition to the building of fishing smacks and passage boats; the latter built to transport goods, produce and timber from ports in the Huon, D'Entrecasteaux Channel, and Ralphs Bay to Hobart Town. The building of the first four steam ferries for the O'May Brothers' River Derwent passenger service is also another highlight of his long and respected career. He also holds the distinction of building the most boats at Battery Point. At least 197 vessels are attributed as being built at Chandler's yard between 1847 and 1899.

The early 1850s saw James Mackey (in partnership with Thomas Cullen and his brother David Mackey) established a shipyard just north of Jacob Chandler's yard. Having learned the craft of shipbuilding from John Watson, the trio built many successful intercolonial and coastal schooners and ketches, and also furnished vessels for the New Zealand coastal trade. When his partners retired, James Mackey continued on with the firm, including launching the steamer *Warrentinna* in 1883. Distinguished as the second-longest serving builder at Battery Point, after 51 years of operation he passed on the reins to his nephew Henry Featherstone in 1902.

Also in the early 1850s John Ross established a shipyard at Battery Point on the Secheron property in the vicinity of the current-day bottom of Finlay Street, just south of Peter Degraves' yard. Here, in 1854, he took a calculated risk, installing Tasmania's first patent slip at a cost £20,000. Capable of accommodating vessels up to 1,500 tons, the slip began operation the following year and proved to be a boon, not only for John Ross personally but also for Hobart Town's maritime community and associated commercial enterprises. Yet in addition to slipping activities, in the 20 years he spent at Battery Point, including operating out of a Napoleon Street site from 1865, John Ross also notably built several large ships and barques, as well as four schooners, many of which were prominent in intercolonial and international trades.

The late 1850s saw John Lucas, another of John Watson's protégés, begin operation of a shipyard along Napoleon Street; between 1872 and 1884 he occupied the neighbouring patent slip property previously established by John Ross. At both sites, in partnership with Robert Jeffrey, he was primarily involved in the repair, painting, cleaning, refit and alteration of vessels, with the building of new vessels supplementing their income. Of these, between 1858 and 1883, 17 vessels were built, including nine schooners and two barques; many of which were employed in intercolonial and international trades. Later on in his career, John Lucas diversified his expertise with the designing and building of several of Hobart's more prominent recreational and racing yachts.

Charles Miller additionally joined the ranks of the Battery Point boat builders during the 1850s, succeeding Joseph Risby at his Napoleon Street yard in 1858. Here he spent the next 31 years building at least 120 boats, including 33 whaleboats, many for interstate or New Zealand-based customers. Like Jacob Chandler he also built vessels for the developing river and coastal fishing trades.

Another tradesman who learned the craft of boat building through apprenticeship at Battery Point was George Whitehouse. Yet his tenure as a Battery Point boat builder, operating his own yard on the Secheron property between 1874 and 1883, was superseded by his involvement in the regional steamer trade. In this enterprise, George Whitehouse heralded the Tasman Peninsula passenger service at a time when regional steam communication and passenger services to this area were in their infancy.

Lachlan 'Lark' Macquarie also operated a boat yard at Battery Point from 1876 to 1884 where he was involved in the building of smaller racing boats, particularly gigs and skiffs, many of which were successful at local regattas and in rowing club races. Following ten years of

Robert Inches' ex-shipyard at Battery Point (c1920s).
Courtesy Maritime Museum of Tasmania (P_2014-1735).

Summary of Ship and Boat Builders of Battery Point (1830 - 1903)

Name	Years of Operation	Number of Vessels*	Type of Vessels	Location
Daniel Callaghan	1830 - 1833	13	4 sailing boats, 2 galley boats, 2 gigs, 1 steam boat, 1 schooner, 1 sloop, 1 barge, 1 cutter, 1 dinghy	Refer to location A on map on page 267
William Williamson	1834 - 1839	8	5 schooners, 3 whaleboats	Refer to location A on map on page 267
	1841 - 1848	10	3 sailing boats, 2 gigs, 2 barques, 2 schooners, 1 brig	
Derwent Ship Building Company (George Bilton, Edward Goldsmith, Andrew Haig, John Meaburn and William Williamson)	1839 - 1841	3	1 schooner, 1 brig, 1 pleasure boat	Refer to locations F and G on map on page 267
John Watson	1839 - 1855	28	12 schooners, 5 barques, 3 boats, 2 steam-powered craft, 2 sailing boats, 1 brigantine, 1 punt, 1 gig, 1 whaleboat	Refer to location I on map on page 267
	1848 - 1851	1	1 barque	Refer to location A on map on page 267
Peter and Henry Degraves	1846 - 1853	9	3 barques, 3 schooners, 1 ship, 1 brig, 1 paddle steamer	Refer to locations B and C on map on page 267
Joseph Risby and family	1844 - 1858	67	24 whaleboats, 23 boats, 6 sculls, 4 gigs, 4 sailing boats, 2 wherries, 1 dinghy, 1 fishing boat, 1 skiff, 1 pleasure boat	Refer to location G on map on page 267
Jacob Chandler	1847 - 1899	197	84 whaleboats, 17 waterman's boats, 17 skiffs, 14 passage boats, 13 pleasure boats, 10 fishing boats, 8 dinghies, 6 gigs, 4 steam ferries, 4 boats, 3 sailing boats, 3 schooners, 3 ketches, 2 wherries, 2 yachts, 2 loading boats, 1 lifeboat, 1 cutter, 1 steam launch, 1 long boat, 1 excursion boat	Refer to location F on map on page 267
James Mackey	1851 - 1902	26	11 schooners, 6 ketches, 3 steam-powered craft, 1 barque, 1 sloop, 1 fishing boat, 1 boat, 1 punt	Refer to location E on map on page 267
John Ross	1851 - 1866	8	3 schooners, 2 barques, 1 steamer, 1 ship, 1 yacht	Refer to location D on map on page 267
	1865 - 1871	2	1 schooners, 1 barque	Refer to location H on map on page 267
John Lucas	1856 - 1872	9	7 schooners, 1 barque, 1 punt	Refer to location I on map on page 267
	1872 - 1884	3	2 schooners, 1 barque, 1 yacht	Refer to location H on map on page 267
Charles Miller	1858 - 1889	120	33 whaleboats, 27 boats, 8 yachts, 7 jolly boats, 6 long boats, 6 dinghies, 5 passage boats, 5 fishing boats, 4 loading boats, 3 schooners, 3 wherries, 2 pleasure boats, 2 gigs, 2 skiffs, 1 ketch, 1 galley boat, 1 surf boat, 1 cobie, 1 waterman's boat, 1 life boat, 1 cutter	Refer to location G on map on page 267
George Whitehouse	1874 - 1883	60	12 skiffs, 10 boats, 9 pleasure boats, 6 whaleboats, 5 sailing boats, 5 ferry boats, 4 yachts, 3 dinghies, 2 waterman's boats, 2 steam launches, 1 loading boat, 1 ketch	Refer to location D on map on next page

* Includes business partners and employees

Name	Years of Operation	Number of Vessels*	Type of Vessels	Location
Lachlan Macquarie	1876 - 1884	73	29 skiffs, 23 gigs, 5 pleasure boats, 5 boats, 3 whaleboats, 3 yachts, 2 fishing boats, 1 ferry boat, 1 dinghy, 1 sailing boat	Refer to location B on map on page 267
Robert Inches	1878 - 1904	19	9 yachts, 4 ketches, 2 steam launches, 1 punt, 1 steamer, 1 oil launch, 1 cutter	Refer to location K on map on page 267
William Bayes	1880 - 1881	5	2 yachts, 1 fishing boat, 1 pleasure boat, 1 whaleboat	Refer to location D on map on page 267
	1885 - 1893	8	3 steam ferries, 1 ferry boat, 1 fishing boat, 1 yacht, 1 loading boat, 1 pleasure boat	Refer to location J on map on page 267
John Bradley	1870	1	1 schooner	Refer to location H on map on page 267
	1872 - 1875	0	--	Refer to location I on map on page 267
Joseph Clinch	1889 - 1894	13	5 whaleboats, 3 lifeboats, 1 fishing boat, 1 waterman's boat, 1 yacht, 1 dinghy, 1 steam yacht	Refer to location G on map on page 267
Solomon Cook	1848 - 1850	9	4 long boats, 4 whaleboats, 1 jolly boat	Refer to location L on map on page 267
Benjamin Dyer	1865 - 1868	3	3 skiffs	Refer to location M on map on page 267
	1869 - 1874	0	--	Refer to location B on map on page 267
Gray and Company	1853 - 1856	0	--	Refer to location C on map on page 267
Henry Hobbs Grubb	1891	3	1 yacht, 1 tender, 1 boat	Refer to location H on map on page 267 **
George Hubbard	1872 - 1881	11	5 passage boats, 3 pleasure boats, 2 waterman's boats, 1 yacht	Refer to location N on map on page 267
Robert Kennedy and Sons	1885 - 1947	2	1 steam dredge, 1 steam launch	Refer to location H on map on page 267
William Tilley	1880 - 1894	1	Yacht	Refer to location I on map on page 267

* Includes business partners and employees
** Likely location

operation, however, Lark Macquarie closed his Battery Point yard, instead opting to travel the state building new vessels to order and undertaking repair work. Still during the period he spent at his site below the Prince of Wales' Battery, he built at least 73 vessels, including 29 skiffs and 23 gigs.

The 1880s saw the relocation from the Huon of another of Battery Point's most revered shipwrights, Robert Inches. Considered one of the finest builders of his era, between 1878 and his untimely death in 1904 Robert Inches built not less than 19 vessels at his Battery Point shipyard, located off Napoleon Street, including nine yachts and four ketches. Further, Inches has the distinction of being one of the first of his cohort to build racing yachts to designs developed by internationally acclaimed designers.

While not the focus of this volume, the late 1890s saw boat builders such as Tucker Abel and Charlie Lucas join the fold; the former having taken over Charles Miller's boat yard in 1897, with the latter, after learning the craft through apprenticeship to Robert Inches, going on to establish his own yard in 1899 on the site previously in the possession of John Watson and John Lucas. Both were enterprising boat builders. Tucker Abel created a niche for himself in the building of motor launches. Yet his time was also earmarked by the hiring out of motor launches and other vessels under the auspices of his Royal Blue Motor Launch Line, as well as the sale of scallops from his boat yard. In comparison, Charlie Lucas' sole passion was boat building. He spent nearly 60 years at Battery Point eking out a living; 37 of them operating his own yard. In a career that saw him build more than 48 recreational vessels, including yachts and motor boats, the outcome of which were flawless and faithful vessels built to pioneering designs, he was intrinsically connected with the growth and legacy of the Royal Yacht of Tasmania and yachting on the Derwent in general. Yet Charlie Lucas also built more

Synopsis

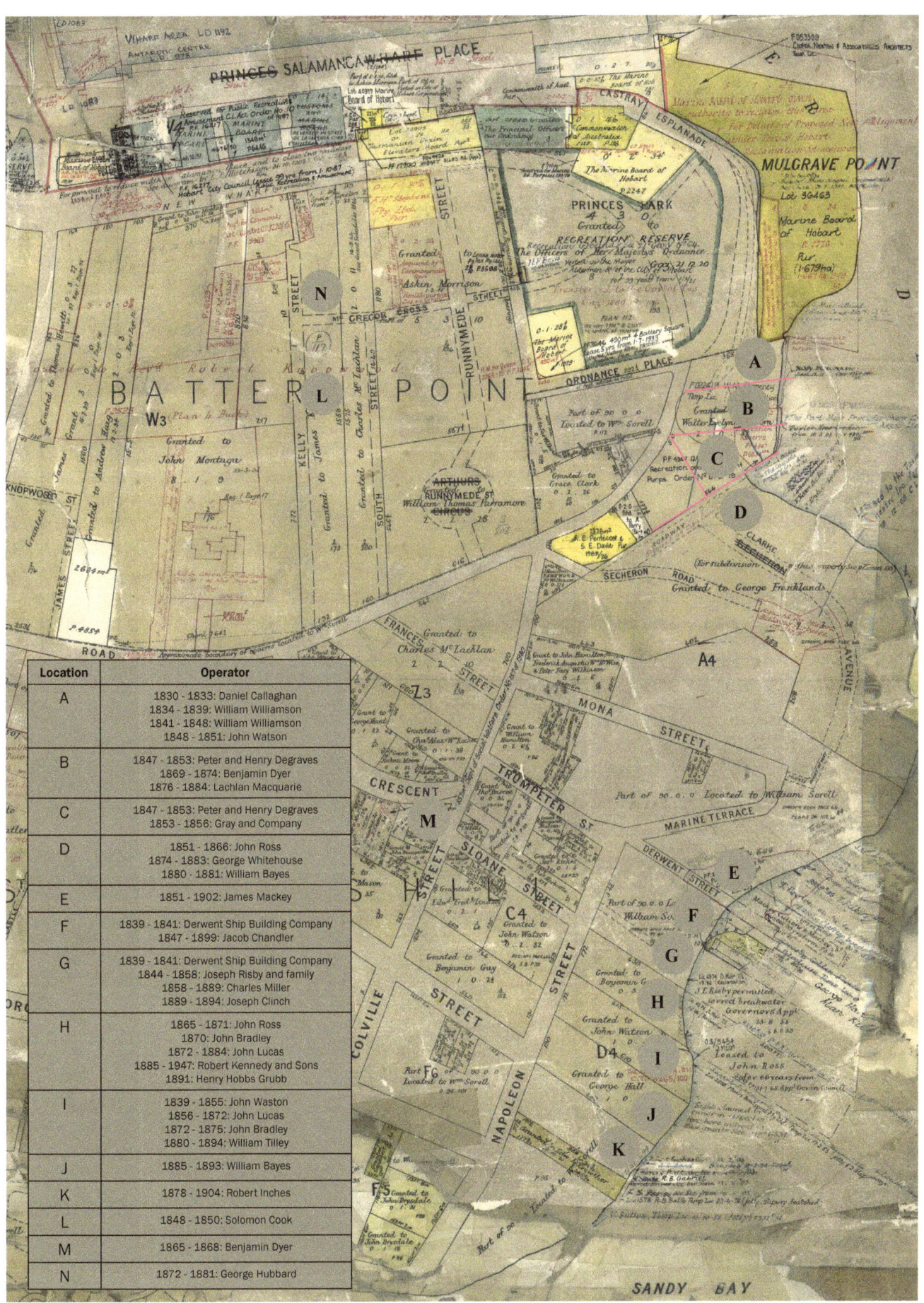

Adapted map of Battery Point, showing location of various boat and ship yards.
Courtesy Tasmanian Archives (AF819/1/135).

Location	Operator
A	1830 – 1833: Daniel Callaghan 1834 – 1839: William Williamson 1841 – 1848: William Williamson 1848 – 1851: John Watson
B	1847 – 1853: Peter and Henry Degraves 1869 – 1874: Benjamin Dyer 1876 – 1884: Lachlan Macquarie
C	1847 – 1853: Peter and Henry Degraves 1853 – 1856: Gray and Company
D	1851 – 1866: John Ross 1874 – 1883: George Whitehouse 1880 – 1881: William Bayes
E	1851 – 1902: James Mackey
F	1839 – 1841: Derwent Ship Building Company 1847 – 1899: Jacob Chandler
G	1839 – 1841: Derwent Ship Building Company 1844 – 1858: Joseph Risby and family 1858 – 1889: Charles Miller 1889 – 1894: Joseph Clinch
H	1865 – 1871: John Ross 1870: John Bradley 1872 – 1884: John Lucas 1885 – 1947: Robert Kennedy and Sons 1891: Henry Hobbs Grubb
I	1839 – 1855: John Waston 1856 – 1872: John Lucas 1872 – 1875: John Bradley 1880 – 1894: William Tilley
J	1885 – 1893: William Bayes
K	1878 – 1904: Robert Inches
L	1848 – 1850: Solomon Cook
M	1865 – 1868: Benjamin Dyer
N	1872 – 1881: George Hubbard

at least 15 fishing boats and commercial ketches, many of which were prominent in the local river and fishing trades.

The dawn of the twentieth century would precipitate a new generation of boat and ship builders, including Henry Featherstone and Tom Purdon, William Lucas and Percy Coverdale. Between 1905 and Tom Purdon's retirement in 1919, Purdon and Featherstone built at least 21 vessels, including eight steamers and eight ketches. Many of these vessels played pivotal roles in local and regional passenger, timber and fishing trades. Following Tom Purdon's retirement in 1919, Henry Featherstone persevered, including launching the schooner *Leprena* and the ketch *Terralinna* in 1922. In 1937 he partnered with his sons, thereby ensuring the longevity of his business.

Like Charlie Lucas, Percy Coverdale also learned the craft of boat building through apprenticeship with Robert Inches. He went on to excel at the building of yachts, cruisers, ketches and fishing boats, building more than 35 vessels in the nearly 50 years he spent at his Battery Point yard. The strength of Percy Coverdale's reputation and the quality of his workmanship saw his vessels coveted by buyers locally and interstate. Many, particularly his racing yachts, were built to innovative designs, helping to advance the modern yacht racing landscape, both locally and interstate. Remaining at his Battery Point yard up until his retirement in 1961, Percy Coverdale's work carried on the legacy of not only his mentor, Robert Inches, and his peers, but it also continued the legacy of all those who had built vessels at Battery Point before him.

The Vessels

While many of the yards primarily concentrated on slip work, between the years 1830 and 1903 more than 720 vessels were built at Battery Point, including 175 whaleboats, 104 gigs and skiffs, 60 pleasure boats and waterman's boats, 53 schooners, 42 yachts, 39 ketches and passage boats, 23 fishing boats, 17 barques, and seven steam ferries. Unfortunately many of the smaller vessels are likely not included in this tally. In general, whaleboats, pleasure boats, skiffs, gigs, loading boats, dinghies and lifeboats, et cetera, were not required to be registered, nor were they routinely mentioned in the press at the time of their construction, unless they were considered novel or unique. Thus estimates of the number of smaller vessels built at Battery Point by boat builders such as Jacob Chandler, Joseph Risby, Charles Miller, George Whitehouse and Lachlan Macquarie are likely extremely conservative compared to the true number of boats each builder actually built.

The largest vessel constructed at Battery Point, in terms of tonnage, was the 562-ton *Tasman*, built by Peter Degraves under the superintendence of John Gray, and launched in 1847. It was the intention of Degraves to build the largest vessel yet built in the colony at the time. Nearly 180 years later, he still holds the record for the largest vessel built at Battery Point.

On a decade-by-decade basis, the output of vessels from Battery Point between the years 1830 to 1903 was remarkable. The 1870s was by far the most active period for the Battery Point boat and ship builders. During this decade, Tasmania's economy was booming, fuelled

View of Battery Point and the Hobart Wharf from the eastern shore of the River Derwent.
Courtesy Tasmanian Archives (NS1013/1/252).

primarily by the newly developed mining industry. There was greater confidence in the state and the standard of living rose. This prosperity resonated to all sectors of the economy, and Hobart Town's ship and boat building industries were stimulated by an increased demand for new vessels, particularly ketches and passage boats to ply the developing river trade, as well as whaleboats to compete in local regattas and private races.

In contrast, demand for new vessels was low during the 1880s and 1890s. Tasmania entered into a recession, unemployment rose, and people fled the state for greener pastures on the mainland. There were sharp decreases in the number of new vessels commissioned. The use of steam power also greatly affected the demand for new passage boats to furnish the river trade, as well as waterman and pleasure boats for use in the local tourist trade.

The 1890s saw the Tasmanian economy continue to decline, fuelled primarily by a downturn in world mineral prices. The recession of the previous decade evolved into a full-blown depression. The Van Diemen's Land Bank collapsed, wages fell and unemployment rose. Yet, the recreational sport of yachting began to emerge during the middle of this decade, and the Battery Point ship and boat builders were thankfully a part of its popularity.

In addition to the construction of vessels, it should be reiterated that almost all of the Battery Point ship and boat builders were employed in the slipping, repair, refit, alteration and overhaul of vessels, particularly of those they had built. This area of their business, combined with the on-sale of vessels and parts, likely remained consistent throughout their careers. Unfortunately it is impossible to estimate the percentage of each builders' time that would have been consumed by these activities compared to the building of new vessels.

Of the vessels still in existence, there are notably at least six. These include the passage boat *Fancy* and the yacht *Maggie* (ex *Edith*), both built by Charles Miller in 1885 and 1886, respectively; and the yacht *Imp* (ex *Claretta*), built by James Davey to the order of Alfred Mitchell and launched from Battery Point in November 1886. Moreover it is probable that two yachts built by Robert Inches remain in existence: the yacht *Fairlie III* was last noted in Italy a decade ago after an extensive restoration while the yacht *Fairlie II* returned to Tasmania in 2023 after many decades spent in both Victoria and New South Wales. This particular craft is currently undergoing restoration at Cygnet. The steam launch *Preana*, built by Robert Inches in 1896, also remains in existence; only in recent years being transferred to Melbourne.

Employees

Owing to a lack of records, it is difficult to find information on the names and years of service of the hundreds and hundreds of business partners, shipwrights, blacksmiths, joiners, sawyers, apprentices and labourers that worked at the various Battery Point boat and ship yards during the nineteenth century. The following list is not at all exhaustive but does inventory those men known to have been employed at one or

more of these yards during this period. Moreover, while some men came into the industry from careers in related fields, others used boat and shipbuilding as a stepping stone to pivot to different opportunities. Still others supplemented their income streams through various ventures, particularly when work was not as brisk and/or the economy was not doing well.

Daniel Callaghan

- James Callaghan

Jacob Chandler

- James Henry Beale[2765]
- John Thomas Chandler
- George Hubbard[2766]
- Henry Hobbs Grubb
- John McGrath[2767]
- William Totham[2768]
- George Whitehouse
- William Whitehouse

Peter Degraves

- Andrew Dalgleish[2769]
- Henry Degraves
- John Gray
- William Griffiths[2770]
- John Hines[2771]
- Mr Martin
- Duncan McKenzie[2772]
- John Moore[2773]
- John Ross
- Thomas White[2774]
- Thomas George Wheatley[2775]
- Robert Wood[2776]

Derwent Ship Building Company

- George Bilton
- Edward Goldsmith
- Andrew Haig
- Samuel Kendall
- John James Meaburn
- William Williams
- William Williamson

Robert Inches

- Alfred Blore
- Percy Coverdale
- Charles Lucas
- J. Ludgrove[2777]
- George Mayne[2778]
- Joseph Mays[2779]
- John Smith[2780]

Robert Kennedy

- Robert Blackwell[2781]
- John Kennedy
- Malcolm Kennedy
- John Lucas
- James William McClymont[2782]

John Lucas

- Thomas Abel[2783]
- Thomas Bayes[2784]
- William Bayes[2785]
- J. Clements[2786]
- Mr Douglas[2787]
- James Eden Heron[2788]
- James Jeffrey[2789]
- Robert Jeffrey
- John Lynch[2790]
- William Lucas
- J. R. McClymont[2791]
- Joseph Smith[2792]
- Thomas Smith[2793]
- John White[2794]
- Mr White[2795]
- Henry Young[2796]

Charles Miller

- Joseph Clinch
- George Luckman
- William Mowatt[2797]
- Charles Wilson[2798]

[2765] *The Advertiser*, 8 June 1864.
[2766] *The Advertiser*, 8 June 1864; *The Advertiser*, 24 October 1864.
[2767] *The Advertiser*, 8 June 1864; *The Mercury*, 15 March 1894.
[2768] *The Advertiser*, 8 June 1864.
[2769] *Colonial Times*, 13 January 1852.
[2770] *The Britannia and Trade's Advocate*, 11 March 1847.
[2771] *Colonial Times*, 13 January 1852.
[2772] *Colonial Times*, 13 January 1852.
[2773] *Colonial Times*, 13 January 1852.
[2774] *Colonial Times*, 13 January 1852.
[2775] *Colonial Times*, 13 January 1852.
[2776] *Colonial Times*, 13 January 1852.

[2777] *Tasmanian News*, 17 January 1893.
[2778] *Tasmanian News*, 14 April 1893.
[2779] *Tasmanian News*, 24 June 1889.
[2780] *Launceston Examiner*, 14 December 1894; *Zeehan and Dundas Herald*, 14 December 1894.
[2781] *Tasmanian News*, 1 May 1888.
[2782] *Tasmanian News*, 13 January 1887.
[2783] *Tasmanian News*, 28 April 1908.
[2784] *The Mercury*, 12 December 1874.
[2785] *The Mercury*, 12 December 1874.
[2786] *The Mercury*, 12 December 1874.
[2787] *The Tasmanian Times*, 23 April 1868.
[2788] *Tribune*, 1 October 1877.
[2789] *The Mercury*, 31 December 1867.
[2790] *The Mercury*, 12 December 1874.
[2791] *The Mercury*, 10 June 1893.
[2792] *Tasmanian News*, 28 April 1908.
[2793] *The Mercury*, 2 July 1881.
[2794] *Tribune*, 24 October 1876.
[2795] *The Mercury*, 27 November 1871.
[2796] *The Mercury*, 5 August 1863.
[2797] *The Mercury*, 9 May 1872.
[2798] *The Mercury*, 14 January 1887.

James Mackey

- James Bailey
- Thomas Cullen
- Henry Featherstone
- Edward Gallahar[2799]
- David Mackey (Jr)
- David Mackey (Sr)
- John Mackey

Joseph Risby

- Charles Miller
- Frederick Gordon Brown[2800]
- Frederick Kidd[2801]
- Samuel Kirkby[2802]
- Joseph Risby
- Thomas Risby (Jr)
- Thomas Risby (Sr)
- William Risby

John Ross

- Charles Bradley
- John Bradley
- John Downie
- Edward Godfrey[2803]
- Alick Harley
- Edward Hennesey[2804]
- William Martin
- J. Mulenhy[2805]
- Mr Ross[2806]
- Edward Williams

William Tilley

- William Bayes
- S. W. McMullen[2807]
- Alfred Tilley
- Edward Williams

John Watson

- James Bailey
- Mr Batches[2808]
- Colin Campbell Carmichael[2809]
- Thomas Cullen
- John Dalgleish
- Charles Dowdell[2810]

- William Duke
- Mr Fairchild
- Edwin Gloster[2811]
- Bill Grey[2812]
- Mr Hicks[2813]
- Henry Jackson[2814]
- Robert Jeffrey
- John Lucas
- David Mackey (Jr)
- David Mackey (Sr)
- James Mackey
- Alexander McGregor
- John McGregor

George Whitehouse

- William Bayes
- William Whitehouse

William Williamson

- James Bailey
- James Bayley
- Martin Cash
- Robert Gray[2815]
- Samuel Kendall
- David Mackey
- Isaac Richardson
- William Sawyer
- John Williams
- William Williams
- William Williamson (Jr)

Casual 'Journeymen' Shipwrights[2816]

- Thomas Abel
- John Ainslo
- Thomas Bayes
- John Dalgleish
- Thomas Davison
- William Drake
- Joseph Hopwood
- Edward Gallagher
- John Gallagher
- Arthur Griffiths
- George Lynch
- James Lynch
- John Lynch
- Patrick Mahar
- Robert Purdy
- Henry Thompson
- Henry Warne
- Edward Williams

[2799] *The Mercury*, 7 September 1874.
[2800] *Colonial Times*, 19 April 1856.
[2801] *Colonial Times*, 19 April 1856.
[2802] *Hobarton Guardian, or, True Friend of Tasmania*, 15 May 1850.
[2803] *The Hobarton Mercury*, 10 October 1855.
[2804] *The Mercury*, 10 October 1862.
[2805] *The Tasmanian Times*, 10 August 1868.
[2806] *The Mercury*, 26 February 1866.
[2807] *The Mercury*, 6 November 1888.
[2808] *The Britannia and Trades' Advocate*, 10 October 1848.
[2809] *Colonial Times*, 3 August 1852.
[2810] *The Britannia and Trades' Advocate*, 10 October 1848.

[2811] *The Tasmanian Colonist*, 3 March 1853.
[2812] *Hobarton Guardian, or, True Friend of Tasmania*, 8 May 1850.
[2813] *Colonial Times*, 21 June 1854.
[2814] *The Tasmanian Colonist*, 3 March 1853.
[2815] *The Hobart Town Daily Mercury*, 22 February 1858.
[2816] *Tasmanian Morning Herald*, 1 January 1866.

Aerial view of Battery Point and the Hobart Wharf (late 1950s).
Courtesy Tasmanian Archives (AA193/1/1064).

Finale

'Our shipbuilders, such men as Mr. Ross, Messrs. Lucas and Jeffrey, and Messrs. McGregor, have proved their ability to turn out ships no port in the world need be ashamed of.'

The Mercury, 14 November 1865.

This book highlights one aspect of Tasmania's maritime history—the commercial boat and ship builders who operated at Battery Point near Hobart during the nineteenth century. Owing to Battery Point's strong boat and ship building history, a separate volume was published in 2017 by the same author on Battery Point's twentieth century builders and their vessels; men such as Charlie Lucas, Percy Coverdale, Athol and Norm Taylor, Max Creese, Jock Muir, Tom Purdon and Henry Featherstone, and Purdon Brothers, who all carried on the legacy of those who had gone before them. Given such rich boat and ship building history centred around Hobart and Tasmania's rivers and coasts, separate volumes could also be written about the Tamar builders, the Huon and Channel builders, and the builders of Hobart's Old Wharf and Domain areas, et cetera.

The boat and ship builders profiled in this book were all spirited, skilled and determined men seemingly with an intuitive predisposition for their craft and a love of all things aquatic. They were immigrants from England, Scotland, including its remote islands, and Ireland. They were the sons and grandsons of free settlers and convicts alike, some arriving in Australia as children, others being born in and around Hobart. Despite these differences, they shared many character traits — vision, enterprise, versatility, innovation, persistence, competitiveness and malleability. Many of them learned the craft of boat and/or ship building through apprenticeship and, with a combination of risk and determination, left to start their own yard. Ensuring that the legacy of their trade carried through in the generations to come, they were also exceptional mentors, particularly of local colonial-born lads.

While the commencement of boat and ship building in Tasmania's colonial era was met with considerable difficulties, including the scarcity of shipwrights and materials and lack of knowledge with regards to endemic timbers, with knowledge, experience and perseverance, the industry not only became well established but also thrived over a number of decades.

Of course there were failures and disappointments, owing to changing trade patterns, advances in technology that benefitted other modes of transport, loss of vessels, and fluctuations in the economy. As such these men endured careers that ebbed and flowed with the tide. Many were on the cusp of financial ruin several times throughout their careers, while others were forced to file for bankruptcy and then seemingly resurrected their careers overnight through new enterprises and being ahead of the curve. Financial realities also meant that many builders supplemented their income with other businesses or moved on to more lucrative ventures. But individually and collectively these men were a success, creating opportunities for themselves and grasping with both hands the opportunities presented to them.

The presence of the Battery Point boat and ship yards, both small and large, was also significant to the local economy. The yards not only employed tens, and in some cases hundreds of men, they also spurred and supported auxiliary businesses, including chandlers, sail makers, foundries, riggers, providores, coopers and waterside workers, et cetera.

To many of these men, boat and ship building was not just a profession, it was their life. They spent their working hours building vessels, their recreational hours sailing and competing in them, and their spare time discussing them. They raced against one another in whaleboat and yacht races, and challenged one another to build and design stronger and safer vessels. When it came to retirement, many of them failed, returning to help others build and/or design vessels at Battery Point or spending their final days walking the Hobart wharves, maintaining associations with their vessels and their customers, while others used their ship and boat building businesses as a stepping stone to further build commercial empires.

A tough, though extremely tight-knit community developed because of the presence of the boat and ship yards at Battery Point. Most builders and their workers lived within walking distance of the yards. In difficult times the community banded together to help those in need. They lost wives, children, parents, siblings; sometimes several family members within a matter of days or weeks. Premature death by diseases now easily curable was common with scarlet fever, typhoid and tuberculoses all taking a toll on the builders and their families. On several occasions family-related deaths occurred in the days leading up to auspicious launches of highly-anticipated vessels. Still, these men persisted; the burden of their loss relegated to private hours away from their yards. Several of these men also suffered depression and were ultimately debilitated by their work, illnesses and injuries leading to early retirement. In all of this life cycle, there was also joy. Births and marriages were celebrated, particularly the intermarriage of their sons and daughters with other family's within Hobart's maritime community; these bonds only strengthening the community's footing.

The yards were happy places on launching days, particularly in the colonial era, with hundreds, and in some cases thousands of spectators on hand to witness the event. Much celebration was had by all; the builders stood tall and deservedly proud. Yet the launch of their vessels from the stocks was often not the end of the builder's relationship with their vessels. Many vessels regularly returned to the cradle to be slipped, repaired, and/or altered. The builders thus became prominent caretakers of the vessels; thereby ensuring their safety and longevity.

Nearing 200 years since the first vessel was launched, the community and camaraderie that the boat and ship building yards instilled on Battery Point is still apparent, perhaps no more so than in the local pub: the Shipwrights Arms. Colloquially referred to as 'Shippies', as the pub nears its 170th birthday this reticent relict stands as a testament to the nautical history of the neighbourhood and the enterprise and modesty of the men who gathered within its walls to sink a pint. Braving the cold winter rains and piercing summer sun on the shore nearby, these men were competitive, determined and tenacious professionals. Yet, the friendship and spirit of this tight-knit community meant that the men stood side-by-side at the local pub celebrating successes, replaying races, antagonising for private matches, commiserating strandings and wrecks, and mourning lost lives.

Overall, the evolution of the boat and ship building yards at Battery Point during the nineteenth century tells the story of Tasmania's maritime history through time. More than 720 vessels were built during this period. Intercolonial trading vessels and whaleboats dominated the landscape initially, followed by river and coastal trading ketches and steamers. Racing and recreational yachts were next off the stocks. All told, the vessels were pivotal in the development of trading routes and new types of craft. Some were even imbued in significant historical moments, from intercolonial gig races and international exhibitions to visits from members of the royal family, as well as the development of organised yachting in Tasmania. This cohort of vessels also remains etched in history, with five, possibly six, of the craft built at Battery Point in the nineteenth century still in existence. These vessels are vital and visible connections between the past and the present. Collectively they serve as tangible links to the success and heritage of Tasmania's maritime history, as well as structural mementoes to the builders themselves. Yet, the Battery Point boat and ship yards perhaps provide the most tangible link to these men and the boats and ships they built. Though succumbed to residential pressure and changing industry dynamics, a few of the yards remain in operation, in much the same state as they did when the colonial builders worked upon them more than a century ago. So too does Mariners Cottage, located at 42 Napoleon Street. One of the oldest buildings in the shipyard precinct, it is believed to have been built between 1839 and the early 1840s either by or for John Watson.

Mariners Cottage, 42 Napoleon Street, Battery Point.
Courtesy Google Maps (2024).

Index

'Our shipbuilders, such men as Mr. Ross, Messrs. Lucas and Jeffrey, and Messrs. McGregor, have proved their ability to turn out ships no port in the world need be ashamed of.'

The Mercury, 14 November 1865.

Aamodt, Hans 122
Abbott, Mr 110
Abbott, W. 102
Abel, Thomas 234, 270, 271
Abel, Tucker 225, 252, 266
Aberdeen 52, 118
Absom, Matthew 33, 40
Acacia 146, 149, 167
Ada 195, 202
Adams, Roy 232
Addison 161
Adelphi 103
Aeolus 218
Agnes 250, 258
Agnew 254, 260
Ailsa 217, 226-228, 232
Ainslo, John 271
Aitkenhead, William 38
Akaroa Boating Club 96
Alabama (ketch) 158, 179, 186
Alabama (skiff) 208, 214
Alabama No. 2 209, 214
Aladdin 169, 258
Albert Packet 137
Albion Foundry 121
Alert (ketch) 125, 133
Alert (schooner) 243
Algerine 240
Alice Maud (fishing boat ex yacht) 259
Alice Maud (passage boat) 250, 258
Alice 169
Allan and Atkins, Messrs 207
Allara 258
Allbeury, John 132
Alligator 5, 38, 117
Allwright, George 235, 260
Amelia J. 256
America 226-228
Amy 167, 210
Anderson, Captain 240, 261
Anderson, Jessie 136
Anglo-Australian Guano Company 113

Ann 18
Annie (brigantine) 99, 110, 111, 122
Annie (sailing boat) 192
Annie (schooner) 55, 59, 61, 122, 161
Annie Hill 158, 180, 187
Annie Stubbs 251, 259
Annie Taylor 161
Annie Ward 104, 114
Aphrodite 202
Appleby and Co., Messrs 101, 113
Appleby Bros. 102, 114
Aquilla 105, 114
Archduke John 241
Archduke Lewis 241
Archer, I. 102
Archer, Isaac 111
Archer, Mr 201
Archer, Richard 111
Archimedes 241
Ariel (cutter) 29
Ariel (schooner) 34, 35, 40, 46
Aristides 256
Armstrong and Gourlay, Messrs 219
Armstrong, H. F. 122, 132, 133, 219
Armstrong, Richard 32
Arnett, G. (Jr) 130
Arthur, George (Lieutenant-Governor) 9, 10, 13, 27, 44, 190
Arthur, Mrs 13
Atalanta (gig) 39
Atalanta (skiff) 208, 214
Atkins, Thomas 89, 104, 113
Atkinson, Edward 132
Atlanta 247
Auguste de Sainson, Louis 14
Auriga 16, 21
Austin, John 94, 109
Austral 247
Australasia Packet 245
Australasian Steam Navigation Company 254
Australian Company 154

Australian Packet 158
Australian 245
Austrian Steam Navigation Company 241
Avon 243

Bailey and Company 118
Bailey, H. W. 194
Bailey, James 118, 176, 271
Baily, H. H. 202
Bain and Dale, Messrs 215
Bain, C. 215
Bainbridge, Thomas 64
Baker, Captain 36, 40
Baker, Mrs 36, 40
Bales, William 174
Bandicoot 44
Bank of Australasia 203
Bank of England 248
Bank of Van Diemen's Land 105
Barclay, John 18
Barnard and Castray, Messrs 234, 259
Barnett, J. 113
Barnett, Joseph 112, 259
Barnett, Moses 105, 115, 258
Barrett, H. S. 132
Barrett, Messrs 159
Barrett, Thomas William 178, 185
Bartley, Mr 18
Barwon Rowing Club 103
Bashful 192
Batches, Mr 271
Battery Point Ratepayers' Association 238
Bayes, Agnes 233
Bayes, Ellen Elizabeth (nee Burrows) 234
Bayes, Lydia 234
Bayes, Sarah (Sr) 233
Bayes, Sarah 233
Bayes, T. 208, 214
Bayes, Thomas (Sr) 233

Bayes, Thomas 234, 245, 270, 271
Bayes, William Alfred (Jr) 234, 237
Bayes, William Alfred 82, 196, 199, 233-237, 257, 259-261, 266, 267
Bayley, James (Captain) 51, 61
Bayley, James 271
Bayly, Jacob 87
Bayly, Michael 87, 88
Baynton, J. 182
Baynton, James 108
Beale, James Henry 270
Beattie, J. W. 62
Beaurais, Louis 18, 21
Belbin and Dowdell, Messrs 146, 148, 149, 180, 186
Belbin, William 61, 148
Belfast Rowing Club 114
Bell, Captain 142, 148
Bell, J. 208, 214
Bell, T. 208, 214
Bell, Thomas 194, 201
Bella Mary 176, 184
Bella Vista 96, 109
Belle Brandon 169
Belle 178, 185
Bellerive Rowing Club 210, 216
Bendall, Captain 160, 220
Bendigo 70, 71, 73
Bennett (brothers) 89
Bennett family 258
Bennett, B. 261
Bennison, E. A. 224, 226, 231, 232
Bentley, Godfrey (Captain) 48, 52, 60, 61
Beppo 76
Berean 238
Berriedale Inn 23
Berry Brown, Andrew E. (Captain) 162
Best, H. E. 102
Bettsworth, Benjamin 221
Biggins, Samuel 37
Bilton, George 30, 31, 39, 76, 265, 270
Bingham, M. 65-67, 71
Binney, W. H. 133
Birch, Thomas (Dr) 4, 5
Bird in Hand Hotel 93, 175
Bishop, Alexander 158, 171
Bishop, Samuel 133
Black Swan 144
Black, James (Captain) 110
Blackwell, Robert 270
Blanche 122
Bloom, William 259
Blore, Alfred 225-227, 232, 270
Blue Jacket 194
Bluebeard 76
Boadicea 151, 154
Bock, A. 110
Bolton, John 112
Boon, William 259
Borneo 257
Bostock, Mr 39
Bowden, Henry 61

Bowden, K. M. 5
Bowser and Company 130, 133
Boys and Hall, Messrs 137
Boys, William 33, 40
Bradley, Charles (Sr) 237
Bradley, Charles 149, 271
Bradley, Elizabeth (nee Purdy) 237-239
Bradley, Helen (nee Fleming) 237
Bradley, James 237
Bradley, John 145, 146, 148, 149, 160, 237-239, 266, 267, 271
Breeze 108
Bremmer, T. W. 226, 232
Bridges, Mr 245
Brier Holme 212, 213
Brisk 112
Britannia 212, 213
Britomart 239
Brock, Henry 33, 36, 40
Brodie, G. S. 137
Bronco 115
Brooker, Lieutenant 175, 184
Brooks, E. A. 225, 232
Brothers 32
Brown, Andrew 108
Brown, Captain 51
Brown, Eliza Jane 166
Brown, Frederick Gordon 271
Brown, James Herrington 207
Brown, Messrs and Company 68, 73, 137
Brown, Thomas and Company 140
Brown, Thomas 45, 67, 68, 73, 148
Brown, William 94, 140, 141, 148, 178, 186
Brownell and Co., Messrs 156, 171
Brownell, James (Captain) 132
Broxam, Graeme 6, 26, 53, 94, 138, 169, 180, 181, 183, 192, 212, 223, 225, 226, 229-231, 240, 243
Bruce, E. A. 133
Bryan, W. 174
Buchanan, E. 209, 215
Buchanan, Peter 15, 21
Buckles, Mr 21
Bundy, W. H. 220
Burbury, Mr 193
Burgess, Captain 55
Burgess, John 114
Burgess, W. 79
Burke, W. 232
Burman, Mr (likely William) 89
Burn, J. H. 192
Burnett, W. 203
Burns, Richard 53
Burns, White and Company 52, 61, 68, 73
Burston, H. 239, 260
Burt, Richard 48
Burton, J. H. 132
Bushton, Timothy 89
Butler, Messrs 10
Butler, P. 195, 202

Butterworth, Jim 228, 232
Buxton, Thomas 174

Cacique 37, 78
Cain, Captain 136
Calamia 195, 202
Calcutta 90
Calder, H. 202, 234, 259, 196
Caledonia 218
Callacombe, John Hills 158
Callaghan, Catherine (nee Hackett) 14
Callaghan, Catherine 20
Callaghan, Daniel 1, 10, 13-21, 23-25, 42, 263, 265, 267, 270
Callaghan, Edward 20
Callaghan, Eugene 14, 15
Callaghan, J. 19
Callaghan, James 16, 19, 21, 243, 270
Callaghan, Margaret 20
Callaghan, Maria 20
Callaghan, Mary (nee Ryan) 14, 18-20
Callaghan, Messrs 16-18
Callaghan, Michael Eugene 20
Callaghan, Michael 14
Calvert family 104
Calvert, C. 113, 114
Calvert, D. 113, 114
Calvert, Robert 105, 115
Camilla 76
Campbell Macquarie 5
Campbell, A. 162, 172
Campbell, D. 162, 172
Cane, A. 209, 215
Canes, Francis 132
Cannaway, Phillip 49, 54
Cape Pigeon 161
Cardiff Coal Company 122, 132, 142, 148
Caress 227
Carin 256
Carmichael, Colin Campbell 271
Carns, Robert 8
Caroline (ketch) 250, 259
Caroline (whaleboat) 190
Caroline and John 183, 188
Caroline May 250, 259
Carter, George 115
Carver, Captain 179, 186
Carver, James (Captain) 111, 126, 133, 155, 171
Carver, John (Captain) 111, 155, 171
Cascade Brewery 62, 65, 66, 71, 72
Cascade 243
Cash, Martin 26, 271
Castle, Henry 126, 221
Castle, Robert 126, 221
Castles, John 78
Castray, Mr 210, 216, 234, 259
Caterpillar 76
Catherine 36
Catholic Church 39
Centipede 46, 76
Chamberlain, Captain 50

Chamberlain, John (Captain) 104, 113
Chambers, C. 216, 226, 232
Chance (fishing boat) 210, 216
Chance (gig) 208, 214
Chancellor, A. E. 261
Chandler, Emma Selina 92, 107
Chandler, Hannah (nee Macbeth) 90, 92
Chandler, Jacob Bayly 77, 83, 87-115, 118, 140, 151, 178, 182, 183, 188-192, 245, 250, 263-265, 267, 268, 270
Chandler, James (born 1866) 98
Chandler, James 244
Chandler, John Thomas 92, 104-107, 110, 111, 270
Chandler, John 122
Chandler, Kezia (nee Cox) 96
Chandler, Marian Ellen 92, 107
Chandler, Martha (nee Macbeth) 96, 98
Chandler, Mary (nee Bayly) 87
Chandler, Mary Selina 90, 92
Chandler, Thomas 87
Chandler, William 90, 96
Chanticleer 161
Chaplin, Edward 174
Chaplin, Eliza 174
Chaplin, Mary Ann 174
Chaplin, Sarah (nee Campbell) 174
Chaplin, T. J. 247, 261
Chapman 256
Chapman, David 223, 231
Chapman, Frederick 252
Chapman, Henry 119, 132
Chapman, Mr 180, 215
Chapman, T. D. and Company 55, 62
Chapman, T. D. 93
Chapman, Thomas 53
Chapman, William 187
Charlotte 15, 16, 18, 21
Chase, George 89
Chase-all 39
Cherry Picker 191, 201
Chessell, Charles 28
Cheverton, George 180, 187
Cheverton, W. H. 236, 261
Cheverton, William G. 123, 133
Cheviot 35
Chingford Mill 173
Chipman, Charles 259
Chipman, Holmes Samuel 168, 172
Chipman, J. 16
Christchurch Rowing Club 176, 184
Church of England 142, 148
Circassian 50, 60, 175, 184
City of Edinburgh 75, 151
City of Hobart Town 51
City of Hobart 79, 85, 102, 122, 139, 142, 144, 158, 161, 178, 185, 239
City of Sydney 217
City School 141
Clara 234, 259
Claretta 260, 269

Clark and Davidson, Messrs 120, 208, 214
Clark family 169
Clark, Alexander 46, 60
Clark, Andrew Inglis 147
Clark, Charles 113
Clark, Francis William 205
Clark, Hugh 45, 60
Clark, John 101
Clark, Mr 209, 214
Clarke brothers 224
Clarke family 10
Clarke, Alfred 224
Clarke, Frederick Norman 217, 224, 226-230, 232
Clarke, George 106, 115, 223, 224, 231, 259
Clarke, Hannah 223
Clarke, J. M. 260
Clarke, J. T. 177, 185
Clarke, Thomas (Jr) 224
Clarke, Thomas Biggs 223
Cleary, W. J. 202
Cleburne, Mr 36, 40
Clematis 160, 161, 220
Clement, Mr 231
Clements, J. 270
Clinch and Luckman, Messrs 183, 239, 240, 260, 261
Clinch, Annie (nee Wright) 239
Clinch, Esther (nee Camp) 239
Clinch, John (Captain) 46, 52, 60, 61, 239
Clinch, Joseph John Charles 169, 239, 240, 260, 261, 266, 267, 270
Clowder, Mr 21
Clutha 217, 227-229, 232
Clytie 259
Cobre 158
Cole, Captain 21
Cole, Henry 55
Coleman, John 216
Coleman, Joseph 111
Colleen Bawn 178, 185
Collicott, J. T. 8
Collin, William 159, 171
Collins, David (Lieutenant-Governor) 3-5
Collins, William 4
Columbia 91, 108
Colvin, Charles 108
Comet 39, 89, 201, 206, 207
Commercial Academy 166
Commercial Bank 138, 139, 145, 147, 169
Commercial Steam Packet Company 240
Commodore 98, 109
Conley, Edward 113
Connecting Link 252
Contest 6, 243
Cook, Colin 162, 172
Cook, Elizabeth (nee Field) 240, 241

Cook, J. 106, 115
Cook, James 39
Cook, Solomon 240, 241, 258, 266, 267
Cookney, George 183, 188
Coolana 168
Cooper, George 48
Copper Reward Company 106, 115
Coquette (sailing boat) 250, 258
Coquette (whaleboat) 111
Coral 210
Corangamite Regional Library
Corporation 52
Cork Mechanics' Institute 13
Cornet 39, 89, 201, 206, 207
Cornhill 138
Coronella 76, 88, 89
Coronet 13
Corsair 208
Cosmopolite 138
Countess of Seafield 176, 184
Countess 209, 215
Coverdale, Percy 1, 231, 268, 270, 273
Cowen, D. (Captain) 124
Cowle, James 161, 163, 166, 167, 172, 180, 187
Cowle, Thomas Pressland 167
Cox and Longwood, Messrs 115
Cracknell, W. 182
Crawford, Robert 259
Creeping Jane 174
Creese, Joseph 260, 261
Creese, Mark 260
Creese, Max 273
Creese, William 260, 261
Crest of the Wave 219
Creswell, E. 209, 215
Crishna 110
Crocker, John (Captain) 26, 38
Crombie, Arthur 243
Cross, August 133
Cross, John 202, 258
Crossland, E. H. 226, 232
Crowther, H. L. 113
Crowther, William (Dr) 34, 35, 98, 109, 122, 132, 163, 178, 185
Crugana 248
Crystal Wave 104, 113
Cullen and Mackey 118-123, 132, 134, 140
Cullen, Thomas 52, 57, 117-123, 130, 132, 134, 263, 271
Cunningham, P. & Co. 113
Cupid (gig) 77, 84, 89
Cupid (skiff) 208, 214
Curlew 77, 84
Currie, Ann 251
Currie, Flora 251
Curtis, William (Sir) 65
Cygnet 190

Daisy 42
Dale, Henry 132
Dalgleish, Andrew 270

Dalgleish, John 59, 169, 256, 271
Dalley, E. 203
Danby, Sarah Ann 174
Dance, Captain 15, 21
Dancing Wave 158
Dandenong 103
Daniel Watson 158
Daphne 225
Dart 53, 54, 118
Dashing Wave 219
Dauntless (cutter) 231, 232
Dauntless (ketch) 221
Davey, James 260, 269
David & Elizabeth 243
David and Jessie 121, 132
Davidson and Clark, Messrs 120, 208, 214
Davidson, Henry 46, 60
Davie Bros., Messrs 247, 261
Davies, Joseph (Captain) 125
Davies, William 113
Davis, George 113
Davis, J. 114
Davis, Miss 69
Davis, Mr 259
Davis, William 244
Davison, Thomas 271
Dawn 159, 171
Daws, T. 79
Dawson, Alexander 50
Dawson, William 30, 39
Decharme, Deborah 65
Decharme, John 65
Degravers, Ann (nee Jones) 63
Degravers, Peter (Dr) 63
Degraves and Macintosh, Messrs 65, 66
Degraves family 63, 68, 70, 135, 137, 143, 205, 208, 213, 242, 243
Degraves, Ann (nee Macintosh) 64
Degraves, Charles 67, 71, 72
Degraves, Deborah 72
Degraves, Ellen 72
Degraves, Frances Deborah 65
Degraves, Henry 36, 37, 63, 68, 69, 71-73, 137, 263, 265, 267, 270
Degraves, Isabella 67
Degraves, John 67, 71, 72, 210
Degraves, Louisa Frances 64, 72
Degraves, Matilda 67
Degraves, Messrs 70
Degraves, Miss 69
Degraves, Peter and Company 64
Degraves, Peter 1, 63-73, 83, 137, 263-265, 267, 268, 270
Degraves, Sophia (born 1808) 64
Degraves, Sophia (born 1816) 65
Degraves, William 67, 71, 72
Delias 76
Denehey, Mr 250, 259
Denman, Andrew 260
Denne, Henry T. 112, 168, 169, 172, 247, 261
Dension Hotel 158

Derwent (barque) 68, 69, 73, 135, 137
Derwent (skiff) 210, 216
Derwent (steamer) 144, 239
Derwent (steamship) 30, 32
Derwent and Tamar Assurance Company 59, 127
Derwent Bank 14
Derwent Belle (gig) 102, 103, 112
Derwent Belle (pleasure boat) 192, 194
Derwent Belle (whaleboat) 111
Derwent Dinghy Sailing Club 231
Derwent Distillery 13
Derwent Iron Smelting Works 208
Derwent Iron Works and Engineering Company 168, 169, 253
Derwent Model Yacht Club 231
Derwent Rowing Club 195, 206, 207-210, 212, 214-216
Derwent Sailing Boat Club See Derwent Sailing Club
Derwent Sailing Club 106, 115, 169, 180, 187, 193, 201, 206, 208, 224, 225, 227, 234, 235, 239, 247, 250, 259, 260
Derwent Ship Building Company 30-33, 39, 76, 90, 265, 267, 270
Derwent Yacht Club 17, 202, 203, 208, 214, 222, 231, 234, 259
Devlin, Arthur 132
Devlin, E. 203
Devon 240, 259, 261
Diamond 21
Diana 30, 31, 39
Dickinson, George 64
Dillon, Charles 93, 96, 98, 109, 110, 114, 191, 192, 201
Dind, William 77, 84
Dixon, Francis 69, 73
Dobbie, W. J. 209, 215
Dobson, Henry 161
Dobson, Mr 136
Doctor 78, 84
Dogherty, Hugh 89
Doherty, Thomas 104, 113
Doig, J. 104, 122
Doig, James 117
Domency, William 120, 132
Doon 240, 261
Douglas Brothers 169
Douglas, Frederick (Captain) 158, 171
Douglas, J. A. 261
Douglas, Mr 270
Dove Inn 241
Dowdell, Charles 61, 146, 148, 149, 180, 186, 271
Dowling, Robert 211
Downie, John 149, 182, 237, 271
Dr Lord's Academy 64
Drake, William 271
Driscoll, Michael 224, 231
Driscoll, Thomas 258
Drysdale, Jane (nee Inches) 221
Drysdale, John 221
Dubuc 4

Duke of Edinburgh 145, 168, 238
Duke of Richmond 256
Duke of York Hotel 174
Duke, Mr 68
Duke, William 50, 271
Duncan, Edward 10
Dunn and Ross, Messrs 136, 137
Dunn, James 132
Dunn, John 89, 135-137
Dunn, Mr 103
Dunn, Thomas 38
Dunning, Mr 259
Dunstan and Boulby, Messrs 261
Dyer, Ann (nee Reay) 242
Dyer, Benjamin Bissell 242
Dyer, Benjamin Reay 71, 242, 258, 266, 267
Dyer, Elizabeth Ann (nee Stewart) 242
Dyer, Janet (nee Munro) 242

E. H. Purden 223, 224, 231
Eamont 31
Eardly-Wilmot, John (Sir) 88, 89
Earl of Kent 111
Easby and Robertson, Messrs 71, 73, 121
Eason, John 25, 32, 37, 38, 117
East India Company 4, 64, 65
Easther, Alfred 104, 113
Eckford, A. 182
Eclipse (fishing boat) 100, 111
Eclipse (gig) 78, 84
Eclipse (schooner) 55, 61
Eclipse (whaleboat) 190
Edinburgh Wine Vaults 23
Edith 173, 182, 183, 188, 269
Edith Alice 220
Edith Ellen 104, 112
Edith Reid 179, 186, 220
Edward and Joseph 104, 112
Edwards, Edward 132
Edwards, J. B. 246
Edwards, W. 258
Einerson Bros. 61
Elbe-Humber Steam Navigation Company 241
Electrolytic Zinc Company 203
Eliza (barge) 237
Eliza (government schooner) 16, 28, 43
Eliza (passage boat) 100, 111
Eliza (schooner) 18
Elizabeth 30
Ella 169, 223
Ellen (gig) 89
Ellen (ship) 174
Ellis, John 94, 109
Elwell, George 100, 111
Elwin, George 194
Emerald Isle 104, 113
Emerald 17, 18, 20
Emeu 121
Emily Downing 169, 254
Emily Ellen 94, 109

Emily 43
Emma Kemp 24
Emma Louise 259
Emma 20
Empress 209, 215
Emu (barque) 68, 73, 243
Emu (steamer) 57, 121, 130, 132
Enchantress 167, 195, 202
Endsor, Francis 113
Enterprise 100, 101, 112
Entwisle, James 241
Erne 166, 167, 172, 180, 187
Esk 163-165, 169, 254
Esperance Belle 244
Esperance 223, 231
Esperanza 36, 40
Ethel May 212
Eucalyptus 96, 130, 137, 138, 148
Eutape 41
Eva (schooner) 119, 132
Eva (skiff) 192
Evans, Alex 203
Evans, Evan 168, 172
Evans, Francis 108
Evans, G. W. 2
Evans, George 94, 109
Evans, H. B. 179, 186
Eveline (passage boat) 113
Eveline (ship) 90, 136
Evelyn 113
Excella 256
Excelsior 179, 186
Express 189, 195, 196, 203, 234

Facy and Company 196, 203
Facy and Fisher, Messrs 111, 159-161, 167, 171, 172, 199, 203, 220
Facy, Hannah 147
Facy, Joseph 147
Facy, Peter 159
Fair Tasmanian 50, 60
Fairchild, Mr 51, 271
Fairland, S. H. 226, 232
Fairley, Rigby and Company Limited 232
Fairlie II 217, 228, 229, 231, 232, 269
Fairlie III 217, 230-232, 269
Fairlie 217, 226, 228, 248
Fairy (schooner) 91, 108
Fairy (yacht) 259
Fairy Queen 111
Fairy Rock 161, 167, 178, 185
Falcon (schooner, 1865) 122, 133
Falcon (schooner, 1877) 126, 127, 133, 169
Fancy 173, 180, 181, 183, 187, 224, 231, 269
Fanny (barquentine) 43
Fanny (schooner) 26, 27, 38
Fanny (ship) 189
Farmer 76
Farmer's Club 167
Faugh-a-Ballagh 71

Faugh-a-Ballah 111, 250
Fay, Margaret 34
Featherstone, C. E. 112
Featherstone, Charles 71
Featherstone, Georgina 93, 105
Featherstone, Henry Inkerman 117, 130, 132, 133, 157, 169, 264, 268, 271, 273
Featherstone, John (Captain) 130, 157
Female Emigration Society 53
Fenton, Mary 19
Ferguson, William 108
Ferry Inn 156, 171, 175, 184
Fife, William (Jr) 217, 226, 227, 229, 230, 232
Fire Fly 55, 137, 138, 148
Fireflash (gig) 103, 112, 210, 216
Fireflash (skiff) 192
Firth, Robert (Captain) 161, 162, 172, 180, 187
Fisher and Facy, Messrs 111, 159-161, 167, 171, 172, 199, 203, 220
Fisher, A. G. 157, 171
Fisher, E. M. 68, 73
Fisher, G. 142, 148
Fisher, J. M. 178, 185
Fisher, Mr 96, 109
Fisher, T. 178, 185
Fisher, William 61, 159
Fleetwing (barge) 122, 220
Fleetwing (skiff) 209, 214
Fleur-de-Lis 192
Florinda 252
Fly 192
Flying Buck 190
Flying Childers 47, 60, 151, 176, 185
Flying Fish 46, 47, 60, 137, 151, 239
Flying Fox 50, 51, 60
Flying Squirrel 45, 46, 60, 76, 239
Foam 223
Forest, Mr 41
Forget-Me-Not 104, 113
Forget-me-not 176, 184
Fortitude 77, 84
Fotheringham, Alexander (Captain) 18-20
Fox 17, 42
Fox, Henry (Sir) 138
Francis 18
Frankland, George 10, 22, 24, 27, 29, 45
Franklin, John (Sir) 27, 28, 44, 45
Frederick, Prince 174
Free Trader 52, 59, 61, 158, 178, 180, 185
Freeman, E. J. 193, 201
Freeman, J. 37
Friend, H. M. (Captain) 42
Friendship (barge) 130
Friendship (barque) 239
Frith family 167
Frith, John 167
Furner, F. H. 203

Gaffin, Mr 196, 203
Galatea (skiff) 192

Galatea (whaleboat) 111
Gales and Company 69, 73
Gales, Robert Gibson 73
Gallagher, Edward 271
Gallagher, John 271
Gallahar, Edward 271
Gannet 239, 260
Gardener, Captain James 33, 40, 68, 73, 84
Garrett, Alfred 45, 46, 60
Garth, J. (Captain) 126
Garth, James 30, 39, 218
Gates and Sons, Messrs 112
Gates, William 236, 261
Gaylor, C. 96, 102, 109
Gazelle (gig) 84
Gazelle (scull) 78, 84
Geeves family 119
Geeves, John 132
Geeves, Osbourne 132
Gellibrand, W. 180, 187, 224, 231
Gellie and Edwards, Messrs 206
Gellie, John 195, 203
Gem 79-81, 85
General Hospital 147, 167, 183, 231
Genevie M. Tucker 255
George III 17, 21
George and Thomas 185
George III, King (HRH) 174
Georgiana 173
Gertrude Lucy 104, 114
Gertrude 234, 259
Gibbs, A. 94
Gibson family 228
Gibson, John 62
Gibson, W. G. (Hon.) 228, 232
Gibson, W. P. 169, 240, 261
Gift (barge) 223, 225
Gift (schooner) 141, 142, 149, 155
Gill, Captain James 26, 38
Gillam, R. 115
Gillespie, David 52, 54
Gippsland Lakes Shipping Company 252
Girard, Francis 18
Gitana 169
Gleam 225
Gleaner 146, 149, 237
Glencoe 110, 179, 186
Glenloth 212
Glenwright, G. T. 258
Gloster, Edwin 271
Godfrey, Edward 271
Godfrey, John 98, 110
Godsiff, Newton and Company, Messrs 180, 187
Golden Fleece Inn 81, 85
Goldie, W. 110
Goldseeker 121
Goldsmith, Edward (Captain) 30, 76, 265, 270
Good Templar 194, 202
Goodwill 111

Goodwin, M. L. 108
Gordon Road Trust 246
Gordon, J. 249
Gorringe, W. G. 232
Goulding, Mr 201
Gourlay, J. R. 159, 171
Gourlay, Mr 219
Government of Britain 156, 171
Government of Hawaii 157, 171
Government of New South Wales 4
Government of New Zealand 176, 184
Government of South Australia 176, 184
Government of Tasmania 56, 81, 84, 85, 96, 98, 110, 141, 143, 147, 169, 175, 180, 184, 187, 210, 215, 261
Government of Van Diemen's Land 46, 60, 66, 77, 79, 84, 87, 91, 108, 218
Government of Victoria 71, 73
Governor Arthur 16, 17, 20, 21
Governor Brisbane 151
Governor Halkett 18
Grace Darling (fishing boat) 104, 113
Grace Darling (schooner) 158, 159, 171
Grace Darling (scull) 79, 85
Grace Darling Hotel 79
Graeme-Evans, A. 75
Grant, James 8, 28, 29
Grasmere 147
Graves, Joseph 130, 133
Gray and Company 243, 266, 267
Gray, Benjamin 243
Gray, John 19, 25, 43, 68, 71, 73, 242-244, 268, 270
Gray, Joseph 244
Gray, Margaret (nee Harper) 243, 244
Gray, Robert 244, 271
Gray, William 243
Gray's Inn 64
Green Man Inn 23
Green, George 103
Green, William 46, 60
Gregory Bros., Messrs 182, 188
Gregory, George 247
Gregson, T. G. (MLC) 206
Greig, Charles 206
Grey, Bill 270
Grierson, P. W. (Captain) 129, 133
Griffin, Edward 251, 259
Griffin, William Henry 182
Griffiths, Arthur 271
Griffiths, Richard 77, 84
Griffiths, William 270
Grubb family 248
Grubb, Alfred Ernest 246
Grubb, Allan Mcleod 247
Grubb, Anne Maria 244
Grubb, Eliza Jane 245
Grubb, Eliza 244
Grubb, Elizabeth Annie 245
Grubb, Elizabeth Thompson (nee Hobbs) 244, 245
Grubb, Elizabeth 244

Grubb, Henrietta Clara Isabel 246
Grubb, Henry (Sr) 244, 245
Grubb, Henry Hobbs 191, 201, 244-248, 261, 266, 267, 270
Grubb, Henry Joseph 246
Grubb, Hugh Benjamin John 246, 248
Grubb, Jane (nee Mcleod) 245-248
Grubb, Mabel Florence Victoria 245
Grubb, Mary Elizabeth 244
Grubb, Mary Jennet 246
Grubb, Susan Priscilla 244
Grubb, Vida Marion 247
Grubb, W. T. 106, 115
Gubbey, George 113
Guesdon, W. A. (Jr) 193, 201
Guesdon, W. A. 52, 61, 108
Guiding Star (barquentine) 167, 169
Guiding Star (schooner) 161, 179, 180, 186, 237
Guildford 249
Gunn, Samuel 1, 3-5
Guthrie, John 45, 60
Guy, Benjamin 25, 55, 76, 143
Guy, F. H. 149
Guy, Jane 143

Hackett family 13-15, 18
Hackett, Bartholomew (born 1830) 14
Hackett, Bartholomew 13
Hackett, Dominick 13
Hackett, James 13-15
Hackett, Maria (nee Donovan) 13
Hackett, William (Sir) 15, 20
Hackett, William Bartholomew (Sir) 15
Hackett, William 13
Haege, H. 46
Haggitt, Cecil 94
Haidee (pleasure boat) 195, 202
Haidee (yacht) 194, 202
Haig, Andrew (Captain) 8, 26, 27, 29-31, 38, 39, 137, 265, 270
Haines, J. 114
Hales, George 115
Halifax Royal Naval Dockyard 135
Hall, Frederick 33, 40
Hall, Henry 167
Hall, Robert Austin (Captain) 126, 127, 129, 133, 187
Hally Bayley 178, 185
Hamilton, Mr 8
Hamilton, W. 37
Hammett, S. A. 242, 258
Hammonia 241
Hanseatic Steam Navigation Company 241
Hanson, John (Captain) 121, 132
Hanson, Max 188
Happy Jack 122
Harbottle, Thomas 54
Harcourt, James 132
Hargraves, John 35, 40
Harlequin (schooner) 19
Harlequin (whaleboats) 77, 80, 84

Harless, George (Jr) 177
Harless, George 177
Harless, Rosa Sarah (nee Miles) 177
Harley, Alexander 217, 218
Harley, Alick 149, 222, 231, 237, 271
Harpley 136
Harrap, Elizabeth Ann (nee Cook) 241
Harrap, John 241
Harriet 58, 156-158, 161, 171, 180, 187
Harriette Nathan 33, 40, 46, 79, 85
Harrington, Ambrose 94
Harris, G. P. 3
Harvey, P. 37
Harvey, Robert 259
Hawden, John 38
Hawkins, William 220, 234
Hayle and Wilson, Messrs 193, 201
Heath, Charles 125, 133
Heather Bell 142
Heatley family 230, 232
Hebe 225, 232
Hector 141, 142, 148
Hedberg, O. H. 132, 225
Hedderwick, Peter 31
Helena Jane 245
Helena 15, 21
Hely, E. 208, 214
Henderson, Messrs D. and W. 162
Henderson, Thomas 154
Henderson, Turner 224
Hennesey, Edward 271
Henrietta 113, 250, 258
Henrietta Elizabeth 104, 113
Henrietta Packet 5
Henry 136
Henry, W. 244
Henty and Company 31, 39
Herbert, Thomas Charles 146, 149
Herbertson, Christina 156, 171, 175, 184
Hero (barge) 161
Hero (waterman's boat) 112
Heron, James Eden 234, 270
Herreshoff, L. F. 88
Herreshoff, Nathaneal Greene 226
Herrington and Son, Messrs 236, 261
Hesione 169
Hesse, George 18
Hewlett, Samuel (Reverend) 90
Hibbard, J. 208, 214
Hicks, Mr 271
Highland and Island Emigration Society 205
Highlander 46
Hill, Lieutenant 15
Hillyard, Mr 188
Hines, John 270
Hinsby, F. 234, 259
Hippolyta 90, 108
Hitchins, Frederick 70, 73
HMS *Beagle* 196, 203
HMS *Galatea* 98
HMS *Orlando* 115
HMS *Rambler* 240, 260

HMS *Renard* 196, 203
HMS *Sulphur* 15, 21
HMS *Wolverine* 196, 203
Hobart City Council 210, 238, 256
Hobart City Mission 130
Hobart Marine Board, see Marine Board of Hobart
Hobart Municipal Council 238
Hobart Police Department 182, 188
Hobart Rowing Club 212
Hobart Sanitary Association 238
Hobart Stock Exchange 238
Hobart Town & Sydney Steam Navigation Company 91
Hobart Town Foot Ball Club 245
Hobart Town Grammar School 49
Hobart Town Mechanics' Institution 13, 14
Hobart Town Police 144
Hodgson, Major-General 194
Hole, Eliza (nee Grubb) 245
Hollis, William 25
Holyman family 178, 185
Holyman, William 178, 185
Holyman, William and Sons 129, 133
Hope (cutter) 98, 110
Hope (fishing smack) 240
Hope (passage boat) 178, 185, 194
Hope (ship) 63, 65
Hopkins, Catherine 124
Hopkins, Henry (Jr) 122-124, 132, 133, 141, 148
Hopkins, Henry 101
Hopwood, Henry (Captain) 155, 158, 161, 171, 172
Hopwood, J. 96, 102, 109
Hopwood, Joseph 271
Horne, Mr 209, 214
Horne, T. 182
Horne, Thomas 10, 24, 46, 243
Houghton, James 174
Howitt, William 90
Hoy, David 35-37, 40, 43
Hubbard, Ann 249
Hubbard, Catherine (nee Burgoyne) 249-251
Hubbard, Catherine Louisa 250
Hubbard, Eliza 249
Hubbard, Elizabeth (nee Reed) 249
Hubbard, Fanny Catherine 249
Hubbard, George Thomas 249, 251
Hubbard, George 109, 111, 248-251, 258, 259, 266, 267, 270
Hubbard, Henry 249
Hubbard, James Edward 249, 251
Hubbard, John Joseph 249
Hubbard, John 249
Hubbard, Mary Ann (nee Martin) 249
Hubbard, Rosa Louisa 249
Hubbard, Thomas 109, 248-250
Hubbard, William Henry 250
Hudspeth, A. 7, 57
Hughes, William 104, 113

Hull, Etherlbert 261
Hume, Mr 210, 215
Hunter, Mr 34
Huon (barge) 218
Huon (steamer) 167, 169
Huon Belle (barge) 122
Huon Belle (racing boat) 197, 203
Huon Chief 170
Huon, Channel and Peninsula Steamship Company Ltd 200, 236
Hutchins School 147, 239
Hutchinson, Thomas 132
Hyacinth 46, 60

Imlay, Alexander 38
Imp 225, 260, 269
Inches and MacLaren, Messrs 218
Inches and Sons, Messrs 220, 221
Inches, Adolphus 222
Inches, Alice Mary (nee Joseph) 220, 221, 227
Inches, Amy Mary Malvina 221, 231
Inches, Ann (nee Reech) 217
Inches, Arthur Robert 220, 221
Inches, Clara 219
Inches, Lillian May 221
Inches, Mary (nee Garth) 217, 218
Inches, Mary Anne 220
Inches, Olive Blanche 221, 231
Inches, Percy Roland 221
Inches, Rebecca (nee Blofield) 219
Inches, Robert 169, 170, 182, 217-232, 235, 264-270
Inches, Robert (Jr) 217
Inches, Robert (Sr) 217
Inches, Robert Horace 222, 231
Inches, Thomas (Jr) 220
Inches, Thomas and Sons 160, 220, 221
Inches, Thomas 217-221, 231
Independence 122
Industry (brig) 46
Industry (cutter) 6
Industry (schooner) 243
Inez 260
Interloper 78, 84
Ionthe 225
Iowa 259
Irazu 223
Irby 169, 254
Iris (sailing boat) 193, 201
Iris (skiff) 111
Iris (whaleboat) 176, 184
Iron Smelting Works 71
Isabel 209, 215
Isabella (barque) 156, 158
Isabella (schooner) 110, 184
Isabella (ship) 43
Isabella Anna 20
Isabella Brown 140, 141, 148, 239
Islander 114
Italy 113
Ivanhoe 94

Jack, E. A. 130, 226
Jackson, George 113
Jackson, Henry 271
Jackson, John 30, 39
Jacobs, George 236, 261
Jacobs, Mr 111
Jacobs, Samuel (Jr) 114, 251, 259
Jacobs, Samuel 112, 114, 210, 215, 250, 258
James, A. 168, 172
James, Arthur 225, 232
James, George 155, 171
James, T. H. 18
Jameson, Mr 229, 232
Jane Cain 136
Jeffrey, Catherine (nee Grady) 154
Jeffrey, Isabella (nee Maclean) 154
Jeffrey, James 154, 270
Jeffrey, Robert Alexander 55, 58, 140, 143, 151, 154-156, 158, 171, 264, 270, 271, 273, 275
Jeffreys, G. 64, 65
Jennings, G. 61
Jennings, Henry 8
Jenny Lind 69, 70, 73, 137
Jessie Nicoll 127
John and Margaret 244
John Frances 79, 85
Johnson, Craven W. 18, 21
Johnson, John 27, 50, 55, 60, 61
Johnston, H. A. 224, 231
Johnston, John 60
Jones, Daniel 114
Jones, H. and Company 256
Jones, John (of Dunedin) 156, 171
Jones, John 61
Jones, Llewellyn (Louis) 104, 114, 178, 185
Jones, Robert 132
Jones, Sarah 83
Jones, W. B. 111
Jones, William Townsend (Captain) 7, 8
Jordan, V. 113
Joseph and Mary 245
Joseph, Benjamin 220
Joseph, Margaret 220
Joubert, J. E. 226, 232
Jubilee 119, 132
Juno 130

Kaa-Ana 169, 240, 261
Kangaroo Point Steam Navigation Company 83
Kangaroo 149, 157, 161
Kassa 169
Kathleen 113
Kelly, James (Captain) 4, 5, 8, 45, 190
Kemp, Dixon 222, 231
Kemsley, J. C. 230, 232
Kendall, Samuel 25, 30, 38, 39, 117, 270, 271
Kennedy, Alexander Donald 252
Kennedy, Angus 252

Kennedy, Ann Currie 252
Kennedy, Catherine McAlister 252
Kennedy, Clavey 252
Kennedy, Colin 252, 256
Kennedy, Duncan William 252
Kennedy, Florinda (nee Aitken) 251, 256
Kennedy, Florinda Marion Aitken 252
Kennedy, John 252, 256, 270
Kennedy, Malcolm 251-254, 256, 270
Kennedy, R. and Sons See Kennedy, Robert and Sons
Kennedy, Robert (Jr) 252
Kennedy, Robert and Sons 169, 182, 188, 233, 247, 252, 253-256, 260, 266, 267, 270
Kennedy, Robert 251-256, 270
Kent 194
Kent, S. 182
Kermode family 10, 119
Kermode, Robert Quayle 119, 221
Kermode, William 9, 10, 24, 45, 118, 119
Kerr, Alexander 55, 61
Kerr, Alexander, and Company 29, 39
Kerr, H. S. 107
Kerr, John 132
Kestrel 122, 133
Kidd, Frederick 271
Kilburn, Douglas Thomas 94, 175, 185
King Billy (barge) 169, 244
King Billy (skiff) 191
King George III (HRH) 107, 174
King Street School 247
King, Mr 105, 112
King, Philip Gidley (Governor) 3, 4
King, Richard 111
Kingfisher 77, 84
Kingston 113, 155, 156, 158, 171, 180, 186
Kinnear 46
Kirby Stephen 64
Kirby, Mr 81, 85
Kirkby, Samuel 271
Knarston, Robert 70, 73
Knight, William 45
Knopwood, Robert (Reverend) 7-9, 75
Kobold 261
Koonya 82, 169, 235, 257, 260
Korunah 114
Kramer, August 33, 35, 36, 40

Lady Bird 109, 250
Lady Brassey 180, 187
Lady Denison (brig) 96, 109, 184
Lady Denison (whaleboat) 77, 90, 91, 108
Lady Emma 68, 69, 73, 79, 85, 137, 176, 184
Lady Franklin (ketch) 197, 203
Lady Franklin (schooner) 26, 27, 38
Lady Griffiths 77, 84
Lady of the Lake 112

Laira 240, 261
Lambert, Mr 215
Lane, James 64
Lang, David 35, 40
Langdale, Robert 104, 114
Langford, J. 259
Larsen, Oscar 212, 213
Launceston Marine Board, see Marine Board of Launceston
Laura Louise 115
Laura 209, 215
Laurel 221, 225
Lavinia 136
Lawler, Captain 136
Lawson, Mr 179, 186
Lawson, W. 5, 43, 47, 50, 55, 64, 135
Ledwell, Mr 201
Lee, Joseph 132
Leisure Hour 201
Lenna 105, 115
Lewis, Charles 90
Lewis, D. 102, 209, 215
Lewis, George 89
Lewis, Neil 90
Lewis, R. 195, 196, 202, 203
Liffey 112
Lillian 114
Lillias 29, 30, 39
Lillie May 224, 231
Lily (barge) 225
Lily (schooner) 161, 162, 167, 172, 179, 180, 186, 187
Linda (skiff) 194, 201
Linda (yacht) 161
Lindsay Samuel (Captain) 148
Lindsay, Captain 140
Lindsay, W. J. 169
Lindsay, W. P. 259
Lion 92
Lister, Captain 19
Little Helena 21
Little Nell 206
Little Wonder 77, 84
Livadia 240
Lloyd, Edward 38
Lloyd, G. 208, 209, 214, 215
Lloyd, J. 208, 209, 214, 215
Lloyds of London 29
Loane, R. W. 5
London Missionary Society 156
Lord Hobart 45
Lord, Walter 64
Lottah 200
Louisa 26, 27, 158
Louise 98, 111, 179, 186
Lovett, Captain 39
Lovett, F. 89
Lovett, Frederick 34
Lovett, Percy 227
Loyteah 240
Lucas and Jeffrey, Messrs 154-158, 273, 275
Lucas family 151

Lucas, Charlie 1, 225, 227, 231, 270, 273
Lucas, Clara 154
Lucas, Edward (Captain) 47
Lucas, Elizabeth Sophia 154
Lucas, Emily Frances 154
Lucas, Ethel Jessie 154
Lucas, Herbert Edwin 154
Lucas, John (Sr) 151
Lucas, John Arthur 154
Lucas, John 55, 58, 59, 68, 73, 140, 143, 147, 150-172, 180, 225, 231, 232, 234, 237, 240, 253, 254, 257, 261, 264-268, 270, 271
Lucas, Marian Elizabeth 154
Lucas, Nathaniel 151, 155
Lucas, Richard 151
Lucas, Robert John 154
Lucas, Sophia (nee Sherburd) 151
Lucas, Sophia (nee Strang) 151, 154, 166
Lucas, Thomas 6, 45, 60, 151, 243
Lucas, William Joseph 111, 154, 170, 209, 214, 231, 270
Luckman family 239
Luckman, A. H. 259
Luckman, Esther (nee Dunkley) 239
Luckman, George Dunkley 183, 239, 240, 260, 261, 270
Luckman, George 239
Luckman, James 25
Luckman, P. 259
Lucretia 247, 261
Lucy Adelaide 239, 261
Ludgrove, J. 225, 270
Lughretta 222, 223, 231
Lurline (ketch) 125, 126, 133, 179, 186
Lurline (passage boat) 104, 113, 225
Lurline (racing boat) 206
Luttrell, Edward 152
Luttrell, W. 94, 109
Lydia 250, 258
Lynch brothers 111
Lynch, George 271
Lynch, James 271
Lynch, John 270
Lynch, Mr 110
Lynch, T. 182
Lynn, R. J. and Company 158, 171

Mabel 180, 182, 187, 240
Macbeth, Eliza 90
Macbeth, William 90
Macintosh, Hugh 63-67
Mackenzie, Henry 209
Mackey and Featherstone, Messrs 130
Mackey, David (Jr) 117-126, 132, 133, 263, 271
Mackey, David (Sr) 117, 118, 270
Mackey, Helen 117
Mackey, J. and D. 123-126, 133, 179
Mackey, James 116-133, 169, 263-265, 267, 271
Mackey, Jane (nee Gracie) 126
Mackey, Margaret (nee Doig) 117

Mackey, Marion (nee McMillan) 118, 130
MacLaren, James 158
MacMeekan, Captain 36
Macmichael, J. C. 183, 188
Macquarie (brigantine) 158
Macquarie (gig) 214
Macquarie, Allan 205, 206
Macquarie, Annie 209
Macquarie, Catherine (nee Mackey) 205, 210
Macquarie, Effy 206
Macquarie, Hector 206
Macquarie, Hugh 206, 209
Macquarie, Lachlan (Governor) 205
Macquarie, Lachlan (Lark) 71, 107, 205-216, 264, 266-268
Maffra 252
Maggie (cutter) 176, 184
Maggie (yacht) 173, 183, 188, 269
Maggie Laurie 94, 140, 141, 148
Maggie Read 105, 115
Mahar, Patrick 271
Maid of Erin 111, 158, 161
Makira 230, 232
Malcolm 178, 179, 185, 186
Manchester 241
Mangana 162, 163
Maning Brothers 53
Manser, Charles 108
Marana 200
Mararoa 226
Margaret (ketch) 202
Margaret (yacht) 188
Margaret Brock 36, 40
Maria (schooner) 6, 25, 243
Maria (whaleboat) 76
Maria Louise 158
Maria Orr 28
Marianne 35
Marie Corelli 130, 133
Marie Laure 161
Marie Louise 122, 132
Marie 235, 240, 260
Marine Board of Hobart 57-59, 61, 121, 127, 133, 141, 169, 170, 180, 182, 186, 187, 199, 238, 240, 256, 258
Marine Board of Launceston 58, 254, 260
Maritime Museum of Tasmania 27, 47, 106, 118, 119, 124, 130, 131, 138-140, 150-153, 160, 168, 170, 179, 182, 194, 196, 199, 224-227, 229, 235, 236, 248, 257, 264
Marquis of Bute 217
Marsh, Henry 119, 132
Marshall 241
Marshall, Thomas 231, 232
Marten 252
Martha Reid 126, 133, 180, 186
Martin Brothers 210, 216
Martin, Allister 188
Martin, Ann 174

Martin, Catherine, see Williamson, Catherine
Martin, Eva Minnie 245
Martin, Jessie (nee Anderson) 137
Martin, Jill 188
Martin, John (Captain) 38
Martin, John (fisherman) 210, 216
Martin, John 245
Martin, Mary Ann 249
Martin, Mr 270
Martin, Sarah Ann 174
Martin, Thomas 174
Martin, W. 115
Martin, William Adam 245
Martin, William 71, 73, 137, 192, 271
Mary Ann 189, 243
Mary Anne 223
Mary Wadley 169
Mary Williams 141, 142, 148
Mary 19, 243
Mason, Alfred 259
Mason, B. R. W. 246
Mason, B. 258
Mason, Joe 247
Mason, Mr 10
Matthews, Anthony 259
Matthison, Henry (Captain) 16
Maweena 200
Maxwell and Smith, Messrs 50, 60, 137, 148
Maxwell, Crawford Mayne 169
May Queen 202
Mayflower 240
Mayne, George 270
Mays, Joseph 270
Mazey, J. 212
McBride, Hugh 61
McCance, J. 182
McClemont, J. 182
McClymont, Charlie 182
McClymont, J. R. 271
McClymont, James William 271
McCormick and O'May, Messrs 224, 231
McCracken, Robert 218
McCulloch, Mary Ann (nee Bruce) 123
McDougall, Messrs 24
McEvoy 122
McEwan, Mr 208, 214
McGrath, John 270
McGregor Brothers 259
McGregor family 60, 68, 73, 169
McGregor, Alexander and Company 240, 260
McGregor, Alexander 59, 140, 271
McGregor, John 1, 271
McGregor, Messrs 273, 275
McInnes, Duncan 137
McIntosh, Captain 161
McKay, Alex 231, 232, 258
McKay, Angus 178, 194
McKay, Donald 104, 105, 112, 115
McKenzie, Duncan 270

McLachlan, Captain 55, 62
McLaren, Eliza Adelaide (nee Garth) 218
McLaren, James 217-219
McLaren, W. 214
McLaren's Hotel 123
McLean, W. 208
Mcleod, Elizabeth (nee Cooper) 245
Mcleod, Hugh 245
McLeod, John (Captain) 125, 133
McMechan, Anthony 137
McMillan, Archibald 118
McMillan, Donald 59, 122, 123, 170
McMillan, Janet (Jessie) 118
McMillan, Janet (nee Fenton) 118
McMullen, S. W. 271
McNaugton, Alexander 53
McPherson, Duncan 39, 44, 45, 55, 60, 154, 160
McPhie, T. 228, 232
McRobie, William 174
Meaburn, John James 30, 76, 265, 270
Medway 13
Melbourne Harbour Trust 71, 73, 252, 253
Melbourne Mechanics' Institution 136
Melbourne Town Council 136
Melbourne University 147
Melbourne 70, 73
Melbourne, Lord 173
Melville, Mr 16, 21
Mercantile Rowing Club 199, 210, 212, 216
Meredith, John 98, 110
Meredith, H. 259
Meredith, Robert 250, 258, 259
Mermaid 234, 259
Merope 239
Mersey Marine Board 254
Michell, Lewis 91, 108
Middleton 53
Midge 191, 201
Mildura 260
Miles, Captain 235, 260
Miles, E. T. 113, 197, 203
Millard, R. 17
Miller family 173, 174
Miller, Alfred Ernest 177, 182
Miller, Charles Henry 58, 82, 96, 143, 173-188, 194, 239, 264-271
Miller, Charles Joseph 173, 174, 178
Miller, Charles Orlando Chaplin 174, 176
Miller, Charles Stuart Campbell 177
Miller, Edith Isabel 178
Miller, Edward Henry 176
Miller, Eleanor Annie 176
Miller, Emma Louise 176
Miller, George 169
Miller, Harriet Ann Elizabeth (nee Martin) 173, 174
Miller, Harriet Sarah 174, 176
Miller, Mary Caroline 174, 176, 182

Miller, R. 182
Miller, Sarah 174
Millewa 195, 202
Milo, Captain 122
Milo, Joseph 133
Minnehaha 206
Minx 254
Miranda (ferry boat) 197, 203
Miranda (schooner) 47, 48, 52, 60, 151
Mischief 208, 214
Miss Degraves 70
Mistral 212
Mitchell, A. J. 259
Mitchell, Alfred 202, 260, 269
Moffat, J. W. 169
Monarch 69, 121, 201
Mongana 200
Montagu, J. 45
Montagu, Justice 77, 84
Montgomery, Henry 106
Montgomery, Maud 106
Moore, Fred 256
Moore, Frederick 37
Moore, Henry 256
Moore, John 270
Moriarty, S. 206
Moriarty, William 42
Morland, Thomas 205, 206, 242, 244, 258
Morling, James 30, 39
Morning Light (dinghy) 234
Morning Light (whaleboat) 96, 109, 190
Morris, Mr 210, 216
Morris, Neil 122
Morrisby, John 75
Morrison, Askin 51, 60, 91, 92
Morse, F. W. 182
Mort & Co. 20
Mortimer, H. W. 30
Moruya Steam Navigation Company 235, 260
Moscheto 53, 59, 61
Moss, Peter 36, 40
Mowatt, William 270
Muir, Jock 273
Muir, John 23
Mulenhy, J. 271
Mulgrave, Earl of 8
Munyard, Joseph 114
Murdoch, James 46, 60
Murdoch, Mrs 182
Murray, R. L. 21
Museums of History New South Wales 70
Museums Victoria 57, 211
Musk, Richard 115
Myall 169
Myrine 223, 240
Myrtle 240, 261
Mystery 94, 176, 184

Nairne, Mr 84
Nanoya 230, 232
Napier family 141, 146, 147
Napier, Eleanor 144, 145
Napier, Hector 145
Napier, Jessie (nee Paterson) 136, 141, 144, 145, 147
Napier, Thomas (Jr) 144
Napier, Thomas 136, 141, 144, 145, 146, 147
Nash, Mike 6, 26, 43, 138, 169, 180, 212, 223, 225, 226, 229, 231, 243
Natal Queen 161, 167, 169
Nathan, Louis 46, 67, 73
Nathan, Moses and Company 33, 40
Nation, George 212
National Archives of Australia 17, 55, 245, 252
National Library of Australia 3, 204, 235
National Library of Ireland 13
National Marine Insurance Company of South Australia 159, 171
National Records of Scotland 23, 154, 251
Native Cherry 76
Native Youth 46, 60, 151
Nautilus 124, 125, 130, 135, 178
Nellie 106, 115, 226
Nemesis 207
Nettle, W. 182
Neva 208, 209, 214, 167
New Norfolk Hospital for the Insane 167
New Town Tannery 115
Newall, Alice (nee Macquarie) 213
Nicholls, H. 169, 240, 261
Nickel, Auguste 230, 232
Nickolls, Frank 258
Nil Desparandum 111
Nimrod 35
Norling, John 114, 231
Norman, L. 59, 93
Norris, Joseph 93
Northern Light 209, 214
Norval 42
Noye, Edward 212, 213
Nubeena Rowing Club 212
Nubeena 199, 200, 236, 261
Nuit, R. W. 80

Oberon 121
O'Boyle, J. 111
O'Brien, Michael 250, 258
Ocean Chief 251
Ocean 135
Oceana 230, 232
Oceania 161, 162, 172, 180, 187
Odd Fellow 77, 84, 91, 108
Oddfellow 225
O'Farrell, R. 45
Offley 98, 109, 111, 154
Ogilvie, Thomas 52, 61
Oldham, Mr 156
Oldham, Peter 60, 93, 108, 138, 148, 184
Oldham, Thomas 121, 122
Oldmeadow, Alfred 225, 232
Oldmeadow, Arthur 225, 232
Oldmeadow, Messrs 169
Olga 225
Olive 229, 230, 232
Olson, Mr 209, 214
O'May Brothers 91, 96, 100-102, 105, 108, 109, 112-114, 195, 235, 260, 263
O'May family 105
O'May, C. 261
O'May, D. 162
O'May, Harry 1
O'May, Messrs 224, 231
O'May, O. 115
O'May, Peter 101, 102
Opposition 46, 76
Oram, H. 15
Orlando 105, 106, 115
Orotovia 41
Orr, Alexander 108
Orr, William 28
Oryx 122
Osprey (ketch) 122, 123, 133
Osprey (waterman's boat) 192
Osprey 103
Otago Yacht Club 178, 185
Owen, H. 208, 214

P. and O. Company 253
Pacific (whaleboat) 77, 84
Pacific (yacht) 195, 202, 241
Paling, Moses 113
Panama (brigantine) 52, 61
Panama (ship) 206
Panic 186
Paragon 191, 201
Parkes, Henry 258
Parliamentary Debating Association 238
Parsons, John 64
Parsons, R. 18, 24, 25, 30, 32, 33, 35, 36, 43-46, 50, 52, 53, 55, 68-70, 78, 91, 117, 119, 120, 121, 137, 142, 159, 218, 243
Paterson, Grace 136
Paterson, James (of Scotland) 136
Paterson, James 112
Paterson, Jessie 136
Paterson, Thomas 157
Paterson, William 136
Patterson, Frederick 37
Patterson, John 136
Patterson, Thomas 30, 39, 156, 171
Paul Pry 89, 98, 110
Peak, Henry 33, 40
Peak, Mr 112
Pearce, E. 209, 215
Pearce, Henry 132
Pearce, John 133
Pearl (passage boat) 104, 112
Pearl (whaleboat) 91, 108
Pearsall, D. W. 232
Peek, Samuel & Co. 19

Pender, F. 261
Pender, William 28
Perkins, John (Hon) 209, 214
Perkins, John 60, 73
Perriman, George 30, 39, 96, 108, 109
Perrin and Company 68, 73
Perry family 193
Perry, Arthur 34, 36, 37, 135
Perry, J. W. 176, 184
Perry, Messr 98, 110
Perry, Mrs 71, 137
Perseverance (sloop) 18, 21
Perseverance (waterman's boat) 96, 109
Pet 114, 167
Petchey, John 27, 28
Peter and James 96, 109
Pethridge, Henry Lander 108
Petrel 122
Pettow, Mr 194, 202
Phantom 94, 158, 175, 184
Philp, J. E. 4
Phoenix (barque) 169
Phoenix (gig) 209, 214
Phyrne 188
Picken, Edwin 39
Pickhaver, Thomas 94, 109
Picnic 96, 109
Picture Victoria 52
Pie, William (Captain) 121, 132
Piggott Brothers 46, 50, 60
Pinafore 189, 196, 199, 203, 234
Pinega 261
Pink, G. H. 35, 40
Pirate 91, 108
Pirie, William 147
Pitfield, William 200
Pitt, Mrs 182
Pixie 226
Planter 98, 110, 167
Plenty and Sons, Messrs 128
Plummer, Henry 206
Polyphemus 206
Port Adelaide Central Methodist Mission 226, 232
Port Huon Fruitgrowers' Association 71
Porter, Mr 258
Portland (schooner) 70, 73
Portland (ship) 154
Potter, John 96, 109
Power, Henry 115
Power, Robert 61
Poynter, James Peek 48, 90
Poynter, Sarah 90
Preana 217, 228, 229, 231, 232, 269
Prentis, Edward 174
Prentis, W. C. 209, 215
Pretty, Edward 115
Pretty, J. 114
Pretty, T. 212, 213
Pride 178, 186
Prince Alfred (HRH), Duke of Edinburgh 98, 100, 145, 191

Prince Alfred Yacht Club 230, 232
Prince Leopold 190
Prince of Wales (cutter) 243
Prince of Wales (skiff) 96, 109
Prince of Wales Hotel 174
Prince Regent 55
Princess 209, 214
Princess Alexandra 191, 201
Progress 114
Prospero 169, 180, 187
Pryde 96, 109
Pryde, George (Captain) 119, 132
Public Works Department 195, 202
Pulfer, William 259
Purcell, Mr 115
Purdon and Featherstone 1, 107, 200, 261
Purdon Brothers 273
Purdon family 237
Purdon, E. H. 223, 231
Purdon, Samuel 237
Purdon, Thomas (Tom) 107, 130, 223, 229, 231, 232, 237, 240, 261, 273
Purdy, Arthur 238
Purdy, Robert 271
Pybus family 230, 232

Queen of Sorell 31, 39
Queen 30, 31, 39
Queen's Orphan School 154, 166, 233

Rachel Thompson 104, 114
Rachel 240, 261
Racquet 114, 248
Rae, R. G. (Captain) 130
Rae, Robert Alexander 130
Rampant Lion 89
Rapp, L. 202
Ratler 240
Rattenbury family 231, 232
Rattenbury, James 114
Rattenbury, Walter 114
Raven, John 136
Read, J. T. 105, 115
Reardon, Michael 119, 132
Rebecca (barge) 218
Rebecca (barque) 19
Reeve, John 48, 60
Reibey, Thomas (Venerable Archdeacon) 142, 148
Reid family 10
Reid, G. F. 8, 126, 133
Reid, Hugh R. 73
Reid, James 191, 201
Reid, Walter and Company 133
Reliance 81
Rennie, Mr 64
Renown 112
Rescue (ketch) 206
Rescue (waterman's boat) 251, 259
Resolute (steam launch) 206
Resolute (steam tug) 221
Resource 42

Result 101, 114
Rex, Robert Richmond 146, 149, 209, 214, 225, 232
Reynolds, T. A. and Company 223, 231, 261
Richardson, C. H. 226, 232
Richardson, Isaac 36, 271
Richardson, Joseph 259
Richardson, Walter Barrett 259
Richmond Packet 243
Rigby, Francis 230, 232
Rimon, James 132
Ringarooma 180, 187
Ringdove 106, 115
Ripple 240
Risby and Brothers 76-78, 84
Risby and Son 46
Risby and Sons 75 76, 82
Risby and Watchorn, Messrs 208, 214
Risby Brothers 71, 90, 91, 106, 115, 173, 224, 232, 235, 240, 257, 260, 263
Risby family 61
Risby, Ann (nee Gibson) 75
Risby, Diana (nee Morrisby) 75
Risby, Edward 75
Risby, Eliza 75
Risby, Elizabeth (nee Birchall) 79
Risby, Henry Edmund 75
Risby, Henry Edward 79
Risby, Isabella (nee Wilson) 79, 83
Risby, Joseph Edward 61, 74-85, 87, 91, 108, 143, 173-175, 178, 179, 182, 183, 186, 263, 264, 265, 267, 268, 271
Risby, Joseph Thomas 79
Risby, Lavinia Rose 75
Risby, Louis John Wilson 83
Risby, Mary Ann 75
Risby, Messrs T. and J. E. 80
Risby, Thomas (Jr) 75-80, 88, 89, 271
Risby, Thomas (Sr) 75, 76, 271
Risby, Thos. and Brothers 76-78
Risby, W. H. I. 75, 78, 73
Risby, William Henry 75
Risby, William 75-78, 271
Ritchie, A. M. 180
Ritchie, Mr 180, 187
Ritchie, Russell 232
Ritchie, W. 194, 202
River Don Trading Company 160, 171
Rob Roy 18
Robert Burns 158, 161
Roberts, D. 247
Roberts, J. A. 261
Roberts, John 158
Roberts, Mr 50
Robin, E. 41-43, 46, 59
Robinson and Lilly, Messrs 142, 148
Robinson, Charles 155, 171
Robinson, George William 155, 171
Robinson, Mr 182
Robinson, W. 111
Roden, William 38
Roe and Passey, Messrs 142, 148

Roland, W. J. 182
Ronald, R. R. 38
Rose of Castile 192
Rose 88, 89, 91, 108, 151
Rosebud 225
Rosny Estates & Ferry Company 203
Rosny 256
Ross, Ernest Sydney 145, 147
Ross, Grace 141, 147
Ross, Hector 139, 141, 147
Ross, Horatio 139
Ross, Jessie 141, 142, 147
Ross, John 1, 68, 69, 71, 73, 98, 134-149, 155, 156, 160, 193, 195, 237, 242, 243, 256-258, 264, 265, 267, 271, 273, 275
Ross, John James (Jr) 137, 141, 144, 147
Ross, Mabel 141, 145, 147
Ross, Margaret 'Maggie' Laurie (nee Paterson) 136, 137, 139-141, 144, 145
Ross, Mr 271
Ross, Percy 139, 141, 147
Ross, Thomas Taylor 135
Rotomahana 112
Rowntree, Amy 7, 9
Royal Blue Motor Launch Line 266
Royal Brighton Yacht Club 169
Royal Charter 72
Royal Hobart Hospital 80
Royal Hotel 246
Royal Naval Dockyard 135
Royal Navy 3, 4, 15, 154
Royal Oak Hotel 23, 174
Royal Society of Van Diemen's Land 53
Royal Sydney Yacht Squadron 226, 232
Royal Tasmanian Botanical Gardens 192
Royal Yacht of Tasmania 266
Royal Yacht Squadron 161
Royalist 105, 115
Rubina (fishing boat) 247
Rubina (waterman's boat) 240, 261
Ruby Louise 106, 115
Runnymede (barque) 51, 52, 61, 114
Runnymede (whaleboat) 91, 108, 192
Russell, Alex 161, 172
Russell, Edward W. 238
Russell, Mr 176, 184
Russell, W. 80, 85
Ryan, Major 28

Salier, George 132
Samuel Cunard 45
Sandfly 105, 106, 115
Sandy Bay Sailing Club 224, 247, 248, 261
Sangwell, Robert 104, 112
Sansom, Henry (Captain) 118
Sapphire 159, 161
Sarah Ann 218
Satanella 103, 112
Saunder, Edward 108
Saunders, Alfred 132
Saunders, Captain 179, 186, 220

Saunders, Mr 126
Saunders, Simon (Captain) 132
Savage Bros. 203
Sawyer, William 33, 271
Sawyers Arms Hotel 257
Schah 76
Schlenk, Anton 160, 171
Schott, J. A. 182
Scotia 32, 237
Scott and Company 228, 232
Scott and Jones, Messrs 178, 185
Scott, A. G. 194, 202
Scott, J. R. (Hon) 178, 186
Scottish Chief 91, 108
Scottish Free Church 205
Scripps, L. 57
Scylla 234, 259
Sea Gull (wherry) 91, 108
Sea Gull (yacht) 93, 94, 108, 111, 122
Sea Queen 214
Seabird 227
Seacroft 105, 115, 225
Seal, Charles 53, 54, 61
Seal, Thomas Edward 158, 171
Sealth, G. R. 125
Secret (cutter) 251, 259
Secret (dinghy) 191, 201
Secret (yacht) 93, 94, 109, 140
Sedwell Jane 167
Setton, Mr 195
Seymour Coal Company 122, 132
Seymour 158
Shamrock 31
Shanley, F. 209, 215
Shannon 122, 158, 161
Sharland, Mr 211, 216
Sharland, W. S. 196, 202
Sharp, J. and Company 229, 232
Shea, Fred 260
Shea, William 18
Sheen, H. 240, 261
Shelahlah 96, 109
Sherburd family 151
Sherrington, Colin (Dr) 188
Sherwood, W. 179, 186
Ship Inn 91, 108
Shipley 248, 249
Shipwrights' Arms 48, 52, 274
Shirley, T. 111, 250
Silver Crest 176, 184
Silver Crown 235, 236, 260
Silver Queen 112
Sime and Ranken 23
Simm, James (Captain) 167
Simpson and Strickland, Messrs 228, 232
Sir Charles Napier 87
Sir Governor Arthur 27
Sir John Franklin 96, 110
Sir William Wallace 79
Sisters (barge) 126
Sisters (schooner) 45, 60, 67
Smail, Alexander 142, 148

Smart family 261
Smart, J. 96, 109
Smart, John 89, 111, 114
Smart, Thomas 114, 261
Smiling Morn 201
Smith, A. F. 197, 203
Smith, Alexander Bruce 156, 171
Smith, Francis 243
Smith, J. 258
Smith, James 243
Smith, John 179, 186, 226, 270
Smith, Joseph 270
Smith, Louis 212
Smith, Messr 50, 60, 137, 148
Smith, Mr 53
Smith, Thomas 10, 15, 24, 25, 27, 31, 32, 36, 37, 63, 263, 270
Smith, W. 182
Smith, W. H. (Captain) 252
Smith, William 89
Snewin, Frederick 252
Sophia 5
Sorell, William 7, 9, 24, 45
South Melbourne Council 253
Southern Cross (barque) 54, 61, 161
Southern Cross (steamer) 112, 114, 145, 161, 167, 177, 180, 185, 187, 259
Spaulding, George 250, 258
Spaulding, W. 231, 232
Spiers, George 258
Spindrift 179, 186, 220
Spode, William 108
Spray (cutter) 224
Spray (fishing boat) 104, 112
Spray (sailing boat) 193, 201
Sprig of Shillelah 19
Spurling, Mr (Jr) 201
Spy 77-79
St Kilda Yacht Club 229, 232
St. Helens 126, 133, 180, 187, 239
St. John's Grammar School 147
Stanfield, Daniel 178, 186
Star (gig) 92, 108
Star (steamer) 241
Star of Tasmania (schooner) 155, 156, 171
Star of Tasmania (waterman's boat) 96, 109
Star of Tasmania Hotel 178
Star of the Sea 192, 194
Star of the South 258
Stark, John 61
Starling (ketch) 126, 127, 133, 187
Starling (waterman's boat) 106, 115
State Library of New South Wales 2, 19, 86, 191
State Library of South Australia 47, 123, 125, 127, 149, 159, 238
State Library of Tasmania 4, 11, 14, 22, 32, 48, 53, 74, 80, 163
State Library of Victoria 6, 10, 97, 100, 146, 252
Steam Boat Company 32

Stevens, T. 55
Stewart, A. T. 185
Stewart, Messr 112
Stone, J. 240, 261
Stone, Richard 212
Storie, Captain 53
Storie, J. W. 46, 60
Storm Bird 157, 171, 240
Stracey, Messr 24
Strachan, James 29, 30, 39
Strang, Jane 154
Strang, Joseph 151
Strang, Robert 154
Strang, Sophia (nee Henderson) 151
Strathmore 220
Strong, James 154
Stuart, A. 216
Stuart, A. T. 194
Stuart, Mr 210, 216
Stubbs, William 251, 259
Success (barge) 118, 132
Success (steam ferry) 101, 113
Sullivan, Peter 258
Sunbeam 225
Sunny South 237
Surprise (cutter) 94
Surprise (steamer) 17
Surprise (yacht) 223, 240, 260
Susan 113
Swansea Packet 161
Sward family 230, 232
Sward, Herbert 229, 232
Sward, William 231
Swift (boat) 81, 85
Swift (ketch) 229, 230, 232
Swift (racing boat) 206
Swiftsure 78, 84
Sword Fish 53, 55, 61, 69, 161, 167, 239
Sydney Rowing Club 102, 103, 209
Sydney 176
Sylph 192
Sylvanus 33, 36, 40
Syme, J. W. 168, 169, 253
Symons, Mr 178, 185
Syren 202
Syrene 240

Talbot, Margharita 251
Tamar Rowing Club 196, 203, 209, 210, 215, 216
Tamar Yacht Club 228
Tamar 210, 216
Tandy, Thomas 91, 108
Tanjil 252
Tara 180, 187
Taranna 188, 199, 200, 234
Tarcoola 236, 256, 261
Tarleton, J. W. (Jr) 247
Tarleton, W. 196, 203
Tarleton, William 192
Tarrina 254, 260
Tas 259
Tasma 106, 115

Tasman (barge) 122, 132
Tasman (fishing boat) 178, 185
Tasman (passage boat) 178
Tasman (sailing boat) 108
Tasman (ship) 63, 68, 72, 243, 262, 268
Tasman (steamer) 161, 179, 180, 186, 187, 209, 239, 243, 258
Tasman (whaleboats) 44, 45, 77, 190
Tasmania 139, 176, 184, 239
Tasmanian Academy 50
Tasmanian Archives 5, 8, 9, 12, 25, 34, 37, 41, 43-45, 48-51, 56, 58, 62, 63, 65, 66, 69, 72, 76, 81, 82, 92, 93, 95, 99, 104, 105, 107, 116, 120, 121, 128, 129, 134, 139, 141-143, 155, 157, 164, 165, 172, 177, 188, 193, 197, 198, 200, 206, 207, 213, 219, 220, 222, 225, 228-230, 233, 244-247, 255, 256, 267, 268, 272
Tasmanian Lass 6, 243
Tasmanian Pyrolignite Company Ltd 71, 143, 193, 208, 242
Tasmanian Steam Navigation (T. S. N.) Company 162
Tasmanian Timber Corporation 230, 232
Tasmanian Yacht Club 93, 94, 108, 109, 140, 148, 175, 184
Tasman's Hotel 197
Taylor, Athol 273
Taylor, J. 108
Taylor, James (Captain) 157
Taylor, Messr 112
Taylor, Norm 273
Taylor, Robert 169
Teazer 136
Terry, W. 202
Tetlow, George 234
Thames (passage boat) 225
Thames (steamer) 35
The Argus Express 79, 85
The Arrow 32, 39
The Dream 178, 185, 194
The Grand Old Duke 174, 175
The Lily 195, 202
The Matchless 39
The Merit 39
The Patent Slip 174
The Prize 15, 21
The Tasman 46, 60
The Wave 15, 21
Theatre Royal 67
Thelma 169, 225, 226, 232
Thistle (barge) 218
Thistle (paddle steamer) 251
Thomas Brown 141, 148
Thomas, Frederick 115
Thomas, Samuel Henry 15, 16, 18, 21
Thompson, Alexander (Dr) 16, 17, 21
Thompson, G. 261
Thompson, Henry 100, 111, 271
Thompson, Jane 38
Thompson, John H. 16, 21
Thompson, T. 215

Thomson, Thomas 168
Three Sisters 180, 186
Tiennah 240
Tiger Cat 89
Tilley and Williams, Messrs 257
Tilley, Alfred 260, 271
Tilley, Anne Abigail (nee Martin) 257
Tilley, Charles 257
Tilley, Edward (the older) 256, 257
Tilley, Edward (the younger) 257
Tilley, Edward James 257
Tilley, Elizabeth Ann (nee Norman) 56, 257
Tilley, George 257
Tilley, John 256, 257
Tilley, Ruby Grace 257
Tilley, William James 235, 236, 256, 257, 260, 266, 267, 271
Tilley, William 257
Timbs, Arthur 260
Tinning, Ernest 132
Tipping, M. 3, 4
Tolman, E. 258
Tommy (sailing boat) 81, 85
Tommy (schooner) 55, 59, 62
Topsy 120, 132
Torphey, Mr 245
Totham, William 270
Townley, W. B. 226, 232
Transit 207
Traveller 78, 84
Travelodge Hotel 49
Travers, S. S. 114
Trial 249
Tri-Color 15, 21
Truganina 29, 31, 39
Tullock, William 158, 171
Turnbull, John 84
Turnbull, Mr 82, 85
Turner, F. 196, 203
Turner, John 113
Turner, T. 191, 201
Twinking Star 158
Twins 122, 238

Uncle Tom 119, 120, 133
Underwood, J. and T. 229, 232
Union Steamship Company of New Zealand 225, 252
Union 37
United Steamship Company 261
University of Paris 63
University of Tasmania 145, 147
Upolu 167, 172
Urquhart, T. H. (Captain) 238

Vampire 162
Van Diemen 45, 60, 76
Van Diemen's Land Bank 269
Van Tromp 55, 61
Veal and Gower, Messrs 180, 187
Velocity 111, 113, 178, 185
Vendetta 223, 224, 226, 231

Ventura 226
Venture 261
Venus (gig) 208, 214
Venus (ketch) 221
Venus (yacht) 257
Verren, William Snell 156, 171
Verrin, William 180, 187
Vesta 167, 168, 172
Vestal 46, 77
Victor 125, 126, 133, 179, 186
Victoria (barge) 161, 240
Victoria (cutter) 244
Victoria (schooner) 43
Victoria Tavern 108
Victorian Railway Department 251, 252
Victory (schooner) 55, 61, 82
Victory (steam ferry) 102, 105, 114
Vigilant 226
Viking 225
Vindictive 93, 108
Violet (skiff) 191, 201
Violet (whaleboat) 112
Vision (skiff) 110, 242, 258
Vision (whaleboat) 192
Vivandiere 209, 215
Vivid 238
Vixen 209, 214
Volant 169, 170, 247, 261

Wagoola 149
Wakefield 167
Walch, James H. B. 219
Walford, Bernard 6, 243
Walker and Gilham, Messrs 225, 232
Walker, Eliza 144
Walker, George 144
Walker, J. B. 4, 5
Walker, T. 21
Wallaby 44, 45
Waller, J. B. 166
Walsh, John 112
Walton, William 156, 171
Wanderer 194
Wanganui 169
Waratah 160, 161, 171, 234
Ward, Peter 188
Ward, Walter 179, 186
Warne, Henry 271
Warrentinna 117, 264, 127-130, 133, 169, 264
Warrington, James 195, 202
Washbourne, Richard 231
Watchorn, Mr 208, 214, 240, 260
Watchorn, W. E. 71
Water Witch 243
Waterhouse, George 59
Waterhouse, Maria (nee Watson) 59
Waterhouse, William 132
Waterwitch 240
Watherstone, John 94, 109
Watson and Sons Shipbuilders 41
Watson, Ann (nee Galley) 41, 42, 55
Watson, Ann Galley 42, 47, 49

Watson, Anne (nee Cunningham) 42, 57
Watson, Eliza 55
Watson, George (Jr) 58
Watson, George Chale 42
Watson, George 41-47, 49, 50, 54, 57, 60, 89, 243
Watson, James 57
Watson, Jane 47, 59
Watson, John (Jr) 58
Watson, John (Sr) 41, 42
Watson, John 1, 36, 41-62, 69, 82, 83, 90, 95, 117, 118, 121, 127, 133, 143, 151, 152, 154, 156, 170, 187, 263-267, 271, 274
Watson, Maria 49, 59
Watson, Mary (nee Middleton) 41-43, 46, 49, 57-59
Watson, Mary Friend 42, 57
Watson, William 58
Watts, Charles 243
Webster family 231
Webster, A. G. 155, 194, 201
Webster, E. H. 93, 169, 260
Websters and Sons 259
Wee Tottie 55
Weiberg brothers 209, 214
Weir, James 91, 108, 110
Weir, William 98, 109, 110
Weld, Frederick (Sir) 180, 187
Welsh, Mr 201
Welstead, Charles 173
Westbrock, T. 201
Westbrook, Messrs 89
Westbrook, Mr 207
Westbrook, Richard 90
Westbrook, Walter 90
Whalers' Return Hotel 34
Whangape 130, 133
Wheatley, Thomas George 270
Whelan family 113
Whirlwind 208, 214
Whitby, George 34, 35
White Hawk 52, 53, 61
White Squall 176, 184
White, Mr 270
White, P. H. 110
White, Thomas 270
Whitehouse and Pitfield, Messrs 200
Whitehouse Brothers 188, 192-197, 199-203, 234, 261
Whitehouse, Edward (Jr) 189, 190
Whitehouse, Edward 189, 190
Whitehouse, Eliza (nee Pegg) 189, 190
Whitehouse, Ernest Edward 192
Whitehouse, Frederick John 192
Whitehouse, G. and W. 185
Whitehouse, George 109, 188-203, 234, 236, 237, 245, 264, 265, 267, 268, 270, 271
Whitehouse, Herbert Edward 192, 200
Whitehouse, John 190
Whitehouse, Linda Louise 192
Whitehouse, Louisa 192

Whitehouse, Martha (nee Bayes) 192, 200
Whitehouse, Robert 190
Whitehouse, Sarah 189, 190
Whitehouse, Susannah 198, 199
Whitehouse, William (Sr) 189
Whitehouse, William George 192, 200
Whitehouse, William 188-203, 234, 236, 270, 271
Whitney, John 57
Whitney, Mary (nee Watson) 57
Who'd Have Thought It 190
Wild Wave (barque) 167, 169
Wild Wave (brig) 176, 184
Wild Wave (schooner) 156, 171
Wilkes Simmons, J. (Reverend) 191, 192, 245
Wilkins, Henry 154
Wilkins, Martha (nee Henderson, nee Lacoste) 151
Wilkinson, Hannah 220
William 59, 61
William and Susan 130
William Hill 55
Williams, E. 182
Williams, Edward 257, 274
Williams, Henry (Captain) 122, 133
Williams, John 32, 271
Williams, Luke 106, 115
Williams, Mr 192
Williams, Thomas 206
Williams, William (Melbourne) 62
Williams, William 30, 180, 270, 271
Williamson, Agnes (nee More or Moir) 23
Williamson, Catherine 37, 38
Williamson, Donald 23
Williamson, George 23
Williamson, Henrietta 23, 38
Williamson, James 23
Williamson, Ramsay (the younger) 37, 38
Williamson, Ramsay 23
Williamson, Sinclair (the younger) 37, 38
Williamson, Sinclair 23, 90
Williamson, William (Jr) 271
Williamson, William 23-40, 63, 67, 90, 117, 118, 263, 265, 267, 270, 271
Williamson, William. & Company 27, 117
Williamstown Borough Council 252
Will-If-I-Can 76
Willing, Percy 248
Willis, Arthur 45
Willis, J. S. 45
Willis, Mr 98, 110
Wilson family 200
Wilson, Charles 258, 270
Wilson, David 178, 185
Wilson, Fleetwood P. 222, 231
Wilson, George 118, 132

Wilson, James Milne 72
Wilson, John 167, 200
Wilson, Robert 168, 172
Wilson, William (Captain) 21
Wilson, William 23
Wilton, Richard 84
Winch, Elizabeth (nee Grubb) 245
Winch, Joseph 245
Windeatt, P. M. 188
Windward 122
Wing, R. 209, 215
Wise, Frederick 132
Witton, Mr 19, 243
Wollomai 252
Wood, James 61
Wood, Robert 270
Woodward, John Herbert 174
Woolnough, Robert 94, 109
Wrathall, Mr 108

Wray, George 243
Wray, Mr 46, 60
Wright, A. 182
Wright, Harold 208, 214
Wright, Howard 208, 214
Wright, Isaac 145, 148, 180, 187
Wright, Messrs 208
Wright, T. S. 180, 187
Wright, Thomas 178, 185
Wright, Valentine 50, 60
Wynaud 192
Wyuna 247, 248

Yankee Bill 258
Yarra 69, 70, 73
Yeoland, W. H. 104, 113
Yolla 224, 225, 232, 240, 260
Young Australia 194, 202
Young Dick 114

Young Tasmania 194, 202
Young, Dart and Mason, Messrs 229, 232
Young, Erle 259
Young, Henry 270
Young, J. R. (Captain) 162
Young, James 236, 261
Young, S. H. 93
Young, T. and J. Messrs 113
Young, Tasman 111
Young, Thomas 104, 112, 243
Young, William 6, 33, 40, 44, 68

Zephyr (brigantine) 158
Zephyr (schooner) 243, 244
Zephyr (yacht) 174, 240